U.S.

A NARRATIVE HISTORY

VOLUME 1: TO 1877

Seventh Edition

The Way You Once Had to Teach History . . .

. . . IS NOW HISTORY!

McGraw-Hill provides INSIGHT® to help you achieve your course goals.

How would your teaching experience change if you could access this information at a glance, either on your computer or tablet device?

1. How are my students performing?

2. How is this particular student performing?

3. How is my section performing?

4. How effective are my assignments?

5. How effective is this particular assignment?

McGraw-Hill's Connect Insight® is a first-of-its-kind analytics tool that distills clear answers to these five questions and delivers them to instructors in at-a-glance snapshots.

Connect Insight's® elegant navigation makes it intuitive and easy-to-use, allowing you to focus on what is important: helping your students succeed.

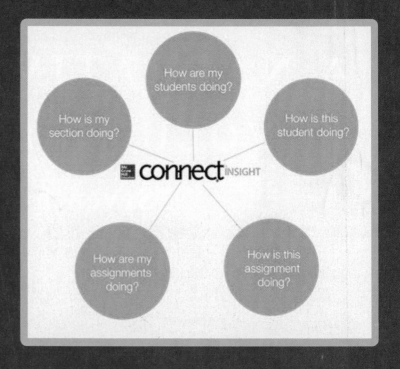

Interactive maps give students a hands-on understanding of geography.

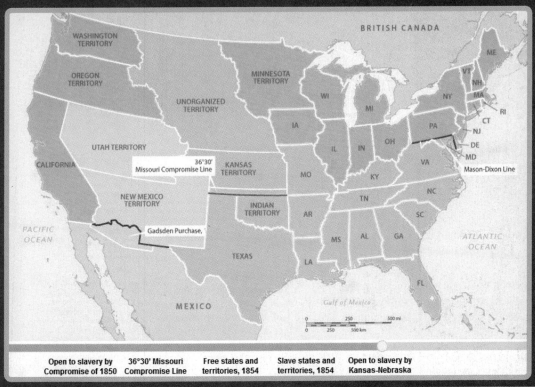

Open to slavery by Compromise of 1850 | 36°30' Missouri Compromise Line | Free states and territories, 1854 | Slave states and territories, 1854 | Open to slavery by Kansas-Nebraska

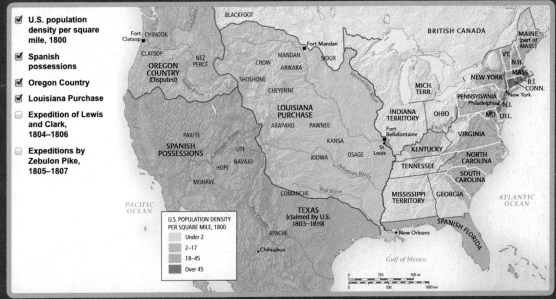

U.S.: A Narrative History offers thirty interactive maps that support geographical as well as historical thinking. These maps appear in both the eBook and Connect History exercises.

For some interactive maps, students click on the boxes in the map legend to see changing boundaries, visualize migration routes, or analyze war battles and election results.

With others, students manipulate a slider to help them better understand change over time.

U.S.: *A Narrative History* is a 21st-century approach to teaching history.

Students study smarter with SmartBook.

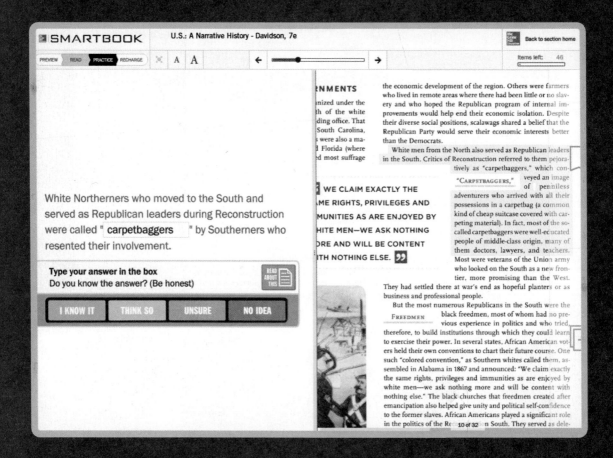

The first and only adaptive reading experience, SmartBook is changing the way students read and learn.

- As the student engages with SmartBook, questions test his or her understanding. In response to the student's answers, the reading experience actually adapts to what the student knows or doesn't know.

- SmartBook highlights the content the student is struggling with, so he or she can focus on reviewing that information.

- By focusing on the content needed to close specific knowledge gaps, the student maximizes the efficiency of his or her study time.

Critical missions promote critical thinking.

What would your students do if they were senators voting on the impeachment of Andrew Johnson?

Or if they were advisers to Harry Truman, helping him decide whether to drop the atomic bomb?

learn about your mission

I have been president for only a few months, assuming the position of Commander in Chief for a nation involved a long, global war. New technology has provided me with an atomic bomb-the world's first nuclear weapon-which could forever change the face of warfare. Now, I must decide whether to use this devastating new weapon to end the war with Japan. One group of advisors, including my chief advisor and long-time mentor, Secretary of State James F. Byrnes, is encouraging me to approve the plan. Another group, including the Under-Secretary of State and expert on Japanese diplomacy, Joseph Grew, advises against it. Here is what I need you to do:

1. Review the information on the following pages-the timeline, the maps, and the documents;
2. Identify important themes and evidence that my advisors have considered in offering their opinions;
3. Write your recommendation concerning whether or not I should use the atomic bomb on Japan, including themes and evidence to support your conclusion.

This is a decision that will shape the future for all humanity; consider it well!

President Harry S Truman

analyze the map

Use the timeline to view changes over time and explore all the information that the map has to offer.

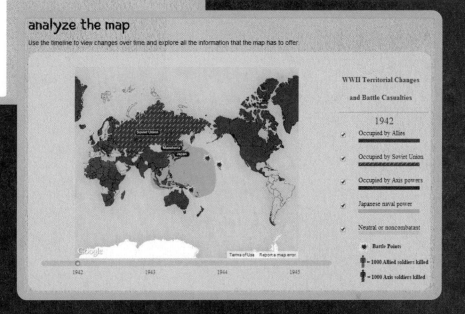

Critical Missions make students feel like active participants in history by immersing them in a series of transformative moments from our past.

As advisers to key historical figures, they read and analyze primary sources, interpret maps and timelines, and write recommendations.

As a follow-up activity in each Critical Mission, students learn to think like historians by conducting a retrospective analysis from a contemporary perspective.

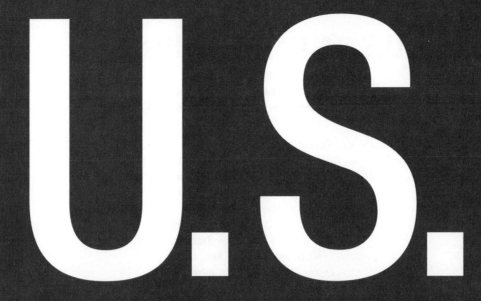

U.S.

A NARRATIVE HISTORY
VOLUME 1: TO 1877
Seventh Edition

James West Davidson

Brian DeLay
University of California, Berkeley

Christine Leigh Heyrman
University of Delaware

Mark H. Lytle
Bard College

Michael B. Stoff
University of Texas, Austin

U.S.: A Narrative History

AUTHORS
James West Davidson   Brian DeLay
Christine Leigh Heyrman   Mark H. Lytle   Michael B. Stoff

SENIOR VICE PRESIDENT, PRODUCTS & MARKETS **Kurt L. Strand**
VICE PRESIDENT, GENERAL MANAGER, PRODUCTS & MARKETS **Michael Ryan**
VICE PRESIDENT, CONTENT DESIGN & DELIVERY **Kimberly Meriwether David**
MANAGING DIRECTOR **Gina Boedeker**
BRAND MANAGER **Laura Wilk**
LEAD PRODUCT DEVELOPER **Rhona Robbin**
EXECUTIVE MARKETING MANAGER **Stacy Ruel Best**
MARKETING MANAGER **April Cole**
DIGITAL PRODUCT ANALYST **John Brady**
DIRECTOR, CONTENT DESIGN & DELIVERY **Terri Schiesl**
PROGRAM MANAGER **Marianne Musni**
CONTENT PROJECT MANAGER **Christine A. Vaughan**
CONTENT PROJECT MANAGER **Emily Kline**
BUYER **Laura M. Fuller**
DESIGN **Matt Backhaus**
CONTENT LICENSING SPECIALIST, IMAGES **Lori Hancock**
CONTENT LICENSING SPECIALIST, TEXT **Beth Thole**
COMPOSITOR **Laserwords Private Limited**
TYPEFACE **10/12 UniMath**
PRINTER **R. R. Donnelley**

U.S.: A Narrative History, Seventh Edition
Published by McGraw-Hill Education, 2 Penn Plaza, New York, NY 10121. Copyright © 2015 by McGraw-Hill Education. All rights reserved. Printed in the United States of America. Previous editions © 2012, 2009. No part of this publication may be reproduced or distributed in any form or by any means, or stored in a database or retrieval system, without the prior written consent of McGraw-Hill Education, including, but not limited to, in any network or other electronic storage or transmission, or broadcast for distance learning.

Some ancillaries, including electronic and print components, may not be available to customers outside the United States.

This book is printed on acid-free paper.

1 2 3 4 5 6 7 8 9 0 RMN/RMN 1 0 9 8 7 6 5 4

ISBN 978-0-07-778042-5 (complete); MHID 0-07-778042-6 (complete)

ISBN 978-0-07-351330-0 (volume 1); MHID 0-07-351330-X (volume 1)

ISBN 978-0-07-778036-4 (volume 2); MHID 0-07-778036-1 (volume 2)

Cover image credits: Miss Ting; Idaho farm; woman weaving; "Our City" lithograph of St. Louis, Janicke and Co. 1859; "Pocahantas Saving the Life of Capt. John Smith,"(detail); "Heart of the Klondike"(detail): The Library of Congress; Caesar Chavez (detail): © Arthur Schatz/Time & Life Pictures/Getty Images; Hopewell Hand: © Heritage Images/Corbis; Freedman's School: © Bettmann/Corbis; "Mandan Dog Sled," Karl Bodmer: © Free Library, Philadelphia/Bridgeman Images; "Tragic Prelude" (detail): © Kansas State Historical Society; "Mrs. Chandler" (detail): Courtesy, National Gallery of Art, Washington, D.C.; Uncle Sam with Banjo: HistoryPicks; View from Space: © NASA/JSC; Buffalo Hunt: Courtesy, National Gallery of Art, Washington.

All credits appearing on page or at the end of the book are considered to be an extension of the copyright page.

Library of Congress Control Number: 2014943610

WHAT'S NEW IN U.S.

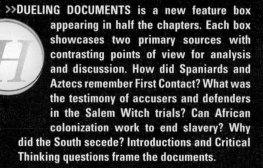

>>**DUELING DOCUMENTS** is a new feature box appearing in half the chapters. Each box showcases two primary sources with contrasting points of view for analysis and discussion. How did Spaniards and Aztecs remember First Contact? What was the testimony of accusers and defenders in the Salem Witch trials? Can African colonization work to end slavery? Why did the South secede? Introductions and Critical Thinking questions frame the documents.

>> **HISTORIAN'S TOOLBOX**, alternating with Dueling Documents, continues to showcase historical images and artifacts, asking students to focus on visual evidence and examine material culture. New items in this edition include an ancient Indian calendar from Chaco Canyon, a plantation owner's list of runaway slaves, a missionary society's lithograph, "The Printer's Angel" and an assortment of costumes worn by the Ku Klux Klan.

>> **GEOGRAPHIC QUESTIONS** have been added to many map captions to reinforce geographic literacy and to connect the maps to the chapter's relevant themes.

>> **END-OF-CHAPTER BIBLIOGRAPHIES** have been updated to reflect new scholarship.

>> **CHAPTER 1, FIRST CIVILIZATIONS OF NORTH AMERICA,** has been revised to adopt the most recent dating of key trends, such as the rise of agriculture; and naming conventions, such as the Ancestral Pueblo (rather than the Anasazi).

>> **CHAPTER 14, WESTERN EXPANSION AND THE RISE OF THE SLAVERY ISSUE,** includes a new section drawing on recent research to explain the attempts, aided by state and federal officials, to exterminate California's Indian population.

>> **CHAPTER 16, TOTAL WAR AND THE REPUBLIC,** features a new section on the consequences of death and suffering arising out of civil war. New material has been added on international diplomacy during the war; and the account of the pivotal battle of Gettysburg has been enlarged.

U.S. BRIEF CONTENTS

Contents

3 COLONIZATION AND CONFLICT IN THE SOUTH 1600–1750

4 COLONIZATION AND CONFLICT IN THE NORTH 1600–1700

NIEUW AMSTERDAM OFTE NUE NIEUW IORX OPT TEYLANT MAN

BOSTON

CHARLES TOWN

7 THE AMERICAN PEOPLE AND THE AMERICAN REVOLUTION 1775–1783

>> **AN AMERICAN STORY:**
"Will He Fight?" 120

8 CRISIS AND CONSTITUTION 1776–1789

9 THE EARLY REPUBLIC 1789–1824

11 THE RISE OF DEMOCRACY
1824–1840

>> **AN AMERICAN STORY:**
"Wanted: Curling Tongs, Cologne, and Silk-Stockings . . ."   **205**

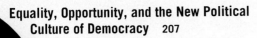

12 AFIRE WITH FAITH
1820–1850

13 THE OLD SOUTH 1820–1860

14 WESTERN EXPANSION AND THE RISE OF THE SLAVERY ISSUE 1820–1850

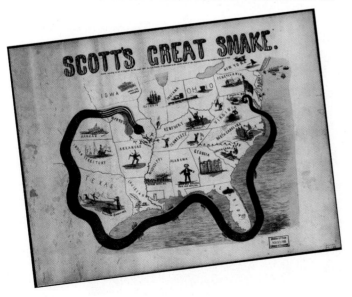

17 RECONSTRUCTING THE UNION 1865–1877

Primary sources help students think critically about history.

DUELING DOCUMENTS

Two primary source documents offer contrasting perspectives on key events for analysis and discussion. Introductions and Critical Thinking questions frame the documents.

Dueling DOCUMENTS

WHO WAS TO BLAME FOR THE BOSTON MASSACRE?

Following the shootings in King Street, Captain Thomas Preston and six of his men stood trial for murder. Two radical patriot lawyers, Josiah Quincy Jr., and future president John Adams, served as defense council. Convinced that Boston must prove itself fair and faithful to the rule of law, both lawyers performed brilliantly. The jury acquitted Preston and four of the soldiers, and convicted two others of manslaughter. The depositions from the trial provide some of our best evidence for how soldiers and Bostonians viewed the standoff differently.

DOCUMENT 1
Deposition of Captain Thomas Preston, March 1770

The mob still increased and were more outrageous, striking their clubs or bludgeons one against another, and calling out, come on you rascals, you bloody backs, you lobster scoundrels, fire if you dare, G-d damn you, fire and be damned, we know you dare not, and much more such language was used. At this time I was between the soldiers and the mob, parleying with, and endeavouring all in my power to persuade them to retire peaceably, but to no purpose. They advanced to the points of the bayonets, struck some of them and even the muzzles of the pieces, and seemed to be endeavouring to close with the soldiers. On which some well-behaved persons asked me if the guns were charged. I replied yes. They then asked me if I intended to order the men to fire. I answered no, by no means, observing to them that I was advanced before the muzzles of the men's pieces, and must fall a sacrifice if they fired; that the soldiers were upon the half cock and charged bayonets, and my giving the word fire under those circumstances would prove me to be no officer. While I was thus speaking, one of the soldiers having received a severe blow with a stick, stepped a little on one side and instantly fired, on which turning to and asking him why he fired without orders, I was struck with a club on my arm, which for some time deprived me of the use of it, which blow had it been placed on my head, most probably would have destroyed me. On this a general attack was made on the men by a great number of heavy clubs and snowballs being thrown at them, by which all our lives were in imminent danger, some persons at the same time from behind calling out, damn your bloods—why don't you fire. Instantly three or four of the soldiers fired, one after another, and directly after three more in the same confusion and hurry. The mob then ran away, except three unhappy men who instantly expired, in which number was Mr. Gray at whose rope-walk the prior quarrels took place; one more is since dead, three others are dangerously, and four slightly wounded. The whole of this melancholy affair was transacted in almost 20 minutes. On my asking the soldiers why they fired without orders, they said they heard the word fire and supposed it came from me. This might be the case as many of the mob called out fire, fire, but I assured the men that I gave no such order; that my words were, don't fire, stop your firing. In short, it was scarcely possible for the soldiers to know who said fire, or don't fire, or stop your firing.

DOCUMENT 2
Deposition of Robert Goddard, March 1770

The Soldiers came up to the Centinel and the Officer told them to place themselves and they formed a half moon. The Captain told the Boys to go home least there should be murder done. They were throwing Snow balls. Did not go off but threw more Snow balls. The Capt. was behind the Soldiers. The Captain told them to fire. One Gun went off. A Sailor or Townsman struck the Captain. He thereupon said damn your bloods fire think I'll be treated in this manner. This Man that struck the Captain came from among the People who were 7 feet off and were round on one wing. I saw no person speak to him. I was so near I should have seen it. After the Capt. said Damn your bloods fire they all fired one after another about 7 or 8 in all, and then the officer bid Prime and load again. He stood behind all the time. Mr. Lee went up to the officer and called the officer by name Capt. Preston, I saw him coming down from the Guard behind the Party. I went to Gaol the next day being sworn for the Grand Jury to see the Captain. Then said pointing to him that's the person who gave the word to fire. He said if you swear that you will ruin me everlastingly. I was so near the officer when he gave the word fire that I could touch him. His face was towards me. He stood in the middle behind the Men. I looked him in the face. He then stood within the circle. When he told 'em to fire he turned about to me. I looked him in the face.

THINKING CRITICALLY

Preston and Goddard come to different conclusions about the shootings but describe similar details (the snowballs, the man who struck Preston). Can details from these two accounts be reconciled? Do they simply have different perspectives on the same event, or do you think one of the depositions must be misleading? Given the tensions these accounts relate, do you think that a violent confrontation between soldiers and Bostonians was inevitable?

WITNESS

Vivid quotes from diaries, letters, and other texts provide a sense of how individuals experienced historical events.

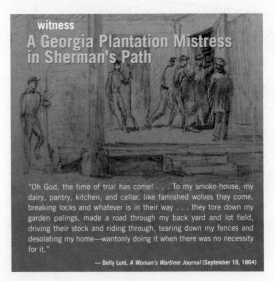

witness
A Georgia Plantation Mistress in Sherman's Path

"Oh God, the time of trial has come! . . . To my smoke-house, my dairy, pantry, kitchen, and cellar, like famished wolves they come, breaking locks and whatever is in their way . . . they tore down my garden palings, made a road through my back yard and lot field, driving their stock and riding through, tearing down my fences and desolating my home—wantonly doing it when there was no necessity for it."

— Dolly Lunt, *A Woman's Wartime Journal* (September 19, 1864)

HISTORIAN'S TOOLBOX

These feature boxes, which alternate with Dueling Documents, showcase historical images and artifacts, asking students to focus on visual evidence and examine material culture. Introductions and Critical Thinking questions frame the images.

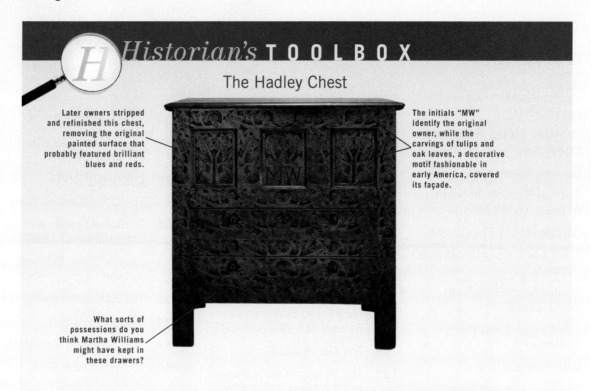

Historian's **TOOLBOX**

The Hadley Chest

Later owners stripped and refinished this chest, removing the original painted surface that probably featured brilliant blues and reds.

The initials "MW" identify the original owner, while the carvings of tulips and oak leaves, a decorative motif fashionable in early America, covered its façade.

What sorts of possessions do you think Martha Williams might have kept in these drawers?

Objects can help historians appreciate complex connections. For example, the first owner of this exuberantly designed cupboard of white oak and pine, Martha Williams, lived in western Massachusetts during the decades around 1700, a time of chronic warfare between the English and their French and Indian allies. Most likely she received the chest as part of her dowry when she married Edward Partridge in 1707, its very solidity assuring this young couple of stability and continuity in a violent and insecure world. Items of similar design have turned up elsewhere in New England, and their first collector dubbed them "Hadley chests," a distinct local craft tradition. This chest and the textiles it probably contained open a window into the sorts of property Anglo-American women retained in marriage and passed down to their descendants. According to historian Laurel Thatcher Ulrich, an artifact such as the Hadley chest "teaches us that material objects were not only markers of wealth but devices for building relationships and lineages over time, and it helps us to understand the cultural framework within which ordinary women became creators as well as custodians of household goods."

THINKING CRITICALLY

Why did Martha Williams have her maiden name emblazoned on the cupboard? Might it have something to do with the restrictive English laws about what women could own in marriage? Do you think women in New Spain or New France would have done the same? What might objects such as these tell us about how women viewed property and identity in British North America?

Source: © Shelburne Museum, Shelburne, Vermont

OPINION

Ideal for class discussion or writing, these questions ask students to offer opinions on debated issues.

Opinion

Does the Electoral College ensure fair outcomes in presidential contests?

List of MAPS

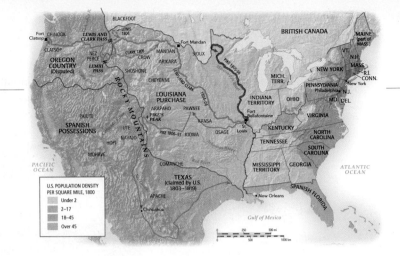

A map of the United States appears on the inside front cover, while a World map appears on the inside back cover.

List of CONNECT HISTORY PRIMARY SOURCE DOCUMENTS

The following primary source documents, carefully selected by the authors to coordinate with this program, are available in Connect History at http://connect.mheducation.com. Documents include an explanatory headnote and are followed by discussion questions.

Choose from many of these documents—or hundreds of others—to customize your print text by visiting McGraw-Hill's Create at www.mcgrawhillcreate.com.

We would like to express our deep appreciation to the following individuals who contributed to the development of our U.S. history programs:

Reviewers of *U.S.: A Narrative History*

Mary Adams,
City College of San Francisco

Chris Bell,
Edmonds Community College

James Blain,
McNeese State University

Roger Bowerman,
Glendale Community College

Jeffrey Brown,
New Mexico State University

Ann Chirhart,
Indiana State University

Bradley Clampitt,
East Central University

Patty Colman,
Moorpark College

Michael Colomaio,
Alfred State University

Clarissa Confer,
California University of Pennsylvania

Cara Converse,
Moorpark College

William Cooley,
Walsh University

Aaron Cowen,
Slippery Rock University

David Cullen,
Collins College, Plano

David Dalton,
College of the Ozarks

Brandon Franke,
Blinn College

Christos Frentzos,
Austin Peay State University

Tabetha Garman,
North East State University

George Gastil,
Grossmont College

Frank Gilbert,
Southeastern Oklahoma State University

Jim Good,
Lone Star College, North Harris

Patricia Gower,
University of the Incarnate Word

Charles Grear,
Prairie View A&M

Devethia Guillory,
Prairie View A&M

Debbie Hargis,
Odessa College

Tom Heiting,
Odessa College

Jennifer Helgren,
University of the Pacific

Jay Hester,
Sierra College

Justin Horton,
Thomas Nelson Community College

Carol Keller,
San Antonio College

Dennis Kortheuer,
California State University, Long Beach

Pat Ledbetter,
Texas College

Mary Lewis,
Jacksonville College

Tammi Littrel,
Chadron State College

Philbert Martin,
San Jacinto College, South

Bob McConaughy,
Austin Community College

James Mills,
University of Texas, Brownsville

Russell Mitchell,
Tarrant County College, Southeast

Michael Namorato,
University of Mississippi

Bret Nelson,
San Jacinto College, North

Alison Ollinger-Riefstahl,
Mercyhurst Northeast College

Stephen Patnodes,
Farmingdale State University

Edward Richey,
University of North Texas

Joaquin Riveya-Martinez,
Texas State University, San Marcos

Stephen Rockenbach,
Virginia State University

Norman Rodriguez,
John Wood Community College

Todd Romero,
University of Houston

Michele Rotunda,
Rutgers University, Newark

Steven Short,
Collin College

Richard Sorrel,
Brookdale Community College

Maureen Melvin Sowa,
Bristol Community College

Jodi Steeley,
Merced Community College

Rita Thomas,
Northern Kentucky University

Richard Trimble,
Ocean County College

Ruth Truss,
University of Montevallo

Salli Vargis,
Georgia Perimeter College

William Wantland,
Mount Vernon Nazarene University

Chad Wooley,
Tarrant County College

About the Authors

James West Davidson received his Ph.D. from Yale University. A historian who has pursued a full-time writing career, he is the author of numerous books, among them *After the Fact: The Art of Historical Detection* (with Mark H. Lytle), *The Logic of Millennial Thought: Eighteenth-Century New England,* and *Great Heart: The History of a Labrador Adventure* (with John Rugge). He is co-editor with Michael Stoff of the *Oxford New Narratives in American History,* in which his own most recent book appears: *'They Say': Ida B. Wells and the Reconstruction of Race.*

Brian DeLay received his Ph.D. from Harvard and is an Associate Professor of History at the University of California, Berkeley. He is a frequent guest speaker at teacher workshops across the country and has won several prizes for his book *War of a Thousand Deserts: Indian Raids and the U.S.-Mexican War.*

Christine Leigh Heyrman is the Robert W. and Shirley P. Grimble Professor of American History at the University of Delaware. She received a Ph.D. in American Studies from Yale University and is the author of *Commerce and Culture: The Maritime Communities of Colonial Massachusetts, 1690–1750.* Her book *Southern Cross: The Beginnings of the Bible Belt* was awarded the Bancroft Prize. She is currently writing a book about evangelical views of Islam in the early nineteenth century.

Mark H. Lytle, a Ph.D. from Yale University, is Professor of History and Chair of the Environmental Studies Program at Bard College. He has served two years as Mary Ball Washington Professor of American History at University College, Dublin, in Ireland. His publications include *The Origins of the Iranian-American Alliance, 1941–1953, After the Fact: The Art of Historical Detection* (with James West Davidson), *America's Uncivil Wars: The Sixties Era from Elvis to the Fall of Richard Nixon,* and most recently, *The Gentle Subversive: Rachel Carson, Silent Spring, and the Rise of the Environmental Movement.* He is also co-editor of a joint issue of the journals *Diplomatic History* and *Environmental History* dedicated to the field of environmental diplomacy.

Michael B. Stoff is Associate Professor of History and Director of the Plan II Honors Program at the University of Texas at Austin. The recipient of a Ph.D. from Yale University, he has been honored many times for his teaching, most recently with election to the Academy of Distinguished Teachers. He is the author of *Oil, War, and American Security: The Search for a National Policy on Foreign Oil, 1941–1947,* co-editor (with Jonathan Fanton and R. Hall Williams) of *The Manhattan Project: A Documentary Introduction to the Atomic Age,* and series co-editor (with James West Davidson) of the *Oxford New Narratives in American History.* He is currently working on a narrative of the bombing of Nagasaki.

1 The First Civilizations of North America

From the air, this serpentine mound fashioned thousands of years ago still stands out in bold relief. Located in southern Ohio, it extends from the snake's coiled tail at the left of the photo to the open mouth at the top right. The snake's tail points toward the winter solstice sunrise, while the mouth is oriented to the summer solstice sunrise.

>> **An American Story**

THE POWER OF A HIDDEN PAST

Stories told about the past have power over both the present and the future. Until recently most students were taught that American history began several centuries ago—with the "discovery" of America by Columbus, or with the English colonization of Jamestown and Plymouth. History books ignored or trivialized the continent's precontact history. But the reminders of that hidden past are everywhere. Scattered across the United States are thousands of ancient archaeological

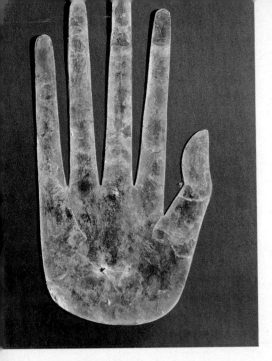

∧ This image of a human hand, discovered in a Hopewell mound, was cut from a single sheet of mica.

sites and hundreds of examples of monumental architecture, still imposing even after centuries of erosion, looting, and destruction.

Man-made earthen mounds, some nearly 5,000 years old, exist throughout eastern North America in a bewildering variety of shapes and sizes. Many are easily mistaken for modest hills, but others evoke wonder. In present-day Louisiana an ancient town with earthworks took laborers an estimated 5 million work hours to construct. In Ohio a massive serpent effigy snakes for a quarter mile across the countryside, its head aligned to the summer solstice. In Illinois a vast, earthen construct covers 16 acres at its base and once reached as high as a 10-story building.

Observers in the colonial and revolutionary eras looked on such sites as curiosities and marvels. George Washington, Thomas Jefferson, and other prominent Americans collected ancient artifacts, took a keen interest in the excavation of mounds, and speculated about the Indian civilizations that created them. Travelers explored these strange mounds, trying to imagine in their mind's eye the peoples who had built them. In 1795 the Reverend James Smith traced the boundaries of a mound wall that was strategically placed to protect a neck of land along a looping river bend in the Ohio valley. "The wall at present is so mouldered down that a man could easily ride over it. It is however about 10 feet, as near as I can judge, in perpendicular height. . . . In one place I observe a breach in the wall about 60 feet wide, where I suppose the gate formerly stood through which the people passed in and out of this stronghold." Smith was astonished by the size of the project. "Compared with this," he exclaimed, "what feeble and insignificant works are those of Fort Hamilton or Fort Washington! They are no more in comparison to it than a rail fence is to a brick wall."

But in the 1830s and 1840s, as Americans sought to drive Indians west of the Mississippi and then confine them on smaller and smaller reservations, many began thinking differently about the continent's ancient sites. Surely the simple and "savage" people just then being expelled from American life could not have constructed such inspiring monuments. Politicians, writers, and even some influential scientists dismissed the claim that North America's ancient architecture had been built by the ancestors of contemporary Indians and instead attributed the mounds to peoples of Europe, Africa, or Asia—Hindus, perhaps, or Israelites, Egyptians, or Japanese. Many nineteenth-century Americans found special comfort in a tale about King Madoc from Wales, who supposedly shipwrecked in the Americas in the twelfth century and had left behind a small but ingenious population of Welsh pioneers who built the mysterious mounds before being overrun by Indians. The Welsh hypothesis seemed to offer poetic justice, because it implied that nineteenth-century Indians were only receiving a fitting punishment for what their ancestors had done to the remarkable mound builders from Wales.

These fanciful tales were discredited in the late nineteenth and early twentieth centuries. In recent decades archaeologists working across the Americas have discovered in more detail how native peoples built the Western Hemisphere's ancient architecture. They have also helped to make clear the degree to which prejudice and politics have blinded European Americans to the complexity, wonder, and significance of America's history before 1492. Fifteen thousand years of human habitation in North America allowed a broad range of cultures to develop, based on agriculture as well as hunting and gathering. In North America a population in the millions spoke hundreds of languages. Cities evolved as well as towns and farms, exhibiting great diversity in their cultural, political, economic, and religious organization. <<

What's to Come

A CONTINENT OF CULTURES

Recent breakthroughs in archaeology and genetics have demonstrated that the first inhabitants of the Americas arrived from Siberia at least 15,500 years ago BP.* Gradually these **nomads** filtered south—ward, some likely following the Pacific coastline in small boats, others making their way down a narrow, glacier—free corridor along the eastern base of the Rocky Mountains and onto the northern Great Plains. There they found and hunted a stunning array of huge mammals, so—called mega—fauna. These animals included mammoths that were twice as heavy as elephants, giant bison, sloths that were taller than giraffes, several kinds of camels, and

> **nomad** a member of a group of people who have no fixed home and who move about, usually seasonally, in pursuit of food, water, and other resources.

terrifying, 8—foot—long lions. Within a few thousand years the descendants of these Siberians, people whom Columbus would wishfully dub "Indians," had spread throughout the length and breadth of the Americas.

This first colonization of the Americas coincided with, and perhaps accelerated, profound changes in the natural world. The last Ice Age literally melted away as warmer global temperatures freed the great reservoirs of water once locked in glaciers. A rise in sea levels inundated the Bering Strait, submerging the land bridge and creating new lakes and river systems. The emergence of new **ecosystems**—climates, waterways, and land environments in which humans interacted with other animals and plants—made for ever—greater diversity. The first human inhabitants of the Americas had fed, clothed, warmed, and armed themselves in part by hunting megafauna, and some combination of overhunting and climate change resulted in the extinction of most of these giants by the end of the Ice Age. As glaciers receded and human populations increased, the first Americans had to adapt to changing conditions. They adjusted by hunting smaller animals with new, more specialized kinds of stone tools and by learning to exploit particular places more efficiently.

> **ecosystem** a community and/or region studied as a system of functioning relationships between organisms and their environments.

So it was that between 10,000 and 2,500 years ago distinctive regional cultures developed among the peoples of the Americas. Those who remained in the Great Plains turned to hunting the much smaller descendants of the now—extinct giant bison; those in the

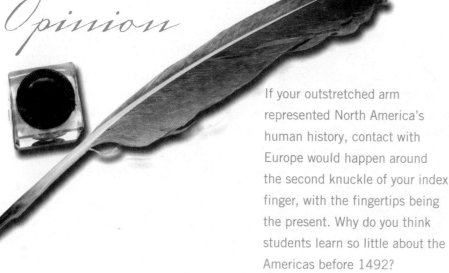

Opinion

If your outstretched arm represented North America's human history, contact with Europe would happen around the second knuckle of your index finger, with the fingertips being the present. Why do you think students learn so little about the Americas before 1492?

---

*Before the Present, used most commonly by archaeologists when the time spans are in multiple thousands of years. This text will also use CE for Common Era, equivalent to the Christian era or AD; BCE is Before the Common Era, equivalent to BC.

deserts of the Great Basin survived on small game, seeds, and edible plants; those in the Pacific Northwest relied mainly on fishing; and those east of the Mississippi, besides fishing and gathering, tracked deer and bear and trapped smaller game animals and birds. Over these same centuries, what once seems to have been an original, common language evolved into regional dialects and eventually into a multitude of distinct languages. Linguistic diversity paced other sorts of divergences, in social organizations, kinship practices, politics, and religion. Technological and cultural unity gave way to striking regional diversity as the first Americans learned how to best exploit their particular environments. Glimpses of these profound changes may be found today in burials, stone tools, and some precious sites of long-term or repeated occupation.

Cultures of Ancient Mexico >> To the south, pioneers in **Mesoamerica** began domesticating plants 10,000 years ago. Over the next several thousand years farmers added other crops, including beans, tomatoes, and especially corn,

Mesoamerica the area stretching from present-day central Mexico southward through Honduras and Nicaragua, in which pre-Columbian civilizations developed.

to an agricultural revolution that would transform life through much of the Americas. Because many crops could be dried and stored, agriculture allowed these first farmers to settle in one place.

By about 1500 BCE farming villages began giving way to larger societies, to richer and more advanced cultures. As the abundant food supply steadily expanded their populations, people began specializing in certain kinds of work. While most continued to labor on the land, others became craftworkers and merchants, architects and artists, warriors and priests. Their built environment reflected this social change as humble villages expanded into skillfully planned urban sites that were centers of trade, government, artistic display, and religious ceremony.

The Olmecs, the first city builders in the Americas, constructed large plazas and pyramidal structures and sculpted enormous heads chiseled from basalt. The Olmec cultural influence gradually spread throughout Mesoamerica, perhaps as a result of the Olmecs' trade with neighboring peoples. By about 100 BCE the Olmecs' example had inspired the flowering of Teotihuacán from a small town in central Mexico into a metropolis of towering pyramids. The city had bustling marketplaces, palaces decorated with mural paintings that housed elite warriors and priests, schools for their children, and sprawling suburbs for commoners. At its height, around 650 CE, Teotihuacán spanned more than 10 square miles and had a population of perhaps a quarter million—larger even than that of Rome at the time.

More impressive still were the achievements of the Mayas, who benefited from their contacts with both the Olmecs and Teotihuacán. In the lowland jungles of Mesoamerica they built cities filled with palaces, bridges, aqueducts, baths, astronomical observatories, and pyramids topped with temples. Their priests developed a written language, their mathematicians discovered the zero, and their astronomers devised a calendar more accurate than any then existing. In its glory, between the third and ninth century CE, the Mayan civilization boasted some 50 urban centers scattered throughout the Yucatán Peninsula, Belize, Guatemala, and Honduras.

But neither the earliest urban centers of the Olmecs nor the glittering city-state of Teotihuacán survived. Even the glories of the Maya had stalled by 900 CE. Like the ancient civilizations of Greece and Rome, they thrived for centuries and then declined. Scholars still debate the reasons for their collapse. Military attack may have brought about their ruin, or perhaps their large populations exhausted local resources.

Mayan grandeur was eventually rivaled in the Valley of Mexico. In the middle of the thirteenth century the Aztecs, a people who had originally lived on Mesoamerica's northern frontiers, swept south and settled in central Mexico. By the end of the fifteenth century they ruled over a vast empire from their capital at Tenochtitlán, an island metropolis of perhaps a quarter of a million people. At its center lay a large plaza bordered by sumptuous palaces and the Great Temple of the Sun. Beyond stood three broad causeways connecting the island to the mainland, many other

⋏ Aztec merchants, or pochtecas, spoke many languages and traveled on foot great distances throughout Mesoamerica and parts of North America. Pictured at left is Yacatecuhtli, Lord Nose, the patron god of merchants. He carries a symbol of the crossroads, with bare footprints. The merchant on the right carries a cargo of quetzal birds.

tall temples adorned with brightly painted carved images of the gods, zoological and botanical gardens, and well–stocked marketplaces. Through Tenochtitlán's canals flowed gold, silver, exotic feathers and jewels, cocoa, and millions of pounds of maize—all trade goods and tribute from the several million other peoples in the region subjugated by the Aztecs.

Unsurpassed in power and wealth, in technological and artistic attainments, theirs was also a highly stratified society. The Aztec ruler, or Chief Speaker, shared governing power with the aristocrats who monopolized all positions of religious, military, and political leadership, while the commoners—merchants, farmers, and craftworkers—performed all manual labor. There were slaves as well, some captives taken in war, others from the ranks of commoners forced by poverty to sell themselves or their children.

Farmers, Potters, and Builders of the Southwest

>> Recent discoveries suggest that Mesoamerican crops and farming techniques began making their way north to the American Southwest as early as 2100 BCE, though it would be nearly two millennia before regional communities fully adopted sedentary agricultural lifestyles. The most successful full–time farmers in the region were the Mogollon and Hohokam peoples, two cultures that flourished in New Mexico and southern Arizona during the first millennium CE. Both tended to cluster their dwellings near streams, which allowed them to adopt the systems of irrigation as well as the maize cultivation of central Mexico. The Mogollon came to be the master potters of the Southwest. The Hohokam pioneered vast and complex irrigation systems in arid southern Arizona that allowed them to support one of the largest populations in precontact North America.

Their neighbors to the north in what is now known as the Four Corners Region of Arizona, Colorado, New Mexico, and Utah, commonly referred to by the term *Anasazi*, are today more properly known as the Ancestral Pueblo peoples. The Ancestral Puebloans adapted corn, beans, and squash to the relatively high altitude of the Colorado Plateau and soon parlayed their growing surplus and prosperity into societies of considerable complexity. Their most stunning achievements were villages of exquisitely executed masonry buildings—apartment–like structures up to four stories high and containing hundreds of rooms at such places as Mesa Verde (Colorado) and Canyon de Chelly (Arizona). Villages in Chaco Canyon (New Mexico), the largest center of Ancestral Puebloan settlement, were linked to the wider region by hundreds of miles of wide, straight roads.

Besides their impressive dwellings, the Ancestral Puebloans filled their towns with religious shrines, astronomical observatories, and stations for sending signals to other villages. Their craftworkers fashioned delicate woven baskets, beautiful feather and hide sashes, decorated pottery, and turquoise jewelry that they traded throughout the region and beyond. For nearly a thousand years this civilization prospered, reaching its zenith between about 900 and 1100 CE. During those three centuries the population grew to approximately 30,000 spread over 50,000 square miles, a total area larger than present–day California.

Chiefdoms of the Eastern Woodlands

>>East of the Mississippi, Indian societies prospered in valleys near great rivers (Mississippi, Ohio, Tennessee, and Cumberland), the shores of the Great Lakes, and the coast of the Atlantic. Everywhere the earliest inhabitants depended on a combination of fishing, gathering, and hunting—mainly deer but also bear, raccoon, and a variety of birds. Around 2500 BCE some groups in the temperate, fertile Southeast began growing the gourds and pumpkins first cultivated by Mesoamerican farmers, and later they also adopted the cultivation of maize. Like the ancient farmers of the Southwest, most Eastern Woodland peoples continued to subsist largely on animals, fish, and nuts, all of which were abundant enough to meet their needs and even to expand their numbers.

Indeed, many of the mysterious earthen mounds that would so fascinate Europeans were built by peoples who did not farm. About 1000 BCE residents of a place now known as Poverty Point in northeastern Louisiana fashioned spectacular earthworks—six semicircular rings that rose 9 feet in height and covered more than half a mile in diameter. Although these structures might have been sites for studying the planets and stars, hundreds of other mounds—built about 2,000 years ago by the Adena and the Hopewell cultures of the Ohio and Mississippi valleys—served as the burial places of their leading men and women. Alongside the corpses mourners heaped their richest goods—headdresses of antlers, necklaces of copper, troves of shells and pearls—rare and precious items imported from as far north as Canada, as far west as Wyoming, and as far east as Florida. All these mounds attest powerfully not only to the skill and sheer numbers of their builders but also to the complexity of these ancient societies, their elaborate religious practices, and the wide scope of their trading networks.

Even so, the most magnificent culture of the ancient Eastern Woodlands, the Mississippian, owed much of its prominence to farming. By the twelfth century CE Mississippians had emerged as the premier city–builders north of the Rio Grande, and their towns radiated for hundreds of miles in every direction from the hub of their trading network at Cahokia, a port city of several thousand located directly across

An Ancient Calendar

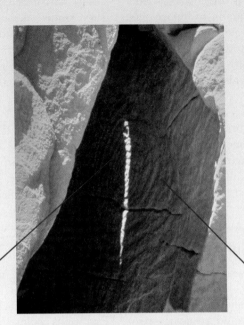

During summer solstice, the spiral is bisected by a single shaft of light.

Why might the Chacoans have used a spiral rather than another image to make this

On a blazing hot summer day in 1977, Anna Sofaer climbed up to the top of Fajada Butte in Chaco Canyon, New Mexico, spotted three sandstone slabs resting carefully against a wall, and walked over to investigate. What she saw against the wall astounded her: a spiral glyph, bisected by a pure shaft of light. An artist and amateur archaeologist, Sofaer had keen interest in how indigenous American cultures harnessed light and shadow in their architecture. Knowing that it was nearly the summer solstice, she recognized instantly that she'd discovered an ancient Anasazi calendar. Later research revealed that the device also marked the winter solstice, the summer and winter equinoxes, and the extremes of the moon's 18–19 year cycle (the major and minor standstills). These discoveries prompted still more research, and scholars now believe that there are structures throughout Chaco Canyon aligned to solar and lunar events.

THINKING CRITICALLY

What practical reasons might there have been to build these sorts of sun and moon calendars? Might there have been cultural, religious, or social purposes to track accurately the movements of the sun and moon?

from present–day St. Louis at the confluence of the Missouri and the Mississippi Rivers. Cahokia's many broad plazas teemed with farmers hauling their corn, squash, and beans and with craftworkers and merchants plying their wares. But what commanded every eye were the structures surrounding the plazas—more than 100 flat–topped pyramidal mounds crowned by religious temples and elite dwellings.

Life on the Great Plains >> Cahokia's size and power depended on consistent agricultural surpluses. Outside the Southwest and the river valleys of the East, agriculture played a smaller role in shaping North American societies. On the Great Plains, for example, some people did cultivate corn, beans, squash,

and sunflowers, near reliable rivers and streams. But more typically Plains communities depended on hunting and foraging, migrating to exploit seasonally variable resources. Plains hunters pursued game on foot; the horses that had once roamed the Americas became extinct after the last Ice Age. Sometimes large groups of people worked together to drive bison over cliffs or to trap them in corrals. The aridity of the plains made it a dynamic and unpredictable place to live. During times of reliable rainfall, bison populations boomed, hunters flocked to the region, and agricultural communities blossomed alongside major rivers. But sometimes centuries passed with lower–than–average precipitation, and families abandoned the plains for eastern river valleys or the foothills of the Rocky Mountains.

Survival in the Great Basin >> Some peoples west of the Great Plains also kept to older ways of subsistence. Among them were the Numic–speaking peoples of the Great Basin, which includes present–day Nevada and Utah, eastern California, and western Wyoming and Colorado. Small family groups scoured their stark, arid landscape for the limited supplies of food it yielded, moving with each passing season to make the most of their environment. Men tracked elk and antelope and trapped smaller animals, birds, even toads, rattlesnakes, and insects. But the staples of their diet were edible seeds, nuts, and plants, which women gathered and stored in woven baskets to consume in times of scarcity. Several families occasionally hunted together or wintered in common quarters, but because the desert heat and soil defied farming, these bands usually numbered no more than about 50 people.

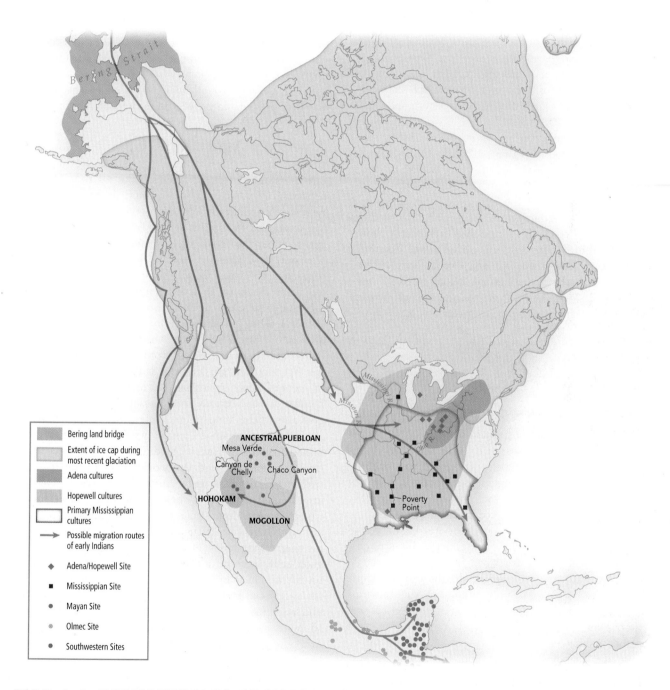

Legend:
- Bering land bridge
- Extent of ice cap during most recent glaciation
- Adena cultures
- Hopewell cultures
- Primary Mississippian cultures
- Possible migration routes of early Indians
- ◆ Adena/Hopewell Site
- ■ Mississippian Site
- ● Mayan Site
- ● Olmec Site
- ● Southwestern Sites

Map labels: Bering Strait, ANCESTRAL PUEBLOAN, Mesa Verde, Canyon de Chelly, Chaco Canyon, HOHOKAM, MOGOLLON, Poverty Point, Mississippi R., Missouri R.

MAP 1.1: EARLY PEOPLES OF NORTH AMERICA

Migration routes across the Bering Strait from Asia were taken by peoples whose descendants created the major civilizations of ancient Americans. The influence of Mesoamerica is most striking among the cultures of the Southwest and the Mississippians.
How would the presence or absence of the ice cap affect the timing of migration over the Bering land bridge?

The Plenty of the Pacific Northwest >> The

rugged stretch of coast from the southern banks of present—day British Columbia to northern California has always been an extraordinarily rich natural environment. Its mild climate and abundant rainfall yield forests lush with plants and game; its bays and rivers teem with salmon and halibut, its oceans with whales and porpoises, and its rocky beaches with seals, otters, abalone, mussels, and clams. Agriculture was unnecessary in such a bountiful place. From their villages on the banks of rivers, the shores of bays, and the beaches of low—lying offshore islands, the ancestors of the Nootkans, Makahs, Tlingits, Tshimshians, and Kwakiutls speared or netted salmon, trapped sea mammals, gathered shellfish, and launched canoes. The largest of these craft, from which they harpooned whales, measured 45 feet bow to stern and nearly 6 feet wide.

By the fifteenth century these fecund lands supported a population of perhaps 130,000. They also permitted a culture with the leisure time needed to create works of art as well as an elaborate social and ceremonial life. The peoples of the Northwest built houses and canoes from red cedar; carved bowls and dishes from red alder; crafted paddles and harpoon shafts, bows, and clubs from Pacific yew; and wove baskets from bark and blankets from mountain goat wool. They evolved a society with sharp distinctions among nobles, commoners, and slaves, the last group being mainly women and children captured in raids on other villages. Non-slaves devoted their lives to accumulating and then redistributing their wealth among other villagers in elaborate potlatch ceremonies in order to confirm or enhance their social prestige.

The Frozen North >> Most of present—day Can-

ada and Alaska was inhospitable to agriculture. In the farthest northern reaches—a treeless belt of Arctic tundra—temperatures fell below freezing for most of the year. The Subarctic, although densely forested, had only about 100 frost—free days each year. As a result, the peoples of both regions survived by fishing and hunting. The Inuit, or Eskimos, of northern Alaska harvested whales from their umiaks, boats made by stretch—ing walrus skin over a driftwood frame and that could bear more than a ton of weight. In the central Arctic they tracked seals. The inhabitants of the Subarc-tic, both Algonquian—speaking peoples in the East and Athapaskan speakers of the West, moved from their summer fishing camps to berry patches in the fall to moose and caribou hunting grounds in the winter.

 REVIEW

How did native cultures differ region to region, and what accounts for these differences?

INNOVATIONS AND LIMITATIONS

The first Americans therefore expressed, governed, and supported themselves in a broad variety of ways. And yet they shared certain core characteristics, including the desire and ability to reshape their world. Whether they lived in forests, coastal regions, jungles, or prairies, whether they inhabited high mountains or low deserts, native communities experimented constantly with the resources around them. Over the course of millennia nearly all the Western Hemi—sphere's peoples found ways to change the natural world in order to improve and enrich their lives.

America's Agricultural Gifts >> No inno-

vation proved more crucial to human history than native manipulation of plants. Like all first farmers, agricultural pioneers in the Americas began experimenting accidentally. Modern—day species of corn, for example, probably derive from a Mesoamerican grass known as teosinte. It seems that ancient peoples gathered teosinte to collect its small grains. By selecting the grains that best suited them and bring—ing them back to their settlements, and by return—ing the grains to the soil through spillage or waste disposal, they unintentionally began the process of domestic cultivation. Soon these first farmers began deliberately saving seeds from the best plants and sowing them in gardens. In this way over hundreds of generations, American farmers transformed the modest teosinte grass into a staple crop that would give rise to the hemisphere's mightiest civilizations.

Indeed, ever since contact with Europe, the great breakthroughs in Native American farming have sus—tained peoples around the world. In addition to corn, the first Americans gave humanity scores of variet—ies of squash, potatoes, beans, and other basic foods. Today plants domesticated by indigenous Americans account for three—fifths of the world's crops, includ—ing many that have revolutionized the global diet. For good or ill, a handful of corn species occupies the cen—ter of the contemporary American diet. In addition to its traditional forms, corn is consumed in chips, breads, and breakfast cereals; corn syrup sweeteners are added to many of our processed foods and nearly all soft drinks; and corn is fed to almost all animals grown to be consumed, even farmed fish.

Other Native American crops have become inte—gral to diets all over the world. Potatoes revolutionized northern European life in the centuries after con—tact, helping to avert famine and boost populations in several countries. Ireland's population tripled in

^ Theodore de Bry, *Florida Indians Planting Maize.* De Bry claimed that this image, produced and published in 1591, was based on a colonist's direct observation. Recently, however, scholars have noted that the image likely contains a variety of inaccuracies. Except for the digging stick, the baskets and tools are all European in design. Moreover, the image suggests that men and women shared agricultural labor, whereas in most American societies this work fell primarily to women and children.

the century after the introduction of potatoes. Beans and peanuts became prized for their protein content in Asia. And in Africa, corn, manioc, and other New World crops so improved diets and overall health that the resulting rise in population may have offset the population lost to the Atlantic slave trade.

Landscapers >>
Plant domestication requires the smallest of changes, changes farmers slowly encourage at the genetic level. But native peoples in the pre-contact Americas transformed their world on grand scales as well. In the Andes, Peruvian engineers put people to work by the tens of thousands, creating an astonishing patchwork of terraces, dykes, and canals designed to maximize agricultural productivity. Similar public-works projects transformed large parts of central Mexico and the Yucatán. Even today, after several centuries of disuse, overgrowth, and even deliberate destruction, human-shaped landscapes dating from the precontact period still cover thousands of square miles of the Americas.

Recently scholars have begun to find evidence of incredible manipulation of landscapes and environments in the least likely places. The vast Amazon rainforest has long been seen by Westerners as an imposing symbol of untouched nature. But it now seems that much of the Amazon was in fact made by people. Whereas farmers elsewhere in the world domesticated plants for their gardens and fields, farmers in the Amazon cultivated food-bearing trees for thousands of years, cutting down less useful species and replacing them with ones that better suited human needs. All told there are more than 70 different species of domesticated trees throughout the Amazon.

At least one-eighth of the nonflooded rain forest was directly or indirectly created by humans. Likewise, native peoples laboriously improved the soil across as much as a tenth of the Amazon, mixing it with charcoal and a variety of organic materials. These managed soils are more than 10 times as productive as untreated soils in the Amazon. Today farmers in the region still eagerly search for the places where precontact peoples enriched the earth.

Native North Americans likewise transformed their local environments. Sometimes they moved forests. Ancestral Puebloans cut down and transported more than 200,000 trees to construct the floors and the roofs of the monumental buildings in Chaco Canyon. Sometimes they moved rivers. By taming the waters of the Salt and the Gila Rivers in present-day Arizona with the most extensive system of irrigation canals anywhere in precontact North America, the Hohokam were able to support large populations in a desert environment. And sometimes they moved the land itself. Twenty-two million cubic feet of earth were moved to construct just one building in the Mississippian city of Cahokia.

Indians also employed fire to systematically reshape landscapes across the continent. Throughout North America's great eastern and western forests, native peoples periodically set low fires to consume under-growth and fallen trees. In this way the continent's first inhabitants managed forests and also animals. Burning enriched the soil and encouraged the growth of grasses and bushes prized by game animals such as deer, elk, beaver, rabbit, grouse, and turkey. The systematic use of fire to reshape forests helped hunters in multiple ways: it increased the overall food supply for grazing animals, it attracted those animal species hunters valued most, and, by clearing forests of ground debris, fire made it easier to track, kill, and transport game. Deliberate burns transformed forests in eastern North America to such an extent that bison migrated

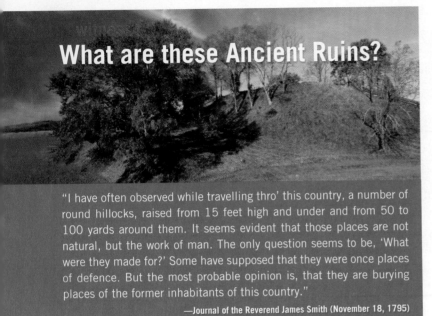

What are these Ancient Ruins?

"I have often observed while travelling thro' this country, a number of round hillocks, raised from 15 feet high and under and from 50 to 100 yards around them. It seems evident that those places are not natural, but the work of man. The only question seems to be, 'What were they made for?' Some have supposed that they were once places of defence. But the most probable opinion is, that they are burying places of the former inhabitants of this country."

—Journal of the Reverend James Smith (November 18, 1795)

from their original ranges on the plains and thrived far to the east. Thus, when native hunters from present-day New York to Georgia brought down a buffalo, they were harvesting a resource that they themselves had helped to create.

The Influence of Geography and Climate

>> No matter how great their ingenuity, the first Americans were constrained by certain natural realities. One of the most important is so basic that it is easy to overlook. Unlike Eurasia, which stretches across the Northern Hemisphere along an east–west axis, the Americas fall along a north–south axis, stretching nearly pole to pole. Consequently, the Americas are broken up by tremendous geographic and climactic diversity, making communication and technology transfer far more difficult than it was in the Old World.

Consider the agricultural revolution in Eurasia. Once plants and animals were first domesticated in the Fertile Crescent around 10,000 years ago, they quickly began spreading east and west. Within 1,500 years these innovations had been adopted in Greece and India. A thousand years later the domesticated plants and animals of the Fertile Crescent had reached central Europe, and from there it took perhaps 200 years for them to be embraced in present–day Spain. Eurasia's east–west axis facilitated these transfers. Locations at roughly the same latitude share the same seasonal variation, have days of the same length, and often have similar habitats and rates of precipitation, making it relatively easy for plants and animals to move from one place to the next.

In contrast, the north–south orientation of the Americas erected natural barriers to plant and animal transfer. Mesoamerica and South America, for example, are about as far apart as the Balkans and Mesopotamia. It took roughly 2,000 years for plants and animals domesticated in Mesopotamia to reach the Balkans. But because Mesoamerica and South America are separated by tropical, equatorial lowlands, it took domesticated plants such as corn several thousand years to jump between the two regions. Sometimes the transfer never happened at all before European contact. South American potatoes would have thrived in central Mexico, but the tropics stopped their northward migration. Equatorial jungles also denied Meso–american societies the llama and the alpaca, domesticated more than 5,000 years ago in the Andes. One wonders what even greater heights the Olmec, Toltec, Mayan, and Aztec civilizations would have achieved if they had had access to these large creatures as draft animals and reliable sources of protein.

Dramatic variations in climate likewise delayed the transfer of agriculture from Mexico to regions north of the Rio Grande. Archaeologists have discovered evidence of 10,000–year–old domesticated squash in a cave in southern Mexico, an indication that agriculture began in the Americas nearly as early as anywhere else in the world. Yet squash and corn were not cultivated in the present–day American Southwest for another 7,000 years, and the region's peoples did not embrace a fully sedentary, agricultural lifestyle until the start of the Common Era. Major differences in the length of days, the growing season, average temperatures, and rainfall between the Southwest and central Mexico meant that farmers north of the Rio Grande had to experiment for scores of generations before they perfected crops suited to their particular environments. Corn took even longer to become a staple crop in eastern North America, which is why we do not see major urban centers arise there until approximately 1000 CE.

By erecting barriers to communication and the spread of technology, then, the predominantly north–south orientation of the Americas made it more difficult for the hemisphere's inhabitants to build on one another's successes. Had American innovations spread as quickly as innovations in Eurasia, the peoples of the Western Hemisphere would likely have been healthier, more numerous, and more powerful than they were when Europeans first encountered them in 1492.

Animals and Illness

>> One other profound difference between the Eurasian world and

∧ Fewer large mammal species were available for domestication in the Americas, perhaps because the first wave of humans on the continent contributed to mass extinctions. Native Americans did domesticate dogs, shown here in a watercolor-and-ink sketch of a Mandan dog sled painted by Karl Bodmer in 1834.

the Americas concerned animals and disease. Most diseases affecting humans originated from domesticated animals, which came inevitably into frequent and close contact with the humans who raised them. As people across Eurasia embraced agriculture and started living with one another and with domesticated animals in crowded villages, towns, and cities, they created ideal environments for the evolution and transmission of infectious disease. For example, measles, tuberculosis, and smallpox all seem to have derived from diseases afflicting cattle.

Eurasians therefore paid a heavy price for living closely with animals. Yet in the long run the continent's terrible illnesses hardened its population. Victims who survived into adulthood enjoyed acquired immunity to the most common diseases: that is, if they had already encountered a particular illness as children, their immune systems would recognize and combat the disease more effectively in the event of reinfection. By the fifteenth century, then, Eurasian bodies had learned to live with a host of deadly communicable diseases.

But Native American bodies had not. With a few important exceptions, including tuberculosis, pneumonia, and possibly herpes and syphilis, human populations in the Western Hemisphere seem to have been relatively free from major communicable pathogens. Insofar as most major diseases emerge from domesticated animals, it is easy enough to see why. Indigenous Americans domesticated turkeys, dogs, Muscovy

ducks, and guinea pigs but raised only one large mammal—the llama or alpaca (breeds of the same species).

This scarcity of domestic animals had more to do with available supply than with the interest or ability of their would-be breeders. The extinction of most species of megafauna soon after humans arrived in the Americas deprived the hemisphere of 80 percent of its large mammals. Those that remained, including modern-day bison, elk, deer, and moose, were more or less immune to domestication because of peculiarities in their dispositions, diets, rates of growth, mating habits, and social characteristics. In fact, of the world's 148 species of large mammals, only 14 were successfully domesticated before the twentieth century. Of those 14 only 1—the ancestor to the llama/alpaca—remained in the Americas following the mass extinctions. Eurasia, in contrast, was home to 13—including the 5 most common and adaptable domestic mammals: sheep, goats, horses, cows, and pigs.

With virtually no large mammals to domesticate, Native Americans were spared the nightmarish effects of most of the world's major communicable diseases—until 1492. After that date European colonizers discovered the grim advantage of their millennia-long dance with disease. Old World infections that most colonizers had experienced as children raged through indigenous communities, usually doing the greatest damage to adults whose robust immune systems reacted violently to the novel pathogens. Often native communities came under attack from multiple diseases at the same time. Combined with the wars that attended colonization and the malnutrition, dislocation, and despair that attend wars, disease would kill native peoples by the millions while European colonizers increased and spread over the land. Despite their ingenuity and genius at reshaping plants and environments to their advantage, native peoples in the Americas labored under crucial disadvantages compared to Europe—disadvantages that would contribute to disaster after contact.

✔ REVIEW

How did the native inhabitants of the Americas transform their environments? What natural constraints put them at a disadvantage to Europeans?

CRISIS AND TRANSFORMATION

With its coastal plains, arid deserts, broad forests, and vast grassy plains, North America has always been a place of tremendous diversity and constant change. Indeed, many of the continent's most dramatic changes took place in the few centuries before European contact. Because of a complex and still poorly understood combination of ecological and social factors, the continent's most impressive civilizations collapsed as suddenly and mysteriously as had those of the Olmecs and the Mayas of Mesoamerica. In the Southwest the Mogollon culture went into eclipse around the twelfth century, the Hohokam and the Ancestral Puebloans by about the fourteenth. In the Eastern Woodlands the story was strikingly similar. Most of the great Mississippian population centers, including the magnificent city of Cahokia, had faded by the fourteenth century.

Enduring Peoples >> The survivors of these crises struggled to construct new communities, societies, and political systems. In the Southwest descendants of the Hohokam withdrew to small farming villages that relied on simpler modes of irrigation. Refugees embarked on a massive, coordinated exodus from the Four Corners region and established new, permanent villages in Arizona and New Mexico that the Spaniards would collectively call the Pueblos. The Mogollon have a more mysterious legacy, but some of their number may have helped establish the remarkable trading city of Paquime in present-day Chihuahua. Built around 1300 Paquime contained more than 2,000 rooms and had a sophisticated water and sewage system unlike any other in the Americas. The city included 18 large mounds, all shaped differently from one another, and three ballcourts reminiscent of those found elsewhere in Mexico. Until its demise sometime in the fifteenth century Paquime was the center of a massive trading network, breeding macaws and turkeys for export and channeling prized feathers, turquoise, seashells, and worked copper throughout a huge region.

The dramatic transformations remaking the Southwest involved tremendous suffering. Southwesterners had to rebuild in unfamiliar and oftentimes less productive places. Although some of their new settlements endure even to this day, many failed. Skeletal analysis from an abandoned pueblo on the Rio Grande, for example, indicates that the average life expectancy was only 16.5 years. Moreover, drought and migrations increased conflict over scarce resources. The most successful new settlements were large, containing several hundred people, and constructed in doorless, defensible blocks, or else set on high mesas to ward off enemy attacks. These changes were only compounded by the arrival of Athapaskan-speaking peoples (known to the Spanish as Apaches and Navajos) in the century or two before contact with Europeans. These hunters and foragers from western Canada and Alaska moved in small bands, were sometimes friendly, sometimes hostile toward different Pueblos, and eventually became key figures in the postcontact Southwest.

In the Eastern Woodlands the great Mississippian chieftainships never again attained the glory of Cahokia, but key traditions endured in the Southeast. In the lower Mississippi valley the Natchez maintained both the temple mound–building tradition and the rigid social distinctions of Mississippian civilization. Below the chief, or "Great Sun," of the Natchez stood a hereditary nobility of lesser "Suns" who demanded respect from the lowly "Stinkards," the common people. Other Muskogean-speakers rejected this rigid and hierarchical social model and gradually embraced a new, more flexible system of independent and relatively **egalitarian** villages that forged confederacies to better cope with outsiders. These groupings would eventually mature into three of the great southeastern Indian confederacies: Creek, Choctaw, and Chickasaw.

egalitarian exhibiting or asserting a belief in the equality of humans in a social, political, or economic context.

To the North lived speakers of Iroquoian languages, roughly divided into a southern faction including Cherokees and Tuscaroras, and a northern faction including the powerful Iroquois and Hurons. Like Muskogean peoples to the South, these Iroquoian communities mixed farming with a hunting/gathering economy and lived in semipermanent towns. The distinctive feature of Iroquois and Huron architecture was not the temple mound but rather the longhouse (some stretching up to 100 feet in length). Each sheltered as many as 10 families.

Algonquian speakers were the third major group of Eastern Woodlands people. They lived along the Atlantic seaboard and the Great Lakes in communities that were generally smaller than those of people speaking Muskogean or the Iroquoian languages. By the fifteenth century the coastal communities from southern New England to Virginia had adopted agriculture to supplement their diets, but those in the colder northern climates with shorter growing seasons depended entirely on hunting, fishing, and gathering plants such as wild rice.

Cultures of equal and even greater resources persisted and flourished during the fifteenth century in the Caribbean, particularly on the Greater Antilles—the islands of present—day Cuba, Haiti and the Dominican Republic, Jamaica, and Puerto Rico. Although the earliest inhabitants of the ancient Caribbean, the Ciboneys, probably came from the Florida peninsula, it was the Tainos, later emigrants from northern South America, who expanded throughout the Greater Antilles and the Bahamas. Taino chiefs known as *caciques*, along with a small number of noble families, ruled island tribes, controlling the production and distribution of food and tools and exacting tribute from the great mass of commoners, farmers, and fisherfolk. Attending to these elites were the poorest Taino peoples—servants who bedecked their masters and mistresses in brilliant diadems of feathers, fine woven textiles, and gold nose and ear pieces and then shouldered the litters on which the rulers sat and paraded their finery.

North America on the Eve of Contact >>By

the end of the fifteenth century, 5 to 10 million people lived north of the Rio Grande—with perhaps another million living on the islands of the Caribbean—and they were spread among more than 350 societies speaking nearly as many distinct languages. (The total precontact population for all of the Americas is estimated at between 57 and 112 million.)

These millions lived in remarkably diverse ways. Some peoples relied entirely on farming; others on hunting, fishing, and gathering; still others on a combination of the two. Some, such as the Natchez and the Iroquois, practiced matrilineal forms of kinship, in which women owned land, tools, and even children. Among others, such as the Algonquians, patrilineal kinship prevailed, and all property and prestige descended in the male line. Some societies, like those of the Great Plains and the Great Basin in the West, the Inuit in the Arctic, and the Iroquoians and Algonquians in the East, were roughly egalitarian, whereas others, like many in the Caribbean and the Pacific Northwest, were rigidly divided into nobles and commoners and servants or slaves. Some, such as the Natchez and the Taino, were ruled by powerful chiefs; others, such as the Algonquians and the Pueblos, by councils of village elders or heads of family clans; still others in the Great Basin, the Great Plains, and the Far North looked to the most skillful hunter or the most powerful shaman for direction. Those people who relied on hunting practiced religions that celebrated their kinship with animals and solicited their aid as guardian spirits, whereas predominantly agricultural peoples sought the assistance of their gods to make the rain fall and the crops ripen.

When Europeans first arrived in North America, the continent north of present—day Mexico boasted an ancient and rich history marked by cities, towns, and prosperous farms. At contact it was a land occupied by several million men, women, and children speaking hundreds of languages and characterized by tremendous political, cultural, economic, and religious diversity. This diversity was heightened by the north-south orientation of the Americas rather than the east—west orientation of Eurasia, since the spread of crops and animals in temperate regions was impeded by the tropical zones of the equator. The isolation from European diseases would make their arrival after 1492 even more devastating. Before 1492, though, the civilizations of North and South America remained populous, dynamic, and diverse.

 REVIEW

What was life like in the Americas on the eve of European contact?

For most of our nation's short history we have not wanted to remember things this way. European Americans have had a variety of reasons to minimize and belittle the past, the works, even the size of the native populations that ruled North America for 99 percent of its human history. In 1830, for example, President Andrew Jackson delivered an address before Congress in which he tried to answer the many critics of his Indian removal policies. Although "humanity has often wept over the fate of the aborigines of this country," Jackson said, the Indians' fate was as natural and inevitable "as the extinction of one generation to make room for another." He reminded his listeners of the mysterious mounds that had so captivated the founding fathers. "In the monuments and fortresses of an unknown people, spread over the extensive regions of the West, we behold the memorials of a once powerful race, which was exterminated, or has disappeared, to make room for the existing savage tribes." Just as the architects of the mounds supposedly met their end at the hands of these "savage tribes," the president concluded, so, too, must Indians pass away before the descendants of Europe. "What good man would prefer a country covered with forests and ranged by a few thousand savages, to our extensive republic, studded with cities, towns, and prosperous farms; embellished with all the improvements which art can devise, or industry execute; occupied by more than twelve millions of happy people, and filled with all the blessings of liberty, civilization, and religion!"

Indeed, stories told about the past have power over both the present and the future. Jackson and many

MAP 1.2: INDIGENOUS NORTH AMERICA, CA. 1500

Establishing the location of native groups in maps of precontact America is always problematic, since many peoples undertook major migrations in the contact period, boundaries between groups were fluid, and names applied to native communities usually differ from what those communities called themselves before colonization. Nonetheless, this map depicts the rough location of some prominent native peoples and their main modes of subsistence on the eve of contact.

California is well suited to farming, yet its large precontact population practiced very little agriculture. Why?

others of his era preferred a national history that contained only a few thousand ranging "savages" to one shaped by millions of indigenous hunters, farmers, builders, and inventors. Yet every generation rewrites its history, and what seems clear from this latest draft is the rich diversity of American cultures on the eve of contact between the peoples of Eurasia, Africa, and the Americas. We are still struggling to find stories big enough to encompass not only Indians from across the continent but also people who have come from all over the world to forge this complex, tragic, and marvelous nation of nations.

CHAPTER SUMMARY

During the thousands of years after bands of Siberian nomads migrated across the Bering Strait to Alaska, their descendants spread throughout the Americas, creating civilizations that rivaled those of ancient Europe, Asia, and Africa.

- Around 1500 BCE Mesoamerica emerged as the hearth of civilization in the Western Hemisphere, a process started by the Olmecs and brought to its height by the Mayas and Aztecs.
- These Mesoamerican peoples devised complex ways of organizing society, government, and religious worship and built cities remarkable for their art, architecture, and trade.
- Both commerce and migration spread cultural influences throughout the hemisphere, notably to the islands of the Caribbean basin and to North America, an influence that endured long after these empires declined.
- The adoption of agriculture gave peoples in the Southwest and the Eastern Woodlands the resource security necessary to develop sedentary cultures of increasing complexity. These cultures eventually enjoyed great achievements in culture, architecture, and agriculture.
- Inhabitants of the Great Plains, the Great Basin, the Arctic, and the Subarctic evolved their own diverse cultures, relying for subsistence on fishing, hunting, and gathering.
- Peoples of the Pacific Northwest boasted large populations and prosperous economies as well as an elaborate social, ceremonial, and artistic life.
- The native inhabitants of the Americas transformed their environments in a variety of ways, from pioneering crops that would eventually feed the world to landscaping mountains and cultivating jungles.
- Nonetheless, natural constraints would leave Native Americans at a disadvantage compared to Europe. The continent's north–south orientation inhibited the spread of agriculture and technology, and a lack of domesticatable animals compared to Europe left Native Americans with little protection against disease.
- For reasons that remain unclear, many of North America's most impressive early civilizations had collapsed by the end of the fifteenth century. In their wake a diverse array of cultures evolved across the continent.
- In the Southwest, Pueblo Indians were joined by Athapaskan–speakers whom Europeans would later call Apaches and Navajos.
- In much of eastern North America, stratified chiefdoms of the Mississippian era gave way to more egalitarian confederacies of independent villages subsisting on farming and hunting.
- Although Americans in the nineteenth, twentieth, and even twenty–first centuries have been slow to recognize the fact, the societies of precontact America were remarkably populous, complex, and diverse. Their influence would continue to be felt in the centuries after contact.

Additional Reading

Scholars in several fields are transforming our understanding of the Americas prior to European contact. The magazine *Archaeology* offers clear explanations of the latest discoveries for nonscientific audiences. For an excellent overview, attentive to controversies among researchers, see Charles C. Mann, *1491: New Revelations of the Americas before Columbus* (2005). For North America specifically, see Alice Beck Kehoe, *America before the European Invasions* (2002). For the Southwest, see Linda S. Cordell and Maxine E. McBrinn, *Archaeology of the Southwest* (2012). For the Eastern Woodlands, see George R. Milner, *The Moundbuilders: Ancient Peoples of Eastern North America* (2005). Roger G. Kennedy, *Hidden Cities: The Discovery and Loss of Ancient North American Civilization* (1994), gives a fascinating account of how white Americans responded to the ruins of ancient American cultures. For the consequences of axis alignment and of domesticated animals, see the captivating work by Jared Diamond, *Guns, Germs, and Steel: The Fates of Human Societies* (1998).

For the cultures of precontact Mexico, see Michael D. Coe and Rex Koontz, *Mexico: From the Olmecs to the Aztecs* (7th ed., 2013). For exhaustive surveys of all regional cultures in North America, see William C. Sturtevant, general editor, *Handbook of North American Indians*, 15 volumes to date (1978–2008).

Significant Events

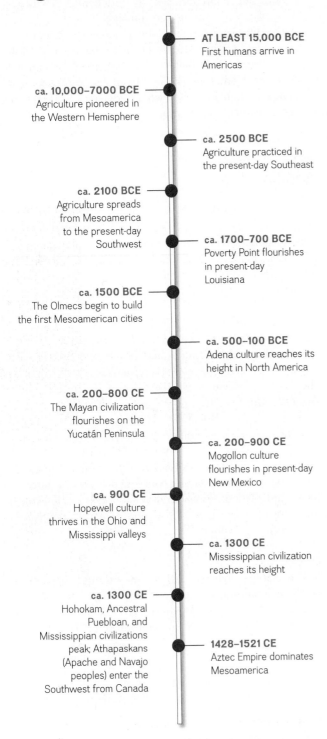

AT LEAST 15,000 BCE
First humans arrive in Americas

ca. 10,000–7000 BCE
Agriculture pioneered in the Western Hemisphere

ca. 2500 BCE
Agriculture practiced in the present-day Southeast

ca. 2100 BCE
Agriculture spreads from Mesoamerica to the present-day Southwest

ca. 1700–700 BCE
Poverty Point flourishes in present-day Louisiana

ca. 1500 BCE
The Olmecs begin to build the first Mesoamerican cities

ca. 500–100 BCE
Adena culture reaches its height in North America

ca. 200–800 CE
The Mayan civilization flourishes on the Yucatán Peninsula

ca. 200–900 CE
Mogollon culture flourishes in present-day New Mexico

ca. 900 CE
Hopewell culture thrives in the Ohio and Mississippi valleys

ca. 1300 CE
Mississippian civilization reaches its height

ca. 1300 CE
Hohokam, Ancestral Puebloan, and Mississippian civilizations peak; Athapaskans (Apache and Navajo peoples) enter the Southwest from Canada

1428–1521 CE
Aztec Empire dominates Mesoamerica

2 Old Worlds, New Worlds

1400–1600

With sails bellying in a gale, this Dutch ship faced the shallows of a rocky coast. Western European sailors risked much as they crossed the Atlantic in search of fish, silver, gold, and other commodities to trade.

>> **An American Story**

FISHING NETS AND FAR HORIZONS

All the world lay before them. Or so it seemed to mariners from England's seafaring "West Country" coasts, pushing toward unknown lands in the far Atlantic.

The scent of the new land came first—not the sight of it, but the smells, perhaps the scent of fir trees wafted from beyond the horizon, delicious to sailors who had felt nothing but the rolling sea for weeks on end. Straightaway the captain would call for a lead to be thrown overboard to sound the depths. At its end was a hollowed-out socket with a bit of tallow in it, so that some of the sea bottom would stick when the lead was hauled up. A good sailing master could tell where he was by what came up—"oozy sand"

17

or perhaps "soft worms" or "popple-stones" as big as beans.

Through much of the fifteenth century the search for cod had drawn West Country sailors north and west, toward Iceland. In the 1480s and 1490s a few English tried their luck farther west. They returned with little to show for their daring until the coming of an Italian named Giovanni Caboto, called John Cabot by the English. Cabot, who hailed from Venice, obtained the blessing of King Henry VII to hunt for unknown lands. From the port of Bristol his lone ship set out to the west in the spring of 1497.

This time the return voyage brought news of a "new-found" island where the trees were tall enough to make fine masts and the codfish were plentiful. After returning to Bristol, Cabot marched off to London to inform His Majesty, received 10 pounds as his reward, and with the proceeds dressed himself in dashing silks. The multitudes of London flocked after him, wondering over "the Admiral"; then Cabot returned triumphantly to Bristol to undertake a more ambitious search for a northwest passage to Asia. He set sail with five ships in 1498 and was never heard from again.

By the 1550s Cabot's island, now known as Newfoundland, attracted 400 vessels annually, fishermen not only from England but also from France, Portugal, and Spain. The harbor of present-day St. John's, Newfoundland, served as the informal hub of the North Atlantic fishery. Sailors from three kingdoms dropped anchor there to take on supplies in the spring, trade with native peoples, or prepare for the homeward voyage in autumn. There was eager conversation at this meeting place, for these seafarers knew as much as anyone—if not more—about the new world of wonders that was opening to Europeans. They were acquainted with names such as Cristoforo Colombo, the Italian from Genoa whom Cabot might have known as a boy. They listened to Portuguese tales of sailing around the Horn of Africa in pursuit of spices and to stories of Indian empires to the south, rich in gold and silver that Spanish treasure ships were bringing home.

Indeed, Newfoundland was one of the few places in the world where so many ordinary folk of different nations could gather and talk, crammed aboard dank ships moored in St. John's harbor, huddled before blazing fires on its beaches, or crowded into smoky makeshift taverns. When the ships sailed home in autumn, the tales went with them, repeated in the tiniest coastal villages by those pleased to have cheated the sea and death one more time. Eager to fish, talk, trade, and take profits, West Country mariners were almost giddy at the prospect of Europe's expanding horizons.

Most seafarers who fished the waters of Newfoundland's Grand Banks remain unknown today. Yet it is well to begin with these ordinary fisherfolk, for the European discovery of the Americas cannot be looked on simply as the voyages of a few bold explorers. Adventurers such as Christopher Columbus and John Cabot were only the most visible representatives of a much larger expansion of European peoples and culture that began in the 1450s. That expansion arose out of a series of gradual but telling changes in the fabric of European society—changes reflected in the lives of ordinary seafarers as much as in the careers of explorers decked out in silks.

Some of these changes were technological, arising out of advances in the arts of navigating and shipbuilding and the use of gunpowder. Some were economic, involving the development of trade networks such as those linking Bristol with ports in Iceland and Spain. Some were **demographic,** bringing

> **demographic** factors relating to the characteristics of populations. Demography is the study of populations, looking at such aspects as size, growth, density, and age distribution.

about a rise in Europe's population after a devastating century of plague. Other changes were religious, adding a dimension of devout belief to the political rivalries that fueled discoveries in the Americas. Yet others were political, making it possible for kingdoms to centralize and extend their influence across the ocean. Portugal, Spain, France, and England—all possessing coasts along the Atlantic—led the way in exploration, spurred on by Italian "admirals" such as Caboto and Colombo, Spanish *conquistadores*—"conquerors"—such as Hernán Cortés and Francisco Pizarro, and English sea dogs such as Humphrey Gilbert and Walter Raleigh. Ordinary folk rode these currents, too. The great and the small alike were propelled by forces that were remolding the face of Europe—and were beginning to remold the face of the world. <<

What's to Come

EURASIA AND AFRICA IN THE FIFTEENTH CENTURY

In 1450, however, the western European kingdoms that would one day dominate much of the world still sat at the fringe of an international economy that revolved around China. By a variety of measures Ming China was the richest, most powerful, and most advanced society in the world. All Eurasia sought Chinese goods, especially spices, ceramics, and silks, and Chinese ships sped these goods to faraway ports. Seven times between 1405 and 1433 China's "treasure fleet"—300 ships manned by 28,000 sailors and commanded by Zheng He (pronounced "Jung Huh")—unfurled its red silk sails off the south China coast and traveled as far as the kingdoms of eastern Africa. The treasure fleet's largest craft were nine-masted junks measuring 400 feet long, sporting multiple decks and luxury cabins. By comparison, Columbus's largest ship in 1492 was a mere 85 feet long, and the crew aboard all three of his ships totaled just 90 men. Political turbulence led Chinese leaders to ground their trading fleet and end the long-distance voyages. But Chinese luxuries, most transported overland, continued to be Eurasia's most sought-after commodities.

The next mightiest powers in the Old World were not European kingdoms but rather huge Islamic empires, especially the Ottomans in the eastern Mediterranean. The Ottomans rose to prominence during the fourteenth and fifteenth centuries, gaining control of critical trade routes and centers of commerce between Asia and Europe. Their greatest triumph came in 1453, when the sultan Mehmet II conquered Constantinople (now Istanbul), the ancient and supposedly impregnable Christian city that straddled Europe and Asia. Mehmet's stunning victory sounded alarms throughout Europe.

Europe's Place in the World >>Europe's rulers had good reason for alarm. Distant from Asia's profitable trade and threatened by the Ottomans' military might, most of the continent remained fractious and vulnerable. During the fourteenth and fifteenth centuries 90 percent of Europe's people, widely dispersed in small villages, made their living from the land. But warfare, poor transportation, and low grain yields all created food shortages, and undernourishment produced a population prone to disease. Under these circumstances life was, to paraphrase the English philosopher Thomas Hobbes, nasty, brutish, and usually short. One-quarter of all children died in the first year of life. People who reached the age of 40 counted themselves fortunate.

⋏ The spread of bubonic plague left Europeans dismayed and desperate. While a priest reads prayers over the bodies being buried in a common grave, a man suddenly taken by the plague writhes in agony. In the background, a cart collects more corpses. And in heaven (*upper left*) St. Sebastian, a Christian martyr, intercedes with God to end the suffering.

It was also a world of sharp inequalities, where nobles and aristocrats enjoyed several hundred times the income of peasants or craftworkers. It was a world with no strong, centralized political authority, where kings were weak and warrior lords held sway over small towns and tiny fiefdoms. It was a world of violence and sudden death, where homicide, robbery, and rape occurred with brutal frequency. It was a world where security and order of any kind seemed so fragile that most people clung to tradition, and more than a few used witchcraft in an attempt to master the chaotic and unpredictable world around them.

But Europe was changing, in part because of a great calamity. Between the late 1340s and the early 1350s bubonic plague—known as the Black Death—swept away one-quarter of Europe's population. Some urban areas lost 70 percent of their people to the disease. The Black Death disrupted both agriculture and commerce, and provoked a spiritual crisis that resulted in violent, unsanctioned religious movements, scapegoating of marginal groups, even massacres of Jews. Although Europeans seem to have met recurrent outbreaks of the disease with less panic, the sickness continued to disrupt social and economic life.

Yet the sudden drop in population relieved pressure on scarce resources. Survivors of the Black Death found that the relative scarcity of workers and consumers made for higher wages, lower prices, and more land. These changes promoted an overall expansion of trade. In earlier centuries Italian merchants had begun encouraging commerce across Europe and tapping into trade from Africa, the Middle East, and, when able, from Asia. By the late fifteenth century Europe's merchants and bankers had devised more efficient ways of transferring the money generated from manufacturing and trade, and established credit in order to support commerce across longer distances. Wealth flowed into the coffers of traders, financiers, and landlords, creating a pool of capital that investors could plow into new technologies, trading ventures, and, eventually, colonial enterprises.

The direction of Europe's political development also laid the groundwork for overseas colonization. After 1450 strong monarchs in Europe steadily enlarged their power at the expense of warrior lords. Henry VII, the founder of England's Tudor dynasty, Francis I of France, and Ferdinand and Isabella of Spain began the trend, forging modern nation-states by extending their political control over more territory, people, and resources. Such larger, more centrally organized states were able to marshal the resources necessary to support colonial outposts and to sustain the professional armies and navies capable of creating and protecting overseas empires.

Africa and the Portuguese Wave >>European expansion began with Africa. For centuries African spices, ivory, and gold had entered the Eurasian market either through ports on the Indian Ocean or through the Sahara Desert and into the Mediterranean Sea. Powerful African kingdoms controlled the routes through which these prized commodities moved, while Islamic expansion in the fifteenth century made competition all the more intense. European merchants yearned to access West African markets directly, by ship. But navigational and shipbuilding technology was not yet up to the challenge of the Atlantic's prevailing currents, which sped ships south along Africa's coast but made the return voyage virtually impossible.

Portugal was the first to solve this problem and tap directly into West African markets, thanks in large part to Prince Henry "the Navigator," as he became known. An ardent Catholic and a man who dreamed of turning back Islam's rising tide, Henry understood that direct commerce with West Africa would allow his kingdom to circumvent the costly trans-Sahara trade. To forward his vision Henry funded exploratory voyages, established a maritime school, and challenged sailors and engineers to conquer the problem of the current. The Portuguese responded by developing the caravel, a lighter, more maneuverable ship that could sail better against contrary winds and in rough seas. More seaworthy than the lumbering galleys of the Middle Ages, caravels combined longer, narrower hulls—a shape built for speed—with triangular lateen sails, which allowed for more flexible steering. The caravel allowed the Portuguese to regularly do what few Europeans had ever done: sail down Africa's west coast and return home. Other advances, including a sturdier version of the Islamic world's astrolabe, enabled Portugal's navigators to calculate their position at sea with unprecedented accuracy.

As the Portuguese pressed southward along the Atlantic rim of sub-Saharan Africa, they began to meet peoples who had never encountered Europeans or even possessed any knowledge of other continents. On catching their first sight of a Portuguese expedition in 1455, villagers on the Senegal River marveled at the strangers' clothing and their white skin. As an Italian member of that expedition recounted, some Africans "rubbed me with their spittle to discover whether my whiteness was dye or flesh."

But the Portuguese were wrong to mistake such acts of innocence for economic or political naïveté. Formidable African chiefdoms and states were eager to trade with Europeans but intent on protecting already established commercial networks. Portugal could not simply take what it wanted from West Africa. With few exceptions, it proved impossible for European powers to colonize territory in West Africa before the nineteenth century, because the region's people were too many and too organized. Furthermore, malaria would kill between one-fourth and one-half of all Portuguese unwise enough to try to stay.

To succeed, the newcomers had to seek partners. As the Portuguese built forts and trading houses on the coast, they gave tribute or taxes to local powers in return for trading privileges. The Portuguese offered textiles, especially, but also raw and worked metal goods, currency (in the form of cowry shells), and beads. In return Africans gave up prized commodities such as gold, ivory, and malaguetta pepper. Portuguese traders also expressed interest in another commodity, one that would reshape the wider Atlantic world: slaves.

Sugar and the Origins of the Atlantic Slave Trade >> Unfree

labor has existed in nearly all human societies. Although the norms, characteristics, and economic importance of slavery have varied widely over time and place, men, women, and children have been held as slaves from before recorded history to the present. (U.S. and international organizations estimate that today there are as many as 27 million people held in some form of labor bondage and that nearly 1 million unfree people are sold across international borders every year.)

By the Middle Ages, elites in Europe had largely abandoned the slave culture of the Roman Empire and relied instead on serfs or peasants for labor. Slaves became more important as status symbols than as workers, and most were young white women. Indeed, the word *slave* comes originally from "Slav"; Slavic girls and women from the Balkans and the coasts of the Black Sea were frequent targets of slave raids.

But European slavery began to change again following the Crusades. In 1099 Christian forces captured Jerusalem from the Seljuk Turks and discovered sugar plantations that the Turks had cultivated in the Holy Land. Crusaders recognized sugar's economic potential. But because sugar required intense work during planting and close tending during the growing season, they found it a difficult commodity to produce. On maturity the crop had to be harvested and processed 24 hours a day to avoid being spoiled. In short, sugar demanded cheap, pliable labor, and the newly arrived crusaders relied in part on slaves.

When Islamic forces under the famed leader Saladin reconquered Jerusalem in the twelfth century, European investors established new plantations on eastern Mediterranean islands. In addition to being labor intensive, though, sugar was a crop that quickly exhausted soils and forced planters to move operations

⌃ The rich, volcanic soils of the Azores, the Canaries, and Madeira proved ideal for growing sugar. These islands in the eastern Atlantic were a stepping-stone to later plantations in the Americas, such as the one pictured in this engraving by Theodore de Bry from 1596.

regularly. Plantations spread to new islands, and by the early 1400s sugar was even being grown in Portugal. As production expanded, planters had to work harder than ever to obtain the necessary labor because of the Black Death and because Turkish conquests restricted European access to the traditional slaving grounds of the eastern Mediterranean and the Balkans.

Thus by the fifteenth century the Portuguese were already producing sugar on slave-run plantations, but they were seeking new cropland and new sources of slaves. Once again Prince Henry's vision enhanced his kingdom's economic interests. While Portugal's merchants were establishing trading posts along the west coast of Africa, Iberian mariners were discovering or rediscovering islands in the eastern Atlantic: the Canaries, Madeira, and the Azores, islands with rich, volcanic soils ideally suited to sugarcane. By the late 1400s sugar plantations were booming on the Atlantic islands, staffed by West African slaves. By 1550 people of African descent accounted for 10 percent of the population of Lisbon, Portugal's capital city.

Now convinced that they could reach coveted Asian markets by sea, ambitious Portuguese mariners sailed their caravels farther and farther south. In 1488 Bartolomeu Dias rounded the Cape of Good Hope on the southern tip of Africa, sailing far enough up that continent's eastern coast to claim discovery of a sea route to India. Ten years later Vasco da Gama reached India itself, and Portugal's interests ultimately extended to Indochina and China.

Portuguese geographers had long felt certain that travel around Africa was the shortest route to the Orient, but an Italian sailor disagreed. Cristoforo Colombo had spent a decade gaining experience from Portugal's master mariners. He also threw himself into research, devouring Lisbon's books on geography and cartography. Columbus (the Latinized version of his name) became convinced that the fastest route to China lay west, across the uncharted Atlantic Ocean. He appealed to Portugal's king to support an exploratory voyage, but royal geographers scoffed at the idea. They agreed that the world was round but insisted (correctly, as it turns out) that the globe was far larger than Columbus had calculated, making any westward route impractical. Almost a decade of rejection had grayed Columbus's red hair, but—undaunted—he packed up in 1485 and took his audacious idea to Spain.

> ✔ **REVIEW**
>
> Why did Europeans begin to develop commercial networks in the Atlantic, and how did the Portuguese operate in Africa?

SPAIN IN THE AMERICAS

He arrived a few years too early. Spain's monarchs, Ferdinand and Isabella, rejected Columbus's offer because they were engaged in a campaign to drive the Muslims out of their last stronghold on the Iberian Peninsula, the Moorish kingdom of Granada. For centuries Arab rulers from Africa had controlled part of present-day Spain and Portugal. But in 1492 Ferdinand and Isabella finally completed what was known as the **Reconquista,** their military reconquest of this territory. Flush with victory, the pair listened to Columbus argue that a westward route to Asia would allow Spain to compete with Portugal and generate enough revenue to continue the reconquest, even into the Holy Land itself. Ignoring the advice of their geographers, the monarchs agreed to his proposal.

 Reconquista military reconquest of the Iberian Peninsula from Islamic Moors of Africa by European Christian rulers.

Columbus's first voyage across the Atlantic could only have confirmed his conviction that he was destiny's darling. His three ships, no bigger than fishing vessels that sailed to Newfoundland, plied their course over placid seas, south from Seville to the Canary Islands and then due west. On October 11, a little more than two months after leaving Spain, branches, leaves, and flowers floated by their hulls, signals that land lay near. Just after midnight a sailor spied cliffs shining white in the moonlight. On the morning of October 12, the *Niña*, the *Pinta*, and the *Santa Maria* set anchor in a shallow sapphire bay, and their crews knelt on the white coral beach. Columbus christened the place San Salvador (Holy Savior).

The Spanish Beachhead in the Caribbean >> Like many men of destiny, Columbus mistook his true destination. At first he confused his actual location, the Bahamas, with an island near Japan. He coasted along Cuba and Hispaniola (today's Haiti and Dominican Republic), expecting at any moment to catch sight of gold-roofed Japanese temples or fleets of Chinese junks. He encountered instead a gentle, generous people who knew nothing of the Great Khan but who welcomed the newcomers profusely. Columbus's journals note that they wore little clothing, but they did wear jewelry—tiny pendants of gold suspended from the nose. He dubbed the Taino people "Indians"—inhabitants of the Indies.

It would take some years before other mariners and geographers understood clearly that these new-found islands and the landmasses beyond them lay between Europe and Asia. One of the earliest geographers to do so was the Florentine Amerigo Vespucci, who first described Columbus's Indies as *Mundus Novus,* a "New World." Rather than dub the new lands "Columbia," a German mapmaker called them "America" in Vespucci's honor. The German's maps proved wildly successful, and the name stuck.

Unlike the kingdoms of West Africa, the Taino chiefdoms lacked the military power to resist European aggression. And Europeans decided that the societies they encountered were better suited to be ruled than partnered with. Moreover, while the newfound islands eventually presented their own threats to European health, they seemed a good deal more inviting than the deadly coast of West Africa. Hints of gold, a seemingly weak and docile population, and a relatively healthy climate all ensured that Columbus's second voyage would be one of colonization rather than commerce. During the 1490s and early 1500s Spanish colonizers imposed a brutal regime on the Tainos, slaughtering native leaders and forcing survivors to toil in mines and fields.

Only a few Spaniards spoke out against the exploitation. Among them was Bartolomé de las Casas, a man who spent several years in the Caribbean, participating in conquests and profiting from native labor. Eventually Las Casas renounced his conduct and, as a

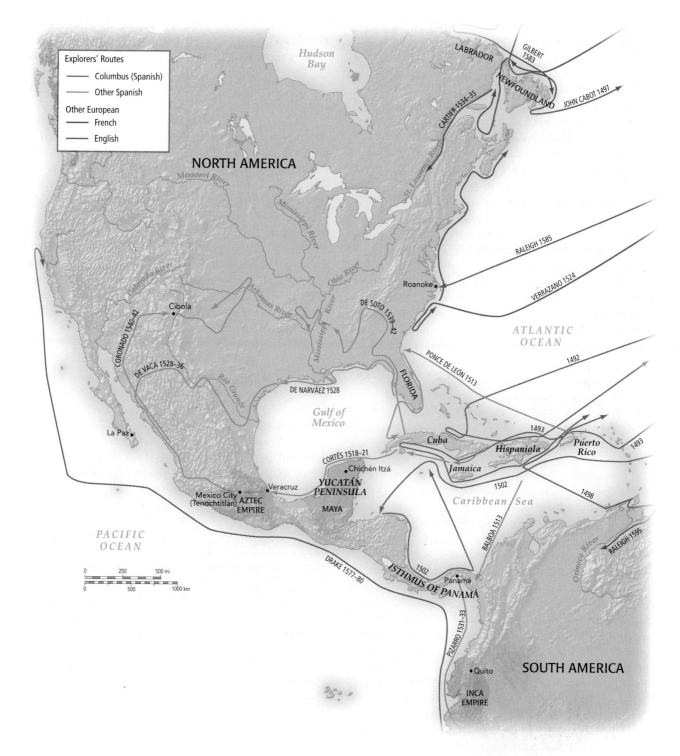

Explorers' Routes
— Columbus (Spanish)
— Other Spanish

Other European
— French
— English

NORTH AMERICA

Hudson Bay

LABRADOR

GILBERT 1583

NEWFOUNDLAND

JOHN CABOT 1497

CARTIER 1534-35

St. Lawrence River

Missouri River

Mississippi River

Colorado River

Arkansas River

Ohio River

Cibola

CORONADO 1540-42

DE VACA 1528-36

Rio Grande

DE NARVÁEZ 1528

DE SOTO 1539-42

RALEIGH 1585

Roanoke

VERRAZANO 1524

ATLANTIC OCEAN

PONCE DE LEÓN 1513

FLORIDA

1492

La Paz

Gulf of Mexico

CORTÉS 1518-21

Chichén Itzá

Cuba

1493

Hispaniola

Puerto Rico

1493

Mexico City (Tenochtitlán)

AZTEC EMPIRE

Veracruz

YUCATÁN PENINSULA

MAYA

Jamaica

1502

Caribbean Sea

1498

PACIFIC OCEAN

BALBOA 1513

RALEIGH 1595

Orinoco River

DRAKE 1577-80

ISTHMUS OF PANAMÁ

1502

Panamá

PIZARRO 1531-33

SOUTH AMERICA

Quito

INCA EMPIRE

0   250   500 mi
0   500   1000 km

MAP 2.1: PRINCIPAL ROUTES OF EUROPEAN EXPLORATION

Dominican friar, became a tireless foe of Spanish cru-elties toward Indians. He railed against the "unjust, cruel, and tyrannical" war waged to force the native peoples into "the hardest, harshest, and most heinous bondage to which men or beasts might ever be bound into." Las Casas's writings, translated throughout Europe and illustrated with gruesome drawings, helped give rise to the "Black Legend" of Spanish atrocities in the Americas.

The warnings had some effect, but not for decades. Within a generation of Columbus's landfall, the Taino population had nearly collapsed from war, overwork, malnutrition, despair, and strange new Eurasian diseases. Ambitious Spaniards began scouring the Caribbean basin, discovering new lands and searching for new populations of Indians to subjugate or enslave in place of the vanishing Tainos. Soon the Bahamas were depopulated by Spanish slavers, and conquests had done to present–day Cuba, Jamaica, and Puerto Rico what they first had done to Hispaniola.

Conquest of the Aztecs >> Would–be conquistadors turned their eyes to the mainland. In 1519 an expedition led by the impetuous Hernán Cortés made contact with native peoples on Mexico's gulf coast. They spoke of an oppressive imperial people who occupied a fantastic city to the west. These were the Aztecs.

Aztecs had much in common with Spaniards. Both societies were predominantly rural, with most inhabitants living in small villages and engaging in agriculture. In both places merchants and specialized craftworkers clustered in cities, organized themselves into guilds, and clamored for protection from the government. Aztec noble and priestly classes, like those in Europe, took the lead in politics and religion, demanding tribute from the common people. Finally, both societies were robustly expansionist, bent on bringing new lands and peoples under their control.

Yet critical differences between these two peoples shaped the outcome of their meeting. The Aztecs lacked the knowledge of ocean navigation, metal tools and weaponry, and firearms. Equally important, the relatively young Aztec Empire had not yet established total control over central Mexico. Formidable peoples remained outside Aztec domination, and conquered city–states within the empire bitterly resented Aztec rule. Cortés exploited that weakness. Massing an army of disgruntled native warriors, he and his men marched inland to the mighty Aztec capital, Tenochtitlán, home to more people (roughly a quarter million) than any city then existing in Europe. When the emperor Moctezuma's ambassadors met Cortés on the road and attempted to appease him with gold ornaments and other gifts, an Indian witness noted that "the Spaniards ... picked up the gold and fingered it like monkeys.... Their bodies swelled with greed." The newcomers were welcomed into the city as honored guests but soon seized Moctezuma and took him captive. For months Cortés ruled the empire indirectly, but the Aztecs drove the Spanish out after Moctezuma's death.

In the midst of this victory the city encountered another foe—smallpox. Geographically isolated from Eurasia and its complex disease environment, the Aztecs and all other native peoples in the Americas lacked the acquired immunity that gave Europeans

virgin soil epidemic epidemic in which the populations at risk have had no previous contact with the diseases that strike them and are therefore immunologically almost defenseless.

a degree of protection against Old World pathogens. The resulting **virgin soil epidemics**—so called because the victims had no previous exposure—took a nightmarish toll. Smallpox claimed millions in central Mexico between 1520 and 1521. This, too, presented Cortés with opportunities. Supported by a massive Indian force, he put Tenochtitlán to siege, killing tens of thousands before the ragged, starving survivors surrendered in August of 1521. The feared Aztec Empire lay in ruins. Conquistadors fanned out from central Mexico, overwhelming new populations and eventually learning of another mighty kingdom to the South. Again relying on political faction, disease, technological advantages, and luck, by 1532 Spaniards under Francisco Pizarro and his brothers had conquered the Inca Empire in South America, which in certain regards outshone even the Aztecs.

The Columbian Exchange >> Virgin soil epidemics, which contributed to the collapse of many Indian populations, were only one aspect of a complex web of interactions between the flora and fauna of the Americas on the one hand and those of Eurasia and Africa on the other. Just as germs migrated along with humans, so did plants and animals. These transfers, begun in the decades after Columbus first landed in the Caribbean,

Columbian exchange transition of people, plants, insects, and microbes between the two hemispheres, initiated when Columbus reached the Americas in 1492.

are known by historians as the **Columbian exchange,** and they had far–reaching effects on both sides of the Atlantic. Europeans brought a host of American crops home with them, as seen in Chapter 1 (page 8). They also most likely brought syphilis, an American disease that broke out across Europe in more virulent form than ever before. Europeans brought to the Americas the horses and large dogs that intimidated the Aztecs; they brought oranges, lemons, figs, and bananas from Africa and the Canary Islands. Escaped hogs multiplied so rapidly that they overran some Caribbean islands, as did European rats.

The Columbian exchange was not a short–lived event. In a host of different ways it reshaped the globe over the next 500 years as travel, exploration, and colonization brought cultures ever closer. Instead of smallpox, today bird flu from Asia or the West Nile virus threatens populations worldwide. But the exchanges of the sixteenth century were often more extreme, unpredictable, and far–reaching, because of the previous isolation of the two hemispheres.

How Did Spaniards and Aztecs Remember First Contact?

The first encounter between the Spaniards under Hernan Cortés and ambassadors of the emperor Moctezuma in 1519 represents a fateful turning point in history. While we have no full contemporary account of that meeting, two remarkable sources present Spanish and Mexican memories of the event written years later. The first selection below was written in the 1560s by one of Cortés's lieutenants, the conquistador Bernal Díaz. The second section comes from a work compiled in the 1540s by the missionary Bernardino de Sahagún, in which indigenous informants recalled Aztec culture, religion, society, and history up to and through the conquest.

DOCUMENT 1
Bernal Díaz

Seeing the big ship with the standards flying they knew that it was there that they must go to speak with the captain; so they went direct to the flagship and going on board asked who was the Tatuan [Tlatoan] which in their language means the chief. Doña Marina who understood the language well, pointed him out. Then the Indians paid many marks of respect to Cortés, according to their usage, and bade him welcome, and said that their lord, a servant of the great Montezuma, had sent them to ask what kind of men we were and of what we were in search. . . . [Cortés] told them that we came to see them and to trade with them and that our arrival in their country should cause them no uneasiness but be looked on by them as fortunate. . . .

[Several days later, one of Montezuma's emissaries] brought with him some clever painters such as they had in Mexico and ordered them to make pictures true to nature of the face and body of Cortés and all his captains, and of the soldiers, ships, sails, and horses, and of Doña Marina and Aguilar, even of the two greyhounds, and the cannon and cannon balls, and all of the army we had brought with us, and he carried the pictures to his master. Cortés ordered our gunners to load the lombards with a great charge of powder so that they should make a great noise when they were fired off. . . . [The emissary] went with all haste and narrated everything to his prince, and showed him the pictures which had been painted. . . .

Source: Bernal Díaz, *The True History of the Conquest of New Spain,* excerpted in Stuart B. Schwartz, ed., *Victors and Vanquished: Spanish and Views of the Conquest of Mexico* (2000), pp. 85–90.

DOCUMENT 2
Fray Bernardino de Sahagún

When they had gotten up into [Cortes's] boat, each of them made the earth-eating gesture before the Captain. Then they addressed him, saying, "May the god attend; his agent Moteucçoma who is in charge in Mexico for him addresses him and says, 'The god is doubly welcome.'"

Then they dressed up the Captain. They put on him the turquoise serpent mask attached to the quetzal-feather head fan, to which were fixed, from which hung the green-stone serpent earplugs. And they put the sleeveless jacket on him, and around his neck they put the plaited green-stone neckband with the golden disk in the middle. On his lower back they tied the back mirror, and also they tied behind him the cloak called a *tzitzilli.* And on his legs they placed the green-stone bands with the golden bells. And they gave him, placing it on his arm, the shield with gold and shells crossing, on whose edge were spread quetzal feathers, with a quetzal banner. And they laid the obsidian sandals before him. . . .

Then the Captain ordered that they be tied up: they put irons on their feet and necks. When this had been done they shot off the cannon. And at this point the messengers truly fainted and swooned; one after another they swayed and fell, losing consciousness. . . . Then [Cortés] let them go.

[Upon returning to Tenochtitlán and reporting to Moteucçoma, he replied] "I will not hear it here. I will hear it at the Coacalco; let them go there." And he gave orders, saying, "Let some captives be covered in chalk [for sacrifice]."

Then the messengers went to the Coacalco, and so did Moteucçoma. There upon the captives died in their presence; they cut open their chests and sprinkled their blood on the messengers. (The reason they did it was that they had gone to very dangerous places and had seen, gazed on the countenances of, and spoken to the gods.) . . .

When this was done, they talked to Moteucçoma, telling him what they had beheld, and they showed him what [the Spaniards'] food was like.

And when he heard what the messengers reported, he was greatly afraid and taken aback, and he was amazed at their food. It especially made him faint when he heard how the guns went off at [the Spaniards'] command, sounding like thunder, causing people to actually swoon, blocking the ears. And when it went off, something like a ball came out from inside, and fire went showering and spitting out. And the smoke that came out had a very foul stench, striking one in the face. And if they shot at a hill, it seemed to crumble and come apart. . . . Their war gear was all iron. They clothed their bodies in iron, they put iron on their heads, their swords were iron, their bows were iron, and their shields were iron.

And the deer that carried them were as tall as the roof. And they wrapped their bodies all over; only their faces could be seen, very white. . . .

And their dogs were huge creatures, with their ears folded over and their jowls dragging. They had burning eyes, eyes like coals, yellow and fiery. . . .

When Moteucçoma heard it, he was greatly afraid; he seemed to faint away, he grew concerned and disturbed.

Source: Fray Bernardino de Sahagún, *Florentine The Codex,* excerpted in Schwartz, ed., *Victors and Vanquished,* pp. 91–99.

THINKING CRITICALLY

How did the Aztecs and the Spaniards communicate? Why does Díaz pay so little attention to the gifts the emissaries brought Cortés? Why might the painters be absent from the Nahua account? What principles of critical thinking should be kept in mind when reading such documents?

⋏ Both the Aztecs and the Spanish tried to understand the new in terms of the familiar. Hence an Aztec artist portrayed Cortés as an Indian with strange clothes and a stranger beard (*left*), whereas a European artist depicted Moctezuma in the style of a Greco-Roman warrior (*right*).

The Crown Steps In >>Proud conquistadors did not long enjoy their mastery in the Americas. Spain's monarchs, who had just tamed an aristocracy at home, were not about to allow a colonial nobility to arise across the Atlantic. The Crown bribed the conquistadors into retirement—or was saved the expense when men such as Francisco Pizarro were assassinated by their own followers. The task of governing Spain's new colonies passed from the conquerors to a small army of officials, soldiers, lawyers, and Catholic bishops, all appointed by the Crown, reporting to the Crown, and loyal to the Crown. Headquartered in urban centers such as Mexico City (formerly Tenochtitlán), an elaborate, centralized bureaucracy administered the Spanish empire, regulating nearly every aspect of economic and social life.

Few Spaniards besides imperial officials settled in the Americas. By 1600 only about 5 percent of the colonial population was of Spanish descent, the other 95 percent being Indian, African, or of mixed heritage. Even by 1800 only 300,000 Spanish immigrants had come to live in the Americas. Indians often remained on the lands that they had farmed under the Aztecs and the Incas, now paying Spanish overlords their taxes and producing livestock for export. More importantly, Indians paid for the new order through their labor, sometimes as slaves but more often through an evolving administrative system channeling native workers to public and private enterprises throughout the Americas. The Spanish also established sugar plantations in the West Indies; these were worked by black slaves who by 1520 were being imported from Africa in large numbers.

Spain's colonies returned even more spectacular profits by the 1540s—the result of huge discoveries of silver in both Mexico and Peru. Silver mining developed into a large-scale capitalist enterprise requiring substantial investment. European investors and Spanish immigrants who had profited from cattle raising and sugar planting poured their capital into equipment and supplies used to mine the silver deposits more efficiently: stamp mills, water-powered crushing equipment, pumps, and mercury. Whole villages of Indians were pressed into service in the mines, joining black slaves and free European workers employed there.

By 1570 the town of Potosí, the site of a veritable mountain of silver, had become larger than any city in either Spain or its American empire, with a population of 120,000. Local farmers who supplied mining centers with food and Spanish merchants in Seville who exported European goods to Potosí profited handsomely. So, too, did the Spanish Crown, which claimed one-fifth of all extracted silver. During the sixteenth century, some 16,000 tons of the precious metal were exported from Spanish America to Europe.

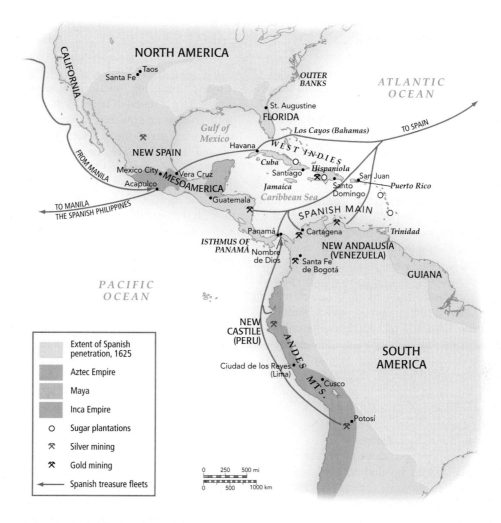

MAP 2.2: SPANISH AMERICA, CA. 1600

By 1600 Spain was extracting large amounts of gold and silver from Mexico and South America, as well as profits from sugar plantations in the Caribbean. Each year, Spanish treasure ships ferried bullion from mines such as the one at Potosí to the Isthmus of Panama, where it was transported by land to the Caribbean coast and from there to Spain. An expedition from Acapulco sailed annually to the Philippines as well, returning with Asian spices and other trade goods.

For an English adventurer looking to capture Spanish silver, which geographic location would be the best place to pick off Spanish treasure ships?

The Search for North America's Indian Empires

>> Riches and glory radicalized Spanish expectations. Would—be conquistadors embarked on an urgent race to discover and topple the next Aztec or Inca Empire, a race to become the next Cortés or Pizarro. The prevailing mood was captured by the portrait of a Spanish soldier that adorns the frontis—piece of his book about the West Indies. He stands with one hand on his sword and the other holding a pair of compasses on top of a globe. Beneath is inscribed the motto "By compasses and the sword/More and more and more and more."

Some of the most ambitious adventurers felt certain that more lands and riches would be found in the North. The Spanish had probed the North American coast up to present—day South Carolina, looking for slaves. But Juan Ponce de León, the con—querer of Puerto Rico, launched the first official expedition to the mainland, which he named Florida in 1513. Everywhere he met armed resistance and was repulsed, because the inhabitants had come to despise Spaniards as slave raiders. Eight years later, he returned, only to be mortally wounded in a battle with Calusa Indians.

Still, the dreams of northern Indian empires per—sisted. In 1528 Pánfilo de Narváez, a red—bearded veteran from the conquest of Cuba, led a major expedition back to Florida. Ignoring advice from his second—in—command, Alvar Núñez Cabeza de Vaca,

Narváez separated from his main force near Tampa Bay and led 300 men on a harrowing march in search of riches. For months Narváez plundered his way through Florida, while the men fell ill or fell victim to Indian archers, whose longbows could bury an arrow six inches into a tree. Disillusioned and desperate, 242 survivors lashed together makeshift rafts and tried to sail along the Gulf Coast to Mexico. Weeks later proud Narváez and most of his men had disappeared at sea, whereas Cabeza de Vaca and a handful of survivors washed up on islands off the Texas coast.

Local Indian groups then turned the tables and made slaves of the Spaniards. After years as prisoners Cabeza de Vaca and three others, including an African slave named Esteban, escaped to make an extraordinary trek across Texas and northern Mexico. Somewhere in present-day Chihuahua they passed through what had been the trading hinterland of Paquime, and Cabeza de Vaca noted an enduring regional commerce in feathers and "green stones"—turquoise. Finally, in July 1536 a shocked party of Spanish slavers stumbled across the four rag-tag castaways and brought them to Mexico City.

The stories the four men told of their ordeal inspired two more massive expeditions to the north. The first, led by Hernán de Soto, scoured the Southeast's agricultural villages searching for gold and taking whatever he wanted: food, clothing, luxury goods, even young women whom he and his men "desired

⚔ As Hernán de Soto traveled through North America, he brought a herd of pigs much like this razorback hog. At times the herd numbered more than 700. The animals were an efficient way of providing protein to the expedition. More than 80 percent of a carcass could be consumed, compared with only 50 percent of a cow or sheep. Hogs could be herded on the march as well, foraging for food as they went. But some anthropologists and historians believe that the hogs were also carriers of disease that migrated to humans. The diseases may have sparked the deaths of thousands of Indians, who lacked the immunity built up by Europeans over centuries of exposure to Eurasian illnesses.

both as servants and for their foul uses...." De Soto's men became the first and last Europeans to glimpse several declining Mississippian chiefdoms, echoes of Cahokia's ancient majesty. Some native communities resisted, inflicting substantial losses on the expedition. Others feigned friendship and sent de Soto to hunt gold in neighboring villages, thus ridding themselves of a great danger and directing it at enemies instead. De Soto's men never found the treasures they sought as they traveled through much of the present-day South (see Map 2.1). But the expedition's cruel and destructive foray did hasten the transformation of the southeastern chiefdoms into decentralized confederacies.

Spanish ambition met a similar fate in the West. In 1539, 29-year-old Francisco Vázquez de Coronado led 300 Spaniards and 1,000 Mexican Indian warriors north into the present-day American Southwest. Coronado was emboldened by tales of cities more wondrous than Tenochtitlán, but his brash confidence began to fail him when instead he found only mud and straw pueblos inhabited by modest farmers. Desperate to turn his hugely expensive expedition to advantage, Coronado sent men in all directions. To the west his scouts were blocked by the vastness of the Grand Canyon. Others traveled east, forcing themselves on the Pueblo peoples of the upper Rio Grande, descendants of the Anasazi. Finally Coronado followed an Indian he dubbed the Turk out onto the Great Plains in search of a rumored kingdom called Quivira. Perhaps the Turk had in mind one of the easternmost Mississippian chiefdoms, but the frustrated conquistador became convinced he had been deceived. He had the Turk strangled somewhere in present-day Kansas and in 1542 returned to Mexico, where Crown authorities tried him for inflicting "great cruelties" on Indians.

Such North American expeditions ruined conquistadors such as Coronado and de Soto, but Spain could afford these blunders. It had taken vast wealth from the Americas, conquered the Western Hemisphere's mightiest peoples, and laid claim to the bulk of the New World. Yet for most of the sixteenth century rival European powers took little interest in the Americas. England's fishermen continued to explore the North Sea, Labrador, and Newfoundland. Portugal discovered and laid claim to Brazil. France launched expeditions along North America's eastern shoreline (Giovanni da Verrazano, 1524) and the St. Lawrence River valley (Jacques Cartier, 1534, 1535, and 1541). These efforts proved important in the long run, but for most of the century Spain could treat the Americas as its own.

Spain owed that luxury, in part, to religious upheaval in Europe. During the second decade of the sixteenth century—the same decade in which Cortés laid siege to Tenochtitlán—religious changes of enormous significance began spreading through Europe.

That revolution in Christianity, known as the Protestant Reformation, occupied European attention and eventually figured as a crucial force in shaping the history of the Americas.

 REVIEW

How did the Spanish respond to the discovery of a "new world"?

RELIGIOUS REFORM DIVIDES EUROPE

During the Middle Ages, the Roman Catholic Church defined what it meant to be a Christian in western Europe. Like other institutions of medieval society, the Catholic Church was a hierarchy. At the top was the pope in Rome, and under him were the descending ranks of other church officials—cardinals, archbishops, bishops. At the bottom of the Catholic hierarchy were parish priests, each serving his own village, as well as monks and nuns living in monasteries and convents. But medieval popes were weak, and their power was felt little in the lives of most Europeans. Like political units of the era, religious institutions of the Middle Ages were local and decentralized.

Between about 1100 and 1500, however, as the monarchs of Europe grew more powerful so, too, did the popes. The Catholic Church acquired land throughout Europe, and its swelling bureaucracy added to church income from tithing (taxes contributed by church members) and from fees paid by those appointed to church offices. In the thirteenth century church officials also began to sell "indulgences." For ordinary believers who expected to spend time after death purging their sins in purgatory, the purchase of an indulgence promised to shorten that punishment by drawing on a "treasury of merit" amassed by the good works of Christ and the saints.

By the fifteenth century the Catholic Church and the papacy had become enormously powerful but increasingly indifferent to popular religious concerns. Church officials meddled in secular politics. Popes and bishops flaunted their wealth, while poorly educated parish priests neglected their pastoral duties. At the same time, popular demands for religious assurance grew increasingly intense.

The Teachings of Martin Luther >> Into this climate of heightened spirituality stepped Martin Luther, who abandoned studying the law to enter a monastery. Like many of his contemporaries, Luther was consumed by fears over his eternal fate. He was convinced that he was damned, and he could not find any consolation in the Catholic Church. Catholic doctrine taught that a person could be saved by faith in God and by his or her own good works—by leading a virtuous life, observing the sacraments (such as baptism, the Mass, and penance), making pilgrimages to holy places, and praying to Christ and the saints. Because Luther believed that human nature was innately evil, he despaired of being able to lead a life that "merited" salvation. If men and women are so bad, he reasoned, how could they ever win their way to heaven with good works?

Luther finally drew on the Bible to break through his despair. It convinced him that God did not require fallen humankind to earn salvation. Salvation, he concluded, came by faith alone, the "free gift" of God to undeserving sinners. The ability to live a good life could not be the *cause* of salvation but its *consequence*: once men and women believed that they had saving faith, moral behavior was possible. Luther elaborated that idea, known as "justification by faith alone," between 1513 and 1517.

Luther was ordained a priest and then assigned to teach at a university in Wittenberg, Germany. He became increasingly critical, however, of the Catholic Church as an institution. In 1517 he posted on the door of a local church 95 theses attacking the Catholic hierarchy for selling salvation in the form of indulgences.

The novelty of this attack was not Luther's open break with Catholic teaching. Challenges to the church had cropped up throughout the Middle Ages. What was new was the passion and force behind Luther's protest. Using the blunt, earthy Germanic tongue, he expressed the anxieties of many devout laypeople and their outrage at the church hierarchy's neglect. The "gross, ignorant asses and knaves at Rome," he warned, should keep their distance from Germany, or else "jump into the Rhine or the nearest river, and take… a cold bath."

The pope and his representatives in Germany at first tried to silence Martin Luther, then excommunicated him. But opposition only pushed Luther toward more radical positions. He asserted that the church and its officials were not infallible; only the Scriptures were without error. Every person, he said, should read and interpret the Bible for himself or herself. In an even more direct assault on church authority, he advanced an idea known as "the priesthood of all believers." Catholic doctrine held that salvation came only through the church and its clergy, a privileged group that possessed special access to God. Luther asserted that every person had the power claimed by priests.

Although Luther had not intended to start a schism within Catholicism, independent Lutheran churches were forming in Germany by the 1520s. During the 1530s Luther's ideas spread throughout Europe, where they were eagerly taken up by other reformers.

The Contribution of John Calvin >> Luther's most influential successor was John Calvin, a French lawyer turned theologian. Calvin agreed with Luther that men and women could not merit their salvation. But, whereas Luther's God was a loving deity who extended his mercy to sinful humankind, Calvin conceived of God as awesome, all–knowing and all–powerful—the controlling force in human history that would ultimately triumph over Satan. To bring about that final victory, to usher in his heavenly kingdom, God had selected certain people as his agents, Calvin believed. These people—"the saints," or "the elect"—had been "predestined" by God for eternal salvation in heaven.

elect in theology, those of the faithful chosen, or "elected" by God for eternal salvation.

Calvin's emphasis on predestination led him to another distinctively Protestant notion—the doctrine of calling. How could a person learn whether he or she belonged to the elect who were saved? Calvin answered: strive to behave like a saint. God expected his elect to serve the good of society by unrelenting work in a "calling," or occupation, in the world. In place of the Catholic belief in the importance of good works, Calvin emphasized the goodness of work itself. Success in attaining discipline and self–control, in bringing order into one's own life and the entire society, revealed that a person might be among the elect.

Calvin fashioned a religion to change the world. Whereas Luther believed that Christians should accept the existing social order, Calvin called on Christians to become activists, reshaping society and government to conform with God's laws laid down in the Bible. He wanted all Europe to become like Geneva, the Swiss city that he had converted into a holy commonwealth in which the elect regulated the behavior and morals of everyone else. And unlike Luther, who wrote primarily for a German audience, Calvin addressed his most important book, *The Institutes of the Christian Religion* (1536), to Christians throughout Europe. Reformers from every country flocked to Geneva to learn more about Calvin's ideas.

French Huguenots and the Birth of Spanish Florida >> The Protestant Reformation shattered the unity of Christendom in western Europe. Spain, Ireland, and Italy remained firmly Catholic. England, Scotland, the Netherlands, Switzerland, and France developed either dominant or substantial Calvinist constituencies. Much of Germany and Scandinavia opted for Lutheranism. As religious groups competed for political power and the loyalties of believers, brutal wars swept sixteenth–century Europe. France experienced some of the worst violence. An influential group of Huguenots (Calvin's French followers) saw in North America a potential refuge from religious persecution. Under Jean Ribault, 150 Huguenots in 1562 established a simple village on Parris Island off present–day South Carolina. That experiment ended in desperation and cannibalism, but two years later Ribault led another, larger group to a site south of present–day Jacksonville, Florida. Here, at Fort Caroline, the Huguenots nurtured a cordial relationship with the local Timucua Indians. It seemed a promising start.

But Spanish authorities in the Caribbean took the Huguenots for a triple threat. First, French pirates had long tried to siphon silver from the Americas by way-laying Spanish galleons as they rode the Gulf Stream up the southeastern coast of North America before turning east toward Spain. With good reason, Spanish administrators feared that Fort Caroline would entrench the threat of piracy. Second, Spain worried that France would take a broader interest in the Americas, perhaps eventually planting colonies in all of North America. Finally, many Spanish Catholics saw Protestantism as a loathsome contagion, to be expunged from Europe and barred from the Americas.

These interlocking concerns prompted Spain to found a permanent colony in Florida under the

⌃ Though both were Protestant reformers, Luther and John Calvin (shown here) were a study in contrasts. Luther was down-to-earth, friendly and emotional. Calvin, on the other hand, was cool and logical—a brilliant thinker whose long, angled face and pointed beard shone with the confidence that he was carrying out God's word.

direction of a focused and unforgiving man named Pedro Menéndez de Avilés. In 1565 Menéndez established a settlement on the coast called St. Augustine (still the United States' oldest continuously occupied, non–Indian settlement). Next he and 500 soldiers slogged through the rain and marsh until they found Fort Caroline. In battle and through later executions the attackers killed Ribault and about 500 of his Huguenots. Flush with victory Menéndez established several more outposts on Florida's Atlantic and Gulf coasts and in 1570 even encouraged a short–lived Jesuit mission just miles from where English colonists would establish Jamestown a generation later. As for the Huguenots, the calamity at Fort Caroline dashed hope that the New World would be their haven. Most had to resign themselves to intensifying persecution in France.

The English Reformation >> While the Reformation racked northern Europe, King Henry VIII of England labored at a goal more worldly than those of Luther and Calvin. He wanted a son, a male heir to continue the Tudor dynasty. When his wife, Catherine of Aragon, gave birth to a daughter, Mary, Henry petitioned the pope to have his marriage annulled in the hope that a new wife would give him a son. This move enraged the king of Spain, who also happened to be Catherine's nephew. He persuaded the pope to refuse Henry's request. Defiantly, England's king proceeded with the divorce nonetheless and quickly married his mistress, Anne Boleyn. He then went further, making himself, not the pope, the head of the Church of England. Henry was an audacious but practical man, and he had little interest in promoting reformist doctrine. Apart from discarding the pope, the Church of England remained essentially Catholic in its teachings and rituals.

England's Protestants gained ground during the six–year reign of Henry's son Edward VI but then found themselves persecuted when Edward's Catholic half–sister Mary became queen in 1553. Five years later the situation turned again, when Elizabeth I (Anne Boleyn's daughter) took the throne, proclaiming herself the defender of Protestantism. Elizabeth was no radical Calvinist, however. A vocal minority of her subjects were reformers of that stripe, calling for the English church to purge itself of bishops, elaborate ceremonies, and other Catholic "impurities." Because of the austerity and zeal of such Calvinist radicals, their opponents proclaimed them "Puritans."

Radical Protestants might annoy Elizabeth as she pursued her careful, moderate policies, but radical Catholics frightened her. She had reason to worry that Spain might use English Catholics to undermine her rule. More ominously, Elizabeth's advisers cautioned that Catholic Ireland to the west would be an ideal base from which Spain or France could launch an invasion of England. Beginning in 1565 the queen encouraged a number of her elite subjects to sponsor private ventures for subduing the native Irish and settling loyal English Protestants on their land. As events fell out, this Irish venture proved to be a prelude to England's bolder attempt to found colonies across the Atlantic.

 REVIEW

What were the major branches of Protestant reform, and how did the religious wars affect the Americas?

ENGLAND'S ENTRY INTO AMERICA

Among the gentlemen eager to win fame and fortune were Humphrey Gilbert and Walter Raleigh, two adventurers with conquistador appetites for more and more. The pair were like most of the English who went to Ireland, ardent Protestants who viewed the native Catholic inhabitants as superstitious, pagan savages: "They blaspheme, they murder, commit whoredome," complained one Englishman, "hold no wedlocke, ravish, steal. . . ." Thus the English found it easy enough to justify their conquest. They proclaimed it their duty to teach the Irish the discipline of hard work, the rule of law, and the truth of Protestant Christianity. And, while the Irish were learning these civilized, English ways, they

Opinion

Do you think religion is only a surface justification or a primary motivation for the religious wars and rivalries of the sixteenth century?

would not be allowed to buy land or hold office or serve on juries or give testimony in courts or learn a trade or bear arms.

When the Irish rebelled at that program of "liberation," the English ruthlessly repressed them, slaughtering not only combatants but civilians as well. Most English in Ireland, like most Spaniards in America, believed that native peoples who resisted civilization and proper Christianity should be subdued at any cost. No scruples stopped Humphrey Gilbert, in an insurgent country, from planting the path to his camp with the severed heads of Irish rebels.

The struggle to colonize and subdue Ireland would serve as a rough model for later English efforts at expansion. The approach was essentially military, like that of the conquistadors. It also set the ominous precedent that Englishmen could treat "savage" peoples with a level of brutal cruelty that would have been inappropriate in wars between "civilized" Europeans. Finding "neither reputation, or profytt" in Ireland, Gilbert, Raleigh, and other West County gentry took their ambition and their Irish education to North America.

The Ambitions of Gilbert, Raleigh, and Wingina >> In 1578 Gilbert got his chance for glory when Elizabeth granted him a royal patent—the first English colonial **charter**—to explore, occupy, and govern any territory in America "not actually possessed of any Christian prince or people." The vague, wildly unrealistic charter ignored the Indian possession of North America and made Gilbert proprietor of all the land lying between Florida and Labrador. In many ways his dreams looked backward. Gilbert hoped to set up a kind of medieval kingdom of his own, where loyal tenant farmers would work the lands of manors, paying rent to feudal lords. Yet his vision also looked forward to a utopian society. He planned to encourage England's poor to emigrate by providing them free land and a government "to be chosen by consent of the people." Elizabeth had high hopes for her haughty champion, but a fierce storm got the better of his ship, and the Atlantic swallowed him before he ever set foot in his American dominions.

charter document issued by a sovereign ruler, legislature, or other authority creating a public or private corporation.

Meanwhile, Gilbert's stepbrother Walter Raleigh had been laying the groundwork for a British–American empire. Raleigh enlisted the talents of Richard Hakluyt, a clergyman, to write an eloquent plea for the English settlement of America, titled *A Discourse Concerning Westerne Planting*. North America's temperate and fertile lands, Hakluyt argued, would not only grow profitable crops, they would also make an

>> John White's sensitive watercolor *Indian Elder or Chief* may well be of Wingina. The portrayal includes the copper ornament worn hanging from his neck, indicating high social status and the presence of an active trade network, since copper is not found on the island. Just as Raleigh had to gauge his strategy in dealing with the Indians, Wingina had to decide how to treat the strange newcomers from across the Atlantic.

excellent base from which to harry the Spanish, search for a northwest passage to Asia, and spread Protestantism. Finally, Hakluyt predicted that because the "Spaniardes have executed most outragious and more then Turkishe crueltes in all the west Indies," Indians would greet Englishmen as liberators.

By the summer of 1584 Raleigh had dispatched an exploratory voyage to the Outer Banks of present-day North Carolina. Expedition leaders made friendly contact with a people known as the Roanoke and ruled by a "weroance," or chief, named Wingina. The enthusiastic Hakluyt envisioned a colony that would become the Mexico of England, full of plantations producing sugar and silk and mountains yielding gold. Elizabeth knighted Raleigh and allowed him to name the new land "Virginia," after his virgin queen.

But Raleigh was not the only one with grand plans. Almost certainly Wingina had encountered or at least heard of Europeans before 1584. Like most coastal groups in the region, his people would have obtained prized European tools and commodities through indirect trade or by scouring wrecked ships. Eager to fortify his own and his people's power, Wingina recognized that friendly relations with the English would give him access to their trade and influence. Perhaps he believed he would act as patron to the newcomers. After all, they knew little of the region, spoke no Indian languages, and even lacked the skills necessary to survive in the area without native assistance. In short, Wingina seems to have welcomed the English because he believed that they could be useful and that they could be controlled. It was a tragic if understandable miscalculation—one that Indian leaders would make again and again in colonial America.

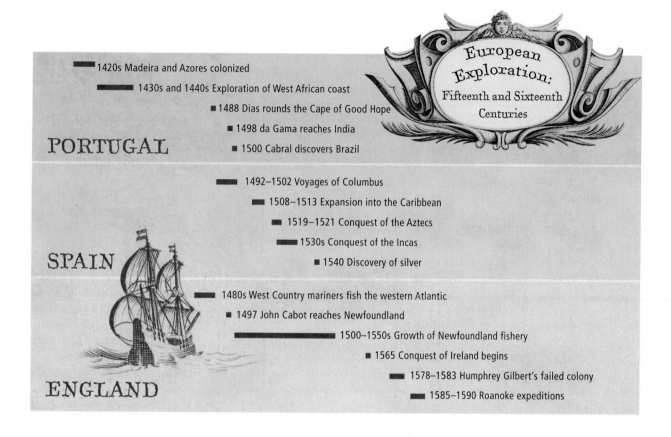

European Exploration: Fifteenth and Sixteenth Centuries

PORTUGAL

1420s Madeira and Azores colonized
1430s and 1440s Exploration of West African coast
1488 Dias rounds the Cape of Good Hope
1498 da Gama reaches India
1500 Cabral discovers Brazil

SPAIN

1492–1502 Voyages of Columbus
1508–1513 Expansion into the Caribbean
1519–1521 Conquest of the Aztecs
1530s Conquest of the Incas
1540 Discovery of silver

ENGLAND

1480s West Country mariners fish the western Atlantic
1497 John Cabot reaches Newfoundland
1500–1550s Growth of Newfoundland fishery
1565 Conquest of Ireland begins
1578–1583 Humphrey Gilbert's failed colony
1585–1590 Roanoke expeditions

Raleigh apparently aimed to establish on Roa—noke a mining camp and a military garrison. In a stroke of genius he included in the company of 108 men a scientist, Thomas Hariot, to study the coun—try's natural resources, and an artist, John White, to make drawings of the Virginia Indians. *A Briefe and True Reporte of the New Found Land of Virginia* (1588), written by Hariot and illustrated by White, served as one of the principal sources about North America and its Indian inhabitants for more than a century. Far less inspired was Raleigh's choice to lead the expedition—two veterans of the Irish campaigns, Sir Richard Grenville and Ralph Lane. Even his fel—low conquistadors in Ireland considered Lane proud and greedy. As for Grenville, he was given to breaking wineglasses between his teeth and then swallowing the shards to show that he could stand the sight of blood, even his own.

The bullying ways of both men quickly alienated the natives of Roanoke. Wingina found the newcomers dis—respectful, haughty, and cruel: when a local stole a cup, the English tried to teach everyone a lesson by torch—ing his village and destroying its corn stores. As suspi—cions and resentments mounted on each side, Wingina tried to regain control of the situation the following summer by meeting with Lane to improve relations. But the meeting was a trap. Lane's men opened fire at the Indian envoys, killed Wingina, and hacked the head from his body. All that averted a massive counterattack was the arrival of England's preeminent privateer, Sir Francis Drake, fresh from freebooting up and down the Caribbean. The settlement's 102 survivors piled onto Drake's ships and put an ocean between themselves and the avenging Roanokes.

A Second Roanoke—and Croatoan >>
Undaunted, Raleigh organized a second expedition to plant a colony farther north, in Chesapeake Bay. He recruited 119 men, women, and children, members of the English middle class, and granted each person an estate of 500 acres. He also appointed as governor the artist John White, who brought along a suit of armor for ceremonial occasions.

White deplored Lane's treachery toward Wingina and hated the senseless violence that had charac—terized the entire endeavor. The artist had spent his time on Roanoke closely observing native peoples, their material cultures, and their customs. His sen—sitive watercolors, especially those featuring women and children, indicate a genuine respect and affection.

White believed that under prudent, moral leaders an English colony could indeed coexist peacefully with American Indians.

Despite his best intentions, everything went wrong. In July of 1587 the expedition's pilot insisted on leaving the colonists at Roanoke Island rather than the Chesapeake. Understandably, the Roanokes took no pleasure in seeing the English return. Sensing that the situation on Roanoke could quickly become desperate, the colonists sent White home to fetch reinforcements.

He returned to England in 1588 just as the massive Spanish navy, the Armada, was preparing an assault on England. Elizabeth enlisted every seaworthy ship and able-bodied sailor to stave off invasion. The Armada was defeated, but White was unable to return to Roanoke Island until 1590. There, he found only an empty fort and a few cottages in a clearing. The sole clue to the colony's fate was an inscription carved on a post: CROATOAN. It was the name of a nearby island off Cape Hatteras.

Had the Roanoke colonists fled to Croatoan for safety? Had they moved to the mainland and joined Indian communities? Had they been killed by Wingina's people? The fate of the "lost colony" remains a mystery, though later rumors suggest that the missing colonists merged with native societies in the interior. His dream of a tolerant, cooperative colony dashed, White sailed back to England, leaving behind the little cluster of cottages, which would soon be overgrown with vines, and his suit of armor, which was already "almost eaten through with rust."

 REVIEW

Why did Elizabeth agree to charter a colony in America, and how successful were the first attempts?

All the world lay before them. Or so it had seemed to the young men from England's West Country who dreamed of gold and glory, conquest and colonization. True, they lived on the fringe of the civilized world in the fifteenth and sixteenth centuries. China remained the distant, exotic kingdom of power and wealth, supplying silks and spices and other luxurious goods. Islamic empires stood astride the land routes from Europe to the east. Nations on the western edge of Europe thus took to the seas. Portugal sent slave and gold traders to Africa, as well as merchants to trade with the civilizations of the Indies. Spanish conquerors such as Cortés toppled Indian empires and brought home mountains of silver. But England's West County sea dogs—would-be conquistadors—met only with frustration. In 1600, more than a century after Columbus's first crossing, not a single English settlement existed in the Americas.

What was left of the freebooting West Country world? Raleigh, his ambition still afire, sailed to South America in quest of a rich city named El Dorado. In 1603, however, Elizabeth's death brought to the English throne her cousin James I, the founder of the Stuart dynasty. The new king arrested the old queen's favorite for treason and imprisoned him for 15 years in the Tower of London. Set free in 1618 at the age of 64, Raleigh returned to South America, his lust for El Dorado undiminished. Along the way he plundered some Spanish silver ships, defying King James's orders. It was a fatal mistake, because England had made peace with Spain. Raleigh lost his head.

James I did not want to harass the king of Spain; he wanted to imitate him. The Stuarts were even more determined than the Tudors had been to enlarge the sphere of royal power. There would be no room in America for a warrior nobility of conquistadors, no room for a feudal fiefdom ruled by the likes of Raleigh or Gilbert. Instead, there would be profitable plantations and colonies managed by loyal, efficient bureaucrats. America would strengthen English monarchs, paving their path to greater power, just as the dominions of Mexico and Peru had enlarged the authority of the Spanish Crown. America would be the making of kings and queens.

Or would it? For some Europeans, weary of freebooting conquistadors and sea rovers, the security that Crown rule and centralized states promoted in western Europe would be enough. But others, men and women who were often desperate and sometimes idealistic, would cast their eyes west across the Atlantic and want more.

CHAPTER SUMMARY

During the late fifteenth century, Europeans and Africans made their first contact with the Americas, where native cultures were numerous and diverse.

- During the fourteenth and early fifteenth centuries, western Europeans were on the fringes of an international economy drawn together by Chinese goods such as spices, ceramics, and silks.
- A combination of technological advances, the rise of new trade networks and techniques, and increased political centralization made Europe's expansion overseas possible.
- Led by Portugal, European expansion began with a push southward along the West African coast, in pursuit of spices, ivory, and gold. As sugar plantations were established in the islands of the eastern Atlantic, a slave trade in Africans became a part of this expansive commerce.

- Spain took the lead in exploring and colonizing the Americas, consolidating a vast and profitable empire of its own in the place of Aztec and Inca Empires. Divisions within Indian empires and the devastating effects of European diseases made Spanish conquest possible.
- The conquistadors who led the Spanish occupation were soon replaced by an elaborate, centralized royal bureaucracy, which regulated most aspects of economic and social life. The discovery of silver provided Spain with immense wealth, while leading to sharply increased mortality among the native population.
- Spanish conquistadors also explored much of the present-day southeastern and southwestern United States. They found no empires, silver mines, or rich empires and were thwarted by the Indian peoples they encountered.
- The Protestant Reformation was inaugurated by Martin Luther in 1517 and carried on by John Calvin, whose more activist theology spread from his headquarters in Geneva outward to England, Scotland, the Netherlands, and the Huguenots in France.
- England, apprehensive of Spain's power, did not turn its attention to exploration and colonization until the 1570s and 1580s. By the time it did, European rivalries were heightened by splits arising out of the Protestant Reformation.
- England's merchants and gentry lent support to colonizing ventures, although early efforts, such as those at Roanoke, failed.

Additional Reading

For ordinary folk in the era of exploration, see Kenneth R. Andrews, *Trade, Plunder, and Settlement* (1985). For Portugal's initial expansion, see Malyn Newitt, *A History of Portuguese Overseas Expansion, 1400–1668* (2004). David Northrup's *Africa's Discovery of Europe, 1450–1850* (2008) explores West Africa's encounter with Europeans. For sugar and expansion, see Philip D. Curtin, *The Rise and Fall of the Plantation Complex* (2nd ed., 1998). The demographic catastrophe that followed contact is explored in Massimo Livi-Bacci, *Conquest: The Destruction of the American Indios* (2008). For telling comparisons between Iberian and English colonialism in the New World, see John Elliott's magisterial *Empires of the Atlantic World: Britain and Spain in America, 1492–1830* (2007). Charles Mann's *1493: Uncovering the New World Columbus Created* (2011) deftly integrates insights from multiple disciplines about the consequences of contact. For Spain in the Caribbean, see David Abulafia, *The Discovery of Mankind* (2008). For an indispensable narrative of Spain's activities in North America, see David J. Weber, *The Spanish Frontier in North America* (1992). Coronado's sojourn is the subject of the exacting work by Richard Flint, *No Settlement, No Conquest* (2008). For the Southeast, see Daniel S. Murphree, *Constructing Floridians* (2006). For a good introduction to the Reformation in England, see Christopher Haigh, *English Reformations* (1993); Eamon Duffy's *The Voices of Morebath* (2001) asks how the Reformation transformed the lives of ordinary people. For early English attempts at colonization, in both Ireland and the Americas, consult the works of Nicholas Canny, as well as Michael Leroy Oberg, *The Head in Edward Nugent's Hand* (2007).

Significant Events

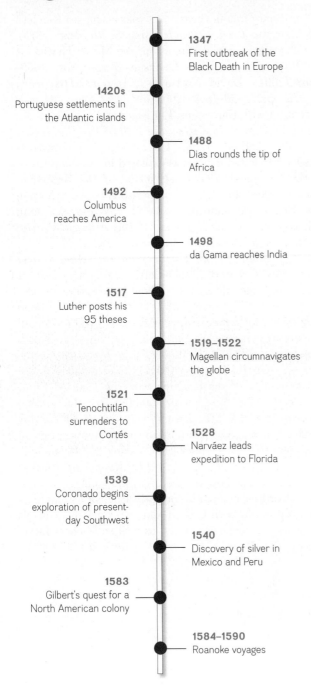

1347
First outbreak of the Black Death in Europe

1420s
Portuguese settlements in the Atlantic islands

1488
Dias rounds the tip of Africa

1492
Columbus reaches America

1498
da Gama reaches India

1517
Luther posts his 95 theses

1519–1522
Magellan circumnavigates the globe

1521
Tenochtitlán surrenders to Cortés

1528
Narváez leads expedition to Florida

1539
Coronado begins exploration of present-day Southwest

1540
Discovery of silver in Mexico and Peru

1583
Gilbert's quest for a North American colony

1584–1590
Roanoke voyages

Colonization & Conflict in the South

1600–1750

This Native American drawing on a canyon wall in present-day Arizona represents the progress of the Spanish into the Southwest. Indians would soon put horses, prominently featured here, to their own uses.

>> An American Story

OUTLANDISH STRANGERS

n the year 1617, as Europeans counted time, on a bay they called the Chesapeake, in a land they named Virginia, the mighty weroance Powhatan surveyed his domain. It had all worked according to plan, and Powhatan, leader of the Pamunkeys, had laid his plans carefully. While in his prime, the tall, robust man had drawn some 30 villages along the Virginia coast into a powerful confederacy numbering nearly 9,000 souls. The natives

^ Pocahontas, daughter of the mighty werowance Powhatan and wife of English colonist John Rolfe, has long fascinated nonnatives. In an image from 1616 (*left*), she is represented as a high-status English lady, stripped of all marks of her native culture save her name, Matoaka (Pocahontas was a nickname). The second image, from the 1993 Disney film, portrays her as a pretty and innocent child of nature. Now as then, we see in her what we want to.

of the Chesapeake, like the peoples who inhabited the length of eastern North America, lived for most of the year in small agricultural villages. As tribute for his protection and leadership Powhatan collected food, furs, and skins from the villagers. He forged alliances with communities too distant or too powerful for him to dominate. He married the daughters of prominent men, dozens in all, to solidify his network of patronage and power.

After 1607 Powhatan was forced to take into account yet another group. The English, as this new people called themselves, came by sea, crammed into three ships. They were 100 men and 4 boys, all clad in heavy, outlandish clothing, many dressed in gaudy colors.

The ships followed a river deep into Powhatan's territory and built a fort on a swampy, mosquito-infested site that they called Jamestown.

Powhatan was not frightened. He knew of these strangers from across the waters. Even amid the bounty of the Chesapeake they failed to feed themselves. With bows and arrows, spears and nets, Indian men brought in an abundance of meat and fish. Fields tended by Indian women yielded generous crops of corn, beans, squash, and melon, and edible nuts and fruits grew wild. Still the English starved, and not just during the first few months of their settlement but for several years afterward. Powhatan could understand why the English refused to grow food. Cultivating crops was women's work—like building houses; or making clothing, pottery, and baskets; or caring for children. And the English settlement included no women until two arrived in the fall of 1608. Yet even after more women came, the English still starved, and they expected—no, they demanded—that Powhatan's people feed them.

And yet these hapless folk put on such airs. They boasted about the power of their god—they had only one—and denounced the Indians'

"devil-worship" of "false gods." They crowed endlessly about the power of their king, James I, who expected Powhatan to become his vassal. Inconceivable—that Powhatan should willingly bow before this King James, the ruler of so small and savage a race! When the Indians made war, they killed the male warriors of rival communities but adopted their women and children. But when Powhatan's people withheld food or defended their land from these invaders, the English retaliated by murdering Indian women and children. Worse, the English could not even keep order among themselves. Too many of them wanted to lead, and they squabbled constantly.

The temptation to wipe out the helpless, troublesome, arrogant tribe of English—or simply to let them starve to death—had been almost overwhelming. But Powhatan allowed the English to survive. Like Wingina before him, he decided that even these barbaric people had their uses. English labor, English trading goods, and, most important, English guns would help quell resistance within his confederacy and subdue his Indian rivals to the west. In 1614 Powhatan cemented his claim on the English and their weapons with the marriage between his favorite child, Pocahontas, and an ambitious Englishman, John Rolfe.

By 1617 events had vindicated Powhatan's strategy of tolerating the English. His chiefdom flourished, ready to be passed on to his brother. Powhatan's people still outnumbered the English, who seldom starved outright now but continued to fight among themselves and sicken and die. Only one thing had changed in the Chesapeake by

1617: the English were clearing woodland along the rivers and planting tobacco.

That was the doing of Powhatan's son-in-law, Rolfe, a man as strange as the rest of the newcomers, all of them eager to store up wealth and worldly goods. Rolfe had been obsessed with finding a crop that could be grown in Virginia and then sold for gain across the sea. When he succeeded by growing tobacco, other English followed his lead. Odder still, not women but men tended the tobacco fields. Here was more evidence of English inferiority. Men wasted long hours laboring when they might supply their needs with far less effort.

In 1617 Powhatan, ruler of the Pamunkeys, surveyed his domain, and sometime in that year, he died. He had lived long enough to see the tobacco fields lining the riverbanks, straddling the charred stumps of felled trees. But perhaps he went to his grave believing that he had done what Wingina had failed to do: bend the English to his purposes. He died before those stinking tobacco weeds spread over the length of his land and sent his hard-won dominion up in smoke.

Wingina and Powhatan were not the only native leaders who dreamed of turning Europeans to their advantage. Across North America, the fleeting if destructive encounters of the sixteenth century gave way to sustained colonialism in the seventeenth. As Europeans began to colonize the edges of North America in earnest, Indian peoples struggled not only to survive and adapt to new realities but also, when possible, to profit from the rapid changes swirling around them.

Those often dramatic changes reflected upheavals under way all across the globe. The tobacco John Rolfe had begun to cultivate was only one of several plantation **monocultures** that Europeans began

> **monoculture** growth of a single crop to the virtual exclusion of all others, either on a farm or more generally within a region.

to establish in their far-flung colonies. Sugar, already flourishing in the Atlantic islands off the coast of West Africa, was gaining a foothold in the islands of the Caribbean. Rice, long a staple in Asia and grown also in Africa, made its way into South Carolina toward the end of the seventeenth century. Because these crops were grown most efficiently on plantations and required intensive labor, African slavery spread during these years, fueled by an expanding international slave trade. Europeans, Africans, and Indians were all, in different ways, caught up in the wrenching transformations. <<

What's to Come

SPAIN'S NORTH AMERICAN COLONIES

Just as Spain had been the first European power to explore North America's interior, so too it led the way in establishing lasting colonies north of Mexico. But while France and especially England eventually established large colonial populations on territory suited to European-style agriculture, Spain confined its northern ventures to the ecologically challenging regions of the upper Rio Grande and coastal Florida. Because economic opportunities and good farmland were abundant elsewhere in Spanish America, few Spaniards migrated to distant and difficult northern

⌃ Like many other Pueblo peoples, the founders of Acoma built their village atop a sandstone mesa to gain protection from enemies. Constructed in the twelfth century CE, Acoma may be the oldest continuously occupied settlement in the present-day United States.

outposts. Even so, Spain's colonial endeavors had tremendous implications for North America's native peoples and for the geopolitics of the continent as a whole.

The Founding of a "New" Mexico >> By the 1590s Coronado's dismal expedition a half–century earlier had been all but forgotten. Again, rumors spread in Mexico about great riches in the North. New Spain's viceroy began casting about for a leader to establish a "new" Mexico as magnificent and profitable as its namesake. He chose Juan de Oñate, son of one of New Spain's richest miners and husband to Isabel de Tolosa Cortés Moctezuma, granddaughter of Hernán Cortés and great–granddaughter of Moctezuma. Ignorant of northern geography and overestimating New Mexico's riches, Oñate proposed to sail ships up the Pacific to Pueblo country, so that twice a year he could resupply his would–be colony and export its expected treasures.

The magnitude of his misconceptions came into focus in 1598, when he led 500 colonists, soldiers, and slaves to the upper Rio Grande. Oñate found modest villages, no ocean, and no significant mineral wealth. Even so, he had come with women and children, with livestock and tools, with artisans and tradesmen, with seeds and books and bibles. He had come to stay. Eager to avoid the violence of earlier encounters, Tewa–speaking Pueblos evacuated a village for the newcomers to use. Many native leaders pledged Oñate their allegiance, Pueblo artisans labored on irrigation systems and other public works for the Spaniards, and Indian women (traditionally the builders in Pueblo society) constructed the region's first Catholic Church.

The colonizers mistook this cautious courtesy for subservience. Oñate's oldest nephew, Juan de Zaldívar, was bolder and cruder than most. At Acoma Pueblo, known today as "Sky City" because of its position high atop a majestic mesa, he brazenly seized several sacred turkeys to kill and eat, answering Indian protests with insults. Outraged, Acoma's men fell upon Zaldívar, killing him and several companions. Fueled by grief and rage, Zaldívar's younger brother Vicente laid siege to Acoma Pueblo, killed perhaps 800 of its residents, and made slaves of several hundred more. The savagery of the Acoma siege and similar repressive measures educated all of the region's native communities about the risks of resistance.

But it was easier to instill terror than grow rich. Desperate to salvage their enterprise, Oñate and key followers toiled on long, fruitless expeditions in search of gold, silver, and cities. Vicente de Zaldívar, the head–strong conqueror of Acoma, tried to domesticate bison as had been done with cattle, rather than search for them on the plains. But the bison—"stubborn animals, brave beyond praise"—quickly broke free of the cottonwood coral his men constructed. Most Spaniards turned to the less hazardous pursuit of farming and husbandry to support their families. Others despaired of securing a living in arid New Mexico and fled back into New Spain.

In 1606 royal authorities recalled Oñate and brought him up on charges of mismanagement and abusing Indians. Meanwhile Spain nearly abandoned "worthless" New Mexico, except that the Franciscans insisted it would be a crime to forsake the thousands of Indians they claimed to have baptized since 1598. Spain's New Mexican outpost continued to struggle along.

The Growth of Spanish Florida >> Franciscans became key actors in Spanish North America. Members of a medieval religious order founded by St. Francis of Assisi, Franciscan monks owned no personal property, remained **celibate,** and survived by begging for alms or accepting donations from wealthy patrons. Franciscans accompanied Columbus on his second voyage, and they began ministering to the Indians of central Mexico soon after Tenochtitlán fell. By the 1570s Spanish authorities started secular–izing central Mexico's missions, transforming them into self–supporting parishes. Franciscans went on to become powerful figures in colonial New Mexico, while Jesuits established several missions in present–day Arizona.

celibate abstaining from sexual intercourse; also unmarried.

For strategic reasons the Crown needed the Franciscans even more in Florida than in New Mexico's distant outposts. As long as pirates or rival colonies on the Atlantic seaboard threatened Spanish shipping, the king had to control Florida. Pedro Menéndez de Avilés did much to secure the peninsula in the 1560s when he destroyed France's Fort Caroline and established several posts on the coast (see Chapter 2). By 1600, however, Menéndez was dead and only St. Augustine endured, with a population of perhaps 500. Spanish Florida needed something more to survive.

To extend his influence the king first offered the peninsula's many native peoples trade privileges and regular diplomatic presents. In return, native leaders promised to support the Spanish in war to and tax their people on behalf of the king. Once these alliances were in place, Indian communities were made to accept Franciscan missions and a few resident soldiers, a policy critical to molding and monitoring native villages. By 1675, 40 missions were ministering to as many as 26,000 baptized Indians. The bishop of Cuba toured Florida and spoke enthusiastically of converts who embraced "with devotion the mysteries of our holy faith." Florida's mission system and network of Indian alliances convinced Spanish authorities that they could maintain their grip on this crucial peninsula.

Popé and the Pueblo Revolt >> As the seventeenth century progressed, New Mexico also seemed to stabilize. Enough Spanish colonists remained to establish a separate town, La Villa Real de la Santa Fe, in 1610. Santa Fe (the second–oldest European town in the United States after St. Augustine) became the hub of Spanish life in New Mexico. Many families settled elsewhere on the Rio Grande, on well–watered lands near Pueblo villages. Economic and political life revolved around a dozen prominent families. By 1675 New Mexico had a diverse colonial population of perhaps 2,500, including Spaniards, Africans, Mexican Indians, mestizos (persons of mixed Spanish–Indian heritage), and mulattoes (of Spanish–African heritage).

This population also included large numbers of Indian captives. Occasionally captives came to Spanish households through war, as after the siege of Acoma. In addition, Spaniards purchased enslaved women and children from other Indians and regularly launched slave raids against so–called enemy Indians such as Utes, Apaches, and Navajos. By 1680 half of all New Mexican households included at least one Indian captive. Depending on age, gender, and the master's disposition, such captives could be treated affectionately as low–status family members or terrorized and abused as disposable human property.

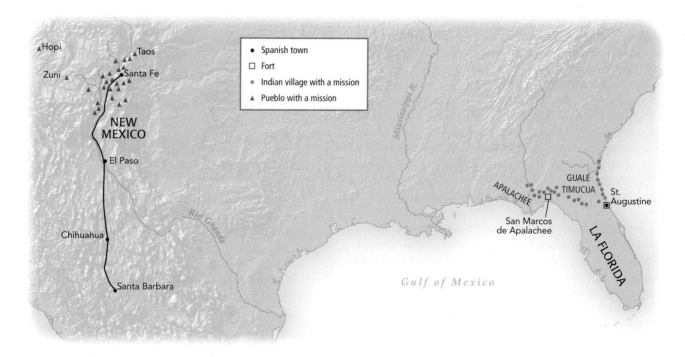

MAP 3.1: SPANISH MISSIONS IN NORTH AMERICA, CA. 1675

From St. Augustine, Spanish missionaries spread into Guale Indian villages in present-day Georgia and westward among the Indians of Timucua, Apalachee, and Apalachicola. In New Mexico, missions radiated outward from the Rio Grande, as distant as Hopi villages in the west. *What was the point of origin from which Spanish missions in New Mexico spread?*

The colonists also extracted labor from Pueblo Indians. Officially Pueblo households had to surrender three bushels of corn and one processed hide or large cotton blanket each year. Pueblos also sometimes labored on public works, and elite Spaniards often exploited their privileges by insisting on more tribute and labor than legally allowed. Still, the populous Pueblos could have satisfied Spanish demands with little difficulty except for other changes in their world. First and most importantly, colonialism meant epidemics. Beginning in the 1620s smallpox killed 70 percent of the population within a generation. Whereas New Mexico boasted about 100 native villages at contact, by 1680 only 30 remained inhabited. Infestations of locusts, severe droughts, and crop failures compounded the crisis. A distraught Franciscan reported starving native men, women, and children "lying dead along the roads, in the ravines, and in their hovels." Mounted Utes, Apaches, and Navajos, embittered by New Mexican slaving and barred from their customary trade in the pueblos, launched punishing raids against the most vulnerable Pueblo villages.

In their deepening misery Pueblos turned to religion—their own. Since 1598 the Franciscans had worked tirelessly to suppress the dances, idols, and ceremonies that long mediated Pueblo relationships with the divine. By the 1670s Pueblo elders were arguing that the calamities of the past decades could be reversed only by rejecting Christianity and returning to the old faith. Franciscans and civil authorities scrambled to extinguish the revival movement, arresting Pueblo leaders, executing two and whipping 43 others in front of large crowds.

One of the 43, a prominent Tewa man known to history as Popé, nursed his wounds in Taos and called for a war against the Spaniards to purify the land. Many individuals and some entire villages refused to participate. But on August 10, 1680, Indians from across New Mexico rose up and began killing Spaniards, pursuing astonished survivors all the way to Santa Fe. Within weeks the desperate Spanish governor, wounded by an arrow in the face and a gunshot to the chest, gathered the remainder of the colonial population and fled south out of New Mexico. The most successful Pan–Indian uprising in North American history, the Pueblo Revolt sent shock waves throughout Spanish America and left the Catholic devout agonizing over what they had done to provoke God's wrath.

 REVIEW

Where and why did Spain establish colonies in North America, and how did native peoples resist colonization?

ENGLISH SOCIETY ON THE CHESAPEAKE

By 1700, then, Spain viewed its situation in the Americas very differently than it had 100 years earlier. The Pueblo Revolt had checked its power at the northern reach of its American possessions. Equally disturbing was the progress of Spain's European rivals in the Americas during the seventeenth century. During the sixteenth, both France and England had envied Spain's American conquests and wealth but did little to compete, beyond preying on Spanish ships and fishing for cod. During the seventeenth century, this would change.

In fact, even by 1600 other European kingdoms were beginning to view overseas colonies as essential to a nation's power and prosperity. They did so in part because of an economic model known as **mercantilism,** which guided Europe's commercial expansion for 200 years. The primary objective of mercantilism was to enrich the nation by fostering a favorable balance of trade. Once the value of exports exceeded the cost of imports, its advocates argued, gold and silver would flow into home ports.

mercantilism European economic doctrine calling for strict regulation of the economy in order to ensure a balance of exports over imports and increase the amount of gold and silver in a nation's treasury.

If a nation could make do without any imports from other countries, so much the better. It was here that the idea of colonies entered the mercantilist scheme. Colonial producers would supply raw materials that the mother country could not produce, while colonial consumers swelled demand for the finished goods and financial services that the mother country could provide. That logic led England's King James I to approve a private venture to colonize the Chesapeake Bay, a sprawling inlet of the Atlantic Ocean fed by more than 100 rivers and streams.

The Virginia Company >> In 1606 the king granted a charter to a number of English merchants, gentlemen, and aristocrats, incorporating them as the Virginia Company of London. The members of the new **joint stock company** sold stock in their venture to English investors, as well as awarding

joint stock company business in which capital is held in transferable shares of stock by joint owners. The joint stock company was an innovation that allowed investors to share and spread the risks of overseas investments.

<< In Jamestown's early years, its military orientation was clear. The fort's heavy palisades and its strategic location upriver and some distance inland underscore the colonists' concern for defense.

imitated their predecessors on Roanoke, bullying Indians for food. Martial law failed to turn the situation around, and skirmishes with native peoples became more brutal and frequent as rows of tobacco plants steadily invaded tribal lands.

a share to those willing to settle in Virginia at their own expense. With the proceeds from the sale of stock, the company planned to send to Virginia hundreds of poor and unemployed people as well as scores of skilled craftworkers. These laborers were to serve the company for seven years in return for their passage, pooling their efforts to produce any commodities that would return a profit to stockholders. If gold and silver could not be found, perhaps North America would yield other valuable commodities—furs, pitch, tar, or lumber. In the spring of 1607—nearly a decade after Oñate had launched Spain's colonies in New Mexico—the first expedition dispatched by the Virginia Company founded Jamestown.

Making the first of many mistakes, Jamestown's 104 men and boys pitched their fort on a swampy inland peninsula in order to prevent a surprise attack from the Spanish. Weakened by bouts of the disease and beset by dysentery, typhoid, and yellow fever, however, they died by the scores.

Even before sickness took its toll, many of Jamestown's colonists had little taste for labor. The gentlemen of the expedition expected to lead rather than to work, while most of the other early settlers were gentlemen's servants and craftworkers who knew nothing about growing crops. Many colonists suffered from malnutrition, which heightened their susceptibility to disease. Only 60 of Jamestown's 500 inhabitants lived through the winter of 1609–1610, known as the "starving time." Desperate colonists unearthed and ate corpses; one settler even butchered his wife. Others

Reform and a Boom in Tobacco >> Determined to salvage their investment, Virginia Company managers in 1618 set in place sweeping reforms. To attract more capital and colonists, the company established a "headright" system for granting land to individuals. Those already settled in the colony received 100 acres apiece. New settlers each received 50 acres, and anyone who paid the passage of other immigrants to Virginia—either family members or servants—received 50 acres per "head." The company also abolished martial law, allowing the planters to elect a representative assembly. Along with a governor and an advisory council appointed by the company, the House of Burgesses had the authority to make laws for the colony. It met for the first time in 1619, beginning what would become a strong tradition of representative government in the English colonies.

The new measures met with immediate success. The free and unfree laborers who poured into Virginia during the 1620s made up the first wave of an English migration to the Chesapeake that numbered between 130,000 and 150,000 over the seventeenth century. Drawn from the ranks of ordinary English working people, the immigrants were largely men, outnumbering women by six to one. Most were young, ranging in age from 15 to 24. Because of their youth, most lacked skills or wealth. Some of those who came to the Chesapeake as free immigrants prospered as Virginia's tobacco economy took off. When in the 1620s demand soared and prices peaked in European markets, colonists with an eye for profit planted every inch of their farms in tobacco and reaped windfalls.

Indentured servants accounted for three—quarters of all immigrants to Virginia. For most, the crossing was simply the last of many moves made in the hope of finding work. Although England's population had been rising since the middle of the fifteenth century, the demand for farm laborers was falling because many landowners were converting croplands into pastures for sheep. The search for work pushed young men and women out of their villages, sending them through the countryside and then into the cities. Down and out in London, Bristol, or Liverpool, some decided to make their next move across the Atlantic and signed **inden—ture.** Pamphlets promoting immigration promised land and quick riches once servants had finished their terms of four to seven years.

indenture contract signed between two parties, binding one to serve the other for a specified period of time.

Even the most skeptical immigrants were shocked at what they found. The death rate in Virginia during the 1620s was higher than that of England during times of epidemic disease. The life expectancy for Chesapeake men who reached the age of 20 was a mere 48 years; for women it was lower still. Servants fared worst of all, because malnutrition, overwork, and abuse made them vulnerable to disease. As masters scrambled to make quick profits, they extracted the maximum amount of work before death carried off their laborers. An estimated 40 percent of servants did not survive to the end of their indentured terms.

War with the Confederacy

>> The expanding cultivation of tobacco also claimed many lives by putting unbearable pressure on Indian land. After Powhatan's death in 1617 leadership of the confederacy passed to Opechancanough, who watched, year after year, as the tobacco mania grew. In March 1622 he coordinated a sweeping attack on white settlements that killed about a quarter of Virginia's colonial population. English retaliation over the next decade cut down an entire generation of young Indian men, drove the remaining Powhatans to the west, and won the colonists hundreds of thousands more acres for tobacco.

News of the ongoing Indian war jolted English investors into determining the true state of their Virginia venture. It came to light that, despite the tobacco boom, the Virginia Company was plunging toward bankruptcy. Nor was that the worst news. Stockholders discovered that more than 3,000 immigrants had not survived the brutal conditions of Chesapeake life. An investigation by James I revealed the grisly truth, causing the king to dissolve the Virginia Company and

witness
The Indian War of 1622

"They came unarmed into our houses . . . yea in some places sat down at Breakfast with our people at their tables, [and] immediately with [our people's] own tools and weapons, either laid down, or standing in their houses, they basely and barbarously murdered, not sparing either age or sex, man, woman, or child . . ."

—Edward Waterhouse, *A Declaration of the State of the Colonie and Affaires in Virginia* (1622)

take control of the colony himself in 1624. Henceforth Virginia would be governed as a royal colony.

As the tobacco boom broke in the 1630s and 1640s, Virginians began producing more corn and cattle. Nutrition and overall health improved as a result. More and more poor colonists began surviving their indenture and establishing modest farms of their own. For women who survived servitude, prospects were even better. With wives at a premium, single women stood a good chance of improving their status by marriage. Even so, high mortality rates still fractured families: one out of every four children born in the Chesapeake did not survive to maturity, and among those children who reached their 18th birthday, one—third had lost both parents to death.

By 1650 Virginia could boast about 15,000 colonists, with more arriving every year. But Virginians looking to expand into more northerly bays of the Chesapeake found their way blocked by a newer English colony.

The Founding of Maryland and the Renewal of Indian Wars

>> Unlike Virginia, established by a private corporation and later converted into a royal colony, Maryland was founded in 1632 by a single aristocratic family, the Calverts. They held absolute authority to dispose of 10 million acres of land, administer justice, and establish a civil government. All these powers they exercised, granting estates, or "manors," to their friends and dividing other holdings into smaller farms for ordinary immigrants. From all these "tenants"—that is, every settler in the colony—the family collected "quitrents" every year, fees for use of the land. The Calverts appointed a governor and a council to oversee their own interests

while allowing the largest landowners to dispense local justice in manorial courts and make laws for the entire colony in a representative assembly.

Virginians liked nothing about Maryland. To begin with, the Calvert family was Catholic and had extended complete religious freedom to all Christians, making Maryland a haven for Catholics. Worse still, the Marylanders were a source of economic competition. Two thousand inhabitants had settled on Calvert holdings by 1640, virtually all of them planting tobacco on land coveted by the Virginians.

Another obstacle to Virginia's expansion was the remnant of the Powhatan confederacy. Hounded for corn and supplies (most colonial fields grew tobacco rather than food), and constantly pressured by the expanding plantation economy, Virginia's native peoples became desperate and angry enough to risk yet another war. Aged Opechancanough sent a new generation of Indians into battle in 1644 against the encroaching Virginia planters. Though his warriors killed several hundred English and brought the frontier to a standstill, Opechancanough was eventually captured and summarily shot through the head. The Powhatan confederacy died with him. Virginia's Indians would never again be in a position to go on the offense against the colony. Over the next decades and centuries, many Indians fled the region altogether. But whole communities remained, quietly determined to continue their lives and traditions in their homeland.

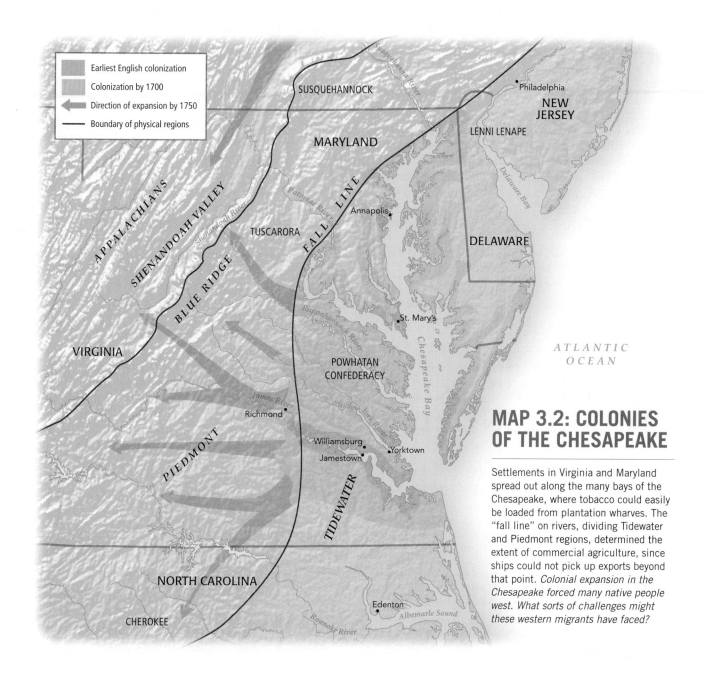

MAP 3.2: COLONIES OF THE CHESAPEAKE

Settlements in Virginia and Maryland spread out along the many bays of the Chesapeake, where tobacco could easily be loaded from plantation wharves. The "fall line" on rivers, dividing Tidewater and Piedmont regions, determined the extent of commercial agriculture, since ships could not pick up exports beyond that point. *Colonial expansion in the Chesapeake forced many native people west. What sorts of challenges might these western migrants have faced?*

Changes in English Policy in the Chesapeake >> Throughout the 1630s and 1640s colonial affairs drew little concern from royal officials. England itself had become engulfed first by a political crisis and then by a civil war.

Outraged at the contempt that King Charles I had shown toward Parliament, disaffected elites and radical Puritans overthrew the king and executed him in 1649. When the "republic" of Oliver Cromwell turned out to be something closer to a military dictatorship, most English were happy to see their throne restored in 1660 to Charles II, the son of the beheaded king. The new monarch was determined that not only his subjects at home but also his American colonies abroad would contribute to England's prosperity. His colonial policy was reflected in a series of regulations passed in the 1660s and 1670s known as the Navigation Acts.

The acts severely restricted colonial trade with Britain's imperial rivals. In this sense they were mercantilistic, designed to ensure that England alone would profit from colonial production and trade. Chesapeake planters chafed under the Navigation Acts. They were used to conducting their affairs as they pleased—and they were often pleased to trade with the Dutch. And, adding to the unhappiness, the new restrictions came just as tobacco prices were dropping. In the effort to consolidate its empire England had unintentionally worsened the economic and social difficulties of Chesapeake society.

REVIEW

How did the Chesapeake colonies support the aims of British mercantilism?

CHESAPEAKE SOCIETY IN CRISIS

By the 1660s overproduction was depressing tobacco prices, and wealthy planters reacted by putting even more prime coastal land into production. Newly freed servants had to either become tenants or try to establish farms to the west in Indian country. Meanwhile, export duties on tobacco paid under the Navigation Acts helped plunge many small planters into crushing debt, and some were forced back into servitude. By 1676 one-quarter of Virginia's free white men remained landless and frustrated.

As the discontent of the poor mounted, so did the worries of big planters. The assembly of the colony lengthened terms of servitude, hoping to limit the number of servants entering the free population. It curbed the political rights of landless men, hoping to stifle opposition by depriving them of the vote. But these measures only set off a spate of mutinies among servants and protests over rising taxes among small planters.

Bacon's Rebellion and Coode's Rebellion >> Tensions came to a head in 1676. The immediate spark to rebellion was renewed fighting between desperate Indians and the expanding colonial population. Virginia's royal governor, William Berkeley, favored building forts to guard against Indians, but frontier farmers opposed his plan as expensive and an ineffective way to defend their scattered plantations. When they clamored for an expedition to punish the Indians, Nathaniel Bacon stepped forward to lead it.

Wealthy and well connected, Bacon had arrived recently from England, expecting to receive every favor from the governor—including permission to trade with the Indians from his frontier plantation. But Berkeley and a few select friends already held a monopoly on the Indian trade. When they declined to include Bacon, he took up the cause of his poorer frontier neighbors. Other recent, well-to-do immigrants who resented being excluded from Berkeley's circle of power and patronage also joined the cause.

In the summer of 1676 Bacon marched into Jamestown with a body of armed men and bullied the assembly into approving his expedition to kill Indians. While Bacon carried out that grisly business, slaughtering friendly as well as hostile natives, Berkeley rallied his supporters and declared Bacon a rebel. Bacon retaliated by turning his forces against those led by the governor. Both sides sought allies by offering freedom to servants and slaves willing to join their ranks. Many were willing: for months the followers of Bacon and

⌄ This ceramic pipe from the 1670s was probably used by an indentured servant or tenant farmer living near Jamestown. Its design, featuring an animal carved around the pipe bowl, combined features typical of pipes made by English colonists, Indians, and African Americans. Virginia during this period experienced unstable relations between the expanding English population, the declining Indian population (due to wars and enslavement), and the growing number of enslaved Africans taking a larger role in the colony.

Berkeley plundered one another's plantations. In September 1676 Bacon reduced Jamestown to a mound of ashes. Only his death from dysentery snuffed out the rebellion.

Political upheaval also shook Maryland, where colonists had long resented the sway of the Calvert family. As proprietors the Calverts and their favorites monopolized political offices, just as Berkeley's circle had in Virginia. Well-to-do planters wanted a share of the Calverts' power. Smaller farmers, like those in Virginia, wanted a less expensive and more representative government. Compounding the tensions were religious differences: the Calverts and their friends were Catholic, but other colonists, including Maryland's most successful planters, were Protestant.

The unrest peaked in July 1689. A former member of the assembly, John Coode, gathered an army, captured the proprietary governor, and then took grievances to authorities in England. There Coode received a sympathetic hearing. The Calverts' charter was revoked and not restored until 1715, by which time the family had become Protestant.

After the rebellions, rich planters in both Chesapeake colonies fought among themselves less and cooperated more. In Virginia older leaders and newer arrivals divided the spoils of political office. In Maryland Protestants and Catholics shared power and privilege. Those arrangements ensured that no future Bacon or Coode would mobilize restless gentlemen against the government. By acting together in legislative assemblies, the planter elite managed to curb the power of royal and proprietary governors for decades.

But the greater unity among the Chesapeake's leading families did little to ease that region's most fundamental problem—the sharp inequality of white society. The gulf between rich and poor planters, which had been etched ever more deeply by the troubled tobacco economy, persisted long after the rebellions of Bacon and Coode. All that saved white society in the Chesapeake from renewed crisis and conflict was the growth of African slavery.

From Servitude to Slavery >> Like the tobacco plants that spread across Powhatan's land, a labor system based on African slavery was an on-the-ground innovation. Both early promoters and planters preferred paying for English servants to importing alien African slaves. Black slaves, because they served for life, were more expensive than white workers, who served only for several years. Because neither white nor black immigrants lived long, cheaper servant labor was the logical choice. The black population of the Chesapeake remained small for most of the seventeenth century, constituting just 5 percent of all inhabitants in 1675.

Africans had arrived in Virginia by 1619, most likely via the Dutch, who dominated the slave trade until the middle of the eighteenth century. The lives of those newcomers resembled the lot of white servants, with whom they shared harsh work routines and living conditions. White and black bound laborers socialized with one another and formed sexual liaisons. They conspired to steal from their masters and ran away together; if caught, they endured similar punishments. There was more common ground: many of the first black settlers did not arrive directly from Africa but came from the Caribbean, where some had learned English and had adopted Christian beliefs. And not all were slaves: some were indentured servants. A handful were free.

A number of changes after 1680 caused planters to invest more heavily in slaves than in servants. First, as death rates in the Chesapeake began to drop, slaves became a more profitable investment. Although they were more expensive to buy than servants, planters could now expect to get many years of work from their bondspeople. Equally important, masters would have title to the children that slaves were now living long enough to have. At the same time, the influx of white servants was falling off just as the pool of available black labor was expanding. When the Royal African Company lost its monopoly on the English slave trade in 1698, other merchants entered the market. The number of Africans sold by British dealers swelled to 20,000 annually.

Would you have opposed slavery if you had lived in the seventeenth century?

Africa and the Atlantic Slave Trade >> From 1492 to 1820, enslaved African migrants outnumbered European migrants to the New World by nearly five to one.

MAP 3.3: SLAVE TRADE ALONG THE GOLD COAST

Toward the end of the seventeenth century, Chesapeake and Carolina planters began importing increasing numbers of slaves. In Africa, the center of that trade lay along a mountainous region known as the Gold Coast, where more than a hundred European trading posts and forts funneled the trade. Despite the heavy trade, only about 4 percent of the total transatlantic slave trade went to North America. *How many different ethnic groups are shown on the map? Would that number be likely to encourage the slave trade, and if so, how?*

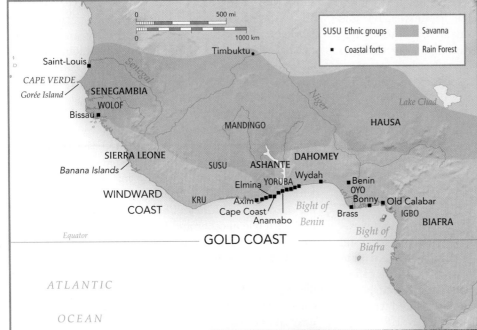

⚐ Katharina, sketched in 1521, was a servant living in the Netherlands. She was probably one of the increasing number of Africans being brought to Europe owing to the growing slave trade.

⚐ Slaves captured in the African interior were marched out in slave "coffles," a forced march in which captives were linked either by chains or by wooden yoke restraints linking two slaves together as they walked.

⚐ Africans found themselves in a variety of conditions in the Americas. Most toiled on plantations. Some, however, like these "watermen" along the James River in Virginia (*far right*), claimed more independence. Still others ran away to Maroon communities in the interior. This armed Maroon (*a runaway slave; near right*) is from Dutch Guiana, where conditions on the plantations were particularly harsh.

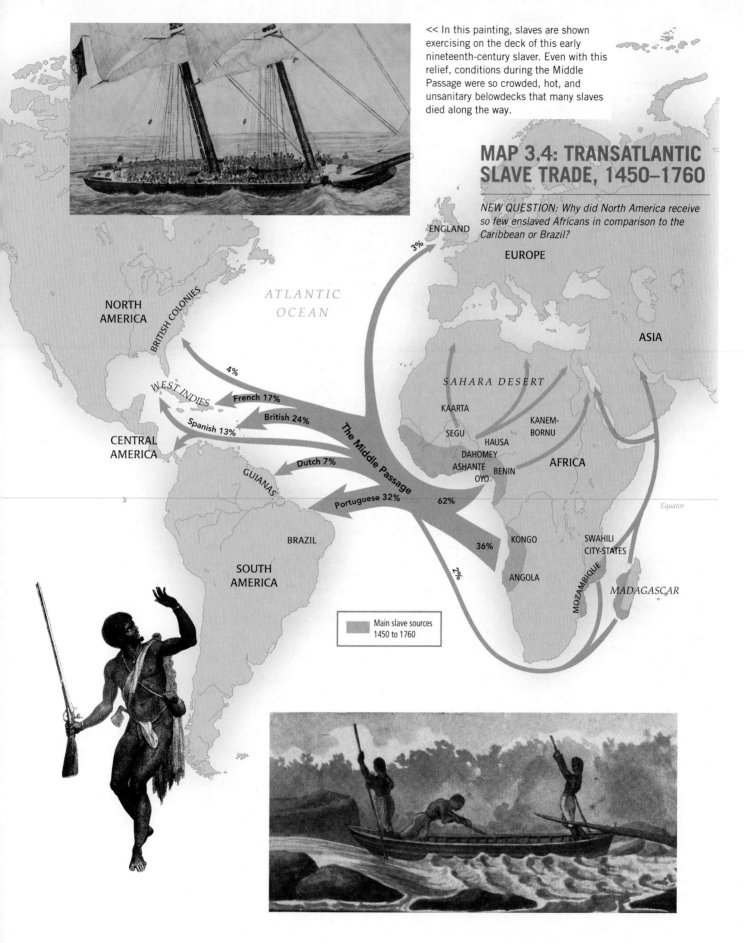

<< In this painting, slaves are shown exercising on the deck of this early nineteenth-century slaver. Even with this relief, conditions during the Middle Passage were so crowded, hot, and unsanitary belowdecks that many slaves died along the way.

MAP 3.4: TRANSATLANTIC SLAVE TRADE, 1450–1760

NEW QUESTION: Why did North America receive so few enslaved Africans in comparison to the Caribbean or Brazil?

ENGLAND

EUROPE

3%

ASIA

ATLANTIC OCEAN

NORTH AMERICA

BRITISH COLONIES

4%

WEST INDIES

French 17%

British 24%

Spanish 13%

Dutch 7%

SAHARA DESERT

KAARTA

SEGU

KANEM-BORNU

HAUSA

DAHOMEY

ASHANTE   BENIN

OYO

AFRICA

CENTRAL AMERICA

GUIANAS

The Middle Passage

Portuguese 32%

62%

Equator

KONGO

SWAHILI CITY-STATES

36%

BRAZIL

2%

ANGOLA

MOZAMBIQUE

MADAGASCAR

SOUTH AMERICA

Main slave sources 1450 to 1760

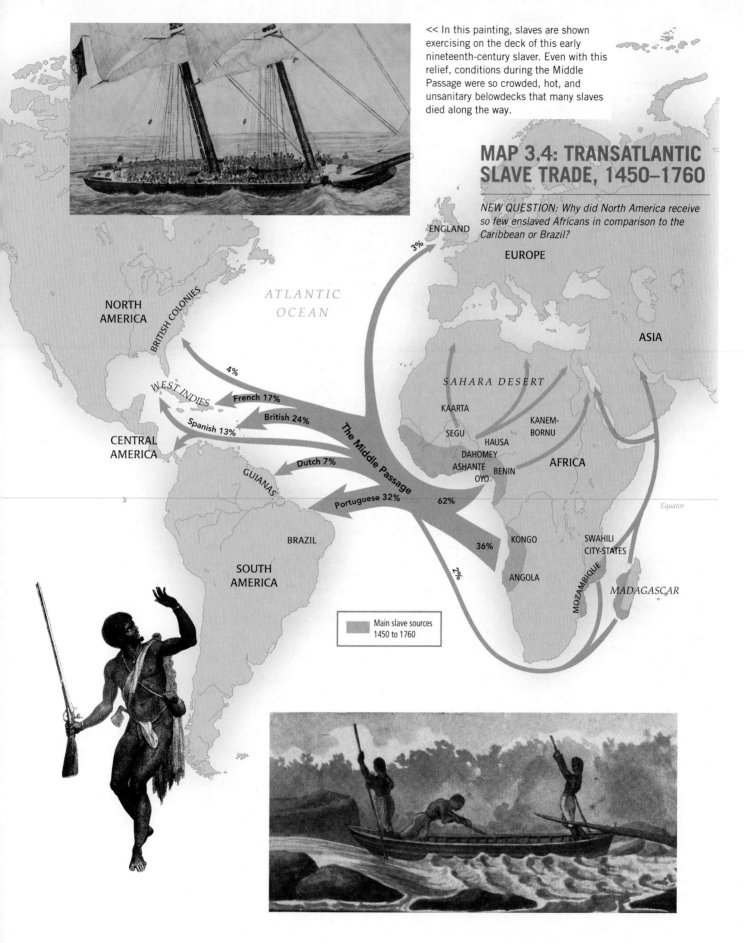

Hip Mask from Benin

These images of mudfish alternate with those of Portuguese merchants. What might the mudfish be meant to symbolize? (Use a few key terms to find answers on the web.)

These pieces of inlaid iron represent medicine-filled incisions that were said to have given Idia metaphysical powers.

Object is hollow at the back; may have been used as receptacle for medicines, as well as a pendant for a hip belt.

This exquisite sixteenth-century ivory mask, now in New York's Metropolitan Museum of Art, graced the neck of Benin's king during ceremonial occasions. Its subtlety and precision suggest that it was produced by Benin's famed guild of royal ivory carvers, specifically for royalty. The object communicates a tremendous amount of visual information. The face itself is a portrait of Idia, mother of Benin's great early sixteenth-century leader Esigie. A powerful political figure in her own right, Idia helped secure the throne for her son and remained an influential adviser throughout his reign. On her head and around her neck are miniature faces of Portuguese merchants who brought great wealth to Benin and enriched and empowered its leaders through the slave trade.

THINKING CRITICALLY

Why pair the mudfish and the Portuguese? Do you think that the artist conceived of the Portuguese merchants as equals? Would you expect Benin's artistic sophistication to shape how the Portuguese regarded the kingdom?

Source: Metropolitan Museum of Art, www.metmuseum.org/toah/ho/08/sfg/ho_1978.412.323.htm.

Put differently, before the twentieth-century, African workers did most of the heavy lifting in the economies of the Americas.

For a century after Columbus's arrival, the traffic in slaves to the Americas had numbered a few thousand annually. But as sugar cultivation steadily prospered after 1600, slave imports rose to 19,000 a year during the seventeenth century and mushroomed to 60,000 a year in the eighteenth century. All told, as many as 21 million people were captured in West and Central Africa between 1700 and 1850: some 9 million among them entered the Americas as slaves, but millions died before or during the Atlantic crossing, and as many as 7 million remained slaves in Africa. Although slavery became indispensable to its economy, British North America played a relatively small role in the Atlantic slave trade. Nine-tenths of all Africans brought to the New World landed in Brazil or the Caribbean islands.

The rapid growth of the trade transformed not only the Americas but also Africa. Slavery became more widespread within African society, and slave trading more central to its domestic and international commerce. Most important, the African merchants and political leaders most deeply invested in the slave trade used their profits for political advantage—to build new chiefdoms and states such as Dahomey, Asante, and the Lunda Empire. Their ambitions and the greed of European slave dealers drew an increasingly large number of Africans, particularly people living in the interior, into slavery's web. By the late seventeenth century, Africans being sold into slavery were no longer only those who had put themselves at risk by committing crimes, running into debt, or voicing unpopular political and religious views. The larger number were instead captives taken by soldiers or kidnappers in raids launched specifically to acquire prisoners for the slave trade, or else desperate refugees captured while fleeing war, famine, and disease. During the decades after 1680, captives coming directly from Africa made up more than 80 percent of all new slaves entering the Chesapeake and the rest of mainland North America. Many were shipped from the coast of Africa that Portuguese explorers had first probed, between the Senegal and Niger Rivers. Most of the rest came from Angola, farther south.

Seized by other Africans, captives were yoked together at the neck and marched hundreds of miles through the interior to coastal forts or other outposts along the Atlantic. There, they were penned in hundreds of prisons, in lots of anywhere from 20 or 30 to more than 1,000. They might be forced to wait for slaving vessels in French *captiveries* below the fine houses of traders on the island of Gorée, or herded into "outfactories" on the Banana Islands upstream on the Sierra Leone River, or perhaps marched into the dank underground slaveholds at the English fort at Cape Coast. Farther south, captives were held in marshy, fever-ridden lowlands along the Bight of Benin, waiting for a slaver to drop anchor. One African, Ottobah Cugoano, recalled finally being taken aboard ship:

> There was nothing to be heard but the rattling of chains, smacking of whips, and the groans and cries of our fellow-men. Some would not stir from the ground, when they were lashed and beat in the most horrible manner.... And when we found ourselves at last taken away, death was more preferable than life, and a plan was concerted amongst us that we might burn and blow up the ship and to perish altogether in the flames.

Worse than the imprisonment was the voyage itself: the so-called Middle Passage, a nightmarish journey across the Atlantic that could take anywhere between three weeks and three months, depending on currents, weather, and where ships disembarked and landed. Often several hundred black men, women, and children were packed below decks, squeezed onto platforms built in tiers spaced so close that sitting upright was impossible. It was difficult to know whether the days or the nights were more hellish. Slaves were taken out and forced to exercise for their health for a few hours each day; the rest of the day, the sun beat down and the heat below the decks was "so excessive," one voyager recalled, that the doctors who went below to examine slaves "would faint away, and the candles would not burn." At night, the slaves "were often heard making a howling melancholy kind of noise," noted a doctor aboard another ship. It was because the slaves, in sleeping, had dreamed "they were back in their own country again, amongst their families and friends" and "when they woke up to find themselves in reality on a slave ship they began to bay and shriek." Historians estimate that for every 85 enslaved Africans that set foot in the Americas, 15 died during the Middle Passage.

After the numb, exhausted survivors reached American ports, they faced more challenges to staying alive. The first year in the colonies was the most deadly for new, "unseasoned" slaves. The sickle-cell genetic trait gave them a greater immunity to malaria than Europeans, but slaves were highly susceptible to respiratory infections. One-quarter of all Africans died during their first year in the Chesapeake, and among Carolina and Caribbean slaves, mortality rates were far higher. In addition to the new disease environment, Africans had to adapt to lives without freedom in a wholly unfamiliar country and culture.

A Changing Chesapeake Society >>

Exchanging a labor system based on servitude for one based on slavery transformed Chesapeake society. Most obviously, the number of Afro-Virginians rose sharply. By 1740, 40 percent of all Virginians were black, and most of those were African-born. Unlike many African men and women who had arrived earlier from the Caribbean, these new inhabitants had little familiarity with English language and culture. This larger, more distinctively African community was also locked into a slave system that was becoming ever more rigid and demeaning. By the late decades of the seventeenth century, new laws made it more difficult for masters to free slaves. Other legislation systematically separated the races by prohibiting free black settlers from having white servants and outlawing interracial marriages and sexual relationships. The legal code fostered **racism** and white contempt for black Virginians in a variety of other ways. While masters were prohibited from whipping their white servants on the bare back, slaves had no

racism discrimination based on inherited physical differences, which according to racist thought separated humans into a few distinct and unequal groups or "races."

such protection. And "any Negro that shall presume to strike any white" was to receive 30 lashes for that rash act.

The new laws both reflected and encouraged racism among white colonists of all classes. Deepening racial hatred, in turn, made it unlikely that poor white planters, tenants, and servants would ever join with poor black slaves to challenge the privilege of great planters. Instead of identifying with the plight of the slaves, the Chesapeake's poorer white residents considered black Virginians their natural inferiors. They could pride themselves on sharing with wealthy white gentlemen the same skin color and on being their equals in the eyes of the law.

The leaders of the Chesapeake colonies cultivated unity among white inhabitants by improving economic prospects for freed servants and lesser planters. The Virginia assembly made provisions for freed servants to get a better start as independent farmers. It lowered taxes, allowing small planters to keep more of their earnings. New laws also gave most white male Virginians a vote in elections, allowing them an outlet to express their grievances. Economic trends toward the end of the seventeenth century contributed to the greater prosperity of small planters, because tobacco prices rose slightly and then stabilized. As a result of Bacon's savage campaign against the Virginia Indians, new land on the frontier became available. Even the domestic lives of ordinary people became more secure as mortality rates declined and the numbers of men and women in the white population evened out. As a result, virtually all men were now able to marry, and families were fragmented less often by the premature deaths of spouses and parents.

After 1700 the Chesapeake evolved into a more stable society. Gone were the bands of wild, landless, young bachelors one step ahead of the law, the small body of struggling lesser planters one step ahead of ruin, and the great mass of exploited servants one step away from rebellion. Virginia and Maryland became colonies of farming families, most of them small planters who owned between 50 and 200 acres. These families held no slaves, or at most two or three. And they accepted, usually without question, the social and political leadership of their acknowledged "superiors," great planters who styled themselves the "gentry."

 REVIEW

Why did slavery replace servitude as the dominant labor system in Virginia and Maryland?

FROM THE CARIBBEAN TO THE CAROLINAS

During the same decade that the English invaded Powhatan's land, they began to colonize the Caribbean, whose islands extended north and west, like beads on a string, from the Lesser Antilles toward the more substantial lands of Puerto Rico, Hispaniola, Jamaica, and Cuba (see Map 3.5). At their long journey's end English sailors found what seemed a paradise: shores rimmed with white sand beaches that rose sharply to coral terraces, then to broad plateaus or mountain peaks shrouded in rain forests. The earliest arrivals came intending not to colonize but to steal from the Spanish. Even after 1604 when some English settled on the islands, few intended to stay.

Yet the English did establish permanent plantation colonies in the West Indies. Beyond that, their Caribbean settlements became the jumping-off points for a new colony on the North American mainland—South Carolina. Because of the strong West Indian influence, South Carolina developed a social order in some ways distinct from that of the Chesapeake colonies. In other ways, however, the development paralleled Virginia and Maryland's path. In both regions, extreme violence, high mortality, and uncertainty gave way to relative stability only over the course of many decades.

Paradise Lost >> The English had traded and battled with the Spanish in the Caribbean since the 1560s. From those island bases English buccaneers conducted an illegal trade with Spanish settlements, sacked the coastal towns, and plundered silver ships bound for Seville. Weakened by decades of warfare, Spain could not hold the West Indies. The Dutch drove a wedge into Caribbean trade routes, and the French and the English began to colonize the islands.

In the 40 years after 1604 some 30,000 immigrants from the British Isles planted crude frontier outposts on St. Kitts, Barbados, Nevis, Montserrat, and Antigua. The settlers—some free, many others indentured servants, and almost all young men—devoted themselves to working as little as possible, drinking as much as possible, and returning to England as soon as possible. They cultivated for export a poor-quality tobacco, which returned just enough profit to maintain straggling settlements of small farms.

Then, nearly overnight, sugar cultivation transformed the Caribbean. In the 1640s Barbados planters learned from the Dutch how to process sugarcane. The Dutch also supplied African slaves to work the cane fields and marketed the sugar for high prices in the Netherlands. Sugar plantations and slave labor rapidly spread to other English and French islands as Europeans developed an insatiable sweet tooth for the once-scarce commodity. Caribbean sugar made more money for England than the total volume of commodities exported by all the mainland American colonies.

Even though its great planters became the richest people in English America, they could not have confused the West Indies with paradise. Throughout the seventeenth century disease took a fearful toll, and island populations grew only because of immigration. In the scramble for land, small farmers were pushed onto tiny plots that barely allowed them to survive.

The desperation of bound laborers posed another threat to British planters. After the Caribbean's conversion to cultivating sugar, African slaves gradually replaced indentured servants in the cane fields. By the beginning of the eighteenth century, resident Africans outnumbered English by four to one. Fear of servant mutinies and slave rebellions frayed the nerves of island masters. They tried to contain the danger by imposing harsh slave codes and inflicting brutal punishments on all laborers. But planters lived under a constant state of siege. One visitor to Barbados observed that whites fortified their homes with parapets from which they could pour scalding water on attacking servants and slaves. During the first century of settlement, seven major slave uprisings shook the English islands.

As more people squeezed onto the islands, some settlers looked for a way out. With all the land in use, the Caribbean no longer offered opportunity to freed servants or even planters' sons. It was then that the West Indies started to shape the history of the American South.

The Founding of the Carolinas >>

The colonization of the Carolinas began with the schemes of Virginia's royal governor, William Berkeley, and Sir John Colleton, a supporter of Charles I who had been exiled to the Caribbean at the end of England's civil war. Colleton saw that the Caribbean had a surplus of white settlers, and Berkeley knew that Virginians needed room to expand as well. Together the two men set their sights on the area south of Virginia. Along with a number of other aristocrats, they convinced Charles II to make them joint proprietors in 1663 of a place they called the Carolinas, in honor of the king.

A few hardy souls from Virginia had already squatted around Albemarle Sound in the northern part of the Carolina grant. The proprietors provided them with a governor and a representative assembly. About 40 years later, in 1701, they set off North Carolina as a separate colony. The desolate region proved a disappointment. Lacking good harbors and navigable rivers, the colony had no convenient way of marketing its produce. North Carolina remained a poor colony, its sparse population engaged in general farming and the production of masts, pitch, tar, and turpentine.

The southern portion of the Carolina grant held far more promise, especially in the eyes of one of its proprietors, Sir Anthony Ashley Cooper, Earl of Shaftesbury. In 1669 Cooper sponsored an expedition of a few hundred English and Barbadian immigrants, who planted the first permanent settlement in South Carolina. By 1680 the colonists had established the center of economic, social, and political life at the confluence of the Ashley and Cooper Rivers, naming the site Charles Town (later Charleston) after the king. Like others before him, Cooper hoped to create an ideal society in America. His utopia was a place where a few landed aristocrats and gentlemen would rule with the consent of many smaller property holders. With his personal secretary, the renowned philosopher John Locke,

MAP 3.5: THE CAROLINAS AND THE CARIBBEAN

The map underscores the geographic link between West Indian and Carolina settlements. Emigrants from Barbados dominated politics in early South Carolina, while Carolinians provided foodstuffs, grain, and cattle to the West Indies. As South Carolinians began growing rice, Caribbean slave ships found it an easy sail north and west to unload their cargoes in Charleston.

The fall line is marked here and on Map 3.2, Colonies of the Chesapeake. What is the fall line? Why is it significant?

Cooper drew up an intricate scheme of government, the Fundamental Constitutions. The design provided Carolina with a proprietary governor and a hereditary nobility who, as a Council of Lords, would recommend all laws to a Parliament elected by lesser landowners.

The Fundamental Constitutions met the same fate as other lordly dreams for America. Instead of peacefully observing its provisions, most of the Carolinians, migrants from Barbados, plunged into economic and political wrangling. They challenged proprietary rule, protested or ignored laws and regulations imposed on them, and rejected the proprietors' relatively benevolent vision of Indian relations. Instead, the colonists fomented a series of Indian slave wars that nearly destroyed the colony altogether.

Carolina, Florida, and the Southeastern Slave Wars

>> Taking wealthy Barbados as the model, the colonists intended to grow Carolina's economy around cash crops tended by African slaves. But before they could afford to establish such a regime, the newcomers needed to raise capital through trade with Indians. Colonists gave textiles, metal goods, guns, and alcohol in exchange for hundreds of thousands of deerskins, which they then exported.

But the trade soon came to revolve around a commodity dearer still. As did most peoples throughout history, southeastern Indians sometimes made slaves of their enemies. Carolina's traders vastly expanded this existing slave culture by turning captives into prized commodities. Convinced that local Indians were physically weaker than Africans and more likely to rebel or flee, colonial traders bought slaves from Indian allies and then exported them to other mainland colonies or to the Caribbean. They found eager native partners in this business. Contact with Europe had unleashed phenomenal changes in interior North America. Epidemics ruined one people and gave advantage to another, new commercial opportunities sparked fierce wars over hunting and trading territories, and many thousands of Indian families became displaced and had to rebuild their lives somewhere new. The chaos, conflict, and movement gave enterprising Indians ample opportunity to enslave weak neighbors and stock Carolina's slave pens.

To ensure a steady supply of slaves, Carolinian merchants courted a variety of Indian allies during the late seventeenth and early eighteenth centuries and encouraged them to raid mission Indians in Spanish Florida. By 1700 Florida's Indian peoples were in sharp decline, and Charles Town's slave traders turned to the large and powerful Creek, Choctaw, Chickasaw, and Cherokee confederacies of the interior, encouraging them to raid one another. Before long the slave wars had a momentum all their own,

extending as far west as the Mississippi River. Even native peoples who deplored the violence and despised the English felt compelled to participate, lest they too become victims.

The trade became central to Carolina's economy, and colonists high and low sought to profit from it. In 1702 Governor James Moore, one of the colony's chief slave traders, launched an audacious raid against Spanish St. Augustine and Florida's missions, returning with hundreds of Indian captives. His campaign inspired still more raids, and over the next few years Creeks, Yamasees, and Englishmen laid waste to 29 Spanish missions, shattering thousands of lives and destroying Spain's precarious system of Indian alliances. By 1706 Spanish authority was once again confined to St. Augustine and its immediate vicinity. Within another 10 years most of Florida had been depopulated of Indians.

It seemed a double victory from Charles Town's perspective. The English had bested a European rival for the Crown and had reaped enormous profits besides. The fragmentary evidence suggests that Carolinians had purchased or captured between 30,000 and 50,000 Indian slaves before 1715. Indeed, before that date South Carolina exported more slaves than it imported from Africa or the Caribbean. But in 1715 Carolina's merchants finally paid a price for the wars that they had cynically fomented for over 40 years.

With Florida virtually exhausted of slaves, the Yamasees grew nervous. Convinced that Carolina would soon turn on them as it had on other onetime allies, the Yamasees struck first. They attacked traders, posts, and plantations on the outskirts of Charles Town, killing hundreds of colonists and dragging scores more to Florida to sell as slaves in St. Augustine. Panicked authorities turned to other Indian peoples in the region but found most had either joined the Yamasees or were too hostile and suspicious to help. Though it lasted only a few months, the Yamasee War finally put an end to the destructive regional slave trade. Animal skins again dominated regional commerce. The powerful southern confederacies grew wary of aligning too closely with any single European power and henceforth sought to play colonies and empires off each other. It was a strategy that would bring them relative peace and prosperity for generations.

White, Red, and Black: The Search for Order

>> As for South Carolina, the Yamasee War set the colony back 20 years. In its aftermath, settlers invested more and more of their resources in African slaves and in the cultivation of rice, a crop that eventually made South Carolina's planters the richest cohort in mainland North America. Unfortunately, South Carolina's swampy coast, so perfectly suited

>> Mulberry Plantation in South Carolina was first carved from coastal swamps in 1714. This painting, done half a century later, shows the Great House visible in the distance, flanked by slave quarters. African slaves skilled in rice cultivation oversaw the arduous task of properly planting and irrigating the crop.

to growing rice, was less suited for human habitation. Weakened by chronic malaria, settlers died in epic numbers from yellow fever, smallpox, and respiratory infections. The European population grew slowly, through immigration rather than natural increase, and numbered only 10,000 by 1730.

Early South Carolinians had little in common but the harsh conditions of frontier existence. Most colonists lived on isolated plantations; early deaths fragmented families and neighborhoods. Immigration after 1700 further intensified the colony's ethnic and religious diversity, adding Swiss and German Lutherans, Scots–Irish Presbyterians, Welsh Baptists, and Spanish Jews. The colony's only courts were in Charles Town; churches and clergy of any denomination were scarce. On those rare occasions when early Carolinians came together, they gathered at Charles Town to escape the pestilential air of their plantations, to sue one another for debt and haggle over prices, or to fight over religious differences and proprietary politics.

Finally, in 1729, the Crown formally established royal government; by 1730 economic recovery had done much to ease the strife. Even more important in bringing greater political stability, the European colonists of South Carolina came to realize that they must unite if they were to counter the Spanish in Florida and the French and their Indian allies on the Gulf Coast.

The growing African population gave European Carolinians another reason to maintain a united front. During the first decades of settlement, frontier conditions and the scarcity of labor had forced masters to allow enslaved Africans greater freedom within bondage. European and African laborers shared chores on small farms. On stock–raising plantations, called "cowpens," African cowboys ranged freely over the countryside. African contributions to the defense of the colony also reinforced racial interdependence and muted European domination. Whenever threats arose— during the Yamasee War, for example—Africans were enlisted in the militia.

European Carolinians depended on African labor even more after turning to rice as their cash crop. In fact, planters began to import slaves in larger numbers partly because of West African skill in rice cultivation. But Europeans harbored deepening fears of the African workers whose labor built planter fortunes. As early as 1708 African men and women had become a majority in the colony, and by 1730 they outnumbered European settlers by two to one. As their colony began to prosper, European Carolinians put into effect strict slave codes like those in the Caribbean that converted their colony into an armed camp and snuffed out the marginal freedoms that African settlers once enjoyed.

The Founding of Georgia >> After 1730 Carolinians could take comfort not only in newfound prosperity and new political harmony but also in the founding of a new colony on their southern border. South Carolinians liked Georgia a great deal more than the Virginians had liked Maryland, because the colony formed a buffer between British North America and Spanish Florida in much the same way that Yamasees and Shawnees had, before the war.

Enhancing the military security of South Carolina was only one reason for the founding of Georgia. More important to General James Oglethorpe and other idealistic English gentlemen was the aim of aiding the "worthy poor" by providing them with land, employment, and a new start. They envisioned a colony of hardworking small farmers who would produce silk and wine, sparing England the need to import those commodities. That dream seemed within reach when George II made Oglethorpe and his friends the trustees of the new colony in 1732, granting them a charter for 21 years. At the end of that time Georgia would revert to royal control.

The trustees did not, as legend has it, empty England's debtors' prisons to populate Georgia. They freed few debtors but recruited from every country in Europe paupers who seemed willing to work hard—and who professed Protestantism. Trustees paid the paupers' passage and provided each with 50 acres of land, tools, and a year's worth of supplies. Settlers who could pay their own way were encouraged to come by being granted larger tracts of land. Much to the trustees' dismay, that generous offer was taken up not only by many hoped–for Protestants but also by several hundred Ashkenazim (German Jews) and Sephardim (Spanish and Portuguese Jews), who established a thriving community in early Savannah.

The trustees were determined to ensure that Georgia became a small farmers' utopia. Rather than selling land, the trustees gave it away, but none of the colony's settlers could own more than 500 acres. The trustees also outlawed slavery and hard liquor in order to cultivate habits of industry and sustain equality among whites. This design for a virtuous and egalitarian utopia was greeted with little enthusiasm by Georgians. They pressed for a free market in land and argued that the colony could never prosper until the trustees revoked their ban on slavery. Because the trustees had provided for no elective assembly, settlers could express their discontent only by moving to South Carolina—which many did during the early decades. As mounting opposition threatened to depopulate the colony, the trustees caved in. They revoked their restrictions on land, slavery, and liquor a few years before the king assumed control of the colony in 1752. Under royal control Georgia continued to develop an ethnically and religiously diverse society, akin to that of South Carolina. Similarly, its economy was based on rice cultivation and the Indian trade.

 REVIEW

How was the colonization of Carolina both distinct from and parallel to that of the Chesapeake?

Empire ... utopia ... independence.... For more than a century after the founding of Oñate's colony on the upper Rio Grande in 1598, those dreams inspired residents of New Mexico, Florida, the Chesapeake, the English Caribbean, the Carolinas, and Georgia. Each of these regions served as staging grounds where kings and commoners, free and unfree, men and women, Native American, European, and African played out their hopes. Their acts were as often filled with desperation as with hope, for conditions were often harsh as the plantation monocultures of sugar and rice spread across the globe.

The dream of an expanding empire faltered for the Spanish, who found few riches in the Southwest and eventually found rebellion. The dream of empire failed, too, when James I and Charles I, England's early Stuart kings, found their power checked by Parliament. And the dream foundered fatally for Indians—for Powhatan's successors, who were unable to resist Old World diseases and land–hungry tobacco planters, and for Yamasees, Shawnees, and the many Indian peoples of Florida who sought to survive, accommodate, or exploit colonialism, but fell to ruin in the end.

English lords had dreamed of establishing feudal utopias in America. But proprietors such as the Calvert family in Maryland and Cooper in the Carolinas found themselves hounded by frontier planters and farmers who sought economic and political power. Georgia's trustees struggled in vain to nurture their dream of a utopia for the poor. The dream of a Spanish Catholic utopia brought by missionaries to the American Southwest dimmed with native resistance and rebellion.

The dream of independence proved the most deceptive of all, especially for the inhabitants of England's colonies. Just a bare majority of the European servant emigrants to the Chesapeake survived to enjoy freedom. The rest were struck down by disease or worn down at the hands of tobacco barons eager for profit. Not only in the Chesapeake but also in the Caribbean and the Carolinas, real independence eluded the English planters. Poorer folk—dependent on richer settlers for land and leadership—deferred to them at church and on election days and depended on them to buy crops or to extend credit. Even the richest planters were dependent on the English and Scottish merchants who supplied them with credit and marketed their crops, as well as on the English officials who made colonial policy.

And everywhere in the American Southeast and Southwest, the lingering dreams of Europeans were realized only through the labor of the least free members of colonial America. That stubborn reality would haunt all Americans who continued to dream of freedom and independence.

CHAPTER SUMMARY

During the seventeenth century, Spain and England moved to colonize critical regions of southern North America.

- Native peoples everywhere in the American South resisted colonization, despite losses from warfare, disease, and enslavement.
- Spanish colonies in New Mexico and Florida grew slowly and faced a variety of threats. By the late seventeenth century, Spanish New Mexico had been lost to the Pueblo Revolt, and Florida's delicate mission system was under siege from English Carolina and its Indian allies.
- Thriving monocultures were established in all of England's southern colonies—tobacco in the Chesapeake, rice in the Carolinas, and sugar in the Caribbean.
- Despite a period of intense enslavement of native peoples, African slavery emerged as the dominant labor system throughout these regions.
- Instability and conflict characterized both Spanish and English colonies in the South for most of the first century of their existence.

Additional Reading

David J. Weber's *Spanish Frontier in North America* (1992) remains indispensable. For New Mexico, see also John L. Kessell's *Spain in the Southwest* (2002); and James F. Brook's pathbreaking *Captives and Cousins* (2002). For Spain in the Southeast, see Paul E. Hoffman's *Florida's Frontiers* (2002); and Daniel S. Murphree's *Constructing Floridians* (2006).

For enduring treatments of early Virginia, see Edmund S. Morgan, *American Slavery, American Freedom* (1975); and Kathleen Brown, *Good Wives, Nasty Wenches, and Anxious Patriarchs* (1996). James D. Rice's *Tales from a Revolution* (2012) explores the multiple perspectives of Indians to Bacon's Rebellion. For Indians in the colonial Southeast, see Gregory A. Waselkov, Peter Wood, and Tom Hatley, eds., *Powhatan's Mantle* (2006). For native Virginia, see also Hellen C. Rountree, *Pocahontas, Powhatan, Opechancanough* (2005).

Recent years have seen a surge in scholarship on African slavery in the New World. David Brion Davis provides a magisterial overview in *Inhuman Bondage* (2006). For British North America, see Ira Berlin, *Many Thousands Gone* (1998); and Philip D. Morgan, *Slave Counterpoint* (1998). The classic account of the British Caribbean remains Richard Dunn's *Sugar and Slaves* (2000 [1972]). Vincent Brown's *Reaper's Garden* (2008) examines the brutalities of the Jamaican slave system. Stephanie Smallwood's *Saltwater Slavery* (2007) provides a haunting portrait of the Middle Passage.

The best overview of South Carolina's development remains Robert Weir, *Colonial South Carolina* (1982). The complexities of Carolina's slave wars are explored in Alan Gallay, *The Indian Slave Trade* (2002). For the topic more broadly, see Christina Snyder, *Slavery in Indian Country* (2010).

Significant Events

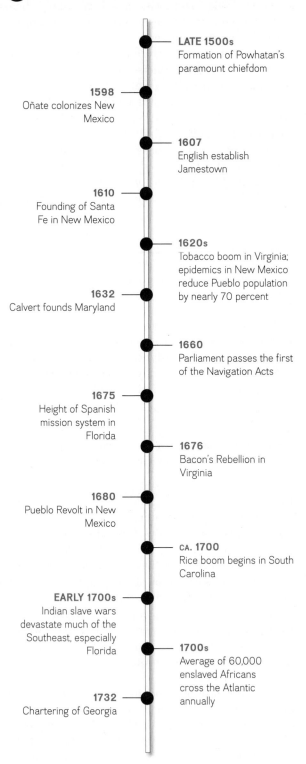

1598
Oñate colonizes New Mexico

LATE 1500s
Formation of Powhatan's paramount chiefdom

1607
English establish Jamestown

1610
Founding of Santa Fe in New Mexico

1620s
Tobacco boom in Virginia; epidemics in New Mexico reduce Pueblo population by nearly 70 percent

1632
Calvert founds Maryland

1660
Parliament passes the first of the Navigation Acts

1675
Height of Spanish mission system in Florida

1676
Bacon's Rebellion in Virginia

1680
Pueblo Revolt in New Mexico

CA. 1700
Rice boom begins in South Carolina

EARLY 1700s
Indian slave wars devastate much of the Southeast, especially Florida

1700s
Average of 60,000 enslaved Africans cross the Atlantic annually

1732
Chartering of Georgia

4 Colonization & Conflict in the North

1600–1700

New Amsterdam—present-day New York City—had a windmill (*left*) and a gallows (*center*) in 1664, when the English captured the outpost from the Dutch.

>> An American Story

BEARS ON FLOATING ISLANDS

They came to her one night while she slept. Into her dreams drifted a small island, and on the island were tall trees and living creatures, one of them wearing the fur of a white rabbit. When she told of her vision, no one took her seriously, not even the shamans and conjurers whose business it was to interpret dreams. No one, that is, until two days later, when the island appeared to all, floating toward shore. On it, as she had seen, were tall trees, and on their branches—bears. Or creatures that looked so much like bears that the men grabbed their weapons and raced to the beach, eager for the good hunt sent by the gods. They were disappointed. The island was not an island at all but a strange wooden ship planted with the trunks of trees. And the bears were not bears at all but a strange sort of men whose bodies were covered with hair. Strangest among them, as she had somehow known, was a man dressed all in white. He commanded great respect among the bearlike men as their "shaman," or priest.

In that way, foretold by the dreams of a young woman, the Micmac Indians in 1869 recounted their people's first encounter with Europeans more than two centuries earlier. Uncannily, the traditions of other northern tribes record similar dreams predicting the European arrival: "large canoes with great white wings like those of a giant bird," filled with pale bearded men bearing "long black tubes."

However Micmacs and other northern Indians first imagined and idealized Europeans, they quickly came to see them as fully human. Traders might bring seemingly wondrous goods, goods that could transform the way labor, commerce, politics, and war functioned in native communities. Yet the traders themselves hardly seemed magical. They could be by turns generous and miserly, brave and frightful, confident and confused, kind and cruel.

Moreover, it soon became clear that these newcomers hailed from different nations, spoke different languages, and often had different goals. English colonists, it seemed, were every day more numerous and wanted nothing so much as land. The French, in contrast, were relatively few and seemed to care for nothing so much as trade—unless it was their Christian God brought with them from across the waters. Strange to say, the Europeans argued over their deity as they did over so many other things. The English, the French, and the Dutch were all rivals, and the Micmacs and others who encountered these new peoples studied them closely and began to make alliances.

Everywhere they went, the newcomers provoked dramatic changes. Thousands of English migrants founded villages and towns throughout the seventeenth century. They not only took up land but also brought animals and plants that changed the way Indians lived. The Dutch, Europe's most powerful commercial nation, planted only a handful of trading settlements along the Hudson River, but they encouraged the Iroquois confederacy to push into rival Indian territories in a quest for furs to trade. Even the French, who claimed to want little more than beaver pelts, brought profound, sometimes cataclysmic changes—changes that would upend the world that natives knew when Europeans were but bears on floating islands. <<

What's to Come

FRANCE IN NORTH AMERICA

Jacques Cartier first explored the land the French would call Canada in 1535, sailing through the Gulf of St. Lawrence. But not until 1605 did the French plant a permanent colony, at Port Royal in Acadia (Nova Scotia). Three years later Samuel de Champlain established Quebec farther up the St. Lawrence valley, to pursue the fur trade with less competition from rival Europeans. Champlain aligned himself with local Montagnais, Algonquians, and, especially, the mighty Hurons—a confederacy of farmers 20,000 strong whose towns near the Georgian Bay straddled a vast trading network.

The Origins of New France >>

The Hurons, Montagnais, and Algonquians had reason to embrace Champlain. Like Europeans elsewhere in North America, the Frenchman came with wondrous textiles, glass, copper, and ironware. At first the Indians treated such things as exotic commodities rather than utilitarian items. Copper kettles, for instance, might be cut into strips for jewelry. But before long, metal tools began transforming native life. The new knives made it far easier to butcher animals; trees could be felled and buildings put up far more easily with iron axes rather than stone; cooking was more efficient with brass kettles that could be placed directly on the fire; flint strike-a-lights eliminated the need to carry hot coals in bounded shells; beads, cloth, needles, and thread allowed for a new level of creative and visual expression; and, because they traveled farther and truer than stone, metal arrowheads made hunters and warriors more deadly than ever before.

For native peoples, all exchanges of goods were bound up in complex social relations. Thus the Montagnais, Algonquians, and Hurons wanted Champlain as a friend as well as a merchant. They persuaded him to accompany them on a campaign against their mutual enemies the Mohawks, one of the five confederated tribes of the Iroquois. Champlain proved his worth in 1609 when he and his Indian companions confronted two hundred Mohawk warriors in what is now upstate New York. The Frenchman strode to the front as the battle was about to begin, raised his musket, and shot dead two Mohawk chiefs. Chaplain's allies let out a joyous cry, for few if any of the warriors had ever seen a gun fired in combat. They drove the remaining Mohawks from the field. It was not the last time European newcomers would alter the balance of power in North America.

The Montagnais, Algonquians, and Hurons became eager trading partners over the next generation. In return for European goods, they provided tens of thousands of otter, raccoon, and especially beaver pelts. The latter went to make fashionable European hats, whereas mink and marten skins were sent to adorn the robes of high-ranking European officials and churchmen. Some of the French derided New France as nothing more than a *comptoir*, a storehouse for the skins of dead animals. Yet Champlain wanted more. He struggled to bring more permanent settlers to Canada and, above all, he looked to bind his native allies firmly to the colonial project. To that end Champlain recruited certain French men and boys to live with Indian families, to learn their language and customs.

Along with these *coureurs de bois*, or "runners in the woods," French authorities engaged Jesuits, members of the Society of Jesus, to establish missions among the Indians. The Jesuits were fired with the passions of the **Counter-Reformation** in Europe, a movement by devout Catholics to correct those abuses that had prompted the Protestant Reformation. At first France's Indian allies tolerated Jesuit missionaries but listened to them little. By the 1630s, however, Champlain began insisting that trading partners allow Jesuits to live among them. More importantly, Christianized Indians got better prices for furs than did their unconverted counterparts. Such policies helped the French pursue what they saw as interlocked economic, strategic, and religious objectives.

Among Champlain's allies the Hurons proved to be the most reluctant to accept European customs and religion. Converts remained relatively few into the 1640s, and the debate over Huron cultural identity increasingly left the confederacy fragmented and vulnerable to enemies.

⌃ French women as well as men in religious orders dedicated their lives to missionary work in Canada. Marguerite Bourgeoys founded a religious community dedicated to the education of young girls.

> **Counter-Reformation** reform movement within the Roman Catholic Church in response to the Protestant Reformation, seeking to reform and reinvigorate the church.

New Netherlands, the Iroquois, and the Beaver Wars

>> If Canada was merely a *comptoir*, it was a profitable one, and the rival Dutch noticed. By around 1600 the Netherlands possessed the greatest manufacturing capacity in the world and had become the key economic power in Europe. Because they enjoyed prosperity and religious freedom at home, few Dutch folk had any desire to plant colonies abroad. But they did want to tap into the wealth flowing out of North America and therefore laid claim to a number of sites around the Connecticut, Delaware, and Hudson Rivers (the last named for the Englishman Henry Hudson, who first explored it for the Dutch in 1609). Most of New Netherlands' few settlers clustered in the village of New Amsterdam on Manhattan Island at the mouth of the Hudson.

More important for the geopolitics of the continent, the Dutch West India Company established a trading outpost 150 miles upriver known as Fort Orange (present-day Albany). By 1630 the powerful Mohawks came to dominate that fort's commerce. Ever since their encounter with Champlain's musket, the Mohawks and the other four members of the **Iroquois League**—the Oneidas, Onondagas, Cayugas, and Senecas—had suffered from their lack of direct access to European tools and weapons. At Fort Orange, the Iroquois finally found that access. As the beaver population, always fragile, collapsed within Iroquois territory, the league used its new weapons to go on the offensive against its northern enemies. To maintain its trading position, it began preying on Huron convoys on its way to Quebec and then selling the plundered pelts to the Dutch.

> **Iroquois League** Indian confederacy consisting of the Mohawks, Oneidas, Onondagas, Cayugas, and Senecas (a sixth nation, the Tuscaroras, would join in 1712). The league exerted enormous influence throughout colonial eastern North America.

<< This undated French engraving depicts something often overlooked or trivialized by European observers: native women's work. Two Iroquois women grind corn into meal while a swaddled infant rests in a backboard.

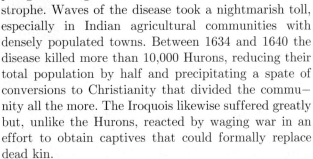
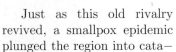

>> The Hurons who became infected with smallpox in the 1630s would have experienced fevers, aches, and vomiting before the telltale spots emerged on their skin. Agonizing pustules would have soon covered them from head to toe, as in this modern photograph, and sometimes the pustules merged into oozing sheets that caused large sections of the victims' skin to peel away from their bodies. The disease claimed millions of lives in the Americas after 1492.

Just as this old rivalry revived, a smallpox epidemic plunged the region into catastrophe. Waves of the disease took a nightmarish toll, especially in Indian agricultural communities with densely populated towns. Between 1634 and 1640 the disease killed more than 10,000 Hurons, reducing their total population by half and precipitating a spate of conversions to Christianity that divided the community all the more. The Iroquois likewise suffered greatly but, unlike the Hurons, reacted by waging war in an effort to obtain captives that could formally replace dead kin.

A second transformative event was the dramatic expansion of the region's arms trade. Reluctant at first to deal in guns, the Dutch at Fort Orange relaxed their policy by the late 1630s in order to obtain more furs. Soon the Iroquois had many times more muskets than the Hurons, whom the French had refused to arm so long as they remained unconverted.

Reeling from disease and internal division, the Hurons saw their world collapsing. In 1648 well-armed Iroquois warriors destroyed three Huron towns. The Hurons made the wrenching decision to burn their remaining towns and abandon their lands for good. Perhaps 2,000 became Iroquois, as either war captives or humble refugees. Others merged with neighboring peoples, while thousands more fled and starved or died of exposure in the harsh winter of 1649–1650.

So began the Beaver Wars, a series of conflicts that transformed the colonial north at least as much as the Indian slave wars had the south. Seeking new hunting grounds and new captives to replenish their diminishing population, Iroquois raiders attacked peoples near and far. After the Hurons, they scattered the nearby Petuns, Eries, and Neutrals—peoples who, like the Hurons, were Iroquoian speakers and could be integrated into Iroquois communities with relative ease. Warriors next moved against non-Iroquoian groups, including Delawares and Shawnees in the

Ohio valley, and even extended their raids south to the Carolinas. To the north they attacked Algonquians in the Canadian Shield, and Abenakis and others in New England.

The Lure of the Mississippi >>

The Beaver Wars continued in fits and starts for the rest of the seventeenth century, provoking a massive refugee crisis as families fled their traditional territories and tried to rebuild their lives. The wars also very nearly ruined New France. About 300 Frenchmen were killed or captured, cutting the colony's meager population in half by 1666. French authorities scrambled to find reliable new partners in the fur trade and became less reluctant to trade guns to Indian allies. In the end, the scope of the conflict and the far—flung movement of refugees led the French to take a more expansive view of the continent and their place in it.

That expansive view was encouraged by the discovery of the Mississippi River. By the 1660s, French traders, priests, and officers were making inroads among refugee villages in the Western Great Lakes, a region the French referred to as the *pays d'en haut,* or "upper country." As they did so, they began exploring the greatest watercourse in North America.

pays d'en haut in the seventeenth century, the lands referred to by the French as the "upper country," the land upriver from Montreal as French fur traders passed into the Great Lakes beyond the southern shores of Lake Ontario.

The Mississippi travels nearly 2,500 miles from its source in present—day Minnesota to the Gulf of Mexico, carrying water from several major rivers and dominating a drainage area larger than the Indian subcontinent in Asia. As the French began exploring in earnest, it dawned on them that the Mississippi valley could be the strategic key to success in North America. French officials courted Indian peoples along the river and its tributaries, employing their hard—won insights into native diplomatic culture along the way. The region's peoples—the Illinois, Shawnees, Quapaws, and others—expressed keen interest in French trade, as well as fear and hatred of their common Iroquois enemies. When René Robert Cavelier, Sieur de La Salle became the first European to descend the river to the Gulf in 1682, he encountered the Natchez, Chickasaws, and others who had not seen Europeans since De Soto and his maniacal march nearly a century and a half before. Other Frenchmen erected trading posts and simple missions, even making contact and tentative alliances with Osages, Arkansas, Ottos, Pawnees, and others west of the great river.

By the early eighteenth century New France had helped broker an uneasy peace between the Iroquois and Indian nations to the west, extended its influence over a vast area, and fortified its colonial core along the St. Lawrence River. In 1700 the colony had scores of simple missions and three modest cities— Quebec, Montreal, and Trois—Rivières—containing a population of about 15,000. Most immigrants to New France eventually returned to Europe, and shortsighted French monarchs insisted that Canada remain Catholic, off limits to France's most obvious emigrants, the Protestant Huguenots. But even with its small colonial population, New France emerged as a powerful player in North America. The French had reason to hope that their strategic and economic alliances with native peoples could help contain the Spanish to the west and limit English expansion from the east.

 REVIEW

What caused the Beaver Wars, and how did the French respond?

THE FOUNDING OF NEW ENGLAND

At first the English regarded the northern part of North America as a place in which only the mad French could see possibility. English fisherfolk who strayed from Newfoundland to the coast of Acadia and New England carried home descriptions of the long, lonely coast, rockbound and rugged. Long winters of numbing cold melted into short summers of steamy heat. There were no minerals to mine, no crops suitable for export, no huge native populations to enslave. The Chesapeake, with its temperate climate and long growing season, seemed a much likelier spot.

But by 1620 worsening conditions at home had instilled in some English men and women the mixture of desperation and idealism needed to settle an uninviting, unknown world. Religious differences among English Protestants became a matter of sharper controversy during the seventeenth century. Along with the religious crisis came mounting political tensions and continuing problems of unemployment and recession. Times were bad—so bad that the anticipation of worse times to come swept English men and women to the shores of New England.

The Puritan Movement >>

The colonization of New England started with a king who chose his enemies unwisely. James I, shortly after succeeding Elizabeth I in 1603, vowed to purge England of all radical Protestant reformers. The radicals James had

Puritans reformers within the Church of England during the sixteenth century, who ultimately formed the Congregationalist and Presbyterian churches. Puritans strove to reform English religion, society, and politics by restricting church membership to the pious and godly and by enlisting the state to enforce a strict moral code.

Presbyterians members of a Protestant denomination that originated in sixteenth-century Britain as part of the Puritan movement. Presbyterians embraced Calvinist beliefs and favored a hierarchical church organization in which individual congregations were guided by presbyteries and synods comprising both laymen and ministers.

Congregationalists members of a Protestant denomination that originated in sixteenth-century Britain as part of the Puritan movement. Congregationalists held that each individual congregation should conduct its own religious affairs, answering to no higher authority.

predestination basis of Calvinist theology and a belief that holds that God has ordained the outcome of all human history before the beginning of time, including the eternal fate of every human being.

in mind were the **Puritans,** most of whom were either Presbyterians or Congregationalists. Although both groups of Puritan reformers embraced Calvin's ideas, they differed on the best form of church organization. Individual **Presbyterian** churches (or congregations) were guided by higher governing bodies of ministers and laypersons. Those in the **Congregationalist** churches, in contrast, believed that each congregation should conduct its own affairs independently, answering to no other authority.

Like all Christians, Protestant and Catholic, the Puritans believed that God was all-knowing and all-powerful. And, like all Calvinists, the Puritans emphasized that idea of divine sovereignty known as **predestination.** At the center of their thinking was the belief that God had ordained the outcome of history, including the eternal fate of every human being. The Puritans found comfort in their belief in predestination, because it provided their lives with meaning and purpose. They felt assured that a sovereign God was directing the fate of individuals, nations, and all of creation. The Puritans strove to play their parts in that divine drama of history and to discover in their performances some signs of personal salvation.

The divine plan, as the Puritans understood it, called for reforming both church and society along the lines laid down by John Calvin. It seemed to the Puritans that England's government hampered rather than promoted religious purity and social order. It tolerated drunkenness, theatergoing, gambling, extravagance, public swearing, and Sabbath-breaking. It permitted popular recreations rooted in pagan custom and superstition—sports such as bear baiting and maypole dancing and festivals such as the celebration of Christmas and saints' days.

Even worse, the state had not done enough to purify the English church of the "corruptions" of Roman Catholicism. The Church of England counted as its members everyone in the nation, saint and sinner alike. To the Puritans, belonging to a church was no birthright. They wished to limit membership and the privileges of baptism and communion to godly men and women. The Puritans also deplored the hierarchy of bishops and archbishops in the Church of England, as well as its elaborate ceremonies in which priests wore ornate vestments. Too many Anglican clergy were "dumb dogges" in Puritan eyes, too poorly educated to instruct churchgoers in the truths of Scripture or to deliver a decent sermon.

Because English monarchs refused to take stronger measures to reform church and society, the Puritans became their outspoken critics. Elizabeth I had tolerated this opposition, but James I would not endure it and intended to rid England of these radicals. With some of the Puritans, known as the Separatists, he seemed to succeed.

The Pilgrim Settlement at Plymouth Colony >>

The Separatists were devout Congregationalists who concluded that the Church of England was too corrupt to be reformed. They abandoned Anglican worship and met secretly in small congregations. From their first appearance in England during the 1570s, the Separatists suffered persecution from the government—fines, imprisonment, and, in a few cases, execution. Always a tiny minority within the Puritan movement, the Separatists were people from humble backgrounds: craftworkers and farmers without influence to challenge the state. By 1608 some had become so discouraged that they migrated to Holland, where the Dutch government permitted complete freedom of religion. But when their children began to adopt Dutch customs and other religions, some Separatists decided to move again, this time to Virginia.

It can only be imagined what fate would have befallen the unworldly Separatists had they actually settled in the Chesapeake during the tobacco boom. But a series of mistakes—including an error in charting the course of their ship, the *Mayflower*—brought the little band far to the north, to a region Captain John Smith had earlier dubbed "New England." In November 1620 some 88 Separatist "Pilgrims" set anchor at a place they called Plymouth on the coast of present-day southeastern Massachusetts. They were sick with scurvy, weak from malnutrition, and shaken by a shipboard mutiny, and neither the site nor the season invited settlement. As one of their leaders, William Bradford, later remembered:

> For summer being done, all things stand upon them with a weatherbeaten face, and the whole country, full of woods and thickets

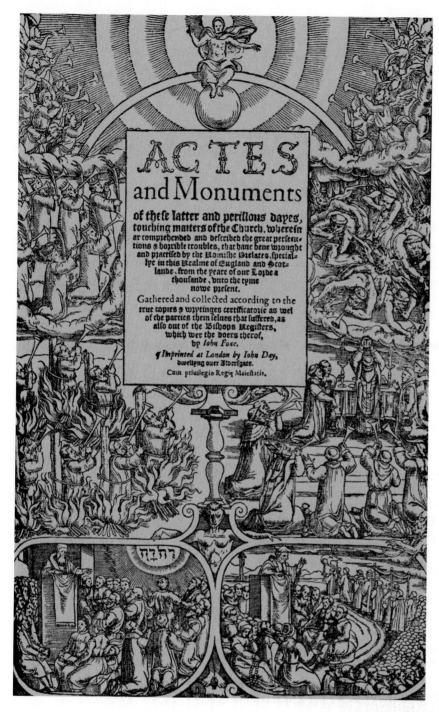

and many did not live long enough to enjoy the distinction. They had arrived too late to plant crops and had failed to bring an adequate supply of food. By the spring of 1621 half the immigrants had died. English merchants who had financed the *Mayflower* voyage failed to send supplies to the struggling settlement. Plymouth might have become another doomed colony except that the Pilgrims received better treatment from native inhabitants than they did from their English backers.

Though they understood it only dimly, the Pilgrims were, in one historian's memorable phrase, the "beneficiaries of catastrophe." Only four years before their arrival coastal New England had been devastated by a massive epidemic, possibly the plague. Losses varied locally, but overall the native coastal population may have been reduced by as much as 90 percent. Abandoned villages lay in ruins up and down the coast, including the village of Patuxet, where the Pilgrims established Plymouth. Years later visitors would still marvel at heaps of unburied human remains dating from the epidemic.

The Wampanoags dominated the lands around Plymouth. Still reeling from loss in 1620 and eager to obtain trade goods and assistance against native enemies, Massasoit, their chief, agreed to help the starving colonists. At first, the peoples communicated through a remarkable Wampanoag named Squanto, who had been kidnapped by English sailors before the epidemic. Taken to Europe, Squanto learned English and returned to America in time to act as a mediator between Massasoit and the newcomers. The Pilgrims accepted Wampanoag hospitality and instruction, and invited native leaders to a feast in honor of their first successful harvest in 1621 (the genesis of the "First Thanksgiving" story).

represented a savage hue. If they looked behind them, there was the mighty ocean which they had passed and was now as a main bar and gulf to separate them from all the civil parts of the world.

For some, the shock was too great. Dorothy Bradford, William's wife, is said to have fallen overboard from the *Mayflower* as it lay anchored off Plymouth. It is more likely that she jumped to her death.

Few Pilgrims could have foreseen founding the first permanent European settlement in New England,

The Pilgrims set up a government for their colony, the framework of which was the Mayflower Compact, drawn up on board ship before landing. That agreement provided for a governor and several assistants to advise him, all to be elected annually by Plymouth's adult males. In the eyes of English law the Plymouth settlers had no clear basis for their land claims or their government, for they had neither a royal charter nor approval from the Crown. But English authorities, distracted by problems closer to home, left the tiny colony of farmers alone.

The Puritan Settlement at Massachusetts Bay

>> Among the Crown's distractions were two groups of Puritans more numerous and influential than the Pilgrims. They included both the Presbyterians and the majority of Congregationalists who, unlike the Pilgrim Separatists, still considered the Church of England capable of being reformed. But the 1620s brought these Puritans only fresh discouragements. In 1625 Charles I inherited his father's throne and all his enemies. When Parliament attempted to limit the king's power, Charles simply dissolved it, in 1629, and proceeded to rule without it. When Puritans pressed for reform, the king began to move against them.

This persecution swelled a second wave of Puritan migration that also drew from the ranks of Congregationalists. Unlike the humble Separatists, these emigrants included merchants, landed gentlemen, and lawyers who organized the Massachusetts Bay Company in 1629. Those able Puritan leaders aimed to build a better society in America, an example to the rest of the world. Unlike the Separatists, they had a strong sense of mission and destiny. They were not abandoning the English church, they insisted, but merely regrouping across the Atlantic for another assault on corruption.

Despite the company's Puritan leanings, it somehow obtained a royal charter confirming its title to most of present-day Massachusetts and New Hampshire. Advance parties in 1629 established the town of Salem on the coast well north of Plymouth. In 1630 the company's first governor, a tough-minded and visionary lawyer named John Winthrop, sailed from England with a dozen other company stockholders and a fleet of men and women to establish the town of Boston. The newcomers intended to build a godly "city on a hill" that would serve as an example to the world.

Once established in the Bay Colony, Winthrop and the other stockholders transformed the charter for their trading company into the framework of government for a colony. The company's governor became the colony's chief executive, and the company's other officers became the governor's assistants. The charter provided for annual elections of the governor and his assistants by company stockholders, known as the freemen. But to create a broad base of support for the new government, Winthrop and his assistants expanded the freemanship in 1631 to include every adult male church member.

The governor, his assistants, and the freemen together made up the General Court of the colony, which passed all laws, levied taxes, established courts, and made war and peace. In 1634 the whole body of the freemen stopped meeting and instead each town elected representatives or deputies to the General Court. Ten years later, the deputies formed themselves into the lower house of the Bay Colony legislature, and the assistants formed the upper house. By refashioning a company charter into a civil constitution, Massachusetts Bay Puritans were well on the way to shaping society, church, and state to their liking.

Contrary to expectations, New England proved more hospitable to the English than did the Chesapeake. The character of the migration itself gave New England settlers an advantage, for most arrived in family groups—not as young, single, indentured servants of the sort whose discontents unsettled Virginia society. The heads of New England's first households were typically freemen—farmers, artisans, and merchants. Most were skilled and literate. Since husbands usually migrated with their wives and children, the ratio of men to women within the population was fairly evenly balanced.

Most of the emigrants, some 21,000, came in a cluster between 1630 and 1642. Thereafter new arrivals tapered off because of the outbreak of the English Civil War. This relatively rapid colonization fostered solidarity, because emigrants shared a common past of persecution and a strong desire to create an ordered society modeled on Scripture.

 REVIEW
Who settled the earliest New England colonies, and why?

Did the Puritans really come to America for religious freedom?

Opinion

STABILITY AND ORDER IN EARLY NEW ENGLAND

Puritan emigrants and their descendants thrived in New England's bracing but healthy climate. The first generation of colonists lived to average age of 70, nearly twice as long as Virginians and 10 years longer than men and women living in England. With 90 percent of all offspring reaching adulthood, the typical family consisted of seven or eight children who came to maturity. Because of low death rates and high birthrates, the number of New Englanders doubled about every 27 years—while the populations of Europe and the Chesapeake barely reproduced themselves. By 1700 New England and the Chesapeake both had populations of approximately 100,000. But, whereas the southern population grew because of continuing emigration and the importation of slaves, New England's expanded primarily through natural increase.

Early emigrants to the Bay Colony carved out an arc of villages around Massachusetts Bay. Within a decade settlers pressed into Connecticut, Rhode Island, and New Hampshire. Connecticut and Rhode Island received separate charters from Charles II in the 1660s, guaranteeing their residents the rights to land and government. New Hampshire, at first part of Massachusetts, became a separate colony in 1679, whereas the handful of hardy souls living along the coast of present-day Maine still accepted the Massachusetts Bay Colony's authority.

Early New Englanders established most of their settlements with an eye to stability and order. Unlike the Virginians, who scattered across the Chesapeake to isolated plantations, most New Englanders established

MAP 4.1: EARLY NEW ENGLAND

Despite some variety among emigrants, New England's English settlements remained relatively homogeneous and stable. Over the years groups of settlers "hived off" from the settlements around Massachusetts Bay, beginning new towns along the Connecticut River, northern and western Connecticut, Long Island, and East Jersey. *Which colony was the only one in New England to attract a significant population of Scots-Irish?*

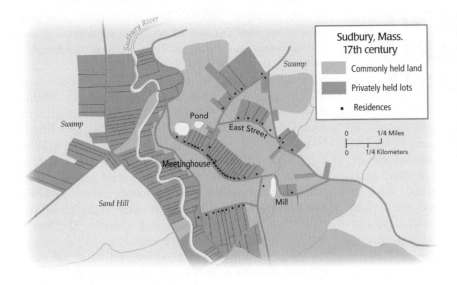

MAP 4.2: SUDBURY, MASSACHUSETTS

Everyday life in New England centered in small towns such as Sudbury, west of Boston. Families lived in houses clustered around the meetinghouse, in contrast to the decentralized plantations of the south. The privately held farm lots were mixed together as well, so that neighbors worked and lived in close contact with one another.
How does the pattern of settlement in Sudbury differ from the pattern of settlement in the Chesapeake region?

tight-knit communities like those they had left behind in England. Each family received a lot for a house along with about 150 acres of land in nearby fields. Farmers left many of their acres uncultivated as a legacy for future generations, for most had only the labor of their own families to work their land. While the Chesapeake abounded with servants, tenant farmers, and slaves, almost every adult male in rural New England owned property. With little hope of prospering through

commercial agriculture, New England farmers also had no incentive to import large numbers of servants and slaves or to create large plantations.

Strong family institutions contributed to New England's order and stability. While the early deaths of parents regularly splintered Chesapeake families, two adult generations were often on hand to encourage order within New England households. Husbands and fathers exacted submission from wives and strict obedience from children. Land gave New England's long-lived fathers great authority over even their grown children; sons and daughters relied on paternal legacies of farms in order to marry and establish their own families.

Whereas churches were few and far between in seventeenth-century Virginia, they constituted the center of community life in colonial New England. Individual congregations ran their own affairs and regulated their own membership. Those wishing to join had to convince ministers and church members that they had experienced a genuine spiritual rebirth or "conversion." Most New Englanders sought and won membership. As majority institutions supported by public taxes, churches had the reach and the resources to oversee public morality, often censuring or expelling wayward neighbors. Still, ministers enjoyed less public power in New England than in the old country. New England's ministers did not serve as officers in the civil government, and the Congregational churches owned no property. In contrast, Catholic and Anglican church officials wielded real temporal power in European states, and the churches held extensive tracts of land.

Finally, New Englanders governed themselves more democratically than did their counterparts in England. Communities throughout the region held regular town meetings of all resident white men. The town fathers generally set the meeting's

<< The Old Ship Meetinghouse, built in Hingham, Massachusetts, in 1681, expresses the importance of hierarchy among New England Puritans. Wealthy families enjoyed the enclosed wooden pews on the ground floor, whereas poorer folk sat on benches in the second-floor gallery. The raised pulpit (*front*) bespeaks the congregation's respect for the authority and learning of the clergy. The American flag, of course, is a modern addition.

agenda and offered advice, but the unanimous consent of townsmen determined all decisions. Colony governments in early New England also evolved into representative and responsive institutions. Typically the central government of each colony, such as the General Court of Massachusetts Bay, consisted of a governor and a bicameral legislature, including an upper house, or council, and a lower house, or assembly. All officials were elected annually by the freemen—white adult men entitled to vote in colony elections. Voting qualifications varied, but the number of men enfranchised made up a much broader segment of society than that in seventeenth-century England.

Communities in Conflict >> Although most New Englanders called themselves Puritans and Congregationalists, the very fervency of their convictions often led them to disagree about how to carry out the teachings of the Bible and the ideas of John Calvin. During the first decades of colonization, such disagreements led to the founding of breakaway colonies. In 1636 Thomas Hooker, the minister of Cambridge, Massachusetts, led part of his congregation to establish the first English settlement in Connecticut. Somewhat more liberal than other Bay Puritans, Hooker favored more lenient standards for church membership. He also opposed the Bay's policy of limiting voting in colony elections to church members. In contrast, New Haven (a separate colony until it became part of Connecticut in 1662) was begun in 1638 by strict Congregationalists who found Massachusetts too liberal.

While Connecticut and New Haven emerged from voluntary migration, enforced exile filled Rhode Island with men and women whose radical ideas unsettled the rest of Massachusetts. Roger Williams, Rhode Island's founder, had come to New England in 1631, serving as a respected minister of Salem. But soon Williams announced that he was a Separatist, like the Pilgrims of Plymouth. He encouraged the Bay Colony to break all ties to the corrupt Church of England. He also urged a more complete **separation of Church and State** than most New Englanders were prepared to accept, and later in his career he endorsed full religious toleration. Finally, Williams denounced the Bay's charter—the legal document that justified Massachusetts's existence—on the grounds that the king had no right to grant land that he had not purchased from the Indians. When Williams boldly suggested that Massachusetts actually inform the king of his mistake, angry authorities prepared to deport him. Instead, Williams fled the colony in the dead of winter to live with the Indians. In 1636 he became the

> **separation of Church and State** principle that religious institutions and their representatives should exercise no civil or judicial powers and that civil governments should give no official sanction, privileges, or financial support to any religious denomination or organization.

founder and first citizen of Providence, later to be part of Rhode Island.

Another charismatic heretic from Massachusetts arrived soon after. Anne Hutchinson, a skilled midwife and the spouse of a wealthy merchant, came to Boston in 1634. Enthusiasm for her minister, John Cotton, started her on a course of explaining his sermons to gatherings of her neighbors—and then to elaborating ideas of her own. The fact that a woman would do such things made the authorities uneasy; they became positively alarmed when they learned that Hutchinson embraced controversial positions on doctrine. Soon a majority of the Bay's ministers accused the popular Hutchinson of holding heretical views. She in turn denounced her detractors, and the controversy escalated. In 1638 the Bay Colony government expelled Hutchinson and her followers for sedition. She settled briefly in Rhode Island before moving on to Long Island, where she died in an Indian attack.

Goodwives and Witches >> If Anne Hutchinson had been a man, her ideas would still have been deemed heretical. However, if she had been a man, she might have found other ways to express her intelligence and magnetism. But life in colonial New England offered women, especially married women, little scope for their talents.

Most adult women were hardworking farm wives who cared for large households of children. Between marriage and middle age, most New England wives were pregnant except when breast-feeding. When they were not nursing or minding children, mothers were producing and preparing much of what was consumed and worn by their families. They planted vegetable gardens and pruned fruit trees, salted beef and pork and pressed cider, milked cows and churned butter, kept bees and tended poultry, cooked and baked, washed and ironed, spun, wove, and sewed. While husbands and sons engaged in farmwork that changed with the seasons, took trips to taverns and mills, and went off to hunt or fish, housebound wives and daughters were locked into a humdrum routine with little time for themselves.

Women suffered legal disadvantages as well. In contrast to New Mexico and Florida with their Spanish civil law traditions, English common law and colonial legal codes accorded married women virtually no control over property. Wives could not sue or be sued, they could not make contracts, and they surrendered to their husbands any property that they had possessed before marriage. Divorce was almost impossible to obtain until the late eighteenth century. Only widows and a few single women had the same property rights as men, but they could not vote in colony elections.

The one arena in which women could attain something approaching equal standing with men was the

ACCUSATIONS AND DEFENSES IN THE SALEM WITCHCRAFT TRIALS

The Salem Witchcraft trials of 1692 set neighbor against neighbor and resulted in the execution of 20 women and men. One of the accused was tavern owner John Proctor, on whom Arthur Miller loosely based the main protagonist in his famous play The Crucible. *The documents below include testimony of three witnesses against Proctor, and his own remarkable response.*

DOCUMENT 1
The Accusations

Sarah Bibber

The Deposition of Sarah Vibber agged about 36 years who testifieth and saith that on the 3 june 1692. Jno: proctor. sen'r came to me and did most greviously torment me by pinching pricking and almost presing me to death urging me to drink: drink as Red as blood which I refusing he did tortor me with variety of tortors and immediatly he vanished away also on the same day I saw Jno: proctor most greviously tortor Susannah Shelden by claping his hands on hir throat and almost choaking hir. also severall times sence Jno: proctor sen'r has most greviously tortored me a grat many times with a variety of tortors

    Sara vibber ownid this har testimony to be the truth on har oath before the Juriars of Inqwest this: 30. of June 1692.

    Jurat in Curia

    (Reverse) Sarah Vibber

Ann Putnam

The Deposistion of Ann putnam Jun'r who testifieth and saith I have often seen the Apperishtion of Jno procktor senr. amongst the wicthes but he did not doe me much hurt tell a little before his examination which was on the 11th of April 1692 and then he sett upon me most greviously and did tortor me most dreadfully also in the time of his examination he afflected me very much: and severall times sence the Apperishtion of John procktor senr, has most greviously tortored me by pinching and allmost choaking me urging me vehemently to writ in his book also on the day of his examination I saw the Apperishtion of Jno: proctor senr goe and afflect and most greviously tortor the bodys of Mistris pope mary walcott Mircy lewes. Abigail williams and Jno: Indian. and he and

his wife and Sarah Cloys keept Elizabeth Hubburd speachless all the time of their examination

(Mask) Ann Putnam

Ann Putman owned what is above written upon oath before and unto the Grand inquest on the 30'th Day of June 1692 (Reverse) Ann puttnam ag't John procter

Mary Warren

The deposition of mary warrin aged 20 y'rs ho testifieth I have seen the apparition of John procter sen'r among the wiches and he hath often tortored me by penching me and biting me and Choakeing me and presing me one my Stomack tell the blood came out of my mouth and all so I saw him tortor Mes poap and marcey lues and John Indian a pon the

---

churches. Puritan women could not become ministers, but after the 1660s they made up the majority of church members. In some churches membership enabled them to vote for ministerial candidates and to voice opinions about admitting and disciplining members. Puritan doctrine itself rejected the medieval Catholic suspicion of women as "a necessary evil," seeing them instead as "a necessary good." Even so, the Puritan ideal of the virtuous woman was a chaste, submissive "helpmeet," a wife and mother who served God by serving men.

Communities sometimes responded to assertive women with accusations of witchcraft. Like most early modern Europeans, New Englanders believed in wizards and witches, men and women who were said to acquire supernatural powers by signing a compact with Satan. A total of 344 New Englanders were charged with witchcraft during the first colonial century, with the notorious Salem Village episode of 1692 producing the largest outpouring of accusations

and 20 executions. More than three—quarters of all accused witches were women, usually middle—aged and older, and most of those accused were regarded as unduly independent. Before they were charged with witchcraft, many had been suspected of heretical religious beliefs, others of sexual impropriety. Still others had inherited or stood to inherit property.

The People in the Way >> Whatever their

political battles, doctrinal disputes, and inequalities, New Englanders were all participants in a colonial project that depended on taking land from other people. At the time of first contact, perhaps 100,000 Algonquin men and women lived in the area reaching from the Kennebec River in Maine to Cape Cod. Like the Puritans, they relied on fishing in spring and summer, hunting year—round, and cultivating and harvesting corn and other crops in spring and fall. To an even greater degree than among the colonists, Indian political authority was local. Within

day of his examination and he hath allso temted me to right in his book and to eat bread which he brought to me which I

Refuseing to doe: Jno proctor did most greviously tortor me with variety of torturs all most Redy to kill me.

Mary Warren owned the above written upon her oath before & unto the Grand inquest on the 30'th Day of June 1692

DOCUMENT 2
The Defense

SALEM-PRISON, July 23, 1692.
Mr. Mather, Mr. Allen, Mr. Moody,
Mr. Willard, and Mr. Bailey.
Reverend Gentlemen.

The innocency of our Case with the Enmity of our Accusers and our Judges, and Jury, whom nothing but our Innocent Blood will serve their turn, having Condemned us already before our Tryals, being so much incensed and engaged against us by the Devil, makes us bold to Beg and Implore your Favourable Assistance of this our Humble Petition to his Excellency, That if it be possible our Innocent Blood may be spared, which undoubtedly otherwise will be shed, if the Lord doth not mercifully step in. The Magistrates, Ministers, Jewries, and all the People in general, being so much inraged and incensed against us by the Delusion of the Devil, which we can term no other, by reason we know in our own Consciences, we are all Innocent Persons. Here are five Persons who have lately confessed themselves to be Witches, and do accuse some of us, of being along with them at a Sacrament, since we were committed into close Prison, which we know to be Lies. Two of the 5 are (Carriers Sons) Youngmen, who would not confess any thing till they tyed them Neck and Heels till the Blood was ready to come out of their Noses, and 'tis credibly believed and reported this was the occasion of making them confess that they never did, by reason they said one had been a Witch a Month, and another five Weeks, and that their Mother had made them so, who has been confined here this nine Weeks. My son William Procter, when he was examin'd, because he would not confess that he was Guilty, when he was Innocent, they tyed him Neck and Heels till the Blood gushed out at his Nose, and would have kept him so 24 Hours, if one more Merciful than the rest, had not taken pity on him, and caused him to be unbound. These actions are very like the Popish Cruelties. They have already undone us in our Estates, and that will not serve their turns, without our Innocent Bloods.

If it cannot be granted that we can have our Trials at Boston, we humbly beg that you would endeavour to have these Magistrates changed, and others in their rooms, begging also and beseeching you would be pleased to be here, if not all, some of you at our Trials, hoping thereby you may be the means of saving the sheeding our Innocent Bloods, desiring your Prayers to the Lord in our behalf, we rest your Poor Afflicted Servants.

JOHN PROCTER, etc.

THINKING CRITICALLY

What patterns do you see in the accusations? What does the language in all four pieces tell you about how members of this community conceived of Satan? How does Proctor try to defend himself? What do you think he was trying to accomplish by comparing the interrogations his son and others faced to "Popish Cruelties"?

each village, a single leader known as the "sachem" or "sagamore" directed economic life, administered justice, and negotiated with other tribes and English settlers. As with New England's town fathers, a sachem's power depended on keeping the trust and consent of his people.

Thus, the newcomers had more in common with their hosts than they cared to admit. But English expansion in the region had to come at someone's expense, and colonists obtained Indian lands in one of three ways. Sometimes they purchased it. Sales varied—they might be free and fair, fraudulent, subtly coerced, or forced through intimidation and violence. Second, colonists eagerly expanded into lands emptied by epidemics. The English often saw God's hand in such events. "Without this remarkable and terrible stroke of God upon the natives," wrote one New Englander after a smallpox epidemic, "[we] would with much more difficulty have found room" to settle.

Third and finally, colonists commonly encouraged and participated in regional wars to obtain native lands. This proved easy enough to do, because, like Europeans, the Indians of New England quarreled frequently with neighboring nations. The antagonism among the English, Spanish, Dutch, and French was matched by the hostilities among the Abenakis, Pawtuckets, Massachusetts, Narragansetts, and Wampanoags of the north Atlantic coast. Epidemics only intensified existing rivalries, because they opened up new opportunities for stronger neighbors to press their advantage.

The English began by aligning with Massasoit and his Wampanoags against other coastal peoples in New England. In 1637 colonial forces joined the Narragansetts in a campaign against the formidable Pequots, who controlled coveted territory in Connecticut. The colonists shocked even their Indian allies when they set fire to the main Pequot village, killing hundreds of men, women, and children. Plymouth's William

Bradford recalled that "it was a fearful sight to see them thus frying in the fire, and the streams of blood quenching the same, and horrible was the stink and scent thereof; but the victory seemed a sweet sacrifice, and they gave the praise thereof to God, who had wrought so wonderfully for them." Several years later the colonists turned against their former allies, joining forces with the Mohegans to intimidate the Narragansetts into ceding much of their territory. Only a few colonists objected to those ruthless policies, among them Roger Williams. "God Land," he warned one Connecticut leader, "will be ... as great a God with us English as God Gold was with the Spaniards."

Metacom's War >> Throughout

these wars, the colonists more or less nurtured their original alliance with Massasoit and his Wampanoags. Indeed, certain colonists tried to bring the two societies closer together. While the impulse to convert was not nearly as strong in New England as in New Spain or New France, a few Englishmen worked tirelessly to bring the word of their God to Indians.

Puritan minister John Eliot began preaching in Algonquian in the 1640s. Over the next two decades he oversaw a project to publish the Scriptures in Algonquian using the Latin alphabet. He also trained scores of native ministers (many of whom became literate) and established seven villages or "praying towns" for Christian Indians. Eliot was not alone. Harvard College defined its mission as "the education of English & Indian youth of this Country" and in 1655 established an Indian college and dormitory on campus. None of these efforts embodied respect for Indian culture or religion. But some New Englanders, at least, wanted to assimilate Indians rather than drive them away.

And yet the colony always grasped for more land. Over time the Puritan–Wampanoag partnership had become a relationship of subordination and suspicion. Rumors of potential native rebellion led colonial authorities to conduct humiliating interrogations and put in place severe rules and restrictions. The colonists' cows and pigs invaded and destroyed Indian fields, provoking innumerable conflicts. When Indians tried to adapt by raising their own cows and pigs, colonial authorities barred them from using common pasture or selling meat in Boston. At the same time, as many as half the dwindling Wampanoags had followed Eliot into the praying towns, threatening tribal unity in a time of mounting crisis.

⚐ Though no images of Metacom survive from his time, in later years artists frequently portrayed him. This image is based on an engraving by Paul Revere.

By 1675 such pressures convinced Massasoit's son and heir, Metacom, whom the English called King Philip, that his nation could be preserved only by chancing war. Complaining that the English were plotting to kill him and other sachems and replace them with Christian Indians more willing to sell land, Metacom rallied most of southern New England's native peoples and laid waste to more than two dozen towns in Plymouth Colony. By the spring of 1676, Metacom's warriors were raiding settlements within 20 miles of Boston. The offensive threatened New England's very existence.

But its momentum could not be sustained. Faced with shortages of food and ammunition, Metacom asked assistance from the Abenakis of Maine and the Mahicans of New York. Both refused. In the summer of 1676 Metacom died in battle; colonial forces brought his severed head to Boston and his hands to Plymouth as trophies. His desperate gamble exhausted native military power in southern New England and virtually destroyed the Wampanoags as a coherent people.

In proportion to population, "King Philip's War" inflicted twice the casualties on New England that the United States as a whole would suffer in the American Civil War. But in the end the region's surviving Indians, Christian or not, found themselves consigned to quiet and often desperate lives on the margins of colonial life.

✓ REVIEW

What were the sources of stability and conflict in early New England?

THE MID-ATLANTIC COLONIES

The inhabitants of the mid–Atlantic colonies—New York, New Jersey, Pennsylvania, and Delaware—enjoyed more secure lives than did most southern colonials. But they lacked the common bonds that lent stability to early New England. Instead, throughout the mid–Atlantic region a variety of ethnic and religious groups vied for wealth from farming and the fur trade and contended bitterly against governments that commanded little popular support.

English Rule in New York >> By the 1660s the Dutch experiment on the mid—Atlantic coast was faltering. While Fort Orange continued to secure furs for the Dutch West India Company, the colonial population remained small and fractious. The company made matters worse by appointing corrupt, dictatorial governors who ruled without an elective assembly. It also provided little protection for outlying Dutch settlements; when it did attack neighboring Indian nations, it did so savagely, triggering terrible retaliations. By the time the company went bankrupt in 1654, it had virtually abandoned its American colony.

Taking advantage of the disarray in New Netherlands, Charles II ignored Dutch claims in North America and granted his brother, James, the Duke of York, a proprietary charter there. The charter granted James all of New Netherlands to Delaware Bay as well as Maine, Martha's Vineyard, and Nantucket Island. In 1664 James sent an invading fleet, whose mere arrival caused the Dutch to surrender.

New York's dizzying diversity would make it difficult to govern. The Duke inherited 9,000 or so colonists: Dutch, Belgians, French, English, Portuguese, Swedes, Finns, and Africans—some enslaved, others free. The colony's ethnic diversity ensured a variety of religions. Although the Dutch Reformed church predominated, other early New Netherlanders included Lutherans, **Quakers,** and Catholics. There were Jews as well, refugees from Portuguese Brazil, who were required by law to live in a ghetto in New Amsterdam. The Dutch resented English rule, and only after a generation of intermarriage and acculturation did that resentment fade. James also failed to win friends among New Englanders who had come to Long Island seeking autonomy and cheap land during the 1640s. He grudgingly gave in to their demand for an elective assembly in 1683 but rejected its first act, the Charter of Liberties, which would have guaranteed basic political rights. The chronic political strife discouraged prospective settlers. By 1698 the colony numbered only 18,000 inhabitants, and New York City, the former New Amsterdam, was an overgrown village of a few thousand.

> **Quakers** Protestant sect, also known as the Society of Friends, founded in mid-seventeenth-century England. The Quakers believed that the Holy Spirit dwelt within each human being and that religious conviction was the source of their egalitarian social practices, which included allowing women to speak in churches and to preach in public gatherings.

The Founding of New Jersey >> Confusion attended New Jersey's beginnings. The lands lying west of the Hudson and east of the Delaware River had been part of the Duke of York's proprietary grant. But in 1664 he gave about 5 million of these acres to Lord Berkeley and Sir George Carteret, two of his favorites who were already involved in the proprietary colonies of the Carolinas. New Jersey's new owners guaranteed settlers land, religious freedom, and a representative assembly in exchange for a small quitrent, an annual fee for the use of the land. The proprietors' terms promptly drew Puritan settlers from New Haven, Connecticut. At the same time, unaware that James had already given New Jersey to Berkeley and Carteret, New York's Governor Richard Nicolls granted Long Island Puritans land there.

More complications ensued when Berkeley and Carteret decided to divide New Jersey into east and west and sell both halves to Quaker investors—a prospect that outraged New Jersey's Puritans. Although some English Quakers migrated to West Jersey, the investors quickly decided that two Jerseys were less desirable than one Pennsylvania and resold both East and West Jersey to speculators. In the end the Jerseys became a patchwork of religious and ethnic groups. Settlers who shared a common religion or national origin formed communities and established small family farms. When the Crown finally reunited East and West as a single royal colony in 1702, New Jersey was overshadowed by settlements not only to the north but now, also, to the south and west.

Quaker Odysseys >> Religious and political idealism similar to that of the Puritans inspired the colonization of Pennsylvania, making it an oddity among the mid—Atlantic colonies. The oddity began with an improbable founder, William Penn. Young Penn devoted his early years to disappointing his distinguished father, Sir William Penn, an admiral in the Royal Navy. Several years after being expelled from college, young Penn finally chose a career that may have made the admiral yearn for mere disappointment: he undertook a lifelong commitment to put into practice Quaker teachings. By the 1670s he had emerged as an acknowledged leader of the Society of Friends, as the Quakers formally called themselves.

The Quakers behaved in ways and believed in ideas that most people regarded as odd. They dressed in a deliberately plain and severe manner. They withheld from their social superiors the customary marks of respect, such as bowing, kneeling, and removing their hats. They refused to swear oaths or to make war. They allowed women public roles of religious leadership. That pattern of behavior reflected their egalitarian ideals, the belief that all men and women shared equally in the "Light Within." Some 40,000 English merchants, artisans, and farmers embraced Quakerism by 1660, and many suffered fines, imprisonment, and corporal punishment.

Since the English upper class has always prized eccentricity among its members, it is not surprising that Penn, despite his Quakerism, remained a favorite of Charles II. More surprising is that the king's favor took the extravagant form of presenting Penn in 1681 with all the land between New Jersey and Maryland. Perhaps the king was repaying Penn for the large sum that his father had lent the Stuarts. Or perhaps the king was hoping to export England's Quakers to an American colony governed by his trusted personal friend.

Penn envisioned that his proprietary colony would provide a refuge for Quakers while producing quitrents for himself. To publicize his colony, he distributed pamphlets praising its attractions throughout the British Isles and Europe. The response was overwhelming: by 1700 its population stood at 21,000. The only early migration of equal magnitude was the Puritan colonization of New England.

Patterns of Growth >> Perhaps half of Pennsylvania's settlers arrived as indentured servants, while the families of free farmers and artisans made up the rest. The majority were Quakers from Britain, Holland, and Germany, but the colonists also included Catholics, Lutherans, Baptists, Anglicans, and Presbyterians. In 1682, when Penn purchased and annexed the Three Lower Counties (later the colony of Delaware), his colony included the 1,000 or so Dutch, Swedes, and Finns living there.

Quakers from other colonies—West Jersey, Maryland, and New England—also flocked to the new homeland. Those experienced settlers brought skills and connections that contributed to Pennsylvania's rapid economic growth. Farmers sowed their rich lands into a sea of wheat, which merchants exported to the Caribbean. The center of the colony's trade was Philadelphia, a superb natural harbor situated at the confluence of the Delaware and Schuylkill Rivers.

In contrast to New England's landscape of villages, the Pennsylvania countryside beyond Philadelphia was dotted with dispersed farmsteads. Commercial agriculture required larger farms, which kept settlers at greater distances from one another. As a result, the county rather than the town became the basic unit of local government in Pennsylvania.

Another reason that farmers did not need to cluster their homes within a central village was that they were at peace with the coastal Indians, the Lenni Lenapes (also called Delawares by the English). Thanks to two Quaker beliefs—a commitment to pacifism and the conviction that the Indians rightfully owned their land—peace prevailed between native inhabitants and newcomers. Before Penn sold any land to colonists, he purchased it from the Indians. He also prohibited the sale of alcohol to the tribe, strictly regulated the fur trade, and learned the language of the Lenni Lenapes. "Not a language spoken in Europe," he remarked, "hath words of more sweetness in Accent and Emphasis than theirs."

"Our Wilderness flourishes as a Garden," Penn declared late in 1683, and in fact, his colony lived up to its promises. New arrivals readily acquired good land on liberal terms, while Penn's Frame of Government instituted a representative assembly and guaranteed all inhabitants the basic English civil liberties and complete freedom of worship.

Quakers and Politics >> Even so, Penn's colony suffered constant political strife. Rich investors whom he had rewarded with large tracts of land and trade monopolies dominated the council, which held the sole power to initiate legislation. That power and Penn's own claims as proprietor set the stage for controversy. Members of the representative assembly battled for the right to initiate legislation. Farmers opposed Penn's efforts to collect quitrents. The Three Lower Counties agitated for separation, their inhabitants feeling no loyalty to Penn or Quakerism.

Penn finally bought peace at the price of approving a complete revision of his original Frame of Government. In 1701 the Charter of Privileges, Pennsylvania's new constitution, stripped the council of its legislative power, leaving it only the role of advising the governor. The charter also limited Penn's privileges as proprietor to the ownership of ungranted land and the power to veto legislation. Thereafter an elective unicameral assembly, the only single-house legislature in the colonies, dominated Pennsylvania's government.

As Pennsylvania prospered, Philadelphia became the commercial and cultural center of England's North American empire. Gradually the interior of Pennsylvania filled with emigrants—mainly Germans and Scots-Irish—who harbored no "odd" ideas about Indian rights, and the Lenni Lenapes and other native peoples were bullied into moving farther west. As for William Penn, he returned to England and spent time in a debtors' prison after being defrauded by his unscrupulous colonial agents. He died in 1718, an ocean away from his American utopia.

 REVIEW

In what ways were the mid-Atlantic colonies more diverse than the other colonies of the period?

⌃ The tidy, productive farmsteads of the Pennsylvania countryside were the basis of that colony's prosperity during the eighteenth century. Their produce fueled the growth of Philadelphia and sustained the expansion of sugar plantations on England's Caribbean islands.

ADJUSTMENT TO EMPIRE

Whatever Penn's personal disappointments, his colony had enjoyed spectacular growth—as had British North America more generally. And yet by the 1680s England's king had reason to complain. Although North America now abounded in places named in honor of English monarchs, the colonies themselves lacked any strong ties to the English state. Until Parliament passed the first Navigation Acts in 1660, England had not even set in place a coherent policy for regulat—ing colonial trade. And the acts had not produced the desired sense of patriotism in the colonies. While Chesapeake planters grumbled over the customs duties levied on tobacco, New Englanders, the worst of the lot, ignored the Navigation Acts altogether and traded openly with the Dutch. Royally appointed proprietors increasingly met defiance in New York, New Jersey, the Carolinas, and Pennsylvania. If England were to prosper from colonies as Spain's monarchs had, the Crown needed to take matters in hand.

The Dominion of New England >> The Crown did so in 1686. At the urging of the new King James II (formerly the Duke of York), the Lords of Trade consolidated the colonies of Connecticut, Plymouth, Massachusetts Bay, Rhode Island, and New Hampshire into a single entity to be ruled by a royal governor and a royally appointed council. By 1688 James had added New York and New Jersey to that domain, called the Dominion of New England. Showing the typical Stuart distaste for representative government, James also abolished all northern colonial

assemblies. The king's aim to centralize authority over such a large territory made the Dominion not only a royal dream but also a radical experiment in English colonial administration.

The experiment failed spectacularly. In England, James II revealed himself to be yet another Stuart who tried to dispense with Parliament and who had embraced Catholicism besides. In a quick, bloodless coup d'état known as the Glorious Revolution, Parliament forced James into exile in 1688. In his place it elevated to the throne his daughter, Mary, and her Dutch husband, William of Orange. Mary was a distinctly better sort of Stuart—a staunch Protestant—and she agreed to rule with Parliament.

William and Mary officially dismembered the Dominion of New England and reinstated representative assemblies everywhere in the northern colonies. Connecticut and Rhode Island were restored their old charters, but Massachusetts received a new charter in 1691. Under its terms Massachusetts, Plymouth,

and present—day Maine were combined into a single royal colony headed by a governor appointed by the Crown rather than elected by the people. The charter also imposed religious toleration and made property ownership rather than church membership the basis of voting rights.

Royal Authority in America in 1700 >>

William and Mary were more politic than James II, but no less interested in revenue. In 1696 Parliament enlarged the number of customs officials stationed in each colony to enforce the Navigation Acts. To prosecute smugglers, Parliament established colonial vice—admiralty courts, tribunals without juries presided over by royally appointed justices. To keep current on colonial matters, the king appointed a new Board of Trade to replace the old Lords of Trade. The new enforcement procedures generally succeeded in discouraging smuggling and channeling colonial trade through England.

⚹ England, in an effort to regulate colonial trade, required all ships bound from America to pass through British ports and pay customs duties. Places such as Plymouth, Liverpool, and Bristol (*shown here*) thrived as a result.

These changes strengthened royal control enough to satisfy England's monarchs for the next half century. By 1700 Virginia, New York, Massachusetts, and New Hampshire all had royal governments. New Jersey, the Carolinas, and Georgia would soon join that list. Royal rule meant that the monarch appointed governors and (everywhere except Massachusetts) also appointed their councils. Royally appointed councils could veto any law passed by a colony's representative assembly, royally appointed governors could veto any law passed by both houses, and the Crown could veto any law passed by both houses and approved by the governor.

Even so, the sway of royal power remained more apparent than real after 1700. The Glorious Revolution asserted once and for all that Parliament's authority—rule by the legislative branch of government—would be supreme in the governing of England. In the colonies, members of representative assemblies grew more skilled at dealing with royal governors and more protective of their rights. They guarded most jealously their strongest lever of power—the right of the lower houses to levy taxes.

The political reality of the assemblies' power reflected a social reality as well. No longer mere outposts along the Atlantic, the colonies of 1700 were becoming more firmly rooted societies. Their laws and traditions were based not only on what they had brought from England but also on the conditions of life in America. That social reality had already blocked Stuart ambitions to shape the future of North America, just as it had thwarted the designs of lordly proprietors and the dreams of religious reformers.

 REVIEW

How did William and Mary try to increase colonial revenue?

Still, the dream of empire would revive among England's rulers in the middle of the eighteenth century—in part because French kings had never abandoned their own imperial visions. France had long been Europe's largest and most populous kingdom. By the 1660s bureaucratic, financial, and political reforms made it the mightiest military power as well. Eager to expand on the continent, France's ambitious king, Louis XIV, unleashed his titanic war machine against his neighbors four times between 1667 and 1714.

Even after 1714 France, England and, to a lesser extent, Spain waged a kind of cold war for a quarter of a century, jockeying for position and influence. Western European monarchs had come to realize that confrontations in North America's vast and distant interior could affect their wars closer to home. [I]n a global chess game, the British had the advan[tage in] numbers: nearly 400,000 subjects in the colonies in 1720, compared with only about 25,000 French spread along a thin line of fishing stations and fur-trading posts, and a meager 5,000 or so Spaniards in New Mexico, Texas, and Florida. But by a considerable margin, native peoples still represented the majority population in North America. Moreover, they still controlled more than 90 percent of its territory. If events in North America could effect the balance of power in Europe, then French and Spanish administrators could still believe that their Indian alliances might yet help them prevail against each other, and, especially, against Britain's booming colonies.

CHAPTER SUMMARY

While the French colonized Canada, the Protestant Reformation in England spurred the colonization of New England and Pennsylvania.

- During the seventeenth century, the French slowly established a fur trade, agricultural communities, and religious institutions in Canada while building Indian alliances throughout the Mississippi drainage.
- Competition over the fur trade in New France and New Netherlands contributed to a devastating series of wars between Iroquois, Hurons, and dozens of other Indian groups.
- Over the same period, English Puritans planted more populous settlements between Maine and Long Island.
- The migration of family groups and a rough equality of wealth lent stability to early New England society, reinforced by the settlers' shared commitment to Puritanism and a strong tradition of self-government.
- The mid-Atlantic colonies also enjoyed a rapid growth of people and wealth, but political wrangling as well as ethnic and religious diversity made for a higher level of social conflict.
- Whereas New Englanders attempted to subdue native peoples, colonists in the mid-Atlantic enjoyed more harmonious relations with the region's original inhabitants, thanks in part to William Penn's Quaker principles.
- The efforts of the later Stuart kings to centralize England's empire ended with the Glorious Revolution in 1688, which greatly reduced tensions between the colonies and the parent country.

Additional Reading

For introductions to French and Indian encounters, see Olive Patricia Dickason, *Canada's First Nations* (1992); and Bruce G. Trigger, *Natives and Newcomers* (1995). Colin G. Calloway's *One Vast Winter Count* (2003) masterfully synthesizes the history of natives and Europeans in early North America west of the Appalachians; and Daniel K. Richter does the same for Eastern North America in *Facing East from Indian Country* (2001). For a history of Dutch America, see Jaap Jacobs, *New Netherland* (2005). Daniel K. Richter's *Ordeal of the Longhouse* (1992) presents a powerful portrait of the Iroquois before, during, and after the Beaver Wars. For important work on Indians in colonial New England, see Jenny Hale Pulsipher, *Subjects unto the Same King* (2008); and David Silverman's *Faith and Boundaries* (2005). To understand the appeal of Puritanism, the best book to read is Charles Cohen, *God's Caress* (1986). For Puritanism in New England, read Stephen Foster's masterly study, *The Long Argument* (1991). And to learn more about the diversity of religious and supernatural views in New England, consult Philip Gura, *A Glimpse of Sion's Glory* (1984); and David Hall, *Worlds of Wonder, Days of Judgment* (1989).

For the everyday lives of northern colonists in New England and New York, rely on Virginia Dejohn Anderson's *New England's Generation* (1991); and Joyce Goodfriend's *Before the Melting Pot* (1991). The best assessment of British imperial policy in the late seventeenth century is Richard R. Johnson, *Adjustment to Empire* (1981). For the complex interplay among English colonialism, environmental change, and Indian power in the Northeast, see William Cronon's classic *Changes in the Land* (1983). The event and memory of "King Philip's War" is the subject of Jill Lepore's *The Name of War* (1998).

Significant Events

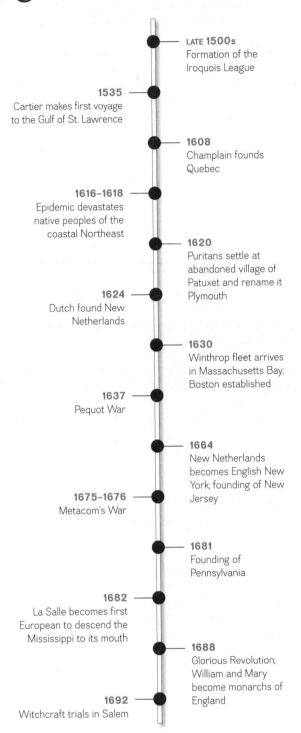

LATE **1500s**
Formation of the
Iroquois League

1535
Cartier makes first voyage
to the Gulf of St. Lawrence

1608
Champlain founds
Quebec

1616–1618
Epidemic devastates
native peoples of the
coastal Northeast

1620
Puritans settle at
abandoned village of
Patuxet and rename it
Plymouth

1624
Dutch found New
Netherlands

1630
Winthrop fleet arrives
in Massachusetts Bay;
Boston established

1637
Pequot War

1664
New Netherlands
becomes English New
York; founding of New
Jersey

1675–1676
Metacom's War

1681
Founding of
Pennsylvania

1682
La Salle becomes first
European to descend the
Mississippi to its mouth

1688
Glorious Revolution;
William and Mary
become monarchs of
England

1692
Witchcraft trials in Salem

The Mosaic of Eighteenth-Century America

1689–1768

A remarkable eighteenth-century painting created on an animal hide portrays the Pawnee surprise attack along the banks of the Platte River in August 1720.

>> **An American Story**

THE TALE OF A TATTOOED TRAVELER

August 13, 1720: Morning sunlight reaches across the junction of the Platte and Loup Rivers in what today is Nebraska. Jean L'Archevêque rises stiffly from where he slept and looks about camp. Spanish soldiers don their wide-brimmed hats, and Pueblo Indian warriors talk softly to one another in the early light. A friar in his habit makes his way around the tents. Don Pedro de Villasur, lieutenant governor of

New Mexico and leader of the party, threads his arms through a bright red officer's coat and orders the soldiers to bring in their horses.

Born in 1672 in Bayonne, France, L'Archevêque had followed a tangled path to that spot in Nebraska. Fleeing family bankruptcy, he was only a boy when he boarded ship to the French Caribbean and joined a scheme to colonize coastal Louisiana. Led by the famous French explorer René Robert Cavelier, Sieur de La Salle (the first European to navigate the immense Mississippi), L'Archevêque and nearly 300 colonists enlisted in the venture had reason for optimism.

But things sometimes go badly for kings and their servants. La Salle and his followers wound up shipwrecked on the coast of present-day Texas and proceeded to starve, sicken, and die. Weakened survivors blamed their leader and in 1687 hatched a plan to be rid of him. Young L'Archevêque seems to have played a part, distracting the great explorer while an accomplice blew his head apart with a musket shot. Jean and the other murderers soon found themselves unhappy guests among Caddo Indians in east Texas. The Caddos tattooed the Frenchmen's faces, carefully inserting a dye made from walnuts into countless tiny cuts. In 1690 Spanish explorers stumbled across L'Archevêque and a companion, ransomed the grateful pair from the Caddos, and sent them off in chains for interrogation in Mexico City, Spain, and then back to Mexico.

L'Archevêque had become a pawn in a high-stakes game. News of La Salle's stillborn colony convinced Spanish officials that they needed to secure their claims on the North American West and stop France from using the region as a base for threatening New Spain and its all too famous silver mines. Crucially, Spain had to reconquer New Mexico. Popé's Pueblo Revolt of 1680 had expelled the Spanish (Chapter 3), but the determined unity of the diverse Pueblo villages collapsed within a dozen years. When Spanish colonists returned in 1692 under Diego de Vargas, they met only fragmented resistance.

In reconquered New Mexico L'Archevêque found his first real home since boyhood. Sent north perhaps because of his facility not only with French but also Indian languages, L'Archevêque prospered in Santa Fe, marrying well and gaining the trust of his neighbors. But eventually the Spanish began hearing complaints from the Plains Apaches about Pawnee raiders armed with French guns. Sensing a threat, in 1719 New Mexico's governor ordered his lieutenant Villasur to take L'Archevêque and a mixed group of Indian and Spanish fighters to confront the French— hence the long trek to the Platte River the following summer, where the men awoke at daybreak on August 13 to do the king's business.

But things sometimes go badly for kings and their servants. Moments after ordering his men to bring in their horses, Villasur heard wild screams as dozens of painted Pawnee warriors rushed his camp. The lieutenant governor was one of the first to die, mouth agape just outside his tent; the well-traveled L'Archevêque fell soon after. Only 13 Spaniards and 40 Pueblo warriors escaped to bring the doleful news to Santa Fe, where for generations residents remembered the ambush as one of the great calamities of their history.

That a merchant's boy from Bayonne, France, could be shipwrecked, recruited to murder, tattooed in Texas, imprisoned in Mexico and Spain, married and made respectable on the upper Rio Grande, and finally shot dead and buried somewhere in Nebraska, testifies in a very personal way to the unpredictable changes roiling eighteenth-century North America. As Europeans established colonies and began competing with one another across the continent, native peoples found life changing at astonishing speed. Europeans, with their animals, plants, technologies, diseases, and designs, sparked a fever pitch of transformation. But Europeans could not predict and did not control the process. Despite their grand ambitions, colonial newcomers often found their own plans upended and their lives reordered by the same forces reworking native life. <<

What's to Come

CRISIS AND TRANSFORMATION IN NORTHERN NEW SPAIN

As European rivals laid claim to more and more of North America, nervous Spanish officials stared at their maps. Around the former Aztec Empire, Spain controlled enormous cities, booming towns, and agricultural villages—a region still home to millions despite waves of epidemics. Though drier and less populated, the lands hundreds of miles north boasted remarkable silver mines. To protect these places from French designs, Spain had to start paying more attention to the blank spaces still farther north on their maps—spaces entirely controlled by Indians.

Defensive Expansion into Texas >>Nowhere did the French seem more menacing than in Texas, one of the many blank spots on Spanish maps. La Salle's adventure could have turned out differently: before his grisly death, the Frenchman pledged to invade northern New Spain with an army of thousands of Indians who, he believed, had "a deadly hatred of the Spaniards." Fearful that another French expedition might actually acquire such an army, in 1690 Spain began establishing missions among the native peoples of Texas. By the early 1720s the Spanish had fortified their claim on Texas with ten Franciscan missions, four presidios (military garrisons), and the beginnings of a civilian settlement on the San Antonio River.

Still, missions disappointed Franciscans and natives alike. Missionaries baptized Indians by the thousands and hoped to create orderly, regimented communities where converts could be shielded from outside influence and taught to be industrious and devout. But Indians insisted on coming and going when they pleased. Many sought the food and sanctuary missions offered, only to leave periodically to rendezvous with kin, hunt, and harvest wild plant foods. Their comings and goings confounded the missionaries. Matters were even worse for Franciscans in east Texas, where sedentary and relatively prosperous Caddos had no need of Spanish crops or protection and preferred to trade with the more liberal French in Louisiana.

However successful they were at retaining autonomy, Indians throughout Texas paid a steep price for any benefits they wrung from missions. Those compelled inside by hunger and insecurity often endured harsh discipline and corporal punishment for disobeying orders. Worse, missions proved ideal vectors for epidemic disease. In the 1730s alone, smallpox killed more than 1,000 mission Indians near San Antonio. Other illnesses became commonplace in what were often filthy, cramped buildings. Children found missions especially dangerous. In eighteenth-century Mission San Antonio, for example, only one in three newborns survived to their third birthday.

Meanwhile, royal administrators encouraged Spanish emigration to Texas—but with little success. In 1731 the province's nonnative population barely amounted to 500 men, women, and children; by 1760 that figure had slightly more than doubled. In 1778 a Franciscan inspector described San Antonio,

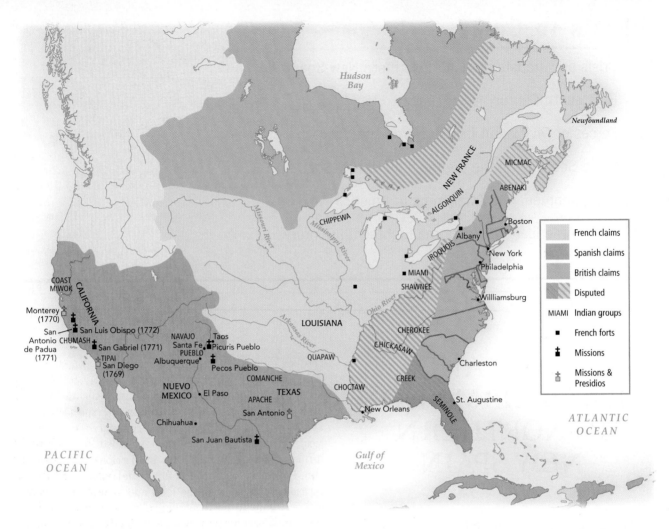

MAP 5.1: EUROPEAN TERRITORIAL CLAIMS IN THE EIGHTEENTH CENTURY

The French, English, and Indian nations all jockeyed for power and position across North America during the eighteenth century. The French expanded their fur trade through the interior, while the English at midcentury began to press the barrier of the Appalachians. But native peoples still controlled the vast majority of the continent and often held the balance of power in interimperial struggles.
What geographic advantages did the French enjoy? And the English?

Texas's major civilian settlement, as "a town so mis—erable that it resembles a most wretched village." He counted "59 houses of stone and mud, and 79 of wood, but all poorly built." After many decades, Spain's push into Texas had created only a slender archipelago of missions, presidios, and a few towns.

Crisis and Rebirth in New Mexico >> Else—where the region remained in the hands of uncon—quered Indians whose regional power only seemed to be expanding. At first Apaches did most to threaten Spain's ambitions in Texas. Their raids thinned Spanish herds, prevented ranching and farming com—munities from expanding, and threatened missions with destruction. Spaniards responded with merci—less slave raids on Apache camps, and the violence escalated.

By the 1730s, however, a new force appeared to eclipse even Apaches. They called themselves Numunuu, "the People." Their enemies came to call them Comanches. Emerging from the foothills of the Rockies in the late sixteenth century, Comanches acquired horses, moved permanently onto the plains, and quickly became some of the most formidable equestrian warriors in history. They allied with Indians who could provide them French guns and ammuni—tion from Louisiana and embarked on a program of territorial expansion. By the mid—eighteenth century Comanches drove most Apaches from the plains and took over their rich bison—hunting territories on the southern plains. Without bison Apaches turned more and more to stealing Spanish animals to survive. Span—iards from Santa Fe to San Antonio soon found them—selves at war with Apaches and Comanches both; New

^ These two Franciscans were regarded as hero-martyrs by their fellow missionaries after Comanches and Wichtas killed them during a 1758 attack on the San Saba mission in Texas.

Mexico often came into conflict with Navajos and Utes as well. Much of northern New Spain became a theater of desolation, abandoned villages up and down the Rio Grande testifying to the limits of Spanish power.

Spaniards accused the "barbarians" of animalistic savagery, but all sides inflicted horrors. Outside the besieged town of Tucson, for example, Lt. Col. Pedro de Allende boasted that he had decapitated a fallen Apache in front of the dead man's comrades and "charged the Apache line single-handed, with the head stuck on his lance." Away from the din of battle a prominent Spaniard noted that his people accuse the Indians of cruelty but added dryly, "I do not know what opinion they would have of us."

By the 1780s nearly everyone had had enough of war. A far-sighted Comanche leader named Ecueracapa helped broker peace with Spanish authorities in 1786, after which the new allies cooperated to entice or threaten Utes, Navajos, and even Apaches into peace as well. Northern New Spain gradually entered a period of relative peace, expansion, and economic growth.

Changes were most dramatic in New Mexico, where Spanish subjects opened up new farms and ranches, enlarged their

>> This *retablo,* or altarpiece, of San Jose (Saint Joseph) is typical of the art produced by the Laguna Santero and his workshop.

flocks and herds, and devoted new energy to local manufacturing. As New Mexico's non-Indian population grew (20,000 by the close of the eighteenth century), new roads funded by the Crown eased the province's isolation. Increased trade allowed caravans to set out from Santa Fe for Chihuahua City once or even twice a year.

Some of the New Mexicans who profited from the newfound opportunities patronized artists and skilled craftsmen. By the late eighteenth century a distinctive New Mexican culture emerged, marked by new traditions in such crafts as woodworking and weaving, as well as in religious art and practice. A master craftsman known only as the Laguna Santero helped define this movement by training local apprentices in his workshop and making pieces for wealthy patrons. The Laguna Santero, his apprentices, and others he inspired began making exquisite portraits of saints on pine boards (*retablos*), hide paintings, elaborate altar screens for churches, and wooden statues of saints (*bultos*)—all art forms still associated with New Mexican folk culture today.

Spanish California >> Spanish California became the empire's last major colonial project in North America. Like the colonies in Texas and Florida, settlement was sparked by anxiety over foreign competition, this time from Russians moving south from Alaska. Though Spaniards first explored the California coast in 1542, not until 1768 did the Crown authorize permanent colonization. A joint expedition of military

men and Franciscans, led by the pragmatic Gaspar de Portolá and the physically frail but iron–willed Friar Junípero Serra, braved shipwrecks, scurvy, and earthquakes to establish ramshackle presidios (military garrisons) and missions at San Diego and Monterey.

Recruiting colonists was difficult. In desperation, officials even scoured the orphanages and prisons of New Spain. Those who journeyed north found the sea voyage difficult and sometimes deadly. The backbreaking overland route from northwestern New Spain had to be abandoned after 1781, when an uprising of Yuma Indians shut down the crossing at the Colorado River. Still, the colony enjoyed modest growth. By 1800 California had two more presidios (at San Francisco and Santa Barbara), three Spanish towns (San José, Los Angeles, and Branciforte, near present–day Santa Cruz), and eighteen Franciscan missions, ministering to 13,000 Indian converts.

Like their colleagues in Texas and Florida, Franciscans in California tried to entice Indians into missions with promises of food, shelter, instruction, and protection. All the while Indians saw the world changing around them. In Monterey, for example, imported pigs, sheep, mules, horses, and cows multiplied at astonishing speed. These animals radiated out from the mission and presidio, overgrazing and annihilating native plants. Soon weeds and plants that Spaniards had unwittingly brought with them spread throughout the region. Pollen analysis of the vegetable matter in adobe from the early nineteenth century indicates that by the time the bricks were made, alien weeds had all but displaced native plants. With their lands transformed by overgrazing and invasive plant species, and their populations diminished by epidemics and hampered by falling birthrates, native families around Monterey abandoned

their villages and either fled to the interior or surrendered to the discipline and danger of mission life. Indians provided labor and food for California's missions, presidios, and three colonial towns.

By 1800 California was home to only 1,800 Hispanic residents. Despite their relative poverty and isolation, they nurtured distinctive traditions ranging from the profound to the comical. In 1835, for example, an American guest recorded something curious at a wedding in Santa Barbara. Amid the singing, dancing, and celebrating, he watched young women knocking off men's sombreros and breaking cologne–filled eggs on their heads. The men were "bound in gallantry to find out the lady and return the compliment, though it must not be done if the person sees you."

English and American visitors to California wrote frequently about the women they encountered there, though usually kept their observations to the superficial. But the most important differences separating women in California from counterparts in Boston and London had nothing to do with dress, hair, dancing, or wedding customs.

Women and the Law in New Spain and British North America

>>Women in California and throughout the Spanish world enjoyed a host of legal rights denied to women in English–speaking realms. When parents died, Spanish law ensured that daughters inherited property equally with sons. English law, in contrast, allowed fathers to craft wills however they wished. If an Englishman died without a will ("intestate"), his eldest son inherited all the land and any buildings on it. Daughters and younger brothers received only a share of the remaining personal property.

In marriage Spanish women retained control over their personal property, and ownership of any dowry (sum of money) they brought into the union. They also maintained the right to buy and sell land and to legally represent themselves in court. Married English women had virtually no control over any kind of property, could not write a will, and could initiate no legal action without a husband's consent. These differences in law persisted into widowhood. Spanish widows were legally entitled not only to their original dowries but also to at least one–half of all property they and their deceased husbands had accumulated in marriage. Their English counterparts had no right to their dowries in widowhood—only to control over a third of their dead husband's property. Even this proved temporary; in contrast to Spanish law, English law maintained that this third share would revert to the deceased *husband's* family upon the widow's death.

witness
Dancing Californians

"[The Fandango] is performed by two persons of different sex who dance either to the Guittar alone or accompanied with the voice; they traverse the room with such nimble evolution, wheeling about, changing sides and smacking with their fingers at every motion; sometimes they dance close to each other, then retire, then approach again, with such wanton attitudes and motions, such leering looks, sparkling eyes & trembling limbs, as would decompose the gravity of a Stoic."

—Archibald Menzies, "California Journal" (1792)

For the poorest women such legal differences meant little. But for those who did have some property or wealth, it mattered a great deal whether they lived in New Spain or British North America.

 REVIEW

Why did Spain establish colonies in Texas and California, and what role did missions play in anchoring the Spanish presence?

EIGHTEENTH-CENTURY NEW FRANCE

Like Spain's vast and sprawling territorial claims in North America, France's imperial ambitions were nothing if not grand. French colonial maps laid claim to the heart of the continent, a massive imperial wedge stretching from Newfoundland southwest to the Mississippi delta, then northwest across the Great Plains and into the cold north woods, and east again through Upper Canada to the North Atlantic.

Colonial Compromises >> Despite these grand claims, most eighteenth–century French Americans continued to live along the St. Lawrence River. They dwelt in farming communities up and down the river valley between the towns of Montreal and Quebec, capital of New France. Jesuit missions also lined the river, ministering to native converts. After a brief boost from colonization in the 1660s and 1670s, the French population grew almost totally through natural increase. Fortunately for France the colonists excelled at natural increase—nurturing large, thriving families and doubling their population every generation.

Those determined enough to endure dark-ness, isolation, and numbing cold in winter, then heat, humidity, and swarming mosquitoes in sum-mer, found life in Canada considerably easier than life in France. Colonists lived longer, more often owned land, and enjoyed greater freedoms than peasants at home. By 1760 the valley contained 75,000 French colonists, soldiers, and priests. Many Canadian house-holds also included Indian slaves: mostly women and children who were captured by other Indians in places as far away as Texas and the Arkansas valley and eventually brought to New France.

To the west and north of New France, in the coun-try known as the *pays d'en haut*, the French venture looked quite different. Here forts and missions rather than farms or towns anchored French ambition. More exactly, the goodwill of Indian peoples provided the anchor. Though certainly willing to use violence, the French in North America recognized that they were too few to secure their interests through force alone. France gained an edge over its rivals in the interior by being useful to Indians, primarily the Algonquian–speaking nations who spread across eastern Canada and the upper Mississippi. French merchants brought coveted European presents and trade goods, while military men, administrators, and Jesuits often medi-ated in conflicts between native groups. Vastly out–numbered by Indians throughout most of the territory that it claimed in North America, France remained deeply dependent on native peoples.

Dependence meant compromise. The two peoples had radically divergent expectations about warfare, trade, marriage, child rearing, religion, food, beauty, and many other areas of life. Few cultural differences seemed as difficult to bridge as those concerning law. In 1706, for example, men associated with a promi-nent Ottawa leader known as Le Pesant killed a priest and a French soldier outside Fort Detroit. Enraged French authorities demanded that Le Pesant be sur-rendered so that he could be tried and, once found guilty, executed for murder. Ottawa leaders coun-tered by offering to replace the dead Frenchmen with Indian slaves. "Raising" the dead this way was a common Ottawa remedy in cases of murder between allies, because it helped avoid a potentially disastrous cycle of blood revenge.

Neither side gave in to the other. Instead, they crafted a novel solution that exemplified the pat-tern of creative, mutual compromises typical of what one scholar has called the "middle ground" char-acterizing French–Indian relations in the *pays d'en haut*. Ottawa leaders turned over Le Pesant to French authorities, whereupon this elderly, obese prisoner miraculously "escaped" just before his execution. Clearly the French and their Ottawa allies came to an understanding. Le Pesant would be surrendered and, once condemned, quietly released. The compromise satisfied both sides more or less and became a model solution to later French–Indian murder cases.

Necessary and inevitable, such compromises none-theless rankled authorities in Paris. In 1731 one such official bemoaned the fact that after more than a cen-tury, colonial administrators in New France had failed to make the "savages" obedient to the Crown. The colony's governor general dashed off a terse reply: "if this has not been done, it is because we have found the task to be an impossible one. Kindly apprise me of any means you should conceive of for securing such obedience."

France on the Gulf Coast >> Forced into uncomfortable compromises in the north, authorities in Paris hoped to establish a colony on the Gulf Coast that could be more profitable, and more French. After La Salle's failure in Texas, it fell to Pierre Le Moyne d'Iberville to establish French Louisiana. A veteran sailor and soldier, d'Iberville spent much of the 1690s attacking British settlements in Newfoundland and the North Atlantic. Sent to the Gulf in 1698, he inaugurated the new colony of Louisiana with a post at Biloxi Bay. D'Iberville's successors established settlements at Mobile Bay and, in 1718, the town of New Orleans. Crown officers and entrepreneurs envisioned an agricultural bonanza, expecting Louisiana to have far more in common with the Caribbean's profitable sugar islands than with the maddening *pays d'en haut*.

Nothing went according to plan. Here, too, Indians forced the French into painful concessions. Louisiana came into conflict with the mighty Chickasaws, and in 1729 the Natchez Indians pushed back, killing or capturing some 500 colonists. Underfunded and usually neglected by the crown, Louisiana's officials became notoriously corrupt and arbitrary. The colony was, according to one observer, a place "without religion, without justice, without discipline, without order, and without police."

More to the point, the Gulf Coast was without many colonists, having acquired a reputation among would-be French migrants as unattractive and unhealthy. When colonists were not fighting Indians, they contended with heat, humidity, hurricanes, droughts, and crop failures, with never-ending battles to turn swamps and forests into farmland, and with the scourges of malaria and yellow fever. By 1731 two-thirds of the French who had journeyed to Louisiana had died or fled. Still, like New Mexico, Canada, California, and Texas, colonial Louisiana persevered and slowly become more populous and more prosperous. Nearly 4,000 French men, women, and children called the colony home by 1746. Their fortunes had in large part come to depend on another, even larger group of newcomers: French Louisiana's African slaves.

Slavery and Colonial Society in French Louisiana

>> Within a year of its founding, New Orleans imported nearly 6,000 slaves—most men, brought directly from Africa. But Louisiana tobacco and, later, indigo proved inferior to the varieties exported from Britain's colonies, and the sudden influx of Africans challenged French control. In 1729 some newly arrived slaves joined forces with the Natchez Indians in their rebellion. The alliance sent waves of panic through the colony, whose population by then had more slaves than free French. The colonists retaliated in a devastating counterattack, enlisting both the Choctaw Indians, rivals of the Natchez, and other enslaved blacks, who were promised freedom in return for their support.

The planters' costly victory persuaded French authorities to stop importing slaves. Nonetheless, blacks continued to make up a majority of all Louisianans, and by the middle of the eighteenth century nearly all were native-born. The vast majority remained enslaved, but their work routines—tending cattle, cutting timber, producing naval stores, manning boats—allowed them relative autonomy of movement. But the greatest prize—freedom—was awarded those black men who served in the French militia, defending the colony from the English and Indians as well as capturing slave runaways. The descendants of these black militiamen would become the core of Louisiana's free black community.

⌃ La Chapelle des Attakapas, located at the Vermilionville living history museum in Lafayette, Louisiana, is a reproduction in the style of churches built in French Louisiana in the eighteenth century. Note the unusual ridge lines on the roof made of cypress shingles. One side was allowed to project above the top of the ridge line in order to provide greater protection against rain blown by the prevailing winds.

Imperial Rivalries >> Male subjects throughout French America stood ready to perform militia duty, formally or informally. They had to. Disputes with Indians proved depressingly common. More to the point, European wars frequently spilled over into North America. In 1689 England joined the Netherlands and the League of Augsburg (several German–speaking states) in a war against France. While the main struggle raged in Europe, French and English colonials, joined by their Indian allies, skirmished in what was known as King William's War. Peace returned in 1697, but only until the Anglo–French struggle resumed with Queen Anne's War, from 1702 to 1713.

For a quarter of a century thereafter the two nations waged a kind of cold war, competing for advantage. At stake was not so much control over people or even territory as control over trade. In North America, France and England vied for access to the sugar islands of the Caribbean, a monopoly on supplying manufactured goods to Spanish America, and dominance of the fur trade. The British had the advantage of numbers: nearly 400,000 subjects in the colonies in 1720, the year of Jean L'Archevêque's death, compared with only about 25,000 French. But this is precisely where France's many compromises paid off. So long as the French maintained their network of alliances with powerful native peoples, British colonies had little chance of expanding west of the Appalachian Mountains.

REVIEW

How did Louisiana differ from French Canada?

FORCES OF DIVISION IN BRITISH NORTH AMERICA

British colonials from Maine to the Carolinas distrusted the French and resented their empire of fish and furs. But the English were preoccupied with their own affairs and, by and large, uninterested in uniting against New France. Indeed, a traveler during the first half of the eighteenth century would have been struck by how hopelessly divided and disunited England's mainland colonies were, split by ethnicity, race, region, wealth, and religion. The British colonies were a diverse and fragmented lot.

Immigration and Natural Increase >> One of the largest immigrant groups—250,000 black men, women, and children—had come to the colonies from Africa in chains. White arrivals included many English immigrants but also a quarter of a million Scots–Irish, the descendants of seventeenth–century Scots who had regretted settling in northern Ireland; perhaps 135,000 Germans; and a sprinkling of Swiss, Swedes, Highland Scots, and Spanish Jews. Most non–English white immigrants were fleeing lives torn by famine, warfare, and religious persecution. All the voyagers, English and non–English, risked the hazardous Atlantic crossing. Many had paid for passage by signing indentures to work as servants in America.

The immigrants and slaves who arrived in the colonies between 1700 and 1775 swelled a colonial American population that was already growing dramatically from natural increase. The birthrate in eighteenth–century America was triple what it is today. Most women bore between five and eight children, and most children survived to maturity.

This astonishing population explosion exemplified a more general global acceleration of population in the second half of the eighteenth century. China's 150 million inhabitants in 1700 had doubled to more than 313 million by century's end. Europe's total rose from about 118 million to 187 million over the same period. The unprecedented global population explosion had several causes. Europe's climate, for one, had become warmer and drier, allowing for generally better harvests. Health and nutrition improved globally with the worldwide spread of Native American crops. Irish farmers discovered that a single acre planted with the American potato could support an entire family. The tomato added crucial vitamins to the Mediterranean diet, and in China the American sweet potato thrived in hilly regions where rice would not grow.

Dramatic population increase in the British colonies, fed by the importation of slaves, immigration, and natural increase, made it hard for colonials to share any common identity. Far from fostering political unity, almost every aspect of social development set Americans at odds with one another. And that process of division and disunity was reflected in the outpouring of new settlers into the backcountry.

Moving into the Backcountry >> To immigrants from Europe weary of war or worn by want, the seaboard's established communities must have seemed havens of order and stability. But by the beginning of the eighteenth century, land scarcity pushed both native–born and newly arrived families to look westward. While descendants of old Yankee families created new

MAP 5.2: NON-ENGLISH SETTLEMENTS IN EIGHTEENTH-CENTURY BRITISH NORTH AMERICA

Many non-English settlers spilled into the backcountry: the Scots-Irish and the Germans followed the Great Wagon Road through the western parts of the middle colonies and southern colonies, while the Dutch and other Germans moved up the Hudson River valley.
In what ways did the concentration of non-English immigrants in the backcountry influence the development of that region?

communities in frontier New England, immigrants from Europe had more luck obtaining land south of New York. By the 1720s German and Scots—Irish immigrants as well as native—born colonists were pouring into western Pennsylvania. Some settled permanently, but others streamed southward into the backcountry of Virginia and the Carolinas, where they encountered native—born southerners pressing westward.

Living in the West could be profoundly isolating. From many farmsteads it was a day's ride to the nearest court—house, tavern, or church. This forced self—sufficiency made the frontier, more than anywhere else in America, a society of equals. Most families crowded into one-room shacks walled with mud, turf, or crude logs. And everyone worked hard.

Social Conflict and the Frontier >>
Ethnic differences heightened sectional tensions between the seaboard's established communities and the frontier. People of English descent predominated along the Atlantic coast, whereas Germans, Scots—Irish, and other white minorities were concentrated in the interior. Many English colonials regarded these new immigrants as culturally inferior and politically subversive. Charles Woodmason, an Anglican missionary in the Carolina backcountry, lamented the arrival of "5 or 6,000 Ignorant, mean, worthless, beggarly Irish Presbyterians, the Scum of the Earth, the Refuse of Mankind," who "delighted in a low, lazy, sluttish, heathenish, hellish life."

German immigrants were generally credited with steadier work habits, as well as higher standards of sexual morality and personal hygiene. But like the clannish Scots—Irish, the Germans preferred to live, trade, and worship among themselves. By 1751 Benjamin Franklin was warning that the Germans would retain their separate language and customs: the Pennsylvania English would be overrun by "the Palatine Boors."

Eighteenth-Century Seaports >>
While most Americans on the move flocked to the frontier, others swelled the populations of colonial cities. By present—day standards such cities were small, harboring from 8,000 to 22,000 citizens by 1750. The scale of seaports remained intimate, too: all of New York City was clustered at the southern tip of Manhattan island, and the length of Boston or Charleston could be walked in less than half an hour.

All major colonial cities were seaports, their waterfronts fringed with wharves and shipyards. By the

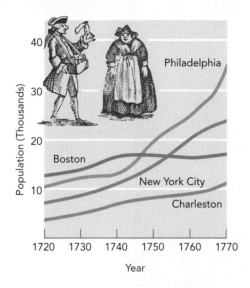

ESTIMATED POPULATION OF COLONIAL CITIES, 1720–1770

Although Boston's population remained stable after 1740, it was surpassed owing to the sharp growth of New York City and, especially, Philadelphia.

1750s the grandest and most populous was Philadelphia, which boasted straight, neatly paved streets, flagstone sidewalks, and three–story brick buildings. Older cities such as Boston and New York had a medieval aspect: most of their dwellings and shops were wooden structures with tiny windows and low ceilings, rising no higher than two stories to steeply pitched roofs. The narrow cobblestone streets of Boston and New York also challenged pedestrians, who competed for space with livestock being driven to the butcher, roaming herds of swine and packs of dogs, clattering carts, carriages, and horses.

Commerce, the lifeblood of seaport economies, was managed by merchants who tapped the wealth of surrounding regions. Traders in New York and Philadelphia shipped the Hudson and Delaware valleys' surplus of grain and livestock to the West Indies. Boston's merchants sent fish to the Caribbean and Catholic Europe, masts to England, and rum to West Africa. Charlestonians exported indigo to English dyemakers and rice to southern Europe.

No large–scale domestic industry produced goods for a mass market: instead, craft shops filled orders for specific items placed by individual purchasers. Some **artisans** specialized in the maritime trades as ship–builders, blacksmiths, and sailmakers. Others, such as butchers, millers, and distillers, processed and packed raw materials for export or served the basic needs of their cities.

> **artisan** skilled craftworker, such as a blacksmith, a cooper, a miller, or a tailor.

On the lowest rung of a seaport's social hierarchy were free and bound workers. Free laborers were mainly young white men and women—journeyman artisans, sailors, fisherfolk, domestic workers, seamstresses, and prostitutes. The ranks of unfree workers included apprentices and indentured servants doing menial labor in shops and on the docks.

Black men and women made up a substantial part of the bound labor force in colonial seaports, but the character of slavery there changed decisively during the mid–eighteenth century. As wars raging in Europe reduced the supply of white indentured servants, colonial cities imported a larger number of Africans. In the two decades after 1730 one–third of all immigrants arriving in New York harbor were black; by 1760 blacks constituted more than three–quarters of all bound laborers in Philadelphia.

Working women found a number of opportunities in port cities. Young single women from poor families worked in wealthier households as maids, cooks, laundresses, seamstresses, or nurses. The highest–paying occupations for women were midwifery and dress-making, and both required long apprenticeships and expert skills. But less than 10 percent of women in seaports worked outside their own homes. Most women spent their workday caring for households: seeing to

⌃ In the mid-eighteenth century, Philadelphia became the largest city in the colonies and the second largest in all the British Empire. Its busy harbor served not only as a commercial hub but also as the disembarkation point for thousands of immigrants.

The Hadley Chest

Later owners stripped and refinished this chest, removing the original painted surface that probably featured brilliant blues and reds.

The initials "MW" identify the original owner, while the carvings of tulips and oak leaves, a decorative motif fashionable in early America, covered its façade.

What sorts of possessions do you think Martha Williams might have kept in these drawers?

Objects can help historians appreciate complex connections. For example, the first owner of this exuberantly designed cupboard of white oak and pine, Martha Williams, lived in western Massachusetts during the decades around 1700, a time of chronic warfare between the English and their French and Indian allies. Most likely she received the chest as part of her dowry when she married Edward Partridge in 1707, its very solidity assuring this young couple of stability and continuity in a violent and insecure world. Items of similar design have turned up elsewhere in New England, and their first collector dubbed them "Hadley chests," a distinct local craft tradition. This chest and the textiles it probably contained open a window into the sorts of property Anglo-American women retained in marriage and passed down to their descendants. According to historian Laurel Thatcher Ulrich, an artifact such as the Hadley chest "teaches us that material objects were not only markers of wealth but devices for building relationships and lineages over time, and it helps us to understand the cultural framework within which ordinary women became creators as well as custodians of household goods."

THINKING CRITICALLY

Why did Martha Williams have her maiden name emblazoned on the cupboard? Might it have something to do with the restrictive English laws about what women could own in marriage? Do you think women in New Spain or New France would have done the same? What might objects such as these tell us about how women viewed property and identity in British North America?

Source: © Shelburne Museum, Shelburne, Vermont

the needs of husbands and children, tending to gardens and domestic animals, and engaged in spinning and weaving—activities crucial to both household and local economies.

While city dwellers—perhaps 1 out of every 20 Americans—endured more ethnic division, poverty, and crime than countryfolk, they had more to do. Plays, balls, and concerts for the wealthiest; taverns, clubs, celebrations, and church services for everyone. Men of every class found diversion in drink and cockfighting. Crowds swarmed to tavern exhibitions of trained dogs or the spectacular waxworks of one John Dyer, featuring "a lively Representation of Margaret, Countess of Herrinburg, who had 365 Children at one Birth."

✔ **REVIEW**

What kinds of divisions led to social tensions and conflicts in British North America?

SLAVE SOCIETIES IN THE EIGHTEENTH-CENTURY SOUTH

Inequalities and divisions between slave and free in the South dwarfed those among seaport dwellers. By 1775 one out of every five Americans was of African ancestry, and more than 90 percent of all black Americans lived in the South, most along the seaboard.

The character of a slave's life depended to a great extent on whether he or she lived in the Chesapeake or the Lower South. Slaves in the low country of South Carolina and Georgia lived on large plantations with as many as 50 other black workers, about half African-born. They had infrequent contact with whites. "They are as 'twere, a Nation within a Nation," observed Francis LeJau, an Anglican priest in the low country. And their work was arduous, for rice required constant cultivation. Black laborers tended young plants and hoed fields in the sweltering summer heat of the mosquito-infested lowlands. During the winter and early spring, they built dams and canals to regulate the flow of water into the rice fields. But the use of the **task system** rather than gang labor widened the window of freedom within slavery. When a slave had completed his assigned task

> **task system** way of organizing slave labor. Masters and overseers of rice and indigo plantations generally assigned individual slaves a daily task, and after its completion, slaves could spend the rest of the day engaged in pursuits of their own choosing.

for the day, one planter explained, "his master feels no right to call upon him."

Most Africans and African Americans in the Chesapeake lived on plantations with fewer than 20 fellow slaves. Less densely concentrated than in the low country, Chesapeake slaves also had more contact with whites. Unlike Carolina's absentee owners, who left white overseers and black drivers to run their plantations, Chesapeake masters actively managed their estates and subjected their slaves to closer scrutiny.

The Slave Family and Community >> The four decades following 1700 marked the heaviest years of slave importation into the Chesapeake and Carolina regions. The newcomers from Africa had to cope not only with the lingering traumas of capture and the Middle Passage but also with alien landscapes, new languages, and new threats. They also had to adjust to their fellow slaves. The "new Negroes" hailed from a number of diverse West African peoples, each with a separate language or dialect and distinctive cultures and kinship systems. Often they had little in common with one another and even less in common with the American-born black minority. Native-born African Americans enjoyed better health, command of English, and experience in dealing with whites. They were also more likely to enjoy a family life, because their advantages probably made them the preferred partners of black women, who were outnumbered two to one by black men. And, since immigrant women waited two or three years before marrying, some immigrant men died before they could find a wife.

After the middle of the eighteenth century, a number of changes fostered the growth of black families and the vitality of slave communities. As slave importations began to taper off, the rate of natural reproduction among blacks started to climb. Gender ratios became more equal. These changes, along with the rise of larger plantations throughout the South, made it easier for black men and women to find partners and start families. Elaborate kinship networks gradually developed, often extending over several plantations in a single neighborhood. And, as the immigrant generations were replaced by native-born offspring, earlier sources of tension and division within the slave community disappeared.

Even so, black families remained vulnerable. If a planter fell on hard times, members of black families might be sold off to different buyers to meet his debts. When an owner died, black spouses, parents, and children might be divided

Was the most critical sectional division in eighteenth-century British North America between North and South or between East and West?

↗ *The Old Plantation* affords a rare glimpse of life in the slave quarters. At this festive gathering, both men and women dance to the music of a molo (a stringed instrument similar to a banjo) and drums.

among surviving heirs. Even under the best circumstances, fathers might be hired out to other planters for long periods or sent to work in distant quarters. Then, as more slaveholders moved from the coast to the interior, black family life suffered. Between 1755 and 1782, masters on the move resettled fully one-third of all adult African Americans living in tidewater Virginia. Most slaves forced to journey west were men and women in their teens and early 20s, who had to begin again the long process of establishing families and neighborhood networks far from kin and friends.

Black families struggling with terrible uncertainties were sustained by the distinctive African American culture evolving in the slave community. The high percentage of native Africans among the eighteenth-century American black population made it easier for slaves to retain homeland traditions. Christianity won few converts, in part because masters feared that baptizing slaves might make them more rebellious but also because African Americans preferred their traditional religions. Slaves also brought agricultural skills and practices from Africa, as well as folktales, music, and dances.

Slave Resistance in Eighteenth-Century British North America >> British North America had no shortage of African Americans who both resisted captivity and developed strategies for survival. Collective attempts at escape were most common among recently arrived Africans. Groups

of slaves, often made up of newcomers from the same tribe, fled inland and formed **Maroon communities** of runaways. These efforts rarely succeeded, because the Maroon settlements were too large to go undetected for long.

More–acculturated blacks turned to subtler subversions, employing what one scholar has called "weapons of the weak." Domestics and field hands alike faked illness, feigned stupidity and laziness, broke tools, pilfered from storehouses, hid in the woods for weeks at a time, or simply took off to visit other plantations. Other slaves, usually escaping bondage as solitary individuals, found a new life as craftworkers, dock laborers, or sailors in the relative anonymity of colonial seaports.

Sometimes slaves rebelled openly. Whites in communities with large numbers of blacks lived in gnawing dread of arson, poisoning, and insurrection. Four slave conspiracies were reported in Virginia during the first half of the eighteenth century. In South Carolina more than two decades of abortive uprisings and insurrection scares culminated in the

Maroon communities groups of escaped slaves, often newly arrived Africans, who fled to the frontiers of colonial settlements in the American South, the Caribbean, and South America.

Stono Rebellion of 1739, the largest slave revolt of the colonial period. Nearly 100 African Americans, led by a slave named Jemmy, seized arms from a store in the coastal district of Stono and killed several white neighbors before they were caught and killed by the colonial militia. But throughout the eighteenth century slave rebellions occurred far less frequently on the mainland of North America than in the Caribbean or Brazil. Whites outnumbered blacks in all of Britain's mainland colonies except South Carolina, and only in Georgia did rebels have a haven for a quick escape—Spanish Florida. Faced with those odds, most slaves reasoned that the risks of rebellion outweighed the prospects for success—and most sought families and opportunities for greater personal freedom within the slave system itself.

✔ **REVIEW**

How did African American culture evolve in the slave community, and what forms did resistance to captivity take?

ENLIGHTENMENT AND AWAKENING IN AMERICA

Where colonists lived, how well they lived, whether they were male or female, native—born or immigrant, slave or free—all these variables fostered distinctive worldviews, differing attitudes and assumptions about the individual's relationship to nature, society, and God. The diversity of colonials' inner lives became even more pronounced during the eighteenth century because of the Enlightenment, an intellectual movement that started in Europe during the seventeenth century.

The Enlightenment in America >> The leading figures of the Enlightenment, the *philosophes*, stressed the power of human reason to promote progress by revealing the laws that governed both nature and society. Isaac Newton in England charted the orbits of the planets and devised a theory of gravity, and John Locke applied reason to the construction of political systems. In France, Voltaire wrote essays, novels, and plays criticizing religion, oppressive governments, and censorship.

Like many devotees of the **Enlightenment,** Benjamin Franklin of Philadelphia was most impressed by its emphasis on useful knowledge and experimentation. He pondered air currents and then invented a stove that heated houses more efficiently. He toyed with electricity and then invented lightning rods to protect buildings in thunderstorms. Other amateur colonial scientists constructed simple telescopes, classified animal species native to North America, or sought to explain epidemics in terms of natural causes.

> **Enlightenment** intellectual movement that flourished in Europe from the mid-1600s through the eighteenth century and stressed the power of human reason to promote social progress by discovering the laws that governed both nature and society.

American colleges helped promote Enlightenment thinking. Although institutions such as Harvard (founded 1636) and Yale (1701) initially focused on training ministers, by the eighteenth century their graduates included lawyers, merchants, doctors, and scientists. Most offered courses in mathematics and the natural sciences, which taught students algebra and such advanced theories as Copernican astronomy and Newtonian physics.

By the middle of the eighteenth century, Enlightenment ideals had given rise to "rational Christianity," which commanded a small but influential following among Anglicans and liberal Congregationalists in the colonies. Their God was not the Calvinists' awesome deity but a benevolent creator who offered salvation to everyone. They believed that God's greatest gift to humankind was reason, which enabled all human beings to follow the moral teachings of Jesus. Some even embraced deism, which rejected the divinity of Jesus and looked to nature rather than the Bible for proof of God's existence.

Enlightenment philosophy and rational Christianity did little to change the lives of most colonials. Few colonial readers had the interest or the background necessary to tackle the learned writings of Enlightenment *philosophes*. The great majority still explained the workings of the world in terms of divine providence rather than natural law. Church attendance ran highest in the northern colonies, where some 80 percent of the population turned out for public worship on the Sabbath. In the South, because of the greater distances involved and the shortage of clergy, about half of all colonials regularly attended Sunday services.

Still, many ministers grew alarmed over the influence of rational Christianity. They also worried about isolated frontier families abandoning Christianity altogether. Exaggerated as these fears may have been, they gave rise to a major religious revival that swept the colonies during the middle decades of the eighteenth century.

The First Great Awakening >> The **Great Awakening,** as the revival came to be called, first appeared in the 1730s among Presbyterians and Congregationalists in the middle colonies and New England. Many ministers in these churches preached an "evangelical" message, emphasizing the need for individuals to experience "a new birth" through religious conversion. Among them was Jonathan Edwards, the pastor of a Congregational church in Northampton, Massachusetts. Edwards's Calvinist preaching combined moving descriptions of God's grace with terrifying portrayals of eternal damnation. "The God that holds you over the pit of hell, much as one holds a spider or some loathsome insect over the fire, abhors you and is dreadfully provoked," he declaimed to one congregation. "There is no other reason to be given, why you have not dropped into hell since you arise in the morning, but that God's hand has held you up."

> **Great Awakening** term used to describe periods of intense religious piety and commitment among Americans that fueled the expansion of Protestant churches.

These local revivals of the 1730s were mere tremors compared to the earthquake of religious enthusiasm that shook the colonies with the arrival in the fall of 1739 of George Whitefield. This handsome (though cross—eyed) "boy preacher" from England electrified

⋀ Benjamin Franklin and George Whitefield portrayed the contrasting facets of Enlightenment and Awakening. Franklin in his 30s appears worldly, sophisticated, and urbane—a look that was just the opposite of the modest, homespun appearance he adopted 30 years later while ambassador to France. The wig, the fancy white sleeves, the dignified tuck of hand in jacket all signify a man of wealth and culture. Whitefield's garb looks not so different, but whereas Franklin was playful, curious, and often disinterested in temperament, Whitefield was so fervent when preaching that many ministers refused to have him in their churches. Instead, he often took to the fields to preach outdoors. He cared little about denominations, only salvation. "Father Abraham, whom have you in heaven?" he called out in one sermon. "Any Episcopalians? No! Any Presbyterians? No! Any Independents or Methodists? No, no, no! Whom have you there? We don't know those names here. All who are here are Christians . . ."

rapidly to the South and its backcountry. From the mid–1740s until the 1770s, scores of new Presbyterian and Baptist churches formed, sparking controversy. Ardent Presbyterians disrupted Anglican worship by loosing packs of dogs in local chapels. County officials, prodded by resentful Anglican parsons, harassed, fined, and imprisoned Baptist ministers.

And so a diverse lot of Americans found themselves continually at odds with one another: arguing over religion and the Enlightenment, conflicted over racial and ethnic tensions, and divided between coastal and backcountry cultures. Benjamin Franklin, a man who made it his business to know, understood the depth of those divisions better than most. Yet even he harbored hopes for political unity among the fractious colonists. After all, most were English. That much they had in common.

crowds from Georgia to New Hampshire during his two–year tour of the colonies. He and his many imitators among colonial ministers turned the church into a theater, enlivening sermons with dramatic gestures, flowing tears, and gruesome depictions of hell. The drama of such performances appealed to people of all classes, ethnic groups, and races. By the time Whitefield sailed back to England in 1741, thousands of awakened souls were joining older churches or forming new ones.

The Aftermath of the Great Awakening >>

Whitefield also left behind a raging storm of controversy. Many "awakened" church members now openly criticized their ministers as cold, unconverted, and uninspiring. To supply the missing fire some laymen—"and even Women and Common Negroes"—took to "exhorting" any audience willing to listen. The most popular ministers became "itinerants," traveling like Whitefield from one town to another.

Northern churches splintered and bickered over the Great Awakening, but the fires of revivalism spread

✔ REVIEW

Describe the different outlooks of Enlightenment and evangelical Christians.

ANGLO-AMERICAN WORLDS OF THE EIGHTEENTH CENTURY

Although most Americans prided themselves on being English, some differences made colonials feel inferior, ashamed of their simplicity when compared with London's sophistication. But they also came to appreciate the greater equality of their society and the more representative character of their governments. If it was good to be English, it was, on balance, better still to be English in America.

English Economic and Social Development

>> The differences between England and America began with their economies. England's huge financial institutions and corporations, its growing factories and profitable mines, and its tenant—based commercial agriculture stood in sharp contrast to the mostly humble economic activity in British North America. England's more developed economy fostered the growth of cities, especially London, a teeming colossus of 675,000 in 1750. In contrast, 90 percent of all eighteenth—century colonials lived in towns of fewer than 2,000. But in another respect, England's more advanced economy drew the colonies and the parent country together. Americans were so eager to acquire British—made commodities that their per capita consumption of imported manufactures rose 120 percent between 1750 and 1773. People of all classes demanded and indulged in such small luxuries as a tin of tea, a pair of gloves, and a bar of Irish soap.

Inequality in England and America

>> Then there were people of no means. In England they were legion. London seethed with filth, crime, and desperate poverty. The poor and the unemployed as well as pick—pockets and prostitutes crowded into its gin—soaked slums, taverns, and brothels. The contrast between the luxuries enjoyed by a wealthy few Londoners and the misery of the many disquieted colonial observers. Ebenezer Hazard, an American Quaker visiting London, knew for certain he was in "a Sink of Sin."

New wealth and the inherited privileges of England's landed aristocracy made for deepening class divisions. Two percent of England's population owned 70 percent of its land. By right of birth, English aristocrats claimed membership in the House of Lords; by custom, certain powerful gentry families dominated the other branch of Parliament, the House of Commons.

⌃ Coffeehouses such as this establishment in London were favorite gathering places for eighteenth-century Americans visiting Britain. Here merchants and mariners, ministers and students, lobbyists and tourists warmed themselves, read newspapers, and exchanged gossip about commerce, politics, and social life.

The colonies had their own prominent families but no titled ruling class holding political privilege by hereditary right. And if England's upper classes lived more splendidly, its lower classes were larger and worse off than those in the colonies. Less than a third of England's inhabitants belonged to the "middling sort" of traders, professionals, artisans, and tenant farmers. More than two–thirds struggled for survival at the bottom of society. In contrast, the colonial middle class counted for nearly three–quarters of the white population. With land cheap, labor scarce, and wages for both urban and rural workers 100 percent higher in America than in England, it was much easier for colonials to accumulate savings and farms of their own.

Colonials were both fascinated and repelled by English society. Benjamin Rush, a Philadelphia physician, felt in the House of Lords as if he "walked on sacred ground." He begged his guide for permission to sit on the throne therein and then sat "for a considerable time." Other colonials gushed over the grandeur of aristocratic estates and imported suits of livery for their servants, tea services for their wives, and wall-paper for their drawing rooms.

But colonials recognized that England's ruling classes purchased their luxury and leisure at the cost of the rest of the nation. In his autobiography Benjamin Franklin painted a devastating portrait of the degraded lives of his fellow workers in a London printshop, who drowned their disappointments by drinking throughout the workday, even more excessively on the Sabbath, and then faithfully observing the holiday of "St. Monday's" to nurse their hangovers. Like Franklin many colonials regarded the idle among England's rich and poor alike as ominous signs of a degenerate nation.

Politics in England and America >> Colonials
were also of two minds about England's government. Although they praised the English constitution as the basis of all liberties, they were alarmed by the actual workings of English politics. In theory, England's **balanced constitution** gave every order of society a voice in government. Whereas the Crown represented the monarchy and the House of Lords the aristocracy, the House of Commons represented the democracy, the people of England.

balanced constitution view that England's constitution gave every part of English society some voice in the workings of its government.

Americans liked to think that their colonial governments mirrored the ideal English constitution. Most colonies had a royal governor who represented the monarch in America and a bicameral (two–house) legislature made up of a lower house (the assembly) and an upper house (or council). The democratically elected assemblies, like the House of Commons, stood for popular interests, whereas the councils, some of which were elected and others appointed, more roughly approximated the House of Lords.

But these formal similarities masked real differences between English and colonial governments. In any showdown with their assemblies most royal governors had to give way, because they lacked the government offices and contracts that bought loyalty. The colonial legislatures possessed additional leverage, since all of them retained the sole authority to levy taxes.

At the same time, widespread ownership of land meant that more than half the colonies' white adult male population could vote. The larger electorate made it more difficult to buy votes. The colonial electorate was also more watchful. Representatives had to reside in the districts that they served, and a few even received binding instructions from their constituents about how to vote.

Most Americans were as pleased with their inexpensive and representative colonial governments as they were horrified by the conduct of politics in England, where webs of patronage and corruption compromised the entire system. John Dickinson, a young Pennsylvanian training as a lawyer in London, was scandalized by a parliamentary election he witnessed in 1754. The king and his ministers had spent over 100,000 pounds sterling to buy support for their candidates, he wrote his father, and "if a man cannot be brought to vote as he is desired, he is made dead drunk and kept in that state, never heard of by his family and friends, till all is over and he can do no harm."

The Imperial System before 1760 >> Few
Britons gave the colonists as much thought as the colonists gave them. Those few who thought about America at all believed that colonials resembled the "savage" Indians more than the "civilized" English. As a London acquaintance remarked to Thomas Hancock, it was a pity Mrs. Hancock had to remain in Boston when he could "take her to England and make her happy with Christians."

The same ignorant indifference contributed to England's haphazard administration of its colonies. Aside from passing an occasional law to regulate trade, restrict manufacturing, or direct monetary policy, Parliament made no effort to assert its authority in America. For the colonies this chaotic and inefficient system of colonial administration left them a great deal of freedom. Even England's regulation of trade rested lightly on the shoulders of most Americans. Southern planters were obliged to send their rice, indigo, and tobacco to Britain only, but they enjoyed favorable credit terms and knowledgeable marketing from English merchants. Colonials were prohibited from finishing iron products and exporting hats and textiles, but they had scant interest in developing

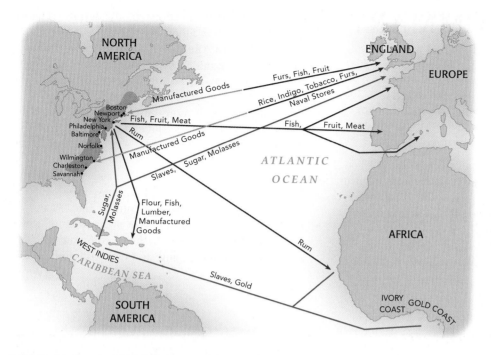

MAP 5.3: OVERSEAS TRADE NETWORKS

Commercial ties to Spain and Portugal, Africa, and the Caribbean sustained the growth of both seaports and commercial farming regions on the British North American mainland and enabled colonials to purchase an increasing volume of finished goods from England.
Why was rum sent from America to Africa? What was the most common product sent from England to the colonies?

domestic industries. Americans were required to import all manufactured goods through England, but by doing so, they acquired high-quality goods at low prices. At little sacrifice, most Americans obeyed imperial regulations.

Following this policy of **benign neglect,** the British Empire rumbled along to the satisfaction of most people on both sides of the Atlantic. Economic growth and political **autonomy** kept most white Americans happy being English, despite their misgivings about the motherland. If imperial arrangements had remained as they were in 1754, the empire might have muddled on indefinitely.

But something important seemed to be changing, both within the British world and in the international order as well. For decades, Europe's imperial wars found their way to America almost as an afterthought. Colonial officials, traders, land speculators, and would-be pioneers regularly seized on news of

> **benign neglect** policy also known as "salutary neglect," pursued by the British Empire in governing its American colonies until the end of the Seven Years' War.
>
> **autonomy** condition of being independent or, in the case of a political structure, the right to self-government.

the latest European conflict as an excuse to attack their Spanish or French or British counterparts in the North American borderlands. The interests of kings and queens had to be served, of course. But by and large it was easier to exploit war for local or personal purposes out on the far margins of Europe's empires. Eastern North America's native peoples likewise sought advantage in these interimperial flare-ups. But for them the stakes were higher. When Indian leaders joined in a fight for profit or revenge, or to please one or another colonial ally, they also put their own people at risk.

As all North Americans learned, however, the outcome of their struggles could be determined by men they would never see: well-heeled diplomats sipping drinks around mahogany tables in European capitals. Victories, defeats, territories won or lost—all this could be and often was undone in treaty talks in Paris, Madrid, or London. The message was clear: great imperial struggles began in Europe and ended in Europe. America followed.

Though few recognized it in 1754, this older model was about to be swept away. That year marked the beginning of yet another imperial war, one begun not in Europe but in the American borderlands. Rather than following events, this time Indians proved decisive to the war's origins, course, and outcome. And rather than the conflict ending with a return to the status quo, this time war would produce changes greater than anyone could have anticipated. In waging the war and managing its aftermath, London would pursue policies that made it difficult—and ultimately impossible—for its American subjects to remain within the empire.

 REVIEW

What were the similarities, differences, and connections between England and America?

CHAPTER SUMMARY

During the eighteenth century Spain, France, and Great Britain competed for power and influence in North America, while native peoples struggled for advantage or simple survival amid profound change. British North Americans grew increasingly diverse, darkening the prospect of political unity.

- Spurred on by imperial rivals, Spain established mission systems in Texas and California. Violence ravaged northern New Spain until the 1780s, when Indian alliances finally allowed for greater prosperity and demographic expansion.
- Underpopulated New France had to seek alliances with Indians. French Louisiana failed to develop into a booming plantation colony despite reliance upon African slave labor.
- In British North America differences erupted among English and non–English immigrants and were compounded by backcountry settlement and the growth of seaports.
- The South became more embattled, too, following massive importation of slaves during the first half of the eighteenth century and a rising tide of black resistance to slavery.
- Religious conflict among colonials was intensified by the spread of Enlightenment ideas and the influence of the Great Awakening of the 1730s.
- Despite their many differences a majority of white colonials took pride in their common English ancestry and in belonging to a powerful empire.

Additional Reading

For early Texas, see Juliana Barr, *Peace Came in the Form of a Woman* (2007). See H. Ross Frank's *From Settler to Citizen* (2000) for economic and social change in New Mexico. Steven Hackel's *Children of Coyote, Missionaries of St. Francis* (2005) is the new standard for colonial California. For France in America during the eighteenth century, see *The People of New France* by Allan Greer (2000). Alan Taylor's *American Colonies* (2001) takes a sweeping, continental perspective on North American history during this era. For women's property rights, see Deborah A. Rosen, "Women and Property across Colonial America: A Comparison of Legal Systems in New Mexico and New York," *William and Mary Quarterly* 60:2 (2003): 355–382.

The effects of ethnic and racial diversity are explored in Bernard Bailyn, *Voyagers to the West* (1986); and Peter Silver, *Our Savage Neighbors* (2007). Philip Morgan's *Slave Counterpoint* (1998) contrasts slave cultures in the early South. For tensions in American seaports, consult Jill Lepore, *New York Burning* (2005); and Gary Nash's *Urban Crucible* (1979).

Nancy Shoemaker, *A Strange Likeness* (2004); and James M. Merrell, *Into the American Woods* (1999), are two compelling accounts of perceived differences. For the expansion of colonial settlement into the eighteenth–century backcountry, begin with Eric Hinderaker and Peter C. Mancall, *At the Edge of Empire* (2003). On religion, see Patricia Bonomi, *Under the Cope of Heaven* (1986); and George Marsden, *Jonathan Edwards* (2003).

Significant Events

1689–1697
King William's War (War of the League of Augsburg)

1690
Spain begins establishing missions in Texas

1698
d'Iberville inaugurates French colony of Louisiana

1702–1713
Queen Anne's War (War of the Spanish Succession)

1729
Natchez revolt against the French

1730s
Comanches move onto the Great Plains with the help of European horses and guns; rise in importation of black slaves in northern colonies

1739
George Whitefield's first preaching tour in America; Stono Rebellion in South Carolina

1766
Tenant Rebellion in New York

1768
Spanish begin to colonize California

6 Imperial Triumph, Imperial Crisis

1754–1776

George Washington was only 22 when he led 200 militiamen and a party of Indians to confront French forces in the Ohio Country in the spring of 1754. He came upon a French detachment at Jumonville Glen, shown in this 2007 photo.

>> **An American Story**

GEORGE WASHINGTON AND THE HALF-KING

Everyone seemed to want something from the Ohio Country. And when so many rivals—assertive, anxious, and aggressive—assembled in one location, it was a situation made for disaster. Young George Washington, deep in the forests of the Ohio Country, learned this lesson in the spring of 1754.

Rich in game and richer still in agricultural potential, the region north of the Ohio River had been a no-man's land for decades following the Beaver Wars. Though the mighty Iroquois had no interest in occupying the territory, they claimed sovereignty over it into the 1750s by right of conquest. By then, however, Delawares, Shawnees, Mingos, and other native peoples had established villages in the territory. If they looked to the Iroquois it was for advice, not orders. Who, then, could claim dominion over the Ohio Country?

European rivalries compounded these uncertainties. By the 1750s both Britain and France saw the lands as vital to their strategic interests. Pennsylvania traders had wandered the territory for years, their reports drawing the interest of land speculators. Wealthy Virginians and Pennsylvanians envisioned colonies in the Ohio Country—schemes London happily encouraged in hopes of weakening New France. In 1745 the Virginia House of Burgesses granted 300,000 acres of land to a newly formed enterprise called the Ohio Company. For their part, the French in Quebec relied on the Ohio lands as a buffer between their own relatively small settlements and the populous British to the east. Anxious, the French built new forts and shored up their Indian alliances.

The British countered. In 1754 Virginia's governor (a major investor in the Ohio Company) ordered 200 militiamen under 22-year-old Lt. Col. George Washington (another investor) to assert British interests in the Ohio Country. Washington's militia marched west with the help of several Indians under the "Half-King" Tanaghrisson, the Iroquois representative for the Ohio Country. Tanaghrisson had grown up near the important forks of the Ohio River (present-day Pittsburgh) and advised the British to build a "strong house" at this key position. Washington, who was intelligent, able, and disciplined but inexperienced and badly out of his depth, soon discovered how little control he had over the circumstances—or even over his own expedition.

To begin with, the French had beaten the Virginians to the forks of the Ohio, where they erected Fort Duquesne. On hearing of the approaching British militia the French commander there dispatched 35 men under an ensign named Jumonville to advise Washington to withdraw. Following Tanaghrisson's lead the British surprised Jumonville's party and fired on it. Badly wounded along with nearly half of his men, the ensign cried out to stop shooting, that he had come only to talk. Once Washington had gotten control of his force, Jumonville tried to hand him a letter from the French commander. But Tanaghrisson stepped in front of the Frenchman, sank a hatchet into his head, ripped his skull apart, and pulled out his brains. Washington staggered back dumbstruck as Tanaghrisson's Indians set about killing the wounded French soldiers.

This was not how it was supposed to happen. Washington hastily retreated some way, threw up a makeshift structure, aptly named "Fort Necessity," and waited for reinforcements from Virginia. About a month later a formidable French force (led by Jumonville's grieving brother) laid siege and quickly compelled Washington's surrender. The Virginians returned home in defeat, bearing the news that the Shawnees, Delawares, and Mingos had either sided with the French or refused to fight. "The chief part" of his men, Washington wrote in dismay, "are almost naked, and scarcely a man has either Shoes, Stockings or Hat." It was an ignominious beginning to a war that would extend for seven years and spread across the entire globe. <<

What's to Come

THE SEVEN YEARS' WAR

Britain and France had come to blows in the back-country before. And Indian peoples had long sought to profit from the imperial rivalry of Europeans and turn it to their own ends. But in the Seven Years' War, bloodshed in the forests of North America for the first time led Europe into war rather than the other way around. And Washington's misadventure set the pattern for the early years of the conflict—years marked by British missteps and British defeats.

Years of Defeat >> The surrender at Fort Necessity only stiffened Britain's resolve to control the Ohio Country. London sent two army divisions under the famed General Edward Braddock to wrest the region from France. France countered with the equivalent of eight divisions to Canada. Unfortunately for the English, General Braddock had all but sealed his doom before even marching into the backcountry. Ignoring American advisers who insisted that Indian alliances

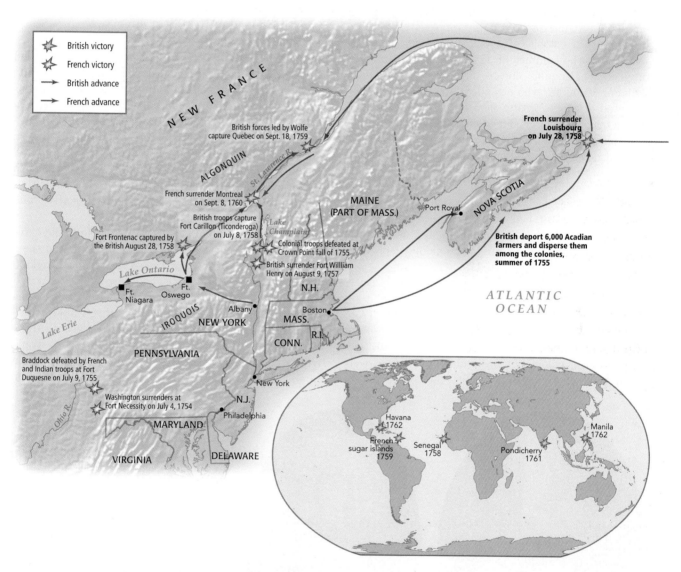

MAP 6.1: THE SEVEN YEARS' WAR

After Washington's surrender and Braddock's defeat in the Pennsylvanian backcountry, the British and the French waged their final contest for supremacy in North America in northern New York and Canada. But the rivalry for empire between France and Britain was worldwide, with naval superiority providing the needed edge to Britain. The British navy isolated French forces in India, winning a victory at Pondicherry, while English offensives captured the French sugar islands in the Caribbean and French trading posts along the West African coast. When Spain entered the war on the side of France, British fleets captured both Havana and the strategic port of Manila in the Philippines. *Which victory sealed the British triumph over New France? Why was the win geographically important?*

would be key to victory, Braddock alienated native leaders and refused to acknowledge their claims to land. His divisions pushed into the Ohio Country with fewer than 10 Indian allies and in 1755 were nearly annihilated by their French and Indian adversaries. The defeat was one of the worst in British military history and cost Braddock his reputation as well as his life. It also sent shock waves through the empire, emboldened the French, and convinced many wavering Indian peoples that the French were the ones to support. Raiding parties began striking backcountry settlements from New York to Virginia; terrified refugees fled east.

Britain's war went from bad to worse, because most British colonials found it difficult to cooperate among themselves. At the start of the war representatives from throughout the colonies attended the so-called Albany Congress in the summer of 1754, designed in part to convince the Iroquois not to ally with New France. Benjamin Franklin, who attended, had larger aims. He presented delegates with a plan for colonial cooperation, in which a federal council made up of representatives from each colony would assume responsibility for a united defense. The Albany delegates were alarmed enough by the wavering Iroquois (who also attended) to accept Franklin's idea. But when they presented the proposal to their legislatures at home, each rejected the Albany Plan of Union. "Everyone cries, a union is necessary," Franklin complained, "but when they come to the manner and form of the union, their weak noodles are perfectly distracted."

London did little to encourage collective self-sacrifice. John Campbell, the Earl of Loudoun, took command of the North American theater in 1756. American soldiers and colonial assemblies alike despised Lord Loudoun. They balked at his efforts to take command over colonial troops and dragged their heels at his high-handed demands for men and supplies.

Meanwhile, the French appointed an effective new commanding general of their forces in Canada, Louis Joseph, the marquis de Montcalm. Montcalm drove southward, capturing key British forts and threatening the security of both New York and New England.

France pressed its advantage in Europe as well, threatening England itself and British holdings throughout the Mediterranean. Meanwhile, the complex system of alliances that was supposed to keep continental Europe at peace began to fail. In August of 1756 Prussia, an English ally, invaded Austria, a French ally. France went to Austria's aid and Prussia suddenly found itself on the defensive, begging London for help. The war was spreading in all directions, none to the advantage of the British Empire.

A Shift in Policy >> British fortunes rebounded only when the veteran English politician William Pitt came out of retirement to direct the war. Pitt was an odd character. Subject to bouts of depression and loathed for his opportunism and egotism, he was nonetheless buoyed by a strong sense of destiny—his own and that of England. France seemed to him the greatest obstacle to this British destiny—and Pitt returned to the political fray charged with energy. "I know that I can save this country," he declared confidently, "and that no one else can."

Pitt unveiled an audacious strategy. He would leave the fighting in Europe to the Prussians but fund them with massive infusions of cash. Meanwhile, England would attack France everywhere else—in the Caribbean, in West Africa, and even in their colonies along the Indian Ocean. Most especially, Pitt would attack them in North America. Indeed, he pledged to drive France out of the continent forever. To do so he would treat the colonials as partners and equals. Pitt recalled Loudoun, pledged to respect the officers in colonial

HATED AND LOVED

<< John Campbell (*left*), the Earl of Loudoun, was a Scottish military man and an aristocrat who expected that colonial soldiers would obey his commands. But colonials and their legislatures resisted his efforts to organize and fund the military campaign. "They have assumed to themselves, what they call Rights and Priviledges, totaly unknown in the Mother Country," he complained. William Pitt (*right*) was no less arrogant ("I know that I can save this country," he declared, "and that no one else can".) But Pitt was willing to treat the colonists as equals and pay handsomely for their services. For Americans' opinion of Pitt, see the porcelain figure on page 110.

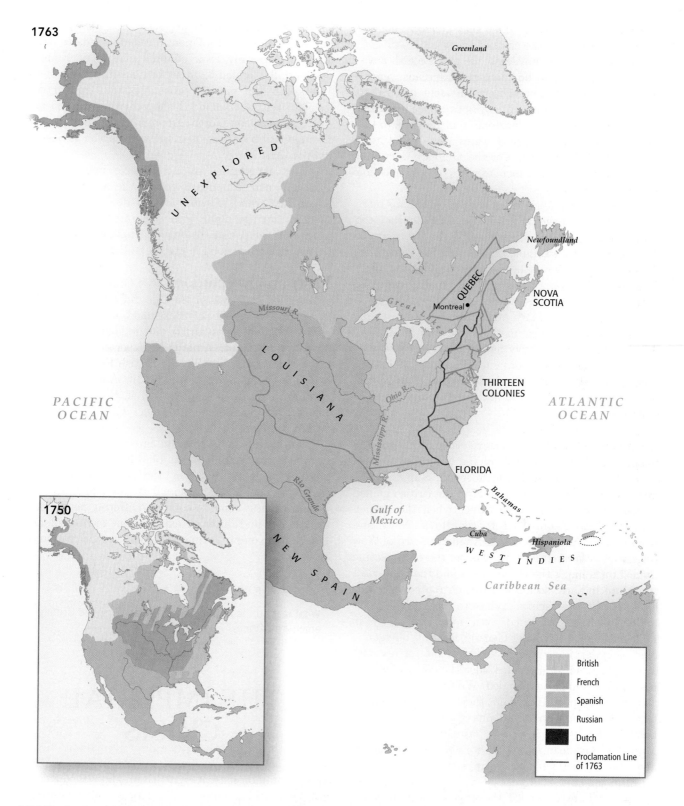

Greenland

U N E X P L O R E D

Newfoundland

QUEBEC

Great La...

Montreal •

NOVA
SCOTIA

Missouri R.

L O U I S I A N A

Ohio R.

THIRTEEN
COLONIES

PACIFIC
OCEAN

ATLANTIC
OCEAN

Mississippi R.

FLORIDA

Rio Grande

Bahamas

Gulf of
Mexico

Cuba

Hispaniola

N E W   S P A I N

W E S T   I N D I E S

Caribbean Sea

1750

	British
	French
	Spanish
	Russian
	Dutch
	Proclamation Line of 1763

MAP 6.2: EUROPEAN CLAIMS IN NORTH AMERICA, 1750 AND 1763

The British victory in the Seven Years' War secured Britain's title to a large portion of the present-day United States and Canada.
What were the major shifts in power among European nations as a result of the Seven Years' War?

militias and, crucially, promised that London—not the colonies—would bear the costs of the war.

Last but certainly not least, the new English government acknowledged how important Indians were to the war effort. The new officers Pitt sent listened to colonial Indian agents and go-betweens, subsidized trade, and approved the distribution of presents to key leaders. These conciliatory gestures were well timed, because the Indian peoples of the Ohio Country and the *pays d'en haut* had increasingly come to question the French alliance.

Though French authorities often took Indians more seriously than did their English counterparts, they too struggled with cultural differences. In the aftermath of joint victories, for example, French officers sometimes felt obliged by European military protocol to deny their Indian allies customary war spoils—captives, plunder, and scalps. Disgruntled native warriors generally took them anyway and often refused to fight for France again. Even more to the point, by 1757 Britain's unsurpassed navy had in place a blockade of the St. Lawrence River that cut off supplies to French Canada. Without arms, ammunition, and metal goods, French authorities found it difficult to maintain their Indian alliances.

Years of Victory >> The reforms galvanized the colonies and turned the tide of the war. Most British North Americans willingly fought for the empire if they were treated as equals. In July 1758 the British gained control of the St. Lawrence River when the French fortress at Louisbourg fell to the Royal Navy and British and colonial troops. In August a force of New Englanders captured Fort Frontenac, thereby isolating French forts lining the Great Lakes and the Ohio valley. More Indians, seeing the French routed from the interior, switched their allegiance to the English.

The British succeeded even more brilliantly in 1759. In Canada Brigadier General James Wolfe gambled on a daring stratagem and won the fortress city of Quebec from Montcalm. Under the cover of darkness naval squadrons landed Wolfe's men beneath the city's steep bluffs, where they scaled the heights to a plateau known as the Plains of Abraham. A fierce battle ensued, and five days later both Wolfe and Montcalm lay dead, along with 1,400 French soldiers and 600 British and American troops. Quebec had fallen to the British. A year later the French surrender of Montreal finally ended the imperial war in North America, although it continued elsewhere around the world for another two years.

The Treaty of Paris, signed in February 1763, put an end to all French claims in North America and confirmed British title to all French territory east of the Mississippi. Spain had foolishly entered the war on France's side in 1762 and quickly lost Havana to

British warships. The treaty restored Cuba to Spain, but at a high price: the Spanish ceded Florida to Britain. It reluctantly took nominal control of France's vast and ill-defined territory of Louisiana, west of the Mississippi, but only to prevent Britain from having it. That territory included the port of New Orleans. In addition to its North America spoils, Britain won several Caribbean islands in the war, as well as Senegal in West Africa.

After generations of inconclusive imperial wars, British North Americans found the victory almost impossibly grand. Towns up and down the Atlantic coast lit up the night with celebratory bonfires and rang with the sounds of clanking tankards and boisterous song. How good it was to be British!

Postwar Expectations >> Grand expectations crowded on the heels of these joyful celebrations. The end of the war, Americans assumed, meant the end of high taxes and access to the fertile lands of the Ohio. Just as important, Americans expected to be given more consideration within the British Empire. Now, as one anonymous pamphleteer put it, Americans would "not be thought presumptuous, if they consider[ed] themselves upon an equal footing" with English in the parent country.

Few in England seemed to agree. British statesmen grumbled that colonial assemblies had been tightfisted when it came to supplying the army. British commanders charged that colonial troops had been lily-livered when it came to combat. Differing perspectives on the war and differing expectations of the colonies' place in the empire primed the postwar generation for crisis.

 REVIEW

What started the Seven Years' War, and how did Britain emerge victorious?

THE IMPERIAL CRISIS

It was common sense. Great Britain had waged a costly war to secure its empire in America; now it needed to consolidate those gains. The empire's North American territory had to be protected, its administration tightened, and its colonies made more profitable for the parent nation. Thus Britain would have to leave a standing army of several thousand troops in America after the Seven Years' War. And, of course, armies needed to be paid for; taxes would be unavoidable.

That the colonists, who benefited most from the great victory, ought to be the ones to pull out their purses for king and country—well, London thought that, too, was common sense.

Pontiac's Rebellion >> British authorities justified the army's continued presence in part by pointing to the various alien peoples that the Crown now had to administer. The army would have to police French

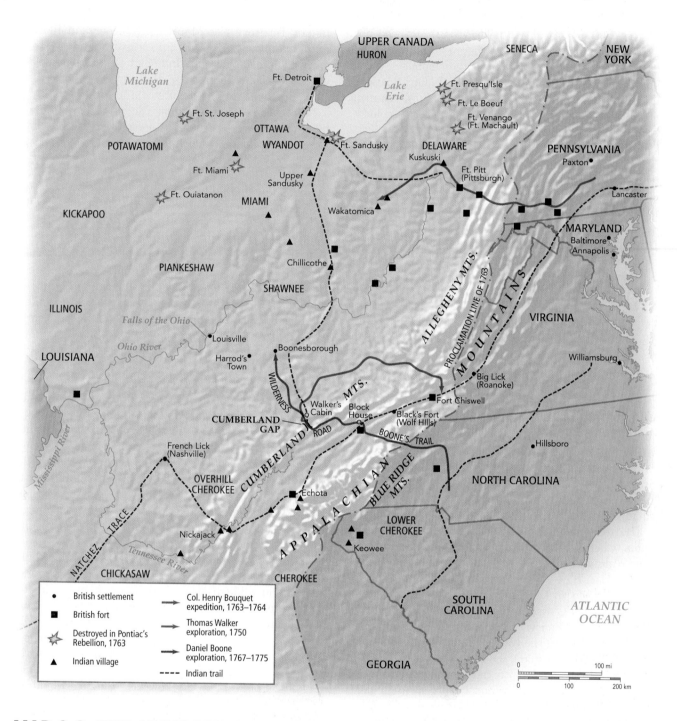

MAP 6.3: THE APPALACHIAN FRONTIER, 1750–1775

Increasingly, land-hungry colonials spilled into the West through the Cumberland Gap, a notch in the chain of mountains stretching the length of the North American interior. A route through the gap was scouted in 1750 by Dr. Thomas Walker and a party of Virginians on behalf of a company of land speculators. In 1763 Indians led by Pontiac seized eight British forts before troops under Colonel Henry Bouquet stopped the offensive. In 1775 Daniel Boone led the first large party of pioneers through the gap to Boonesborough, in present-day Kentucky. *How did efforts to expand American settlement west of the Appalachians help spark conflict between the British and the American colonists?*

colonists in Canada, Spaniards in Florida, and, most especially, dozens of formidable native peoples west of the Appalachians. General Jeffery Amherst, the top British officer in North America, believed Indian troubles could be avoided if military and civil authorities simply projected strength. With the French no longer on the continent, Amherst believed, Britain need not purchase Indian friendship with presents, subsidized trade, and tiresome diplomatic ceremonies. When knowledgeable colonists insisted that Indian relations hinged on such practices, Amherst scoffed. "When men of what race soever behave ill," the general scolded, "they must be punished but not bribed."

Still reeling from the war, Indian peoples reacted to Britain's triumphal attitude and the new westward surge of speculators and colonists with a religious revival that cut across tribal lines. The Delaware holy man Neolin told followers that God, or the Master of Life, believed his native children should "drive [the British] out, make war on them ... they know me not, and are my enemies. Send them back to the lands I have created for them...."

Pontiac, a charismatic Ottawa chief, embraced Neolin's message of Indian unity and organized attacks against British forts in the summer of 1763. Shawnees, Mingos, Potawatomis, Wyandots, and other Indian peoples in the Ohio Country, working with Pontiac or independently, captured every British fort west of Detroit by early July. Backcountry settlements from Pennsylvania to Virginia came under attack, leaving hundreds of colonials dead and hundreds more fleeing east. Determined to assert British rule, an enraged Amherst sent troops west to attack Indian forces and native villages. He also authorized the commander at Fort Pitt to give Indians blankets from the forts' infirmary, where several men had been stricken with smallpox.

Hatreds mounted on all sides. In western Pennsylvania, where Indian raids had taken an especially grim toll, a number of Scots-Irishmen calling themselves the "Paxton Boys" set out to purge the colony of Indians altogether. In December of 1763 they burst into a small village of Christian Indians, killed six people, and burned the settlement to the ground. Fourteen other inhabitants fled to the town of Lancaster, which gave them protective custody. Leading a mob the Paxton Boys forced their way into the safe house and massacred all 14 men, women, and children with broadswords. Colonists and natives alike were increasingly willing to simplify difference and see all "Indians" or all "whites" as despicable enemies.

Officials in London blamed Pontiac's Rebellion on bad leadership and replaced General Amherst. More important, the crown issued the Proclamation of 1763, which significantly transformed colonial policy.

Presents and respectful diplomacy were to resume, and the Crown appointed two Indian superintendents (one in South Carolina and the other in New York) to oversee good relations. Most critically, colonial settlement was to cease west of the Appalachians. A so-called proclamation line reserved all western lands as Indian Territory (see Map 6.2). (Quebec and Florida were exceptions, divided into eastern and western halves, for colonials and Indians.) Restricting westward movement might ease Indian fears, the British hoped, and so stave off future conflicts.

However sensible and just the Proclamation Line might have seemed from the perspective of the Ohio Country or London, most British colonists viewed it as a betrayal by their own government. Many wondered why they had fought and sacrificed in the war against France, if all the territory they helped win was set aside for Indians.

George Grenville's New Measures >> If Pontiac's Rebellion and the Proclamation of 1763 had been the only postwar disappointments colonists faced, that would have been trouble enough. But George Grenville, the first lord of the treasury, also confronted the dismal financial consequences of the Seven Years' War.

Britain's national debt had doubled in the decade after 1754. Adding to that burden was the drain of supporting troops in the colonies. As matters stood, heavy taxes were already triggering protests among hard-pressed Britons. Americans, in contrast, paid comparatively low taxes to their colonial governments and little in trade duties to the empire. Indeed, Grenville discovered that the colonial customs service paid out four times more in salaries to its collectors than it gathered in duties. Rampant bribery and tax evasion allowed merchants to avoid existing duties on foreign molasses, for example, which New England merchants imported to make rum.

George Grenville reasoned that if Americans could pay out a little under the table to protect an illegal trade, they would willingly pay a little more to go legitimate. Parliament agreed. In April 1764 it passed the Revenue Act, commonly called the Sugar Act. This **tariff** actually lowered the duty on foreign molasses from six to three pence a gallon. This time, however, the tax would be scrupulously collected, ships would be tightly monitored to make sure they complied, and violators would be tried in admiralty courts, far harsher than typical colonial courts.

tariff duty on trade, the purpose of which is primarily to regulate the flow of commerce rather than to raise a revenue.

Parliament approved other proposals by Grenville, all designed to improve British finances. The Currency

Act of 1764 prohibited the colonies from making their paper money legal tender. That prevented Americans from paying their debts to British traders in currency that had fallen to less than its face value. The Quartering Act of 1765 obliged any colony in which troops were stationed to provide suitable accommodations. That contributed to the cost of keeping British forces in America. Finally, in March 1765 Parliament passed the Stamp Act.

The Stamp Act placed **taxes** on legal documents, customs papers, newspapers, almanacs, college diplomas, playing cards, and dice. After November 1, 1765, all these items had to bear a stamp signifying that their possessor had paid the tax. Violators of the Stamp Act, like those disobeying the Sugar Act, were to be tried without juries in admiralty courts. The English had been paying a similar tax for nearly a century, so Grenville expected few objections. Little did he understand the colonial viewpoint.

> **taxes** duty on trade (known as external taxation) or a duty on items circulating within a nation or a colony (known as internal taxation) intended primarily to raise a revenue rather than to regulate the flow of commerce.

⋏ British grenadier

The Beginning of Colonial Resistance >>

Like other Britons, colonials in America accepted a maxim laid down by the English philosopher John Locke: property guaranteed liberty. Property, in this view, was not merely real estate, or wealth, or material possessions. It was the source of strength for every individual, providing the freedom to think and act independently. It followed from this close connection between property, power, and liberty that no people should be taxed without consenting—either personally or through elected representatives. The power to tax was the power to destroy, by depriving a person of property. Yet both the Sugar Act and the Stamp Act were taxes passed by members of Parliament, none of whom had been elected by colonials.

Like the English, colonials also prized the right of trial by jury as one of their basic constitutional liberties. Yet both the Sugar Act and the Stamp Act would prosecute offenders in the admiralty courts, not in local courts, thus depriving colonials of the freedom claimed by all other English men and women.

The concern for protecting individual liberties was only one of the convictions shaping the colonies' response to Britain's new policies. Equally important was their deep suspicion of power itself, a preoccupation that colonials shared with a minority of radical English thinkers. These radicals were known by a variety of names: the Country Party, the Commonwealthmen, and the **Opposition.** They drew their inspiration from the ancient tradition of **classical republicanism,** which held that representative government safeguarded liberty more reliably than either monarchy or oligarchy did. Underlying that judgment was the belief that human beings were driven by passion and insatiable ambition. One person (a monarch), or even a few people (an oligarchy), could not be entrusted with governing, because they would inevitably become corrupted by power and turn into despots. Even in representative governments, the people were obliged to watch those in power at all times. The price of liberty was eternal vigilance.

> **the Opposition** diverse group of political thinkers and writers in Great Britain, also known as the Country Party and the Commonwealthmen, who elaborated the tradition of classical republicanism from the late seventeenth century through the eighteenth century.

> **classical republicanism** emphasized that all rulers needed to be watched because of a tendency for power to corrupt human nature.

The Opposition believed that the people of England were not watching their rulers closely enough. During the first half of the eighteenth century, they argued, the entire executive branch of England's government—monarchs and their ministers—had been corrupted by their appetite for power. Proof of their ambition could be found in the bloated state bureaucracy, the massive standing army, and the rising taxes. The Opposition warned that a sinister conspiracy originating in the executive branch of government threatened English liberty.

Opposition writers were more or less ignored in England, but colonial leaders revered them. The Opposition's view of politics confirmed colonial anxieties about England, doubts that ran deeper after 1763. Parliament's attempt to tax the colonies and the quartering of a standing army on the frontier smacked of a corrupt plot to enslave the colonies.

Britain's attempt to raise revenue after 1763 was a disaster of timing, not just psychologically but also economically. By then the colonies were in the throes of a recession. The boom produced in America by government spending during the war had collapsed once British subsidies were withdrawn. Colonial response to the Sugar Act reflected these painful postwar trends. New England merchants led the opposition, objecting to the Sugar Act principally on economic grounds.

But with the passage of the Stamp Act, the terms of the imperial debate widened. The new act took money from the pockets of anyone who made a will, filed a deed, traded out of a colonial port, bought a newspaper, consulted an almanac, graduated from college, took a chance at dice, or played cards. More important, the Stamp Act served notice that Parliament claimed the authority to tax the colonies directly.

Riots and Resolves >> That unprecedented assertion provoked an unprecedented development: the first display of colonial unity. During the spring and summer of 1765, American assemblies passed resolves denying Parliament's authority to tax the colonies. That right belonged to colonial assemblies alone, they argued, by the law of nature and by the liberties guaranteed in colonial charters and in the British constitution.

Virginia's assembly, the House of Burgesses, took the lead in protesting the Stamp Act, prodded by Patrick Henry. Just 29 years old in 1765, Henry had tried his hand at planting in western Virginia before recognizing his real talent—demagoguery. Blessed with the eloquence of an evangelical preacher, the dashing charm of a southern gentleman, and a mind uncluttered by much learning, Henry parlayed his popularity as a smooth-talking lawyer into a place among the Burgesses. He took

his seat just 10 days before introducing the Virginia Resolves against the Stamp Act.

The Burgesses passed Henry's resolutions upholding their exclusive right to tax Virginians. Other assemblies followed suit, affirming that the sole right to tax Americans resided in their elected representatives. In October 1765 delegates from nine colonies convened in New York, where they prepared a joint statement of the American position and petitioned the king and Parliament to repeal both the Sugar Act and the Stamp Act.

Meanwhile, colonial leaders turned to the press to arouse popular opposition to the Stamp Act. Disposed by the writings of the English Opposition to think of politics in conspiratorial terms, they warned that Grenville and the king's other ministers schemed to deprive the colonies of their liberties by unlawfully taxing their property. The Stamp Act was only the first step in a sinister plan to enslave Americans. In response the merchants of Boston, New York, and Philadelphia agreed to stop importing English goods in order to pressure British traders to lobby for repeal. In every colony organizations emerged to ensure that the Stamp Act, if not repealed, would never be enforced.

The new resistance groups, which styled themselves the "Sons of Liberty," consisted of traders, lawyers, and prosperous artisans. With great success, they organized the lower classes of the seaports in opposition to the Stamp Act. The sailors, dockworkers, poor artisans, apprentices, and servants who poured into the streets resembled mobs that had been organized from time to time earlier in the century. Previous riots against houses of prostitution, merchants who hoarded goods, or supporters of smallpox inoculation had not been spontaneous, uncontrolled outbursts. Crowds chose their targets and their tactics carefully and usually carried out the communal will with little personal violence.

Opinion

Were the Whigs right to worry about the dangers of a standing army? If so, does our standing army pose a danger today?

↑ The Stamp Act riots had their roots in raucous demonstrations by "people out of doors," as such crowds were known during the eighteenth century. One annual celebration, the anti-Catholic "Pope's Day," was held every year in Boston. In this engraving boys dressed as devil's imps accompany a cart bearing an effigy of the pope. In the 1760s effigies of tax collectors and royal officials appeared instead.

In every colonial city the mobs of 1765 burnt the stamp distributors in effigy, insulted them on the streets, demolished their offices, and attacked their homes. One hot night in August 1765 a mob went further than the Sons of Liberty had planned. They all but leveled the stately mansion of Thomas Hutchinson, the unpopular lieutenant governor of Massachusetts and the brother–in–law of the colony's stamp distributor. The destruction stunned Bostonians, especially the Sons of Liberty, who resisted Britain in the name of protecting private property. Thereafter they took care to keep crowds under tighter control. By the first of November, the day the Stamp Act took effect, most of the stamp distributors had resigned.

Repeal of the Stamp Act >> Meanwhile,
repeal of the Stamp Act was already underway back in England. The man who came—unintentionally—to America's relief was George III. The young king was a good man, industrious and devoted to the empire, but he was also immature and not particularly bright. Insecurity made him an irksome master, and he ran through ministers rapidly. By the end of 1765 George had replaced Grenville with a new first minister, the Marquis of Rockingham. Opposed to the Stamp Act from the outset, Rockingham secured its repeal in March 1766.

The Stamp Act controversy demonstrated to colonials how similar in political outlook they were to one another and how different they were from the British. Most fundamentally, Americans agreed about the meaning of representation. To counter colonial objections to the Stamp Act, Grenville and his supporters

had claimed that Americans were virtually represented, because each member of Parliament stood for the interests of the whole empire. But colonials put little stock in the theory of **virtual representation.** After all, living an ocean away, their interests differed significantly from those of Britons. They insisted on **actual representation,** emphasizing that elected officials were directly accountable to their constituents.

Americans also agreed that Parliament had no legitimate right to tax the colonies. Colonials conceded Parliament's right to legislate and to regulate trade for the good of the whole empire. But taxation, in their view, was the free gift of the people through their representatives—who were not sitting in Parliament.

Members of Parliament brushed aside colonial petitions and resolves, all but ignoring these constitutional arguments. To make its own authority clear, Parliament accompanied the repeal of the Stamp Act with a Declaratory Act, asserting that it had the power to make laws for the colonies "in all cases whatsoever." In fact, the Declaratory Act clarified nothing. Did Parliament understand the power of legislation to include the power of taxation?

virtual representation view that representation is not linked to election but rather to common interests. During the imperial crisis, the British argued that Americans were virtually represented in Parliament, even though colonials elected none of its members.

actual representation view that the people can be represented only by a person whom they have actually elected to office.

The Townshend Acts >> In the summer of 1766
George III—again unintentionally—gave the colonies what should have been an advantage by changing ministers yet again. The king replaced Rockingham with William Pitt, who enjoyed great favor among colonials for his leadership during the Seven Years' War and for his opposition to the Stamp Act. Almost alone among British politicians, Pitt had grasped and approved the colonists' constitutional objections to taxation. During Parliament's debate over repeal of the Stamp Act, Grenville asked sarcastically, "Tell me when the colonies were emancipated?" Pitt immediately shot back, "I desire to know when they were made slaves!"

If the man who believed that Americans were "the sons not the bastards of England" had been well enough to govern, matters between Great Britain and the colonies might have turned out differently. But almost immediately after Pitt took office his health collapsed, and power passed into the hands of Charles Townshend, the chancellor of the exchequer, who wished only to raise more revenue. In 1767 Townshend persuaded Parliament to tax the lead, paint, paper, glass, and tea that Americans imported from Britain. Then he used revenue from these new tariffs to pay the salaries of many royal officials serving in the colonies.

This was a change—and an important one. Previously, governors and other officers such as customs collectors and judges had received their salaries from colonial legislatures. The assemblies lost that crucial leverage when Townshend used the revenues to pay those bureaucrats directly. Royal officials depended less, now, on coming to terms with American legislators. Finally, in order to ensure more effective enforcement of all the duties on imports, Townshend created an American Board of Customs Commissioners, who appointed a small army of new customs collectors. He also established three new vice–admiralty courts in Boston, New York, and Charleston to bring smugglers to justice.

The Resistance Organizes >> In Townshend's efforts to centralize the administration of the empire, Americans saw new evidence that they were not being treated like the English. A host of newspapers and pamphlets took up the cry against taxation. The most widely read publication, "A Letter from a Farmer in Pennsylvania," was the work of John Dickinson—who was, in fact, a Philadelphia lawyer. He urged Americans to protest the Townshend duties by consuming fewer imported English luxuries. The virtues of hard work, thrift, and home manufacturing, Dickinson argued, would bring about repeal.

As Dickinson's star rose over Philadelphia, the Townshend Acts also shaped the destiny of another man farther north. Samuel Adams was a leader in the Massachusetts assembly, one whose rise had been unlikely. Adams's earlier ventures as a merchant ended in bankruptcy; his stint as

>> John Dickinson of Philadelphia

a tax collector left all of Boston in the red. But he proved a consummate political organizer and agitator. First his enemies and later his friends claimed that Adams had decided on independence for America as early as 1768. In that year he persuaded the assembly to send to other colonial legislatures a circular letter condemning the Townshend Acts and calling for a united American resistance.

As John Dickinson and Samuel Adams whipped up public outrage, the Sons of Liberty again organized the opposition in the streets. Customs officials, like the stamp distributors before them, became targets of popular hatred. But the customs collectors gave as good as they got. Using the flimsiest excuses, they seized American vessels for violating royal regulations. With cold insolence they shook down American merchants for what amounted to protection money. The racketeering in the customs service brought tensions in Boston to a flash point in June 1768 after officials seized and condemned the *Liberty*, a sloop belonging to one of the city's biggest merchants, John Hancock. Several thousand Bostonians vented their anger in a night of rioting, searching out and roughing up customs officials.

The new secretary of state for the colonies, Lord Hillsborough, responded to the *Liberty* riot by sending two regiments of troops to Boston. In the fall of 1768 the redcoats, like a conquering army, paraded into town under the cover of warships lying off the harbor. In the months that followed, citizens bristled when challenged on the streets by armed soldiers. Even more disturbing to Bostonians was the execution of British military justice on the Common. British soldiers were whipped savagely for breaking military discipline, and desertion was punished by execution.

The *Liberty* riot and the arrival of British troops in Boston pushed colonial assemblies to coordinate their resistance more closely. Most legislatures endorsed the Massachusetts circular letter of protest sent to them by Samuel Adams. They promptly adopted agreements not to import or to consume British goods. The reluctance among some merchants to revive nonimportation in 1767 gave way to greater enthusiasm by 1768, and by early 1769 such agreements were in effect throughout the colonies.

The Stamp Act crisis had also called forth intercolonial cooperation and tactics such as nonimportation. But the protests against the Townshend Acts raised the stakes by creating new institutions to carry forward the resistance. Subscribers to the nonimportation agreements established "committees of inspection" to enforce the ban on trade with Britain. The committees publicly denounced merchants who continued to import, vandalized their warehouses, forced them to stand

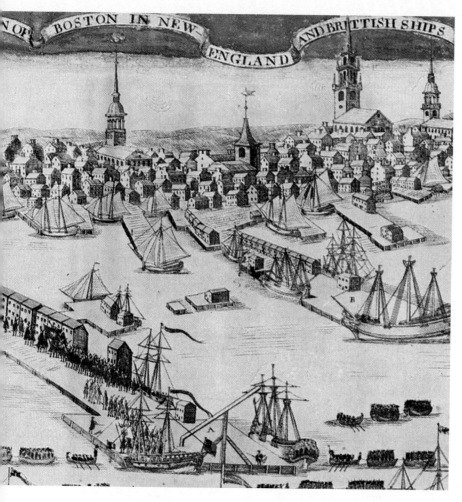

BOSTON IN NEW-ENGLAND AND BRITTISH SHIPS

↑ Like a swarm of angry bees, British troops disembark on one of Boston's long wharves in 1768. American colonials who had cheered the triumphs of British soldiers only a few years earlier now complained bitterly about the presence of a standing army designed to intimidate them.

journalist and a leading politician of the Opposition. Both men charged the king's ministers with corrupting the political life of the British Isles. The doings of political rebels even in distant Poland and Turkey engaged colonial sympathies, too. But perhaps the international cause dearest to American lovers of liberty was the fate of Corsica.

For years this tiny island off the coast of Italy had fought for its independence, first from the Italian state of Genoa and then from France, which bought the island in 1768. The leader of the Corsican rebellion, Pascal Paoli, hoped that England would rally to defend Corsica's freedom, if only to keep France from seizing this strategic Mediterranean outpost. But British statesmen had no intention of going to war with France over mere Corsica, and when French troops routed his rebel army, Paoli fled to exile in England in 1769. Adding insult to injury this "greatest man of earth," as he was lionized, began to hobnob with British nobles. He even accepted a pension of 1,000 pounds a year from George III. The moral of the sad story, according to more than one colonial newspaper, was that British corruption pervaded not only the empire but all of Europe. Within a few years Europeans sympathizing with these notions would cross the Atlantic to fight in the American Revolution.

under the gallows, and sometimes resorted to tar and feathers.

After 1768 the resistance also brought a broader range of colonials into the politics of protest. Artisans, who recognized that nonimportation would spur domestic manufacturing, began to organize as independent political groups. In many towns women took an active part in opposing the Townshend duties. The "Daughters of Liberty" took to heart John Dickinson's advice: they wore homespun clothing instead of English finery, served coffee instead of tea, and boycotted shops selling British goods.

The International Sons of Liberty >> The resistance after 1768 grew broader in another sense. Many of its supporters in the colonies felt a new sense of kinship with freedom fighters throughout Europe. Eagerly they read about the doings of men such as Charles Lucas, an Irish newspaper editor and member of the Irish Parliament, and John Wilkes, a London

The Boston Massacre >> Meanwhile, the situation in Boston deteriorated steadily. British troops found themselves regularly cursed by citizens and occasionally pelted with stones, dirt, and human excrement. The British regulars were particularly unpopular among Boston's laboring classes, because they competed with them for jobs. Off-duty soldiers moonlighted as maritime laborers, and they sold their services at rates cheaper than the wages paid to locals. By 1769 brawls between British regulars and waterfront workers broke out frequently.

With some 4,000 redcoats enduring daily contact with some 15,000 Bostonians under the sway of Samuel Adams, what happened on the night of March 5, 1770, was nearly inevitable. A crowd gathered around the customshouse for the sport of heckling the 10 soldiers who guarded it. The redcoats panicked and fended off insults and snowballs with live fire, hitting 11 rioters and killing 5. Adams and other propagandists seized on the incident. Labeling the bloodshed "the Boston

WHO WAS TO BLAME FOR THE BOSTON MASSACRE?

Following the shootings in King Street, Captain Thomas Preston and six of his men stood trial for murder. Two radical patriot lawyers, Josiah Quincy Jr., and future president John Adams, served as defense council. Convinced that Boston must prove itself fair and faithful to the rule of law, both lawyers performed brilliantly. The jury acquitted Preston and four of the soldiers, and convicted two others of manslaughter. The depositions from the trial provide some of our best evidence for how soldiers and Bostonians viewed the standoff differently.

DOCUMENT 1
Deposition of Captain Thomas Preston, March 1770

The mob still increased and were more outrageous, striking their clubs or bludgeons one against another, and calling out, come on you rascals, you bloody backs, you lobster scoundrels, fire if you dare, G-d damn you, fire and be damned, we know you dare not, and much more such language was used. At this time I was between the soldiers and the mob, parleying with, and endeavouring all in my power to persuade them to retire peaceably, but to no purpose. They advanced to the points of the bayonets, struck some of them and even the muzzles of the pieces, and seemed to be endeavouring to close with the soldiers. On which some well-behaved persons asked me if the guns were charged. I replied yes. They then asked me if I intended to order the men to fire. I answered no, by no means, observing to them that I was advanced

before the muzzles of the men's pieces, and must fall a sacrifice if they fired; that the soldiers were upon the half cock and charged bayonets, and my giving the word fire under those circumstances would prove me to be no officer. While I was thus speaking, one of the soldiers having received a severe blow with a stick, stepped a little on one side and instantly fired, on which turning to and asking him why he fired without orders, I was struck with a club on my arm, which for some time deprived me of the use of it, which blow had it been placed on my head, most probably would have destroyed me. On this a general attack was made on the men by a great number of heavy clubs and snowballs being thrown at them, by which all our lives were in imminent danger, some persons at the same time from behind calling out, damn your

bloods—why don't you fire. Instantly three or four of the soldiers fired, one after another, and directly after three more in the same confusion and hurry. The mob then ran away, except three unhappy men who instantly expired, in which number was Mr. Gray at whose rope-walk the prior quarrels took place; one more is since dead, three others are dangerously, and four slightly wounded. The whole of this melancholy affair was transacted in almost 20 minutes. On my asking the soldiers why they fired without orders, they said they heard the word fire and supposed it came from me. This might be the case as many of the mob called out fire, fire, but I assured the men that I gave no such order; that my words were, don't fire, stop your firing. In short, it was scarcely possible for the soldiers to know who said fire, or don't fire, or stop your firing.

DOCUMENT 2
Deposition of Robert Goddard, March 1770

The Soldiers came up to the Centinel and the Officer told them to place themselves and they formed a half moon. The Captain told the Boys to go home least there should be murder done. They were throwing Snow balls. Did not go off but threw more Snow balls. The Capt. was behind the Soldiers. The Captain told them to fire. One Gun went off. A Sailor or Townsman struck the Captain. He thereupon said damn your bloods fire think I'll be treated in this manner. This Man that struck the Captain came from among the People who were 7 feet off and were round on one wing. I saw no person speak to him. I was so near I should have seen it. After the Capt. said Damn your bloods

fire they all fired one after another about 7 or 8 in all, and then the officer bid Prime and load again. He stood behind all the time. Mr. Lee went up to the officer and called the officer by name Capt. Preston, I saw him coming down from the Guard behind the Party. I went to Gaol the next day being sworn for the Grand Jury to see the Captain. Then said pointing to him that's the person who gave the word to fire. He said if you swear that you will ruin me everlastingly. I was so near the officer when he gave the word fire that I could touch him. His face was towards me. He stood in the middle behind the Men. I looked him in the face. He then stood within the circle. When he told 'em

to fire he turned about to me. I looked him in the face.

THINKING CRITICALLY

Preston and Goddard come to different conclusions about the shootings but describe similar details (the snowballs, the man who struck Preston). Can details from these two accounts be reconciled? Do they simply have different perspectives on the same event, or do you think one of the depositions must be misleading? Given the tensions these accounts relate, do you think that a violent confrontation between soldiers and Bostonians was inevitable?

Massacre," they publicized that "atrocity" through-out the colonies. The radical Boston *Gazette* framed its account in an eye-catching black-bordered edition headed with a drawing of five coffins.

While Townshend's policies spurred the resistance in America, the obvious finally dawned on Parliament. They recognized that Townshend's duties on imported English goods only discouraged sales to colonials and encouraged them to manufacture at home. The argument for repeal was overwhelming, and the way had been cleared by the unexpected death of Townshend. In 1770 his successor, Lord North, convinced Parliament to repeal all the Townshend duties except the one on tea, allowing that tax to stand as a source of revenue and as a symbol of Parliament's authority.

Resistance Revived >> Repeal of the Townshend duties took the wind from the sails of American resistance for more than two years. But the controversy between England and the colonies had not been resolved. Colonials still paid taxes on molasses and tea, taxes to which they had not consented. They were still subject to trial in admiralty courts, which operated without juries. They still lived with a standing army in their midst. Beneath the banked fires of protest smoldered the live embers of Americans' political inequality. Any shift in the wind could fan those embers into flames.

The wind did shift, quite literally, on Narragansett Bay in 1772, running aground the *Gaspee*, a British naval schooner in hot pursuit of Rhode Island smugglers. Residents of nearby Providence quickly celebrated the *Gaspee*'s misfortune by burning it down to the waterline. Outraged British officials sent a special commission to look into the matter, intending once again to bypass the established colonial court system. The arrival of the Gaspee Commission reignited the imperial crisis, and in America, once again, resistance flared.

It did so through an ingenious mechanism, the **committees of correspondence.** Established in all the colonies by their assemblies, the committees drew up statements of American rights and grievances, distributed those documents within and among the colonies, and solicited responses from towns and counties. The brainchild of Samuel Adams, the committee structure formed a new communications network, one that fostered an intercolonial agreement on resistance to British measures. The strategy succeeded, and not only among colonies. The committees spread the scope of the resistance from colonial seaports into rural areas, engaging farmers and other country folk in the opposition to Britain.

> **committees of correspondence** strategy devised by Samuel Adams in 1772 to rally popular support among American colonials against British imperial policies.

⋀ While the new political activism of some American women merely amused male leaders of the resistance, it inspired the scorn of some defenders of British authority. When the women of Edenton, North Carolina, renounced imported tea, this British cartoon mocked them. Can you find at least five details in the drawing used by the artist to insult the Americans?

The committees had much to talk about when Parliament passed the Tea Act in 1773. The law was an effort to bail out the bankrupt East India Company by granting that corporation a monopoly on the tea trade to Americans. Because the company could use agents to sell its product directly, cutting out the middlemen, it could offer a lower price than that charged by colonial merchants. Thus, although the Tea Act would hurt American merchants, it promised to make tea cheaper for ordinary Americans. Still, many colonials saw the act as Parliament's attempt to trick them into accepting its authority to tax the colonies. They set out to deny that power once and for all.

In the early winter of 1773 popular leaders in Boston called for the tea cargoes to be returned immediately to England. On the evening of December 16, thousands of Bostonians, as well as farmers from the surrounding countryside, packed into the Old South Meetinghouse. Some members of the audience knew what Samuel Adams planned for the evening's agenda, and they awaited their cue. It came when Adams told the meeting that they could do nothing more to save their country. War whoops rang through the meetinghouse, the crowd spilled onto the streets and out to the waterfront, and the Boston Tea Party commenced.

From the throng emerged 50 men dressed as Indians to disguise their identities. The party boarded three vessels docked off Griffin's Wharf, broke open casks containing 90,000 pounds of tea, and brewed a beverage worth 10,000 pounds sterling in Boston harbor.

The Empire Strikes Back >> The Boston Tea Party proved to British satisfaction that the colonies aimed at independence. Lord North's assessment was grim: "We are now to dispute whether we have, or have not, any authority in that country." To reassert its authority, Parliament passed the Coercive Acts, dubbed in the colonies the "Intolerable Acts." The first of these came in March 1774, after hearing of the Tea Party, when Parliament passed the Boston Port Bill, closing that harbor to all oceangoing traffic until such time as the king saw fit to reopen it. And George, Parliament announced, would not see fit until colonials paid the East India Company for their losses.

During the next three months Parliament approved three other "intolerable" laws designed to punish Massachusetts. The Massachusetts Government Act handed over the colony's government to royal officials. Even convening town meetings would require royal permission. The Impartial Administration of Justice Act permitted any royal official accused of a crime in Massachusetts to be tried in England or in another colony. The Quartering Act allowed the housing of British troops in uninhabited private homes, outlying buildings, and barns—not only in Massachusetts but in all the colonies.

Many colonials saw the Coercive Acts as proof of a plot to enslave the colonies. In truth, the taxes and duties, laws and regulations of the past decade *were* part of a deliberate design—a plan to centralize the administration of the British Empire that seemed only common sense to British officials. But those efforts by the king's ministers and Parliament to run the colonies more efficiently and profitably were viewed by more and more Americans as a sinister conspiracy against their liberties.

For colonials the study of history confirmed that interpretation, especially their reading of the histories written by the English Opposition. The Opposition's favorite historical subject was the downfall of republics, whether those of ancient Greece and Rome or more recent republican governments in Venice and Denmark. The lesson of their histories was always the same: power overwhelmed liberty, unless the people remained vigilant. The pattern, argued radicals, had been repeated in America over the previous dozen years: costly wars waged; oppressive taxes levied to pay for them; standing armies sent to overawe citizens; corrupt governors, customs collectors, and judges appointed to enrich themselves by enforcing the measures. Everything seemed to fit.

Week after week in the spring of 1774, reports of legislative outrages came across the waters. Shortly after approving the Coercive Acts, Parliament passed the Quebec Act, which established a permanent government in what had been French Canada. Ominously, it included no representative assembly. Equally ominous to Protestant colonials, the Quebec Act officially recognized the Roman Catholic Church and extended the bounds of the province to include all land between the Mississippi and Ohio Rivers. Suddenly New York, Pennsylvania, and Virginia found themselves bordering a British colony whose subjects had no voice in their own government.

With the passage of the Coercive Acts, many more colonials came to believe not only that ambitious men plotted to enslave the colonies but also that those conspirators included almost all British political leaders. At the time of the Stamp Act and again during the agitation against the Townshend Acts, most colonials had confined their suspicions to the king's ministers. By 1774 members of Parliament were also implicated in that conspiracy—and a few radicals were wondering aloud about George III.

As alarm deepened in the wake of the Coercive Acts, one colony after another called for an intercolonial congress—like the one that had met during the Stamp Act crisis—to determine the best way to defend their freedom. But many also remained unsettled about where the logic of their actions seemed to be taking them: toward a denial that they were any longer English.

 REVIEW

How did British colonial policy change after the Seven Years' War, and in what ways did colonial Americans resist it?

TOWARD THE REVOLUTION

By the beginning of September 1774, when 55 delegates to the First Continental Congress gathered in Philadelphia, the news from Massachusetts was grim. The colony verged on anarchy, it was reported, as its inhabitants resisted the enforcement of the Massachusetts Government Act.

In the midst of this atmosphere of crisis, the members of Congress also had to take one another's measure. Many of the delegates had not traveled outside their own colonies. (All but Georgia sent representatives.) Although the delegates encountered a great deal of diversity, they quickly discovered that they esteemed the same traits of character, attributes that they called "civic virtue." These traits included simplicity and self—reliance, industry and thrift, and above all, an unselfish commitment to the public good. Most members of the Congress also shared a common mistrust of England, associating the mother country with vice, extravagance, and corruption. Still, the delegates had some misgivings about those from other colonies. Massachusetts in particular brought with it a reputation—well deserved, considering that Samuel Adams was along—for radical action and a willingness to use force to accomplish its ends.

The First Continental Congress

>> As the delegates settled down to business, their aim was to reach agreement on three key points: How were they to justify the rights they claimed as American colonials? What were the limits of Parliament's power? And what were the proper tactics for resisting the Coercive Acts? Congress quickly agreed on the first point. The delegates affirmed that the law of nature, the colonial charters, and the British constitution provided the foundations of American liberties. This position was what most colonials had argued since 1765.

On the two other issues, Congress charted a middle course between the demands of radicals and the reservations of conservatives. Since the time of the Stamp Act, most colonials had insisted that Parliament had no authority to tax the colonies. But later events had demonstrated that Parliament could undermine colonial liberties by legislation as well as by taxation. The suspension of the New York legislature, the Gaspee Commission, and the Coercive Acts all fell into this category. Given those experiences, the delegates adopted a Declaration of Rights and Grievances on October 14, 1774, asserting the right of the colonies to tax and legislate for themselves. The Declaration of Rights thus limited Parliament's power over Americans more strictly than colonials had a decade earlier.

By denying Parliament's power to make laws for the colonies, the Continental Congress blocked efforts of the most conservative delegates to reach an accommodation with England. Their leading advocate, Joseph Galloway of Pennsylvania, proposed a plan of union with Britain similar to the one set forth by the Albany Congress in 1754. Under it, a grand council of the colonies would handle all common concerns, with any laws it passed subject to review and veto by Parliament. For its part, Parliament would have to submit for the grand council's approval any acts it passed affecting America. A majority of delegates judged that Galloway left Parliament too much leeway in legislating for colonials, and they rejected his plan.

Although the Congress denied Parliament the right to impose taxes or to make laws, delegates stopped short of declaring that it had no authority in the colonies. They approved Parliament's regulation of trade, but only because of the interdependent economy of the empire. And although some radical pamphleteers were attacking the king for plotting against American liberties, the Congress acknowledged the continuing allegiance of the colonies to George III. In other words, the delegates called for a return to the situation that had existed in the empire before 1763, with Parliament regulating trade and the colonies exercising all powers of taxation and legislation.

On the question of resistance, the Congress satisfied the desires of its most radical delegates by drawing up the Continental Association, an agreement to cease all trade with Britain until the Coercive Acts were repealed. They agreed that their fellow citizens would immediately stop drinking East India Company tea and that by December 1, 1774, merchants would no longer import goods of any sort from Britain. A ban on the export of American produce to Britain and the West Indies would go into effect a year later, during September 1775—the lag being a concession to southern rice and tobacco planters, who wanted to market crops already planted.

The Continental Association provided for the total cessation of trade, but Samuel Adams and other radicals wanted bolder action. They received help from Paul Revere, a Boston silversmith who had long provided newspapers with lurid engravings showing British abuses. On September 16 Revere galloped into Philadelphia bearing a copy of resolves drawn up by Bostonians and other residents of Suffolk County. The Suffolk Resolves, as they were called, branded the Coercive Acts as unconstitutional and called for civil disobedience to protest them. The Congress endorsed the resolves, as Adams had hoped. But it would not approve another part of the radicals' agenda—preparing for war by authorizing proposals to strengthen and arm colonial militias.

Thus the First Continental Congress steered a middle course. Although determined to bring about repeal of the Coercive Acts, it held firm in resisting any revolutionary course of action. If British officials had responded to its recommendations and restored the status quo of 1763, the war for independence might have been postponed—perhaps indefinitely. However, even though the Congress did not go to the extremes urged by the radicals, its decisions drew colonials farther down the road to independence.

The Last Days of the British Empire in America

>> Most colonials applauded the achievements of the First Continental Congress. They expected that the Association would bring about a speedy repeal of the Coercive Acts. But fear that the colonies were moving toward a break with Britain led others to denounce the doings of the Congress. Conservatives were convinced

that if independence were declared, chaos would ensue. Colonials, they argued, would quarrel over land claims and sectional tensions and religious differences, as they had so often in the recent past. Without Britain to referee such disputes, they feared, the result would be civil war, followed by anarchy.

The man in America with the least liking for the Continental Congress sat in the hottest seat in the colonies, that of the governor of Massachusetts. General Thomas Gage watched as royal authority crumbled in Massachusetts and the rebellion spread to other colonies. In June 1774 a desperate Gage dissolved the Massachusetts legislature, only to see it re-form, on its own, into a Provincial Congress. That new body assumed the government of the colony in October and began arming the militia. Gage then started to fortify Boston and pleaded for more troops—only to find his fortifications damaged by saboteurs and his requests for reinforcements ignored by Britain.

Outside Boston, royal authority fared no better. Farmers in western Massachusetts forcibly closed the county courts, turning out royally appointed justices and establishing their own tribunals. Popularly elected committees of inspection charged with enforcing the Association took over towns everywhere in Massachusetts, not only restricting trade but also regulating every aspect of local life. The committees called on townspeople to display civic virtue by renouncing "effeminate" English luxuries such as tea and fine clothing and "corrupt" leisure activities such as dancing, gambling, and racing. The committees also assigned spies to report on any citizen unfriendly to the resistance. "Enemies of American liberty" risked being roundly condemned in public or beaten and pelted with mud and dung by hooting, raucous mobs.

Throughout the other colonies a similar process was under way. During the winter and early spring of 1775 provincial congresses, county conventions, and local committees of inspection were emerging as revolutionary governments, replacing royal authority at every level. As the spectacle unfolded before General Gage, he concluded that only force could subdue the colonies. It would take more than he had at his command, but reinforcements might be on the way. In February 1775 Parliament had approved an address to the king declaring that the colonies were in rebellion.

The Fighting Begins >> As spring came to Boston the city waited. A band of artisans, organized as spies and express riders by Paul Revere, watched General Gage and waited for him to act. On April 14 word from Lord North finally arrived: Gage was to seize the leaders of the Provincial Congress, an action that would behead the rebellion, North said. Gage knew better than to believe North—but he also knew that he had to do something.

On the night of April 18 the sexton of Boston's Christ Church hung two lamps from its steeple. It was a signal that British troops had moved out of Boston and were marching toward the arms and ammunition stored by the Provincial Congress in Concord. As the lamps flashed the signal, Revere and a comrade, William Dawes, rode out to arouse the countryside.

When the news of a British march reached Lexington, its Minuteman militia of about 70 farmers, chilled and sleepy, mustered on the Green at the center of the small rural town. Lexington Green lay directly on the road to Concord. About four in the morning 700 British troops massed on the Green, and their commander, Major John Pitcairn, ordered the Lexington militia to disperse. The townsmen, outnumbered and overawed, began to obey. Then a shot rang out—whether the British or the Americans fired first is unknown—and then two volleys burst from the ranks of the redcoats. With a cheer the British set off for Concord, five miles distant, leaving eight Americans dead on Lexington Green.

By dawn hundreds of Minutemen from nearby towns were surging into Concord. The British entered at about seven in the morning and moved, unopposed, toward their target, a house lying across the bridge that spanned the Concord River. While three companies of British soldiers searched for American guns and ammunition, three others, posted on the bridge, had the misfortune to find those American arms—borne by the rebels and being fired with deadly accuracy. By noon the British were retreating to Boston.

The narrow road from Concord to Boston's outskirts became a corridor of carnage. Pursuing Americans fired on the column of fleeing redcoats from the cover of fences and forests. By the end of April 19 the British had sustained 273 casualties; the Americans, 95. It was only the beginning. By evening of the next day some 20,000 New England militia had converged on Boston for a long siege.

Common Sense >> The bloodshed at Lexington Green and Concord's North Bridge committed colonials to a course of rebellion—and independence. That was the conclusion drawn by Thomas Paine, who urged other Americans to join the rebels.

Paine himself was hardly an American. He was born in England, first apprenticed as a corsetmaker, appointed later a tax collector, and fated finally to become midwife to the age of republican revolutions. Paine came to Philadelphia late in 1774, set up as a journalist, and made the American cause his own. "Where liberty is, there is my country," he declared. In January 1776 he wrote a pamphlet to inform colonials of their identity as a distinct people and their destiny as a nation. *Common Sense* enjoyed tremendous popularity and wide circulation, selling 120,000 copies.

^ Amos Doolittle engraved this scene of retreating British troops after the skirmishes at Lexington and Concord. As the engraving makes clear, American militia took advantage of the stone fences to provide cover as sharpshooters picked off the retreating redcoats.

After Lexington and Concord Paine wrote, as the imperial crisis passed "from argument to arms, a new era for politics is struck—a new method of thinking has arisen." That new era of politics for Paine was the age of republicanism. He denounced monarchy as a foolish and dangerous form of government, one that violated the dictates of reason as well as the word of the Bible. By ridicule and remorseless argument, he severed the ties of colonial allegiance to the king. *Common Sense* scorned George III as "the Royal Brute of Britain," who had enslaved the chosen people of the new age—the Americans.

Nor did Paine stop there. He rejected the idea that colonials were or should want to be English. The colonies occupied a huge continent an ocean away from the tiny British Isles—clear proof that nature itself had fashioned America for independence. England lay locked in Europe, doomed to the corruption of an Old World. America had been discovered anew to become an "asylum of liberty."

Many Americans had liked being English, but being English hadn't worked. Perhaps that is another way of saying that over the course of nearly two centuries colonial society and politics had evolved in such a way that for Americans an English identity no longer fit.

The radicals in America viewed this change in identity in terms of age-old conspiracies that repeated themselves throughout history. First, the people of a republic were impoverished by costly wars—as the colonists could appreciate after the Seven Year's War. Then the government burdened the people with taxes to pay for those wars—as in the case of the Sugar Act or the Stamp Act or the Townshend duties. Next, those in power stationed a standing army in the country, pretending to protect the people but actually lending military force to their rulers. The rhetoric of the Opposition about ministerial conspiracies gave such talk a fervid quality that, to some modern ears, may seem an exaggeration.

Take away the rhetoric, however, and the argument makes uncomfortable sense. The British administration began its "backwoods" war with France, intending to limit it to the interior of North America. But the war aims of William Pitt—the leader Americans counted as their friend—grew with every victory, turning the conflict into a world war, driving France out of India and attacking Spain's colonies in the Philippines and Cuba. Peace came only once Britain and the major powers had bankrupted their treasuries. Conspiracy may not have been at the heart of the plan. But wars must be paid for. And so began the effort to regulate and bring order to Britain's "ungrateful" colonies.

In America, colonials were ungrateful precisely because their political institutions made the rights of "freeborn Britons" more available to ordinary citizens than they were in the nation that had created those liberties. Ironically, perhaps most Americans had succeeded *too* well at becoming English, regarding themselves as political equals entitled to basic constitutional freedoms. The imperial crisis made clear that despite all that the English and Americans shared, they stood fundamentally at odds over the distribution of political power. The call to arms at Lexington and Concord made retreat impossible.

On that point Paine was clear. It was the destiny of Americans to be republicans, not monarchists. It was the destiny of Americans to be independent, not subject to British dominion. It was the destiny of Americans to be American, not English. That, according to Thomas Paine, was common sense.

 REVIEW

What course of events had occurred by the mid-1770s to transform nonimportation and political protest into organized rebellion?

CHAPTER SUMMARY

Following its victory in the Seven Years' War Britain adopted policies designed to administer new territories and boost revenue. But these policies provoked a colonial backlash that led ultimately to the Revolutionary War.

- French and Indian forces did well at first during the Seven Years' War, as British policies alienated colonials and Indians alike.
- But William Pitt's reforms galvanized the colonies, won Britain Indian allies, and triumphed over France throughout the continent.
- Partly in response to Pontiac's Rebellion, Britain moderated its Indian policies and, with the Proclamation of 1763, forbade all colonial settlement west of the Appalachians.
- The new measures passed by Parliament in the early 1760s—the Proclamation of 1763, the Sugar Act, the Stamp Act, the Currency Act, and the Quartering Act—were all designed to generate revenue and bind the colonies more closely to the empire.
- These new measures deflated American expectations that they would be treated equally and violated what they held to be their right to consent to taxation, their right to trial by jury, and their right to freedom from standing armies.
- Although Parliament repealed the Stamp Act in the face of colonial protests, it reasserted its authority to tax Americans by passing the Townshend Acts in 1767.

- The Coercive Acts of 1774 led Americans to conclude that British actions in the past decade were part of a plot to enslave Americans by depriving them of property and liberty.
- At the First Continental Congress, delegates resisted both radical demands to mobilize for war and conservative appeals to reach an accommodation. The Congress denied Parliament any authority in the colonies except the right to regulate trade; it also drew up the Continental Association, an agreement to cease all trade with Britain until the Coercive Acts were repealed.
- When General Thomas Gage sent troops from Boston in April 1775 to seize arms being stored at Concord, the first battle of the Revolution took place.

Additional Reading

Fred Anderson, *Crucible of War* (2000), offers a magisterial account of the Seven Years' War; and Gregory Evans Dowd, *War under Heaven* (2002), explores the implications of that conflict for American Indians. *The Stamp Act Crisis* (1953) by Edmund S. Morgan and Helen M. Morgan remains the clearest and most vivid portrayal of that defining moment. For American resistance after the Stamp Act, see Pauline Maier, *From Resistance to Revolution* (1972); and to understand that struggle as lived and recalled by a Boston artisan, read Alfred F. Young's engaging book *The Shoemaker and the Tea Party* (1999). Two key interpretations of the logic of revolutionary resistance in Massachusetts and Virginia are Robert Gross, *The Minutemen and Their World* (1976); and Timothy Breen, *Tobacco Culture* (1985). A more recent study by Breen, *The Marketplace Revolution* (2005), sheds light on the role of a transatlantic consumer culture in fueling tensions within the British Empire.

Bernard Bailyn, *The Ideological Origins of the American Revolution* (1967), remains the classic study of the English Opposition and republican political thought in America. For biographies of eighteenth-century Americans who led—or opposed—the resistance to Britain see Pauline Maier, *The Old Revolutionaries* (1980); Bailyn's *The Ordeal of Thomas Hutchinson* (1974); and two biographies of Thomas Paine (both published in 2006) by Harvey Kaye and Craig Nelson.

Significant Events

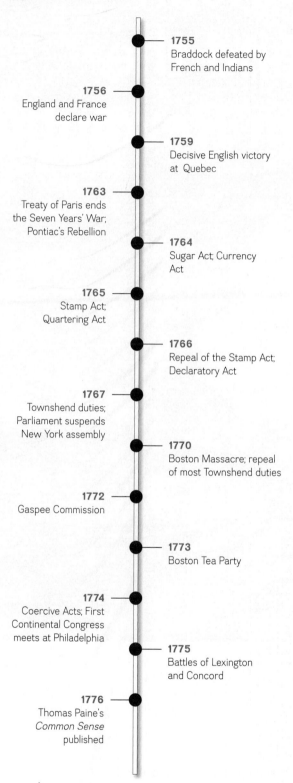

1755
Braddock defeated by
French and Indians

1756
England and France
declare war

1759
Decisive English victory
at Quebec

1763
Treaty of Paris ends
the Seven Years' War;
Pontiac's Rebellion

1764
Sugar Act; Currency
Act

1765
Stamp Act;
Quartering Act

1766
Repeal of the Stamp Act;
Declaratory Act

1767
Townshend duties;
Parliament suspends
New York assembly

1770
Boston Massacre; repeal
of most Townshend duties

1772
Gaspee Commission

1773
Boston Tea Party

1774
Coercive Acts; First
Continental Congress
meets at Philadelphia

1775
Battles of Lexington
and Concord

1776
Thomas Paine's
Common Sense
published

7 The American People and the American Revolution

1775–1783

On June 17, 1775, colonials flocked to the rooftops and upper windows of their Boston homes to witness the British attack on Breed's Hill across the water on nearby Charlestown.

CHARLES TOWN

BOSTON

>> **An American Story**

"WILL HE FIGHT?"

From a high place somewhere in the city—Beacon Hill, perhaps, or Copse Hill—General Thomas Gage looked down on Boston. Through a spyglass his gaze traveled over the church belfries and steeples, the roofs of brick and white frame houses. Finally he fixed his sights on a figure far in the distance across the Charles River. The man was perched atop a crude fortification on Breed's Hill, an elevation lying just below Bunker Hill on the Charlestown peninsula. Gage took the measure of his enemy: an older man, past middle age, a sword swinging beneath his homespun coat, a broad-brimmed hat shading his eyes. As he passed the spyglass to his ally, an American loyalist, Gage asked Abijah Willard if he knew the man on the fort. Willard peered across the Charles and identified his own brother-in-law, Colonel William Prescott. A veteran of the Seven Years' War, Prescott was now a leader in the rebel army laying siege to Boston.

"Will he fight?" Gage wondered aloud.

"I cannot answer for his men," Willard replied, "but Prescott will fight you to the gates of hell."

Fight they did on June 17, 1775, both William Prescott and his men. The evening before, three regiments had followed the colonel from Cambridge to Breed's Hill—soldiers drawn from the thousands of militia who had surrounded British-occupied Boston after the bloodshed at Lexington and Concord. Through the night they dug trenches and built up high earthen walls atop the hill. At the first light of day a British warship spotted the new rebel outpost and opened fire. By noon barges were ferrying British troops under Major General William Howe across the half mile of river that separated Boston from Charlestown. The 1,600 raw rebel troops tensed at the sight of scarlet-coated soldiers streaming ashore, glittering bayonets grasped at the ready. The rebels were farmers and artisans, not professional

soldiers, and they were frightened out of their wits.

But Prescott and his men held their ground. The British charged Breed's Hill twice, and Howe watched in horror as streams of fire felled his troops. Finally, during the third British frontal assault, the rebels ran out of ammunition and were forced to withdraw. Redcoats poured into the rebel fort, bayoneting its handful of remaining defenders. By nightfall the British had taken Breed's Hill and the rest of the Charlestown peninsula. They had bought a dark triumph at the cost of 228 dead and 800 wounded.

The cost came high in loyalties as well. The fighting on Breed's Hill fed the hatred of Britain that had been building since April. Throughout America preparations for war intensified: militia in every colony mustered; communities stockpiled arms and ammunition. Around Charlestown civilian refugees fled the countryside, abandoning homes and shops set afire by the British shelling of Breed's Hill. "The roads filled with frightened women and children, some in carts with their tattered furniture, others on foot fleeing into the woods," recalled Hannah Winthrop, one of their number.

The bloody, indecisive fight on the Charlestown peninsula known as the Battle of Bunker Hill actually took place on Breed's Hill. And the exchange between Thomas Gage and Abijah Willard that is said to have preceded the battle may not have taken place. But the story has persisted in the folklore of the

American Revolution. Whether it really happened or not, the conversation between Gage and Willard raised the question that both sides wanted answered: Were Americans willing to fight for independence from British rule? It was one thing, after all, to oppose the British ministry's policy of taxation. It was another to support a rebellion for which the ultimate price of failure was hanging for treason. And it was another matter entirely for men to wait nervously atop a hill as the seasoned troops of their own "mother country" marched toward them with the intent to kill.

Indeed, the question "Will they fight?" was revolutionary shorthand for a host of other questions concerning how ordinary Americans would react to the tug of loyalties between long-established colonial governments and a long-revered parent nation and monarch. For slaves, the question revolved around their allegiance to masters who spoke of liberty or to their masters' enemies who promised liberation. For those who led the rebels, it was a question of strengthening the resolve of the undecided, coordinating resistance, instilling discipline—translating the will to fight into the ability to do so. And for those who believed the rebellion was a madness whipped up by artful politicians, it was a question of whether to remain silent or risk speaking out, whether to take up arms for the king or flee. All these questions were raised, of necessity, by the act of revolution. But the barrel of a rifle shortened them to a single, pointed question: Will you fight? <<

What's to Come

THE DECISION FOR INDEPENDENCE

The delegates to the Second Continental Congress gathered at Philadelphia on May 10, 1775, just one month after the battles at Lexington and Concord. They had to determine whether independence or reconciliation offered the best way to protect the liberties of their colonies. Yet during the spring and summer of 1775, even strong advocates of independence did not openly seek a separation from Britain. If independence was to be achieved, radicals needed to forge greater agreement among Americans. Moderates and conservatives harbored deep misgivings about independence: they had to be brought along slowly.

The Second Continental Congress >> To

bring them along, Congress adopted the "Olive Branch Petition" in July 1775, which affirmed American loyalty to George III and asked the king to disavow the policies of his principal ministers. At the same time, Congress issued a declaration denying that the colonies aimed at independence. Yet, less than a month earlier, Congress had authorized the creation of a rebel military force, the **Continental Army,** and had issued paper money to pay for the troops.

Continental Army main rebel military force, created by the Second Continental Congress in July 1775 and commanded by George Washington.

A Congress that sued for peace while preparing for war was a puzzle that British politicians did not even try to understand, least of all Lord George Germain. A tough−minded statesman charged with colonial affairs, he was determined to subdue the rebellion by force. George III proved just as stubborn: he refused to receive the Olive Branch Petition. By the end of that year Parliament had shut down all trade with the colonies and had ordered the Royal Navy to seize colonial merchant ships on the high seas. In November 1775 Virginia's royal governor, Lord Dunmore, offered freedom to any slaves who would join the British. During January of the next year he ordered the shelling of Norfolk, Virginia, reducing that town to smoldering rubble.

British belligerence withered the cause of reconciliation within Congress and the colonies. Support for independence gained more momentum from the overwhelming reception of *Common Sense* in January 1776. On June 7 Virginia's Richard Henry Lee offered the motion "that these United Colonies are, and of right ought to be, free and independent States . . . and that all political connection between them and the State of Great Britain is, and ought to be, totally dissolved."

The Declaration >> Congress postponed a final

vote on Lee's motion until July. Some opposition still lingered among delegates from the middle colonies, and a committee appointed to write a declaration of independence needed time to complete its work. That committee included some of the leading delegates in Congress: John Adams, Benjamin Franklin, Connecticut's Roger Sherman, and New York's Robert Livingston. But the man who did most of the drafting was a young planter and lawyer from western Virginia.

Thomas Jefferson was just 33 years old in the summer of 1776 when he withdrew to his lodgings on the outskirts of Philadelphia, pulled a portable writing desk onto his lap, and wrote the statement that would explain American independence to a "candid world." In the document's brief opening section

⌃ This painting, which commemorated the signing of the Declaration of Independence, shows Benjamin Franklin (*seated center*) weighing the consequences of the action he and his colleagues are about to undertake. John Hancock, the president of the Congress, is reported to have remarked, "We must be unanimous; there must be no pulling different ways; we must all hang together." Franklin is said to have rejoined, "Yes, we must indeed all hang together, or most assuredly, we shall all hang separately."

Jefferson set forth a general justification of revolution that invoked the "self−evident truths" of human equality and "unalienable rights" to "life, liberty, and the pursuit of happiness." These natural rights had been "endowed" to all persons "by their Creator," the Declaration pointed out; thus there was no need to appeal to the narrower claim of the "rights of Englishmen."

While the first part of the Declaration served notice that Americans no longer considered themselves English, its second and longer section denied England any authority in the colonies. In its detailed history of American grievances against the British Empire, the Declaration referred only once to Parliament. Instead, it blamed George III for a "long train of abuses and usurpations" designed to achieve "absolute despotism." Congress adopted the Declaration of Independence on July 4, 1776.

The colonies thus followed the course set by common sense into the storms of independence. To those Britons who took a wide view of their empire, the decision for independence made no sense, and their perplexity is understandable. Since the end of the Seven Years' War Britain had added to its overseas dominion a vast and diverse number of subjects formerly under French rule— Native Americans, French Catholic Canadians, peoples of African descent in the Caribbean. And then there was India: part Hindu, part Muslim,

most of it ruled by the East India Company. What better, more efficient way to regulate this sprawling empire than to bring all its parts under the rule of a sovereign Parliament? What other way could the empire endure and prosper— and fend off future challenges from Catholic, monarchical France? British officials took it for granted that colonials could not be granted the same rights as Britons: an empire firmly based on hierarchy was needed to hold chaos at bay. Most colonial elites agreed with the logic of that position—East India Company officials, Bengal nabobs, Canadian traders and landlords. Only the leading men in Britain's original 13 colonies would not go along.

American Loyalists >> But the sentiment for independence was not universal. Those who would not back the rebellion, supporters of the king and Parliament, numbered perhaps one−fifth of the population in 1775. While they proclaimed themselves **"loyalists,"** their rebel opponents dubbed them "tories." That division made the Revolution a conflict pitting Americans against one another as well as the British.

> **loyalists** supporters of the king and Parliament and known to the rebels as "tories."

Predictably, the king and Parliament commanded the strongest support in colonies that had been wracked by internal strife earlier in the eighteenth century. In New York, New Jersey, and Pennsylvania, tenants who lived on land controlled by proprietors rebelled from time to time over the quit-rents they were required to pay their landlords. Tenant riots plagued New Jersey in the 1740s, and New York's Hudson valley manors took up arms in 1757 and more violently in 1766. In the Carolinas, settlers in western counties took matters into their own hands when eastern legislators ignored their needs, serving out vigilante justice in South Carolina and taking over corrupt county courts in North Carolina, in movements known as "the Regulation." These quarrels reignited during the Revolution, with old enemies taking opposite sides. To win support against Carolina's rebels, whose ranks included most wealthy coastal planters, western loyalist leaders played on ordinary settlers' resentments of privileged easterners. Grievances dating back to the 1760s also influenced the revolutionary allegiances of former land rioters of New York and New Jersey. If their old landlord opponents opted for the rebel cause, the tenants took up loyalism.

Other influences also fostered allegiance to Britain. Government officials who owed their jobs to the empire, major city merchants who depended on British trade, and Anglicans living outside the South retained strong ties to the parent country. Loyalists were also disproportionately represented among recent emigrants from the British Isles.

MAP 7.1: PATTERNS OF ALLEGIANCE

Although most New Englanders rallied behind the rebel cause, support for the Revolution was not as widespread in the middle colonies and southern colonies.
According to the text, what disputes among Americans encouraged loyalism to flourish? Locate these regions on the map.

Many who took up the king's cause had not lacked sympathy for the resistance. Loyalist leaders such as Joseph Galloway and Daniel Leonard had opposed the Stamp Act in 1765 and disapproved of imperial policy thereafter. It was not until the crisis reached a fever pitch in 1774 that more colonials cast their lot with the king. Worse than British taxation, in their view, was the radicalism of American resistance—the dumping of tea into Boston harbor, the forming of the Association, and the defying of royal authority.

Such acts of defiance touched what was for loyalists the rawest nerve: a deep-seated fear of the divisions and instability of colonial society. Without the British around to maintain order, they warned, differences among Americans would result in civil war. It would take the passage of less than a century for such fears to be borne out by events—the Union divided and the North and South locked in a fratricidal war.

Although a substantial minority, loyalists never became numerous enough anywhere to pose a serious threat to the Revolution. A more formidable threat was posed by the British army. And the greatest threat of all was posed by those very Americans who claimed that they wanted independence. For the question remained: Would they fight?

 REVIEW

What were the arguments for and against independence, and how did the advocates for independence prevail?

THE FIGHTING IN THE NORTH

In the summer of 1775 Americans who wished to remain neutral probably outnumbered either loyalists or rebels. From the standpoint of mere survival, staying neutral made more sense than fighting for independence. Even the most ardent advocates of American rights had reason to harbor doubts, given the odds against the rebel colonists defeating the armed forces of the British Empire.

Perhaps no friend of American liberty saw more clearly how slim the chances of a rebel victory were than George Washington. Yet June of 1775 found him, then 43 years old, attending the deliberations of the Second Continental Congress and dressed—a bit conspicuously—in his officer's uniform. Washington was the most celebrated American veteran of the Seven Years' War who remained young enough to lead a campaign. Better still, as a southerner he could bring his region into what thus far had remained mostly New England's fight. Congress

readily appointed him commander in chief of the newly created Continental Army.

The Two Armies at Bay >> Thus did Washington find himself, only a month later, looking to bring order to the rebel forces around Boston. He knew he faced a formidable foe, for the king's troops were seasoned professionals. An aristocratic officer corps drilled and disciplined rank-and-file soldiers, men drawn mainly from the bottom of British society, into a savage fighting machine. At the height of the campaign in America, reinforcements brought the number of British troops to 50,000, strengthened by some 30,000 Hessian mercenaries from Germany and the support of half the ships in the British navy, the largest in the world.

Washington was more modest about the army under his command, and he had much to be modest about. At first Congress recruited his fighting force of 16,600 rebel "regulars," the Continental Army, from the ranks of local New England militia bands. Although enlistments swelled briefly during the patriotic enthusiasm of 1775, for the rest of the war Washington's Continentals suffered chronic shortages of men and supplies. Most men preferred to fight instead as members of local militia units, the "irregular" troops who turned out to support the regular army whenever British forces came close to their neighborhoods.

The general reluctance to join the Continental Army created a host of difficulties for its commander and for Congress. Washington could not create an effective fighting force out of militias that mustered occasionally or men who enlisted for short stints in the Continental Army. But his desire for a professional military establishment clashed with the preferences of most republican leaders. They feared standing armies and idealized "citizen-soldiers"—men of selfless civic virtue who volunteered whenever needed—as the backbone of the common defense.

Only the dwindling number of volunteers gradually overcame republican fears of standing armies. In September 1776 Congress set terms in the Continental Army at a minimum of three years or for the duration of the war and assigned each state to raise a certain number of troops. They offered every man who enlisted in the army a cash bounty and a yearly clothing issue; enlistees for the duration were offered 100 acres of land as well. Still the problem of recruitment persisted. Less than a year later Congress recommended that the states adopt a draft, but Congress had no authority to compel the states to meet their troop quotas.

Even in the summer of 1775, before enlistments fell off, Washington was worried. As his Continentals laid siege to British-occupied Boston, most officers provided no real leadership, and the men under

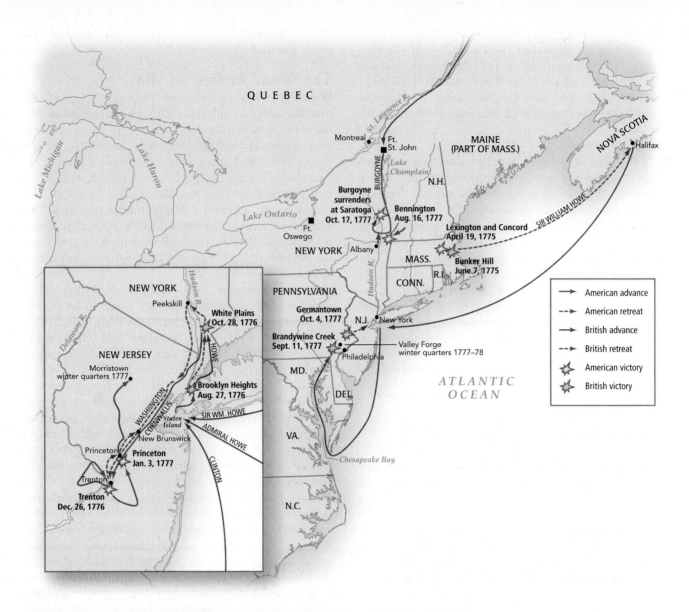

MAP 7.2: THE FIGHTING IN THE NORTH, 1775–1777

After the British withdrew from Boston in 1775, they launched an attack on New York City the following year. Washington was forced to retreat northward, then across the Hudson and south into New Jersey and Pennsylvania, before surprising the British at Trenton and Princeton. Burgoyne's surrender at Saratoga in 1777 marked a turning point in the war.

If General Howe had moved forces toward Albany, could he and General Burgoyne have split rebel New England from the rest of the former colonies? If so, how?

their command shirked their duties. They slipped away from camp at night; they left sentry duty before being relieved; they took potshots at the British; they tolerated filthy conditions in their camps.

While Washington strove to impose discipline on his Continentals, he also attempted, without success, to rid himself of "the Women of the Army." When American men went off to fight, their wives usually stayed at home. To women then fell the sole responsibility for running farms and businesses, raising children, and keeping households together. They helped to supply the troops by sewing clothing,

making blankets, and saving rags and lead weights for bandages and bullets. Other women on the home front organized relief for the widows and orphans of soldiers and protests against merchants who hoarded scarce commodities.

But the wives of poor men who joined the army were often left with no means to support their families. Thousands of such women—1 for every 15 soldiers—drifted after the troops. In return for half–rations, they cooked and washed for the soldiers; and after battles, they nursed the wounded, buried the dead, and scavenged the field for clothing and equipment.

Laying Strategies >> At the same time that he tried to discipline the Continentals, Washington designed a defensive strategy to compensate for their weakness. To avoid exposing raw rebel troops on "open ground against their Superiors in number and Discipline," he planned to fight the British from strong fortifications. With that aim in mind, in March 1776, Washington barricaded his army on Dorchester Heights, an elevation commanding Boston harbor from the south. That maneuver, which allowed American artillery to fire on enemy warships, confirmed a decision already made by the British to evacuate their entire army from Boston and sail for Halifax, Nova Scotia.

Britain had hoped to reclaim its colonies with a strategy of strangling the resistance in Massachusetts. But by the spring of 1776 they saw clearly that more was required than a show of force against New England. Instead, the situation called for Britain to wage a conventional war in America, capturing major cities and crushing the Continental forces in a decisive battle. Military victory, the British believed, would enable them to restore political control and reestablish imperial authority.

The first target was New York City. General William Howe and Lord George Germain, the British officials now charged with overseeing the war, chose that seaport for its central location and—they hoped—its large loyalist population. Howe's army intended to move from New York City up the Hudson River, meeting with British troops under General Sir Guy Carleton coming south from Canada. Either the British drive would lure Washington into a major engagement, crushing the Continentals or, if unopposed, the British offensive would cut America in two, smothering resistance to the south by isolating New England.

Unfortunately for the British, the strategy was sounder than the men placed in charge of executing it. Concern for preserving manpower addicted General Howe to caution, when daring more would have carried the day. Howe's brother, Admiral Lord Richard Howe, the head of naval operations in America, also stopped short of pressing the British advantage, owing to his personal desire for reconciliation. The reluctance of the Howe brothers to fight became the formula for British frustration in the two years that followed.

The Campaigns in New York and New Jersey

>> By mid–August of 1776, 32,000 British troops, including 8,000 **Hessians**—the largest expeditionary force of the eighteenth century—faced Washington's army of 23,000, which had marched from Boston to take up positions on Long Island. At dawn on August 22 the

> **Hessians** German soldiers who fought with the British army during the American Revolution.

Howe brothers launched their offense, pushing the rebel army back across the East River to Manhattan. After lingering on Long Island for a month the Howes again lurched into action, ferrying their forces to Kip's Bay, just a few miles south of Harlem. When the British landed, the handful of rebel defenders at Kip's Bay fled—straight into the towering wrath of Washington, who happened on the scene during the rout. For once the general lost his habitual self–restraint, flogged both officers and men with his riding crop, and came close to being captured himself. But the Howes remained reluctant to hit hard, occupying New York City but letting Washington's army escape from Manhattan to Westchester County.

Throughout the fall of 1776 General Howe's forces followed as Washington's fled southward across New Jersey. On December 7, the British nipping at their heels, the rebels crossed the Delaware River into Pennsylvania. There Howe stopped, pulling back most of his army to winter in New York City and leaving the Hessians to hold the British line of advance along the New Jersey side of the Delaware River.

Although the retreat through New York and New Jersey had shriveled rebel strength to only 3,000 men, Washington decided that the campaign of 1776 was not over. On a snowy Christmas night, the Continentals floated back across the Delaware, picked their way over roads sleeted with ice, and finally slid into Hessian–held Trenton at eight in the morning. One thousand German soldiers, still recovering from their spirited Christmas celebration and caught completely by surprise, quickly surrendered. Washington's luck held on January 3, 1777, when the Continentals defeated British troops on the outskirts of Princeton, New Jersey.

During the winter of 1776–1777 the British lost more than battles: they alienated the very civilians whose loyalties they had hoped to ensure. In New York City the presence of the main body of the British army brought shortages of food and housing and caused constant friction between soldiers and city dwellers. In the New Jersey countryside still held by the Hessians, the situation was more desperate. Forced to live off the land, the Germans aroused resentment among local farmers by seizing "hay, oats, Indian corn, cattle, and horses, which were never or but very seldom paid for," as one loyalist admitted. The Hessians ransacked and destroyed homes and churches; they kidnapped and raped young women.

Many neutrals and loyalists who had had enough of the king's soldiers now took their allegiance elsewhere. Bands of **militia** on Long Island, along the Hudson River, and all over New Jersey rallied to support the Continentals.

> **militia** local defense band of civilians comprising men between the ages of 16 and 65 whose military training consisted only of occasional gatherings known as musters.

Capturing Philadelphia >> By the summer of 1777 General Howe had decided to goad the Americans into battle by capturing Philadelphia. In early August the redcoats disembarked on the Maryland shore and headed for Philadelphia. Washington engaged Howe twice—in September at Brandywine Creek and in October in an early dawn attack at Germantown— but both times the rebels were beaten back. He had been unable to prevent the British occupation of Philadelphia.

But in Philadelphia, as in New York, British occupation created hostility as the flood of troops jacked up prices for food, fuel, and housing. Philadelphians complained of redcoats looting their shops, trampling their gardens, and harassing them on the streets.

Even worse, the British march through Maryland and Pennsylvania had outraged civilians, who fled before the army and then returned to find their homes and barns bare, their crops and livestock gone. Everywhere Howe's men went in the middle states, they left in their wake Americans with compelling reasons to support the rebels. Worst of all, just days after Howe marched his occupying army into Philadelphia in the fall of 1777, another British commander in North America surrendered his entire army to rebel forces at Saratoga, New York.

Disaster for the British at Saratoga >> The calamity that befell the British at Saratoga was the doing of a glory—mongering general, John "Gentleman Johnny" Burgoyne. After his superior officer, Sir Guy Carleton, bungled a drive into New York in 1776, Burgoyne won approval to command another attack from Canada. The following summer he set out from Quebec with a force of 9,500 redcoats, 2,000 women and children, and a baggage train that included the commander's silver dining service, his dress uniforms, and numerous cases of champagne. As Burgoyne's entourage lumbered southward, a handful of Continentals and a horde of New England militia assembled several miles below Saratoga at Bemis Heights under the command of General Horatio Gates.

On September 19 Gates's rebel scouts, nested high in the trees, spied the glittering bayonets of Burgoyne's approaching force. Benedict Arnold, a brave young officer, led several thousand rebels into battle at a clearing at Freeman's Farm. At the end of the day British reinforcements finally pushed the rebels back from a battlefield piled high with the bodies of soldiers from both sides. Burgoyne tried to flee to Canada but got no farther than Saratoga, where he surrendered his army to Gates on October 17.

Saratoga changed everything. With Burgoyne's surrender, the rebels succeeded in convincing France that, with a little help, the Americans might well reap the fruits of victory.

✔ **REVIEW**

What challenges did the Continental Army face between 1775 and 1777?

THE TURNING POINT

France had been waiting for revenge against Britain ever since its humiliating defeat in the Seven Years' War. And for some years a scheme for evening the score had been taking shape in the mind of the French foreign minister, Charles Gravier de Vergennes. He reckoned that France might turn discontented colonials into willing allies against Britain.

The American Revolution as a Global War >> Vergennes wanted to make certain that the rift between Britain and its colonies would not be reconciled and that the rebels in America stood a fighting chance. Although France had been secretly supplying the Continental Army with guns and ammunition since the spring of 1776, Vergennes would go no further than covert assistance.

Congress approached their former French enemies with equal caution. Would France, the leading Catholic monarchy in Europe, make common cause with the republican rebels? A few years earlier American colonials had fought against the French in Canada; only recently they had renounced a king, and for centuries they had overwhelmingly adhered to Protestantism.

But the string of defeats dealt the Continental Army during 1776 convinced Congress that they needed the French. In November Congress appointed a three—member commission to negotiate not only aid from France but also a formal alliance. Its senior member was Benjamin Franklin, who enchanted all

>> The French public's infatuation with Benjamin Franklin knew no bounds. They particularly delighted in his rustic dress and styled him a representative of "frontier" America. He appears in this guise on a terra cotta medallion created in 1777 by Jean-Baptiste Nini, an Italian artist living in Paris.

of Paris when he arrived sporting a simple fur cap and a pair of spectacles. Hailing Franklin as a homespun sage, Parisians stamped his face on everything from the top of snuffboxes to the bottom of chamber pots.

Still, Franklin understood that mere popularity could not produce the alliance sought by Congress. It was only news that Britain had surrendered an entire army at Saratoga that convinced Vergennes that the rebels could actually win. In February 1778 France signed a treaty of commerce and friendship and a treaty of alliance, which Congress approved in May. Under the terms of the treaties, both parties agreed to accept nothing short of independence for America. The alliance left the British no choice other than to declare war on France. Less than a year later Spain joined France, hoping to recover territory lost to England in earlier wars.

Winding Down the War in the North >> The Revolution widened into a global war after 1778. Preparing to fight France and Spain dictated a new British strategy in America. No longer could the British concentrate on crushing the Continental Army; instead, they would disperse their forces to fend off challenges all over the world. In May Sir Henry Clinton replaced William Howe as commander in chief and received orders to withdraw from Philadelphia to New York City.

Only 18 miles outside Philadelphia, at Valley Forge, Washington and his Continentals were assessing their own situation. Some 11,000 rebel soldiers had passed a harrowing winter in that isolated spot, starving for want of food, freezing for lack of clothing, huddling in miserable huts, and hating the British who lay 18 miles away in Philadelphia. The army also cursed their fellow citizens, for its misery resulted from congressional disorganization and civilian indifference. Congress lacked both money to pay and maintain the army and an efficient system for dispensing provisions to the troops. Most farmers and merchants preferred to supply the British, who could pay handsomely, than to do business with financially strapped Congress. What little did reach the army often was food too rancid to eat or clothing too rotten to wear. Perhaps 2,500 perished at Valley Forge, the victims of cold, hunger, and disease.

Why did civilians who supported the rebel cause allow the army to suffer? Probably because by the winter of 1777 the Continentals came mainly from social classes that received little consideration at any time. The respectable, propertied farmers and artisans who had laid siege to Boston in 1775 had stopped enlisting. Serving in their stead were single men in their teens and early 20s, some who joined the army out of desperation, others who were drafted, still others who were hired as substitutes for the affluent. The landless sons of farmers, unemployed laborers, drifters,

petty criminals, vagrants, indentured servants, slaves, even captured British and Hessian soldiers—all men with no other means and no other choice—were swept into the Continental Army. The social composition of the rebel rank and file had come to resemble that of the British army. It is the great irony of the Revolution: a war to protect liberty and property was waged by those Americans who were poorest and least free.

The beginning of spring in 1778 brought a reprieve. Supplies arrived at Valley Forge, and so did a fellow calling himself Baron von Steuben, a penniless Prussian soldier of fortune. Although Washington's men had shown spirit and resilience ever since Trenton, they still lacked discipline and training. Those defects and more von Steuben began to remedy. Barking orders and spewing curses in German and French, the baron (and his translators) drilled the rebel regiments to march in formation and to handle their bayonets like proper Prussian soldiers. By the summer of 1778 morale had rebounded.

Spoiling for action after their long winter, Washington's army, now numbering nearly 13,500, harassed Clinton's army as it marched overland from Philadelphia to New York. On June 28 at Monmouth Courthouse, a long, confused battle ended in a draw. After both armies retired for the night, Clinton's forces slipped away to safety in New York City. Washington pursued, but he lacked the numbers to launch an all-out assault on New York City.

During the two hard winters that followed, resentments mounted among the rank and file over spoiled food, inadequate clothing, and arrears in pay. The army retaliated with **mutinies.** Between 1779 and 1780, officers managed to quell uprisings in three New England regiments.

> **mutiny** refusal of rank-and-file soldiers to follow the commands of their superior officers.

But in January 1781 both the Pennsylvania and the New Jersey lines mutinied outright and marched on Philadelphia, where Congress had reconvened. Order returned only after Congress promised back pay and provisions and Washington put two ringleaders in front of a firing squad.

War in the West >> The battles between Washington's Continentals and the British made the war in the West seem, by comparison, a sideshow of attacks and counterattacks that settled little. American fighters, such as George Rogers Clark, captured outposts such as Kaskaskia and Vincennes without materially affecting the outcome of the war. Yet the conflict sparked a tremendous upheaval in the West, both from the dislocations of war and from the disease that spread in war's wake.

The disruptions were so widespread because the "War for Independence" had also become a war involving the

THE ALLIES._ *Par nobile Fratrum!*

<< While both sides in the Revolution sought Indian allies, the American rebels sensationalized the efforts of British leaders to enlist Native Americans. Stories and images featuring British and Indian cruelty to American victims stirred debate even back in Britain. In this 1780 cartoon printed in London, the prime minister, Lord North, joins with Indians in feasting on a child, an act of cannibalism that revolts even a dog. The archbishop of York approaches, hypocritically promising to make God's ways "known upon Earth" as his porter, professing that "we are hellish good Christians," carries boxes of scalping knives, tomahawks, and crucifixes. This propaganda fueled the hatred of Indians by Americans who expanded westward after the Revolution.

imperial powers of Britain, France, and Spain. Those European powers and the United States pressed Indian tribes to become allies and attacked them when they did not. Caught in the crossfire, some Indian nations were pushed to the brink of their own civil war, splitting into pro–American or pro–British factions.

Indians understood that the pressures of war always threatened to deprive them of their homelands. "You are drawing so close to us that we can almost hear the noise of your axes felling our Trees," one Shawnee told the Americans. Thousands fled the raids and counter–raids, while whole villages relocated. Hundreds made their way even beyond the Mississippi, to seek shelter in territory claimed by Spain.

The political instability was vastly compounded by a smallpox epidemic that broke out first among American troops besieging Quebec in 1775. The disease soon spread to Washington's troops in New England and then south along the coast; it eventually reached New Orleans and leapt to Mexico City by the autumn of 1779. From New Orleans it spread via fur traders up the Mississippi River and across the central plains, and from New Spain northward as well. By the time the pandemic burned out in 1782, it had felled over 130,000. By contrast, the Revolutionary War caused the deaths of some 8,000 soldiers while fighting in battle and another 13,000 from disease, including the mortality from smallpox.

The Home Front in the North >> By 1779 most northern civilians along the eastern seaboard gained a respite from the war. But disease and military demands disrupted family economies throughout the countryside. The seasons of intense fighting drew men off into military service just when their labor was most needed on family farms. Wives and daughters were left

to assume the work of husbands and sons while coping with loneliness, anxiety, and grief. Often enough the disruptions, flight, and loss of family members left lasting scars. Two years after she fled before Burgoyne's advance into upstate New York, Ann Eliza Bleecker confessed to a friend, "I muse so long on the dead until I am unfit for the company of the living."

Despite these hardships, many women vigorously supported the revolutionary cause in a variety of ways. The Daughters of Liberty joined in harassing those who opposed the rebel cause. One outspoken loyalist found himself surrounded by angry women who stripped off his shirt, covered him with molasses, and plastered him with flower petals. In more genteel fashion, groups of well–to–do women collected not only money but also medicines, food, and pewter to melt for bullets.

✓ **REVIEW**

How did the Revolution become a global war, and what were conditions like for both soldiers and civilians?

THE STRUGGLE IN THE SOUTH

By the autumn of 1778 the British had come to believe that their most vital aim was to regain their colonies in the mainland South. The Chesapeake and the Carolinas were more profitable to the empire and more strategically important, being so much closer to rich British sugar islands in the West Indies. Inspired by this new "southern strategy," Clinton dispatched forces to the Caribbean and Florida. In addition, the British laid plans for a new offensive drive into the Carolinas and Virginia.

English politicians and generals believed that the war could be won in the South. Loyalists were numerous, they believed, especially in the backcountry, where resentment of the seaboard, a rebel stronghold, would breed readiness among frontier folk to take up arms for the king at the first show of British force. And southern rebels—especially the vulnerable planters along the coast—could not afford to turn their guns away from their slaves. So, at least, the British theorized. All that was needed, they concluded, was for the British army to establish a beachhead in the South and then, in league with loyalists, drive northward, pacifying the population while pressing up the coast.

The Siege of Charleston >> The southern strategy worked well for a short time in a small place.

In November 1778 Clinton sent 3,500 troops to Savannah, Georgia. The resistance in the tiny colony quickly collapsed, and a large number of loyalists turned out to help the British. Encouraged by that success, the British moved on to South Carolina.

During the last days of 1779 an expedition under Clinton himself set sail from New York City. Landing off the Georgia coast, his troops mucked through the swamps to the peninsula lying between the Ashley and Cooper Rivers. At the tip of that neck of land stood Charleston, and the British began to lay siege. By then an unseasonably warm spring had set in, making the area a heaven for mosquitoes and a hell for human beings. Sweltering and swatting, redcoats weighted down in

their woolen uniforms inched their siegeworks toward the city. By early May Clinton's army had closed in, and British shelling was setting fire to houses within the city. On May 12 Charleston surrendered.

Clinton sailed back to New York at the end of June 1780, leaving behind 8,300 redcoats to carry the British offensive northward to Virginia. The man charged with leading that campaign was his ambitious and able subordinate Charles, Lord Cornwallis.

The Partisan Struggle in the South >> Cornwallis's task in the Carolinas was complicated by the bitter animosity between rebels and loyalists there. Many Carolinians had taken sides years before Clinton's conquest of Charleston. In the summer and fall of 1775 the supporters of Congress and the new South Carolina revolutionary government mobbed, tortured, and imprisoned supporters of the king in the backcountry. These attacks only hardened loyalist

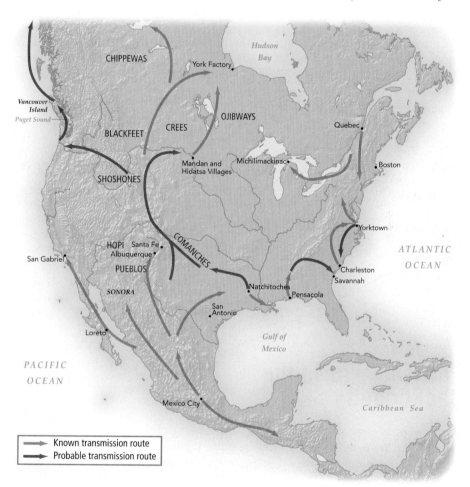

MAP 7.3: THE SMALLPOX PANDEMIC, 1775–1782

Smallpox spread across North America beginning late in 1775 as American forces attacked the city of Quebec in Canada. The routes of transmission give only a rough idea of the disease's impact, as it moved down the eastern seaboard and around the Gulf of Mexico, and then penetrated the interior, where the scattered surviving data make the pandemic harder to track. But the ravages of smallpox, combined with the disruptions sparked by the western raids of the Revolutionary War, placed severe stress on Indian peoples all across the continent. *How can you tell that smallpox was a European disease? Where are the two major points from which the disease first spreads?*

resolve: roving bands seized ammunition, broke their leaders out of jail, and besieged rebel outposts. But within a matter of months, a combined force of rebel militias from the coast and the frontier managed to defeat loyalist forces in the backcountry.

With the fall of Charleston in 1780 the loyalist movement on the frontier returned to life. Out of loyalist vengefulness and rebel desperation issued the brutal civil war that seared the southern backcountry after 1780. Neighbors and even family members fought and killed one another as members of roaming rebel and tory militias. The intensity of **partisan warfare** in the backcountry produced unprecedented destruction. All of society, observed one minister, "seems to be at an end. Every person keeps close on his own plantation. Robberies and murders are often committed on the public roads.... Poverty, want, and hardship appear in almost every countenance."

partisan warfare armed clashes among political rivals, typically involving guerrilla fighting and the violent intimidation of civilians by militias.

Cornwallis, when confronted with the chaos, erred fatally. He did nothing to stop his loyalist allies or his own troops from mistreating civilians. A Carolina loyalist admitted that "the lower sort of People, who were in many parts originally attached to the British Government, have suffered so severely...that Great Britain has now a hundred enemies, where it had one before."

A growing number of civilians outraged by the king's men cast their lot with the rebels. That upsurge of popular support enabled Francis Marion, the "Swamp Fox," and his band of white and black raiders to cut British lines of communication between Charleston and the interior. It mobilized the "over–the–mountain men," a rebel militia in western Carolina, who claimed victory at the Battle of King's Mountain in October

witness
Partisan War in the Backcountry

"I was invited by some of my comrades to go and see some of the prisoners. We went to where six were standing together. Some discussion was taking place, I heard some of our men cry out, 'Remember Buford' [a rebel soldier killed by loyalists], and the prisoners were immediately hewed to pieces with broadswords. At first I bore the scene without any emotion, but upon a moment's reflection, I felt such horror as I never felt before nor have since . . ."

—Moses Hall, *Description of a Battle's Aftermath in North Carolina* (February 1781)

1780. By the end of 1780 these successes had persuaded most civilians that only the rebels could restore order.

If rebel fortunes prospered in the partisan struggle, they faltered in the conventional warfare being waged at the same time in the South. In August 1780 the Continentals commanded by Horatio Gates lost a major engagement to the British force at Camden, South Carolina. In the fall of 1780 Congress replaced Gates with Washington's candidate for the southern command, Nathanael Greene, an energetic, 38–year–old Rhode Islander and a veteran of the northern campaigns.

Greene Takes Command >> Greene bore out Washington's confidence by grasping the military situation in the South. He understood the needs of his 1,400 hungry, ragged, and demoralized troops and instructed von Steuben to lobby Virginia for food and clothing. He understood the importance of the rebel militias and sent Lieutenant Colonel Henry "Light horse Harry" Lee to assist Marion's raids. He understood the weariness of southern civilians and prevented his men from plundering the countryside.

Above all, Greene understood that his forces could never hold the field against the whole British army. That led him to break the first rule of conventional warfare: he divided his army. In December 1780 he dispatched to western South Carolina a detachment of 600 men under the command of Brigadier General Daniel Morgan of Virginia.

Back at the British camp Cornwallis worried that Morgan and his rebels, if left unchecked, might rally the entire backcountry against the British. However, Cornwallis reckoned that he could not commit his entire army to the pursuit of Morgan's men, for then Greene and his troops might retake Charleston. The only solution, unconventional to be sure, was for Cornwallis to divide his army. That he did, sending Lieutenant Colonel Banastre Tarleton and 1,100 men west after Morgan. Cornwallis had played right into Greene's hands: the rebel troops might be able to defeat a British army split into two pieces. For two weeks Morgan led Tarleton's troops on a breakneck chase across the Carolina countryside. In January 1781 at an open meadow called Cowpens, Morgan routed Tarleton's force.

Now Cornwallis took up the chase. Morgan and Greene joined forces and agreed to keep going north until the British army wore out. Cornwallis finally stopped at Hillsboro, North Carolina, but few local loyalists responded to his call for reinforcements. To ensure that loyalist ranks remained thin, Greene decided to make a show of force near the tiny village of Guilford Courthouse. On a brisk March day the two

MAP 7.4: THE FIGHTING IN THE SOUTH, 1780–1781

In December 1780 Nathanael Greene made the crucial decision to split his army, sending Daniel Morgan west, where he defeated the pursuing Banastre Tarleton at Cowpens. Meanwhile, Greene regrouped and replenished at Cheraw, keeping Cornwallis off balance with a raid (*dotted line*) toward Charleston and the coast. Then, with Cornwallis in hot pursuit, Greene and Morgan rejoined at Salisbury, retreating into Virginia. Cornwallis was worn down in this vain pursuit and lost three-quarters of the troops he began with before finally abandoning the Carolina campaign.

What was General Nathanael Greene's risky strategy, according to the text? And how does the map show that strategy?

sides joined battle, each sustaining severe casualties before Greene was forced to retreat. But the high cost of victory convinced Cornwallis that he could not put down the rebellion in the Carolinas.

Although Nathanael Greene's command provided the Continentals with effective leadership in the South, it was the resilience of rebel militias that thwarted the British offensive in the Carolinas. Many Continental Army officers complained about the militia's lack of discipline, its habit of melting away when home-sickness set in or harvest approached, and its record of cowardice under fire in conventional engagements. But when set the task of ambushing supply trains and dispatch riders, harrying bands of local loyalists, or making forays against isolated British outposts, the militia came through. Many southern civilians refused to join the British or to provide the redcoats with

food and information because they knew that once the British army left their neighborhoods, the rebel militia would always be back. The Continental Army in the South lost many conventional battles, but the militia kept the British from restoring political control over the backcountry.

African Americans in the Age of Revolution >> The British also lost in the Carolinas because they did not seek greater support from those southerners who would have fought for liberty with the British: African American slaves.

Black Americans, virtually all in bondage, made up one-third of the population between Delaware and Georgia. Since the beginning of the resistance to Britain, white southerners had worried that the watchwords of liberty and equality would spread to the slave quarters. Gripped by the fear of slave rebellion, southern revolutionaries began to take precautions. Marylanders disarmed black inhabitants and issued extra guns to the white militia. Charlestonians hanged and then burned the body of Thomas Jeremiah, a free black who was convicted of spreading the word to others that the British "were coming to help the poor Negroes."

Southern whites fully expected the British to turn slave rebelliousness to their strategic advantage. As early as 1775 Virginia's royal governor, Lord Dunmore, confirmed white fears by offering to free any slave who joined the British. When Clinton invaded the South in 1779 he renewed that offer. According to Janet Schaw, an Englishwoman visiting her brother's North Carolina plantation, the neighbors had heard that loyalists were "promising every Negro that would murder his master and family he should have his Master's plantation" and that "the Negroes have got it amongst them and believe it to be true."

But in Britain there was overwhelming opposition to organizing support among African Americans. British leaders dismissed Dunmore's ambitious scheme to raise a black army of 10,000 and another plan to create a sanctuary for black loyalists on the southeastern coast. Turning slaves against masters, they recognized, was not the way to retain the support of white southern loyalists.

Runaways

What is implied by the tallying of children ["girls" and "boys"] with slave women?

What is the significance of the list specifying occupations for some of the slave men?

How does the number of female runaways compare with that of males? Children with adults?

"A List of Negroes That Went Off to Dunmore," dated April 14, 1776, Library of Virginia, Richmond.

Americans in earlier centuries were inveterate listmakers, providing present-day historians with a rich trove of evidence. College students recorded the titles of books they read; ministers noted the Bible passages on which they preached; clerks kept count of church members; tax assessors enumerated household members and the rates owed and paid; probate court officers inventoried the possessions of the dead, often down to chipped crockery and broken tools. But the roster of slaves shown above is an extraordinary list, drawn up not on account of their master's death but because these 87 men, women, and children had fled their Virginia plantation, emboldened by Lord Dunmore's promise of freedom. It is impossible to know whether they ran away in small groups, stealing off over a period of several months between 1775 and 1776, or whether they ran away in larger companies within the space of a few days. But we do know that throughout Virginia, as on this plantation, women and children made up a significant percentage of the runaways.

THINKING CRITICALLY

For what purposes might the Virginia master have composed this list? Why are slave artisans so well represented among the men on this list? Why were slave women and their children willing to risk escape in such large numbers?

Even so, southern fears of insurrection made the rebels reluctant to enlist black Americans as soldiers. At first, Congress barred African Americans from the Continental Army. But as the rebels became more desperate for manpower, policy changed. Northern states actively encouraged black enlistments, and in the Upper South, some states allowed free men of color to join the army or permitted slaves to substitute for their masters.

Slaves themselves sought freedom from whichever side seemed most likely to grant it. Perhaps 10,000 slaves took up Dunmore's offer in 1775 and deserted their masters, and thousands more flocked to Clinton's forces after the fall of Charleston.

For many runaways the hope of liberation proved an illusion. Although some served the British army as laborers, spies, and soldiers, many died of disease in army camps (upward of 27,000 by one estimate) or were sold back into slavery in the West Indies. About 5,000 black soldiers served in the revolutionary army in the hope of gaining freedom. In addition, the number of runaways to the North soared during the Revolution. In total perhaps 100,000 men and women—nearly a fifth of the total slave population—attempted to escape bondage. Their odysseys to freedom took some to far–flung destinations: loyalist communities in Nova Scotia, a settlement established by the British in Sierra Leone on the West African coast, even the Botany Bay penal colony in Australia.

> ✔ **REVIEW**
>
> Why did the British fail to achieve their military and political goals in the South?

THE WORLD TURNED UPSIDE DOWN

Despite his losses in the Carolinas, Cornwallis still believed that he could score a decisive victory against the Continental Army. The theater he chose for that showdown was the Chesapeake. During the spring of 1781 he and his army joined forces along the Virginia coast with the hero of Saratoga and newly turned loyalist, Benedict Arnold. Embarrassed by debt and disgusted by Congress's shabby treatment of the Continental Army, Arnold had started exchanging rebel secrets for British money in 1779 before defecting outright in 1780. By June of 1781 Arnold and Cornwallis were fortifying a site on the tip of the peninsula formed by the York and James Rivers, a place called Yorktown.

Meanwhile, Washington and his French ally, the comte de Rochambeau, met in Connecticut to plan a major attack. Rochambeau urged a coordinated land–sea assault on the Virginia coast. Washington insisted instead on a full–scale offensive against New York City. Just when the rebel commander was about to have his way, word arrived that a French fleet under the comte de Grasse was sailing for the Chesapeake to blockade Cornwallis by sea. Washington's Continentals headed south.

Surrender at Yorktown >> By the end of September, 7,800 Frenchmen, 5,700 Continentals, and 3,200 militia had sandwiched Yorktown between the devil of an allied army and the deep blue sea of French warships. "If you cannot relieve me very soon," Cornwallis wrote to Clinton, "you must expect to hear the worst."

⌄ On September 30, 1780, a wagon bearing this two-faced effigy was drawn through the streets of Philadelphia. The effigy represents Benedict Arnold, who sits between a gallows and the devil. Note the similarities between this piece of street theater and the demonstrations mounted on Pope's Day several decades earlier, shown on page 109.

The British navy did arrive—but seven days after Cornwallis surrendered to the rebels on October 19, 1781.

It need not have ended at Yorktown, but timing made all the difference. At the end of 1781 and early in 1782 the British army received setbacks in the other theaters of the war: India, the West Indies, and Florida. The French and the Spanish were everywhere in Europe as well, gathering in the English Channel, planning a major offensive against Gibraltar. The cost of the fighting was already enormous. British leaders recognized that the rest of the empire was at stake and set about cutting their losses in America.

The Treaty of Paris, signed on September 3, 1783, was a diplomatic triumph for the American negotiators: Benjamin Franklin, John Adams, and John Jay. They dangled before Britain the possibility that a generous settlement might weaken American ties to France. The British jumped at the bait. They recognized the independence of the United States and agreed to ample boundaries for the new nation: the Mississippi River on the west, the 31st parallel on the south, and the present border of Canada on the north. American negotiators then persuaded a skeptical France to approve the treaty by arguing that, as allies, they were bound to present a united front to the British. When the French finally persuaded Spain, the third member of the alliance, to reduce its demands on Britain for territorial concessions, the treaty became an accomplished fact. The Spanish settled for Florida and Minorca, an island in the Mediterranean.

Those present at Yorktown on that clear autumn afternoon in 1781 watched as the British second-in-command to Cornwallis (who had sent word that he was "indisposed") surrendered his superior's sword. He offered the sword first, in a face-saving gesture, to the French commander Rochambeau, who politely refused and pointed to Washington. But the American commander in chief, out of a mixture of military protocol, nationalistic pride, and perhaps even wit, pointed to his second-in-command, Benjamin Lincoln.

 REVIEW

How did the United States manage to prevail in the war and in the treaty negotiations?

Some witnesses recalled that British musicians arrayed on the Yorktown green played "The World Turned Upside Down." Their recollections may have been faulty, but the story has persisted as part of the folklore of the American Revolution. The world had, it seemed, turned upside down with the coming of American independence. The colonial rebels shocked the British with their answer to the question "Would they fight?"

The answer had been yes—but on their own terms. By 1777 most propertied Americans avoided fighting in the Continental Army. Yet whenever the war reached their homes, farms, and businesses, many Americans gave their allegiance to the new nation by turning out with rifles or supplying homespun clothing, food, or ammunition. They rallied around Washington in New Jersey, Gates in upstate New York, Greene in the Carolinas. Middle-class American men fought, some from idealism, others out of self-interest, but always on their own terms, as members of the militia. These citizen-soldiers turned the world upside down by defeating professional armies.

Of course, the militia did not bear the brunt of the fighting. That responsibility fell to the Continental Army, which by 1777 drew its strength from the poorest ranks of American society. Yet even the Continentals, for all their desperation, managed to fight on their own terms. Some asserted their rights by raising mutinies, until Congress redressed their grievances. All of them, as the Baron von Steuben observed, behaved differently than European soldiers did. Americans followed orders only if the logic of commands was explained to them. The Continentals, held in contempt by most Americans, turned the world upside down by sensing their power and asserting their measure of personal independence.

Americans of African descent dared as much and more in their quests for liberty. Whether they chose to escape slavery by fighting for the British or the Continentals or by striking out on their own as runaways, their defiance, too, turned the world upside down. Among the tens of thousands of slaves who would not be mastered was one Henry Washington, a native of Africa who became the slave of George Washington in 1763. But Henry Washington made his own declaration of independence in 1776, slipping behind British lines and serving as a corporal in a black unit. Thereafter, like thousands of former slaves, he sought to build a new life elsewhere in the Atlantic world, settling first in Nova Scotia and finally in Sierra Leone. By 1800 he headed a community of former slaves who were exiled to the outskirts of that colony for their

Opinion

Would the American colonies have won their independence without the military assistance of France?

determined efforts to win republican self—government from Sierra Leone's white British rulers. Like Thomas Paine, Henry Washington believed that freedom was his only country.

In all those ways a revolutionary generation turned the world upside down. They were a diverse lot—descended from Indians, Europeans, and Africans, driven by desperation or idealism or greed—but joined, even if they did not recognize it, by their common struggle to break free from the rule of monarchs or masters. What now awaited them in the world of the new United States?

CHAPTER SUMMARY

The American Revolution brought independence to Britain's former colonies after an armed struggle that began in 1775 and concluded with the Treaty of Paris in 1783.

- When the Second Continental Congress convened in the spring of 1775, many of the delegates still hoped for reconciliation—even as they approved the creation of the Continental Army.
- The Second Continental Congress adopted the Declaration of Independence on July 4, 1776, hoping that they could count on a majority of Americans to support the Revolution.
- The British scored a string of victories in the North throughout 1776 and 1777, capturing both New York and Philadelphia.
- The British suffered a disastrous defeat at the Battle of Saratoga in October 1777, which prompted France to openly ally with the American rebels soon thereafter.
- By 1780 Britain aimed to win the war by claiming the South and captured both Savannah, Georgia, and Charleston, South Carolina.
- The Continental Army in the South, led by Nathanael Greene, foiled the British strategy, and

Cornwallis surrendered after the Battle of York—town in 1781.
- Except for the first year of fighting, the rank and file of the Continental Army was drawn from the poorest Americans, whose needs for food, clothing, and shelter were neglected by the Continental Congress.

Additional Reading

The outstanding military histories of the American Revolution are Don Higginbotham, *The War for American Independence* (1971); and Robert Middlekauff, *The Glorious Cause, 1763 to 1789* (1982). Both provide a wealth of detail about battles, contending armies, and the role of militias and civilian populations in the fighting. For a compelling treatment of the lives of soldiers in the Continental Army, read Caroline Cox, *A Proper Sense of Honor* (2004); and to become better acquainted with their commander—in—chief, turn to *His Excellency: George Washington* (2004) by Joseph Ellis. Colin Calloway, *The American Revolution in Indian Country* (1995), offers a fine summary of the role of American Indians in that conflict. Benjamin Franklin's efforts to secure an alliance with France come in for lively chronicling by Stacy Schiff in *A Great Improvisation* (2005). Impressive interpretations of the war's impact on American society include Charles Royster, *A Revolutionary People at War* (1979); and John Shy, *A People Numerous and Armed* (1976). Sylvia Frey offers a thoughtful history of African Americans during this era in *Water from the Rock* (1991); and Cassandra Pybus, *Epic Journeys of Freedom* (2006), recounts the experiences of runaway slaves who seized on the wartime crisis to gain liberty. The role of women in revolutionary America receives excellent coverage in Carol Berkin, *Revolutionary Mothers* (2005); and in Mary Beth Norton's classic study, *Liberty's Daughters* (1980).

Significant Events

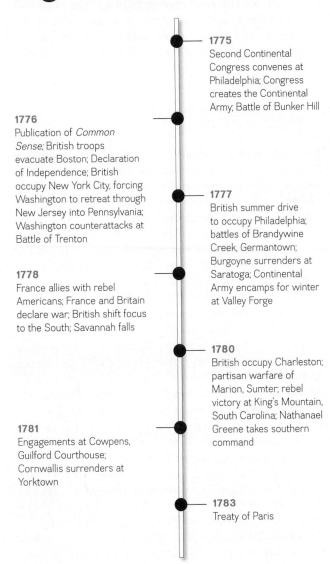

1775
Second Continental Congress convenes at Philadelphia; Congress creates the Continental Army; Battle of Bunker Hill

1776
Publication of *Common Sense*; British troops evacuate Boston; Declaration of Independence; British occupy New York City, forcing Washington to retreat through New Jersey into Pennsylvania; Washington counterattacks at Battle of Trenton

1777
British summer drive to occupy Philadelphia; battles of Brandywine Creek, Germantown; Burgoyne surrenders at Saratoga; Continental Army encamps for winter at Valley Forge

1778
France allies with rebel Americans; France and Britain declare war; British shift focus to the South; Savannah falls

1780
British occupy Charleston; partisan warfare of Marion, Sumter; rebel victory at King's Mountain, South Carolina; Nathanael Greene takes southern command

1781
Engagements at Cowpens, Guilford Courthouse; Cornwallis surrenders at Yorktown

1783
Treaty of Paris

8 Crisis and Constitution

1776–1789

South Carolina's low country supplies the background for this portrait of a wealthy Charleston couple, John Purves and his wife, Anne Pritchard Purves. John saw military service in both the state militia and the Continental Army; Anne, with her classically draped dress, evokes the goddess of Liberty. What do you make of the expressions on the couple's faces?

>> An American Story

"THESE UNITED STATES"

"I am not a Virginian, but an American," Patrick Henry declared in the Virginia House of Burgesses. Most likely he was lying. Certainly no one listening took him seriously, for the newly independent colonists did not identify themselves as members of a nation. They would have said, as did Thomas Jefferson, "Virginia, Sir, is my country." Or as John Adams wrote to another native son, "Massachusetts is our country." Jefferson and Adams were men of wide political vision and experience: both were leaders in the Continental Congress and more inclined than most to think nationally. But like other members of the revolutionary generation, they identified deeply with their home states and even more deeply with their home counties and towns.

It followed that allegiance to the states, not the Union, determined the shape of the first republican political experiments.

For a decade after independence the revolutionaries were less committed to creating an American nation than to organizing 13 separate state republics. The Declaration of Independence referred explicitly not to the United States but to these United States. It envisioned not one republic so much as a federation of 13.

Only when peace was restored during the decade of the 1780s were Americans forced to face some unanswered questions raised by their revolution. The Declaration proclaimed that these "free and independent states" had "full power to levy war, conclude peace, contract alliances, establish commerce." Did that mean that New Jersey could sign a trade agreement with France, excluding the other states? If the United States were to be more than a loose federation, how could it assert power on a national scale? Similarly, American borderlands to the west presented problems. If these territories were settled by Americans, would they eventually join the United States? Go their own ways as independent nations? Become new colonies of Spain or England?

Such problems were more than political; they were rooted in social realities. For a political union to succeed, the inhabitants of 13 separate states had to start thinking of themselves as Americans. When it came right down to it, what united a Vermont farmer working his rocky fields and a South Carolina gentleman presiding over a vast rice plantation? What bonds existed between a Kentuckian rafting the Ohio River and a Salem merchant sailing to China for porcelain?

And in a society in which all citizens were said to be "created equal," social inequalities had to be confronted. How could women participate in the Revolution's bid for freedom if they were not free to vote or to hold property? How would free or enslaved African Americans live in a republic based on equality? How could black Americans feel a bond with white Americans when so often the only existing bonds had been forged with chains?

To such questions there were no final answers in 1781. There was ferment, excitement, and experimentation as 13 states each sought to create their governments anew; as Americans—or rather, Virginians and New Yorkers and Georgians and citizens of other countries—began to imagine how the revolutionary virtue of equality might transform their societies. But as the decade progressed, the sense of crisis deepened. <<

What's to Come

REPUBLICAN EXPERIMENTS

constitution framework of government establishing the contract between rulers and ruled.

After independence was declared in July 1776, many of America's best political minds turned to draw up **constitutions** for their individual states. In truth, the state constitutions were crucial republican experiments, the first efforts at establishing a government of and by the people. All the revolutionaries agreed that the people—not a king or a few privileged aristocrats—should rule. Yet they were equally certain that republican governments were best suited to small territories. They believed that the new United States was too sprawling and its people too diverse to be safely consolidated into a single national republic. They feared, too, that the government of a

⋏ Americans responded to independence with rituals of "killing the king," as did this New York crowd in 1776, which is pulling down a statue of George III. Americans also expressed their mistrust of monarchs by establishing state governments with weak executive branches.

large republic would inevitably grow indifferent to popular concerns, being distant from many of its citizens. Without being under the watchful eye of the people, representatives would become less accountable to the electorate and turn tyrannical. A federation of small state republics, they reasoned, would stand a far better chance of enduring.

The State Constitutions >> The new state constitutions retained the basic form of their old colonial governments, most providing for a governor and a bicameral legislature. But most states dramatically changed the balance of power among the different branches of government.

From the republican perspective in 1776, the greatest problem of any government lay in curbing executive power. What had driven Americans into rebellion was the abuse of authority by the king and his appointed officials. To ensure that the executive could never again threaten popular liberty, the new states either accorded almost no power to their governors or abolished that office. The governors had no authority to convene or dissolve the legislature. They could not veto the legislatures' laws, grant land, or erect courts. Most important, governors had few powers to appoint other state officials. All these limits were designed to deprive the executive of any patronage or other form of influence over the legislature.

What the state governors lost, the legislatures gained. To ensure that those powerful legislatures truly represented the will of the people, the new state constitutions called for annual elections and required candidates for the legislature to live in the district they represented. Many states even asserted the right of voters to instruct the men elected to office how to vote

on specific issues. Although no state granted universal manhood suffrage, most reduced the amount of property required of qualified voters. Finally, state supreme courts were also either elected by the legislatures or appointed by an elected governor.

With all power vested in popular assemblies, a majority of voters within a state could do whatever they wanted, unchecked by governors or courts—which opened the door for legislatures to turn as tyrannical as governors. But the revolutionaries brushed that prospect aside: republican theory assured them that the people possessed a generous share of civic virtue, the capacity for selfless pursuit of the general welfare.

In an equally momentous change, the revolutionaries insisted on written state constitutions. Whenever government appeared to exceed the limits of its authority, Americans wanted to have at hand the written contract between rulers and ruled. When eighteenth-century Englishmen used the word *constitution*, they meant the existing arrangement of government—not an actual document but a collection of parliamentary laws, customs, and precedents. But Americans believed that a constitution should be a written code that stood apart from and above government, a yardstick against which the people measured the performance of their rulers. After all, they reasoned, if Britain's constitution had been written down, available for all to consult, would American rights have been violated?

From Congress to Confederation >> While Americans lavished attention on their state constitutions, the national government nearly languished during the decade after 1776. With the coming of independence the Second Continental Congress conducted the common business of the federated states. It created and maintained the Continental Army, issued currency, and negotiated with foreign powers.

Although Congress acted as a central government by common consent, it lacked any legal basis for its authority. To redress that need, in July 1776 Congress appointed a committee to draft a constitution for a national government. The urgent business of waging the war made for delay, but Congress approved the first national constitution in November 1777. It took four more years—until February 1781—for all of the states to ratify these Articles of Confederation.

The Articles of Confederation provided for a government by a national legislature—essentially a continuation of the Second Continental Congress. That body had the authority to declare war and make peace, conduct diplomacy, regulate Indian affairs, appoint military and naval officers, and requisition men from the states. In affairs of finance it could coin money and issue paper currency. Extensive as these responsibilities were, Congress could not levy taxes or even regulate trade. The crucial power of the purse rested entirely with the states, as did the final power to make and execute laws. Even worse, the national government had no distinct executive branch. Congressional committees, constantly changing in their membership, not only had to make laws but had to administer and enforce them as well.

Those weaknesses appear more evident in hindsight. For Congress in 1777 it was no easy task to frame a new government in the midst of a war. And most American leaders in the 1770s had given little thought to federalism, the means by which political power could be divided among the states and the national government. In any case, creating a strong national government would have antagonized many Americans, who after all had just rebelled against the distant, centralized authority of Britain's king and Parliament.

Guided by republican political theory and by their colonial experience, American revolutionaries created a loose confederation of 13 independent state republics under a nearly powerless national government. They succeeded so well that the United States almost failed to survive its first decade of independence. The problem was that lessons from the colonial past were not always useful guides to postwar realities. Only when events forced Americans to think nationally did they begin to consider the possibility of reinventing "these United States"—this time under the yoke of a truly federal republic.

REVIEW

What political concerns shaped the first constitutions?

THE TEMPTATIONS OF PEACE

The surrender of Cornwallis at Yorktown in 1781 marked the end of military crisis in America. But as the threat from Britain receded, so did the source of American unity. The many differences among Americans, most of which lay submerged during the struggle for independence, surfaced in full force. Those domestic divisions, combined with challenges to the new nation from Britain and Spain, created conflicts that neither the states nor the national government proved equal to handling.

⌃ As the stumps dotting the landscape indicate, western farmers first sought to "improve" their acreage by felling trees. But their dwellings were far less substantial than those depicted in this idealized sketch of an "American New Cleared Farm." And although some Indians guided parties of whites into the West, as shown in the foreground, more often they resisted white encroachment. For that reason dogs, here perched placidly in canoes, were trained to alert their white masters to the approach of Indians.

The Temptations of the West >> The greatest opportunities and the greatest problems for postwar Americans awaited in the rapidly expanding West. With the boundary of the new United States now set at the Mississippi River, more settlers spilled across the Appalachians, planting farmsteads and towns throughout Ohio, Kentucky, and Tennessee. By 1790 places that had been almost uninhabited by whites in 1760 held more than 2.25 million people, one-third of the nation's population.

After the Revolution, as before, western settlement fostered intense conflict. American claims that its territory stretched all the way to the Mississippi were by no means taken for granted by European and Indian powers. The West also confronted Americans with questions about their own national identity: Would the newly settled territories enter the nation as states on an equal footing with the original 13 states? Would they be ruled as dependent colonies? The fate of the West, in other words, constituted a crucial test of whether "these" United States could grow and still remain united.

Foreign Intrigues >> Both the British from their base in Canada and the Spanish in Florida and Louisiana hoped to chisel away at American borders. Their considerable success in the 1780s exposed the weakness of Confederation diplomacy.

Before the ink was dry on the Treaty of Paris, Britain's ministers were secretly instructing Canadians to maintain their forts and trading posts inside the United States' northwestern frontier. They reckoned—

correctly—that with the Continental Army disbanded, the Confederation could not force the British to withdraw.

The British also made mischief along the Confederation's northern borders, mainly with Vermont. For decades Ethan Allen and his Green Mountain Boys had waged a war of nerves with neighboring New York, which claimed Vermont as part of its territory. After the Revolution the British tried to woo Vermont into their empire as a province of Canada, a flirtation that pressured Congress into granting Vermont statehood in 1791.

The loyalty of the southwestern frontier was even less certain. By 1790 more than 100,000 settlers had poured through the Cumberland Gap to reach Kentucky and Tennessee. But the commercial possibilities of the region depended entirely on access to the Mississippi and the port of New Orleans, since it was far too costly to ship southwestern produce over the rough trails east across the Appalachians. And the Mississippi route was still dominated by the Spanish, who controlled Louisiana as well as forts along western Mississippi shores as far north as St. Louis. The Spanish, seeing their opportunity, closed the Mississippi to American navigation in 1784. That action prompted serious talk among southwesterners about seceding from the United States and joining Spain's empire.

The Spanish also tried to strengthen their hold on North America by making common cause with the Indians. Of particular concern to both groups was protecting Spanish Florida from the encroachment of American settlers filtering south from Georgia. Florida's governor complained that those backwoods folk were "distinguished from savages only in their color, language, and the superiority of their depraved cunning and untrustworthiness." So Spanish colonial officials responded eagerly to the overtures of Alexander McGillivray, a young Indian leader whose mother was of French–Creek descent and whose father was a Scots trader. His efforts brought about a treaty of alliance between the Creeks and the Spanish in 1784, quickly followed by similar alliances with the Choctaws and the Chickasaws.

MAP 8.1: WESTERN LAND CLAIMS, 1782–1802

The Confederation's settlement of conflicting western land claims was an achievement essential to the consolidation of political union. Some states asserted that their original charters extended their western borders to the Mississippi River. A few states, such as Virginia, claimed western borders on the Pacific Ocean. *Which states claimed western lands that they eventually ceded to the Confederation?*

Disputes among the States

>> As if foreign intrigues were not divisive enough, the states continued to argue among themselves over western land claims. The old royal charters for some colonies had extended their boundaries all the way to the Mississippi and beyond. (See Map 8.1). But the charters were often vague, granting both Massachusetts and Virginia, for example, undisputed possession of present–day Wisconsin. In contrast, other charters

limited state boundaries to within a few hundred miles of the Atlantic coast. **"Landed" states** such as Virginia wanted to secure control over the large territory granted by their charters. **"Landless" states** (which included Maryland, Delaware, Pennsylvania, Rhode Island, and New Jersey) called on Congress to restrict the boundaries of landed states and to convert western lands into a domain administered by the Confederation.

landed states and landless states some of the 13 colonies that became the United States had originally been granted land whose western boundaries were vague or overlapped the land granted to other colonies. During the Confederation period, the so-called "landless" states had boundaries that were firmly drawn on all sides, such as Maryland and New Jersey. "Landed" states possessed grants whose western boundaries were not fixed.

The landless states lost the opening round of the contest over ownership of the West. The Articles of Confederation acknowledged the old charter claims of the landed states. Then Maryland, one of the smallest landless states, retaliated by refusing to ratify the Articles. Since every state had to approve the Articles before they were formally accepted, the fate of the United States hung in the balance. One by one the landed states relented. The last holdout, Virginia, in January 1781 ceded its charter rights to land north of the Ohio River.

The More Democratic West >> An even greater source of contention concerned the sort of men westerners elected to political office. The state legislatures of the 1780s were both larger and more democratic in their membership than the old colonial assemblies were. Before the Revolution no more than a fifth of the men serving in the assemblies were middle-class farmers or artisans; government was almost exclusively the domain of the wealthiest merchants, lawyers, and planters. After the Revolution twice as many state legislators were men of moderate wealth. The shift was more marked in the North, where middle-class men predominated among representatives. But in every state some men of modest means, humble background, and little formal education attained political power.

State legislatures became more democratic in membership mainly because as backcountry districts grew, so did the number of their representatives. Since western districts tended to be less developed economically and culturally, their leading men were less rich and cultivated than the seaboard elite.

But many eastern republican gentlemen, while endorsing government by popular consent, doubted whether ordinary people were fit to rule. The problem, they contended, was that the new western legislators concerned themselves only with the narrow interests of their constituents, not with the good of the whole state. As Ezra Stiles, the president of Yale College, observed, the new breed of politicians were those with "the all-prevailing popular talent of coaxing and flattering," who "whenever a bill is read in the legislature ...instantly thinks how it will affect his constituents." And if state legislatures could not rise above petty bickering and narrow self-interest, how long would it be before civic virtue and a concern for the general welfare simply withered away?

The Northwest Territory >> Such fears of "democratic excess" also influenced policy when Congress debated what to do with the **Northwest Territory.** Carved out of the land ceded by the states to the national government, the Northwest Territory comprised the present-day states of Ohio, Indiana, Illinois, Michigan, and Wisconsin. With so many white settlers moving into these lands, Congress dealt with the issue of expansion by adopting three ordinances.

Northwest Territory present-day states of Ohio, Indiana, Illinois, Michigan, and Wisconsin.

The first, drafted by Thomas Jefferson in 1784, divided the Northwest Territory into 10 states, each to be admitted to the Union on equal terms as soon as its population equaled that in any of the existing states. In the meantime, Jefferson provided for democratic self-government of the territory by all free adult males. A second ordinance of 1785 set up an efficient mechanism for dividing and selling public lands. The Northwest Territory was surveyed into townships of six miles square. Each township then was divided into 36 lots of one square mile, or 640 acres.

Congress waited in vain for buyers to flock to the land offices it established. The cost of even a single lot—$640—was too steep for most farmers. Disappointed by the shortage of buyers and desperate for money, Congress finally accepted a proposition submitted by a private company of land speculators that offered to buy some 6 million acres in present-day southeastern Ohio. That several members of Congress numbered among the company's stockholders no doubt added to enthusiasm for the deal.

The transaction concluded, Congress calmed the speculators' worries that incoming settlers might enjoy too much self-government by scrapping Jefferson's democratic design and substituting the Northwest Ordinance of 1787. That ordinance provided for a period in which Congress held sway in the territory through its appointees—a governor, a secretary, and three judges. When the population reached 5,000 free adult males a legislature was to be established, although its laws required the governor's approval. A representative could sit in Congress but had no vote. When the population reached 60,000 the inhabitants might apply for statehood, and the whole Northwest Territory was to be divided into not less than three or more than five states. The ordinance outlawed slavery

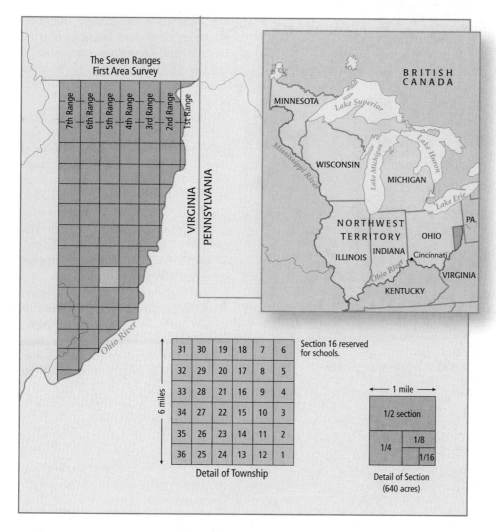

MAP 8.2: THE ORDINANCE OF 1785

Surveyors entered the Northwest Territory in September 1785, imposing on the land regular grids of six square miles to define new townships, as shown on this range map of a portion of Ohio. Farmers purchased blocks of land within townships, each one mile square, from the federal government or from land speculators.

throughout the region, but it provided for the return of fugitive slaves to the South. It also guaranteed basic rights—freedom of religion and trial by jury—and provided for the support of public education.

With the Northwest Ordinance in place, Congress had succeeded in extending republican government to the West and incorporating the frontier into the new nation. The Republic now had an orderly way to expand its federation of states in a way that minimized the tensions between the genteel East and the democratic West that had plagued the colonies and the Confederation throughout much of the eighteenth century. Yet ironically, the new ordinance served to heighten tensions in a different way. By limiting the spread of slavery in the northern states, Congress deepened the critical social and economic differences between the North and South, evident already in the 1780s.

The consequences of the new territorial system were also significant for hundreds of thousands of the continent's other inhabitants. In the short term the ordinance ignored completely the rights of the Shawnee, Chippewa, and other Indian peoples who lived in the region. In the long term the system "laid the blueprint," as one historian noted, for bringing new lands into the United States. The ordinance thus accelerated the pressures on Indian lands and aggravated the social and geographic dislocations already set in motion by disease and the western conflicts of the Revolutionary War.

Slavery and Sectionalism >> When white Americans declared their independence, they owned nearly half a million black Americans. African Americans of the revolutionary generation, most of them enslaved, constituted 20 percent of the total population of the colonies in 1775, and nearly 90 percent of them lived in the South. Yet few political leaders directly confronted the issue of whether slavery should be permitted to exist in a truly republican society.

When political discussion did stray toward the subject of slavery, southerners—especially ardent republicans—bristled defensively. Theirs was a difficult position, riddled with contradictions. On the one hand, they had condemned parliamentary taxation as tantamount to political "slavery" and had rebelled, declaring that all men were "created equal." On the other hand, enslaved African Americans formed the basis of the South's plantation economy. To surrender slavery, southerners believed, would be to usher in economic ruin.

Some planters in the Upper South resolved the dilemma by freeing their slaves. Such decisions were made easier by changing economic conditions in the Chesapeake. As planters shifted from tobacco toward

↑ In 1787 in Philadelphia, the year delegates to the Constitutional Convention met, Richard Allen and Absalom Jones founded Bethel African Methodist Episcopal Church. The first church was a former blacksmith's shop that the members hauled to a site they purchased on Sixth Street. By the time this illustration was created in 1829, a more spacious building had replaced the first church.

the immediate or gradual abolition of slavery. Freedom for most northern African Americans came slowly, but by 1830 there were fewer than 3,000 slaves out of a total northern black population of 125,000.

The Revolution, which had been fought for liberty and equality, did little to change the status of most black Americans. By 1800 more enslaved African Americans lived in the United States than had lived there in 1776. Slavery continued to grow in the Lower South as the rice culture of the Carolinas and Georgia expanded and as the new cotton culture spread westward.

Still, a larger number of slaves than ever before became free during the war and in the decades following, whether through military service, successful escape, manumission, or gradual emancipation. All these developments fostered the growth of free black communities, especially in the Upper South and in northern cities. By 1810 free African Americans made up 10 percent of the total population of Maryland and Virginia. The composition of the postwar free community changed as well. Before independence most free blacks had been either mulattoes—the offspring of interracial unions—or former slaves too sick or aged to have value as laborers. In contrast, the free population of the 1780s were darker skinned, younger, and healthier. This group injected new vitality into black communal life, organizing independent schools, churches, and mutual benefit societies for the growing number of "free people of color."

wheat, a crop demanding much less labor, Virginia and Maryland liberalized their manumission statutes, laws providing for freeing slaves. Between 1776 and 1789 most southern states also joined the North in prohibiting the importation of slaves, and a few antislavery societies appeared in the Upper South. But no southern state legally abolished slavery. Masters defended their right to hold human property in the name of republicanism.

Eighteenth-century republicans regarded property as crucial, because it provided a man and his family with security, status, and wealth. More important, it provided a measure of independence: to be able to act freely, without fear or favor of others. People without property were dangerous, republicans believed, because the poor could never be politically independent. Southern defenders of slavery thus argued that free, propertyless black people would pose a political threat to the liberty of propertied white citizens. Subordinating the human rights of blacks to the property rights of whites, southern republicans reached the paradoxical conclusion that their freedom depended on keeping African Americans in bondage.

The North followed a different course. Because its economy depended far less on slave labor, black emancipation did not run counter to powerful economic interests. Antislavery societies, the first founded by the Quakers in 1775, spread throughout the northern states during the next quarter century. Over the same period the legislatures of most northern states provided for

peculiar institution euphemism for slavery, perhaps revealing in its use. Peculiar also suggests the contradiction with the ideals of the Declaration of Independence, that "all men are created equal."

After the Revolution slavery ceased to be a national institution. It became the **"peculiar institution"** of a single region, the American South.

Wartime Economic Disruption

>> With the outbreak of the Revolution, Americans had suffered an immediate loss of the manufactured goods, markets, and credit that Britain had formerly supplied. Matters did not improve with the coming of peace. France and Britain flooded the new states with their manufactures, and postwar Americans, eager for luxuries, indulged in a most unrepublican spending spree. The flurry of buying left some American merchants and consumers as deeply in debt as their governments. When loans from private

citizens and foreign creditors such as France had proved insufficient to finance the fighting, both Congress and the states had printed paper money—a whopping total of $400 million. The paper currency was backed only by the government's promise to redeem the bills with money from future taxes, since legislatures balked at the unpopular alternative of levying taxes during the war. For the bills to be redeemed the United States had to survive, so by the end of 1776, when Continental forces sustained a series of defeats, paper money started to depreciate dramatically. By 1781 it was virtually without value, and Americans coined the expression "not worth a Continental."

The printing of paper money, combined with a wartime shortage of goods, triggered an inflationary spiral of scarcer and scarcer goods costing more and more worthless dollars. In this spiral, creditors were gouged by debtors, who paid them back with depreciated currency. At the same time, soaring prices for food and manufactured goods eroded the buying power of wage earners and small farmers. And the end of the war brought on demands for prompt repayment from the new nation's foreign creditors as well as from soldiers seeking backpay and pensions.

Congress could do nothing. With no power to regulate trade, it could neither dam the stream of imported goods rushing into the states nor stanch the flow of gold and silver to Europe to pay for these items. With no power to prohibit the states from issuing paper money, it could not halt depreciation. With no power to regulate wages or prices, it could not curb inflation. With no power to tax, it could not reduce the public debt. Efforts to grant Congress greater powers met with determined resistance from the states.

Within states, too, economic problems aroused discord. Some major merchants and large commercial farmers had profited handsomely during the war by selling supplies to the American, British, and French armies at high prices. Eager to protect their windfall, they lobbied state legislatures for an end to inflationary monetary policies. That meant passing high taxes to pay wartime debts, a paper currency that was backed by gold and silver, and an active policy to encourage foreign trade.

Less affluent men fought back, pressing legislatures for programs that met their needs. Western farmers, often in debt, urged the states to print more paper money and to pass laws lowering taxes and postponing the foreclosure of mortgages. Artisans opposed merchants by calling for protection from low-priced foreign imports that competed with the goods they produced. They set themselves against farmers as well by demanding price regulation of the farm products they consumed. In the continuing struggle the state legislatures became the battleground of competing economic factions.

As the 1780s wore on, conflicts mounted. As long as the individual states remained sovereign, the Confederation was crippled—unable to conduct foreign affairs effectively, unable to set coherent economic policy, unable to deal with discontent in the West. Equally dismaying was the discovery that many Americans, instead of being selflessly concerned for the public good, selfishly pursued their private interests.

 REVIEW

What challenges did the West pose for the new republic?

REPUBLICAN SOCIETY

The war for independence transformed not only America's government and economy but also its society and culture. Inspired by the Declaration's ideal of equality, some Americans rejected the subordinate position assigned to them under the old colonial order. Westerners, newly wealthy entrepreneurs, urban artisans, and women all claimed greater freedom, power, and recognition. The authority of the traditional leaders of government, society, and the family came under a new scrutiny; the impulse to defer to social superiors became less automatic. The new assertiveness demonstrated how deeply egalitarian assumptions were taking root in American culture.

The New Men of the Revolution >> The Revolution gave rise to a new sense of social identity and a new set of ambitions among several groups of men who had once accepted a humbler status. The war also offered opportunities to aspiring entrepreneurs everywhere, and often they were not the same men who had prospered before the war. At a stroke, independence swept away the prominence of loyalists, whose ranks included an especially high number of government officials, large landowners, and major merchants. And while loyalists found their properties confiscated by revolutionary governments, other Americans grew rich. Many northern merchants gained newfound wealth from privateering or military contracts. Commercial farmers in the mid-Atlantic states prospered from the high food prices caused by wartime scarcity and army demand.

The Revolution effected no dramatic redistribution of wealth. Indeed, the gap between rich and poor increased during the 1780s. But the Revolution's republican ideals of equality and experience emboldened city artisans to demand a more prominent role in politics. Calls for men of their own kind to represent them in government came as a rude shock to such gentlemen as South Carolina's William Henry Drayton, who balked at sharing power with men "who were never in a way to study" anything except "how to cut up a beast in the market to best advantage, to cobble an old shoe in the neatest manner, or to build a necessary house." The journeymen who worked for master craftsmen also exhibited a new sense of independence, forming new organizations to secure higher wages.

But the greatest gains came to those men newly enriched by the war and by the opportunities of independence. Representative of this aspiring group was William Cooper, a Pennsylvania Quaker who did not support the Revolution but in its aftermath strove to transform himself from a wheelwright into a gentleman. He hoped to effect that change through another: the transformation of thousands of acres of hilly, heavily forested land around Otsego Lake in upstate New York into wheat—producing farms clustered around a market village called Cooperstown. Yankee emigrants fleeing the shrinking farms of long—settled New England made Cooper's vision a reality and made him the leading land developer of the 1790s. But the influx of white settlement radically altered the environment of what had once been part of Iroquoia. Farmers killed off panthers, bears, and wolves to protect their livestock. Grain farming leeched nutrients from the thin topsoil, forcing farmers to clear more trees, and as the forest barrier fell, weeds and insects invaded. By the beginning of the nineteenth century, the children of many small farmers were migrating to western New York and northern Ohio.

Similar scenarios played out on frontiers throughout the new United States. And everywhere, too, men like William Cooper demanded and received social recognition and political influence. Even though some, like Cooper, never lost the crude manners that betrayed humble origins, they styled themselves as the "aristocracy of merit" enshrined by republican ideals.

The New Women of the Revolution >> Not
long after the fighting with Britain had broken out, Margaret Livingston of New York wrote to her sister Catherine, "You know that our Sex are doomed to be obedient in every stage of life so that we shant be great gainers by this contest." By war's end, however, Eliza Wilkinson from rural South Carolina was complaining boldly to a woman friend: "The men say we have no business with political matters... it's not our sphere.... [But] I won't have it thought that because we are the weaker Sex (as to bodily strength my dear) we are Capable of nothing more, than minding the Dairy... surely we may have enough sense to give our Opinions."

What separated Margaret Livingston's resignation from Eliza Wilkinson's confidence was the Revolution. Wilkinson had managed her parents' plantation during the war and defended it from British marauders. Other women discovered similar reserves of skill and resourcefulness. When soldiers returned home, some were surprised to find their wives and daughters, who had been running family farms and businesses, less submissive and more self—confident.

But American men had not fought a revolution for the equality of American women. In fact, male revolutionaries gave no thought to the role of women in the new nation, assuming that those of the "weaker sex" were incapable of making informed and independent political decisions. Most women of the revolutionary generation agreed that the proper female domain was the home, not the public arena of politics. Still, the currents of the Revolution occasionally left gaps that allowed women to display their political interests. When a loosely worded provision in the New Jersey state constitution gave the vote to "all free inhabitants" owning a specified amount of property, white widows and single women went to the polls. Only in 1807 did the state legislature close the loophole.

Mary Wollstonecraft's Vindication >> In
the wake of the Revolution there also appeared in England a book that would become a classic text of modern feminism, Mary Wollstonecraft's *A Vindication of the Rights of Woman* (1792). Attracting a wide, if not widely approving, readership in America as well, it called not only for laws to guarantee women civil and political equality but also for educational reforms to ensure their social and economic equality.

Wollstonecraft dashed off *Vindication* in six short months. She charged that men deliberately conspired to keep women in "a state of perpetual childhood" by giving them inferior, frivolous educations. That encouraged young girls to fixate on fashion and flirtation and made them "only anxious to inspire love, when they ought to cherish a nobler ambition, and by their abilities and virtues exact respect." Girls, she proposed, should receive the same education as boys, including training that would prepare them for careers in medicine, politics, and business. No woman should have to pin her hopes for financial security on making a good marriage, Wollstonecraft argued. On the contrary, well—educated and resourceful women capable of supporting themselves would make the best wives and mothers, assets to the family and the nation.

Vindication might have been written in gunpowder rather than ink, given the reaction it aroused on both sides of the Atlantic. Even so, Wollstonecraft won many defenders among both men and women, who sometimes publicly and more often privately expressed

A Woman's Compass

A woman drinking spirits as her baby tumbles from her lap.

A woman crying, pointing to letters on a table. Was she jilted by a lover? Other possibilities?

A woman at hard labor in prison.

A woman being apprehended by the authorities. For prostitution? Drunkenness? Debt?

Could there be any more eloquent testimony to the anxieties aroused by the newly confident (and sometimes outspoken) women of postrevolutionary America? Much like jokes, idealized images (for example, the smiling woman within the compass) can point historians toward areas of tension and conflict in the past. In this illustration, the four scenes displayed outside the compass send even clearer signals. Published sometime between 1785 and 1805 and titled "Keep Within Compass," the illustration celebrates domesticity and wifely devotion while also warning women tempted to stray from that straight and narrow path. It promises a contented and prosperous life—lovely home, thriving garden, swishy silk dress, killer hat, and even a pet squirrel—to the woman "whose bosom no passion knows." But woe betide her erring sisters who strayed from the path of virtue, disgracing themselves as well as the men in their lives! Those twin themes proved equally popular in American novels published during the decades around 1800.

THINKING CRITICALLY

Is the kind of virtue promoted by the illustration similar to or different from the republican understanding of virtue? What accounts for the concern about the virtue of women in the decades around 1800? Why did the virtue of women loom so large, since they had few legal or political rights?

"Keep Within Compass," illustration, ca. 1785–1805, Winterthur Museum.

their agreement with her views. Among them was the Philadelphia Quaker Elizabeth Drinker, who confided to her diary that "in very many of her sentiments, she ...speaks my mind."

Seduction Literature and the Virtues of Women

>> The decades around 1800 also witnessed a heightened concern for the chastity of women. Books, magazines, and newspapers on both sides of the Atlantic overflowed with cautionary tales of young white women who were seduced or coerced into surrendering their virginity by unscrupulous "rakes," only to be abandoned by these faithless lovers, disowned by their families for becoming pregnant out of wedlock, and finally reduced to beggary or prostitution.

"Seduction literature" sent the unmistakable message that young women must preserve their sexual purity. Women were equipped with greater self-control by nature, authors advised, and they were obliged to inspire the same restraint in their suitors, because men were naturally passionate and impulsive. Depicting women as the guardians of sexual virtue marked a major shift in cultural attitudes, because for centuries before, most male writers had insisted that women were the more dangerous sex, their insatiable lust and deceitful ways luring men into sin.

Republican Motherhood and Education for Women

>> In the new republic, the new image of women as the upholders of private virtue met with an enthusiastic reception, especially among those who believed that wives and mothers had an obligation to encourage republican virtue in their husbands and children. That view, known as **"republican motherhood,"** inspired many educational reformers in the revolutionary generation. Philadelphian Benjamin Rush argued that only educated and independent-minded women could raise the informed and self-reliant citizens that a republican government required, while New Englander Judith Sargent Murray urged the cultivation of women's minds to encourage self-respect. Their efforts contributed to the most dramatic change in the lives of women after the war—the spread of female literacy.

Between 1780 and 1830 the number of American colleges and secondary academies rose dramatically, and some of these new institutions were devoted to educating women. Not only did the number of schools

republican motherhood redefinition of the role of women promoted by many American reformers in the 1780s and 1790s, who believed that the success of republican government depended on educated and independent-minded mothers who would raise children to become informed and self-reliant citizens.

↑ A devoted mother with her daughter from the 1790s: but note the generation gap. While the mother holds fancy needlework in her lap, her daughter looks up from an opened book. Many women—especially younger women—in the decades around 1800 chose to include books in their portraits, indicating that literacy and education were becoming essential to their identity and self-esteem.

for women increase, but these schools also offered a solid academic curriculum. By 1850—for the first time in American history—there were as many literate women as there were men.

The Revolution also prompted some states to reform their marriage laws, making divorce somewhat easier, although it remained extremely rare. But although women won greater freedom to divorce, married women still could not sue or be sued, make wills or contracts, or buy and sell property. Any wages they earned went to their husbands; so did all personal property that wives brought into a marriage; so did the rents and profits of any real estate they owned. Despite the high ideals of "republican motherhood," most women remained confined to the "domestic sphere" of the home and deprived of the most basic legal and political rights.

The Attack on Aristocracy

>> Why wasn't the American Revolution more revolutionary? Independence secured the full political equality of white men who owned property, but women were still deprived of political rights, African Americans of human rights. Why did the revolutionaries stop short of extending equality to the most unequal groups in American society—and with so little sense that they were being inconsistent?

In part, the lack of concern was rooted in republican ideas themselves. Republican ideology viewed property as the key to independence and power. Lacking property, women and black Americans were easily consigned to the custody of husbands and masters.

Then, too, prejudice played its part: the perception of women and blacks as naturally inferior beings.

But revolutionary leaders also failed to press for greater equality because they conceived their crusade in terms of eliminating the evils of a European past dominated by kings and aristocrats. They believed that the great obstacle to equality was monarchy—kings and queens who bestowed hereditary honors and political office on favored individuals and granted legal privileges and monopolies to favored churches and businesses. These artificial inequalities posed the real threat to liberty, most republicans concluded. In other words, the men of the Revolution were intent on attaining equality by leveling off the top of society. It did not occur to most republicans that the cause of equality could also be served by raising up the bottom—by attacking the laws and prejudices that kept African Americans enslaved and women dependent.

The most significant reform of the republican campaign against artificial privilege was the dismantling of state–supported churches. Most states had a religious establishment. In New York and the South, it was the Anglican Church; in New England, the Congregational Church. Since the 1740s, dissenters who did not worship at state churches had protested laws that taxed all citizens to support the clergy of established denominations. After the Revolution, as more dissenters became voters, state legislators gradually abolished state support for Anglican and Congregational churches.

Not only in religious life but in all aspects of their culture, Americans rejected inequalities associated with a monarchical past. In that spirit reformers attacked the Society of Cincinnati, a group organized by former officers of the Continental Army in 1783. The society, which was merely a social club for veterans, was forced to disband for its policy of passing on its membership rights to eldest sons. In this way, critics charged, the Society of Cincinnati was creating artificial distinctions and perpetuating a hereditary warrior nobility.

Today many of the republican efforts at reform seem misdirected. While only a handful of revolutionaries worked for the education of women and the emancipation of slaves, enormous zeal went into fighting threats from a monarchical past that had never existed in America. Yet the threat from kings and aristocrats was real to the revolutionaries—and indeed remained real in many parts of Europe. Their determination to sweep away every shred of formal privilege ensured that these forms of inequality never took root in America.

 REVIEW

How did the Revolution alter American society?

FROM CONFEDERATION TO CONSTITUTION

While Americans from many walks of life sought to realize the republican commitment to equality, Congress wrestled with the problem of preserving the nation itself. With the new republic slowly rending itself to pieces, some political leaders concluded that neither the Confederation nor the state legislatures were able to remedy the basic difficulties facing the nation. But how could the states be convinced to surrender their sovereign powers? The answer came in the wake of two events—one foreign, one domestic—that lent momentum to the cause of strengthening the central government.

The Jay-Gardoqui Treaty >> The international episode that threatened to leave the Confederation in shambles was a debate over a proposed treaty with Spain. In 1785 southwesterners still could not legally navigate the Mississippi and still were threatening to secede from the union and annex their territory to Spain's American empire. To shore up southwestern loyalties, Congress instructed its secretary of foreign affairs, John Jay, to negotiate an agreement with Spain preserving American rights to navigate on the Mississippi River. But the Spanish emissary, Don Diego de Gardoqui, sweet–talked Jay into accepting a treaty by which the United States would give up all rights to the Mississippi for 25 years. In return Spain agreed to grant trading privileges to American merchants.

Jay, a New Yorker, knew more than a few northern merchants who were eager to open new markets. But when the proposed treaty became public knowledge, southwesterners denounced it as nothing short of betrayal. The treaty was never ratified, but the hostility stirred up during the debate revealed the strength of sectional feelings. Only a decade later, when the Senate ratified a treaty negotiated with Spain by Thomas Pinckney in 1796, did Americans gain full access to the Mississippi.

Shays's Rebellion >> On the heels of this humiliation by Spain came an internal conflict that challenged the notion that individual states could maintain order in their own territories. The trouble erupted in western Massachusetts, where many small farmers were close to ruin. Yet they still had to pay mortgages on their farms, still had other debts, and were perpetually short of money. In 1786 the lower house of the Massachusetts legislature obliged the farmers with a package of relief measures. But creditors in eastern Massachusetts, determined to safeguard their own investments, persuaded the upper house to defeat the measures.

In the summer of 1786 western farmers responded, demanding that the upper house of the legislature be abolished and that the relief measures go into effect. That autumn 2,000 farmers rose in armed rebellion, led by Captain Daniel Shays, a veteran of the Revolution. They closed the county courts to halt creditors from foreclosing on their farms and marched on the federal arsenal at Springfield. The state militia quelled the uprising by February 1787, but the insurrection left many in Massachusetts and the rest of the country thoroughly shaken.

Daniel Shays's rebels were no impoverished rabble. They were reputable members of western communities who wanted their property protected and believed that government existed to provide that protection. The Massachusetts state legislature had been unable to safeguard the property of farmers from the inroads of recession or to protect the property of creditors from the armed debtors who closed the courts. It had failed, in other words, to fulfill the most basic aim of republican government.

Other states with discontented debtors feared what the example of western Massachusetts might mean for the future of the Confederation itself. But by 1786 Shays's Rebellion supplied only the sharpest jolt to a movement for reform that was already under way. Even before the rebellion, a group of Virginians had proposed a meeting of the states to adopt a uniform system of commercial regulations. Once assembled at Annapolis in September 1786, the delegates from five states agreed to a more ambitious undertaking. They called for a second, broader meeting in Philadelphia, which Congress approved, for the "express purpose of revising the Articles of Confederation."

Framing a Federal Constitution >> It was the
wettest spring anyone could remember. The 55 men who traveled over muddy roads to Philadelphia in May 1787 arrived drenched and bespattered. Fortunately, most of the travelers were men in their 30s and 40s, young enough to survive a good soaking. Since most were gentlemen of

some means—planters, merchants, and lawyers with powdered wigs and prosperous paunches—they could recover from the rigors of their journey in the best accommodations offered by America's largest city.

The delegates came from all the states except Rhode Island. The rest of New England supplied shrewd backroom politicians—Roger Sherman and Oliver Ellsworth from Connecticut and Rufus King and Elbridge Gerry, Massachusetts men who had learned a trick or two from Sam Adams. The middle states marshaled much of the intellectual might: two Philadelphia lawyers, John Dickinson and James Wilson; one Philadelphia financier, Robert Morris; and the aristocratic Gouverneur Morris. From New York there was Alexander Hamilton, the mercurial and ambitious young protégé of Washington. South Carolina provided fiery orators Charles Pinckney and John Rutledge.

It was "an assembly of the demigods," gushed Thomas Jefferson, who, along with John Adams, was serving as a diplomat in Europe when the convention met. In fact, the only delegate who looked even remotely divine was the convention's presiding deity. Towering a full half foot taller than most of his colleagues, George Washington displayed his usual self-possession from a chair elevated on the speaker's platform where the delegates met, in the Pennsylvania State House. At first glance, the delegate of least commanding presence was Washington's fellow Virginian, James Madison. Short and slightly built, the 36-year-old Madison had no profession except hypochondria.

But he was an astute politician and a brilliant political thinker who, more than anyone else, shaped the framing of the federal Constitution.

The delegates from 12 different states had two things in common: they were all men of considerable political experience, and they all recognized the need for a stronger national union. So when the Virginia delegation introduced Madison's outline for a new central government, the convention was ready to listen.

The Virginia and New Jersey Plans >> What
Madison had in mind was a truly national republic, not a confederation of independent states. His "Virginia Plan" proposed a central government with three branches: legislative, executive, and judicial. Furthermore, the legislative branch, Congress, would possess the power to

⌃ James Madison, the scholar and statesman whose ideas and political skill shaped the Constitution.

veto all state legislation. In place of the Confederation's single assembly, Madison substituted a bicameral legislature, with a lower house elected directly by the people and an upper house chosen by the lower from nominations made by state legislatures. Representatives to both houses would be apportioned according to population—a change from practice under the Articles, in which each state had a single vote in Congress. Madison also revised the structure of government that had existed under the Articles by adding an executive, who would be elected by Congress, and an independent federal judiciary.

After two weeks of debate over the Virginia Plan, William Paterson, a lawyer from New Jersey, presented a less radical counterproposal. While his "New Jersey Plan" increased Congress's power to tax and to regulate trade, it kept the national government as a unicameral assembly, with each state receiving one vote in Congress under the policy of equal representation. The delegates took just four days to reject Paterson's plan. Most endorsed Madison's design for a stronger central government.

Even so, the issue of apportioning representation continued to divide the delegates. While smaller states pressed for each state's having an equal vote in Congress, larger states backed Madison's provision for basing representation on population. Underlying the dispute over representation was an even deeper rivalry between southern and northern states. While northern and southern populations were nearly equal in the 1780s, and the South's population was growing more rapidly, the northern states were more numerous. Giving the states equal votes would put the South at a disadvantage. Southerners feared being outvoted in Congress by the northern states and felt that only proportional representation would protect the interests of their section.

That division turned into a deadlock as the wet spring burned off into a blazing summer. The stifling heat was made even worse because the windows remained shut, to keep any news of the proceedings from drifting out onto the Philadelphia streets.

The Deadlock Broken >> Finally, as the heat wave broke, so did the political stalemate. On July 2 a committee headed by Benjamin Franklin suggested a compromise. States would be equally represented in the upper house of Congress, each state legislature appointing two senators to six-year terms. That satisfied the smaller states. In the lower house of Congress, which alone could initiate money bills, representation was to be apportioned according to population. Every 30,000 inhabitants would entitle a state to send one representative for a two-year term. A slave was to count as three-fifths of a free person in the calculation of population, and the slave trade was to continue until 1808. That satisfied the larger states and the South.

By the end of August the convention was prepared to approve the final draft of the Constitution. The delegates agreed that the executive, now called the president, would be chosen every four years. Direct election seemed out of the question—after all, how could citizens in South Carolina know anything about a presidential candidate who happened to live in distant Massachusetts, or vice versa? But if each state chose presidential electors, either by popular election or by having the state legislature name them, those eminent men would likely have been involved in national politics, have known the candidates personally, and be prepared to vote wisely. Thus the Electoral College was established, with each state's total number of senators and representatives determining its share of electoral votes.

An array of other powers ensured that the executive would remain independent and strong: the president would have command over the armed forces, authority to conduct diplomatic relations, responsibility to nominate judges and officials in the executive branch, and the power to veto congressional legislation. Just as the executive branch was made independent, so, too, the federal judiciary was separated from the other two branches of government. Madison believed that this clear **separation of powers** was essential to a balanced republican government.

> **separation of powers** principle that each branch of government—the legislature (Congress), the executive (the president), and the judiciary (the Supreme Court)—should wield distinct powers independent from interference or infringement by other branches of government.

Madison's only real defeat came when the convention refused to give Congress veto power over state legislation. Still, the new bicameral national legislature enjoyed

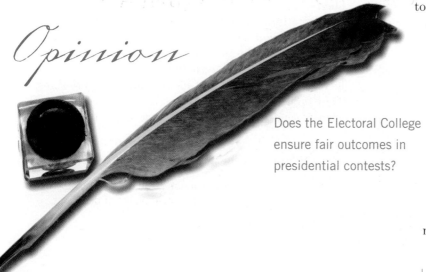

Opinion

Does the Electoral College ensure fair outcomes in presidential contests?

much broader authority than Congress had under the Confederation, including the power to tax and to regulate commerce. The Constitution also limited the powers of state legislatures, prohibiting them from levying duties on trade, coining money or issuing paper currency, and conducting foreign relations. The Constitution and the acts passed by Congress were declared the supreme law of the land, taking precedence over any legislation passed by the states. And changing the Constitution would not be easy. Amendments could be proposed only by a two-thirds vote of both houses of Congress or in a convention requested by two-thirds of the state legislatures. Ratification of amendments required approval by three-quarters of the states.

On September 17, 1787, 39 of the 42 delegates remaining in Philadelphia signed the Constitution. Charged only with revising the Articles, the delegates had instead written a completely new frame of government. And to speed up ratification, the convention decided that the Constitution would go into effect after only nine states had approved it. They further declared that the people themselves—not the state legislatures—would pass judgment on the Constitution in special ratifying conventions. To serve final notice that the new central government was a republic of the people and not merely another confederation of states, Gouverneur Morris of Pennsylvania hit on a happy turn of phrase to introduce the Constitution. "We the People," the document begins, "in order to form a more perfect union..."

Ratification

>> With grave misgivings on the part of many, the states called for conventions to decide whether to ratify the new Constitution. Those with the gravest misgivings—the Anti-Federalists, as they came to be called—voiced familiar republican fears. Older and less cosmopolitan than their **Federalist** opponents, the Anti-Federalists drew on their memories of the struggle with England to frame their criticisms of the Constitution. Expanding the power of the central government at the expense of the states, they warned, would lead to corrupt and arbitrary rule by new aristocrats. Extending a republic over a large territory, they cautioned, would separate national legislators from the interests and close oversight of their constituents.

federalism governing principle established by the Constitution in which the national government and the states divide power.

Madison responded to these objections in *The Federalist Papers*, a series of 85 essays written with Alexander Hamilton and John Jay during the winter of 1787–1788. He countered Anti-Federalist concerns over the centralization of power by pointing out that each separate branch of the national government would keep the others within the limits of their legal authority. That mechanism of **checks and balances** would prevent the executive from oppressing the people while preventing the people from oppressing themselves.

checks and balances mechanism by which each branch of government—executive, legislative, and judicial—keeps the others within the bounds of their constitutional authority.

To answer Anti-Federalist objections to a national republic, Madison drew on the ideas of an English philosopher, David Hume. In his famous 10th essay in *The Federalist Papers*, Madison argued that in a great republic "the Society becomes broken into a greater variety of interests, of pursuits, of passions, which check each other." The larger the territory, the more likely it was to contain multiple political interests and parties, so that no single faction could dominate. Instead, each would cancel out the others.

The one Anti-Federalist criticism Madison could not get around was the absence of a national bill of rights. Opponents insisted on an explicit statement of rights to prevent the freedoms of individuals and minorities from being violated by the federal government. Madison finally promised to place a bill of rights before Congress immediately after the Constitution was ratified.

Throughout the early months of 1788 Anti-Federalists continued their opposition. But they lacked the articulate and influential leadership that rallied behind the Constitution and commanded greater access to the public press. In the end, too, Anti-Federalist fears of centralized power proved less compelling than Federalist prophecies of the chaos that would follow if the Constitution were not adopted.

By the end of July 1788 all but two states had voted in favor of ratification. The last holdout, Rhode Island, finally came aboard in May 1790, after Madison had carried through on his pledge to submit a Bill of Rights to the new Congress. Indeed, these 10 amendments—ratified by enough states to become part of the Constitution by the end of 1791—proved to be the Anti-Federalists' most impressive legacy. The Bill of Rights set the most basic terms for defining personal liberty in the United States. Among the rights guaranteed were freedom of religion, the press, and speech, as well as the right to assemble and petition and the right to bear arms. The amendments also established clear procedural safeguards, including the right to a trial by jury and protection against illegal searches and seizures. They prohibited excessive bail, cruel and unusual punishment, and the quartering of troops in private homes.

✔ REVIEW

What short-term crises precipitated the Constitutional Convention, and what were the main points of debate at that meeting?

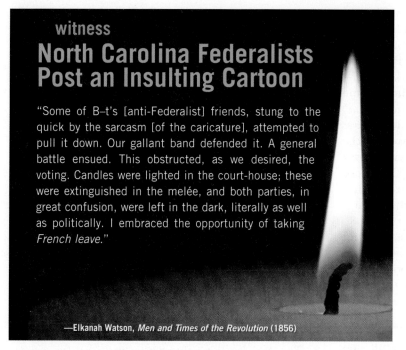

North Carolina Federalists Post an Insulting Cartoon

"Some of B—t's [anti-Federalist] friends, stung to the quick by the sarcasm [of the caricature], attempted to pull it down. Our gallant band defended it. A general battle ensued. This obstructed, as we desired, the voting. Candles were lighted in the court-house; these were extinguished in the melée, and both parties, in great confusion, were left in the dark, literally as well as politically. I embraced the opportunity of taking *French leave*."

—Elkanah Watson, *Men and Times of the Revolution* (1856)

Within the life span of a single generation, Americans had declared their independence twice. In many ways the political freedom claimed from Britain in 1776 was less remarkable than the intellectual freedom from the Old World that Americans achieved by agreeing to the Constitution. The Constitution represented a triumph of the imagination—a challenge to many beliefs long cherished by western Europe's republican thinkers.

Revolutionary ideals had been deeply influenced by the conflicts of British politics, in particular the Opposition's warnings about the dangers of executive power. Those concerns at first committed the revolutionaries to making legislatures supreme. In the end, though, Americans ratified a constitution that provided for an independent executive and a balanced government. The Opposition's fears of distant, centralized power had at first prompted the revolutionaries to embrace state sovereignty. But in the Constitution, Americans established a national government with authority independent of the states. Finally, the common sense among all of western Europe's republican theorists—that large national republics were an impossibility—was rejected by Americans, making the United States an impossibility that still endures.

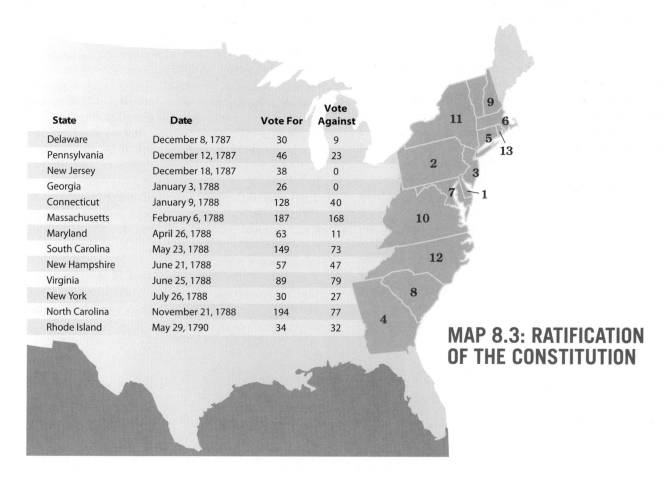

State	Date	Vote For	Vote Against
Delaware	December 8, 1787	30	9
Pennsylvania	December 12, 1787	46	23
New Jersey	December 18, 1787	38	0
Georgia	January 3, 1788	26	0
Connecticut	January 9, 1788	128	40
Massachusetts	February 6, 1788	187	168
Maryland	April 26, 1788	63	11
South Carolina	May 23, 1788	149	73
New Hampshire	June 21, 1788	57	47
Virginia	June 25, 1788	89	79
New York	July 26, 1788	30	27
North Carolina	November 21, 1788	194	77
Rhode Island	May 29, 1790	34	32

MAP 8.3: RATIFICATION OF THE CONSTITUTION

What, then, became of the last tenet of the old republican creed—the belief that civic virtue would sustain popular liberty? The hard lessons of the war and the crises of the 1780s withered confidence in the capacity of Americans to sacrifice their private interests for the public welfare. Many came to share Washington's sober view that "the few ... who act upon Principles of disinterestedness are, comparatively speaking, no more than a drop in the Ocean." The Constitution reflected the new recognition that interest rather than virtue shaped the behavior of most people most of the time and that the clash of diverse interest groups would remain a constant of public life.

Yet Madison and many other Federalists did not believe that the competition between private interests would somehow result in policies fostering public welfare. That goal would be met instead by the new national government acting as "a disinterested and dispassionate umpire in disputes between different passions and interests in the State." The Federalists looked to the national government to fulfill that role, because they trusted that a large republic, with its millions of citizens, would yield more of that scarce resource—disinterested gentlemen dedicated to serving the public good. Such gentlemen, in Madison's words, "whose enlightened views and virtuous sentiments render them superior to local prejudices," would fill the small number of national offices.

Not all the old revolutionaries agreed. Anti-Federalists drawn from the ranks of ordinary Americans still believed that common people were more virtuous and gentlemen more interested than the Federalists allowed. "These lawyers and men of learning, and moneyed men, that talk so finely," complained one Anti-Federalist, would "get all the power and all of the money into their own hands, and then they will swallow up all us little folks." Instead of being dominated by enlightened gentlemen, the national government should be composed of representatives from every social class and occupational group.

The narrow majorities by which the Constitution was ratified reflected the continuing influence of such sentiments, as well as fear that the states were surrendering too much power. That fear made Patrick Henry so ardent an Anti-Federalist that he refused to attend the Constitutional Convention in 1787, saying that he "smelt a rat." "I am not a Virginian, but an American,"

Henry had once declared. Most likely he was lying. Or perhaps Patrick Henry, a southerner and a slaveholder, could see his way clear to being an "American" only as long as sovereignty remained firmly in the hands of the individual states. Henry's convictions, 70 years hence, would rise again to haunt the Union.

CHAPTER SUMMARY

Leading Americans would give more thought to federalism, the organization of a United States, as the events of the postrevolutionary period revealed the weaknesses of the state and national governments.

- For a decade after independence the revolutionaries were less committed to creating a single national republic than to organizing 13 separate state republics, each dominated by popularly elected legislatures.
- The Articles of Confederation provided for a government by a national legislature but left the crucial power of the purse, as well as all final power to make and execute laws, entirely to the states.
- Many conflicts in the new republic were occasioned by westward expansion, which created both international difficulties with Britain and Spain and internal tensions over the democratization of state legislatures.
- In the wake of the Revolution, ordinary Americans struggled to define republican society: workers began to organize; some women claimed a right to greater political, legal, and educational opportunities; and religious dissenters called for disestablishment.
- In the mid-1780s the political crisis of the Confederation came to a head, prompted by the controversy over the Jay-Gardoqui Treaty and Shays's Rebellion.
- The Constitutional Convention of 1787 produced an entirely new frame of government that established a truly national republic and provided for a separation of powers among a judiciary, a bicameral legislature, and a strong executive.
- The Anti-Federalists, opponents of the Constitution, softened their objections when promised a Bill of Rights after ratification, which was incorporated into the Constitution by 1791.

Additional Reading

The work of Gordon Wood is indispensable for under—standing the transformation of American politics and culture during the 1780s and thereafter; see especially *The Creation of the American Republic* (1969) and *The Radicalism of the American Revolution* (1992). To understand the arguments in favor of the Constitution, consult Garry Wills, *Explaining America* (1981); and to appreciate the contributions of its opponents, read Saul Cornell, *The Other Founders* (1999); and the classic writings of Cecilia Kenyon collected in *Men of Little Faith* (2003).

To explore the meaning of republicanism for American women, see two fine studies by Linda Kerber, *Women of the Republic* (1980) and *No Constitutional Right to Be Ladies* (1998); as well as Rosemarie Zagarri's superb biography of Mercy Otis Warren, *A Woman's Dilemma* (1995). For a vivid sense of how the 1780s transformed local society and politics in one Massachusetts county, read John Brooke, *The Heart of the Commonwealth* (1991); and for a fascinating tale of how the Revolution made one ordinary man's life extraordinary, enjoy Alan Taylor, *William Cooper's Town* (1995). The best accounts of how the Revolution's legacy affected the lives of African Americans in the North include Shane White, *Somewhat More Independent* (1991); and Joan Pope Melish, *Disowning Slavery* (1998).

Significant Events

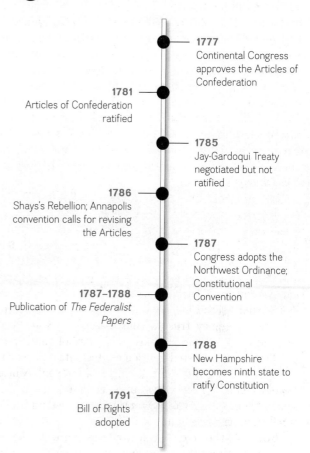

1777
Continental Congress approves the Articles of Confederation

1781
Articles of Confederation ratified

1785
Jay-Gardoqui Treaty negotiated but not ratified

1786
Shays's Rebellion; Annapolis convention calls for revising the Articles

1787
Congress adopts the Northwest Ordinance; Constitutional Convention

1787–1788
Publication of *The Federalist Papers*

1788
New Hampshire becomes ninth state to ratify Constitution

1791
Bill of Rights adopted

9

The Early Republic

1789–1824

Fourth of July parades helped citizens define the identity of their young republic. This New York parade was led by the Tammany Society, which rejected the aristocratic leanings of the Federalist Party.

>> An American Story

"I FELT MYSELF MAD WITH PASSION"

One spring evening in 1794 General John Neville was riding home from Pittsburgh with his wife and granddaughter. As they went up a hill, his wife's saddle started to slip, so Neville dismounted. As he adjusted the strap, he heard the clip-clop of an approaching horse. A rider galloped up and in a gruff voice asked, "Are you Neville the excise officer?" "Yes," Neville replied, without turning around.

"Then I must give you a whipping!" cried the rider and leapt from his horse. He grabbed Neville by the hair and lunged at his throat. Breaking free, Neville finally managed to knock the man down: he recognized his attacker as Jacob Long, a local farmer. After Long fled, Neville resumed his journey, badly shaken.

John Neville was not accustomed to such treatment. As one of the wealthiest men in the area, he expected respect from those of lower social rank. And he had received it—until becoming embroiled in a controversy over the new "whiskey tax" on distilled spirits. In a frontier district like western Pennsylvania, farmers regularly distilled their grain into whiskey for barter and sale. Not surprisingly, the **excise tax,** passed

> **excise tax** internal tax placed on the production or sale of a commodity, usually a luxury item or nonessential.

by Congress in 1791, was notoriously unpopular. Still, Neville had accepted an appointment to be one of the tax's regional inspectors. For three years he had endured threats as he enforced the law, but this roadside assault showed that popular hostility was rising.

As spring turned to summer the grain ripened, and so did the people's anger. In mid-July a federal marshal arrived to serve summonses to a number of farmer-distillers who had not paid taxes. One, William Miller, squinted at the paper and was amazed to find the government ordering him to appear in court—hundreds of miles away in Philadelphia—in little more than

^ In this antigovernment cartoon, a devil's imp with horns and barbed tail offers to escort a tax collector—the Exciseman—to his master. Like the Stamp Act riots of the Revolutionary period, protesters in western Pennsylvania against the excise tax ritually hanged tax collectors in effigy (*left*).

a month. Even worse, the papers claimed he owed $250.

And there, next to this unknown federal marshal, stood the unyielding John Neville.

"I felt myself mad with passion," recalled Miller. "I thought $250 would ruin me; and . . . I felt my blood boil at seeing General Neville along to pilot the sheriff to my very door." Word of the marshal's presence brought 30 or 40 laborers swarming from a nearby field. Armed with muskets and pitchforks, they forced Neville and the marshal to beat a hasty retreat.

Next morning the local militia company marched to Neville's estate. A battle ensued, and the general, aided by his slaves, beat back the attackers. A larger group, numbering 500 to 700, returned the following day to find Neville fled and his home garrisoned by a group of soldiers from nearby Fort Pitt. The mob burned down most of the outbuildings and, after the soldiers surrendered, torched Neville's elegantly furnished home.

Throughout the region that summer, marauding bands roamed the countryside, burning homes and

attacking tax collectors. While the greatest unrest flared in western Pennsylvania, farmers in the western districts of several other states also defied federal officials and refused to pay the tax, thus launching a full-scale "Whiskey Rebellion" in the summer of 1794.

Alexander Hamilton, a principal architect of the strong federal government established by the Constitution, knew a challenge to authority when he saw one: "Shall there be a government, or no government?" So did an alarmed George Washington, now president and commander in chief of the new republic, who led an army of 13,000 men—larger than that he had commanded at Yorktown against the British—into the Pennsylvania countryside.

That show of force cowed the Pennsylvania protesters, snuffing out the Whiskey Rebellion. But the riots and rebellion deepened fears for the future of the new republic. As Benjamin Franklin remarked in 1788, Americans were skilled at overthrowing governments, but only time would tell whether they were any good at sustaining them. By 1794 Franklin's warning seemed prophetic.

Federalists such as Washington and Hamilton—supporters of a powerful national government—had high hopes for their newly created republic. Stretching over some 840,000 square miles in 1789, it was approximately four times the size of France, five times the size of Spain, ten times the size of Great Britain. Yet the founders of the republic knew how risky it was to unite such a vast territory. Yankee merchants living along Boston wharves had economic interests and cultural traditions distinct from those of backcountry farmers who raised hogs, tended a few acres of corn, and distilled whiskey. Even among farmers, there was a world of difference between a South Carolina planter who shipped tons of rice to European markets and a New Hampshire family whose stony fields yielded barely enough to survive. Could the new government established by the Constitution provide a framework strong enough to unite such a socially diverse nation? Within a decade national political leaders split into two sharply opposed political parties, drawing ordinary men and women into civic life.

Social and political divisions within the nation were sharpened by currents of global change, both across the Atlantic and westward across the continent. After 1789 an increasingly bloody revolution in France sharpened old rivalries, and as Europe plunged into war, Americans were torn in their loyalties. Britain also determined to make Americans fight for their independence once again, while in the West, Spain and later France pressured white settlers beyond the Appalachians. Indian nations, buffeted by disease and dislocation, sought to unite in a confederacy west of the Appalachian Mountains.

In short, the early republic was a fragile creation, buffeted by changes beyond its borders and struggling to create a stable government at home. During the nation's first three decades its survival depended on balancing the interests of a socially and economically diverse population. <<

What's to Come

1789: A SOCIAL PORTRAIT

When the Constitution went into effect, the United States stretched from the Atlantic Ocean to the Mississippi River. The first federal census, compiled in 1790, counted approximately 4 million people, divided about evenly between the northern and southern states. Only about 100,000 settlers lived beyond the Appalachians in the Tennessee and Kentucky territories, which were soon to become states.

Within the Republic's boundaries were two major groups that lacked effective political influence: African Americans and Indians. In 1790 black Americans numbered 750,000, almost one-fifth the total population. More than 90 percent lived in the southern states from Maryland to Georgia; most were slaves who worked on tobacco and rice plantations, but there were free blacks as well. The census did not count the number of Indians living east of the Mississippi. North of the Ohio, the powerful Miami Confederacy discouraged settlement, while to the south, five strong, well—organized tribes—the Creeks, Cherokees, Chickasaws, Choctaws, and Seminoles—dominated the region from the Appalachians to the Mississippi River.

That composition would change as the white population continued to double about every 22 years. Immigration contributed only a small part to this astonishing growth. On average, fewer than 10,000 Europeans arrived annually between 1790 and 1820. The primary cause was natural increase, since, on average, American white women gave birth to nearly eight children each. As a result, the United States had an unusually youthful population: in 1790 almost half of all white Americans were under 16 years old. The age at first marriage was about 25 for men, 24 for women—and three or four years younger in newly settled areas—which contributed to the high birthrate.

This youthful, growing population remained overwhelmingly rural. Only 24 towns and cities boasted 2,500 or more residents, and 19 out of 20 Americans lived outside them. In fact, more than 80 percent of American families in 1800 were engaged in agriculture. In such a rural environment the movement of people, goods, and information was slow. Few individuals used the expensive postal system, and most roads were still little more than dirt paths hacked through the forest. In 1790 the country had 92 newspapers, but they were published mostly in towns and cities along major avenues of transportation.

Life in isolated regions contrasted markedly with that in bustling urban centers, such as New York and Philadelphia. But the most basic division in American society was not between the cities and the countryside, important as that was. What would divide Americans most broadly over the coming decades was the contrast between **semi—subsistence** and commercial ways of life. Semisubsistence farmers lived on the produce of their own land and labor. Americans in the commercial economy were tied more closely to the larger markets of a far—flung world.

> semisubsistence economy economy in which individuals and families produce most of what they need to live on.

Semisubsistence and Commercial Economies

>> Most rural white Americans in the interior of the northern states and the backcountry of the South lived off the produce of their own land. Wealth in those areas, although not distributed equally, was spread fairly broadly. And subsistence remained the goal of most white families. "The great effort was for every farmer to produce anything he required within his own family," one European visitor noted. In such an economy women played a key role. Wives and daughters had to be skilled in making such articles as candles, soap, clothing, and hats, since the cost of buying them was steep.

With labor scarce and expensive, farmers also depended on their neighbors to help clear fields, build

homes, and harvest crops. If a farm family produced a small surplus, it usually exchanged it locally rather than selling it for cash in a distant market. In this barter economy, money was seldom seen and was used primarily to pay taxes and purchase imported goods.

Indian economies were also based primarily on subsistence. In the division of labor women raised crops, while men fished or hunted—not only for meat but also for skins to make clothing. Because Indians followed game more seasonally than did white settlers, they moved their villages to several different locations over the course of a year. But both whites and Indians in a semisubsistence economy moved periodically to new fields after they had exhausted the old ones. Indians exhausted agricultural lands less quickly, because they planted beans, corn, and squash in the same field, a technique that better conserved soil nutrients.

Despite the image of both the independent "noble savage" and the self—reliant yeoman farmer, virtually no one in the backcountry operated within a truly self—sufficient economy. Although farmers tried to grow most of the food their families ate, they normally bought salt, sugar, and coffee, and they often traded with their neighbors for food and other items. In addition, necessities such as iron, glass, lead, and gunpowder had to be purchased, and many farmers hired artisans to make shoes and weave cloth. Similarly, Indians were enmeshed in the wider world of European commerce, exchanging furs for iron tools or clothing and ornamental materials.

Outside the backcountry, Americans were tied much more closely to a **commercial economy.** Here, merchants, artisans, and even farmers did not subsist on what they produced but instead sold goods or services in a wider market and lived on their earnings. Cities and towns, of course, played a key part in the commercial economy. But so did the agricultural regions near the seaboard and along navigable rivers.

> commercial economy economy in which individuals are involved in a network of markets and commercial transactions. Such economies are often urban, where goods and services are exchanged for money and credit; agricultural areas are also commercial when crops and livestock are sold in markets rather than consumed by those who grew or raised them.

For commerce to flourish, goods had to move from producers to market cheaply enough to reap profits. Water offered the only cost—effective transportation over any distance; indeed, it cost as much to ship goods a mere 30 miles over primitive roads as to ship by boat 3,000 miles across the Atlantic to London. Cost—effective transportation was available to the planters of the Tidewater South, and city merchants used their access to the sea to establish trading ties to the West Indies and Europe. But urban artisans and workers were also linked to

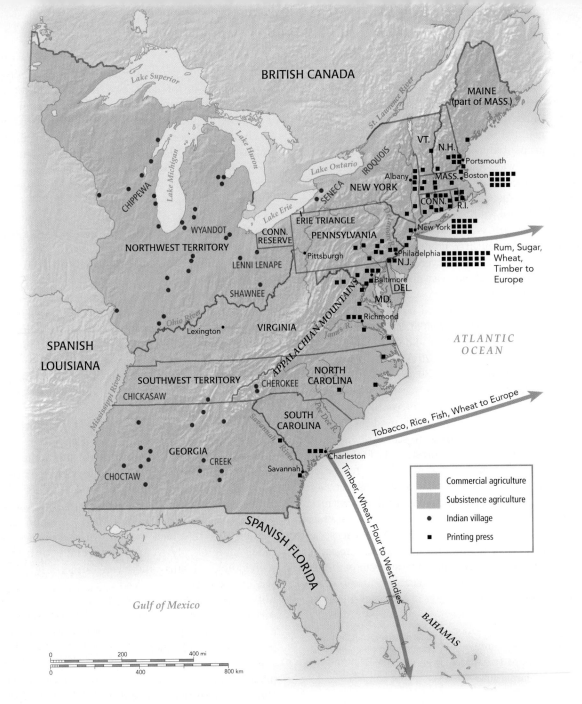

MAP 9.1: SEMISUBSISTENCE AND COMMERCIAL AMERICA, 1790

To prosper, a commercial economy demanded relatively cheap transportation to move goods. Thus in 1790 American commerce was confined largely to settled areas along the coast and to navigable rivers below the fall line. Because commerce depended on an efficient flow of information and goods, newspapers flourished in these areas.
What was the geographic boundary for the western border of commercial agriculture in the early republic?

this market economy, as were many farm families in the Hudson valley, southeastern Pennsylvania, and southern New England.

In commercial economies, wealth was less equally distributed. By 1790 the richest 10 percent of Americans living in cities and in the plantation districts of the Tidewater South owned about 50 percent of the wealth. In the backcountry the top 10 percent was likely to own 25 to 35 percent of the wealth.

The Constitution and Commerce >>In many ways the fight over ratification of the Constitution represented a struggle between the commercial and the subsistence—oriented elements of American society. Urban merchants and workers as well as commercial farmers and planters generally rallied behind the Constitution. They took a broader, more cosmopolitan view of the nation's future, and they had a more favorable view of government power.

Americans who remained a part of the semisubsistence **barter economy** tended to oppose the Constitution. More provincial in outlook, they feared con

centrated power, were suspicious of cities and commercial institutions, opposed aristocracy and special privilege, and in general just wanted to be left alone.

And so in 1789 the United States embarked on its new national course, with two rival visions of the direction that the fledgling Republic should take. Which vision would prevail—a question that was as much social as it was political—increasingly divided the generation of revolutionary leaders in the early republic.

 REVIEW

Describe the semisubsistence and commercial economies of the United States in 1789, and explain their differing visions of how the country should develop.

THE NEW GOVERNMENT

⚊ As Washington traveled from his plantation at Mount Vernon to New York, to be inaugurated as president, he was treated nearly as a god. At Trenton, where he had won a victory after his famous crossing of the Delaware River, maidens scattered flowers in his path as he proceeded through an archway festooned with flowers and evergreens. Philadelphia went one better and dangled a boy above him, to lower a crown of laurel onto Washington's head. The general was so mortified by the attention that he snuck out of town the next morning an hour before a cavalry guard arrived to escort him.

Whatever the Republic was to become, Americans agreed that George Washington personified it. When the first Electoral College cast its votes, Washington was unanimously elected, the only president in history so honored. John Adams became vice president. Loyalty to the new republic, with its untried form of government and diversity of peoples and interests, rested to a great degree on the trust and respect Americans gave Washington.

Washington Organizes the Government >>

George Washington realized that as the first occupant of the executive office, everything he did was fraught with significance. "I walk on untrodden ground," he commented. "There is scarcely any part of my conduct which may not hereafter be drawn into precedent."

The Constitution made no mention of a cabinet. Yet the drafters of the Constitution, aware of the experience of the Continental Congress under the Articles of Confederation, clearly assumed that the president would have some system of advisers. Congress authorized the creation of four departments—War, Treasury, State, and Attorney General—whose heads were to be appointed with the consent of the Senate. Washington's most important choices were Alexander Hamilton as secretary of the treasury and Thomas Jefferson to head the State Department. Washington gradually excluded Adams from cabinet discussions, and any meaningful role for the vice president, whose duties were largely undefined by the Constitution, soon disappeared.

The Constitution created a federal Supreme Court but beyond that was silent about the court system. The Judiciary Act of 1789 set the size of the Supreme Court at 6 members; it also established 13 federal district courts and 3 circuit courts of appeal. Supreme Court justices spent much of their time serving on these circuit courts, a distasteful duty whose long hours "riding the circuit" caused one justice to grumble that Congress had made him a "traveling postboy." The Judiciary Act made it clear that federal courts had the right to review decisions of the state courts and specified cases over which the Supreme Court would have original jurisdiction. Washington appointed John Jay of New York, a staunch Federalist, as the first chief justice.

Hamilton's Financial Program >> When

Congress called on Alexander Hamilton to prepare a report on the nation's finances, the new secretary of the treasury undertook the assignment eagerly.

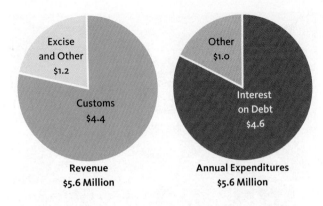

Revenue
$5.6 Million

Annual Expenditures
$5.6 Million

HAMILTON'S FINANCIAL SYSTEM

Under Hamilton's financial system, more than 80 percent of federal revenues went to pay the interest on the national debt of over $75 million. Note that most of the revenue came from tariff duties (customs).

A brilliant thinker and an ambitious politician, he did not intend to be a minor figure in the new administration. Convinced that human nature was fundamentally selfish, Hamilton was determined to link the interests of the wealthy with those of the new government. He also intended to use federal power to encourage manufacturing and commerce in order to make the United States economically strong and independent of Europe.

Neither goal could be achieved until the federal government solved its two most pressing financial problems: revenue and credit. Without revenue it could not be effective. Without credit—the faith of merchants and other nations that the government would repay its debts—it would lack the ability to borrow. Hamilton proposed that all $52 million of the federal debt, much of it generated by the Revolutionary War, be paid in full (or funded). He also recommended that the federal government assume responsibility for the remaining $25 million in debts that individual states owed—a policy of "assumption." He intended with these twin policies to put the new federal government on a sound financial footing and enhance its power by increasing its need for revenue and making the wealthy look to the national government, not the states. Hamilton also proposed a series of excise taxes, including a controversial 25 percent levy on whiskey, to help meet government expenses.

After heated debate Congress deadlocked over funding and assumption. Finally, at a dinner with Hamilton, Jefferson and James Madison of Virginia agreed to support his proposal if, after 10 years in Philadelphia, the permanent seat of government would be located in the South, on the Potomac River between Virginia and Maryland. Aided by this understanding, funding and assumption passed Congress. In 1791 Congress also approved a 20-year charter for the first Bank of the United States. The bank would hold government deposits and issue banknotes that would be received in payment of all debts owed the federal government. Congress proved less receptive to the rest of Hamilton's program, although a limited tariff to encourage manufacturing and several excise taxes, including the one on whiskey, won approval.

The passage of Hamilton's program caused a permanent rupture among supporters of the Constitution. Madison, who had collaborated closely with Hamilton in the 1780s, broke with his former ally over funding and assumption. Jefferson finally went over to the opposition when Hamilton announced plans for a national bank. Eventually the two warring factions organized themselves into political parties: the Republicans, led by Jefferson and Madison, and the Federalists, led by Hamilton and Adams.[1] But the division emerged slowly over several years.

Hamilton's program promoted the commercial sector at the expense of semisubsistence farmers. Thus it rekindled many of the concerns that had surfaced during the struggle over ratification of the Constitution. The ideology of the Revolution had stressed that republics inevitably contained groups who sought power in order to destroy popular liberties and overthrow the republic. To some Americans, Hamilton's program seemed a clear threat to establish a privileged and powerful financial aristocracy—perhaps even a monarchy.

Who, after all, would benefit from the funding proposal? During and after the Revolution, the value of notes issued by the Continental Congress dropped sharply. Speculators had bought up most of these notes for a fraction of their face value from small farmers and workers. If the government finally paid back the debt, speculators would profit accordingly. Equally disturbing, members of Congress had been purchasing the notes before the adoption of Hamilton's program. Nearly half the members of the House owned U.S. securities, a dangerous mimicking of Britain, where the Bank of England's loans to many members of Parliament gave the bank great political influence.

Fears were heightened, because Americans had little experience with banks: only three existed in the country when the Bank of the United States was chartered. One member of Congress expressed a common attitude when he said that he would no more be caught entering a bank than a house of prostitution. Then, too, banks and commerce were a part of the urban environment that rural Americans so distrusted. Although Hamilton's opponents admitted that a certain amount of commerce was necessary, they believed that it should remain subordinate. Hamilton's program, in contrast, encouraged manufacturing and urbanization,

---

[1] The Republican Party of the 1790s, sometimes referred to as the Jeffersonian Republicans, is not to be confused with the modern-day Republican Party, which originated in the 1850s.

developments that history suggested were incompatible with liberty and equality.

After Congress approved the bank bill, Washington hesitated to sign it. When he consulted his cabinet, Jefferson stressed that the Constitution did not specifically authorize Congress to charter a bank. Both he and Madison upheld the idea of strict construction—that the Constitution should be interpreted narrowly and the federal government restricted to powers expressly delegated to it. Otherwise, the federal government would be the judge of its own powers, and there would be no safeguard against the abuse of power.

Hamilton countered that the Constitution contained implied as well as enumerated powers. He particularly emphasized the clause that permitted Congress to make all laws "necessary and proper" to carry out its duties. A bank would be useful in carrying out the enumerated powers of regulating commerce and maintaining the public credit; Congress thus had a right to decide whether to establish one. In the end Washington accepted Hamilton's arguments and signed the bill.

Economically Hamilton's program was a success. The government's credit was restored, and the national bank ended the inflation of the previous two decades and created a sound currency. In addition, Hamilton's theory of implied powers and broad construction gave the nation the flexibility necessary to respond to unanticipated crises.

The Emergence of Political Parties >>

Members of the revolutionary generation fervently hoped that political parties would not take root in the United States. "If I could not go to heaven but with a party, I would not go at all," remarked Jefferson. Influenced by radical English republican thought, American critics condemned parties as narrow interest groups that placed selfishness and party loyalty above a concern for the public good. Despite Americans' distrust of such institutions, however, the United States became the first nation to establish truly popular parties.

Social conditions encouraged the rise of parties. Because property ownership was widespread, the nation had a broad **suffrage.** During the American Revolution legislatures lowered property requirements in many states, increasing the number of voters still further. If party members hoped to hold office, they had to offer a program attractive to the broader voting public. When parties acted as representatives of economic and social interest groups, they became one means by which a large electorate could make its feelings known. In addition, the United States had the highest literacy rate in the world and the largest number of newspapers, further encouraging political interest and participation. Finally, the fact that well-known patriots of the Revolution headed both the Federalists and the Republicans helped defuse the charge that either party was hostile to the Revolution or the Constitution.

[**suffrage** right to vote.

Americans and the French Revolution >>

While domestic issues first split the supporters of the Constitution, it was a crisis in Europe that pushed the nation toward political parties. Americans had hoped that their revolution would spark similar movements for liberty on the European continent, and in fact the American Revolution was only one of a series of revolutions in the late eighteenth century that shook the Western world, the most important of which began in France in 1789. There a rising population and the collapse of government finances sparked a challenge to royal authority that became a mass revolution. The French revolutionary ideals of "liberty, equality, and fraternity" eventually spilled across Europe.

Americans first hailed the French Revolution. Many rejoiced to learn that the Bastille prison had been stormed and that a new National Assembly had abolished feudal privileges and adopted the Declaration of the Rights of Man. But by 1793 American enthusiasm for the Revolution had cooled after radical elements instituted a reign of terror, executing the king and queen and many of the nobility. The French Republic even outlawed Christianity and substituted the worship of Reason. Finally in 1793 republican France and monarchical England went to war. Americans were deeply divided over whether the United States should continue its old alliance with France or support Great Britain.

⌃ The execution of King Louis XVI by guillotine left Americans divided over the French Revolution.

Hamilton and his allies viewed the French Revolution as sheer anarchy. French radicals seemed to be destroying the very institutions that held civilization together: the church, social classes, property, law and order. The United States, Hamilton argued, should renounce the 1778 treaty of alliance with France and side with Britain. By contrast, Jefferson and his followers supported the treaty and regarded France as a sister republic. They believed that despite deplorable excesses, its revolution was spreading the doctrine of liberty.

Washington's Neutral Course >> Washington, for his part, was convinced that in order to prosper, the United States must remain independent of European quarrels and wars. Thus he issued a proclamation of American neutrality and tempered Jefferson's efforts to support France.

Under international law, neutrals could trade with belligerents—nations at war—as long as the trade had existed before the outbreak of hostilities and did not involve war supplies. But both France and Great Britain refused to respect the rights of neutrals in the midst of their desperate struggle. They began intercepting American ships and confiscating cargoes. In addition, Britain, which badly needed manpower to maintain its powerful navy, impressed into service American sailors it suspected of being British subjects.

Britain also continued to maintain the western forts it had promised to evacuate in 1783, and it closed the West Indies, a traditional source of trade, to American ships.

Recognizing that the United States was not strong enough to challenge Britain militarily, Washington sent John Jay to negotiate the differences between the two countries. Although Jay did persuade the British to withdraw their troops from the Northwest, he could gain no other concessions. Disappointed, Washington nonetheless submitted Jay's Treaty to the Senate. After a bitter debate, the Senate narrowly ratified it in June 1795.

The Federalists and the Republicans Organize >> Thus events in Europe contributed directly to the rise of parties in the United States by stimulating fears over the course of American development. By the mid–1790s both sides were organizing on a national basis. Hamilton took the lead in coordinating the Federalist Party, which grew out of the voting bloc in Congress that had enacted his economic program. Increasingly, Washington drew closer to Federalist advisers and policies and became the symbol of the Federalist Party, although he clung to the vision of a **nonpartisan** administration—one that stood above any party.

nonpartisan avoiding any ties to a political party.

The guiding genius of the opposition movement was Hamilton's onetime colleague James Madison. Jefferson, who resigned as secretary of state at the end of 1793, became the symbolic head of the party, much as Washington reluctantly headed the Federalists. But it was Madison who orchestrated the Republican strategy and lined up their voting bloc in the House. The disputes over Jay's Treaty and over the whiskey tax in 1794 and 1795 gave the Republicans popular issues, and they began organizing on the state and local levels. Republican leaders had to be careful to distinguish between opposing the administration and opposing the Constitution. And they had to overcome the ingrained idea that an opposition party was seditious.

As more and more members of Congress allied themselves with one faction or the other, voting became increasingly partisan. By 1796 even minor matters were decided by partisan votes. Gradually, party organization extended all the way from the national level to local communities.

The 1796 Election >> As long as Washington remained head of the Federalists, they enjoyed a huge advantage. But in 1796 the weary president, stung by the abuse heaped on him by the opposition press,

announced that he would not accept a third term. In doing so he set a two–term precedent that future presidents followed until Franklin Roosevelt. In his Farewell Address, Washington warned against the dangers of parties and urged a return to the earlier nonpartisan system. That vision, however, had become obsolete: parties were an effective way of expressing the interests of different social and economic groups within the nation. When the Republicans chose Thomas Jefferson to oppose John Adams, the possibility of a constitutional system without parties ended.

The framers of the Constitution did not anticipate that political parties would run competing candidates for both the presidency and the vice presidency. Thus they provided that, of the candidates running for president, the one with the most electoral votes would win and the one with the second highest number would become vice president. But Hamilton strongly disliked both Adams and Jefferson. Ever the intriguer, he tried to manipulate the electoral vote so that the Federalist vice presidential candidate, Thomas Pinckney of South Carolina, would be elected president. In the ensuing confusion Adams won with 71 electoral votes, and his rival, Jefferson, gained the vice presidency with 68 votes.

Federalist and Republican Ideologies >>

The fault line between Federalists and Republicans reflected basic divisions in American life. Geographically, the Federalists were strongest in New England, with its commercial ties to Great Britain and its powerful tradition of hierarchy and order. Farther south, the party became progressively weaker. Of the southernmost states, the Federalists enjoyed significant strength only in aristocratic South Carolina. The Republicans won solid support in semisubsistence areas such as the West, where farmers were only weakly involved with commerce. The middle states were closely contested, although the most cosmopolitan and commercially oriented elements remained the core of Federalist strength.

In other ways, each party looked both forward and backward: toward certain traditions of the past as well as toward newer social currents that would shape America in the nineteenth century.

Most Federalists viewed themselves as a kind of natural aristocracy making a last desperate stand against the excesses of democracy. They clung to the notion that the upper class should rule over its social and economic inferiors. In supporting the established social order, most Federalists opposed unbridled individualism. In their view, government should regulate individual behavior for the good of society and protect property from the violent and unruly.

Yet the Federalists were remarkably forward–looking in their economic ideas. They sensed that the

United States would become a major economic and military power only by government encouragement of economic development.

The Republicans, in contrast, looked backward to the traditional revolutionary fear that government power threatened liberty. The Treasury, they warned, was corrupting Congress, the army would enslave the people, and interpreting the Constitution broadly would make the federal government all–powerful. Nor did Republican economic ideals anticipate future American development. For the followers of Madison and Jefferson, agriculture—not commerce or manufacturing—was the foundation of American liberty and virtue. Republicans also failed to appreciate the role of financial institutions in promoting economic growth, condemning speculators, bank directors, and holders of the public debt.

Yet the Jeffersonians were more farsighted in matters of equality and personal liberty. Their faith in the people put them in tune with the emerging egalitarian temper of society. They embraced the virtues of individualism, hoping to reduce government to the bare essentials. And they looked to the West—the land of small farms and a more equal society—as the means to preserve opportunity and American values.

 REVIEW

What fostered the intense political loyalties of the 1790s?

THE PRESIDENCY OF JOHN ADAMS

As president, John Adams became the head of the Federalists, although in many ways he was out of step with his party. Unlike Hamilton, Adams felt no pressing need to aid the wealthy, nor was he fully committed to Hamilton's commercial–industrial vision. As a revolutionary leader who in the 1780s had served as American minister to England, Adams also opposed any alliance with Britain.

Increasingly, Adams and Hamilton clashed over policies and party leadership. Part of the problem stemmed from personalities. Adams was so thin–skinned that it was difficult for anyone to get along with him, and Hamilton's intrigues in the 1796 election had not improved relations between the two men. Although Hamilton had resigned from the Treasury Department in 1795, key members of Adams's cabinet regularly turned to the former secretary for advice. Indeed, they opposed Adams so often that the frustrated president sometimes dealt with them, according to Jefferson, "by dashing and trampling his wig on the floor."

The Naval War with France >> Adams began his term trying to balance relations with both Great Britain and France. Because the terms of Jay's Treaty were so favorable to the British, the French in retaliation set their navy and privateers to raiding American shipping. To resolve the conflict Adams dispatched three envoys to France in 1797, but the French foreign minister demanded a bribe before negotiations could even begin. The American representatives refused, and when news of these discussions became public, it became known as the XYZ Affair.

In the public's outrage over French bribery, Federalist leaders saw a chance to retain power by going to war. In 1798 Congress repudiated the French alliance of 1778 and enlarged the army and navy. Republicans suspected that the real purpose of the army was not to fight the French army—none existed in North America—but to crush the opposition party and establish a military despotism. All that remained was for Adams to whip up popular feeling and lead the nation into war.

But Adams feared he would become a scapegoat if his policies failed. Furthermore, he distrusted standing armies and preferred the navy as the nation's primary defense. So an unofficial naval war broke out between the United States and France as ships in each navy raided the fleets of the other, while Britain continued to impress American sailors and seize ships suspected of trading with France.

Suppression at Home >> Meanwhile, Federalist leaders attempted to suppress disloyalty at home. In the summer of 1798 Congress passed several measures known together as the Alien and Sedition Acts. The Alien Act authorized the president to arrest and deport aliens suspected of "treasonable" leanings. Although never used, the act directly threatened immigrants who had not yet become citizens, many of whom were prominent Jeffersonians. To limit the number of immigrant voters—again, most of them Republicans—Congress increased the period of residence required to

naturalization act of granting full citizenship to someone born outside the country.

become a **naturalized** citizen from 5 to 14 years. But the most controversial law was the Sedition Act, which established heavy fines and even imprisonment for writing, speaking, or publishing anything of "a false, scandalous and malicious" nature against the government or any officer of the government.

Because of the partisan way it was enforced, the Sedition Act quickly became a symbol of tyranny. Federalists convicted and imprisoned a number of prominent Republican editors, and several Republican papers ceased publication. In all, 25 people were arrested under the law and 10 convicted and imprisoned.

Previously, most Americans had agreed that newspapers should not be restrained before publication but that they could be punished afterward for sedition. Jefferson and others now argued that the American government was uniquely based on the free expression of public opinion, and thus criticism of the government was not a sign of criminal intent. Only overtly seditious acts, not opinions, should be subject to prosecution. The courts eventually endorsed this view, adopting a new, more absolute view of freedom of speech guaranteed by the First Amendment.

Virginia and Kentucky Resolutions >> The Republican–controlled legislatures of Virginia and Kentucky each responded to the crisis of 1798 by passing a set of resolutions. Madison secretly wrote those for Virginia, and Jefferson those for Kentucky. These resolutions proclaimed that the Constitution was a compact among sovereign states that delegated strictly limited powers to the federal government. When the government exceeded those limits and threatened the liberties of citizens, states had the right to interpose their authority. In the 1830s the two resolutions would serve as the precedent for state efforts to nullify federal laws.

But Jefferson and Madison were not ready to rend a union that had so recently been forged. The two men intended for the Virginia and Kentucky resolutions only to rally public opinion to the Republican cause. They opposed any effort to resist federal authority by force.

The Election of 1800 >> With a naval war raging on the high seas and the Alien and Sedition Acts sparking debate at home, Adams shocked his party by negotiating a peace treaty with France. It was a courageous act, because Adams not only split his party in two but also ruined his own chances for reelection by driving Hamilton's pro–British wing of the party into open opposition. But the nation benefited, as peace returned.

With the Federalist Party split, Republican prospects in 1800 were bright. Again the party chose Jefferson to run against Adams, along with Aaron Burr for vice president. Sweeping to victory the Republicans won the presidency, as well as control of both houses of Congress for the first time. Yet the election again demonstrated the fragility of the fledgling political system. Jefferson and Burr received an equal number of votes, but the Constitution did not distinguish between the votes for president and vice president. With the election tied, the decision lay with the House of Representatives, where each state was allotted one vote. Because Burr refused to step aside for Jefferson, the election remained deadlocked for almost a week,

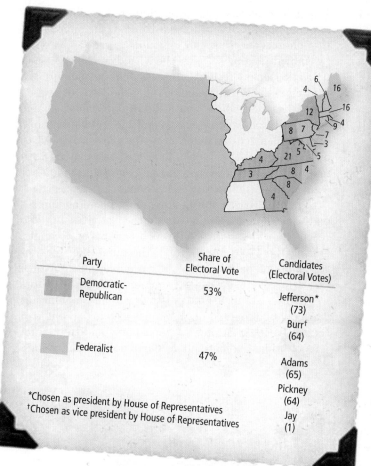

Party	Share of Electoral Vote	Candidates (Electoral Votes)
Democratic-Republican	53%	Jefferson* (73)
		Burr† (64)
Federalist	47%	Adams (65)
		Pickney (64)
		Jay (1)

*Chosen as president by House of Representatives
†Chosen as vice president by House of Representatives

MAP 9.2: ELECTION OF 1800

until the Federalists decided that Jefferson represented the lesser of two evils. They allowed his election on the 36th ballot. In 1804 the Twelfth Amendment corrected the problem of a tie, specifying that electors were to vote separately for president and vice president.

John Marshall and Judicial Review >>

Having lost both the presidency and the control of Congress in 1800, the Federalists took steps to shore up their power before Jefferson took office. They did so by expanding the size of the federal court system, the one branch of the federal government that they still controlled. The Judiciary Act of 1801 created 6 circuit courts and 16 new judgeships. Federalists justified these "midnight appointments" (executed by Adams in the last weeks of his term) on the grounds that the expanding nation required a larger judiciary.

Among Adams's last-minute appointments was that of William Marbury as justice of the peace for the District of Columbia. When James Madison assumed the office of secretary of state under the new administration, he found a batch of undelivered commissions, including Marbury's. Wishing to appoint loyal Republicans to these posts, Jefferson instructed Madison

not to hand over the commissions, whereupon Marbury sued. The case of *Marbury v. Madison* went directly to the Supreme Court in 1803.

Chief Justice John Marshall, a Federalist and one of Adams's late-term appointments, actually ruled in favor of Madison—but in a way that strengthened the power of the federal courts. Marshall affirmed the right of the Supreme Court to review statutes and interpret the meaning of the Constitution. "It is emphatically the province of and duty of the judicial department to say what the law is," he wrote in upholding the doctrine of **judicial review.** In Marshall's view, the Court "must of necessity expound and interpret" the Constitution and the laws when one statute conflicted with another or when a law violated the framework of the Constitution.

Marshall and his colleagues later asserted the power of the Court to review the constitutionality not only of federal but also of state laws. In fact, during his long tenure as chief justice (over 30 years), John Marshall extended judicial review to all acts of government.

> **judicial review** doctrine set out by Chief Justice John Marshall in *Marbury v. Madison,* that the judicial branch of the federal government possesses the power to determine whether the laws of Congress or the actions of the executive branch violate the Constitution.

As John Adams left office, he looked back with mixed feelings on the 12 years that the Federalist Party had held power. Under Washington's firm leadership and his own, his party had made the Constitution a workable instrument of government. The Federalists had proved that a republican form of government was compatible with stability and order. They had established economic policies that brought a return of prosperity. Washington had established the principle of American neutrality in foreign affairs, which became an accepted ideal by both parties for decades to come.

But most Federalists took no solace in such reflections, because the forces of history seemed to be running against them. In the election of 1800 they stood as the champions of order and hierarchy, of government by the wellborn, of a society in which social betters guided their respectful inferiors. They had waged one last desperate battle to save their disintegrating world—and had lost. Power had fallen into the hands of the ignorant rabble, led by that demagogue Thomas Jefferson.

 REVIEW

Why did John Adams lose the election of 1800?

THE POLITICAL CULTURE OF THE EARLY REPUBLIC

Such extreme views poisoned the political atmosphere of the early republic. Two distinct parties had emerged during the 1790s, but both longed to reestablish a one–party system. Neither Federalists nor Republicans could accept the novel idea that political parties might peacefully resolve differences among competing social, geographic, and economic interests. Instead, each party regarded its opponents as a dangerous faction of ambitious men striving to increase their wealth and power at the expense of republican liberty.

What resulted was a political culture marked by verbal and, at times, physical violence. Republicans accused Washington and Hamilton of being British agents and monarchists; Federalists denounced Jefferson as an atheist and his partisans as a pack of "blood–drinking cannibals." The leading Republican newspaper editor in Philadelphia plunged into a street brawl with his Federalist rival; two members of Congress slugged it out on the floor of the House of Representatives. Mobs threatened the leaders of both parties, and at the height of the crisis of 1798–1799, Adams smuggled guns into his home for protection.

Popular Participation in Political Festivals >> The deepening divisions among national leaders also encouraged ordinary Americans to take an interest in politics. Beginning in the 1790s and for decades thereafter, activists in cities and villages everywhere in the new republic organized grand festivals to celebrate American patriotism and the glories of the Republicans or the Federalists. That grassroots movement democratized the conduct of politics by educating men and women, white and black, voters and nonvoters alike, about the issues of the day. In doing so, such activities encouraged strong partisan loyalties.

Holidays such as the Fourth of July and Washington's Birthday became prime occasions for local party leaders to rally their fellow citizens. They hosted celebrations that began with parades in which marchers, hoisting banners to identify their particular trade, militia company, or social club, processed through the main street to a church, meeting hall, or public square. There the assembled throng of marchers and onlookers sang patriotic songs, recited prayers, and listened to the reading of the Declaration of Independence, all capped by a rousing sermon or political oration. Then the party started: in the North, taverns and hotels hosted community banquets; in the South, the crowds flocked to outdoor barbecues. Everywhere, the feasts ended with many toasts to the glories of republican liberty and, of course, to the superiority of Federalists or Republicans.

These local celebrations not only made an impact on those who were able to attend the festivities but also reached a wider audience through newspaper accounts. During the 1790s and beyond, the number of local or regional newspapers in the new republic mushroomed, but their coverage was far from objective. Most editors were either staunch Federalists or ardent Republicans who could be counted on to publish glowing accounts of the festivities sponsored by their party and to instruct a much wider audience about party policies and values.

∧ In 1821 these "victuallers"—suppliers of food—rode along the streets of Philadelphia in a typical celebration. The butchers wear traditional white frocks as they ride ahead of a two-story float. In the thriving market economy, butchers displayed civic pride as they hauled more than 86,000 pounds of beef, pork, lamb, and other foods to the market in 100 carts.

CAN THIS MARRIAGE BE SAVED?

Proponents of providing women with greater educational opportunities—here identified as "The Female Advocate"—often held ideals of marriage that differed dramatically from those embraced by conservative Americans such as Samuel Jennings, a Methodist minister and the founder of a medical college in Baltimore.

DOCUMENT 1
"The Female Advocate" on the Virtues of an Educated Wife

How greatly doth a man of science [knowledge] misjudge in choosing a companion for life, if he selects one from the class of ignorant and untaught, that he may, by this mean, the more securely retain his favorite supremacy. Is it not a total blindness to the ideas of refined happiness, arising from a reciprocity of sentiments and the exchange of rational felicity, as well as an illiberal prejudice, thus to conduct? Shall a woman be kept ignorant, to render her more docile in the management of domestic concerns? How illy capable is such a person of being a companion for a man of refinement? How miserably capable of augmenting his social joys, or managing prudently the concerns of a family, or educating his children? Is it not of the utmost consequence, that the tender mind of the youth receive an early direction for future usefulness? And is it

not equally true, that the first direction of a child necessarily becomes the immediate and peculiar province of the woman? And may I not add, is not a woman of capacious and well stored mind, a better wife, a better widow, a better mother, and a better neighbor; and shall I add, a better friend in every respect. . . .

When women, no longer the humble dependent, or the obsequious slave, but the companion and friend, is party to an attachment founded on mutual esteem, then, and not till then, does man assume his intended rank in the scale of creation. . . .

Suppose one who has from her youth been indoctrinated and habituated to sentiments of female inferiority, one who has never been suffered to have an opinion of her own, but on the reverse, has been taught, and accustomed to rely, and implicitly believe, right or wrong, on her

parents, guardians, or husband. What will be the consequence of this, in a situation when deprived of the counsel of either or all of them, she is necessitated to act for herself, or be exposed to the fraudulence of an unfriendly world? Perhaps she is left a widow with a large property and a flock of small dependent children? But where have they to look for protection, or on whom to rely, but on their insufficient, helpless mother? How poorly capable is she to fill the vacancy, and act to her tender babes and orphans, in their bereaved situation, as is absolutely necessary, both father and mother? How incapable also is she of assisting in the settlement and adjustment of the estate; how liable to fraud, and how probable to be injured by unreal or exaggerated debts.

Source: The Female Advocate, Written by a Lady (New Haven, 1801).

DOCUMENT 2
Samuel K. Jennings on the Virtues of a Submissive Wife

As it is your great wish and interest, to enjoy much of your husband's company and conversation, it will be important to acquaint yourself with his temper, his inclination, and his manner, that you may render your house, your person, and your disposition quite agreeable to him. . . .

Your choice in forming the connexion [marriage], was at best a passive one. Could you have acted the part of a courtier and made choice of a man whose disposition might have corresponded precisely with yours, there would have been less to do afterwards. But under present circumstances, it is your interest to adapt yourself to your husband, whatever may be his peculiarities.

Again, nature has made man the stronger, the consent of mankind has given him superiority over his wife, his inclination is, to claim his natural and acquired rights. He of course expects from you a degree of

condescension, and he feels himself the more confident of the propriety of his claim, when he is formed, that St. Paul adds to his authority its support. "Wives submit to your own husbands, as unto the Lord, for the husband is the head of his wife."

In obedience then to this precept of the gospel, to the laws of custom and of nature, you ought to cultivate a cheerful and happy submission. . . .

Do not suppose, that my plan implies that the husband has nothing to do. So far from this he is bound "To love and cherish his wife, as his own flesh." But I repeat, this obligation seems, in a great degree, to rest on the condition of a loving and cheerful submission on the part of the wife. Here again perhaps you object and say, "Why not the husband, first shew a little condescension as well as the wife?" I answer for these plain reasons. It is not

his disposition; it is not the custom but with the henpecked; it is not his duty; it is not implied in the marriage contract; it is not required by law or the gospel.

Source: Samuel K. Jennings, The Married Lady's Companion, or Poor Man's Friend (New York, 1808).

THINKING CRITICALLY

How did "The Female Advocate" advise men to choose their wives? How to behave as husbands? Why did she believe that her advice served the best interests of men? On what grounds did Samuel Jennings argue that women should submit to their husbands?

African American Celebrations >> African Americans, too, were drawn to political festivals, but unlike white women, they discovered that party organizers were determined to keep them away. In the years after 1800, bullies often drove black men and women from Fourth of July celebrations with taunts, threats, and assaults. James Forten, a leading citizen of Philadelphia's African American community, complained that because of the hostility of drunken whites, "black people, upon certain days of public jubilee, dare not to be seen" on the streets after noon.

The growing free black population of northern cities countered that opposition by organizing celebrations to express their own political convictions. They established annual holidays to celebrate the abolition of the slave trade in Britain and the United States as well as the successful slave revolt in the Caribbean that resulted in the founding of Haiti in 1804. Those acts of defiance—the spectacle of blacks marching down the main streets with banners flying and bands of music playing, and of black audiences cheering orators who publicly condemned slavery—only inflamed racial hatred and opposition among many whites.

But African Americans continued to press for full citizenship by persuading sympathetic white printers to publish poetry, slave narratives, and pamphlets composed by black authors. The strategy of those writings was to refute racist notions by drawing attention to the intelligence, virtue, and patriotism of black American women and men, both free and enslaved. Typical was the autobiography of Venture Smith, the first slave narrative published in the United States (1798), which followed his captivity as a young boy in West Africa through his lifelong struggle in New England to purchase his own freedom and that of his wife and children. Hardworking and thrifty, resourceful and determined to better himself and his family, Venture Smith's story invited white readers to conclude that he was as true a republican and a self-made man as Benjamin Franklin.

Women's Civic Participation >> The new republic's political festivals and partisan newspapers aimed to woo the loyalty of white adult males who held enough property to vote. But they also sought the support of white women, some of whom joined in the crowds and even took part in the parades. In one New Jersey village the folks lining the parade route cheered as "16 young ladies uniformed in white with garlands in their hats" marched past, playing a patriotic anthem on their flutes. Federalists and Republicans alike encouraged women's involvement on those occasions, hoping that displays of approval from "the American Fair" would encourage husbands and male admirers to support their parties.

Many women seized on such opportunities for greater civic involvement. True, the law excluded most from taking direct part in voting and governing, but those prohibitions did not prevent women from taking an active interest in politics and voicing their opinions. When a female guest in a best-selling novel of the 1790s (the first by an American woman) "simpered" that their sex should not meddle with politics, her hostess shot back, "Why then should the love of our country be a masculine passion only? Why should government, which involves the peace and order of society, of which we are a part, be wholly excluded from our observation?"

 REVIEW

In what ways did politics become more participatory during the 1790s?

JEFFERSON IN POWER

The growing political engagement of ordinary white Americans played an important role in electing Thomas Jefferson to the presidency. He later referred to his election as "the Revolution of 1800," asserting that it "was as real a revolution in the principles of our government as that of 1776 was in its form." That claim exaggerates: Jefferson's presidency did little to enhance political rights or social opportunities of white women or African Americans. Even so, during the following two decades Republicans did set the United States on a more democratic course. And in their dealings with Britain and France, as well as with the Indian tribes of the West, Republican administrations defined, for better and worse, a fuller sense of American nationality.

The New Capital City >> Thomas Jefferson was the first president to be inaugurated in the new capital, Washington, D.C. In 1791 George Washington had commissioned Pierre Charles L'Enfant, a French architect and engineer who had served in the American Revolution, to draw up plans for the new seat of government. L'Enfant designed a city with broad avenues, statues and fountains, parks and plazas, and a central mall. Because the Federalists believed that government was the paramount power in a nation, they had intended that the city would be a new Rome—a cultural, intellectual, and commercial center of the Republic.

The new city fell far short of this grandiose dream. It was located in a swampy river bottom near the head of the Potomac, and the surrounding hills rendered the spot oppressively hot and muggy during the summer. The streets were filled with tree stumps and became seas of mud after a rain. Much of the District was wooded, and virtually all of it remained unoccupied.

When the government moved to its new residence in 1800, the Senate chamber, where Jefferson took the oath of office, was the only part of the Capitol that had been completed.

This isolated and unimpressive capital city reflected the new president's attitude toward government. Distrustful of centralized power of any kind, Jefferson deliberately set out to remake the national government into one of limited scope that touched few people's daily lives. The states rather than the federal government were "the most competent administrators for our domestic concerns," he asserted in his inaugural address. Ever the individualist, he recommended a government that left people "free to regulate their own pursuits of industry and improvement."

Jefferson's Philosophy

>> Jefferson was a product of the Enlightenment, with its faith in the power of human reason to improve society and decipher the universe. He considered "the will of the majority" to be "the only sure guardian of the rights of man," which he defined as "life, liberty, and the pursuit of happiness." Although he conceded that the masses might err, he was confident they would soon return to correct principles. His faith in human virtue exceeded that of most of the founding generation, yet in good republican fashion, he feared those in power, even if they had been elected by the people. Government seemed to Jefferson a necessary evil at best.

To Jefferson agriculture was a morally superior way of life. "Those who labour in the earth are the chosen people of God, if ever he had a chosen people," he wrote in *Notes on the State of Virginia* (1787). Jefferson praised rural life for nourishing the honesty, independence, and virtue so essential in a republic.

Although Jefferson asserted that "the tree of liberty must be refreshed from time to time by the blood of patriots and tyrants," he was no radical. Although he wanted to give the vote to a greater number of Americans, he embraced the traditional republican idea that voters should own property. Republican theorists had long argued that property owners were more economically independent and therefore less likely to be bribed or swayed by demagogues. One of the largest slaveholders in the country, he increasingly muffled his once-bold condemnation of slavery, and in the last years of his life he reproached critics of the institution who sought to prevent it from expanding westward.

Slaveholding aristocrat and apostle of democracy, lofty theorist and pragmatic politician, Jefferson was a complex, at times contradictory, personality. But like most politicians he was flexible in his approach to problems and tried to balance means and ends. And like most leaders he quickly discovered that he confronted very different problems in power than he had in opposition.

Jefferson's Economic Policies

>> The new president quickly proceeded to cut spending and to reduce the size of the government. He also abolished the internal taxes enacted by the Federalists, including the controversial excise on whiskey, and thus was able to get rid of all tax collectors and inspectors. Land sales and tariff duties would supply the funds needed to run the scaled-down government.

The most serious spending cuts were made in the military branches. Jefferson slashed the army budget in half, decreasing the army to 3,000 men. In a national emergency, he reasoned, the militia could defend the country. Jefferson reduced the navy even more, halting work on powerful frigates authorized during the naval war with France.

By such steps Jefferson made significant progress toward paying off Hamilton's national debt. Still, he did not entirely dismantle the Federalists' economic program. Funding and assumption could not be reversed—the nation's honor was pledged to paying these debts, and Jefferson understood the importance of maintaining the nation's credit. More surprising, Jefferson argued that the national bank should be left to run its course until 1811, when its charter would expire. In reality, he expanded the bank's operations and, in words reminiscent of Hamilton, advocated tying banks and members of the business class to the government by rewarding those who supported the Republican Party. In effect, practical politics had triumphed over agrarian economics.

 REVIEW

How does Jefferson compare to the Federalist presidents who preceded him?

WHITES AND INDIANS IN THE WEST

For all his pragmatism Jefferson still viewed the lands stretching from the Appalachians to the Pacific through the perspective of his agrarian ideals. America's vast spaces provided enough land to last for a thousand generations, he predicted in his inaugural address, enough to transform the United States into "an empire of liberty."

The Miami Confederacy Resists >> That optimistic vision contrasted sharply with the views of most Federalists, who feared the West as a threat to social order and stability. In the 1790s they had good reason to fear. British troops refused to leave their forts in the Northwest, and Indian nations still controlled most of the region. Recognizing that fact, the United States conceded that Indian nations had the right to negotiate as sovereign powers. North of the Ohio, leaders of the Miami Confederacy, composed of eight tribes, stoutly refused to sell their homelands without "the united voice of the confederacy."

In response the Washington administration sent 1,500 soldiers in 1790 under General Josiah Harmar to force the Indians to leave by burning their homes and fields. The Miami Confederacy, led by Blue Jacket and Little Turtle, roundly defeated the whites. Harmar was court-martialed, the nation embarrassed, and a second expedition organized the following year under General Arthur St. Clair. This force of over 2,000 was again routed by Little Turtle, whose warriors killed 600 and wounded another 300. The defeat was the worst in the history of Indian wars undertaken by the United States. (In contrast, Custer's defeat in 1876 counted 264 fatalities.)

President Washington dispatched yet another army of 2,000 to the Ohio valley, commanded by "Mad Anthony" Wayne, an accomplished general. At the Battle of Fallen Timbers in August 1794, Wayne won a decisive victory, breaking the Indians' hold on

the Northwest. In the Treaty of Greenville (1795), the tribes **ceded** the southern two-thirds of the area between Lake Erie and the Ohio River, opening it up to white families. Federalists were still not eager to see the land settled. Although they allowed the sale of federal land, they kept the price high, with a required purchase of at least 640 acres—more than four times the size of most American farms.

cede to give up possession of.]

Once in power, Jefferson and the Republicans encouraged settlement by reducing the minimum tract that buyers could purchase (to 320 acres) and by offering land on credit. Sales boomed. By 1820 more than 2 million whites lived in a region they had first entered only 50 years earlier. From Jefferson's perspective, western expansion was a blessing economically, socially, and even politically, because most of the new westerners were Republican.

Doubling the Size of the Nation >> With Spain's colonial empire weakening, Americans were confident that before long they would gain control of Florida and the rest of the Mississippi, either through purchase or by military occupation. Spain had already agreed, in Pinckney's Treaty (see page 151), to allow Americans to navigate the lower Mississippi River. But in 1802 Spain suddenly retracted this right. More alarming, word came that France was about to take control of Louisiana—the territory lying between the Mississippi River and the Rocky Mountains—after a secret agreement with Spain. Under the leadership of Napoleon Bonaparte, France had become the most powerful nation on the European continent, with the military might to protect its new colony and to block American expansion.

Jefferson dispatched James Monroe to Paris to join Robert Livingston, the American minister, in negotiating the purchase of New Orleans and West Florida from the French and thus securing control of the Mississippi. The timing was fortunate: with war looming again in Europe, Napoleon lost interest in Louisiana. He needed money, and in April 1803 he offered to sell not just New Orleans but all of Louisiana to the United States. This proposal flabbergasted Livingston and Monroe. Their instructions said nothing about acquiring all of Louisiana, and they had not been authorized to spend what the French demanded. But here was an opportunity to expand dramatically the boundaries of the United States. Pressed for an immediate answer, Livingston and Monroe took a deep breath and, after haggling over a few details, agreed to purchase Louisiana for approximately $15 million. In one fell swoop the American negotiators had doubled the country's size by adding some 830,000 square miles.

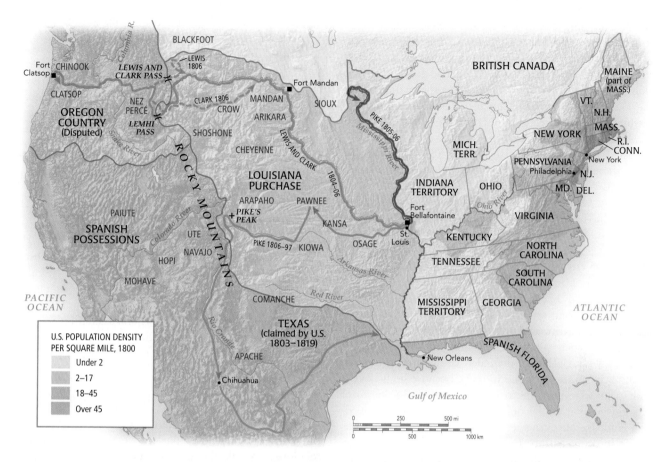

MAP 9.3: EXPLORATION AND EXPANSION: THE LOUISIANA PURCHASE

The vast, largely uncharted Louisiana Purchase lay well beyond the most densely populated areas of the United States. The Lewis and Clark expedition, along with Lieutenant Zebulon Pike's exploration of the upper Mississippi River and the Southwest, opened the way for westward expansion.

What territory did the Lewis and Clark expedition traverse in addition to the Louisiana Purchase? What territory did the Pike expedition traverse?

While Jefferson was pleased at the prospect of acquiring so much territory, he found the legality of the act troubling. The Constitution, after all, did not authorize the acquisition of territory by treaty. In the end, the president sent the treaty to the Senate for ratification, noting privately, "The less we say about constitutional difficulties the better." Once again pragmatism triumphed over theory.

Even before the Louisiana Purchase was completed, Congress secretly funded an expedition up the Missouri River to the Pacific. Leading that party were Meri-wether Lewis, Jefferson's secretary, and William Clark, a younger brother of George Rogers Clark. Jefferson instructed them to make detailed observations of the soil, climate, rivers, minerals, and plant and animal life. They were also to investigate the practicabil-ity of an overland route to the Pacific and engage in diplomacy with the Indians along the way. By push-ing onward to the Pacific Lewis and Clark would

strengthen the American title to Oregon, which several nations claimed but none effectively occupied.

In the spring of 1804 Lewis and Clark left St. Louis and headed up the Missouri River with 48 men. They laboriously hauled their boats upstream to present-day North Dakota, where they spent the winter with the Mandan Indians. The next spring, they headed west again. Only with great difficulty did the expedi-tion pass the rugged mountains ahead of the winter snows and then float down first the Snake and then the Columbia River to the Pacific.

The western country Lewis and Clark traversed had been shaken by momentous changes over the pre-vious quarter of a century. The trade routes across the plains and through the mountains circulated goods in greater quantities than ever before. Horses and guns in particular upset older Indian ways, making tribes more mobile and more dangerous. Lewis and Clark's expedition spotted Spanish horse gear from Mexico in villages along the upper Missouri River, guns from French traders to the northeast, and British teapots along the Columbia River. Most disruptive to these western lands was smallpox, which had made its way along the same trade routes ever since the pandemic of the 1780s (see page 131). The disease decimated Indian populations and forced many tribes to resettle.

After a bleak winter in Oregon the expedition returned home over the Rockies in 1806. It brought back thousands of plant and animal specimens and produced a remarkably accurate map of its journey. Lewis and Clark had crossed a continent disrupted by change. In the century to come the changes would only accelerate.

Pressure on Indian Lands and Culture >>

East of the Mississippi, white settlers continued to flood into the backcountry. Jefferson endorsed the policy that Indian tribes either would have to assimilate into American culture by becoming farmers and abandoning their seminomadic hunting or would have to move west. Jefferson defended these alternatives as in the best interests of the Indians, because he believed that otherwise they faced extermination. But he also recognized that by becoming farmers they would need less land. He encouraged the policy of selling goods on credit in order to lure Indians into debt. "When these debts get beyond what the individuals can pay," the president observed, "they become willing to lop them off by a cession of lands."

Between 1800 and 1810, whites pressed Indians into ceding more than 100 million acres in the Ohio River valley. The loss of so much land devastated Indian cultures and transformed their environment by reducing hunting grounds and making game and food scarce. "Stop your people from killing our game," the Shawnees complained in 1802 to federal Indian agents. "They would be angry if we were to kill a cow or hog of theirs, the little game that remains is very dear to us." Tribes also became dependent on white trade to obtain blankets, guns, metal utensils, alcohol, and decorative beads. To pay for these goods with furs Indians often overtrapped, which forced them to invade the lands of neighboring tribes, provoking wars.

The strain produced by white expansion led to alcoholism, growing violence among tribe members, family disintegration, and the collapse of the clan system designed to regulate relations among different villages. The question of how to deal with white culture became a matter of anguished debate. While some Native Americans attempted to take up farming and accommodate to white ways, for most the course of assimilation proved unappealing and fraught with risk.

White Frontier Society >>

Whites faced their own problems on the frontier. In the first wave of settlement came backwoods families who cleared a few acres of forest by girdling the trees, removing the brush, and planting corn between the dead trunks. Such settlers were mostly squatters without legal title to their land. As a region filled up, these pioneers usually sold their improvements and headed west again.

Taking their place, typically, were young single men from the East, who married and started families. These pioneers, too, engaged in semisubsistence agriculture, except those lucky few whose prime locations allowed them to transport their crops down the Ohio and Mississippi Rivers to New Orleans for shipment to distant markets. But many frontier families struggled, moving several times but never managing to rise from the ranks of squatters or tenant farmers to become independent landowners. Fledgling western communities lacked schools, churches, and courts, and inhabitants often lived miles distant from even their nearest neighbors.

The Beginnings of the Second Great Awakening >>

This hardscrabble frontier proved the perfect tinder for sparking a series of dramatic religious revivals in the decades surrounding 1800. What lit the fire were missionary efforts by major Protestant churches—particularly the Baptists and the Methodists—who sent their ministers to travel the countryside on horseback and to preach wherever they could gather a crowd. Often those religious meetings took place outdoors and drew eager hearers from as far as 100 miles away, who camped for several days in makeshift tents to listen to sermons and to share in praying and singing hymns.

Thus was born a new form of Protestant worship, the camp meeting, which drew national notice after a mammoth gathering at Cane Ridge, Kentucky, in

Opinion

Was there any strategy that Indian nations between the Appalachians and the Mississippi could have adopted to halt white expansion?

↟ Tents ringed the central area of a camp meeting where benches faced the preachers' platform. What does this illustration of an 1837 camp meeting suggest about gender relations and religious experience?

August 1801. At a time when the largest city in the state had only 2,000 people, more than 10,000 men, women, and children, white and black, flocked there to hear dozens of ministers preaching the gospel. Many in the crowd were overwhelmed by powerful religious feelings, some shrieking and shaking over guilt for their sins, others laughing and dancing from their high hopes of eternal salvation.

Some Protestant ministers denounced the "revival" at Cane Ridge and elsewhere as yet another instance of the ignorance and savagery of westerners. Other ministers were optimistic: they saw frontier camp meetings as the first sign of a Protestant Christian renewal that would sweep the new republic. Their hopes set the stage for what would come to be called the Second Great Awakening, a wave of religious revivals that swept throughout the nation after 1800 (see Chapter 12).

The Prophet, Tecumseh, and the Pan-Indian Movement >> Native peoples also turned to religion to meet the challenges of the early national frontier. Indeed, in traditional Indian religions they found the resource to revitalize their cultures by severing all ties with the white world. During the 1790s a revival led by Handsome Lake took hold among the Iroquois, following the loss of most of the Iroquois lands and the collapse of their military power in western New York. Later Lalawethika, also known as the Prophet, sparked a religious renewal among the Shawnees. The Prophet's early life was bleak: he was a poor hunter and as a child accidentally blinded himself in the right eye with an arrow; the ridicule of his fellow tribe members drove him to alcoholism. Suddenly, in

April 1805 he lapsed into a trance so deep that he was given up for dead. When he revived he spoke of being reborn. From this vision and others he outlined a new creed for the Shawnees.

Taking a new name—Tenskwatawa (Open Door)—he urged the Shawnees to renounce whiskey and white goods and return to their old ways of hunting with bows and arrows, eating customary foods such as corn and beans, and wearing traditional garb. The Shawnees could revitalize their culture, the Prophet insisted, by condemning intertribal violence, embracing monogamous marriage, and rejecting the idea of private instead of communal property. Except for guns, which could be used in self-defense, his followers were to discard all items made by whites. Intermarriage with white settlers was forbidden.

Setting up headquarters in 1808 at the newly built village of Prophetstown in Indiana, Tenskwatawa led a wider revival among the tribes of the Northwest. Just as thousands of white settlers traveled to Methodist or Baptist camp meetings in the woods, where preachers denounced the evils of liquor and called for a return to a pure way of life, so thousands of Indians from northern tribes traveled to the Prophet's village for inspiration. Many were concerned about the threatened loss of Indian lands.

Whereas Tenskwatawa's strategy of revitalization was primarily religious, his older brother Tecumseh turned to political and military solutions. William Henry Harrison described Tecumseh as "one of those uncommon geniuses which spring up occasionally to produce revolutions and overturn the established order of things." Tall and athletic, an accomplished hunter and warrior, Tecumseh traveled throughout the Northwest, urging tribes to forget ancient rivalries and unite to protect their lands. Just as Indian nations in the past had adopted the strategy of uniting in a confederacy, Tecumseh's alliance brought together the Wyandot, Chippewa, Sauk and Fox, Winnebago, Potawatomi, and other tribes on an even larger scale.

But the campaign for Pan-Indian unity ran into serious obstacles. Often, Tecumseh was asking tribes to unite with their traditional enemies in a common cause. When he headed south in 1811 he encountered greater resistance. Compared with northern tribes, most southern tribes were more prosperous, were more acculturated, and felt less immediate pressure on their land from whites. His southern mission ended largely in failure.

To compound Tecumseh's problems, while he was away a force of Americans under Governor Harrison defeated the Prophet's forces at the Battle of Tippecanoe in November 1811 and destroyed Prophetstown. As a result Tecumseh became convinced that the best way to contain white expansion was to play off the Americans against the British, who still held forts in

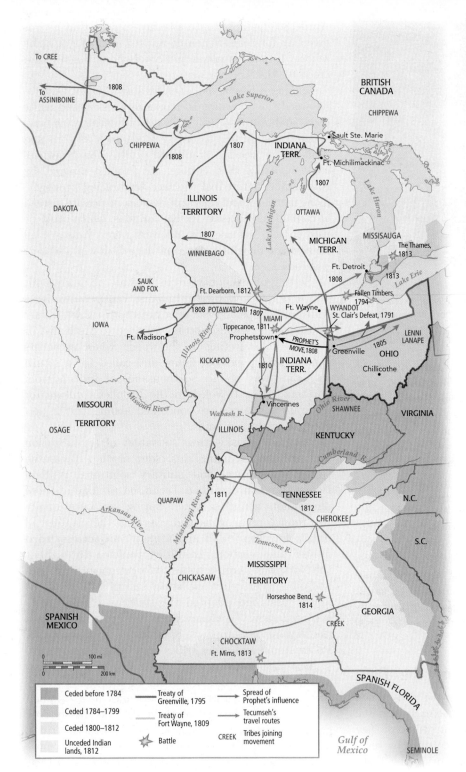

With land cessions and white western migration placing increased pressure on Indian cultures after 1790, news of the Prophet's revival fell on eager ears. It spread especially quickly northward along the shores of Lake Michigan and westward along Lake Superior and the interior of Wisconsin. Following the Battle of Tippecanoe, Tecumseh eclipsed the Prophet as the major leader of Indian resistance, but his trips south to forge political alliances met with less success.

How far south did Tecumseh travel in his attempt to unite Indian resistance?

THE SECOND WAR FOR AMERICAN INDEPEN-DENCE

As Tecumseh worked to achieve a Pan–Indian alliance, Jefferson encountered his own difficulties in trying to achieve American political unity. The president hoped to woo all but the most extreme Federalists into the Republican camp. His reelection in 1804 showed how much progress he had made, as he defeated Federalist Charles Cotesworth Pinckney and carried 15 of 17 states. With the Republicans controlling three–quarters of the seats in Congress, one–party rule seemed at hand.

But events across the Atlantic complicated the efforts to unite Americans. Only two weeks after Napoleon agreed to sell Louisiana to the United States, war broke out between France and Great Britain. As in the 1790s the United States found itself caught between the world's two greatest powers. Jefferson insisted that the nation should remain neutral in a European war. But the policies he proposed to maintain neutrality sparked sharp divisions in American society and momentarily revived the two–party system.

the Great Lakes region. Indeed, by 1811 the United States and Great Britain were on the brink of war.

✓ REVIEW

How did Jefferson's presidency shape the settlement of the West?

In the past Jefferson had not shrunk from the use of force in dealing with foreign nations—most notably the Barbary States of North Africa—Algiers, Morocco, Tripoli, and Tunis. During the seventeenth and eighteenth centuries their corsairs plundered the cargo of enemy ships and enslaved the crews. European nations found it convenient to pay tributes to the Barbary States so their ships could sail unmolested. But both Jefferson and John Adams disliked that idea. The "policy of Christendom" of paying tribute, complained Adams, "has made Cowards of all their Sailors before the Standard of Mahomet [Mohammed]."

By the time John Adams became president he had subdued his outrage and agreed to tributes. But when Tripoli increased its demands in 1801 President Jefferson sent a squadron of American ships to force a settlement. In 1803 Tripoli captured the USS *Philadelphia*. Only the following year did Lieutenant Stephen Decatur repair the situation by sneaking into Tripoli's harbor and burning the vessel. The American blockade that followed forced Tripoli to give up its demands for tribute. Even so, the United States continued paying tribute to the other Barbary States until 1816.

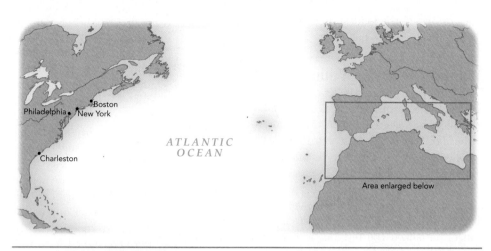

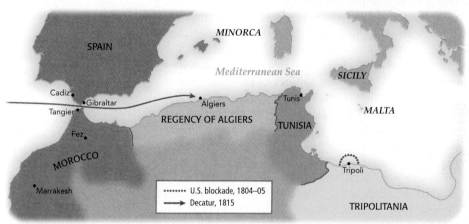

MAP 9.5: THE UNITED STATES AND THE BARBARY STATES, 1801–1815

The young United States, like many European powers, found its trading vessels challenged by the Barbary States of Morocco, Algiers, Tunis, and Tripoli. When the pasha of Tripoli declared war on the United States in 1801, Jefferson dispatched a force that blockaded Tripoli to bring the war to an end in 1805. Tribute paid to the other Barbary States continued until 1816, after a new naval force, led by Captain Stephen Decatur, forced the ruler of Algiers to end the practice.
What cultural factors made Jefferson and Adams reluctant to pay tribute to the Barbary States?

The Embargo >> Jefferson was willing to fight the Barbary States, but he drew back from declaring war against Britain or France. Between 1803 and 1807 Britain seized more than 500 American ships; France more than 300. The British navy also impressed into service thousands of sailors, some who were deserters from England's fleet but others who were native-born Americans. Despite such harrassment, Jefferson pursued a program of "peaceable coercion" designed to protect neutral rights without war. His proposed **embargo** not only prohibited American ships from trading with foreign ports but also stopped the export of all American goods. The president was confident that American exports were so essential to the two belligerents that they would quickly agree to respect American neutral rights. In December 1807 Congress passed the Embargo Act.

> **embargo** government act prohibiting trade with a foreign country or countries, usually to exert economic pressure.

Jefferson had seriously miscalculated. France did not depend on American trade and so managed well enough, while British ships quickly took over the carrying trade as American vessels lay idle. Under the embargo, both American imports and exports plunged. As the center of American shipping, New England port cities protested the loudest, and their merchants smuggled behind officials' backs.

Madison and the Young Republicans >>

Following Washington's example Jefferson did not seek a third term. A caucus of Republican members of Congress selected James Madison to run against Federalist Charles Cotesworth Pinckney. Madison triumphed easily, although in discontented New England, the Federalists picked up 24 seats in Congress.

Few men have assumed the presidency with more experience than James Madison, yet his tenure as president proved disappointing. Despite his intellectual brilliance, he lacked the force of leadership and the inner strength to impose his will on less capable men.

With a president reluctant to fight for what he wanted, leadership passed to Congress. The elections of 1810 swept in a new generation of Republicans, led by the magnetic 34-year-old Henry Clay of Kentucky, who gained the rare distinction of being elected Speaker in his first term. These younger Republicans were more nationalistic than the generation led by Jefferson and Madison. They sought an ambitious program of economic development and were aggressive expansionists, especially those from frontier districts. Their willingness to go to war earned them the name of War Hawks. Though they numbered fewer than 30 in Congress, they quickly became the driving force in the Republican Party.

The Decision for War >> During Jefferson's final week in office in early 1809 Congress repealed the Embargo Act. The following year Congress authorized trade with France and England but decreed that if one of the two belligerents agreed to stop interfering with American shipping, trade with the other would be prohibited.

Given these circumstances, Napoleon outmaneuvered the British by announcing that he would put aside the French

>> Where the Prophet centered his attempts at Indian unity on religious renewal, his brother Tecumseh, pictured here, took a political approach to the Indian revitalization movement. Advocating political unity in order to preserve Indian lands and cultures, Tecumseh was the dominant figure among Indians east of the Mississippi until he died fighting alongside the British in the War of 1812.

trade regulations. Madison took the French emperor at his word and reimposed a ban on trade with England. French raiders continued to seize American ships, but American anger focused on the British, who then seized many more ships and continued to impress American sailors. Finally, on June 16, 1812, the British ministry suspended the searches and seizures of American ships.

The concession came too late. Two days earlier, unaware of the change in policy, Congress granted Madison's request for a declaration of war against Britain. The vote was mostly along party lines, with every Federalist voting against war. By contrast, members of Congress from the South and the West clamored most strongly for war. Their constituents were consumed with a desire to seize additional territory in Canada or in Florida (owned by Britain's ally Spain). In addition, they accused the British of stirring up hostility among the Indian tribes.

Perhaps most important, the War Hawks were convinced that Britain had never truly accepted the verdict of the American Revolution. To them, American independence—and with it republicanism—hung in the balance. For Americans hungering to be accepted in the community of nations, nothing rankled more than still being treated by the British as colonials.

With Britain preoccupied by Napoleon, the War Hawks expected an easy victory. In truth, the United States was totally unprepared for war. Crippled by Jefferson's cutbacks, the navy was unable to lift the British blockade of the American coast, which bottled up the country's merchant marine and most of its navy. As for the U.S. Army, it was small and poorly led. When Congress moved to increase its size to 75,000, even the most hawkish states failed to meet their quotas. Congress was also reluctant to levy taxes to finance the war.

A three-pronged American invasion of Canada from Detroit, Niagara, and Lake Champlain failed dismally in 1812. Americans fared better the following year, as both sides raced to build a navy on the strategically located Lake Erie. Led by Commander Oliver Hazard Perry, American forces won a decisive victory at Put-In Bay in 1813.

As the United States struggled to organize its forces, Tecumseh sensed that his long-awaited opportunity had come to drive Americans out of the western territories. "Here is a chance . . . such as

MAP 9.6: THE WAR OF 1812

After the American victory on Lake Erie and the defeat of the western Indians at the Battle of the Thames, the British adopted a three-pronged strategy to invade the United States, climaxing with an attempt on New Orleans. But they met their match in Andrew Jackson, whose troops marched to New Orleans after fighting a series of battles against the Creeks and forcing them to cede a massive tract of land.
Why did so much of the fighting in the War of 1812 take place on the northern borders of the United States?

will never occur again," he told a war council, "for us Indians of North America to form ourselves into one great combination." Allying with the British, Tecumseh traveled south in the fall to talk again with his Creek allies. To coordinate an Indian offensive for the following summer, he left a bundle of red sticks with eager Creek soldiers. They were to remove one stick each day from the bundle and attack when the sticks had run out.

Some of the older Creeks were more acculturated and preferred an American alliance. But about 2,000 younger "Red Stick" Creeks launched a series of attacks, climaxed by the destruction of Fort

Mims along the Alabama River in August 1813. Once again, the Indians' lack of unity was a serious handicap, as warriors from the Cherokee, Choctaw, and Chickasaw tribes, traditional Creek enemies, allied with the Americans. At the Battle of Horseshoe Bend in March 1814, General Andrew Jackson and his Tennessee militia soundly defeated the Red Stick Creeks. Jackson promptly dictated a peace treaty under which the Creeks ceded 22 million acres of land in the Mississippi Territory. They and the other southern tribes still retained significant landholdings, but Indian military power had been broken in the South, east of the Mississippi.

Farther north, in October 1813, American forces under General William Henry Harrison defeated the British and their Indian allies at the Battle of the Thames. In the midst of heavy fighting Tecumseh was killed. With him died any hope of a Pan–Indian movement.

The British Invasion >> As long as the war against Napoleon continued, the British were unwilling to divert army units to North America. But in 1814 Napoleon was at last defeated. Free to concentrate on America the British devised a coordinated strategy to invade the United States in the northern, central, and southern parts of the country. The main army headed south from Montreal but was checked when Americans destroyed the British fleet on Lake Champlain.

Meanwhile, a smaller British force captured Washington and burned several public buildings, including the Capitol and the president's home. To cover the scars of this destruction, the executive mansion was painted with whitewash and became known as the White House. The burning of the capital was a humiliating event: President Madison and his wife, Dolley, were forced to flee. But the defeat had little military significance. The principal British objective was Baltimore, where for 25 hours their fleet bombarded Fort McHenry in the city's harbor. When Francis Scott Key saw the American flag still flying above the fort at dawn, he hurriedly composed the verses of "The Star Spangled Banner," which was eventually adopted as the national anthem.

The third British target was New Orleans, where a formidable army of 7,500 British troops was opposed by a hastily assembled force commanded by Major General Andrew Jackson. The Americans included regular soldiers; frontiersmen from Kentucky and Tennessee; citizens of New Orleans, including several companies of free African Americans; Choctaw Indians; and a group of pirates. Jackson's outnumbered and ill–equipped forces won a stunning victory, which made the general an overnight hero.

In December 1814, while Jackson was organizing the defense of New Orleans, New England Federalists met in Hartford to map strategy against the war. Angry as they were, the delegates still rejected calls for secession. Instead, they proposed a series of amendments to the Constitution that showed their displeasure with the government's economic policies and their resentment of the South's national political power.

To the convention's dismay its representatives arrived in Washington to present their demands just as news of Andrew Jackson's victory was being trumpeted on the streets. The celebrations badly undercut the Hartford Convention, as did news from across the Atlantic that American negotiators in Ghent, Belgium, had signed a treaty ending the war. Hostilities had ceased, technically, on Christmas Eve 1814, two weeks before the Battle of New Orleans. Both sides were relieved to end the conflict, even though the Treaty of Ghent left unresolved the issues of impressment, neutral rights or trade.

America Turns Inward >> The return of peace hard on the heels of Jackson's victory sparked a new confidence in many Americans. The new nationalism sounded the death knell of the Federalist Party, for even talk of secession at the Hartford Convention had tainted the party with disunion and treason. In the 1816 election Madison's secretary of state, James Monroe, resoundingly defeated Federalist Rufus King of New York. Four years later Monroe ran for reelection unopposed.

Monroe's Presidency >> The major domestic challenge that Monroe faced was the renewal of sectional rivalries in 1819, when the Missouri Territory applied for admission as a slave state. Before the controversy over Missouri erupted, slavery had not been a major issue in American politics. Congress had debated the institution when it prohibited the African slave trade in 1808, the earliest year this step could

⋀ Young Henry Clay of Kentucky promoted the Missouri Compromise.

be taken under the Constitution. But lacking any specific federal legislation to stop it, slavery had crossed the Mississippi River into the Louisiana Purchase. Louisiana entered the Union in 1812 as a slave state, and in 1818 Missouri, which had about 10,000 slaves in its population, asked permission to come in, too.

In 1818 the Union contained 11 free and 11 slave states. As the federal government became stronger and more active, both the North and the South worried about maintaining their political power. The North's greater population gave it a majority in the House of Representatives, 105 to 81. The Senate, of course, was evenly balanced, because each state had two senators regardless of population. But Maine, which previously had been part of Massachusetts, requested admission as a free state. That would upset the balance unless Missouri came in as a slave state.

Representative James Tallmadge of New York disturbed this delicate state of affairs when in 1819 he introduced an amendment that would establish a program of gradual emancipation in Missouri. For the first time Congress directly debated the morality of slavery, often bitterly. The House approved the Tallmadge amendment, but the Senate refused to accept it, and the two houses deadlocked.

When Congress reconvened in 1820, Henry Clay of Kentucky promoted what came to be known as the Missouri Compromise. Under its terms Missouri was admitted as a slave state and Maine as a free state. In addition, slavery was forever prohibited in the remainder of the Louisiana Purchase north of 36°30' (the southern boundary of Missouri). Clay's proposal, the first of several sectional compromises he would engineer in his long career, won congressional approval and Monroe signed the measure, ending the crisis. But southern fears for the security of slavery and northern fears about its spread remained. Monroe's greatest achievements were diplomatic, accomplished largely by his talented secretary of state, John Quincy Adams, the son of President John Adams. An experienced diplomat, Adams thought of the Republic in continental terms and was intent on promoting expansion to the Pacific. Such a vision required dealing with Spain, which had never recognized the legality of the Louisiana Purchase. In addition, between 1810 and 1813 the United States had occupied and unilaterally annexed Spanish West Florida.

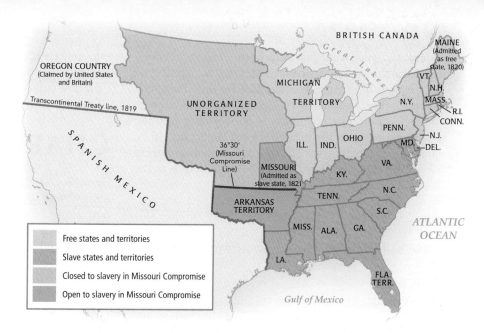

MAP 9.7: THE MISSOURI COMPROMISE AND THE UNION'S BOUNDARIES IN 1820

But Spain was preoccupied with events farther south in the Americas. In the first quarter of the nineteenth century its colonies one after another revolted and established themselves as independent nations. These revolutions increased the pressure on the Spanish minister to America, Luis de Onís, to come to terms with the United States. So, too, did Andrew Jackson, who marched into East Florida and captured several Spanish forts in 1818. Jackson had exceeded his instructions, but Adams understood the additional pressure this aggression put on Onís and refused to disavow it.

Fearful that the United States might next invade Texas or other Spanish territory, Spain agreed to the Transcontinental Treaty in February 1819. Its terms set the boundary between American and Spanish territory all the way to the Pacific. Spain not only gave up its claims to the Pacific Northwest but also ceded Florida. In order to obtain the line to the Pacific, the United States abandoned its contention that Texas was part of the Louisiana Purchase.

More important, the United States also came to terms with Great Britain. Following the War of 1812 the British abandoned their connections with the western Indian tribes and no longer attempted to block American expansion to the Rocky Mountains. In a growing spirit of cooperation the countries agreed in 1818 to the 49th parallel as the northern boundary of the Louisiana Purchase and also to joint control of the Oregon Territory for 10 years, subject to renewal.

In his annual message to Congress, on December 2, 1823, Monroe also announced that the United States would not interfere with already established European colonies in the Western Hemisphere. But any intervention in the new republics of Latin America, he warned, would be considered a hostile act: "The American continents . . . are henceforth not to be considered as subjects for future colonization by any European powers." The essence of this policy was the concept of two worlds, one old and one new, each refraining from interfering in the other's affairs. American public opinion hailed Monroe's statement and then promptly forgot it. Only years later would it be referred to as the Monroe Doctrine.

 REVIEW

What were the causes of the War of 1812?

The three decades after 1789 demonstrated how profoundly events in the wider world could affect life within the United States, shaping its politics, its boundaries, its economy—its future.

The French Revolution contributed to splintering the once–united leaders of the American Revolution into two rival parties. The wars that followed, between France and England, deepened the divisions between Federalists and Republicans and prompted both parties to mobilize the political loyalties of ordinary white American men and women. Napoleon's ambitions to conquer Europe handed Jefferson the Louisiana Territory, while British efforts to reclaim its American empire tempted some New Englanders to secede from the Union and encouraged Tecumseh's hopes of mounting a Pan–Indian resistance on the frontier. The Haitian Revolution in the Caribbean prompted free blacks in northern cities to protest racial inequalities and slavery within the United States.

But by the 1820s most white Americans paid less attention to events abroad than to expanding across the vast North American continent. Jefferson had dreamed of an "empire of liberty," delighting in expansion as the means to preserve a nation of small farmers. But younger, more nationalistic Republicans had a different vision of expansion. They spoke of internal improvements, protective tariffs to foster American industries, roads and canals to link farmers with towns, cities, and wider markets. These new Republicans were not aristocratic, like the Federalists of old. Still, their dream of a national, commercial republic resembled Franklin's and Hamilton's more than Jefferson's. They had seen how handsomely American merchants and commercial farmers profited when European wars swelled demand for American wheat and cotton. They looked to profit from speculation in land, the growth of commercial agriculture, and new methods of industrial manufacturing. If they

represented the rising generation, what would be the fate of Crèvecoeur's semisubsistence farm communities? The answer was not yet clear.

CHAPTER SUMMARY

Basic social divisions between the commercial and semisubsistence regions shaped the politics of the new United States. Between 1789 and the 1820s the first parties emerged and, along with them, a more popular and participatory political culture. Over the same decades Indian confederacies mounted a sustained resistance to westward expansion, while events in Europe deepened divisions among Federalists and Republicans and threatened the very existence of the fledgling American republic.

- The first party to organize in the 1790s was the Federalists, led by Alexander Hamilton and George Washington.
- Divisions over Hamilton's policies as secretary of the treasury led to the formation of the Republicans, led by James Madison and Thomas Jefferson.
- The commercially minded Federalists believed in order and hierarchy, supported loose construction of the Constitution, and wanted a powerful central government to promote economic growth.
- The Republican Party, with its sympathy for agrarian ideals, endorsed strict construction of the Constitution, wanted a less active federal government, and harbored a strong fear of aristocracy.
- The French Revolution, the XYZ Affair, the naval war, and the Alien and Sedition Acts also deepened the partisan division between Federalists and Republicans during the 1790s. The Federalists' controversial domestic and foreign policies, internal divisions, and hostility to the masses eventually led to their downfall.
- Before becoming president, Jefferson advocated the principles of agrarianism, limited government, and strict construction of the Constitution. But once in power, he failed to dismantle Hamilton's economic program and promoted western expansion by acquiring Louisiana from France.
- Chief Justice John Marshall proclaimed that the courts were to interpret the meaning of the Constitution (judicial review), a move that helped the judiciary emerge as an equal branch of government.
- Lewis and Clark produced the first reliable information and maps of the Louisiana territory. The lands they passed through had been transformed over the previous 25 years by disease, dislocation, and the arrival of horses and guns.

- The Shawnee prophet Tenskwatawa and his brother Tecumseh organized the most important Indian resistance to the expansion of the new republic, but the movement collapsed with the death of Tecumseh during the War of 1812.
- France and Britain both interfered with neutral rights, and the United States went to war against Britain in 1812.
- After 1815 a surge in American nationalism was reinforced by Britain's recognition of American sovereignty and the Monroe Doctrine's prohibition of European intervention in the Western Hemisphere. But the Missouri crisis foreshadowed growing sectional rivalries.

Additional Reading

Two good overviews of early national politics are Stanley Elkins and Eric McKitrick's *The Age of Federalism* (1993); and James Roger Sharp, *American Politics in the Early Republic* (1993). Another approach to understanding the politics of this period is to read about the lives of leading political figures: among the best are Joseph Ellis's biographies of John Adams (*Passionate Sage*, 1993) and Thomas Jefferson (*American Sphinx*, rev. ed., 1998); and two biographies of Alexander Hamilton by Ron Chernow and Gerald Stourzh. To become better acquainted with the popular political culture of the early republic, consult *Beyond the Founders* (2004), a superb collection of essays edited by Jeffrey Pasley, Andrew W. Robertson, and David Waldstreicher. For an engaging narrative about the political influence exerted by white women, see Catherine Allgor, *Parlor Politics* (2000); and for rich descriptions of the social and political interactions among whites, African Americans, and Indians in the new republic, see Joshua Rothman, *Notorious in the Neighborhood* (2003); and John Wood Sweet, *Bodies Politic* (2003). To gain a fuller understanding of the lives of both Indians and western frontier settlers, rely on Gregory Evans Dowd, *A Spirited Resistance* (1993); John Mack Faraghers, *Sugar Creek* (1986); Adam Rothman, *Slave Country* (2005); Alan Taylor, *William Cooper's Town* (1995); and R. David Edmunds, *The Shawnee Prophet* (1983).

Significant Events

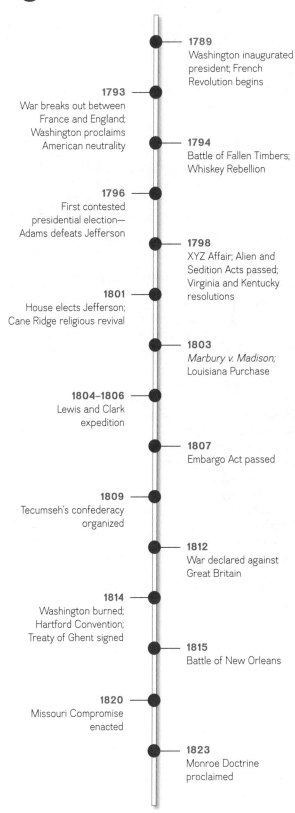

1789 Washington inaugurated president; French Revolution begins

1793 War breaks out between France and England; Washington proclaims American neutrality

1794 Battle of Fallen Timbers; Whiskey Rebellion

1796 First contested presidential election—Adams defeats Jefferson

1798 XYZ Affair; Alien and Sedition Acts passed; Virginia and Kentucky resolutions

1801 House elects Jefferson; Cane Ridge religious revival

1803 *Marbury v. Madison*; Louisiana Purchase

1804–1806 Lewis and Clark expedition

1807 Embargo Act passed

1809 Tecumseh's confederacy organized

1812 War declared against Great Britain

1814 Washington burned; Hartford Convention; Treaty of Ghent signed

1815 Battle of New Orleans

1820 Missouri Compromise enacted

1823 Monroe Doctrine proclaimed

10 The Opening of America

1815–1850

New York's Erie Canal transformed many inland settlements into commercial centers. This canal boat is named after the first inland boom-town in America, Rochester.

>> An American Story

FROM BOOM TO BUST WITH ONE-DAY CLOCKS

In the years before the Civil War, the name of Chauncey Jerome could be found traced in neat, sharp letters in a thousand different places across the globe: everywhere from the fireplace mantels of southern planters to the log cabins of Illinois farmers, and even in Chinese trading houses. For Chauncey Jerome was a New England clockmaker whose clever and inexpensive machines had conquered the markets of the world.

As a boy Jerome had apprenticed himself to a carpenter, but after serving in the War of 1812 he decided to try clock-making. For years he eked out a living peddling his products from farmhouse to farmhouse, until 1824, when his career took off thanks to a "very showy" bronze looking-glass clock. Between 1827 and 1837 Jerome's factory produced more clocks than any other in the country. But when the Panic of 1837 struck, Jerome had to scramble to avoid financial ruin.

Looking for a new opportunity, he set out to produce an inexpensive brass "one-day" clock—so called because its winding mechanism kept it running that long. Traditionally, the works of these clocks were made of wood, and the wheels and teeth had to be painstakingly cut by hand. Jerome's brass version proved more accurate and cheaper to boot. Costs came down further when he began to use interchangeable parts and combined his operations for making cases and movements within a single factory in New Haven, Connecticut. By systematically organizing the production process, Jerome brought the price of a good clock within the reach of ordinary people. So popular were the new models that desperate competitors began attaching Jerome labels to their own inferior imitations.

Disaster loomed again in 1855 when Jerome took on several unreliable partners. Within a few years his business faltered, then failed. At

<< Peddlers like this one helped spread the market economy to every corner of the United States. Early in his career, Chauncey Jerome himself peddled his clocks from farmhouse to farmhouse.

the age of 62 the once-prominent business leader found himself working again in a clock factory as an ordinary mechanic. He lived his last years in poverty.

Chauncey Jerome's life spanned the transition from the master-apprentice system of production to the beginnings of mechanization and the rise of the factory system. By 1850 the notion of independent American farmers living mainly on what they themselves produced had become a dream of the past. In its place stood a commercial republic in which a full-blown national market encompassed most settled areas of the country.

The concept of the market is crucial here. Americans tied themselves to one another eagerly, even aggressively, through the mechanism of the free market. They sold cotton or wheat and bought manufactured cloth or brass one-day clocks. They borrowed money

not merely to buy a house or farm but also to speculate and profit. They relied, even in many rural villages, on cash and paper money instead of bartering for goods and services. American life moved from less to more specialized forms of labor. It moved from subsistence-oriented to commercially oriented outlooks and from face-to-face local dealings to impersonal, distant transactions. It shifted from the mechanically simple to the technologically complex and from less dense patterns of settlement on farms to more complex arrangements in cities and towns. Such were the changes Chauncey Jerome witnessed—indeed, changes he helped to bring about himself, with his clocks that divided the working days of Americans into more disciplined, orderly segments.

As these changes took place, Jerome sensed that society had taken on a different tone—that the marketplace and its ethos had become dominant. "It is all money and business, business and money which make the man now-a-days," he complained. "Success is every thing." The United States, according to one foreign traveler, had become "one gigantic workshop, over the entrance of which there is the blazing inscription 'No admission here except on business.'" <<

What's to Come

THE NATIONAL MARKET ECONOMY

The national market economy began to develop following the War of 1812. As the United States entered a period of unprecedented economic expansion, the economy became varied enough to grow without relying on international trade. Before the war, if European nations suddenly stopped purchasing American commodities such as tobacco and timber, the domestic economy faltered. Since so many Americans remained rural and primarily self–sufficient, they could not absorb any increase in goods produced by American manufacturers.

But the War of 1812 marked an important turning point in the creation and expansion of a domestic market. First the embargo and then the war itself stimulated manufacturing, particularly in textiles. In addition, war had also bottled up capital in Europe. When peace was restored, this capital flowed into the United States to take advantage of new investment opportunities. Finally, the war experience led the federal government to adopt policies designed to spur economic expansion.

The New Nationalism >> After the war with Britain, leadership passed to a new generation of the Republic—younger men such as Henry Clay, John C. Calhoun, and John Quincy Adams. Each was an ardent nationalist eager to use federal power to promote development. Increasingly dominant within the Republican Party, they advocated the "New Nationalism," a set of economic policies designed to help all regions prosper and bind the nation more tightly together.

Even James Madison saw the need for increased federal activity, given the problems the government experienced during the war. The national bank had closed its doors in 1811 when its charter expired, and the result had been financial chaos. With Madison's approval Congress in 1816 chartered the Second Bank of the United States for a period of 20 years. Madison also agreed to a mildly protective tariff to aid young American industries by raising the price of competing foreign goods. Finally, Madison supported federal aid for internal improvements such as roads, canals, and bridges, since the war had demonstrated how cumbersome it was to move troops or supplies overland.

The Cotton Trade >> The most important spur to American economic development after 1815 was the growing cotton trade. By the end of the eighteenth century, southern planters had discovered that short–fiber cotton would grow in the lower part of the South. But the cotton contained sticky green seeds that could not be easily separated from the lint by hand, until a mechanical engine, or "cotton gin," patented by Eli Whitney, was developed to do the job. With a slave now able to clean 50 pounds of cotton a day (compared with only 1 pound by hand), and with prices high on the world market, cotton production in the Lower

Opinion

Did the national market economy benefit most Americans?

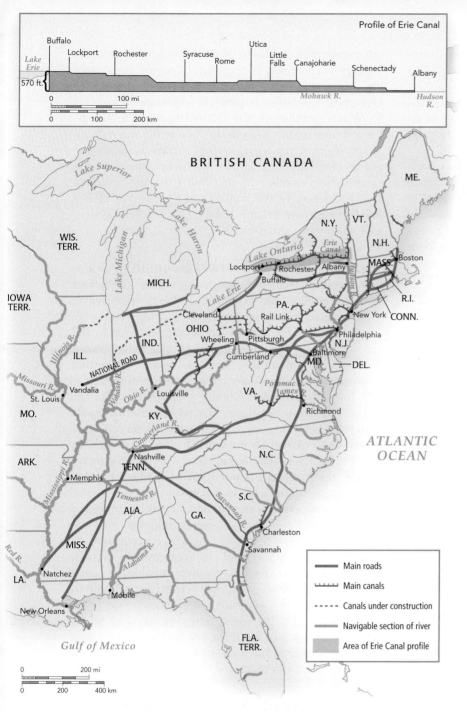

Profile of Erie Canal

MAP 10.1: THE TRANSPORTATION NETWORK OF A MARKET ECONOMY, 1840

Canals played their most important role in the Northeast, where they linked eastern cities to western rivers and the Great Lakes. Steamboats were most crucial in the extensive river systems of the South and the West.
What accounts for the concentration of canals in the northern states?

As for the North, its factories increasingly made money by turning raw cotton into cloth, while northern merchants reaped profits from shipping the cotton and then reshipping the textiles. Planters used the income they earned to purchase foodstuffs from the West and goods and services from the Northeast.

The Transportation Revolution >>

For a market economy to become truly national, a transportation network linking various parts of the nation was essential. The economy had not become self-sustaining earlier partly because the only way to transport goods cheaply was by water. Thus trade was limited largely to coastal and international markets, for even on rivers, bulky goods moved easily in only one direction: downstream.

After 1815 all that changed. From 1825 to 1855—the span of a single generation—the cost of transportation on land fell 95 percent, while its speed increased five-fold. As a result, new regions were drawn quickly into the market.

Canals attracted considerable investment capital, especially after the success of the Erie Canal. Built between 1818 and 1825 the canal stretched 364 miles from Albany on the Hudson River to Buffalo on Lake Erie. Its construction by the state was an act of faith, for in 1816 the United States had only 100 miles of canals, none longer than 28 miles. But within a few years of opening, the Erie Canal paid for itself. It reduced the cost of shipping a ton of goods from Buffalo to New York City from more than 19 cents a mile to less than 3 cents. Where the canal's busy traffic passed, settlers flocked, and towns such as Rochester and Lockport sprang up and thrived by moving goods and serving markets. The steady flow of goods eastward gave New York City the dominant position in the scramble for control of western trade.

New York's commercial rivals, like Philadelphia and Baltimore, were soon frantically trying to build their own canals to the West. Western states such as Ohio and Indiana, convinced that their prosperity depended on cheap transportation, constructed canals to link interior regions with the Great Lakes. By 1840 the nation had completed more than 3,300 miles of canals at a cost of about $125 million. Almost half of that amount came from state governments.

South soared. By 1840 the South produced more than 60 percent of the world supply, and cotton accounted for almost two-thirds of all American exports.

Because of its vast expanse, the United States depended particularly on river transportation. But shipping goods downstream from Pittsburgh to New Orleans took 6 weeks, and the return journey required 17 weeks or more. Steamboats reduced the time of an upstream trip from New Orleans to Louisville from 90 to 8 days while cutting costs by 90 percent.

Robert Fulton in 1807 demonstrated the commercial possibilities of propelling a boat with steam when his ship, the *Clermont*, traveled from New York City to Albany on the Hudson River. But steamboats had the greatest effect on transportation on western rivers, where the flat-bottomed boats could haul heavy loads even in low water.

The first significant railroads appeared in the 1830s, largely as feeder lines to canals. Soon enough, cities and towns saw that their future depended on having good rail links. The country had only 13 miles of track in 1830, but 10 years later railroad and canal mileage were almost exactly equal (3,325 miles). By 1850, the nation had a total of 8,879 miles. Railroad rates were usually higher, but railroads were twice as fast as steamboats, offered more direct routes, and could operate year-round. Although railroads increasingly dominated the transportation system after 1850, canals and steamboats were initially the key to creating a national market.

Revolution in Communications >> What rail and steam engines did for transportation, Samuel F. B. Morse's telegraph did for communications. Morse in 1837 patented a device that sent electrical pulses over a wire, and before long, telegraph lines fanned out in all directions, linking various parts of the country in instantaneous communication. The new form of communication sped business information, helped link the transportation network, and enabled newspapers to provide readers with up-to-date news.

Indeed, the invention of the telegraph and the perfection of a power press in 1847 by Robert Hoe and his son Richard revolutionized journalism. The mechanical press sharply increased the speed with which sheets could be printed over the old hand method and brought newspapers within economic reach of ordinary families. Hoe's press had a similar impact on book publishing, since thousands of copies could be printed at affordable prices.

The Postal System >> A national market economy depended on mass communications to transmit commercial information and bring into contact producers and sellers separated by great distances. Although postage was relatively expensive, the American postal system subsidized the distribution of newspapers and helped spread other forms of commercial information. Indeed, in the years before the Civil War, the postal system employed more laborers than did any

other enterprise in the country. Although the system's primary purpose was to promote commerce, the system had a profound social impact by accustoming people to long-range and even impersonal communication.

When traveling in the United States in 1831, the French commentator Alexis de Tocqueville was amazed at the scope of the postal system. "There is an astonishing circulation of letters and newspapers among these savage woods," he reported from the Michigan frontier. Although the British and French post offices handled a greater volume of mail, the American system was much more extensive.

Agriculture in the Market Economy >> The new forms of transportation had a remarkable effect on farm families: they became linked ever more tightly to a national market system. Given cheap transportation, farmers increased their output in order to sell the surplus at distant markets. In this shift toward commercial agriculture, farmers began cultivating more acres, working longer hours, and adopting scientific farming methods, including crop rotation and the use of manures as fertilizer. Instead of bartering goods with neighbors, they more often paid cash or depended on banks to extend them credit. Instead of marketing crops themselves, they began to rely on regional merchants. Like southern planters, western wheat farmers increasingly sold in a world market.

As transportation and market networks connected more areas of the nation, they encouraged regional specialization. The South increasingly concentrated on staple crops for export, and the West grew foodstuffs, particularly grain. Eastern farmers, unable to compete with the wheat yields of western farms, shifted to producing fruits, vegetables, and dairy products for rapidly growing urban areas. The cities of the East no longer looked primarily to the sea for their trade; they looked to southern and western markets. That, indeed, was a revolution in markets.

John Marshall and the Promotion of Enterprise >> A national market system also needed a climate favorable to investment. Under the leadership of Chief Justice John Marshall, the Supreme Court became the branch of the federal government most aggressive in protecting the new forms of business central to the growing market economy.

Marshall, who presided over the Court from 1801 to 1835, convinced his colleagues to uphold the sanctity of private property and the power of the federal government to promote economic growth. In the case of *McCulloch v. Maryland* (1819) the Court upheld the constitutionality of the Second Bank of the United States. Just as Alexander Hamilton had argued in the debate over the first national bank, Marshall

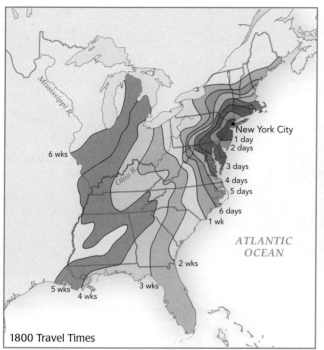

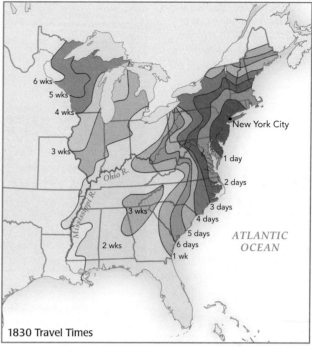

1800 Travel Times

1830 Travel Times

MAP 10.2: TRAVEL TIMES TO NEW YORK, 1800 AND 1830

emphasized that the Constitution gave Congress the power to make all "necessary and proper" laws to carry out its delegated powers. If Congress believed that a bank would help it meet its responsibilities, such as maintaining the public credit and regulating the currency, then the bank was constitutional. By upholding Hamilton's doctrine of implied powers, Marshall enlarged federal power to an extraordinary degree.

He also encouraged a more freewheeling commerce in *Gibbons v. Ogden* (1824), which gave Marshall a chance to define the greatest power of the federal government in peacetime, the right to regulate interstate commerce. In striking down a steamboat monopoly granted by the state of New York, the chief justice gave the term *commerce* the broadest possible definition, declaring that it covered all commercial dealings and that Congress's power over interstate commerce could be "exercised to its utmost extent." The result was increased business competition throughout society.

At the heart of most commercial agreements were private contracts, made between individuals or companies. Marshall took an active role in defining contract law, which was then in its infancy. The case of *Fletcher v. Peck* (1810) showed how far he was willing to go to protect private property. The justices unanimously struck down a Georgia law that struck down a land grant to a group of speculators that had bribed the legislature to get it. A grant was a contract, Marshall declared, and since the Constitution forbade states to impair "the obligation of contracts,"

the legislature could not interfere with the grant once it had been made. Although the framers of the Constitution probably meant contracts to refer only to agreements between private parties, Marshall made no distinction between public and private agreements, thereby greatly expanding the meaning of the contract clause.

The most celebrated decision Marshall wrote on the contract clause was in *Dartmouth College v. Woodward*, decided in 1819. This case arose out of the attempt by New Hampshire to alter the college's charter of 1769. The Court overturned the state law on the grounds that state charters were also contracts and could not be altered by later legislatures. By this ruling Marshall intended to protect **corporations,** which conducted business under charters granted by individual states.

> **corporation** business entity that has been granted a charter granting it legal rights, privileges, and liabilities distinct from the individual members that are a part of it.

Thus the Marshall Court sought to encourage economic risk-taking by protecting property and contracts, by limiting state interference, and by creating a climate of business confidence.

 REVIEW

Describe the workings of the national market economy and the ways in which it was shaped by the revolutions in transportation and communications.

A RESTLESS TEMPER

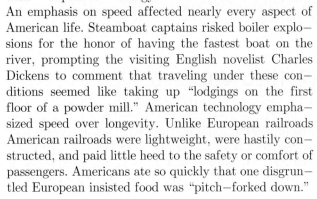

Between 1815 and 1850 the nation reverberated with explosive energy. An emphasis on speed affected nearly every aspect of American life. Steamboat captains risked boiler explosions for the honor of having the fastest boat on the river, prompting the visiting English novelist Charles Dickens to comment that traveling under these conditions seemed like taking up "lodgings on the first floor of a powder mill." American technology emphasized speed over longevity. Unlike European railroads American railroads were lightweight, were hastily constructed, and paid little heed to the safety or comfort of passengers. Americans ate so quickly that one disgruntled European insisted food was "pitch-forked down."

Population Growth >> If the economic hallmark of this new order was the growth of a national market, there were social factors that also contributed to American restlessness. The American population continued to double about every 22 years—more than twice the rate of Great Britain. The census, which stood at fewer than 4 million in 1790, surpassed 23 million in 1850. Although the birthrate peaked in 1800, it declined only slowly before 1840.

From 1790 to 1820 natural increase accounted for virtually all of the country's population growth. But immigration, which had been disrupted by the Napoleonic Wars in Europe, revived after 1815. In the 1830s some 600,000 immigrants arrived, more than double the number in the quarter century after 1790.

The Restless Movement West >> The vast areas of land opened for settlement absorbed much of the burgeoning population. As settlers streamed west, speculation in western lands reached frenzied proportions. Whereas only 68,000 acres of the public domain had been sold during the year 1800, sales peaked in 1818, at a staggering 3.5 million acres.

The Panic of 1819 sent sales and prices crashing, and in the depression that followed many farmers lost their farms. Congress reacted by abolishing credit sales of federal land and demanding payment in cash, but it tempered this policy by lowering the price of the cheapest lands to $1.25 an acre and reducing the minimum tract to 80 acres.

Even so, speculators purchased most of the public lands sold, since there was no limit on the amount of acreage an individual or a land company could buy. These land speculators played a leading role in settlement of the West. To hasten sales they usually sold land partially on credit—a vital aid to poorer farmers. They also provided loans to purchase needed tools and supplies. Many farmers became speculators themselves, buying up property in the neighborhood and selling it to latecomers at a tidy profit.

Given such rapid settlement, geographic mobility became one of the most striking characteristics of the American people. The 1850 census revealed that nearly half of all native-born free Americans lived outside the state where they had been born. The typical American "has no root in the soil," visiting Frenchman Michel Chevalier observed, but "is always in the mood to move on, always ready to start in the first steamer that comes along from the place where he had just now landed."

It was the search for opportunity, more than anything else, that accounted for such restlessness. In 1851 a new railroad line bypassed the village of Auburn, Illinois. Despite the village's handsome location, residents quickly abandoned it in order to live in the new town that sprang up around the depot, even though that land was swampier. A neighboring farmer purchased the old village and plowed up the streets, and Auburn reverted to a cornfield.

⋏ This traffic jam in New York City conveys the rapid pace and impatient quality of American life in the first half of the nineteenth century. "In the streets all is hurry and bustle," one European visitor to the city reported. "Carts, instead of being drawn by horses at a walking pace, are often met at a gallop, and always in a brisk trot. . . . The whole population seen in the streets seem to enjoy this bustle and add to it by their own rapid pace, as if they were all going to some place of appointment, and were hurrying on under the apprehension of being too late."

Urbanization >> Even with the growth of a national market, the United States remained a rural nation. Nevertheless, the four decades after 1820 witnessed the fastest rate of urbanization in American history. As a result the ratio of farmers to city dwellers steadily dropped, from 15 to 1 in 1800 to 5.5 to 1 in 1850. Improved transportation, the declining productivity of many eastern farms, the beginnings of industrialization, and the influx of immigrants all stimulated the growth of cities.

The most urbanized area of the country was the Northeast, where in 1860 more than a third of the population lived in cities.[1] Important urban centers such as St. Louis and Cincinnati arose in the West. The South, with only 10 percent of its population living in cities, was the least urbanized region.

 REVIEW

What were the effects of population growth and movement in the United States during the first half of the nineteenth century?

THE RISE OF FACTORIES

It was an isolated life, growing up in rural, hilly Vermont. But stories of the textile factories that had sprung up in Lowell and other towns in Massachusetts reached even small villages, such as Barnard. Fifteen−year−old

---

[1]The Northeast included New England and the mid−Atlantic states (New York, Pennsylvania, and New Jersey). The South comprised the slave states plus the District of Columbia.

Mary Paul was working there as a domestic servant when, in 1845, two friends helped her find her first job at the Lowell mills. "I am in need of clothes which I cannot get about here," she explained to her farm-bound father. After four years she returned home, but now found "countryfied" life too confining, and before long she left her rural hometown—this time for good.

Mary Paul was one of thousands of rural Americans whose lives were fundamentally altered by the economic transformations of the young republic. The changes in her lifestyle and her working habits demonstrated that the new factories and industries needed more than technological innovation to run smoothly. Equally crucial, labor needed to be reorganized.

Technological Advances >> Before 1815 manufacturing had been done in homes or shops by skilled artisans. As master craftworkers they imparted the knowledge of their trades to apprentices and **journeymen.** In addition, women often worked in their homes part-time under the putting-out system, making finished articles from raw material supplied by merchant capitalists. After 1815 this older form of manufacturing began to give

journeyman person who has served an apprenticeship in a trade or craft and who is a qualified worker employed by another person.

way to factories with machinery tended by unskilled or semiskilled laborers.

From England came many of the earliest technological innovations. But Americans often improved on the British machines. "Everything new is quickly introduced here," one visitor commented in 1820. "There is no clinging to old ways; the moment an American hears the word 'invention' he pricks up his ears." From 1790 to 1860 the United States Patent Office granted more patents than England and France combined.

The first machines required highly skilled workers both to build and to repair them. Eli Whitney had a better idea. Having won a contract to produce 10,000 rifles for the government, he developed machinery that would mass-produce parts that were interchangeable from rifle to rifle. Such parts had to be manufactured to rigid specifications, but once the process was perfected, these parts allowed a worker to assemble a rifle quickly with only a few tools. Simeon North applied the same principle to the production of clocks, and Chauncey Jerome followed North's example and soon surpassed him.

Textile Factories >> The factory system originated in the Northeast, where capital, water power, and transportation facilities were available. As in England, the production of cloth was the first manufacturing

⌃ St. Louis, a major urban center that developed in the West, depended on the steamboat to sustain its commerce, as this 1859 illustration makes clear.

>> Mill workers, Lowell. "I am in need of clothes which I cannot get about here," Mary Paul had told her father in rural Vermont. Indeed, these workers wear the textiles they helped produce in factories like Lowell's, each pattern slightly different.

process to use the new technology on a large scale. Eventually all the processes of manufacturing fabrics were brought together in a single location, and machines did virtually all the work.

In 1820 a group of wealthy Boston merchants known as the Boston Associates set up operations at Lowell, Massachusetts, which soon became the nation's most famous center of textile manufacturing. Its founders intended to avoid the misery that surrounded English factories by combining **paternalism** with high profits. Instead of relying primarily on child labor or a permanent working class, the Lowell mills employed daughters of New England farm families. Female workers lived in company boardinghouses under the watchful eye of a matron. To its many visitors, Lowell presented an impressive sight, with huge factories and well-kept houses. Female workers were encouraged to attend lectures and use the library; they even published their own magazine, the *Lowell Offering*.

The reality of factory life, however, involved strict work rules and long hours of tedious, repetitive work. At Lowell, for example, workers could be fined for lateness or misconduct, such as talking on the job, and the women's morals in the boardinghouses were strictly guarded. Work typically began at 7 A.M. (earlier in the summer) and continued until 7 at night, six days a week. With only 30 minutes for the noon meal, many workers had to run to the boardinghouse and back to avoid being late. Winter was the "lighting up" season, when work began before daylight and ended after dark. The only light after sunset came from whale oil lamps that filled the long rooms with smoke.

Although the labor was hard the female operators earned from $2.40 to $3.20 a week, wages considered good by the standards of the time. (Domestic servants and seamstresses were paid less than $1.00 a week.) The average "mill girl" was between 16 and 30 years

> **paternalism** attitude or policy of treating individuals or groups in a fatherly manner, by providing for their needs without granting them rights or responsibilities.

old. Most were not working to support their families back home on the farm; instead, they wanted to accumulate some money for perhaps the first time in their lives and sample some of life's pleasures. "I must . . . have something of my own before many more years have passed," Sally Rice wrote in rejecting her parents' request that she return home to Somerset, Vermont. "And where is that something coming from if I go home and earn nothing?"

Like Rice, few women in the mills intended to work permanently. The majority stayed no more than five years before getting married. The sense of sisterhood that united women in the boardinghouses made it easier for farm daughters to adjust to the stress and regimen the factory imposed on them.

As competition in the textile industry intensified, factory managers tried to raise productivity. In the mid-1830s the mills began to increase the workloads and speed up the machinery. Even these changes failed to maintain previous profits, and on several occasions factories cut wages. The ever-quickening pace of work finally provoked resistance among the women in the mills. Several times in the 1830s wage cuts sparked strikes in which a minority of workers walked out. In the 1840s workers' protests focused on the demand for a 10-hour day.

As the mills expanded a smaller proportion of the workers lived in company boardinghouses, and moral regulations were relaxed. But the greatest change was a shift in the workforce from native-born females to Irish immigrants, including men and children. The Irish, who made up only 8 percent of the Lowell workforce in 1845, amounted to almost half by 1860. Desperately poor and eager for any work, they did not view their situation as temporary. Wages continued to decline, and a permanent working class took shape.

Lowell and the Environment >> Lowell was a city built on water power. Early settlers had used the power of the Merrimack River to run mills, but never on the scale of the textile factories. As the market spread Americans came to link progress with the fullest use of the environment's natural resources.

By 1836 Lowell had seven canals, with a supporting network of locks and dams, to govern the Merrimack's flow and distribute water to the city's 26 mills. As more

MAP 10.3: DEVELOPMENT OF THE LOWELL MILLS

As more mills were built at Lowell the demand increased for water to power them. By 1859 the mills drew water from lakes 80 to 100 miles upstream, including Winnipesaukee, Squam, and Newfound. The map at left shows the affected watersheds. In the city of Lowell (*right*), a system of canals was enlarged over several decades. The photograph shows Pawtucket Canal as it has been preserved at Lowell National Historical Park. Rail links tied Lowell and Boston together.

How did the mills at Lowell, Massachusetts, affect both farmers and other mills in New Hampshire?

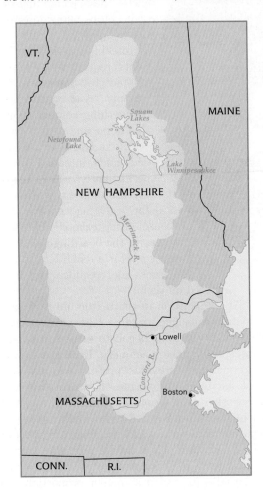

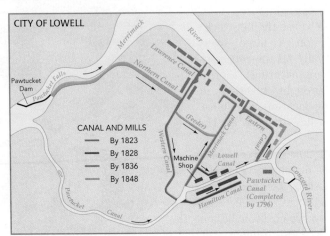

and more mills were built, at both Lowell and other sites, the Boston Associates erected dams at several points along the river to store water and divert it into power canals for factories. At Lawrence they constructed the largest dam in the world at the time, a 32–foot–high granite structure that spanned 1,600 feet across the river. But even dammed, the Merrimack's waters proved insufficient. So the Associates gained control of over 100 square miles of New Hampshire lakes that fed the river system. Damming these lakes provided a regular flow of water, especially in the drier summer months.

By regulating the river's waters, the Associates made the Merrimack valley the nation's greatest industrial center in the first half of the nineteenth century. But not all who lived there benefited. By raising water levels the dams flooded farmlands, blocked the transportation of logs downstream, and damaged mills upstream

by reducing the current. The dams also devastated the fish population by preventing upstream spawning, while factories routinely dumped their wastes into the river to be carried downstream, eventually contaminating water supplies. Epidemics of typhoid, cholera, and dysentery increased, so that by midcentury Lowell had a reputation as a particularly unhealthy city.

Industrial Work >> The creation of an industrial labor force that was accustomed to working in factories did not occur easily. Previously, artisans had worked within the home. Apprentices were considered part of the family, and masters were responsible not only for teaching their apprentices a trade but also for providing them some education and for supervising their moral behavior. Journeymen knew that if they perfected their skill, they could become respected master artisans with their own shops. And skilled artisans worked not by the clock, at a steady pace, but rather in bursts of intense labor alternating with greater leisure.

The factory changed that. Factory goods were not so finished or elegant as those done by hand, and pride in artisanship gave way to rates of productivity. At the same time, workers were required to discard old habits, because industrialism demanded a worker who was sober, dependable, and self−disciplined. Absenteeism, lateness, and drunkenness hurt productivity and disrupted the regular factory routine. Thus industrialization not only produced a fundamental change in the way work was organized but also transformed the very nature of work.

With the loss of personal freedom also came the loss of standing in the community. The master−apprentice relationship gave way to factories' sharp separation of workers from management. Few workers rose through the ranks to supervisory positions, and even fewer could set up their own businesses, as many artisans dreamed. Even well−paid workers sensed their decline in status.

The Labor Movement >> In this newly emerg−ing economic order workers sometimes organized to protect their rights and traditional ways of life. Craft−workers such as carpenters, printers, and tailors formed unions, and in 1834 individual unions came together in the National Trades' Union.

Union leaders argued that labor was degraded in America: workers endured long hours, low pay, and low status. Unlike most American social thinkers of the day, they accepted the idea of conflict between differ−ent classes. They did not believe that the interests of workers and employers could be reconciled, and they blamed the plight of labor on monopolies, especially banking and paper money, and on machines and the factory system.

If the unions' rhetoric sounded radical, the solutions they proposed were moderate. Reformers agitated for public education, abolition of imprisonment for debt, political action by workers, and effective unions as the means to guarantee social equality and restore labor to its former honored position. Proclaiming the repub−lican virtues of freedom and equality, they attacked special privilege, denounced the lack of equal opportu−nity, and decried workers' loss of independence.

The labor movement gathered some momentum in the decade before the Panic of 1837, but in the depression that followed, labor's strength collapsed. During hard times few workers were willing to strike or engage in collective action. Nor did skilled craftwork−ers, who spearheaded the union movement, feel a par−ticularly strong bond with semiskilled factory workers and unskilled laborers. More than a decade of agitation did finally win the 10−hour day for some workers by the 1850s, and the courts also recognized workers' right to strike, but these gains had little immediate impact.

Workers were united in resenting the industrial system and their loss of status, but they were divided by ethnic and racial antagonisms, gender, conflicting religious perspectives, occupa−tional differences, party loyalties, and disagreements over tac−tics. For them, the factory and industrialism were not agents of opportunity but reminders of their loss of independence and a measure of control over their lives.

Sam Patch and a Worker's "Art" >> Some fought against the loss of independence in unusual ways. The waterfalls that served as a magnet for capitalists build−ing mills also attracted their workers. Such cascades were places to visit during off−hours to picnic, swim, fish, or laze about. And for those with

⌃ Waterfalls at mill towns, like this one in Pawtucket, Rhode Island, were places to swim, fish, and relax, as the people do in the foreground. Jumpers like Sam Patch leaped off the Pawtucket bridge and also off the roof of a nearby building into the foamy froth.

nerve, the falls provided a place to show off skills in a different way. Every mill town had its water-fall jumpers, with their own techniques to survive the plunge (knees bent, chest thrust forward). No jumper won more fame than Sam Patch, a young man who had begun working at the Pawtucket mills at the age of seven.

Patch gained wider attention when he jumped at Passaic Falls, New Jersey, where a mill owner was opening a private park that charged admission, in order to keep away "the lazy, idle, rascally" and lower-class riff-raff. Workers who resented this undemocratic practice rejoiced when Patch spoiled the park's opening by leaping 70 feet into the foam-ing water. Thousands of ordinary folk cheered him from outside the park. Eventually Patch's daring led him to the biggest challenge of all: Niagara Falls. Twice he leapt more than 80 feet into the cascade's churning waters. But he drowned a month later when he dared Genesee Falls in another mill town along the Erie Canal—Rochester, New York. Still, his fame persisted for decades. Leaping waterfalls was "an art which I have knowledge of and courage to perform," he once declared defiantly. In a market economy where skilled "arts" were being replaced by machine labor, Sam Patch's acts were a defiant protest against the changing times.

 REVIEW

What factors contributed to the beginnings of industrialization in the United States?

SOCIAL STRUCTURES OF THE MARKET SOCIETY

Thousands of miles beyond Lowell's factory gates a different class of Americans roamed who at first appeared unconnected to the bustle of urban mar-kets. These were the legendary mountain men, who flourished from the mid-1820s through the mid-1840s. Traveling across the Great Plains, along upland streams, and over the passes of the Rockies, outdoors-men such as Jim Bridger, Jedediah Smith, and James Walker wore buckskin hunting shirts, let their hair grow to their shoulders, and stuck pistols and toma-hawks in their belts. Wild and exotic, the mountain men became romantic symbols of the American quest for individual freedom.

Yet these wanderers, too, were tied to the emerg-ing market society. The mountain men hunted beaver pelts and shipped them east, to be turned into fancy hats for gentlemen. The fur trade was not a sporting event but a business, dominated by organizations such as John Jacob Astor's American Fur Company, and the trapper was the agent of an economic structure that stretched from the mountains to eastern cities and even to Europe. Most of these men went into the wil-derness not to flee civilization but to make money. Of those who survived the fur trade, most returned and took up respectable new careers as shopkeepers, trad-ers, ranchers, politicians, and even bankers. They, like farmers, were expectant capitalists for whom the West was a land of opportunity.

The revolution in markets, in other words, affected Americans from all walks of life: mountain men as well as merchants, laborers as well as farmers. Equally critical, it restructured American society as a whole.

Economic Specialization >> To begin with, the spread of the market produced greater special-ization. Transportation networks made it possible for farmers to concentrate on producing certain crops, while factories could focus on making a single item such as cloth or shoes. Within factories, the division of labor meant that the process of manufacturing an item became more specialized, broken down into less skilled tasks.

This process evolved at different rates. Textiles and milling were completely mechanized, while other sec-tors of the economy, such as shoes and men's clothing, depended little on machinery. Moreover, large factories were the exception rather than the rule. Still, the ten-dency was toward more technology, greater efficiency, and increasing specialization.

Specialization had consequences at home as well as in the workplace. The average eighteenth-century American woman produced items such as thread, cloth, clothing, and candles in the home for family use. As factories spread, however, household manufactur-ing all but disappeared, and women lost many of the economic functions they had previously performed in the family unit. Again, textiles are a striking example. Between 1815 and 1860 the price of cotton cloth fell from 18 to 2 cents a yard, and because it was also smoother and more brightly colored than homespun, most women purchased cloth rather than making it themselves. Similarly, the development of ready-made men's clothing reduced the amount of sewing women did, especially in urban centers.

Materialism >> European visitors were struck dur-ing these years by how much Americans were preoc-cupied with material goods. The new generation did not

<< Indians and fur traders mixed at Fort Laramie, Wyoming, maintained by the government as a way station for the burgeoning fur trade of the 1830s. The scene looks exotic, but the fur trade was a serious and extensive business that stretched from the Rocky Mountains to eastern cities and to Europe beyond.

invent materialism, but the spread of the market after 1815 made it much more evident. "I know of no country, indeed," Tocqueville commented, "where the love of money has taken stronger hold on the affections of men."

In a nation that had no legally recognized aristocracy, no established church, and class lines that were only informally drawn, wealth became the most obvious symbol of status. Materialism reflected more than a desire for goods and physical comfort. It represented a quest for respect and recognition. The esteem of the founding generation for intellectual achievement was mostly lost in the scramble for wealth that seemed to consume the new generation.

Wealth and the Emerging Middle Class >>

In the years after 1815 a new middle class took shape in American society. A small class of shopkeepers, professionals, and master artisans had existed earlier, but the creation of a national market economy greatly expanded its size and influence. As specialization increased, office work and selling were more often physically separated from the production and handling of merchandise. Businesspeople, professionals, storekeepers, clerks, office workers, and supervisors began to think of themselves as a distinct social group. Members of the growing middle class had access to more education and enjoyed greater social mobility. They were paid not only more but differently. A manual worker might earn $300 a year, paid as wages computed on an hourly basis. Professionals received a yearly salary and might make $1,000 a year or more.

Middle–class neighborhoods, segregated along income and occupational lines, also began to develop in towns and cities. In larger cities improved transportation enabled middle–class residents to move to surrounding suburbs and commute to work. Leisure also became segregated, as separate working–class and middle–class social organizations and institutions emerged.

As middle–class Americans accumulated greater wealth, they were able to consume more. Thus material goods became emblems of success and status—as clockmaker Chauncey Jerome sadly discovered when his business failed and his wealth vanished. Indeed, this materialistic ethos was most apparent in the middle class, as they strove to set themselves apart from other groups in society.

Furthermore, as American society became more specialized after 1815, greater extremes of wealth appeared. As the new markets created fortunes for the few, the factory system lowered the wages of workers by dividing labor into smaller, less skilled tasks. At the upper end of the social scale, wealth was most highly concentrated in large eastern cities and in the cotton kingdom of the South. Still, throughout the nation the tendency was for the rich to get richer and own a larger share of the community's total wealth. By 1860, 5 percent of American families owned more than

THE MARKET AND EQUALITY: SHE SAID, HE SAID

Frances Wright, a Scotswoman who would later make her career in America as an advocate of slaves, workers, and women, made her first trip in 1819 at the age of 23 and found much to celebrate. Alexis de Tocqueville, 25 when he arrived in the United States in 1831, agreed that white Americans were the freest people in the world, but he described their pursuit of equality as elusive and paradoxical.

DOCUMENT 1
Equality Secures Liberty: Frances Wright

The universal spread of useful and practical knowledge, the exercise of great political rights, the ease and, comparatively, the equality of condition give to this people [Americans] a quality peculiar to themselves. Every hand is occupied, and every head is thinking, not only of the active business of human life (which usually sits lighter upon this people than many others), but of matters touching the general weal of a vast empire. Each man being one of a sovereign people is not only a politician but a legislator—a partner, in short, in the grand concern of the state . . . one engaged in narrowly inspecting its operations, balancing its accounts, guarding its authority, and judging of its

interests. A people so engaged are not those with whom a lounger might find it agreeable to associate: he seeks amusement, and he finds business. . . .

It is not very apparent that public virtue is peculiarly requisite for the preservation of political equality; envy might suffice for this: You shall not be greater than I. Political equality is, perhaps, yet more indispensable to preserve public virtue than public virtue to preserve it; wherever an exclusive principle is admitted, baleful passions are excited. Divide a community into classes, and insolence is entailed upon the higher, servility or envy, and often both united, upon the lower. . . .

In all republics, ancient or modern, there has been a leaven of aristocracy. America fortunately had, in her first youth, virtue sufficient to repel the introduction of hereditary honors. . . .

Liberty is here secure, because it is equally the portion of all. The state is liable to no convulsions, because there is nowhere any usurpations to maintain, while every individual has an equal sovereignty to lose.* No king will voluntarily lay down his scepter, and in a democracy all men are kings.

Source: Frances Wright, *Views of Society and Manners in America* (London, 1821).

*"A grievous exception to this rule is found in the black slavery of the commonwealths of the South."

DOCUMENT 2
Equality Promotes Anxiety: Alexis de Tocqueville

In America I saw the freest and most enlightened men, placed in the happiest circumstances which the world affords; it seemed to me as if a cloud habitually hung upon their brow, and I thought them serious and almost sad even in their pleasures.

It is strange to see with what feverish ardor the Americans pursue their own welfare; and to watch the vague dread that constantly torments them lest they should not have chosen the shortest path which may lead to it.

A native of the United States clings to this world's goods as if he were certain never to die; and he is so hasty in grasping at all within his reach, that one would suppose he was constantly afraid of not living long enough to enjoy them. He clutches everything, he holds nothing fast, but soon loosens his grasp to pursue fresh gratifications.

In the United States a man builds a house to spend his latter years in it, and he sells it before the roof is on; he plants a garden, and lets it [rents it] just as the trees are coming into bearing; he brings a field into tillage, and leaves other men to gather the crops; he embraces a profession, and gives it up; he settles in a place, which he soon afterward leaves, to carry his changeable longings elsewhere. If his private affairs leave him any leisure, he instantly plunges into the vortex of politics; and if at the end of a year of unremitting labor he finds he has a few days' vacation, his eager curiosity whirls him over the vast extent of the United States, and he will travel fifteen hundred miles in a few days, to shake off his happiness. Death at length overtakes him, but it is before he is weary of his bootless chase of that complete felicity which is for ever on the wing.

At first sight there is something surprising in this strange unrest of so many happy men, restless in the midst of abundance. The spectacle itself is, however, as old as the world; the novelty is to see a whole people furnish an exemplification of it. . . .

The equality of conditions leads by a still straighter road to several of the effects which I have here described. When all the privileges of birth and fortune are abolished, when all professions are accessible to all, and a man's own energies may place him at the top of any one of them, an easy and unbounded career seems open to his ambition, and he will readily persuade himself that he is born to no vulgar destinies. But this is an erroneous notion, which is corrected by daily experience. The same equality which allows every citizen to conceive these lofty hopes, renders all the citizens less able to realize them; it circumscribes their powers on every side, while it gives freer scope to their desires. Not only are they themselves powerless, but they are met at every step by immense obstacles, which they did not at first perceive. They have swept away the privileges of some of their fellow-creatures which stood in their way: but they have opened the door to universal competition. . . .

Among democratic nations men easily attain a certain equality of conditions; they can never attain the equality they desire. It perpetually retires from before them, yet without hiding itself from their sight, and in retiring draws them on. At every moment they think they are about to grasp it; it escapes at every moment from their hold."

Source: Alexis de Tocqueville, *Democracy in America* (1835, 1840).

THINKING CRITICALLY

What did Frances Wright admire about Americans? How does she think political equality will help preserve public virtue? How did Alexis de Tocqueville account for the restless ambition of Americans? According to Tocqueville, what was the paradox of pursuing equality?

50 percent of the nation's wealth. In villages where the market revolution had not penetrated, wealth tended to be less concentrated.

In a market society, the rich were able to build up their assets, because those with capital were in a position to increase it dramatically by taking advantage of new investment opportunities. Although a few men, such as Cornelius Vanderbilt and John Jacob Astor, vaulted from the bottom ranks of society to the top, most of the nation's richest individuals came from wealthy families.

Social Mobility >> The existence of great fortunes is not necessarily inconsistent with the idea of **social mobility** or property accumulation. Although the gap between the rich and the poor widened after 1820, even the incomes of

> **social mobility** movement of individuals from one social class to another.

most poor Americans rose, because the total amount of wealth produced in America had become much larger. From about 1825 to 1860 the average per-capita income almost doubled, to $300. Voicing the popular belief, a New York judge proclaimed, "In this favored land of liberty, the road to advancement is open to all."

Social mobility existed in these years, but not as much as contemporaries boasted. Most laborers—or more often their sons—did manage to move up the social ladder, but only a rung or two. Few unskilled workers rose higher than to a semiskilled occupation. Even the children of skilled workers normally did not escape the laboring classes to enter the middle-class ranks of clerks, managers, or lawyers. For most workers, improved status came in the form of a savings account or homeownership, which gave them some security during economic downswings and in old age.

A New Sensitivity to Time >> It was no accident that Chauncey Jerome's clocks spread throughout the nation along with the market economy. The new methods of doing business involved a new and stricter sense of time. Factory life necessitated a more regimented schedule, where work began at the sound of a bell, workers kept machines going at a constant pace, and the day was divided into hours and even minutes.

Clocks began to invade private as well as public space. With mass production ordinary families could now afford clocks, and even farmers became more sensitive to time as they were integrated into the market.

 REVIEW

What was the effect of the new market economy on social structure and values in the United States during the first half of the nineteenth century?

PROSPERITY AND ANXIETY

As Americans watched their nation's frontiers expand and its market economy grow, many began to view history in terms of continuous improvement. The path of commerce, however, was not steadily upward. Rather, it advanced in a series of wrenching **boom-and-bust cycles:** accelerating growth, followed by a crash, and then depression.

> **boom-and-bust cycle** periods of expansion and recession or depression that an economy goes through. Also referred to as *business cycle.*

The country remained extraordinarily prosperous from 1815 until 1819, only to sink into a depression that lasted from 1819 to 1823. During the next cycle the economy expanded slowly during the 1820s, followed by frenzied speculation in the 1830s. Then came the inevitable contraction in 1837, and the country suffered an even more severe depression from 1839 to 1843. The third cycle followed the same pattern: gradual economic growth during the 1840s, frantic expansion in the 1850s, and a third depression, which began in 1857 and lasted until the Civil War. In each of these "panics"

<< This mock banknote illustrates the anxieties often felt in times of "bust," when the value of currencies plummeted and it was difficult to tell whether the banks that issued paper money were solvent.

thousands of workers were thrown out of work, over-extended farmers lost their farms, and many businesses closed their doors.

In such an environment, prosperity and personal success seemed all too fleeting. Because Americans believed the good times would not last—that the bubble would burst and another "panic" set in—their optimism was often tinged by insecurity and anxiety. They knew too many individuals like Chauncey Jerome, who had been rich and then lost all their wealth in a downturn.

The Panic of 1819 >> The initial shock of this boom—and—bust psychology came with the Panic of 1819, the first major depression in the nation's history. From 1815 to 1818 cotton had commanded truly fabulous prices on the Liverpool market. In this heady prosperity the federal government extended liberal credit for land purchases, and the new national bank encouraged merchants and farmers to borrow in order to catch the rising tide.

But in 1819 the price of cotton collapsed and took the rest of the economy with it. Once the inflationary bubble burst, land values, which had been driven to new heights by the speculative fever, plummeted 50 to 75 percent almost overnight. As the economy went slack, so did the demand for western foodstuffs and eastern manufactured goods and services, pushing the nation into a severe depression. Because the market economy had spread to new areas, the downturn affected not only city folk but rural Americans as well. New cotton planters in the Southwest, who were most vulnerable to the ups and downs of the world market, were especially hard hit.

 REVIEW

In what ways did the new market economy shape the hopes and fears of Americans during the first half of the nineteenth century?

As depression spread in the years following 1819, most Americans could not guess that the ups and downs of the boom—and—bust cycle would continue through the next three decades, their swings made sharper by the growing networks of the market economy both nationally and internationally. But the interconnections between buyers and sellers did feed both prosperity and panic. Farmers and factories specialized in order to sell goods to distant buyers. Canals and railroads widened the network, speeding products, information, and profits. And as markets tied distant lands more tightly together, international events contributed to the business cycles.

It was the Liverpool market in England, in fact, that bid the price of American cotton to its high at over 32 cents. Then in 1816 and 1817 English textile manufacturers, looking for cheaper cotton, began to import more cotton from India, plummeting the price of New Orleans cotton to 14 cents. Broader changes also hurt American markets. The French and the British had been at war with each other for decades—more than 100 years, if the imperial wars of the seventeenth and eighteenth centuries were counted. In 1814 and 1815 the major powers of Europe hammered out a peace at the Congress of Vienna, one that lasted, with only minor interruptions, until the coming of World War I in 1914. When Europe had been at war, American farmers had found a ready market abroad. With thousands of European soldiers returning to their usual work as farmers, demand for American goods dropped.

The stresses of the Panic of 1819 shook the political system at home, too. As the depression deepened and hardship spread, Americans viewed government policies as at least partly to blame. The postwar nationalism, after all, had been based on the belief that government should stimulate economic development through a national bank and protective tariff, by improving transportation, and by opening up new lands. As Americans struggled to make sense of their new economic order, they looked to take more direct control of the government that was so actively shaping their lives. During the 1820s the popular response to the market and the Panic of 1819 produced a strikingly new kind of politics in the Republic.

CHAPTER SUMMARY

By uniting the country in a single market, the new market economy transformed the United States during the quarter century after 1815.

- The federal government promoted the creation of a market through a protective tariff, a national bank, and internal improvements.
- The development of new forms of transportation, including canals, steamboats, and eventually rail-roads, allowed goods to be transported cheaply on land.
- The Supreme Court adopted a pro–business stance that encouraged investment and risk–taking.
- Economic expansion generated greater national wealth, but it also brought social and intellectual change.
  - ▶ Americans pursued opportunity, embraced a new concept of progress, viewed change as normal, developed a strong materialist ethic, and con-sidered wealth the primary means to determine status.
  - ▶ Entrepreneurs reorganized their operations to increase production and sell in a wider market.
- The earliest factories were built to serve the textile industry, and the first laborers in them were young women from rural families.
  - ▶ Factory work imposed on workers a new disci-pline based on time and strict routine.
  - ▶ Workers' declining status led them to form unions and resort to strikes, but the depression that began in 1837 destroyed these organizations.
- The new market economy distributed wealth much more unevenly and left Americans feeling alterna-tively buoyant and anxious about their social and economic status.
- Social mobility existed, but it was more limited than popular belief claimed.
- The economy lurched up and down in a boom–and–bust cycle.
- In hard times Americans looked to the government to relieve economic distress.

Additional Reading

The best study of early–nineteenth–century U.S. history is Daniel Walker Howe, *What Hath God Wrought* (2009). For a provocative overview of the economic changes during this period and their impact on society and culture, consult Charles Sellers, *The Market Revolution* (1991). Then dip into two fine anthologies of essays: Melvin Stokes and Stephen Con-way, eds., *The Market Revolution in America* (1996); and Scott C. Martin, ed., *Cultural Change and the Market Revolution in America, 1789–1860* (2005). The best recent book on the transportation revolu-tion is John Larson, *Internal Improvements* (2001); and for a fascinating study of the role played by the postal system in linking Americans, see Richard John, *Spreading the News* (1995). There are many fine studies of urban social classes during the first half of the nineteenth century, and among the best are Sean Wilentz, *Chants Democratic* (1984), which traces the formation of New York City's working class; and Stuart Blumin, *The Emergence of the Middle Class* (1989). To understand the market economy's affect on rural society, read John Mack Faragher's vivid account of the transformation of a farming community in frontier Illinois, *Sugar Creek* (1986); and Robert Shalhope, *A Tale of New England* (2003), which traces the for-tunes of a Vermont farmer and his family.

There is also no shortage of excellent books explor-ing the relationship between the market revolution and American culture during the first half of the nine-teenth century. Begin with Karen Halttunen's clas-sic study of middle–class culture, *Confidence Men and Painted Women* (1982); and a more recent study, Thomas Augst, *The Clerk's Tale* (2003); and then turn to Paul Johnson's lively exploration of working–class culture, *Sam Patch, the Famous Jumper* (2003). To celebrate any occasion, treat yourself to Stephen Nissenbaum, *The Battle for Christmas* (1996). And to console yourself in between celebrations, turn to Scott Sandage, *Born Losers: A History of Failure in America* (2005).

Significant Events

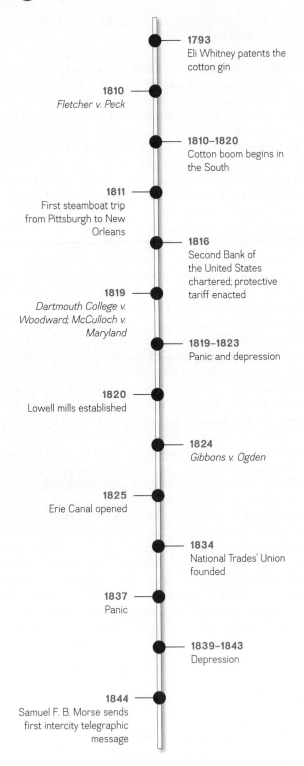

1793
Eli Whitney patents the cotton gin

1810
Fletcher v. Peck

1810–1820
Cotton boom begins in the South

1811
First steamboat trip from Pittsburgh to New Orleans

1816
Second Bank of the United States chartered; protective tariff enacted

1819
Dartmouth College v. Woodward; McCulloch v. Maryland

1819–1823
Panic and depression

1820
Lowell mills established

1824
Gibbons v. Ogden

1825
Erie Canal opened

1834
National Trades' Union founded

1837
Panic

1839–1843
Depression

1844
Samuel F. B. Morse sends first intercity telegraphic message

11 The Rise of Democracy

1824–1840

As citizens give their oath to an election judge at this county election, party workers dispense free drinks, offer party tickets (*center, below the banner*), and keep a tally of who has voted (the man sitting on the steps). One groggy voter has to be held up as he stands in line.

>> An American Story

"WANTED: CURLING TONGS, COLOGNE, AND SILK-STOCKINGS . . ."

The notice, printed in a local newspaper, made the rounds in the rural Pearl River district of Mississippi.

A traveler, the advertisement announced, had lost a suitcase while fording the Tallahala River. The contents included "6 ruffled shirts, 6 cambric handkerchiefs, 1 hair-brush, 1 toothbrush, 1 nail-brush . . ."

As the list went on, the popular reaction would inevitably shift from amusement to disdain: "1 pair curling tongs . . . 1 bottle Cologne, 1 [bottle] rose-water, 4 pairs silk stockings, and 2 pairs kid gloves." The howls of derision that filled the air could only have increased on learning that anyone finding said trunk was requested to contact the owner—Mr. Powhatan Ellis of Natchez.

Powhatan Ellis was no ordinary backcountry traveler. Born into a genteel Virginia family, Ellis had moved in 1816 to the raw Southwest to enlarge his fortune. With his cultivated tastes and careful dress, he upheld the tradition of the gentleman politician. In Virginia he would have commanded respect: indeed, in Mississippi he had been appointed district judge and U.S. senator. But for the voters along the Pearl River the advertisement for his trunk of ruffled shirts, hair oils, and fancy "skunkwater" proved to be the political kiss of death. His opponents branded him an aristocrat and a dandy, and his support among the piney woods farmers evaporated faster than a morning mist along Old Muddy on a sweltering summer's day.

No one was more satisfied with this outcome than the resourceful Franklin E. Plummer, one of Ellis's political enemies. For in truth, although the unfortunate Powhatan Ellis had lost a trunk fording a stream, he had not placed the advertisement trying to locate it. That was the handiwork of Plummer, who well understood the new playing field of American politics in the 1820s. Born in New England Plummer had made his way as a young man to the new state of Mississippi, where he set himself up as an attorney, complete with a law library of three books, and was quickly elected to the legislature.

Plummer's ambition soon extended beyond the state capital, and in 1830 he announced his candidacy for Congress. In his campaign he portrayed himself as the champion

ELECTIONEERING IN MISSISSIPPI.

⌃ Franklin Plummer campaigning.

of the people battling the aristocrats of Natchez. Contrasting his humble background with that of his wealthy opponent, Plummer proclaimed: "We are taught that the highway to office, distinction and honor, is as free to the meritorious poor man, as to the rich; to the man who has risen from obscurity by his own individual exertions, as to him who has inherited a high and elevated standing in society, founded on the patrimony of his ancestors." Taking as his slogan "Plummer for the People, and the People for Plummer," he was easily elected.

As long as Plummer maintained his image as one of the people, he remained invincible. But when he was a candidate for the U.S. Senate, his touch deserted him. Borrowing money from a Natchez bank, he purchased

a stylish coach, put his servant in a uniform, and campaigned across the state. Aghast at such aristocratic pretensions, his followers promptly abandoned him. He died in 1852 in obscurity and poverty. Ah, Plummer! Even the trustiest tribune of the people may succumb to the temptations of power and commerce. In fact, Franklin Plummer was being pulled two ways by the forces transforming American society. The growth of commerce opened up opportunities for more and more Americans during the quarter century after 1815. Through his connections with bankers and the well-to-do, Plummer saw the opportunity to accumulate wealth and to gain status and respect.

Yet at the same time that new markets were producing a more **stratified,** unequal

stratified layered; in this case, according to class or social station.]

society, the nation's politics were becoming more democratic. The new political system that developed after 1820 differed from that of the early republic. Just as national markets linked the regions of America economically, the new system of national politics with its mass electioneering techniques involved more voters than ever before. Plummer's world reflected that more egalitarian

political culture patterns, habits, institutions, and traits associated with a political system.]

political culture. But the relationship between the new equalities of politics and the new opportunities of the market was an uneasy one. <<

What's to Come

EQUALITY, OPPORTUNITY, AND THE NEW POLITICAL CULTURE OF DEMOCRACY

Middle– and upper–class Europeans who visited the United States during these decades were especially sensitive to the egalitarian quality of American life. To begin with, they discovered that only one class of seats was available on stagecoaches and railcars. These were filled according to the rough–and–ready rule of first come, first served. In steamboat dining rooms or at country taverns, everyone ate at a common table, sharing food from the same serving plates. As one upper–class gentleman complained: "The rich and the poor, the educated and the ignorant, the polite and the vulgar, all herd on the cabin floor, feed at the same table, sit in each others laps, as it were." Indeed, the democratic "manners" of Americans seemed positively shocking. In Europe social inferiors would speak only if spoken to. But Americans felt free to strike up a conversation or to shake hands with anyone, including total strangers.

Americans were proud of such democratic behavior, which they viewed as a valued heritage of the Revolution. The keelboaters who carried the future King Louis–Philippe of France on a trip down the Mississippi made their republican feelings plain when the keelboat ran aground. "You kings down there!" bellowed the captain. "Show yourselves and do a man's work, and help us three–spots pull off this bar!" The ideology of the Revolution made it clear that, in the American deck of cards at least, "three–spots" counted as much as jacks, kings, and queens. Kings were not allowed to forget that—and neither was Franklin Plummer.

By equality, Americans did not mean equality of wealth or property. "I know of no country where profounder contempt is expressed for the theory of permanent equality of property," Alexis de Tocqueville wrote. Nor did equality mean that all citizens had equal talent or capacity. In the end, what Americans upheld was equality of opportunity, not equality of condition. "True republicanism requires that every man shall have an equal chance—that every man shall be free to become as unequal as he can," one American commented. In an economy that could go bust as well as boom, Americans agreed that one primary objective of government was to safeguard opportunity. Thus the new politics of democracy walked hand in hand with the new opportunities of the market.

The stately James Monroe, with his powdered hair and buckled shoes and breeches, was not part of the new politics. But in 1824 as he neared the end of his second term, a host of new leaders in the Republican Party looked to succeed him. The Republican congressional caucus finally settled on William H. Crawford of Georgia as the party's presidential

↑ Oyster houses were the sports bars of antebellum America, and the preferred sport was politics. Newspapers expressed strong party loyalties, inspiring the man at the right to harangue his skeptical friend.

nominee. Condemning "King Caucus" as undemocratic, three other Republicans, all ardent nationalists, refused to withdraw from the race: Secretary of State John Quincy Adams; John C. Calhoun, Monroe's secretary of war; and Henry Clay, the Speaker of the House.

None of these men bargained on the sudden emergence of another Republican candidate, Andrew Jackson, the hero of the Battle of New Orleans. Because of his limited experience, no one took Jackson's candidacy seriously at first, including Jackson himself. But soon the general's supporters and rivals began receiving reports of his popularity. Savvy politicians flocked to his standard, but it was the people who first made Jackson a serious candidate.

The Election of 1824 >> Calhoun eventually dropped out of the race, but none of the four remaining candidates received a majority of the popular vote. Still, Jackson led the field and also finished first in the Electoral College. Under the terms of the Twelfth Amendment, the House was to select a president from the top three candidates. Henry Clay, who finished fourth and was therefore eliminated, met privately with Adams and then rallied the votes in the House needed to put Adams over the top.

Two days later Adams announced that Clay would be his secretary of state, the usual stepping-stone to the presidency. Jackson and his supporters promptly charged that there had been a "corrupt bargain" between Adams and Clay. Before Adams had even assumed office, the 1828 race was under way.

More significant, the election of 1824 shattered the old party system. Henry Clay and John Quincy Adams began to organize a new party, known as the National Republicans to distinguish it from Jefferson's old party. For the next decade the political system continued to evolve. By the mid-1830s the National Republicans gave way to the Whigs, a political party that also drew members from another party that flourished briefly, the Anti-Masons.[1] The Democrats as the other major party came together under the leadership of Andrew Jackson. Once established, this second party system dominated the nation's politics until the 1850s.

Social Sources of the New Politics >> Why was it that a new style and new system of politics emerged in the 1820s? Part of the answer lay in the Panic of 1819. During the depression that followed, many Americans became convinced that government policy had aggravated, if not actually produced, hard times. Consequently, they decided that the government had a responsibility to relieve distress and promote prosperity.

The connection made between government policy and economic well-being stimulated rising popular interest in politics during the 1820s. Agitation mounted, especially at the state level, for government to enact debtor relief and provide other forms of assistance. Elections became the means through which the majority expressed its policy preferences, by voting for candidates pledged to specific programs. The older idea that representatives should be independent, voting their best judgment, gave way to the notion that representatives were to carry out the will of the people, as expressed in the results of elections.

Opinion

Did the period between the American Revolution and the 1830s bring about a significant democratization in American politics?

---

[1]The Anti-Masons had led a campaign against the Freemasons or Masons, a fraternal order whose members shared the Enlightenment belief in the power of reason but whose secret meetings and rituals seemed aristocratic and undemocratic to many Americans.

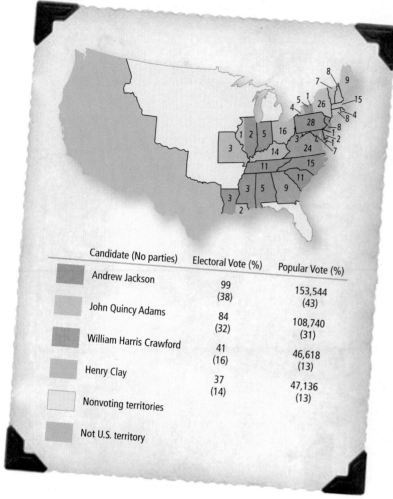

Candidate (No parties)	Electoral Vote (%)	Popular Vote (%)
Andrew Jackson	99 (38)	153,544 (43)
John Quincy Adams	84 (32)	108,740 (31)
William Harris Crawford	41 (16)	46,618 (13)
Henry Clay	37 (14)	47,136 (13)
Nonvoting territories		
Not U.S. territory		

MAP 11.1: ELECTION OF 1824

With more citizens championing the "will of the people," pressure mounted to open up the political process. Most states eliminated property qualifications for voting in favor of white manhood suffrage, under which all adult white males were allowed to vote (see Map 11.3). Similarly, property requirements for officeholders were reduced or dropped.

Presidential elections became more democratic as well. By 1832 South Carolina was the only state where the legislature rather than the voters still chose presidential electors. Parties began to hold conventions as a more democratic method of nominating candidates and approving a platform. And because a presidential candidate had to carry a number of states in different sections of the country, the backing of a national party, with effective state and local organizations, became essential.

The democratic winds of change affected European societies and eventually other areas of the world as well. In no other major country, however, were

these reforms achieved as early and with as little resistance as in the United States. Suffrage provides a good example. In Britain, in response to growing demonstrations and the cautionary example of the French monarchy's overthrow in 1830, Parliament approved the Reform Bill of 1832, which enfranchised a number of property holders and gave Britain the broadest electorate in Europe. Yet in fact, only about 15 percent of the adult males in Britain enjoyed the right of suffrage after the bill's passage. Even Britain's second Reform Act (1867) enfranchised only about one-third of the adult males. Likewise, virtually all the Latin American republics established in the 1820s and 1830s imposed property requirements on voting or forbade certain occupational groups, such as servants and peasants, to vote.

As the new reforms went into effect in the United States, voter turnout soared. Whereas in the 1824 presidential election only 27 percent of eligible voters had bothered to go to the polls, in 1840, 78 percent cast ballots, probably the highest turnout in American history.

All these developments favored the emergence of a new type of politician: one whose life was devoted to party service and whose living often depended on public office. As the number of state internal improvement projects increased during the 1820s, so did the number of government jobs that could support party workers. No longer was politics primarily the province of the wealthy, who spent only part of their time on public affairs. Instead, political leaders were more likely to come from the middle ranks of society, especially outside the South. As Franklin Plummer demonstrated, a successful politician now had to mingle with the masses and voice their feelings—requirements that put the wealthy elite at a disadvantage.

Politics became mass entertainment, with campaign hoopla frequently overshadowing issues. Parades, massive rallies, and barbecues were used to rouse voters, and treating to drinks became an almost universal campaign tactic. ("The way to men's hearts is down their throats," quipped one Kentucky vote-getter.) Although politicians talked often about principles, political parties were pragmatic organizations, intent on gaining and holding power.

The Jacksonian era has been called the Age of the Common Man, but such democratic tendencies had distinct limits. Women and slaves were not allowed to vote, nor could free African Americans (except in a few states) or Indians. Nor did the parties always deal effectively with (or even address) basic problems in society. Despite such limitations, however, popular political parties provided an

∧ Democratic reforms of the 1820s and 1830s brought a new sort of politician to prominence, one whose life was devoted to party service and whose living often depended on public office. This cartoon from 1834 shows the downside of the new situation. Andrew Jackson sports the wings, horns, and tail of a devil as he dangles the rewards of various political offices above a clamoring group of eager job-seekers.

essential mechanism for peacefully resolving dif—ferences among competing interest groups, regions, and social classes.

 REVIEW

In what ways did the political culture of the 1820s and 1830s differ from that of the 1780s and 1790s?

JACKSON'S RISE TO POWER

When he assumed the presidency in 1825, John Quincy Adams might have worked to create a mass—based party. On the state level, the new democratic style of politics was already making headway. But Adams, a talented diplomat and a great secretary of state, had hardly a political bone in his body. Cold and tactless, he could build no popular support for the ambitious and often farsighted programs he proposed. His pro—posals that government promote not only manufac—turing and agriculture but also the arts, literature, and science left his opponents aghast.

Nor would Adams take any steps to gain reelection. Henry Clay finally undertook to organize the National Republicans, but with a reluctant candidate he labored under serious handicaps. The new style of politics came into its own nationally only when Andrew Jack—son swept to power at the head of a new party, the Democrats. During the campaign, he remained vague about his position on many issues, and the 1828 race descended into a series of personal attacks, splattering mud on all involved. But Jackson emerged victorious, with enormous majorities behind him in the South.

Jackson's stubborn determination shines through in this portrait painted in 1835. "His passions are terrible," Jefferson noted. "When I was President of the Senate, he was Senator, and he could never speak on account of the rashness of his feelings. I have seen him attempt it repeatedly, and as often choke with rage."

President of the People

>> The election of 1828 marked the beginning of politics as Americans have practiced it ever since, with two disciplined national parties actively competing for votes, emphasizing personalities over issues, and resorting to mass electioneering techniques. Yet in terms of public policy, the meaning of the election was anything but clear. The people had voted for Jackson as a national hero without any real sense of what he would do with his newly won power.

The first president from west of the Appalachians, Jackson was a man of action, and though he had a quick mind, he had little use for learning. His troops had nicknamed him Old Hickory out of respect for his toughness, but that strength sometimes became arrogance, and he could be vindictive and a bully. Over the course of his turbulent career he had fought several duels, one of which left a bullet embedded for the rest of his life within inches of his heart. For all his flaws, however, Jackson was a shrewd politician. He knew how to manipulate men and could be affable or abusive as the occasion demanded. He also displayed a keen sense of public opinion, reading the shifting national mood better than any of his contemporaries.

As the nation's chief executive Jackson defended the **spoils system,** under which government jobs were awarded to political supporters. Replacing officials regularly was

a democratic reform, he insisted: the practice would guard against insensitive bureaucrats who presumed that they held their positions by right. The cabinet, he believed, existed more to carry out his will than to offer counsel. Throughout his term he insisted on his way—and usually got it.

> **spoils system** practice of rewarding loyal party members with jobs in government.

The Political Agenda in the Market Economy

>> Jackson took office at a time when the market economy was expanding throughout America and the nation's population was spreading geographically. The three major problems his administration faced were directly caused by the resulting growing pains.

First, the demand for new lands put continuing pressure on Indians, whose valuable cornfields and hunting grounds could produce marketable commodities such as cotton and wheat. Second, as the economies of the North, South, and West became more specialized, their rival interests forced a confrontation over the tariff. And finally, the booming economy focused attention on the role of credit and banking in society and on the new commercial attitudes that were a central part of the developing market economy. The president attacked all three issues in his characteristically combative style.

✓ **REVIEW**

What were the most pressing problems faced by President Andrew Jackson?

DEMOCRACY AND RACE

>> Is this a southern belle whose father owned a cotton plantation? Perhaps, but the young woman is a Chickasaw Indian. Her elegant hair and fashionable dress suggest the complexity of cultural relations in the Old Southwest, where some Indians had acculturated to white ways, owning plantations and even slaves. This woman was among the thousands of Indians removed to territory west of the Mississippi during the first half of the nineteenth century.

As a planter Jackson benefited from the international demand for cotton that was drawing new lands into the market. He had gone off to the Tennessee frontier in 1788, a rowdy, ambitious young man who could afford to purchase only one slave. Caught up in the speculative mania of the frontier, he became a prominent land speculator, established himself as a planter, and, by the time he became president, owned nearly 100 slaves. His popularity derived not only from defeating the British but also from opening extensive tracts of valuable Indian lands to white settlement.

Even so, in 1820 an estimated 125,000 Indians remained east of the Mississippi River. In the Southwest the Choctaws, Creeks, Cherokees, Chickasaws, and Seminoles retained

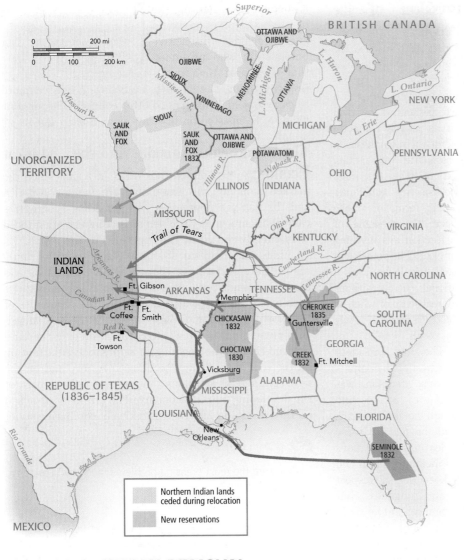

MAP 11.2: INDIAN REMOVAL

During Jackson's presidency the federal government concluded nearly 70 treaties with Indian tribes in the Old Northwest as well as in the South. Under their terms, the United States acquired approximately 100 million acres of Indian land.
Which Indian nation was the latest to be removed to western lands? Why?

millions of acres of prime agricultural land in the heart of the cotton kingdom. Led by Georgia, southern states demanded that the federal government clear these titles.

As white pressure for removal intensified, a shift in the attitude toward Indians and toward race in general occurred. In the past whites most often had attributed cultural differences among whites, blacks, and Indians to the environment. Increasingly after 1815 the dominant white culture stressed "innate" racial differences that could never be erased. A growing number of Americans began to argue that the Indian was a permanently inferior savage who blocked progress.

Accommodate or Resist? >> The clamor among southern whites for removal placed the southwestern tribes in a difficult situation. Understandably, they

rejected the idea of abandoning their lands. They diverged, however, over how to respond. Among the Cherokees, mixed–bloods led by John Ross argued that a program of accommodation— of adopting white ways— would best stave off removal. After a bitter struggle Ross prevailed, and in 1827 the Cherokees adopted a written constitution modeled after that of the United States. They also enacted the death penalty for any member who sold tribal lands to whites without consent of the governing general council. Developing their own alphabet, they published a bilingual newspaper, the *Cherokee Phoenix*.

The division between traditionalists and those favoring accommodation reflected the fact that Indians too had been drawn into a web of market relationships. As more Cherokee families began to sell their surplus crops, they ceased to share property communally as in the past. Cherokee society became more stratified and unequal, just as white society had, and economic elites dominated the tribal government. Nor were the Cherokees untouched by the cotton boom. Some tribal leaders, particularly half–bloods who could deal easily with white culture, became wealthy planters who owned many black slaves and thousands of acres of cotton land. Largely of mixed ancestry, slave-holders were the driving force behind acculturation.

As cotton cultivation expanded among the Cherokees, slavery became harsher and a primary means of determining status, just as in southern white society. The general council passed several laws forbidding intermarriage with blacks and excluding blacks and mulattoes from voting or holding office. Ironically, at the same time that white racial attitudes toward Indians were deteriorating, the Cherokees' view of African Americans drew closer to that of white society.

Trail of Tears >> As western land fever increased and racial attitudes hardened, Jackson prodded

Congress to provide funds for Indian removal. At the same time, the Georgia legislature declared Cherokee laws null and void and decreed that tribal members would be tried in state courts. In 1830 Congress finally passed a removal bill.

But the Cherokees brought suit in federal court against Georgia's actions. In 1832 in the case of *Worcester v. Georgia*, the Supreme Court, in an opinion written by Chief Justice John Marshall, ruled that Georgia had no right to extend its laws over Cherokee territory. Pronouncing Marshall's decision "stillborn," Jackson ignored the Court's edict and went ahead with plans for removal.

Although Jackson assured Indians that they could be removed only voluntarily, he paid no heed when state governments harassed tribes into surrendering lands. Under the threat of coercion, the Choctaws, Chickasaws, and Creeks reluctantly agreed to move to tracts in present–day Oklahoma. In the process land–hungry schemers cheated tribal members out of as much as 90 percent of their land allotments.

The Cherokees held out longest, but to no avail. In order to deal with more pliant leaders of the tribe, Georgia authorities kid–napped Chief John Ross, who had led the resistance to relocation, and threw him into jail. Ross was finally released but not allowed to negotiate the treaty, which stipulated that the Chero–kees leave their lands no later than 1838. When that time came, most refused to leave. In response, Presi–dent Martin Van Buren had the U.S. Army round up resistant members and force them, at bayonet point, to join the westward march. Of the 15,000 who traveled this Trail of Tears, approx–imately one–quarter died along the way of exposure, disease, and exhaustion.

Some Indians chose resistance. In the Old Northwest a group of the Sauk and Fox led by Black Hawk recrossed the Mississippi into Illinois in 1832 and were crushed by federal troops and the militia. More successful was the resistance of a minority of Seminoles led by Osceola. Despite Osceola's death the Seminoles held out until 1842 in the Florida Everglades before being subdued and removed. In the end, only a small number of southern tribe members were able to escape removal.

In his Farewell Address in 1837, Jackson defended his policy by piously asserting that the eastern tribes had been finally "placed beyond the reach of injury or oppression, and that [the] paternal care of the Gen–eral Government will hereafter watch over them and protect them." Indians, however, knew the bitter truth of the matter. Without effective political power, they were at the mercy of the pressures of the marketplace and the hardening racial attitudes of white Americans.

MAP 11.3: THE SPREAD OF WHITE MANHOOD SUFFRAGE

White manhood suffrage became the norm during the Jacksonian era, but in a number of states free black males who had been voting by law or by custom lost the right to vote. After 1821 a $250 property requirement disenfranchised about 90 percent of adult black males in New York. *What prompted the disenfranchisement of free blacks?*

Free Blacks in the North >> Unlike with Indian removal, the rising discrimination against free African Americans did not depend directly on presidential action. Still, it was Jackson's Democratic Party, which was in the vanguard of promoting white equality, that was also the most strongly proslavery and the most hostile to black rights. The intensifying racism that accompanied the emergence of democracy in American life bore down with particular force on free African Americans.

Before the Civil War, the free black population remained small: about 171,000 in 1840. Although those numbers amounted to less than 2 percent of the North's population, most states enacted laws to keep African Americans in an inferior position. (For a discussion of free African Americans in the South, see page 257.)

Most black northerners lacked meaningful political rights. Black men could vote on equal terms with whites in only five New England states. New York imposed a property requirement only on black voters, which disenfranchised the vast majority. Moreover, in New Jersey, Pennsylvania, and Connecticut, African American men lost the right to vote after having previously enjoyed that privilege.

⌃ The confident air of this African American, displayed in a daguerreotype (an early photographic process), suggests the dignity free blacks maintained in the face of unrelenting hostility and discrimination.

Blacks in the North were also denied basic civil rights that whites enjoyed. Five states forbade them to testify against whites, and either law or custom kept African Americans from juries everywhere except in Massachusetts. In addition, several western states passed black exclusion laws prohibiting free African Americans from emigrating to the state. These laws were seldom enforced, but they were available to harass the free black population.

Segregation, or the physical separation of the races, was widely practiced in the free states. African Americans were excluded from public transportation or assigned to separate sections. Throughout the North they could not go into most hotels and restaurants, and if permitted to enter theaters and lecture halls, they sat in the corners and balconies. In white churches they sat in separate pews and took communion after white members. In virtually every community black children were excluded from the public schools or forced to attend overcrowded and poorly funded separate schools. Commented one English visitor: "We see, in effect, two nations—one white and another black—growing up together . . . but never mingling on a principle of equality."

Discrimination pushed African American males into the lowest-paying and most unskilled jobs: servants, sailors, waiters, and common laborers. African American women normally continued working after marriage, mostly as servants, cooks, laundresses, and seamstresses, since their wages were critical to the family's survival. Blacks were willing strikebreakers, because white workers, fearing economic competition and loss of status, were overtly hostile and excluded them from trade unions. A number of antiblack riots erupted in northern cities during these years. Driven into abject poverty, free blacks in the North suffered from inadequate diet, were more susceptible to disease, and in 1850 had a life expectancy 8 to 10 years shorter than that of whites.

The African American Community >> Free blacks had long suffered from such oppression and injustice. Between the Revolution and the War of 1812, they had responded by founding schools, churches, and mutual aid societies to sustain their communities. Some, like Paul Cuffe, sought to escape white prejudice entirely by establishing settlements of free blacks in West Africa. The Quaker son of a West African father and a Wampanoag Indian mother, Cuffe became a sea captain, and in 1816 his merchant ship brought 38 free black New Englanders to settle in West Africa. Cuffe's venture drew white sympathizers who formed the American Colonization Society (ACS) and founded Liberia in West Africa in 1821–1822. Several state legislatures in the North and the Upper South as well as all the major Protestant churches endorsed ACS plans to encourage free black emigration, but its members were an unlikely and unstable coalition. Some opposed

AFRICAN COLONIZATION: HOPING FOR THE BEST AND SUSPECTING THE WORST

Henry Clay owned 50 slaves who worked his Kentucky plantation, but he was a lifelong advocate of gradual emancipation and a founder of the American Colonization Society in 1816. He explained his support in 1827. David Walker, a militant leader of the northern free black community, singled out Clay and other colonizationists for sharp criticism.

DOCUMENT 1
In Favor of Colonization: Henry Clay

Numbers of the free African race among us are willing to go to Africa. . . . Why should they not go! Here they are in the lowest state of social gradation; aliens—political, moral, social aliens—strangers though natives. There they would be in the midst of their friends, and their kindred, at home, though born in a foreign land, and elevated above the natives of the country, as much as they are degraded here below the other classes of the community. . . .

What is the true nature of the evil of the existence of a portion of the African race in our population? It is not that there are some, but that there are so many among us of a different caste, of a different physical, if not moral, constitution, who never can amalgate with the great body of our population. Here . . . the African part of our population bears so large a proportion to the residue, of European origin, as to create the most lively apprehension, especially in some quarters of the Union. Any project, therefore, by which, in a material degree, the dangerous element in the general mass can be diminished or rendered stationary, deserves deliberate consideration.

The Colonization Society has never imagined it to be practicable . . . to transport the whole of the African race within the limits of the United States. Nor is that necessary to accomplish the desirable objects of domestic tranquility, and render us one homogeneous people. Let us suppose . . . that the whole population at present of the United States, is twelve millions of which ten may be estimated of the Anglo-Saxon and two of the African race. If there could be annually transported from the United States an amount of the African portion equal to the annual increase of the whole of that caste, while the European race should be left to multiply, we should find at the termination of the period . . . that the relative proportion would be as twenty to two. And if the process were continued, during the second term of duplication, the proportion would be forty to two—one which would eradicate every cause of alarm or solicitude from the breasts of the most timid.

Source: Henry Clay, Speech at the Annual Meeting of the American Colonization Society, Washington, January 30, 1827, In *The Works of Henry Clay,* ed. Calvin Colton (New York, 1904).

DOCUMENT 2
Against Colonization: David Walker

Here is demonstrative proof, of a plan got up, by a gang of slaveholders to select the free people of colour from among the slaves, that our more miserable brethren may be the better secured in ignorance and wretchedness, to work their farms and dig their mines, and thus go on enriching the Christians with their blood and groans. What our brethren could have been thinking about, who have left their native land and home and gone away to Africa. I am unable to say. This country is as much ours as it is the whites, whether they will admit it or not they will see and believe it by and by. They tell us about prejudice—what have we to do with it? Their prejudices will be obliged to fall like lightning to the ground, in succeeding generations: not, however, with the will and consent of all the whites, for some will be obliged to hold on to the old adage, viz: the blacks are not men, but were made to be an inheritance to us and our children for ever!!!!!! I hope the residue of the coloured people, will stand still and see the salvation of God and the miracle which he will work for our delivery from wretchedness under the Christians!!!!!! . . .

I shall give an extract from the letter of that truly Reverend Divine, (Bishop [Richard] Allen) of Philadelphia, respecting this trick . . . he says, "Dear Sir, I have been for several years trying to reconcile my mind to the Colonizing of Africans in Liberia, but there have always been and there still remain great and insurmountable objections against the scheme. . . . Can we not discern the project of sending the free people of colour away from their country? Is it not for the interest of the slaveholders to select the free people of colour out of the different states, and send them to Liberia? Will it not make their slaves uneasy to see free men of colour enjoying liberty? It is against the law in some of the Southern States, that a person of colour should receive an education, under a severe penalty. . . . See the thousands of foreigners emigrating to America every year: and if there be ground sufficient for them to cultivate, and bread for them to eat, why would they wish to send the *first tillers* of the land away? Africans have made fortunes for thousands, who are yet unwilling to part with their services; but the free must be sent away, and those who remain must be *slaves.* I have no doubt that there are many good men who do not see as I do, and who are for sending us to Liberia; but they have not duly considered the subject—they are not men of colour. This land which we have watered with our *tears* and *our blood* is now our *mother country,* and we are well satisfied to stay where wisdom abounds and the gospel is free."

Source: David Walker *Appeal to the Coloured Citizens of the World* (1829).

THINKING CRITICALLY

What were Henry Clay's concerns about free African Americans? Why did he regard colonization as a viable solution to the problems he believed African Americans posed to the United States? What did David Walker and Richard Allen believe to be the true intentions of the colonizationists? Do you believe that they accurately assessed those motives?

slavery and hoped that colonization would encourage manumissions and gradual emancipation, while others believed that ridding the nation of free blacks would secure the future of slavery.

Even as white support for colonization swelled during the 1820s, black enthusiasm for emigration diminished. Many African American leaders in the North were turning to more–confrontational tactics: they advocated resistance to slavery and condemned racism and inequality. Among the most outspoken of this new, more militant generation was David Walker, whose *Appeal to the Colored Citizens of the World* (1829) denounced colonization and urged slaves to use violence to end bondage.

Racism Strikes a Deeper Root >> What

prompted greater militancy among African Americans after the 1820s was also the growth of an increasingly virulent racism among whites. Ironically, the success of efforts to promote education, religious piety, and temperance within the free black community threatened many lower–class whites and intensified their resentment of African Americans. That animosity found vent in race riots, which erupted in Pittsburgh, Boston, Cincinnati, and New Haven.

The depth of racism in the culture could be seen in the rise of the minstrel show, the most popular form of entertainment in Jacksonian America. Originating in the 1830s and 1840s, these shows played to packed houses in cities and towns throughout the nation. They featured white actors performing in blackface, whose skits dealt in the broadest of racial stereotypes, ridiculing blacks as physically different and portraying them as buffoons.

Minstrelsy's greatest success came in northern cities. Its basic message was that African Americans could not cope with freedom and therefore did not belong in the North. Slaves were portrayed as happy and contented, whereas free blacks were caricatured either as strutting dandies or as helpless ignoramuses. Drawing its patrons from workers, Irish immigrants, and the poorer elements in society, minstrelsy assured these white champions of democracy that they remained superior.

The unsettling economic, social, and political changes of the Jacksonian era heightened white Americans' fear of failure, which stimulated racism. The popular yet unrealistic expectation was that any white man might become rich. Yet in fact, 20 percent or more of white adult males of this era never accumulated any property. Their lack of success prompted them to relieve personal tensions through increased hostility toward their black neighbors. The power of racism in Jacksonian America stemmed at least in part from the fact that equality remained part of the nation's creed while it steadily receded as a social reality.

 REVIEW

In what ways did Indians and free African Americans attempt to protect their communities in Jacksonian America?

THE NULLIFICATION CRISIS

Indian removal and antiblack discrimination provided one answer to the question of who would be given equality of opportunity in America's new democracy: Indians and African Americans would not. The issue of nullification raised a different, equally pressing question. As the North, South, and West increasingly specialized economically in response to the market revolution, how would a democratic system of government help various regions or interest groups to accommodate their differences?

The Growing Crisis in South Carolina >>

South Carolina had been particularly hard–hit by the depression of 1819. When prosperity returned to the rest of the nation, many of the state's cotton planters still suffered. With lands exhausted from years of cultivation, they could not compete with the fabulous yields of frontier planters in Alabama and Mississippi.

Under these difficult conditions, South Carolinians increasingly blamed federal tariffs for their miseries. When Congress raised the duty rates in 1824, they attacked the tariff as an unfair tax. After all, they sold their cotton on the open market for a price that went up and down, without any tariff protection. But tariffs artificially raised the price of finished goods southerners imported from abroad (including cotton textiles) in order to benefit New England merchants. Other southern states opposed the 1824 tariff as well, though none so vehemently.

The one southern state in which black inhabitants outnumbered whites, South Carolina had also been growing more sensitive about the institution of slavery. In 1822 Denmark Vesey, a daring and resourceful free black carpenter in Charleston, secretly organized a plan to seize control of the city and raise the standard of black liberty. At the last moment, white officials thwarted the conspiracy and executed Vesey and his chief lieutenants; nevertheless, white South Carolinians were convinced that other conspirators still lurked in their midst. As an additional measure of security, they began to push for stronger constitutional protection of slavery. After all, the constitutional doctrine of broad construction and implied powers had already been used to justify higher protective tariffs. What was to prevent it from being used to end slavery?

When Congress, over the protests of the state's representatives, raised the duty rates still higher in 1828 with the so-called Tariff of Abominations, South Carolina's legislature published the *South Carolina Exposition and Protest*, which outlined for the first time the theory of nullification. Only later was it revealed that its author was Jackson's own vice president, John C. Calhoun.

Calhoun was the most impressive intellect of his political generation. During the 1820s the South Carolina leader made a slow but steady journey away from nationalism toward an extreme states' rights position. When he was elected Jackson's vice president, South Carolinians assumed that tariff reform would be quickly forthcoming. But Jackson and Calhoun soon quarreled, and Calhoun lost all influence in the administration.

In his theory of nullification Calhoun argued that the Union was a compact between sovereign states. Thus the people of each state, acting in special conventions, had the right to nullify any federal law that exceeded the powers granted to Congress under the Constitution. In response, Congress could either repeal the law or propose a constitutional amendment expressly giving it the power in question. If the amendment was ratified, the nullifying state could either accept the decision or exercise its ultimate right as a sovereign state and secede from the Union.

In 1830 Senator Daniel Webster of Massachusetts responded that the Union was not a compact of sovereign states. The people, and not the states, he argued, had created the Constitution. "It is the people's constitution, the people's government, made for the people, made by the people, and answerable to the people." Webster also insisted that the federal government did not merely act as the agent of the states but had sovereign powers in those areas where it had been delegated responsibility.

The Nullifiers Nullified >> When Congress passed another tariff in 1832 that failed to give the state any relief, South Carolina's legislature called for the election of delegates to a popular convention, which overwhelmingly adopted an ordinance in November that declared the tariffs of 1828 and 1832 "null, void, and no law, nor binding upon this state, its officers or citizens" after February 1, 1833.

Jackson, who had spent much of his life defending the nation, was not about to tolerate any defiance of his authority or the federal government's. In his Proclamation on Nullification, issued in December 1832, he insisted that the Union was perpetual and that under the Constitution, no state had the right to secede. To reinforce his announced determination to enforce the tariff laws, Congress passed the Force Bill, reaffirming the president's military powers.

Yet Jackson was also a skillful politician. At the same time that he threatened South Carolina, he urged Congress to reduce the tariff rates. With no other state willing to follow South Carolina's lead, Calhoun reluctantly agreed to a compromise tariff in 1833. South Carolina's convention repealed the nullifying ordinance, and the crisis passed.

Calhoun's doctrine had proved too radical for the rest of the South. Even so, the controversy convinced many southerners that they were becoming a permanent minority. "We are divided into slave-holding and non-slave-holding states," concluded nullifier William Harper, "and this is the broad and marked distinction that must separate us at last." As that feeling of isolation grew, it was not nullification but the threat of secession that ultimately became the South's primary weapon.

 REVIEW

What were the issues being contested in the debate over nullification?

THE BANK WAR

Jackson understood well the political ties that bound the nation. He grasped much less firmly the economic and financial connections that linked regions of the country through banks and national markets. His clash with the Second Bank of the United States led to the greatest crisis of his presidency.

The National Bank and the Panic of 1819 >>Chartered by Congress in 1816 for a 20–year period, the Second Bank of the United States suffered from woeful mismanagement. At first it helped fuel the speculative pressures in the economy. Then it turned about–face and sharply contracted credit by calling in loans when the depression hit in 1819. Critics viewed the Bank's policies not as a consequence but as the cause of the financial downswing. To many Americans, the Bank had already become a monster.

The psychological effects of the Panic of 1819 were almost as momentous as the economic. The shock of the depression made the 1820s a time of soul–searching, during which many uneasy farmers and workers came to view the hard times as punishment for having lost sight of the old virtues of simplicity, frugality, and hard work. For these Americans, banks were a symbol of the commercialization of American society and the rapid passing of a simpler way of life.

In 1823 Nicholas Biddle, a rich 37–year–old Phila–delphia businessman, became president of the national bank. Biddle was intelligent and thoroughly familiar with the banking system, but he was also impossibly arrogant and politically dense. He set out to use the bank to reg–ulate the amount of credit available in the economy, and thereby provide the nation with a sound currency.

The government regularly deposited its revenues in the national bank. These revenues were paid largely in banknotes (paper money) issued by state–chartered banks. If Biddle believed that a state bank had issued more notes than was safe, he presented them to that bank and demanded they be redeemed in **specie** (gold or silver). Because banks did not have enough spe–cie reserves to back all the paper money they issued, the only way a state bank could continue to redeem its notes was to call in its loans and reduce the amount of its notes in circulation. This action had the effect of lessening the amount of credit in the economy. But if Biddle felt that a bank's credit policies were reasonable, he simply returned the state banknotes to circulation without presenting them for redemption.

specie coined money of gold or silver; also referred to as hard money or hard currency. In contrast, banknotes, or notes, are paper money or paper currency.

Under Biddle's direction the Bank became a finan–cial colossus with enormous power over state banks and over the economy. Yet Biddle used this power responsibly to provide the United States a sound paper currency, which the expanding economy needed.

Although the Bank had strong support in the busi–ness community, workers complained that they were often paid in **depreciated** state banknotes that could be redeemed for only a portion of their face value, a prac–tice that cheated them of their full wages. They called for a "hard money" currency of only gold and silver. Hard–money advocates viewed bankers and financiers as profiteers who manipulated the paper money system to enrich themselves at the expense of honest, hardworking farmers and laborers.

depreciated decreased in value owing to market conditions.

The Bank Destroyed >>Jackson's own experiences left him with a deep distrust of banks and paper money. In 1804 his Tennessee land speculations had brought him to the brink of bankruptcy, from which it took years of painful struggle to free himself. Reflecting on his per–sonal situation, he became convinced that banks and paper money threatened to corrupt the Republic.

As president, Jackson periodically called for reform of the banking system, but Biddle refused even to consider curbing the Bank's powers. Already distracted by the nullification controversy, Jackson warned Bid–dle not to inject the bank issue into the 1832 campaign. When Biddle went ahead and applied for a renewal of the Bank's charter in 1832, four years early, Jack–son was furious. "The Bank is trying to kill me," he stormed, "but I will kill it."

Despite the president's opposition, Congress passed a recharter bill in the summer of 1832. Immediately, Jack–son vetoed it as unconstitutional (rejecting Marshall's earlier ruling in *McCulloch v. Maryland*). Condemning the Bank as an agent of special privilege, the president pledged to protect "the humble members of society—the farmer, mechanics, and laborers" against "the advance–ment of the few at the expense of the many."

When Congress failed to override Jackson's veto, the Bank became a central issue of the 1832 cam–paign. Jackson's opponent was Henry Clay, a National Republican who eagerly accepted the financial support of Biddle and his bank. Clay went down to defeat, and, once reelected, Jackson was determined to move boldly. He believed that as a private corporation the Bank wielded a dangerous influence over government policy and the economy, and he was justly incensed over its interference in the election.

To cripple the Bank, the president simply ordered all the government's federal deposits withdrawn. Since such an act clearly violated federal law, Jackson was forced to transfer one secretary of the treasury and fire another

before he finally found an ally, Roger Taney, willing to take the job and carry out the edict. Taney (pronounced "Taw–ney") gradually withdrew the government's funds while depositing new revenues in selected state banks.

Biddle fought back by deliberately precipitating a brief financial panic in 1833, but Jackson refused to budge. Eventually Biddle had to relent, and Jackson's victory was complete. When the Bank's charter expired in 1836, no national banking system replaced it.

Jackson's Impact on the Presidency >>Jack–son approached the end of his administration in triumph. Indian removal was well on its way to completion, the nullifiers had been confounded, and the "Monster Bank" had been destroyed. In the process Jackson immeasur–ably enlarged the power of the presidency. "The Presi–dent is the direct representative of the American people," he lectured the Senate when it opposed him. "He was elected by the people, and is responsible to them." With this declaration Jackson redefined the character of the presidential office and its relationship to the people.

Jackson also converted the veto into an effective presidential power. During his two terms in office he vetoed 12 bills, compared with only 9 for all previ–ous presidents combined. Moreover, where his prede–cessors had vetoed bills only on strict constitutional grounds, Jackson felt free to block laws simply because he thought them bad policy. The threat of such action became an effective way to shape pending legislation to his liking, a tactic that fundamentally strengthened the power of the president over Congress. The development of the modern presidency began with Andrew Jackson.

"Van Ruin's" Depression >> With the con–trols of the national bank removed, state banks rap–idly expanded their activities, including the printing of more money. As the cur–rency expanded, so did the number of banks: from 329 in 1829 to 788 in 1837. A spiraling **inflation** set in as prices rose 50 percent after 1830 and interest rates by half as much.

> **inflation** increase in the overall price of goods and services over an extended period of time; or a simi–lar decrease over time of the purchasing power of money.

As prices soared so did speculative fever. By 1836 land sales, which had been only $2.6 million four years earlier, approached $25 million. Almost all these lands were bought entirely on credit with banknotes. In July 1836 Jackson issued the Specie Circular, which decreed that the government would accept only specie for the purchase of public land. Land sales plummeted, but the speculative pressures in the economy were already too great.

During Jackson's second term, his opponents had gradually come together in a new party, the Whigs. Led by Henry Clay, they charged that "King Andrew I" had dangerously concentrated power in the presidency. The Whigs also embraced Clay's "American System," designed to spur national economic development through a protective tariff, a national bank, and federal aid for internal improvements. In 1836 the Democrats nominated Martin Van Buren, who triumphed over three Whig sectional candidates.

Van Buren had less than two months in office to savor his triumph before the speculative mania collapsed, and with it the economy. After a brief recovery, the bottom fell out of the international cotton market in 1839, and the country entered a serious depression. It was not until 1843 that the economy revived.

Public opinion identified hard times with the policies of the Democratic Party. Since he continued to oppose a new national bank, Van Buren instead persuaded Congress in 1840 to create an Independent Treasury to hold the government's funds. Its offices were forbidden to accept paper currency, issue any banknotes, or make any loans. The government's money would be safe, as Van Buren intended, but it would also remain unavailable to banks to make loans and stimulate the economy. Whigs, in contrast, hoped to encourage manufacturing and revive the economy by passing a protective tariff, continuing state internal improvement projects, protecting corporations, and expanding the banking and credit system.

As the depression deepened, thousands of workers were unemployed, and countless businesses failed. Nationally, wages fell 30 to 50 percent. "Business of all kinds is completely at a stand," wrote New York business and civic leader Philip Hone in 1840, "and the whole body politic sick and infirm, and calling aloud for a remedy."

The Whigs Triumph >> For the 1840 presidential campaign the Whigs turned to William Henry Harrison, who had defeated the Shawnee Indians at Tippecanoe, to oppose Van Buren. In the midst of the worst depression of the century, Whigs employed the democratic electioneering techniques that Jackson's supporters had perfected. They hailed Harrison as a man of the people while painting Van Buren as a dandy and an aristocrat who wore a corset, ate off gold plates with silver spoons, and used

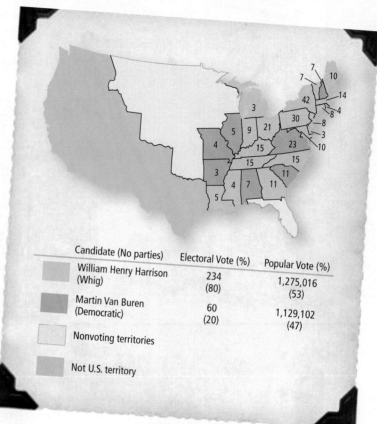

MAP 11.4: ELECTION OF 1840

Candidate (No parties)		Electoral Vote (%)	Popular Vote (%)
	William Henry Harrison (Whig)	234 (80)	1,275,016 (53)
	Martin Van Buren (Democratic)	60 (20)	1,129,102 (47)
	Nonvoting territories		
	Not U.S. territory		

cologne. Whig rallies featured hard cider and log cabins to reinforce Harrison's image as a man of the people. Ironically, Harrison had been born into one of Virginia's most aristocratic families and was living in a 16–room mansion in Ohio. But the Whig campaign, by casting the election as a contest between aristocracy and democracy, was perfectly attuned to the prevailing national spirit.

In the campaign of 1840 Whigs also prominently involved women, urging them to become politically informed in order to morally instruct their husbands. Women attended Whig rallies, conducted meetings, made speeches, and wrote campaign pamphlets, activities previously performed solely by men. Democrats were uneasy about this innovation, yet had no choice but to follow suit. Within a few years the presence of women at party rallies was commonplace.

The election produced a record turnout, with nearly four–fifths of the eligible voters going to the polls. Although the popular vote was fairly close (Harrison led by about 150,000 votes out of 2.4 million cast), in the Electoral College he won an easy victory, 234 to 60.

The "log cabin" campaign marked the final transition from the deferential politics of the Federalist era to the egalitarian politics that had emerged in the wake of the Panic of 1819. As the *Democratic Review* conceded after the Whigs' victory in 1840, "We have taught them how to conquer us."

 **REVIEW**

Why did Jackson oppose the Second Bank of the United States?

THE JACKSONIAN PARTY SYSTEM

It is easy, given the hoopla of democratic campaigning, to be distracted from the central fact that the new political system was directly shaped by the social and economic strains of an expanding nation. Whigs and Democrats held different attitudes toward the changes brought about by the market, banks, and commerce.

Democrats, Whigs, and the Market >> The
Democrats tended to view society as a continuing conflict between "the people"—farmers, planters, and workers—and a set of greedy aristocrats. They charged that this "paper money aristocracy" of bankers, stock jobbers, and investors manipulated the banking system for their own profit. For Democrats, the Bank War became a battle to restore the old Jeffersonian Republic with its values of simplicity, frugality, hard work, and independence.

Jackson understood the dangers private banks posed to a democratic society. Yet Democrats, in effect, wanted the rewards and goods that the market offered without sacrificing the features of a simple agrarian republic. They wanted the wealth that the market produced without the competitive society, the complex dealings, the dominance of urban centers, and the loss of independence that came with it.

Whigs were more comfortable with the market. They envisioned no conflict between farmers and mechanics on the one hand and businesspeople and bankers on the other. The government's responsibility was to provide a well-regulated economy that guaranteed opportunity

for citizens of ability. In such an economy, banks and corporations were not only useful but necessary.

Whigs and Democrats also disagreed over how active government should be. Despite Andrew Jackson's inclination to be a strong president, Democrats as a rule believed in limited government. Government's role in the economy was to promote competition by destroying monopolies and special privileges. In keeping with this philosophy, Democrats also rejected the idea that moral beliefs were the proper sphere of government action. Religion and politics, they believed, should be kept clearly separate, and they generally opposed humanitarian legislation.

The Whigs, in contrast, viewed government power positively. They believed that it should be used to protect individual rights and public liberty, and that it had a special role where individual effort was ineffective. By regulating the economy and competition, the government could ensure equal opportunity. Indeed, for Whigs the concept of government promoting the general welfare went beyond the economy. Northern Whigs in particular also believed that government power should be used to foster the moral welfare of the country. They were much more likely to favor temperance or antislavery legislation and aid to education. Whigs portrayed themselves not only as the party of prosperity but also as the party of respectability and proper behavior.

The Social Bases of the Two Parties >> In
some ways the social makeup of the two parties was similar. To be competitive Whigs and Democrats both had to have significant support among farmers, the largest group in society, and workers. Neither party could carry an election by appealing exclusively to the rich or the poor.

The Whigs, however, enjoyed disproportionate strength among the business and commercial classes, especially following the Bank War. Whigs appealed to planters who needed credit to finance their cotton and rice trade in the world market, to farmers who were eager to sell their surpluses, and to workers who wished to improve their

<< Whigs drew strongly from the business and commercial classes who were eager to improve themselves. This daguerrotype is said to be of the merchant Cyrus Field, a Whig with a strong commercial vision who partnered with other entrepreneurs to lay a telegraph cable across the Atlantic.

social position. Democrats attracted farmers isolated from the market or uncomfortable with it, workers alienated from the emerging industrial system, and rising entrepreneurs who wanted to break monopolies and open the economy to newcomers like themselves. The Whigs were strongest in the towns, cities, and rural areas that were fully integrated into the market economy, whereas Democrats dominated areas of semisubsistence farming that were more isolated and languishing economically. Attitude toward the market, rather than economic position, was more important in determining party affiliation.

Religion and ethnic identities also shaped partisanship. As the self–proclaimed "party of respectability," Whigs attracted the support of high–status native–born church groups, including Congregationalists and Unitarians in New England and Presbyterians and Episcopalians elsewhere. The party also attracted immigrant groups that most easily merged into the dominant Anglo–Protestant culture, such as the English, Welsh, and Scots. Democrats, however, recruited more Germans and Irish, whose more lenient observance of the Sabbath and (among Catholics) use of parochial schools generated native–born hostility. Democrats appealed to the lower–status Baptists and Methodists, particularly in states where they earlier had been subjected to legal disadvantages. Both parties also attracted freethinkers and the unchurched, but the Democrats had the advantage because they resisted demands for temperance and sabbatarian laws, such as the prohibition of Sunday travel. In the few states where they could vote, African Americans were solidly Whig in reaction to the Democratic Party's strong racism and hostility to black rights.

 REVIEW

What were the major differences between the Whigs and the Democrats?

In the Americas as well as in Europe, the rise of democratic governance and the spread of market economies evolved roughly in tandem over the same half century. Andrew Jackson's triumph was only the latest in a series of upheavals stretching back to the American and French Revolutions of the eighteenth century. Latin America, too, experienced democratic revolutions. From 1808 to 1821 Spain's American provinces declared their independence one by one, taking inspiration from the writings of Jefferson and Thomas Paine as well as the French *Declaration of the Rights of Man*. Democracy did not always root itself in the aftermath of these revolutions, but democratic ideology remained a powerful social catalyst.

In the United States the parallel growth of national markets and democratic institutions exhibited a similarly checkered history. If Jackson championed the cause of the "common people," he also led the movement to displace Indians from their lands. A poor white American might vote for "Old Hickory" at the same time that he took comfort that African Americans could never rise as high as he in an increasingly racist society. Furthermore, the advance of markets created social strains, including the increasing impoverishment of the labor force in the North and the growing gap in society between the richest and the poorest.

Still, Americans had evolved a system of democratic politics to deal with the conflicts that the new order produced. The new national parties, like the new markets, had become essential structures uniting the American nation. They advanced an ideology of equality and opportunity, competed vigorously with one another, and mobilized large numbers of ordinary Americans in the political process. Along with the market, democracy had become an integral part of American life.

CHAPTER SUMMARY

Beginning in the 1820s the United States experienced a democratic revolution that was identified with Andrew Jackson.

- The rise of democracy was stimulated by the Panic of 1819, which caused Americans to look toward both politicians and the government to address their needs.
- The new political culture of democracy included the use of conventions to make nominations, the celebration of the wisdom of the people, the adoption of white manhood suffrage, and the acceptance of political parties as essential for the working of the constitutional system.
- The new politics had distinct limits, however. Women were not given the vote, and racism intensified.
  - ▶ The eastern Indian tribes were forced to move to new lands west of the Mississippi River.
  - ▶ Free African Americans found themselves subject to increasingly harsh discrimination and exclusion.
- In politics Andrew Jackson came to personify the new democratic culture. Through his forceful leadership he significantly expanded the powers of the presidency.
  - ▶ Jackson threatened to use force against South Carolina when it tried to nullify the federal tariff using John C. Calhoun's theory of

nullification—that is, that a state convention could nullify a federal law.

- ▶ In response nationalists advanced the idea of the perpetual Union. The compromise of 1833, which gradually lowered the tariff, ended the crisis.
- ▶ Jackson vetoed a bill to recharter the Second Bank of the United States and destroyed it by removing its federal deposits.
- ▶ Under President Martin Van Buren, the nation entered a severe depression.
- Capitalizing on hard times and employing the dem-ocratic techniques pioneered by the Democrats, the Whigs gained national power in 1840.
- By 1840 the two parties had developed different ideologies.

    - ▶ The Whigs were more comfortable with the mechanisms of the market and linked commerce with progress.
    - ▶ The Democrats were uneasy about the market and favored limited government.

Additional Reading

The most comprehensive reinterpretation of antebel-lum political history from Jackson to Lincoln is Sean Wilentz, *The Rise of Democracy* (2005). For a broader perspective on the evolution of American political cul-ture throughout the nineteenth century, see Glenn Altschuler and Stuart Blumin, *Rude Republic* (2000). A good interpretation of Jacksonian politics is Harry Watson, *Liberty and Power* (1990); and important discussions of party ideologies include Marvin Meyers, *The Jacksonian Persuasion* (1957); Daniel Walker Howe, *The Political Culture of American Whigs* (1979); and Lawrence Frederick Kohl, *The Politics of Individualism* (1988). For the history of the Whig Party, the book to read is Michael Holt, *The Rise and Fall of the American Whig Party* (1999).

The best account of the nullification crisis is still William Freehling, *Prelude to the Civil War* (1966); and Robert Remini offers a succinct analysis of the banking controversy in *Andrew Jackson and the Bank War* (1967). Paul Goodman, *Towards a Christian Republic* (1988), is the most valuable study of Anti-Masonry. On Indian removal in the South, see John Ehle, *The Trail of Tears* (1997); and Robert Remini, *Andrew Jackson and His Indian Wars* (2001).

Significant Events

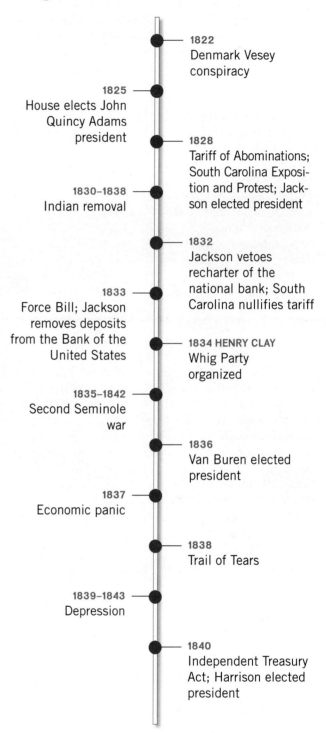

1822 Denmark Vesey conspiracy

1825 House elects John Quincy Adams president

1828 Tariff of Abominations; South Carolina Exposi-tion and Protest; Jack-son elected president

1830–1838 Indian removal

1832 Jackson vetoes recharter of the national bank; South Carolina nullifies tariff

1833 Force Bill; Jackson removes deposits from the Bank of the United States

1834 HENRY CLAY Whig Party organized

1835–1842 Second Seminole war

1836 Van Buren elected president

1837 Economic panic

1838 Trail of Tears

1839–1843 Depression

1840 Independent Treasury Act; Harrison elected president

12 Afire with Faith

1820–1850

Bursting with energy and enthusiasm, Methodists head toward a camp meeting in 1819.

>> **An American Story**

THE BEECHERS AND THE KINGDOM OF GOD

n 1826 the Reverend Lyman Beecher was probably the most celebrated minister of the Republic, and the pulpit of Hanover Street Church was his to command. Beecher looked and spoke like a pious farmer, but every Sunday he was transformed when he mounted the pulpit of Boston's most imposing church. From there he would blaze forth denunciations of dancing, drinking, dueling, and "infidelity," all the while punctuating his sermon with pump-handle strokes of the right hand.

Nor were Beecher's ambitions small. His goal was nothing less than to bring the kingdom of Christ to the nation and the world. Like many ministers Beecher had studied the intriguing final book of the New Testament, the Revelation to John. The Revelation foretold in the latter days of Earth a glorious millennium—a thousand years of peace and triumph—when the saints would rule and evil would be banished from the world. Beecher was convinced that the long-awaited millennium might well begin in the United States.

To usher in the kingdom of God, entire communities and even nations would have to be swept with the fire of **millennialism.** Toward that

> **millennialism** belief in the thousand-year reign of Christ predicted in the New Testament's final book, the Revelation to John.

end Beecher joined other Protestant ministers in supporting a host of religious reforms and missionary efforts. By 1820 they had formed voluntary organizations devoted to a wide range of activities: blanketing the United States with tracts and bibles, educating young men for the ministry, sending missionaries to every corner of the globe, promoting Sunday schools for children, ministering to sailors and the poor, reforming drunkards, and stopping business on the Sabbath. To Beecher the organizations constituting this loosely united "Benevolent Empire" were signs of the coming kingdom.

As the new pastor at Hanover Street, Beecher also directed his righteous artillery on a host of evils

⌃ Lyman Beecher (*center*) with his family in 1855. Five of his six sons, all of whom were ministers, stand in back. In front, daughters Catharine (holding his arm to steady it for the long exposure) and Isabella are on the left; Harriet, the author of *Uncle Tom's Cabin,* is at the far right.

that seemed to be obstructing God's kingdom. With scorn he attacked Unitarians, whose liberal, rational creed rejected the divinity of Jesus. In Boston, Unitarians were mainly upper class and cultured. But he also denounced what he viewed as sinful pastimes of the lower class: playing cards, gambling, and drinking. And he denounced Roman Catholic priests and nuns as superstitious, devious agents of "Antichrist."

Beecher's efforts at "moral reform" antagonized many immigrants and other working people who enjoyed liquor or lotteries. In disdain they referred to Hanover Street Church, with its imposing stone tower, as Beecher's "stone jug." After all, it was there that its pastor drank most deeply of his religious spirits. In 1830 a blaze broke out in the basement of his church, and some of the locals had their revenge. Firefighters stood by and made jokes about "Old Beecher" and hellfire as flames cracked the stone tower from top to bottom and the splendid structure burned into ruins.

Any fire, real or spiritual, is unpredictable as it spreads from one scrap of tinder to the next. That proved to be the case with reform

movements of the 1820s and 1830s as, in subsequent decades, they moved in diverging, sometimes contradictory, ways. What did it mean, after all, to make a heaven on earth?

Lyman Beecher embodied the spirit of antebellum evangelical Protestantism. At the core of evangelicalism was the conviction that divine grace brought about a new birth, one that enabled belief in Jesus Christ. That conviction also committed the individual convert to reforming his or her own vices as well as the faults of others. But evangelicalism was changing over the course of Beecher's lifetime, and, as it changed, so did its influence on Christian believers. Early-nineteenth-century evangelical leaders such as Beecher sought to convert individuals through revivals and then to turn their energies toward reforming others through the voluntary associations of the Benevolent Empire. Their conservative aim, as he expressed it, was to restore America to "the moral government of God."

But the next generation of evangelical leaders—including Beecher's own children—sought not merely to convert individuals to Christianity but also to reform the most fundamental institutions structuring American society: slavery, the family, and the political and legal subordination of women. By the 1840s they were joined by many other believers in faiths both secular and religious— Unitarians and Transcendentalists, Shakers and socialists. All were afire with the faith that they could radically remake the United States. <<

THE TRANSFORMATION OF AMERICAN EVANGELICALISM

Before about 1800, most American **evangelicals** embraced the doctrines of Calvinism (see pages 30–31).

evangelicals Christian believers who work actively to spread the "good news," or gospel of Jesus as recounted in the New Testament of the Bible.

They believed that God had determined which individuals were destined to be damned or saved and that no human effort could alter those eternal fates. But by the beginning of the nineteenth century, such propositions seemed increasingly unreasonable to the American heirs of a revolution that celebrated human equality, free will, and reason. As a result, a growing number of evangelicals moved toward an outlook that, although not denying the sinfulness of human nature and the necessity of divine grace for salvation, granted more power to free will and human effort. That more democratic belief—that all men and women might choose and win salvation, that each individual should take an active responsibility for redemption—came to characterize the religious views of most evangelicals among the ranks of Congregationalists, Presbyterians, Baptists, and Methodists over the course of the Second Great Awakening. In turn, their more optimistic assessment of human potential fostered revivals and ambitious programs for reforming individuals and society.

Charles Grandison Finney and Modern Revivalism >> The man who embodied this transformed evangelicalism was Charles Grandison Finney, the founder of modern revivalism. In 1821, as a young man, Finney experienced a soul–shattering conversion that led him to give up his law practice to become an itinerant minister. Eventually he was ordained in the Presbyterian Church, although he lacked any formal theological training. He first attracted national attention when in the mid–1820s and early 1830s he conducted a series of spectacular revivals in the booming port cities along the new Erie Canal.

Like George Whitefield before him, Finney had an entrancing voice that carried great distances. His success also resulted from his use of special techniques—"the new measures." These new measures had been developed during the frontier revivals of the Second Great Awakening (pages 176–177). Finney's contribution was to popularize the techniques and use them systematically. He held "protracted meetings" night after night to build up excitement. Speaking boldly and bluntly, he prayed for sinners by name, encouraged women to testify in public gatherings, and placed those struggling with conversion on the "anxious bench" at the front of the church. Whereas the leaders of the first Great Awakening (pages 93–94) had regarded revivals as god–sent outpourings of grace, Finney viewed them as the consequence of human agency. Like most other antebellum evangelical revivalists, Finney endorsed free will and preached that all men and women who wanted to could be saved.

With salvation within reach of every individual, what might be in store for society at large? "If the church would do her duty," Finney confidently predicted, "the millennium may come in this country in three years."

The Appeal of Evangelicalism >> The revivals of the Second Great Awakening drew converts from every segment of American society. Men, women, and children, whites, African Americans, and Indians, northerners and southerners, slave and free—all joined evangelical churches in unprecedented numbers during

CENTRAL PART OF BUFFALO STREET, ROCHESTER, N. Y.

view shows the central part of the city, near the junction of State and Exchange streets, with Buffalo street. The spire of the Court House is seen on the right; part of the Methodist church, and other public buildings, on the left.

⤊ In the winter of 1830–1831, Charles Finney preached frequently in Rochester, the nation's first inland boomtown.

the opening decades of the nineteenth century. Evangelicalism proved a potent and protean faith, one that could be adapted to answer both the spiritual strivings and needs and the temporal anxieties and sufferings of diverse groups.

In the North middle–class white men under intense pressure from the market economy—lawyers, merchants, and manufacturers—found comfort in evangelicalism's celebration of human ability. It provided them the assurance that they could contend with so many economic uncertainties in their lives. The emerging urban working class, struggling to stay afloat in the face of industrialization, found in evangelicalism's moral code a discipline centered on self–control and self–improvement. Rural southerners—planters and farmers alike—found their mastery over wives, children, and blacks confirmed by evangelical teachings. And white men of all classes, in North and South, found that church membership and the reputation it conferred for sobriety, honesty, and respectability often helped them to get ahead in a rootless, competitive society.

Blacks, both free and enslaved, also joined antebellum churches in impressive numbers, even as they continued to forge a distinctive and liberating faith by infusing evangelicalism with African religious traditions. Increasing racial tensions led to the formation of

more black Methodist and Baptist churches in northern and southern cities. The most important was the African Methodist Episcopal (AME) Church, organized at Philadelphia in 1816. Richard Allen, a former Delaware slave who bought his freedom, became that denomination's first bishop. But as reformers challenged the institution of slavery more openly, many southern white communities, especially in the Deep South, suppressed independent black churches after 1820. Black evangelical churches continued to grow in the North, however, and to serve as organizing centers for the swelling African American opposition to slavery. By 1856 the AME Church boasted some 20,000 members.

Women, Marriage, and Conversion >>

Despite the prominence of men as both clerical and lay leaders in the Second Great Awakening, it was women—black and white, northern and southern—whose presence dominated antebellum revivals and churches. In most revivals female converts outnumbered males by about three to two. Usually the first convert in a family was a woman, and many men who converted were related to women who had come forward earlier.

Women played an important role in the Awakening partly because of changes in their own social universe. Instead of parents arranging the marriages of

A Slave's Conversion Experience

"I stopped, dropped the plow, and started running, but the voice kept on speaking to me saying, 'Fear not, my little one, for behold! I come to bring you a message of truth.' Everything got dark, and I was unable to stand any longer. I began to feel sick, and there was a great roaring. I tried to cry and move but I was unable to do either."

—Mortimer, a former slave (1930s).

the Methodists emerging as the largest Protestant denomination in both the North and the South. Observers such as French visitor Alexis de Tocqueville noted the striking contrast with Europe, where adherence to Christianity was declining sharply over the same decades.

Not only their sheer numbers but also their institutional presence made evangelicals a formidable force. Their organizations to distribute tracts and bibles, organize Sunday schools and staff missions, encourage temperance and promote Sabbath observance all operated at a national level; the only other institutions able to make such a claim were the Second Bank of the United States and the post office. Evangelical publications dominated the markets for both religious periodicals and books.

Few were more aware of the scope of evangelicalism's sway than the Reverend Lyman Beecher. Earlier in his career Beecher had lamented the collapse of state-supported Congregationalist religious establishments throughout New England. But looking back in later years, he realized that the churches did not need government support to figure as powerful forces in the United States. To his delight Beecher concluded that evangelicals had, in fact, gained "deeper influence" since disestablishment "by voluntary efforts, societies, missions, and revivals."

their children, couples were beginning to wed more often on the basis of affection. Under such conditions a woman's prospects for marriage became less certain, and in older areas such as New England and the coastal South the migration of so many young men to the West compounded this uncertainty. Yet marriage was deemed important for a woman's happiness, and it remained essential for her economic security.

The unpredictability of these social circumstances drew young women toward religion, especially those between the ages of 12 and 25. Joining a church heightened a young woman's feeling of initiative and gave her a sense of purpose. By establishing respectability and widening her social circle of friends, church membership also enhanced her chances of marriage. And before and after marriage, it opened opportunities to participate in benevolent and reform associations that took women outside the domestic circle and into a realm of public activism.

The Significance of the Second Great Awakening

>> As a result of the Second Great Awakening, the dominant form of Christianity in America became evangelical Protestantism. Membership in the major Protestant churches—Congregational, Presbyterian, Baptist, and Methodist—soared during the first half of the nineteenth century. By 1840 about half the adult population was connected to some church, with

 REVIEW

How did evangelical Protestants change their doctrines to appeal to new social conditions in the early decades of the nineteenth century?

REVIVALISM AND THE SOCIAL ORDER

How right Beecher was. The revivals of the Second Great Awakening sparked profound and lasting consequences. Its effects went well beyond the churching of hundreds of thousands of American men, women, and children and the spectacular growth of evangelical Protestant denominations. Religious commitment fundamentally reshaped antebellum society, because, to keep the fervor afire, Beecher, Finney, and their fellow revivalists channeled the energies of converts into

The Printer's Angel

Printing press, other printers

What is indicated by these mosques and minarets?

A girl in the United States— What is conveyed by her reading a scroll similar to the one in the angel's hands?

And the gospel must first be published among all nations.

The American Tract Society (ATS), one of the many evangelical Protestant voluntary associations founded in the early nineteenth century, celebrated its mission with this illustration. An allegorical rendering of the power of print to convert the world, it shows an angel delivering a scroll, presumably God's word inscribed in the Bible, to a printer's outstretched hands. Although other voluntary associations printed bibles, the ATS produced millions of tracts, small booklets narrating experiences of religious conversion or inculcating moral lessons. Children in the United States, especially those attending Sunday schools, were among the ATS's target audiences: tracts aimed at boys and girls were often illustrated with woodcuts and covered in brightly colored paper. By 1850 millions of copies of children's tracts had flown off the ATS presses, along with millions more for children and adults translated into several languages. As the mother and son shown in the right-hand corner indicate, the ATS shared the aim of other Protestant voluntary associations to hasten the millennium by persuading Jews and Muslims, pagans and Roman Catholics, to embrace the beliefs of evangelical Protestants.

Illustration from the American Tract Society; updated (American Antiquarian Society).

THINKING CRITICALLY

What message is conveyed by positioning a Protestant church and a Muslim mosque on opposite sides of the illustration? Why are a woman and a boy—but no adult men—the recipients of tracts in the lower-right scene? Does this image of an angel recall any biblical scene often depicted by Roman Catholic artists? Why would the Protestant illustrator wish to evoke that association?

---

a host of benevolent organizations and reform societ-ies. But zealous evangelicals did a great deal more than teach Sunday school at home and dispatch missionaries abroad. As early as the 1820s and 1830s their activism was already affecting three aspects of American cul-ture: drinking habits, ideals of women and the family, and Protestant attitudes toward a growing number of Roman Catholics.

The Temperance Movement >> The tem-perance campaign, a reform dear to the heart of Lyman Beecher and other evangelical clergy, effected

a sweeping change in the personal habits of a large number of Americans.

Until the middle of the eighteenth century, most colonials (and Europeans) considered spirits an essen-tial supplement to their diet. But alcohol consump-tion soared after the Revolution, so that by 1825 the average American over the age of 15 consumed seven gallons of absolute alcohol a year, the highest level in American history and nearly triple present-day levels.

Led largely by clergy, the temperance movement at first focused on drunkenness and did not oppose mod-erate drinking. But in 1826 the American Temperance

Consumption of spirits in gallons

^ Beginning in 1790 per capita levels of drinking steadily rose until 1830, when the temperance movement produced a sharp decline over the next two decades.
What is the range between the highest and lowest years of consumption of spirits, in gallons per capita? Can you research the present average in the United States?

Society was founded, taking voluntary abstinence as its goal. As the movement gained momentum, annual per–capita consumption of alcohol dropped sharply. By 1845 it had fallen below two gallons a year.

The temperance movement lasted longer and attracted many more supporters than other reforms did. Its success came partly for social reasons. Democracy necessitated sober voters; factories required sober workers. In addition, temperance attracted the upwardly mobile—professionals, small businesspeople, and skilled artisans eager to improve their social standing. Finally, temperance advocates stressed the suffering that men inflicted on women and children, and thus the movement appealed to women as a means to defend the home and carry out their domestic mission.

Ideals of Women and the Family >> Evangelicals also contributed substantially to a new ideal of womanhood. The ideal was promoted by the clergy and female authors in sermons, advice manuals, magazine articles, and novels during the first half of the nineteenth century. Called the "cult of **domesticity**"or "true womanhood" or "evangelical woman–hood," that ideal cast wives and mothers as the "angels" of their households. Women were singularly suited to serve as dispensers of love, comfort, and moral instruction to husbands and children. The premise of that new ideal was that men and women, by their very nature, inhabited separate spheres. The rough–and–tumble world of business and politics was the proper province of husbands and fathers, while women ruled the domestic sphere of home and family. "Love is our life our reality, business yours," Mollie Clark told one suitor.

domesticity devotion to home life, and a woman's place at the center of that life.

This new ideal also held that women were by nature morally stronger and more religious than men. That view reversed the negative medieval and early modern views of women as the sinful daughters of the temptress Eve, more passionate by nature and thus less morally restrained and spiritually inclined than men. But the new ideal also held antebellum women to a higher standard of sexual purity. A man's sexual infidelity, although hardly condoned, brought no lasting shame. But a woman who engaged in sexual relations before marriage or was unfaithful afterward was threatened with everlasting disgrace. Under this new double standard women were to be pure, passionless, and passive: they were to submerge their identities in those of their husbands.

Spokespersons for the new ideal of womanhood and the notion of separate spheres directed their message mainly at elite and middle–class women. And that message found an impressionable audience among wives and daughters in the urbanizing Northeast. There the separation of the workplace from the home was most complete. As a result of industrialization, many men worked outside the home, while the rise of factories also led to a decline in part–time work such as spinning, which women had once performed to supplement family income. Home manufacturing was no longer essential, because, except on the frontier, families could easily purchase the articles that women previously had made, such as cloth, soap, and candles. This growing separation of the household from the workplace in the Northeast made it that much easier for the home to be idealized as a place of "domesticity," a haven away from the competitive, workaday world, with the mother firmly at its center.

The celebration of domesticity was not unique to the United States. Indeed, this redefinition of women's roles was more sweeping in Europe, because previously

↑ As business affairs grew increasingly separate from the family in the nineteenth century, the middle-class home became a female domain. A woman's role as a wife and mother was to dispense love and moral guidance to her husband and her children. As this domestic scene makes clear, she was at the very center of the world of the family.

middle—class women had left the task of child—raising largely to hired nurses and governesses. By midcentury these mothers devoted much more time to domestic duties, including rearing the children. Family size also declined, both in France and in England. The mid—dle class was most numerous in England; indeed, the importance of the middle class in Britain during Queen Victoria's reign (1837–1901) gave these ideals the label **Victorianism.**

> **Victorianism** constellation of middle-class values attributed to the proper virtues of Britain's Queen.

As elite and middle—class homes came to be seen as havens of moral virtue, those domestic settings devel—oped a new structure and new set of attitudes closer in spirit to those of the modern family. The pressures to achieve success led middle—class young adults to delay marriage, since a husband was expected to have the financial means to support his wife. Smaller family size resulted, since wives, especially those among the urban middle class, began to use birth control to space chil—dren farther apart and to minimize the risks of preg—nancy. In addition, it has been estimated that before 1860 one abortion was performed for every five or six live births. With smaller families, parents could tend more carefully to their children's success. Increasingly, middle—class families took on the expense of addi—tional education to prepare their sons for a career in business. They also frequently equalized inheritances rather than favoring the eldest son or favoring sons over daughters.

Expanding Public Roles for Women >>Most
women in the United States did not have time to make domesticity the center of their lives. Farmers' wives and enslaved women had to work constantly, whereas lower—class families could not get by without the wages of female members. Still, some elite and middle—class women tried to live up to the new ideals, though many found the effort confining. "The great trial is that I have nothing to do," one complained. "Here I am with abundant leisure and capable, I believe, of accom—plishing some good, and yet with no object on which to expend my energies."

In response to those frustrations Lyman Beech—er's eldest daughter, Catharine (who never married), made a career out of assuring women that the proper care of household and children was their sex's crucial responsibility. Like the earlier advocates of "republican motherhood," Catharine Beecher supported women's education and argued that women exercised power as moral guardians of the nation's future. She also wrote several books on efficient home management.

But many women yearned to exert moral author—ity outside the confines of their households. Ironi—cally, the new host of benevolent and reform societies offered them just that opportunity. Devout wives and daughters, particularly those from middle—class fami—lies, flocked to these voluntary associations, many of which had separate women's chapters. By serving in such organizations, they gained the practical experi—ence of holding office on governing boards, conduct—ing meetings, drafting policy statements, organizing reform programs, and raising money.

Evangelicalism thus enabled women to enter public life and to make their voices heard in ways that were socially acceptable. After all, evangelical teachings affirmed that they were the superior sex in piety and morality, a point often invoked by those very women who devoted much of their time to benevolence and reform. They justified such public activism as merely the logical extension of their private responsibility to act as spiritual guides to their families.

Protestants and Catholics >>

Women's piety and spiritual influence were surely on the mind of Isaac Bird one Saturday morning in the autumn of 1819. A devout evangelical preparing for the ministry, he had wandered into a Roman Catholic church in Boston and now watched with rapt attention a ritual, conducted entirely in Latin, in which two women "took the veil" and became nuns. Bird often visited Boston on his vacations to proselytize its poorest inhabitants. Many were Catholics, as he noted, some of them recent Irish and German immigrants and others African American. It troubled Bird, this gathering presence of devout Catholics.

Protestants had a long history of animosity toward Roman Catholics, especially in New England. But before the beginning of the nineteenth century, the number of Catholics had been small: by 1815 there were only 150,000 scattered throughout the United States, and they often had little access to priests or public worship.

That had begun to change by 1820. French–Canadian Catholic immigrants were filtering into New England in growing numbers, and there began what would become during the 1840s and 1850s an influx of Catholic immigrants from the British Isles and German–speaking countries. By 1830 the Catholic population had jumped to 300,000, and by 1850 it accounted for 8 percent of the U.S. population—the same proportion as Presbyterians. As these newcomers settled in eastern cities and on western frontiers, there were an increasing number of priests, nuns, and churches to minister to their spiritual needs.

The differences between Roman Catholicism and Protestantism—especially evangelicalism—were substantial. Where evangelicals stressed the inward transformation of conversion as essential to salvation, Catholics emphasized the importance of outward religious observances, such as faithfully attending mass and receiving the sacraments. Where evangelicals insisted that individuals read the Bible to discover God's will, Catholics urged their faithful to heed church teachings and traditions. Where Catholics believed that human suffering could be a penance paving the way toward redemption, evangelicals regarded it as an evil to be alleviated. Where evangelicals looked toward an imminent millennium, Catholics harbored no such expectation and played almost no role in antebellum benevolence and reform movements.

To Protestants many elements of Catholicism seemed superstitious and even subversive. They rejected the Catholic doctrine of transubstantiation, which held that the bread and wine consecrated by the priest during mass literally turned into the body and blood of Jesus Christ. They condemned as idolatry the Catholic veneration of the Virgin Mary and the saints. They regarded Catholic nuns and convents as threats to the new ideals of womanhood and domesticity. They found it amiss that Catholic laymen had no role in governing their own parishes and dioceses, entrusting that responsibility entirely to priests and bishops.

But the worst fears of Protestants fastened on what they saw as the political dangers posed by Catholics, especially immigrants. Alarmed as Irish and German settlers poured into the West, Lyman Beecher warned that "the world has never witnessed such a rush of dark—minded population from one country to another, as is now leaving Europe and dashing upon our shores." Beecher foresaw a sinister plot hatched by the pope to snuff out American liberty. For what else would follow in a nation overwhelmed by Catholicism, "a religion which never prospered but in alliance with despotic government, has always been and still is the inflexible enemy of liberty of conscience and free enquiry, and at this moment is the mainstay of the battle against republican institutions?"

It was all the more appalling to evangelicals, then, that some Protestants found Catholic teachings appealing: so attractive that some 57,000 converted to Catholicism in the 30 years after 1830. In response to those defections many Protestants, believing that converts were drawn by the artistic beauties of Catholic worship, began to include in their churches recognizably Catholic elements such as the symbol of the cross, the use of candles and flowers, organ and choir music, stained glass windows, and Gothic architecture.

Other Protestants attacked Catholicism directly. Writing under the name "Maria Monk," a team of evangelical ministers produced a lurid account of life in a convent, replete with sex orgies involving priests and nuns and a cellar planted with dead babies. Published in 1836 this publication outsold every book except *Uncle Tom's Cabin* in the years before the Civil War. And with anti—Catholic sentiment running so high, predictably, there was violence. In 1834 a mob in Charlestown, Massachusetts, burned a convent to the ground. Both the sisters and their students escaped injury but, during the summer of 1844 in Philadelphia, two separate outbreaks of anti—Catholic violence left 14 people dead, as well as two churches and three dozen homes in smoldering ruins.

Most antebellum Protestants condemned violence against Catholics. But anti—Catholicism had emerged as a defining feature of American Protestant identity, and the alienation of the two groups ran deep, enduring far into the twentieth century.

 REVIEW

In what ways did transcendentalism shape the themes of writers of the American Renaissance? Who were the major communitarian reformers of the era?

^ The Reverend Lyman Beecher's Hanover Street Church—his "stone jug"—was an early example of Gothic Revival architecture, with its medieval stone battlements atop a massive tower and pointed windows. Such a church stood in stark contrast with the plain Congregational meetinghouses of the Puritans. On the one hand, Beecher railed against the evils of Catholicism. On the other, he recognized the attraction of such imposing architecture. "If you want to get martins about your house," he commented, comparing his own church flock to the swallows who were so particular about where they nested, "you must put up a martin box."

VISIONARIES

Increasingly hostile to Roman Catholics, evangelicals also stood at odds with other groups in antebellum America who envisioned new ways of improving individuals and society. Although they often expressed optimism about the prospects for human betterment, these other reformers—Unitarians and Transcendentalists, socialists and communitarians—otherwise had little in common with evangelicals.

The Unitarian Contribution >> During the opening decades of the nineteenth century, the religious division among Americans that produced the fiercest debates pitted evangelicals against deists, Unitarians, and other rational Christians. A majority only in eastern Massachusetts, Unitarians denied the divinity of Jesus while affirming the ability and responsibility of humankind to follow his moral teachings. Disdainful of the emotionalism of revivals, they were also inclined to interpret the Bible broadly rather than literally. To

most Americans such views were so suspect that the presidents who adhered to Unitarianism—John Adams, Thomas Jefferson, and John Quincy Adams—did not wish to publicize their beliefs.

Despite their many differences, Unitarians shared with evangelicals an esteem for the power of human free will and a commitment to the goal of social betterment. Small though their numbers were, Unitarians made large contributions to the cause of reform. One, Boston schoolteacher Dorothea Dix, took the lead in creating state-supported asylums to treat the mentally ill, who were often chained, beaten, and kept in cages. Samuel Gridley Howe promoted education for the blind and deaf, and Horace Mann strove to give greater access to public schooling to children of poor and working-class families.

From Unitarianism to Transcendentalism >>
A new philosophic outlook—transcendentalism—blossomed in the mid-1830s, when a number of Unitarian clergy such as George Ripley and Ralph Waldo Emerson resigned their pulpits, loudly protesting the

↑ In the summer of 1858, members of the cultural Saturday Club of Boston made an excursion to the Adirondacks to observe nature. In *Philosopher's Camp*, painted by William J. Stillman, who organized the expedition, a group on the left dissects a fish under the supervision of the famous scientist Louis Agassiz. Alone at the center of the painting stands Ralph Waldo Emerson, in a contemplative mood.

church's teachings as dry, bloodless, and self–satisfied. The new "Transcendentalist Club" attracted a small following among other discontented Boston intellec–tuals, including Margaret Fuller, Bronson Alcott, and Orestes Brownson.

Transcendentalism emphasized feeling over rea–son, seeking a spiritual communion with nature. In following this course tran–scendentalists mirrored the beliefs of Romanticism, a European movement that arose as a reaction to the Enlightenment. As the name suggested, transcendental–ists sought to go beyond or to rise above—specifically above reason and beyond the material world. As part of creation, every human being contained a spark of divinity, Emerson avowed. Transcendentalists also shared in Romanticism's glorification of the individ–ual. "Trust thyself. Every heart vibrates to that iron string," Emerson advised. If freed from the constraints of traditional authority, the individual possessed infi–nite potential. Like the devout at Finney's revivals, who sought to improve themselves and society, lis–teners who flocked to Emerson's lectures were infused with the spirit of optimistic reform.

In extolling nature, other American writers wor–ried that the advance of civilization, with its market economy and crowded urban centers, might destroy the natural simplicity of the land. In 1845 Henry David Thoreau built a cabin on the edge of Walden Pond in Concord, living by himself for 16 months

transcendentalism a philo-sophical and religious movement that embraced intuition, emotion, and the divine spark within the indi-vidual as the path to tran-scend, or move beyond, the material world.

to demonstrate the advantages of self–reliance. His experiences became the basis for *Walden* (1854), which eloquently denounced Americans' frantic competition for material goods and wealth. Only in nature, Tho–reau argued, could one find true independence, liberty, equality, and happiness. Voicing the anti–institutional impulse of Romanticism, he took individualism to its antisocial extreme.

In contrast to Thoreau, who prized isolation, Walt Whitman embraced American society in its infinite variety. A journalist and laborer in the New York City area, Whitman was inspired by the common people, whose "manners, speech, dress, friendships . . . are unrhymed poetry." In taking their measure in *Leaves of Grass* (1855), he pioneered a new, modern form of poetry, unconcerned with meter and rhyme and filled with frank imagery and sexual references.

Utopian Communities >> Evangelicals, Uni–tarians, and writers such as Thoreau and Whit–man focused their attention on how individuals might be saved, improved, fulfilled. But some antebellum believers, both secular and religious, sought to remake society at large by forming communities intended as examples to the rest of the world.

Even some transcendental individualists attempted a utopian venture. During the early 1840s Emerson's friend George Ripley organized Brook Farm, a com–munity near Boston where members could live "a more wholesome and simple life than can be led amid the pressure of our competitive institutions." But predict–ably, these Romantic individualists could not sustain the group cooperation essential for success.

Some secular thinkers shared the transcendentalists' view that competition, inequality, and acquisitiveness were corrupting American society. Among those critics were socialists, and their goal was to defend the interests of American workers from the ravages of industrialization. The most influential was Robert Dale Owen, the unlikely founder of America's first socialist community. A Welsh industrialist who had made a fortune manufacturing textiles, Owen then turned to realizing his vision of a just society—one in which property was held in common and work equally shared. Such a benign social environment, he believed, would foster tolerant, rational human beings capable of self–government. What better place than America to make this dream come true?

Initially, Owen received a warm reception. John Quincy Adams not only attended both lectures that Owen delivered at the Capitol but also displayed a model of his proposed community in the White House. A few months later about 900 volunteers flocked to Owen's community at New Harmony, Indiana. But alas, most lacked the skills and commitment to make it a success, and bitter factions soon split the settlement. Owen made matters worse by announcing that he rejected both the authenticity of the Bible and the institution of marriage. New Harmony dissolved in 1827, but Owen's principles inspired nearly 20 other short–lived experiments.

The United States was a poor proving–ground for socialist experiments. Wages were too high and land too cheap for such communities to interest most Americans. And individualism was too strong to foster a commitment to cooperative action. Communities founded by believers in religious rather than secular faiths proved far more enduring. Their common spiritual convictions muted individualism, and their charismatic leaders held divisions at bay.

Among the most successful of these religiously based communal groups were the Shakers. Ann Lee, the illiterate daughter of an English blacksmith, believed that God had a dual nature, part male and part female, and that her own life would reveal the feminine side of the divinity, just as Christ had revealed the masculine. In 1774 she led a small band of followers to America. Her followers sometimes shook in the fervent public demonstration of their faith—hence the name Shakers.

As the Second Great Awakening crested, recruits from revivals swelled Shaker ranks, and their new disciples founded about 20 villages. Members held the community's property in common, worked hard, and lived simply. Convinced that the end of the world was at hand and that there was no need to perpetuate the human race, Shakers practiced celibacy. Men and women normally worked apart, ate at separate tables in silence, entered separate doorways, and had separate living quarters. Elders typically assigned tasks by gender, with women performing household chores and men laboring in the fields, but leadership of the church was split equally between men and women. Lacking any natural increase, membership began to decline after 1850, from a peak of about 6,000 members.

The Mormon Experience >> The most spectacularly successful antebellum religious community—one that mushroomed into a denomination whose followers now number in the millions around the world—was the Church of Jesus Christ of Latter–day Saints. The Mormons, as they are generally known, took their rise from the visions of a young man named Joseph Smith in Palmyra, in western New York, where the religious fires of revivalism often flared. The son of a poor farmer, Smith was robust, charming, almost hypnotic in his appeal. In 1827, at the age of only 22, he announced that he had discovered and translated a set of golden tablets on which was written the Book of Mormon. The tablets told the story of a band of Hebrews who in biblical times journeyed to America, splitting into two groups, the Nephites and Lamanites. The Nephites established a Christian civilization, only to be exterminated by the Lamanites, whose descendants were said to be the Indians of the Americas. Seeking to reestablish the true church, Smith gathered a group of devoted followers.

Like nineteenth–century evangelicalism, Mormonism proclaimed that salvation was available to all. Mormon culture also upheld the middle–class values of hard work, thrift, and self–control. It partook of the optimistic, materialist attitudes of American society. And by teaching that Christ would return to rule the earth, it shared in the hope of a coming millennial kingdom.

Yet Mormonism was less an outgrowth of evangelicalism than of the primitive gospel movement, which sought to reestablish the ancient church. In restoring

<< The Mormon temple at Nauvoo, Illinois, was adorned with this sun stone and other celestial carvings drawn from a dream vision by Joseph Smith. The image resembles some of the astronomical symbols popularized by the Masons, a fraternal order whose secret rituals and symbols were hotly debated in western New York, where Smith grew up.

theocracy system of government by priests or clergy claiming divine inspiration or guidance.

what Smith called "the ancient order of things," he created a **theocracy** uniting church and state, reestablished biblical priesthoods and titles, and adopted temple rituals.

Like Roman Catholics, the Mormons drew bitter opposition—and armed attacks. Smith's unorthodox teachings provoked persecution wherever Smith and his followers went, first to Ohio and then to Missouri. Mob violence finally hounded him out of Missouri in 1839. Smith then established a new holy city, which he named Nauvoo, located on the Mississippi River in Illinois.

Reinforced by a steady stream of converts from Britain, Nauvoo became the largest city in Illinois, with a population of 10,000 by the mid–1840s. There Smith introduced the most distinctive features of Mormon theology, including baptism for the dead, eternal marriage, and polygamy, or plural marriage. As a result, Mormonism increasingly diverged from traditional Christianity and became a distinct new religion. To bolster his authority as a prophet, Smith established a theocratic political order under which church leaders controlled political offices and governed the community, with Smith as mayor.

Neighboring residents, alarmed by the Mormons' growing political power and reports that church leaders were practicing polygamy, demanded that Nauvoo's charter be revoked and the church suppressed. In 1844, while in jail for destroying the printing press of dissident Mormons in Nauvoo, Smith was murdered by an anti–Mormon mob. In 1846 the Mormons abandoned Nauvoo, and the following year Brigham Young, Smith's successor, led them westward to Utah.

RADICAL REFORM

Late in the fall of 1834 Lyman Beecher was in the midst of his continuing efforts to "overturn and overturn" on behalf of the kingdom of God. He had left Boston for Cincinnati to assume leadership of Lane Seminary. The school had everything that an institution for training ministers to convert the West needed—everything, that is, except students. In October 1834 all but 8 of Lane's 100 scholars had departed after months of bitter fighting with Beecher and the trustees over the issue of abolition.

Beecher knew the source of his troubles: a scruffy, magnetic convert of Finney's revivals named Theodore Dwight Weld. Weld had been firing up his classmates over the need to end slavery immediately. He had been influenced by the arguments of William Lloyd Garrison, whose abolitionist writings had sent shock waves

across the entire nation. Indeed, Beecher's troubles at Lane Seminary provided only one example of how the flames of reform could spread along paths not anticipated by those who had kindled them.

The Beginnings of the Abolitionist Movement >> William Lloyd Garrison symbolized the transition from a moderate antislavery movement to the more militant abolitionism of the 1830s. A sober, religious youngster deeply influenced by his Baptist mother, Garrison in the 1820s edited a newspaper sympathetic to many of the new reforms. In 1829 he was enlisted in the antislavery cause by Benjamin Lundy, a Quaker who edited a Baltimore antislavery newspaper, *The Genius of Universal Emancipation*. Calling for a gradual end to slavery, Lundy supported colonization, hoping to overcome southern fears of emancipation by transporting free black Americans to Africa.

Garrison went to Baltimore to help edit Lundy's paper, and for the first time he encountered the opinions of free African Americans. To his surprise Garrison discovered that most of them strongly opposed the colonization movement as proslavery and antiblack. Under their influence Garrison soon developed views far more radical than Lundy's. Within a year of moving to Baltimore the young firebrand was convicted of libel and imprisoned. On his release Garrison hurried back to Boston, determined to publish a new kind of antislavery journal.

On January 1, 1831, the first issue of *The Liberator* appeared, and abolitionism was born. Repudiating gradual emancipation and embracing "immediatism," Garrison insisted that slavery end at once. He denounced colonization as a racist, antiblack movement and upheld the principle of racial equality. To those who suggested that slaveowners should be compensated for freeing their slaves, Garrison was firm. Southerners ought to be convinced by "moral suasion" to renounce slavery as a sin. Virtue was its own reward.

Garrison attracted the most attention, but other abolitionists spoke with equal conviction. Lewis Tappan and his brother Arthur, two New York City silk merchants, boldly placed their wealth behind a number of humanitarian causes, including abolitionism. Angelina and Sarah Grimké, the daughters of a South Carolina planter, left their native state to speak against the institution.

To abolitionists, slavery was a moral, not an economic, question. The institution seemed a contradiction of the principle of the American Revolution that all human beings had been created with natural rights. Abolitionists condemned slavery because of the breakup of marriages and families by sale, the harsh punishment of the lash, slaves' lack of access to education, and the sexual abuse of black women. Most

⋀ Black abolitionist Frederick Douglass (*second from left at the podium*) was only 1 of nearly 50 runaway slaves who appeared at an abolitionist convention held in August 1850 in Cazenovia, New York. The question of whether women should be allowed to take active roles in the movement fractured antislavery advocates and sparked women reformers to speak out more strongly for women's rights.

of all they denounced slavery as outrageously contrary to Christian teaching. As one Ohio antislavery paper declared: "We believe slavery to be a sin, always, everywhere, and only, sin—sin, in itself." So persistent were abolitionists in their religious objections that they forced the churches to face the question of slavery head—on. In the 1840s the Methodist Church and the Baptist Church each split into northern and southern organizations over the issue.

The Spread of Abolitionism >> After helping organize the New England Anti—Slavery Society in 1832, Garrison joined with Lewis Tappan and Theodore Weld the following year to establish a national organization, the American Anti—Slavery Society. It coordinated a loosely affiliated network of state and local societies. During the years before the Civil War, perhaps 200,000 northerners belonged to an abolitionist society.

Abolitionists were concentrated in the East, especially New England, and in areas that had been settled by New Englanders, such as western New York and northern Ohio. The movement was not strong in cities or among businesspeople and workers. Most abolitionists were young, being generally in their 20s and 30s when the movement began, and had grown up in rural areas and small towns in middle—class families. Intensely religious, many had been profoundly affected by the revivals of the Second Great Awakening.

Theodore Weld was cut from this mold. After enrolling in Lane Seminary in 1833, he promoted immediate abolitionism among his fellow students.

When Lyman Beecher assumed the Lane presidency a year later, he confronted a student body dominated by committed immediatists.

The radicalism of Lane students was also made clear in their commitment to racial equality. Unlike some abolitionists, who opposed slavery but disdained blacks as inferior, Lane students mingled freely with Cincinnati's free black community. Alarmed by rumors in the summer of 1834 that the town's residents intended to demolish the school, Beecher and Lane's trustees forbade any discussion of slavery on campus, restricted contact with the black community, and ordered students to return to their studies. All except a few left the school and enrolled at Oberlin College, which agreed to their demands for guaranteeing freedom of speech and admitting black students.

Free African Americans, who made up the majority of subscribers to Garrison's *Liberator*, provided important support and leadership for the movement. Frederick Douglass assumed the greatest prominence. Having escaped from slavery in Maryland, he became an eloquent critic of its evils. Other important black abolitionists included Martin Delany, William Wells Brown, William Still, and Sojourner Truth. Aided by many other African Americans, these men and women battled against racial discrimination in the North as well as slavery in the South.

A network of antislavery sympathizers also developed in the North to convey runaway slaves to Canada and freedom. Although not as extensive or as tightly organized as contemporaries claimed, the Underground Railroad hid fugitives and transported them northward from one station to the next. Free African Americans, who were more readily trusted by wary slaves, played a leading role in the Underground Railroad. One of its most famous conductors was Harriet Tubman, an escaped slave who repeatedly returned to the South and eventually escorted more than 200 slaves to freedom.

Opponents and Divisions >> The drive for immediate abolition faced massive obstacles within American society. With slavery increasingly important to their region's economy, southerners forced opponents of slavery to flee north. In the North, where racism was equally entrenched, abolitionism provoked bitter resistance.

On occasion northern resistance turned violent. A Boston mob seized Garrison in 1835 and paraded him with a rope around his body before he was finally rescued. And in 1837 in Alton, Illinois, Elijah Lovejoy was murdered when he tried to protect his printing press from an angry crowd. The leaders of these mobs were not from the bottom of society but, as one of

⌃ In this playbill advertising a dramatic production of *Uncle Tom's Cabin,* vicious bloodhounds pursue the light-skinned runaway slave Eliza, who clutches her child as she frantically leaps to safety across the ice-choked Ohio River.

their victims noted, were "gentlemen of property and standing" who reacted to the threat that abolitionists posed to their prosperity.

The antislavery cause was also hindered by divisions among reformers. Lyman Beecher conceived of sin in terms of individual immorality, not unjust social institutions. But to the abolitionists, America could never become a godly nation until slavery was abolished. Among them was Beecher's daughter, Harriet Beecher Stowe, who in the 1850s wrote the most successful piece of antislavery literature in the nation's history, *Uncle Tom's Cabin.* Yet the abolitionists themselves splintered, shaken by the opposition they encountered and unable to agree on the most effective response. More conservative reformers wanted to work within established institutions, using the churches and political action to end slavery. But for Garrison and his followers, the mob violence demonstrated that slavery was only part of a deeper national disease, whose cure required the overthrow of American institutions and values.

By the end of the decade Garrison had worked out a program for the total reform of society. He embraced perfectionism and pacifism, urged members to leave the churches, and called for an end to all government.

Condemning the Constitution as proslavery—"a covenant with death and an agreement with hell"—he publicly burned a copy one July 4th. This platform was radical enough on all counts, but the final straw for Garrison's opponents was his endorsement of women's rights as an inseparable part of abolitionism.

The Women's Rights Movement >>American women were kept out of most jobs, denied political rights, and given only limited access to education beyond the elementary grades. When a woman married, her husband became the legal representative of the marriage and gained complete control of her property. If a marriage ended in divorce, the husband was awarded custody of the children. Any unmarried woman was made the ward of a male relative.

When abolitionists divided over the issue of female participation in their societies, women found it easy to identify with the situation of slaves, since both were victims of male tyranny. Sarah and Angelina Grimké took up the cause of women's rights after they were criticized for speaking to audiences that included men as well as women. Sarah responded with *Letters on the Condition of Women and the Equality of the Sexes* (1838), arguing that women deserved the same rights as men.

Two abolitionists, Elizabeth Cady Stanton and Lucretia Mott, launched the women's rights movement after they were forced to sit behind a curtain at a world antislavery convention in London. In 1848 Stanton and Mott organized a conference in Seneca Falls, New York, that attracted about a hundred supporters. The meeting issued a Declaration of Sentiments, modeled after the Declaration of Independence, that began, "All men and women are created equal."

The Seneca Falls Convention called for educational and professional opportunities for women, laws giving them control of their property, recognition of legal equality, and repeal of laws awarding the father custody of the children in divorce. The most controversial proposal, and the only resolution that did not pass unanimously, was one demanding the right to vote. The Seneca Falls Convention set forth the arguments and the program for the women's rights movement for the remainder of the century.

In response, several states gave women greater control over their property, and a few made divorce easier or granted women the right to sue in courts. But disappointments and defeats outweighed these early victories. Still, many of the important leaders in the crusade for women's rights who emerged after the Civil War had already taken their places at the forefront of the movement. They included Stanton, Susan B. Anthony, Lucy Stone, and—as Lyman Beecher by now must have expected—one of his daughters, Isabella Beecher Hooker.

The Schism of 1840 >> It was Garrison's position on women's rights that finally split antislavery ranks already divided over other aspects of his growing radicalism. The showdown came in 1840 at the national meeting of the American Anti–Slavery Society, when delegates debated whether women could hold office in the organization. By packing the convention, Garrison carried the day. His opponents, led by Lewis Tappan, resigned to found the rival American and Foreign Anti–Slavery Society.

The schism of 1840 lessened the influence of abolitionism as a reform movement. Although abolitionism heightened moral concern about slavery, it failed to convert the North to its program, and its supporters remained a tiny minority. Despite the considerable courage of its leaders, the movement lacked a realistic, long–range plan for eliminating such a deeply entrenched institution.

 REVIEW

What helped to spark the growth of an abolitionist movement? What factors caused the movement to splinter?

REFORM SHAKES THE PARTY SYSTEM

The crusading idealism of reformers inevitably collided with the hard reality that society could not be perfected by converting individuals. A growing number of frustrated reformers were abandoning the principle of voluntary persuasion and looking to government coercion to achieve their goals.

The Turn toward Politics >> Politicians did not particularly welcome the new interest. Because the Whig and Democratic Parties both drew on evangelical and nonevangelical voters, heated moral debates over the harmful effects of drink or the evils of slavery threatened to detach regular party members from their old loyalties and disrupt each party's unity. The strong opposition of German and Irish immigrants to temperance stimulated antiforeign sentiment among reformers and further divided both party coalitions, particularly the Democrats.

Because women could not vote, they felt excluded when the temperance and abolitionist movements turned to electoral action to accomplish their goals. By the 1840s female reformers increasingly demanded the right to vote as the means to change society. Nor were men blind to what was at stake: one reason they so strongly resisted female suffrage was because it would give women real power.

The political parties could resist the women's suffrage movement, because most of its advocates lacked the right to vote. Less easily put off were temperance reformers. Although drinking had significantly declined in American society by 1840, it had hardly been eliminated. In response, temperance advocates proposed state laws that would outlaw the manufacture and sale of alcoholic beverages. Their first major triumph came in 1851. The Maine Law, as it was known, authorized search and seizure of private property in that state and provided stiff penalties for selling liquor. In the next few years a number of states enacted similar laws, although most were struck down by the courts or later

Did the status of women improve in the United States between the American Revolution and the Civil War?

⋀ Elizabeth Cady Stanton, one of the instigators and guiding spirits at the Seneca Falls Convention, photographed with two of her children about that time.

repealed. Prohibition remained a controversial political issue throughout the century.

Although prohibition was temporarily defeated, the issue badly disrupted the Whig and Democratic Parties. It greatly increased party switching and brought to the polls a large number of new voters, including many "wets" who wanted to preserve their right to drink. By dissolving the ties between so many voters and their parties, the temperance issue played a major role in the eventual collapse of the Jacksonian party system in the 1850s.

Abolitionism and the Party System >>

Slavery proved even more divisive. In 1835 abolitionists distributed more than a million pamphlets, mostly in the South, through the post office. Former senator Robert Hayne led a Charleston mob that burned sacks of U.S. mail containing abolitionist literature, and postmasters in other southern cities refused to deliver the material. Andrew Jackson's administration allowed southern states to censor the mail, leading abolitionists to protest that their civil rights had been violated. In reaction, the number of antislavery societies in the North nearly tripled.

With access to the mails impaired, abolitionists began flooding Congress with petitions against slavery. Asserting that Congress had no power over the institution, angry southern representatives demanded action, and the House in response adopted the so-called gag rule in 1836. It automatically tabled without consideration any petition dealing with slavery. But southern leaders had made a tactical blunder. The gag rule allowed abolitionists not only to attack slavery but also to speak out as defenders of white civil liberties. The appeal of the antislavery movement was broadened, and in 1844 the House finally repealed the controversial rule.

Many abolitionists outside Garrison's circle began to feel that an antislavery third party offered a more effective means of attacking slavery. In 1840 these political abolitionists founded the Liberty Party and nominated for president James Birney, a former slaveholder who had converted to abolitionism. Birney received only 7,000 votes, but the Liberty Party was the seed from which a stronger antislavery political movement would grow. From 1840 onward, abolitionism's importance would be in the political arena rather than as a voluntary reform organization.

✔ REVIEW

How did reform movements create instability in the political system?

The ferment of reform during the decades from 1820 to 1850 reflected a multitude of attempts to deal with transformations working through not just the United States but also Europe. Abolition was potentially the most dangerous of the trans–Atlantic reforms, because slavery was so deeply and profitably intertwined with the industrial system. Slave labor produced cotton for the textile factories of New England, Great Britain, and Europe. Plantation economies supplied the sugar, rice, tea, and coffee that were a part of European and American diets. Revolutionary France had abolished slavery in 1794, but Napoleon reinstated it, along with the slave trade. Great Britain outlawed the trade in 1808 (as did the United States) and then freed nearly 800,000 slaves in its colonies in 1834.

Any move for emancipation in the United States seemed out of the question, and as late as 1840 abolition lacked the power to threaten the political system. But the growing northern concern about slavery highlighted differences between the two sections. Despite the strength of evangelicalism in the South, the reform impulse spawned by the revivals found little support there, since reform movements were discredited by their association with abolitionism. The party system confronted the difficult challenge of holding together sections that, although sharing much, were also diverging in important ways. To the residents of both sections, the South increasingly appeared to be a unique society with its own distinctive way of life.

CHAPTER SUMMARY

The Jacksonian era produced the greatest number of significant reform movements in American history.

- The Second Great Awakening, which preached the doctrine of salvation available to all and the coming of the millennium, encouraged revivals and reform.
- Revivals drew converts from every segment of American society and spoke to their spiritual needs.
- Women were most prominent among revival converts.
- The Second Great Awakening made evangelicals the dominant religious subculture in the United States.
- Benevolence and reform societies decisively changed drinking habits and the ideals of womanhood and the family.
- Evangelical religious fervor also fueled anti-Catholicism.
- Unitarianism and transcendentalism, which emphasized the unlimited potential of each individual, also strengthened reform.
- Utopian communities sought to establish a model society for the rest of the world to follow.
- Mormons developed a following and drew persecution.
- Abolitionism precipitated both strong support and violent opposition, and the movement split in 1840.
- Temperance, abolitionism, and women's rights movements each turned to political action to accomplish their goals.
- Although it survived, the party system was seriously weakened by these reform movements.

Additional Reading

Good introductions to antebellum evangelical religion and reform include Robert Abzug, *Cosmos Crumbling* (1994); Charles Hambrick–Stowe, *Charles G. Finney and the Spirit of American Evangelicalism* (1996); and Bertram Wyatt–Brown, *Lewis Tappan and the Evangelical War Against Slavery* (1971). For suggestive analyses of the relationship between antebellum evangelicalism and the sweeping changes in economic and political life, consult Richard Carwardine, *Evangelicals and Politics in Antebellum America* (1997); Candy Gunther Brown, *The Word in the World* (2004); and Paul Johnson and Sean Wilentz, *The Kingdom of Matthias* (1994). The best studies of the role of women in evangelical churches and reform societies are Anne Boylan, *The Origins of Women's Activism* (1988); Lori Ginzberg, *Women and the Work of Benevolence* (1990); and Nancy Hewitt, *Women's Activism and Social Change* (1984). To understand the link between reformist activism and the early women's rights movement, begin with Lori Ginzberg, *Untidy Origins* (2005); and Nancy Isenberg, *Sex and Citizenship in the United States* (1998).

Despite the dominant influence of evangelical Protestants, both Roman Catholics and Mormons attracted a growing number of adherents during the antebellum period. For a fascinating account of the origins and rise of Mormonism, see John Brooke, *The Refiner's Fire* (1996); and for a compelling account of how American Protestants responded to the growth of Roman Catholicism after the 1830s, see Ryan Smith, *Gothic Arches, Latin Crosses* (2006). To explore the reasons why a small but influential minority of nineteenth-century Americans rejected all forms of Christianity in favor of agnosticism or atheism, rely on James Turner, *Without God, Without Creed* (1985).

Significant Events

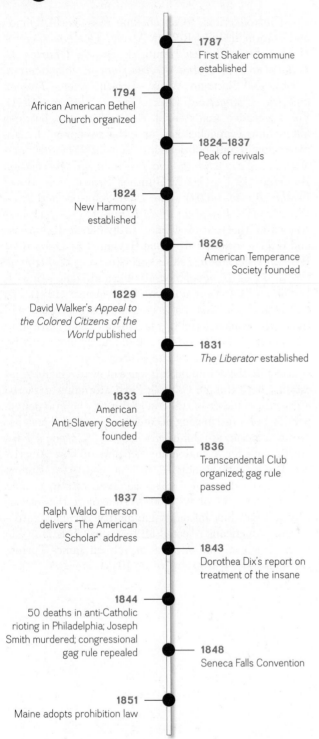

1787
First Shaker commune established

1794
African American Bethel Church organized

1824–1837
Peak of revivals

1824
New Harmony established

1826
American Temperance Society founded

1829
David Walker's *Appeal to the Colored Citizens of the World* published

1831
The Liberator established

1833
American Anti-Slavery Society founded

1836
Transcendental Club organized; gag rule passed

1837
Ralph Waldo Emerson delivers "The American Scholar" address

1843
Dorothea Dix's report on treatment of the insane

1844
50 deaths in anti-Catholic rioting in Philadelphia; Joseph Smith murdered; congressional gag rule repealed

1848
Seneca Falls Convention

1851
Maine adopts prohibition law

13 The Old South

1820–1860

This Louisiana plantation contained the sort of deep woods and bayous to which the slave Octave Johnson fled to escape the harsh life of slavery. In this painting the woods also provide a space apart, where the black community is attending a slave burial.

>> An American Story

WHERE IS THE REAL SOUTH?

The impeccably dressed Colonel Daniel Jordan, master of 261 slaves at Laurel Hill, strolls down his oak-lined lawn to the dock along the Waccamaw River, a day's journey north of Charleston, to board the steamship *Nina.* On Fridays it is Colonel Jordan's custom to visit the exclusive Hot and Hot Fish Club, founded by his fellow low-country planters, to play a game of lawn bowling or billiards and be waited on by black servants in livery as he sips an iced mint julep. For Colonel Jordan, this is the South.

Several hundred miles to the west another steamboat, the *Fashion,* makes its way along the Alabama River. One of the passengers is upset by the boat's slow pace. He has been away from his plantation in the Red River country of Texas and is eager to get back. "Time's money, time's money!" he mutters. "Time's worth more'n money to me now; a hundred percent more, 'cause I left my niggers all alone; not a damn white man within four mile on 'em." When asked what

A seller of chicken legs and rolls at the Richmond railway station in 1860. Modern viewers are likely to note the woman's proud, jaunty appearance. But the British traveler who sketched her betrayed the prejudices of his day, describing such vendors as "Negro girls, of the most tawdry dress and of extreme vulgarity."

they are doing, since the cotton crop has already been picked, he says, "I set 'em to clairin', but they ain't doin' a damn thing. . . . But I'll make it up, I'll make it up when I get thar, now you'd better believe." For this Red River planter, time is money and cotton is his world— indeed, cotton is what the South is all about. "I am a cotton man, I am, and I don't car who knows it," he proclaims. "I know cotton, I do. I'm dam' if I know anythin' but cotton."

At the other end of the South the slave Sam Williams works in the intense heat of Buffalo Forge, an iron-making factory in the Shenandoah Valley. As a refiner, Williams heats pig iron in white-hot coals, then slings the ball of glowing metal onto an anvil, where he pounds it with huge, water-powered hammers to remove the impurities. Ambitious and hardworking, he earns extra money (at the same rate paid to whites) for any iron he produces beyond his weekly quota. His wife, Nancy, in charge of the dairy, earns extra money, too. Their savings at the local bank total more than $150. The income helps them keep their family intact in an unstable environment: they know that their owner is unlikely to sell away slaves who work so hard. For Sam and Nancy Williams, family ties, worship at the local Baptist church, and socializing with their fellow slaves are what make life important.

In the bayous of the Deep South, only a few miles from where the Mississippi delta meets the Gulf, Octave Johnson hears the dogs coming. For over a year Johnson has been a runaway slave. He fled from a Louisiana plantation when the overseer threatened to whip him for staying in bed. To survive, he hides in the swamps four miles behind the plantation—stealing turkeys, chickens, and pigs and trading with other slaves. As uncertain as this life is, nearly 30 other slaves have joined him over the past year.

When the pack of hounds bursts upon them, the slaves do not flee but kill as many dogs as possible. Then they plunge into the bayou, and as the hounds follow, alligators make short work of another six. ("Alligators [prefer] dog flesh to personal flesh," he explains later.) For Octave Johnson the real South is a matter of weighing one's prospects between the uncertainties of alligators and the overseer's whip— and deciding when to say no.

Ferdinand Steel and his family are not forced, by the flick of the lash, to rise at five in the morning. They rise because the land demands it. Steel, in his 20s, owns 170 acres of land in Carroll County, Mississippi. His life is one of continuous hard work, caring for the animals and tending the crops. His mother, Eliza, and sister, Julia, have plenty to keep them busy: making soap, fashioning dippers out of gourds, sewing.

The Steel family grows cotton, too, but not with the single-minded devotion of the planter aboard the *Fashion*. Self-sufficiency and family security always come first, and Steel's total crop amounts to only five or six bales. His profit is never enough for him to consider buying even one slave—but the cotton means cash, and cash means that he can buy things he needs in town. Though fiercely independent, Steel and his scattered neighbors help one another raise houses, clear fields, shuck corn, and quilt. They depend on one another and are bound together by blood, religion, obligation, and honor. For small farmers such as Ferdinand Steel, these ties constitute the real South.

The portraits could go on: different people, different Souths, all of them real. Such contrasts underscore the difficulty of trying to define a regional identity. Encompassing in 1860 the 15 slave states plus the District of Columbia, the South was a land of great social and geographic diversity.

Yet despite its many differences of people and geography, the South was bonded by ties so strong, they eventually outpulled those of the nation itself. At the heart of this unity was an agricultural system that took advantage of the region's warm climate and long growing season. Most important, this rural agricultural economy was based on the institution of slavery, which had far-reaching effects on all aspects of southern society. It shaped not only the culture of the slaves themselves but also the lives of their masters and mistresses, and even of farm families and herders in the hills and backwoods, who saw few slaves from day to day. To understand the Old South, then, we must understand how the southern agricultural economy and the institution of slavery affected the social class structure of both white and black southerners. <<

What's to Come

THE SOCIAL STRUCTURE OF THE COTTON KINGDOM

The spread of cotton stimulated the nation's remarkable economic growth after the War of 1812. Demand spurred by the textile industry sent the price of cotton soaring on the international market, and white southerners scrambled into the fresh lands of the Southwest to reap the profits to be made in the cotton sweepstakes.

↟ An army worm on a cotton ball.

The Cotton Environment >> This new cultivation dramatically transformed the South's landscape, denuding countless acres covered with vines, brush, and trees. Cotton also imposed a demanding work discipline on slaves, who cultivated hundreds of acres, as well as white farming families, who tended many fewer. Typically they planted the newly cleared land in corn for a year, just long enough for tree stumps to decompose. In the next spring season, a heavy plow pulled by oxen or mules cleaved the fields into deep furrows, followed by workers who pitched cottonseed between the ridges. Then began the battle to protect the sprouting plants from weather, insects, and fungi. It was crucial to thin the excess cotton shoots in the spring and to yank out weeds throughout the summer. In years of heavy rains when such competing vegetation flourished, masters put even their house slaves into the fields.

But the greatest and most ingenious efforts went into defeating the dreaded army worm, for infestations of those caterpillars could strip an entire district of cotton. During a summer in the 1850s slaves on one plantation dug a deep trench between the cotton fields hoping to halt the pest's progress. Into it the army worms tumbled, "in untold millions," one observer reported, until the trench's bottom "for nearly a mile in extent, was a foot or two deep in [a] living mass of animal life." Then the slaves hitched a team of oxen to a heavy log and, as they pulled it through the ditch, "it seemed to float on a crushed mass" of army worms.

MAP 13.1: COTTON AND OTHER CROPS OF THE SOUTH

By 1860 the cotton kingdom extended across the Lower South into the Texas prairie and up the Mississippi River valley. Tobacco and hemp were the staple crops of the Upper South, where they competed with corn and wheat. Rice production was concentrated in the swampy coastal region of South Carolina and Georgia as well as the lower tip of Louisiana. The sugar district was in southern Louisiana.
Why was rice growing concentrated in coastal regions? Which staple crop predominated in the South, according to the map?

The Boom Country Economy >>The difficulties of cultivation did little to discourage white southerners' enthusiasm for cotton. Letters, newspapers, and
word of mouth all brought tales of the Black Belt region
of Alabama, where the dark, rich soil was particularly suited to growing cotton, and of the tremendous
yields from the soils along the Mississippi River's broad
reaches. "The Alabama Feaver rages here with great
violence and has carried off vast numbers of our Citizens," a North Carolinian wrote in 1817. A generation
later, in the 1830s, immigrants were still "pouring in
with a ceaseless tide," but by the 1840s residents were
leaving Alabama and Mississippi for even fresher cotton
lands along the Red River and up into Texas. By the
eve of the Civil War nearly a third of the total cotton
crop came from west of the Mississippi River. As Senator James Henry Hammond of South Carolina boasted
in 1858, cotton was king in the Old South: its primary
export and the major source of southern wealth.

As cotton transformed the boom country of the Deep
South, agriculture in the **Upper South** also adjusted.

Upper South the border
states (Delaware, Maryland,
Kentucky, and Missouri)
and Virginia, North Carolina,
Tennessee, and Arkansas.

Deep South South Carolina,
Georgia, Florida, Alabama,
Mississippi, Louisiana, and
Texas.

Scientific agricultural practices reversed the decline in
tobacco, which had begun
in the 1790s. More impor-
tant, farmers in the Upper
South made wheat and corn
their major crops. Because
the new crops required less
labor, slaveholders in the
Upper South sold their surplus slaves to planters in
the **Deep South.** There, eager buyers paid as much as
$1,500 in the late 1850s for a prime field hand.

Southern prosperity, however, masked basic problems in the economy. Much of the South's new wealth
resulted from migration of its population to more-fertile
western lands. The amount of prime agricultural land
was limited, and once it was settled, the South could not
sustain its rate of expansion. Furthermore, the single-
crop agriculture practiced by southern farmers (especially in tobacco and corn) rapidly wore out the soil.
Wheat production in the Upper South helped to restore

soils, but because farmers now plowed fields rather than using the hoe, this shift accelerated soil erosion. In addition, reliance on a single crop increased toxins and parasites in the soil, making southern agriculture more vulnerable than diversified agriculture was.

Perhaps the most striking environmental consequence of the expansion of southern society was the increase in disease. Epidemic diseases such as malaria, yellow fever, and cholera were brought to the area by Europeans. The clearing of land—which increased runoff, precipitated floods, and produced pools of stagnant water—encouraged their spread, especially in the Lower South.

The Rural South >> The Old South, then, was expanding, dynamic, and booming economically. But the region remained over-whelmingly rural, with 84 percent of its labor force engaged in agriculture in 1860, compared with 40 percent in the North. Conversely, the South produced only 9 percent of the nation's manufactured goods. Efforts to diversify the South's economy made little headway in the face of the high profits from cotton. With so little industry, few cities developed in the South. North Carolina, Florida, Alabama, Mississippi, Arkansas, and Texas did not contain a single city with a population of 10,000.

As a rural society the South showed far less interest in education. Most wealthy planters opposed a state-supported school system, because they hired tutors or sent their children to private academies. Georgia in 1860 had only one county with a free school system, and Mississippi had no public schools outside its few cities. The 1850 census showed that among native-born white citizens, 20 percent were unable to read and write. In the middle states the figure was 3 percent; in New England, only 0.4 percent.

Distribution of Slavery >> Even more than agrarian ways, slavery set the South apart. Whereas in 1776 slavery had been a national institution, by 1820 it was confined to the states south of Pennsylvania

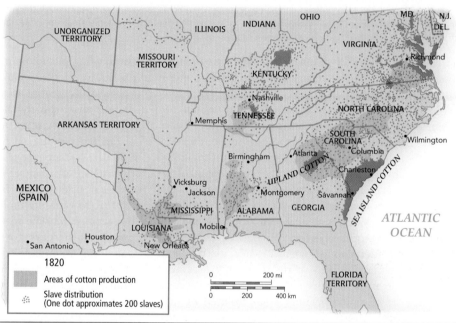

1820

▨ Areas of cotton production

⠿ Slave distribution (One dot approximates 200 slaves)

MAP 13.2: THE SPREAD OF SLAVERY, 1820–1860

Between 1820 and 1860 the slave population of the South shifted south and westward, concentrating especially heavily in coastal South Carolina and Georgia, in the Black Belt of central Alabama and Mississippi (so named because of its dark, rich soil), and in the Mississippi valley. *Comparing this map with Map 13.1, was a heavy concentration of slaves associated with only some of the South's staple crops? What factors contributed to a heavy concentration of slaves?*

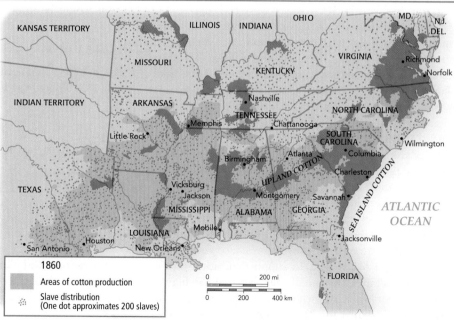

1860

▨ Areas of cotton production

⠿ Slave distribution (One dot approximates 200 slaves)

^ In this romanticized Currier and Ives print of a cotton plantation, field hands are waist-deep in cotton while other slaves haul the picked cotton to be ginned and then pressed into bales. Mounted on a horse, an overseer rides through the field supervising the work, while the owner and his wife look on. Picking began as early as August and continued in some areas until late January. Because the bolls ripened at different times, a field had to be picked several times.

and the Ohio River. The South's "peculiar institution" bound white and black southerners together in a multitude of ways.

Slaves were not evenly distributed throughout the region. More than half lived in the Deep South, where African Americans outnumbered white southerners in both South Carolina and Mississippi by the 1850s. Elsewhere in the Deep South, the black population exceeded 40 percent in all states except Texas. In the Upper South, in contrast, whites greatly outnumbered blacks. Only in Virginia and North Carolina did the slave population top 30 percent.

Geography determined some of this distribution. In areas of fertile soil, flat or rolling countryside, and good transportation, slavery and the plantation system dominated. In the pine barrens, areas isolated by lack of transportation, and hilly and mountainous regions, small family farms and few slaves were the rule.

Almost all enslaved African Americans, male and female, worked in agricultural pursuits, with only about 10 percent living in cities and towns. On large plantations a few slaves were domestic servants, and others were skilled artisans—blacksmiths, carpenters, or bricklayers—but most toiled in the fields.

Slavery as a Labor System >> Slavery was, first and foremost, a system to manage and control labor. The plantation system, with its extensive estates and large labor forces, could never have developed without slavery. Slaves represented an enormous capital investment, worth more than all the land in the Old South. Furthermore, slavery remained a highly profitable investment. The average slaveowner spent perhaps $30 to $35 a year to support an adult slave; some expended as little as half that. Even at the higher cost of support, a slaveowner took about 60 percent of the annual wealth produced by a slave's labor. For

those who pinched pennies and drove slaves harder, the profits were even greater.

By concentrating wealth and power in the hands of the planter class, slavery shaped the tone of southern society. Planters were not aristocrats in the European sense of having special legal privileges or formal titles of rank. Still, the system encouraged southern planters to think of themselves as a landed gentry upholding the aristocratic values of pride, honor, family, and hospitality.

Public opinion in Europe and in the North grew increasingly hostile to the peculiar institution, causing white southerners to feel like an isolated minority defending an embattled position. Yet they clung tenaciously to slavery, because it was the base on which the South's economic growth and way of life rested. As one Georgian observed on the eve of the Civil War, slavery was "so intimately mingled with our social conditions that it would be impossible to eradicate it."

 REVIEW

How did the cotton economy shape the South's environment and labor system?

CLASS STRUCTURE OF THE WHITE SOUTH

Once a year around Christmastime, James Henry Hammond gave a dinner for his neighbors at his South Carolina plantation, Silver Bluff. The richest man for miles around as well as an ambitious politician, the aristocratic

Hammond used these dinners to put his neighbors under personal obligation to him as well as to receive the honor and respect he believed his due. In addition, Hammond hired his neighbors to perform various tasks and allowed them to use his grist mill and gin their cotton. His less affluent neighbors recognized Hammond's social rank, but they, too, displayed a strong personal pride. After their superior ungraciously complained about the inconvenience of these services, only three of his neighbors came to his Christmas dinner in 1837, a snub that enraged him. As Hammond's experience demonstrated, class relations among whites in the Old South were a complex blend of privilege, patronage, and equality.

The Slaveowners >>

In 1860 the region's 15 states had a population of 12 million, of which roughly two-thirds were white, one-third were black slaves, and about 2 percent were free African Americans. Of the 8 million white southerners, only about a quarter either owned slaves or were members of slaveowning families. Moreover, most slaveowners owned only a few slaves. If one uses the census definition of a planter as a person who owned 20 or more slaves, only about 1 out of every 30 white southerners belonged to families of the planter class. A planter of consequence, however, needed to own at least 50 slaves, and there were only about 10,000 such families—less than 1 percent of the white population. This privileged group made up the aristocracy at the top of the southern class structure. Owners of large numbers of slaves were very rare;

only about 2,000 southerners, such as Colonel Daniel Jordan, owned 100 or more slaves. Although limited in size, the planter class nevertheless owned more than half of all slaves and controlled more than 90 percent of the region's total wealth.

Tidewater and Frontier >>

Southern planters shared a commitment to preserve slavery as the source of their wealth and stature. Yet in other ways they were a diverse group. On the one hand, the tobacco and rice planters of the Atlantic Tidewater were part of a settled region and a culture that reached back 150 to 200 years. States such as Mississippi and Arkansas, in contrast, had rawer and more-volatile societies, since most non-Indian residents had flooded into the region after 1815.

It was along the Tidewater, especially the bays of the Chesapeake and the South Carolina coast, that the legendary "Old South" was born. Here, masters erected substantial homes, some—especially between Charleston and Columbia—the classic white-pillared mansions in the Greek Revival style. An Irish visitor observed that in Maryland and Virginia the great planters lived in "a style which approaches nearer to that of the English country gentleman than what is to be met with anywhere else on the continent." As in England, the local gentry often served as justices of the peace, and the Episcopal Church remained the socially accepted road to heaven. Here, too, family names continued to be important in politics.

While the newer regions of the South boasted of planters with cultivated manners, as a group the cotton lords were a different breed. Whatever their background, these entrepreneurs had moved west for the reason so many other white Americans had: to make their fortunes. By and large the cotton gentry were men of ordinary backgrounds who had risen through hard work, aggressive business tactics, and good luck. For them the cotton boom and the exploitation of enslaved men and women offered the chance to move up in a new society that lacked an entrenched elite.

"Time's money, time's money." For men like the impatient Texan, time was indeed money, slaves were capital, and cotton by the bale signified cash in hand. This business orientation was especially apparent in the cotton kingdom, where planters sought to maximize their profits and constantly reinvested their returns in land and slaves. And while most planters ranked among the richest citizens in America, the homes of the newer cotton gentry were often simple one- or two-story unpainted wooden frame houses. Some were even log cabins. "If you wish to see people worth millions living as [if] they were not worth hundreds," advised one southwestern planter in 1839, "come to the land of cotton and negroes." Practical men, few of the new cotton lords had absorbed the culture and learning of the traditional country gentleman.

Non-slaveowners, 75% of white population

Free blacks **2%**

Slaves **32%**

Whites **66%**

Slaveowners 25% of white population

50+ slaves
20–49 slaves
10–19 slaves
1–9 slaves

SOUTHERN POPULATION, 1860

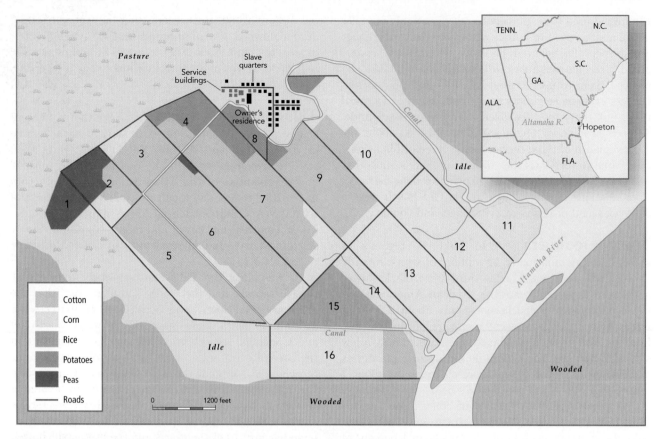

MAP 13.3: A PLANTATION LAYOUT, HOPETON, GEORGIA

Often covering a thousand acres or more, a plantation was laid out like a small village and contained several fields and usually extensive uncleared woods. Somewhere near the master's "big house" were the quarters—slave cabins clustered along one or more streets. Service buildings might include a smokehouse, stables, a gin house (for cotton) or a rice mill, and an overseer's dwelling. Like most large plantations, Hopeton produced a considerable amount of foodstuffs, but it grew both rice and cotton as staples. Most plantations concentrated on a single cash crop.

The Master at Home >> Whether supervising a Tidewater plantation or creating a cotton estate on the Texas frontier, the master had to coordinate a complex agricultural operation. He gave daily instructions concerning the work to be done, settled disputes between slaves and the overseer, and generally handed out rewards and penalties. In addition, the owner made the critical decisions for planting, harvesting, and marketing the crops as well as for investments and expenditures.

In performing his duties the plantation owner was supposed to be the "master" of his crops, his family, and his slaves. Defenders of slavery often held up this paternalistic ideal—the care and guidance of dependent "children"—and maintained that slavery promoted a genuine bond of affection between the caring master and his loyal slaves. In real life, however, the forces of the market made this paternalistic ideal less evident. Even in the Tidewater, planters were concerned with money and profits. Indeed, some of the most brutal forms of slavery existed on rice plantations. Except for a few domestic servants, owners of large plantations generally had little contact with their slaves. Nor could paternalism mask the reality that slavery everywhere rested on violence, racism, and exploitation.

The Plantation Mistress >> Upper–class white women in the South, like those in the North, grew up with the ideal of domesticity, reinforced by the notion of a paternalistic master who was lord of the plantation. But the plantation mistress soon discovered that the daily demands placed on her made that ideal hard to fulfill.

In her youth a genteel lady enjoyed a certain amount of leisure. But once married and the mistress of a plantation, she discovered the magnitude of her responsibilities. Nursing the sick, making clothing, tending the garden, caring for the poultry, and overseeing every aspect of food preparation were all her domain. She also supervised and planned the work of the domestic servants. After taking care of breakfast, one harried Carolina mistress recounted that she "had

⋀ Sarah Pierce Vick, the mistress of a plantation near Vicksburg, Mississippi, pauses to speak to one of her slaves, who may be holding feed for her horse. A plantation mistress had many duties and, while enjoying the comforts brought by wealth and status, often found her life more difficult than she had anticipated before marriage.

the [sewing] work cut out, gave orders about dinner, had the horse feed fixed in hot water, had the box filled with cork: . . . now I have to cut out the flannel jackets." Sarah Williams, the New York bride of a North Carolina planter, admitted that her mother–in–law "works harder than any Northern farmer's wife I know."

Unlike female reformers in the North, upper–class southern women did not openly challenge their role, but some found their sphere confining. The greatest unhappiness stemmed from the never–ending task of managing slaves. One southern mistress confessed she was frightened at being "always among people whom I do not understand and whom I must guide, and teach and lead on like children." Yet without the labor of slaves, the lifestyle of these women was an impossibility.

Many white women also despised the widespread double standard for sexual behavior. A man who fathered illegitimate children by slave women suffered no social or legal penalties, even in the case of rape (southern law did not recognize such a crime against slave women), whereas a white woman guilty of adultery lost all social respectability. One planter's wife spoke of "violations of the moral law that made mulattoes as common as blackberries," and another recalled, "I saw slavery . . . teemed with injustice and shame to all womankind and I hated it."

Some white women drew a parallel between their situation and that of the slaves. Both were subject to male dominance, and independent–minded women found the subordination of marriage difficult. Susan

Dabney Smedes, in her recollection of growing up on an Alabama plantation, recalled that "it was a saying that the mistress of a plantation was the most complete slave on it."

Still, plantation mistresses were unwilling to forgo the material comforts that slavery made possible. Moreover, racism was so pervasive within American society that the few white southern women who privately criticized the institution displayed little empathy for the plight of slaves themselves, including black women. Whatever the burdens of the plantation mistress, they were hardly akin to the bondage of slavery itself.

Yeoman Farmers >> In terms of numbers, yeoman farm families were the backbone of southern society, accounting for well over half the southern white population. These farmers owned no slaves and farmed the traditional 80 to 160 acres, like northern farmers. About 80 percent owned their own land. They settled almost everywhere in the South, except in the rice and sugar districts and valuable river bottomlands of the Deep South, which were monopolized by large slaveowners. Like Ferdinand Steel, most were semisubsistence farmers who raised primarily corn and hogs, along with perhaps a few bales of cotton or some tobacco, which they sold to obtain the cash needed to buy items like sugar, coffee, and salt. Yeoman farmers lacked the wealth of planters, but they had a pride and dignity that earned them the respect of their richer neighbors.

While southern farmers led more isolated lives than did their northern counterparts, their social activities were not very different. Religion played an important role at camp meetings held in late summer, after the crops were laid by and before harvest time. As in the North, neighbors also met to exchange labor and tools. The men rolled logs to clear fields of dead trees, women met for quilting bees, and adults and children alike would gather to shuck corn. Court sessions, militia musters, political rallies—these, too, were occasions that brought rural folk together.

Since yeoman farmers lacked cheap slave labor, good transportation, and access to credit, they could not compete with planters in the production of staples. In the North urban centers became a market for small farmers to sell their staple crops, but in the South the lack of towns limited this internal market. Thus, although southern yeoman farmers were not poor, they suffered from a chronic lack of money and the absence of conveniences that northern farm families enjoyed. Josiah Hinds, who hacked a farm out of the isolated woods of northern Mississippi, worried that his children were growing up "wild." He complained that "education is but little prized by my neighbours," who were satisfied "if the corn and cotton grows to perfection . . .

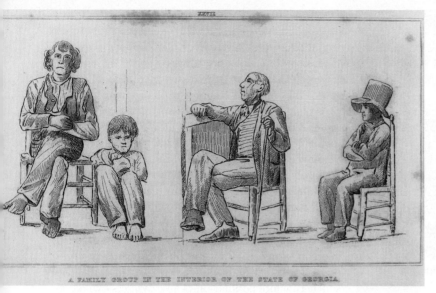

A FAMILY GROUP IN THE INTERIOR OF THE STATE OF GEORGIA.

<< A majority of white southerners were members of non-slaveholding yeoman farm families. Ruggedly independent, these families depended on their own labor and often lived under primitive conditions. Basil Hall, an Englishman traveling through the South in 1827 and 1828, sketched members of this Georgia family with the aid of a camera lucida, an optical device that projected an image from real life onto paper, where it could be traced with accuracy.

[and] brings a fare price, and hog meat is at hand to boil with the greens."

In some ways, then, the worlds of the yeoman farmers and the upper–class planters were not only different but also in conflict. Still, a hostility between the two classes did not emerge. Yeoman farmers admired planters and hoped that one day they would join the gentry. Furthermore, they accepted slavery as a means of controlling African Americans as members of an inferior social caste based on race. "Now suppose they was free," one poor farmer told Frederick Law Olmsted, a northern visitor. "You see they'd all think themselves as good as we." Racism and fear of black people were sufficient to keep non–slaveholders loyal to southern institutions.

Poor Whites >> The poorest white southerners were confined to land that no one else wanted. They lived in rough, windowless log cabins located in the remotest areas and were often squatters without title to the land they were on. The men spent their time hunting and fishing, while women did the domestic work, including what farming they could manage. Circumstances made their poverty difficult to escape. Largely illiterate, they suffered from malnutrition stemming from a monotonous diet of corn, pork, and whiskey, and they were afflicted with malaria and hookworm, diseases that sapped their energy. Other white southerners referred to them scornfully as crackers, white trash, sand–hillers, and clay–eaters.

The number of poor whites in the Old South is difficult to estimate. There may have been as few as 100,000 or as many as a million; probably they numbered about 500,000, or a little more than 5 percent of the white population.

Because poor whites traded with slaves, exchanging whiskey for stolen goods, contemptuous planters often bought them out simply to rid the neighborhood of them. For their part, poor whites keenly resented planters, but their hostility toward African Americans was even stronger. Poor whites refused to perform any work commonly done by slaves and vehemently opposed ending slavery. Emancipation would remove one of the few symbols of their status—that they were, at least, free.

✔ REVIEW

What was the relationship between the South's great planters and yeoman farmers?

THE PECULIAR INSTITUTION

Slaves were not free. That overwhelming fact must be understood before anything is said about the kindness or the cruelty individual slaves experienced; before any consideration of healthy or unhealthy living conditions; before any discussion of how slave families coped with hardship, rejoiced in shared pleasures, or worshiped in prayer. The lives of slaves were affected day in and day out, in big ways and small, by the basic reality that slaves were not their own masters. The master determined a slave's workload, whether a slave could

Opinion

What role did race play in maintaining the institution of slavery? Could a system of white or Indian slavery have existed as easily?

visit a nearby plantation, and whether a slave family remained intact. Whatever slaves wanted to do, they always had to consider the response of their masters.

When power is distributed as unequally as it was between masters and slaves, every action on the part of the enslaved involves a certain calculation, conscious or unconscious. The consequences of every act, of every expression or gesture, have to be considered. In that sense, the line between freedom and slavery penetrated every corner of a slave's life, and it was an absolute and overwhelming distinction.

One other stark fact reinforced the sharp line between freedom and slavery: slaves were distinguished on the basis of color. While the peculiar institution was an economic system of labor, it was also a **caste system** based on race. The color line of slavery made it easier to defend the institution and win the support of yeoman farmers and poor white southerners, even though in many ways the system held them back. Hence slavery must be understood on many levels: not only as an economic system but also as a racial and cultural one, in terms of not only its outward conditions of life and labor but also the inner demands it made on the soul.

> **caste system** system of social stratification separating individuals by various distinctions, among them heredity, rank, profession, wealth, and race.

Work and Discipline >> The conditions slaves
encountered varied widely, depending on the size of the farm or plantation, the crop being grown, the personality of the master, and whether he was an absentee owner. On small farms, slaves worked in the fields alongside their owners and had much closer contact with whites. On plantations, in contrast, most slaves dealt primarily with the overseer, who was paid by the size of the harvest he brought in and was therefore often harsh in his approach.

House servants and the drivers, who supervised the field hands, received the highest status, and skilled artisans such as carpenters and blacksmiths were also given special recognition. The hardest work was done by the field hands, both men and women.

Some planters organized their slaves in the gang system, in which a white overseer or a black driver supervised gangs of 20 to 25 adults. Although this approach extracted long hours of reasonably hard labor, the slaves had to be constantly supervised, and shirkers were difficult to detect. Other planters preferred the task system, under which each slave was given a specific daily assignment to complete, after which he or she was finished for the day. This system allowed slaves to work at their own pace, gave them an incentive to work carefully, and freed overseers from having to closely supervise the work. But slaves resisted vigorously if masters tried to increase the workload. The task system was most common in the rice fields, whereas the gang system predominated in the cotton districts. Many planters used a combination of the two systems.

During cultivation and harvest, slaves were in the field 15 to 16 hours a day, eating a noonday meal there and resting before resuming labor. Work was uncommon on Sundays, and frequently only a half day was required on Saturdays. Even so, the routine was taxing. "I am never caught in bed after day light nor is any body else on the place," an Arkansas cotton planter reported, "and we continue in the cotton fields when we can have fair weather till it is so dark we can't see to work."

Often masters rewarded hardworking slaves, but the threat of punishment was always present. Slaves could be denied passes; their food allowance could be reduced; and if all else failed, they could be sold. The most common instrument of punishment was the whip. The frequency of its use varied from plantation to plantation, but few slaves escaped the lash entirely. "We have to rely more and more on the power of fear," planter James Henry Hammond acknowledged. "We are determined to continue masters, and to do so we have to draw the rein tighter and tighter day by day to be assured that we hold them in complete check."

Slave Maintenance >> Planters generally bought
rough, cheap cloth for slave clothing and each year gave adults at most only a couple of outfits and a pair of shoes. Some planters provided well-built housing, but more commonly slaves lived in cramped, poorly built cabins that were leaky in wet weather, drafty in cold, and furnished with only a few crude chairs or benches and a table, perhaps a mattress filled with corn husks or straw, and a few pots and dishes. To keep medical expenses down, slaveowners treated sick slaves and called in a doctor only for serious cases. On average a slaveowner spent less than a dollar a year on medical care for each slave.

Nevertheless, the United States was the only slave society in the Americas where the slave population increased naturally—indeed, at about the same rate as for the white population. Even so, infant mortality among slaves was more than double that of the white population; for every 1,000 live births among southern slaves, more than 200 died before the age of 5. For those who survived infancy, enslaved African Americans had a life expectancy about 8 years less than that of white Americans. As late as 1860 fewer than two-thirds of slave children survived to the age of 10.

Resistance >> Given the wide gulf between free-
dom and slavery, it was only natural that slaves resisted the bondage imposed on them. The most radical form of resistance was rebellion, which occurred repeatedly in

⋏ Slaves resisted their masters by fleeing to nearby swamps or forests. Masters often used specially trained dogs to track them. Those shown here were imported from Cuba, and Zachary Taylor, who was elected president of the United States in 1848, was among the planters who imported them.

witness

Resistance and Discipline on a Cotton Plantation

"October 4, 1839. Boy Lewis came in last night [after having run away for five days]—gave him the worst whipping I ever gave any young negro. I predict he will not run away *soon*. Building a jail for him, Dennis, and Ginny Jerry—intend jailing them from Saturday nights 'till Monday mornings."

—Bennet H. Barrow, a Florida Planter, Diary Entry (October 4, 1839)

slave societies in the Americas. In Latin America slave revolts were relatively frequent, involving hundreds and even thousands of slaves and pitched battles in which large numbers were killed. The most success-ful slave revolt occurred in France's sugar—rich colony, Saint—Domingue (the western part of the Caribbean island of Hispaniola). There, free blacks who had fought in the Ameri-can Revolution because of France's alliance with the United States brought back the ideals of freedom and equality. The bru-tally overworked population of half a mil-lion slaves received further encouragement from the example of the French Revolu-tion. Led by Toussaint L'Ouverture, black slaves established Haiti in 1804, the sec-ond independent republic in the Western Hemisphere.

Elsewhere, Jamaica averaged one significant revolt every year from 1731 to 1823, and in 1823 thousands rose in Guiana. Jamaica witnessed an upris-ing of some 20,000 slaves in 1831. These revolts were savagely suppressed. And in Brazil, which had the largest num-ber of slaves outside the United States, the government took 50 years to bring under control a colony of some 20,000 fugitive slaves who had sought refuge in the mountains.

In contrast, slave revolts were rare in the United States. Unlike in Latin America, in the Old South whites outnumbered blacks, the government was much more powerful, a majority of slaves were native–born, and family life was stronger. Slaves recognized the odds against them, and many potential leaders became fugitives instead. What is remarkable is that American slaves revolted at all.

Early in the nineteenth century several well–organized uprisings were barely thwarted. In 1800 Gabriel Prosser, a slave blacksmith, recruited perhaps a couple hundred slaves to march on Richmond and capture the governor. But a few conspirators betrayed the plot, and Prosser and other leaders were captured and executed. Denmark Vesey's conspiracy in Charleston in 1822 met a similar fate.

The most famous slave revolt, led by a literate slave preacher named Nat Turner, was spontaneous. Turner, who lived on a farm in southeastern Virginia, was given unusual privileges by his master, whom he described as a kind and trusting man. A religious mystic, Turner became convinced that God had selected him to punish white people through "terror and devastation." One night in 1831 following an eclipse of the sun, he and six other slaves stole out and murdered Turner's master and family. Recruiting some 70 slaves as they went, Turner's band killed 57 white men, women, and children. But the revolt was crushed within 48 hours, and Turner was eventually captured, tried, and executed. Even so, the uprising left white southerners uneasy. Turner had seemed a model slave, yet who could read a slave's true emotions behind the mask of obedience?

Few slaves followed Turner's violent example. But there were subtle ways of resisting a master's authority. Most dramatically, slaves could run away. With the odds stacked heavily against them, few runaways escaped safely to freedom except from the border states. More frequently, slaves fled to nearby woods or swamps. Some runaways stayed out only a few days; others, like Octave Johnson, held out for months.

Many slaves resisted by abusing their masters' property. They mishandled animals, broke tools and machinery, misplaced items, and worked carelessly in the fields. Slaves also sought to trick the master by feigning illness or injury and by hiding rocks in the cotton they picked. Slaves complained directly to the owner about an overseer's mistreatment, thereby attempting to drive a wedge between the two.

The most common form of resistance was theft. Slaves raided the master's smokehouse, secretly slaughtered his stock, and killed his poultry. Slaves often distinguished between "stealing" from one another and merely "taking" from white masters. "Dey always done tell us it was wrong to lie and steal," recalled Josephine Howard, a former slave in Texas, "but why did the white folks steal my mammy and her mammy? They lives . . . over in Africy. . . . That's the sinfulles' stealin' there is."

Slaves learned to outwit their masters, one former bondsman testified, by wearing an "impenetrable mask" around whites: "How much of joy, of sorrow, of misery and anguish have they hidden from their tormentors." Frederick Douglass, the most famous fugitive slave, explained that "as the master studies to keep the slave ignorant, the slave is cunning enough to make the master think he succeeds."

 REVIEW

In what ways did slaves resist their oppression?

SLAVE CULTURE

Trapped in bondage, slaves could at least forge a culture of their own by combining strands from their African past with customs that evolved from their life in America. This slave culture was most distinct on big plantations, where the large slave population lived farther apart from white scrutiny.

The Slave Family >> Maintaining a sense of family was one of the most remarkable achievements of African Americans in bondage, given the obstacles they faced. Southern law did not recognize slave marriages as legally binding, nor did it allow slave parents complete authority over their children. Black women faced the possibility of rape by the master or overseer without legal recourse, and husbands, wives, and children had to live with the fear of being sold and separated. From 1820 to 1860 more than 2 million slaves were sold in the interstate slave trade. Perhaps 600,000 husbands and wives were separated by such sales.

Still, family ties remained strong, as slave culture demonstrated. The marriage ceremony among slaves varied from a formal religious service to jumping over the broomstick in front of the slave community to nothing more than the master's giving verbal approval. Whatever the ceremony, slaves viewed the ritual as a public affirmation of the couple's commitment to their new duties and responsibilities. Rather than adopting white norms, slaves developed their own moral code concerning sexual relations and marriage. Although young slaves often engaged in premarital sex, they were expected to choose a partner and become part of a stable family. It has been estimated that at least one in five slave women had one or more children before marriage, but most of these mothers eventually married. "The negroes had their own ideas of morality, and they held them very strictly," the daughter of a Georgia planter recalled. "They did not consider it wrong for a girl to have a child before she married, but afterwards were very strict upon anything like infidelity on her part."

The traditional nuclear family of father, mother, and children was the rule, not the exception, among slaves. Women did the indoor work such as cooking, washing, and sewing, and men performed outdoor chores, such as gathering firewood, hauling water, and tending the animals and garden plots. The men also hunted and fished to supplement the spare weekly rations. "My old daddy...caught rabbits, coons an' possums," recalled Louisa Adams of North Carolina. "He would work all day and hunt at night."

Songs and Stories of Protest and Celebration >>

In the songs they sang, slaves expressed some of their deepest feelings about life. "The songs of the slave represent the sorrows of his heart," commented Frederick Douglass. Surely there was bitterness as well as sorrow when slaves sang:

> We raise the wheat
> They give us the corn
> We bake the bread
> They give us the crust
> We sift the meal
> They give us the husk
> We peel the meat
> They give us the skin
> And that's the way
> They take us in

Yet songs were also central to the celebrations held in the slave quarters: for marriages, Christmas revels, and after harvest time. And a slave on the way to the fields might sing, "Saturday night and Sunday too/ Young gals on my mind."

>> Students of this painting by Christian Friedrich Mayr speculate that the participants in this Kitchen Ball at White Sulphur Springs included both free blacks and slaves who had accompanied their masters to this resort in present-day West Virginia (then part of Virginia).

Slaves expressed themselves through stories as well as song. Most often these folktales used animals as symbolic models for the predicaments in which slaves found themselves. In the best known of these, the cunning Brer Rabbit was a weak fellow who used his wits to defeat larger animals, such as Brer Fox and Brer Bear. Such stories, whether direct or symbolic, taught the young how to survive in a hostile world.

The Lord Calls Us Home >>

Religion stood at the center of slave culture. Slaveowners encouraged a carefully controlled form of religion among slaves. "Church was what they called it," one former slave protested, "but all that preacher talked about was for us slaves to obey our masters and not to lie and steal. Nothing about Jesus was ever said and the overseer stood there to see that the preacher talked as he wanted him to talk." In response, some slaves rejected all religion.

Most, however, sought a Christianity beyond the control of the master. On many plantations they met secretly at night, when they would break into rhythmic singing and dancing, modeled on the ring shout of African religion. Even in regular services, observers noted the greater emotion of black worshipers. "The way in which we worshiped is almost indescribable," one slave preacher recalled. "The singing was accompanied by a certain ecstasy of motion, clapping of

hands, tossing of heads, which would continue without cessation about half an hour." In an environment where slaves, for most of the day, were prevented from expressing their deepest feelings, such meetings provided a satisfying emotional release.

Although secret religious meetings were important, the religious experience of most enslaved African Americans occurred mainly within the regular white-controlled churches of the South. Perhaps a million slaves were included in the southern churches before the Civil War, especially in the Methodist and Baptist Churches. Indeed, in some areas, slaves were a majority in local congregations. As a result most slaves worshiped together with their masters rather than in separate services. At one point during the regular service ministers delivered a special message to the slaves, but they also heard the same sermon as whites, with its emphasis on faith and salvation. The churches were also the one institution in the South where blacks were accorded a measure of equality. Black members were held to the same standards of conduct as whites, were subject to the same church discipline, and were allowed to testify in court against whites.

Religion also provided slaves with values to guide them through their lives and give them a sense of self-worth. Slaves learned that God one day would raise the poor and downtrodden to honor and glory. Just as certainly, on the final Day of Judgment, masters would be punished for their sins. "This is one reason why I believe in hell," a former slave declared. "I don't believe a just God is going to take no such man as my former master into His Kingdom."

Again, song played a central role. Slaves sang religious "spirituals" at work and at play as well as in religious services. Seemingly meek and otherworldly, the songs often contained a hidden element of protest. Frederick Douglass disclosed that when slaves sang longingly of "Canaan, sweet Canaan," they were thinking not only of the Bible's Promised Land but of the North and freedom.

Religion, then, served not only to comfort slaves after days of toil and sorrow. It also strengthened the sense of togetherness and common purpose and held out the promise of eventual freedom in this world and the next. Having faith that "some of these days my time will come" was one of the most important ways that slaves coped with bondage and resisted its pressure to rob them of their self-esteem.

The Slave Community >> While slaves managed to preserve a culture of their own, they found it impossible to escape fully from white control. In terms of social hierarchy, the prestige of a slave driver rested ultimately on the authority of the white master, and skilled slaves and house servants often felt superior to other slaves, an attitude masters promoted. Light-skinned slaves sometimes deemed their color a badge of superiority. Fanny Kemble recorded that one woman begged to be relieved of field labor, which she considered degrading, "on 'account of her color.'"

Despite these divisions the realities of slavery and white racism inevitably drove black people closer together in a common bond and forced them to depend on one another to survive. Excluded from the individualistic society of whites, slaves out of necessity created a community of their own.

Free Black Southerners >> Of the 4 million African Americans living in the South in 1860, only 260,000—about 7 percent—were free. More than 85 percent of them lived in the Upper South. Free black southerners were also much more urban than either the southern white or slave populations. In 1860 almost a third of the free African Americans in the Upper South, and more than half in the Lower South, lived in towns and cities. As a rule, free African Americans were more literate than slaves, and they were disproportionately female and much more likely to be of mixed ancestry.

Most free black southerners lived in rural areas, although usually not near plantations. A majority eked out a living farming or in low-paying unskilled jobs, but some did well enough to own slaves themselves. In 1830 about 3,600 did, although commonly their "property" was their wives or children, purchased because they could not be emancipated under state laws. A few, however, were full-blown slaveowners.

The boundary sometimes blurred between free and enslaved African Americans. Sally Thomas of Nashville was technically a slave, but in the 1830s and 1840s her owner allowed her to ply her trade as a laundress and keep some of her wages. (She used $350 of these savings to purchase the freedom of one of her sons.) The boundary stretched especially for African Americans working along rivers and the seashore in the fishing trades, as pilots or seamen, or as "watermen" ferrying supplies and stores in small boats. Under such conditions, laborers preserved more freedom and initiative than most agricultural workers.

Along Albemarle Sound in North Carolina, free blacks and slaves flocked from miles around to "fisherman's courts," a kind of annual hiring fair. Amid an atmosphere of drinking, carousing, cockfighting, and boxing, men who ran commercial fishing operations signed up workers. The crews would then go down to the shore in late February or early March to net vast schools of fish, working around the clock. A single team might haul 100,000 herring onto the beach in four to seven hours. Women and children then headed, gutted, cleaned, and salted the fish. A good "cutter" might head tens of thousands of herring a day. In such settings African Americans, both free and slave, could share news with folk they did not regularly see.

Following Nat Turner's Rebellion of 1831, southern legislatures increased the restrictions placed on free African Americans. They were forbidden to enter a new state, had to carry their free papers, could not assemble when they wished, were subject to a nightly curfew, often had to post a bond and be licensed to work, and could not vote, hold office, or testify in court against white people.

Free African Americans occupied an uncertain position in southern society, well above black slaves but distinctly beneath even poorer white southerners. They were victims of a society that had no place for them.

 REVIEW

In what ways did the culture and communities created by blacks help to sustain them in slavery?

SOUTHERN SOCIETY AND THE DEFENSE OF SLAVERY

While the South was a remarkably diverse region, it was united above all by the institution of slavery. As the South's economy became more dependent on slave–produced staples, slavery became more central to the life of the South, to its culture and its identity.

The Virginia Debate of 1832 >> During the Revolution the leading critics of slavery were southerners—Jefferson, Washington, Madison, and Patrick Henry among them. But beginning in the 1820s, in the wake of the controversy over admitting Missouri as a slave state, southern leaders became more aggressive in defending slavery. The turning point occurred in the early 1830s, when the South found itself increasingly under attack. It was in 1831 that William Lloyd Garrison began publishing his abolitionist newspaper, *The Liberator*. That was also the year Nat Turner led his revolt, which frightened so many white southerners.

In response to the Turner insurrection, a number of Virginia's western counties, where there were few slaves, petitioned the legislature in 1832 to adopt a program for gradual emancipation. In the end, however, the legislature refused. The debate represented the last significant attempt of white southerners to take action against slavery. Instead, during the 1830s

and 1840s southern leaders defended slavery as a good, not just for white but for black people. As John C. Calhoun proclaimed in 1837, "I hold that in the present state of civilization, where two races…are brought together, the relation now existing in the slaveholding states between the two is, instead of an evil, a good—a positive good."

The Proslavery Argument >> White southern leaders justified slavery in a variety of ways. Ministers argued that none of the biblical prophets or Christ himself had ever condemned slavery. Defenders of the institution pointed out that classical Greece and Rome also depended on slavery. They even cited John Locke, that giant of the Enlightenment, who had recognized slavery in the constitution he drafted for the colony of Carolina. African Americans belonged to an intellectually and emotionally inferior race, slavery's defenders argued, and therefore lacked the ability to care for themselves.

Proslavery writers sometimes argued that slaves in the South lived better than factory workers in the North. Masters cared for slaves for life, whereas northern workers had no claim on their employer when they were unemployed, old, or no longer able to work. In advancing this argument, white southerners exaggerated the material comforts of slavery and minimized the average worker's living conditions—to say nothing, of course, about the incalculable psychological value of freedom. Still, to many white southerners, slavery seemed a more humane system of labor relations.

Defenders of slavery did not really expect to convert northerners. Their target was more often slaveowners themselves. As Duff Green, a southern editor, explained, "We must satisfy the consciences, we must allay the fears of our own people. We must satisfy them that slavery is of itself right—that it is not a sin against God—that it is not an evil, moral or political. In this way only," he went on, "can we prepare our own people to defend their institutions."

Closing Ranks >> Not all white southerners could quell their doubts. Still, in the decades before the Civil War, few outside the border states contended that slavery was wrong. And white southerners who did oppose slavery found themselves harassed, assaulted, and driven into exile. Southern mobs destroyed the presses of antislavery papers. Southern mails were forcibly closed to abolitionist propaganda. Southerners such as James Birney and Sarah and Angelina Grimké had to leave their native region to carry on the fight against slavery from the free states.

Increasingly, too, slavery entered the national political debate. Before 1836 Andrew Jackson's popularity in the South blocked the formation of a

George Washington, Slaveholder

This image is a lithograph of a painting. What's a lithograph? (Well worth it to Google "lithograph")

A young neighbor, perhaps Washington's overseer or a yeoman or tenant farmer

Washington's two step-grandchildren

Washington himself. Why so formally dressed for the hay field?

Advocates of the proslavery argument made strategic use of anecdotes and images portraying George Washington as the master of Mount Vernon, his plantation—without mentioning that, upon his death, his will freed all his slaves. Based on a painting of 1851, this 1853 lithograph and others conveying a similar proslavery message found their way into thousands of southern parlors and libraries before the Civil War. (Historians of technology tell us that lithography came into widespread use in the early nineteenth century, allowing for the cheap mass production of images as well as print.) Such stories and pictures portrayed Washington as a benevolent patriarch—a father to his slaves as well as to his country—and depicted slavery as a benevolent institution. At the center of this scene, a group of hale, neatly outfitted black men refresh themselves with water brought by a slave woman, demurely dressed right up to her head covering. Judging by the riding crop in his hand and the horse (far left), Washington has just dismounted, perhaps to give some instructions to his overseer, a young man who holds not a whip but a rake—to help the slaves with the hay-gathering.

THINKING CRITICALLY

What is the significance of placing whites in the foreground of the painting? What point was the artist making by drawing Washington's two step-grandchildren happily at play in the left corner? What was the artist implying by portraying Washington and the young man (who is plainly of lesser status), talking with easy familiarity?

Credit: Claude Regnier after Junius Brutus Stearns, Life of George Washington: the Farmer (lithograph, 1853) LIBRARY OF CONGRESS

competitive two–party system. The rise of the abolitionist movement in the 1830s, however, left many southerners uneasy, and when the Democrats nominated the northerner Martin Van Buren in 1836, southern Whigs charged that Van Buren could not be counted on to meet the abolitionist threat to slavery. The Whigs made impressive gains in the South in 1836, carrying several states and significantly narrowing the margin between the two parties.

During the Jacksonian era, most southern political battles did not revolve around slavery. Still, southern politicians in both parties had to be careful about being the least bit critical of slavery or southern institutions. They knew quite well that, even if their constituents were not so fanatical as John Calhoun in the defense of the peculiar institution, southern voters overwhelmingly supported slavery.

✓ REVIEW
How did white southerners defend slavery as a positive good?

As the past several chapters have made clear, two remarkable transformations were sweeping the world in the first half of the nineteenth century. The first was a series of political upheavals leading to increased democratic participation in many nation–states. The second, the Industrial Revolution, applied machine labor and technological innovation to commercial and agricultural economies.

Although it is common to identify the Industrial Revolution with New England's factories and the North's cities, that revolution transformed the rural South, too. Cotton could not have become king without the demand created by textile factories or without the ability to "gin" the seeds out of cotton by Eli Whitney's invention. Nor could cotton production flourish without industrial advances in transportation, which allowed raw materials to be shipped worldwide. As for democratic change, the suffrage was extended in Britain by the Reform Bill of 1832, and popular uprisings spread across Europe in 1830 and 1848. In the United States, white southerners and northerners participated in the democratic reforms of the 1820s and 1830s.

The Industrial Revolution and democratic revolution thus transformed the South as well as the North, though in different ways. Increasingly, slavery became the focus of disputes between the two sections. The Industrial Revolution's demand for cotton increased the demand for slave labor and the profits to be gained from it. Yet the spread of democratic ideology worldwide increased pressure to abolish slavery. France and Britain had already done so. In eastern Europe the near–slavery of feudal serfdom was being eliminated as well: in 1848 within the Hapsburg Empire; in 1861 in Russia; in 1864 in Romania.

By the mid–1840s the contradictory pressures of the Industrial Revolution and democratic revolution were beginning to sharpen, as the United States embarked on a new program of westward expansion that thrust the slavery issue into the center of politics. Americans were forced to debate how much of the newly won territory should be open to slavery; and in doing so, some citizens began to question whether the Union could permanently endure, half slave and half free.

CHAPTER SUMMARY

The Old South was a complex, biracial society that increasingly diverged from the rest of the United States in the years before 1860.

- Southerners placed heavy emphasis on agriculture and upheld the superiority of the rural way of life. Few cities and towns developed.
- Southern commercial agriculture produced staple crops for sale in northern and European markets: tobacco, sugar, rice, and, above all, cotton.
- As southern agriculture expanded into the fresh lands of the Deep South, the slave population moved steadily westward and southward.
- Slavery played a major role in shaping the class structure of the Old South.
- Ownership of slaves brought privilege and status, and the largest slaveowners were extraordinarily wealthy.
- Planters on the older eastern seaboard enjoyed a more refined lifestyle than did those on the new cotton frontier.
- Most slaveowners owned only a few slaves, and the majority of southern whites were non–slaveowning yeoman farmers. Slavery hurt non–slaveholding whites economically, but class tensions were muted in the Old South because of racial fears.
- The institution of slavery was both a labor system and a social system, regulating relations between the races.
- Slaves resisted bondage in many ways, ranging from the subtle to the overt. Slave revolts, however, were rare.
- Slaves developed their own culture, in which the family, religion, and songs played key roles in helping them cope with the pressures of bondage.
- As slavery increasingly came under attack, white southerners rallied to protect their peculiar institution. They developed a set of arguments defending slavery as a positive good.
- Many Americans, in both the North and the South, shared the same values: personal independence, social egalitarianism, evangelical Protestantism. But beginning in the mid–1840s with renewed westward expansion, the slavery issue increased sectional tensions.

Additional Reading

The reports of Frederick Law Olmsted, who traveled through the South in the 1850s, make a fascinating jumping-off point for a first look at the region. Much of Olmsted's material is conveniently collected in Lawrence Powell, ed., *The Cotton Kingdom* (1984). A contrasting approach to traveling about is to stay at one plantation, as Erskine Clarke does in his brilliant *Dwelling Place: A Plantation Epic* (2005).

Frank Owsley's *Plain Folk of the Old South* (1949), about southern yeoman farmers, is still useful and can be supplemented by Samuel C. Hyde Jr., ed., *Plain Folk of the South Revisited* (1997). The lives of upper-class southern white women and their servants are analyzed in Elizabeth Fox-Genovese, *Within the Plantation Household* (1988); whereas Victoria E. Bynum, *Unruly Women* (1992), deals with white and black women of lower status.

The best exploration of slavery as a labor system remains Kenneth M. Stampp, *The Peculiar Institution* (1956); but the most perceptive treatment of slave culture is Eugene D. Genovese, *Roll, Jordan, Roll* (1974). John Hope Franklin and Loren Schweninger, *Runaway Slaves* (1999), detail an important aspect of slave resistance. Walter Johnson, *Soul by Soul: Life Inside the Antebellum Slave Market* (1999), provides a concrete and chilling view of the trade that helped sustain the "peculiar institution." Ira Berlin, *Slaves Without Masters* (1974), is an excellent account of free black southerners. As for the political and ideological aspects of slavery, consult Drew Faust, *A Sacred Circle* (1977); and William J. Cooper Jr., *The Politics of Slavery* (1978).

Significant Events

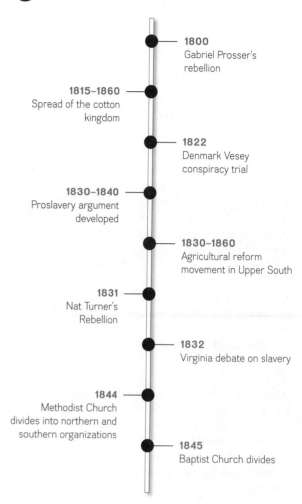

1800
Gabriel Prosser's rebellion

1815–1860
Spread of the cotton kingdom

1822
Denmark Vesey conspiracy trial

1830–1840
Proslavery argument developed

1830–1860
Agricultural reform movement in Upper South

1831
Nat Turner's Rebellion

1832
Virginia debate on slavery

1844
Methodist Church divides into northern and southern organizations

1845
Baptist Church divides

14 Western Expansion and the Rise of the Slavery Issue
1820–1850

The Hidatsa Indians retreated to these well-insulated earth lodges in the forested and more-sheltered river bottoms to escape the fierce winter storms of the Great Plains. The Hidatsa survived on stores of dried beans, corn, squash, and meat. Swiss artist Karl Bodmer painted this scene after a visit in 1833–1834.

>> An American Story

STRANGERS ON THE GREAT PLAINS

At first the Crows, Arapahos, and other Indians of the Great Plains paid little attention to the new people moving out from the forests far to the east. For as long as they could remember these peoples had called the plains their own. But the new arrivals were not to be taken lightly. Armed with superior weapons and bringing with them a great many women and children, they seemed to have an unlimited appetite for land. They attacked the villages of the Plains Indians, massacred women and children, and forced defeated tribes to live on reservations.

The invaders who established this dominance were *not* the strange "white men," who also came from the forest. During the 1830s and early 1840s whites were still few in number. The more dangerous people—the ones who truly worried the Plains tribes—were the Sioux.

Westward expansion is usually told as a one-dimensional tale, centering on the wagon trains pressing on toward the Pacific. But frontiers are the transition zones between different cultures or environments, and during the nineteenth century those in the West were constantly shifting. Frontiers moved not only east to west, as with the European and the Sioux migrations, but also south to north, as Spanish culture diffused, and west to east, as Asian immigrants came to California.

Furthermore, frontiers marked not only human but also animal boundaries. Horses, cattle, and pigs—species imported from Europe—moved across the continent, often in advance of European settlers. These animals transformed the way Indian peoples lived. Frontiers could also be technological, as in the case of trade goods and firearms. Moreover, disease moved across the continent with disastrous consequences for natives who had not acquired immunity to European microorganisms.

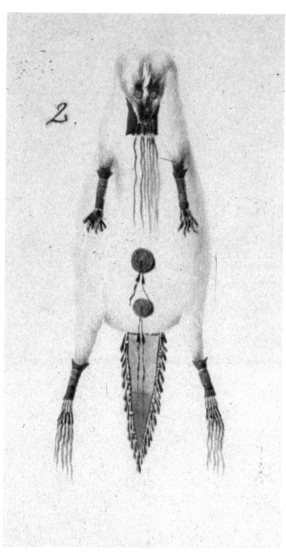

⋏ Pouch made from a white skunk skin. The skin, as well as the decorative beads, were obtained from a white trapper. The pouch probably held tobacco or other trade items.

Three frontiers revolutionized the lives of the Sioux: those of the horse, the gun, and disease. The horse frontier spread ahead of European settlement from the southwest, where horses had first been imported by the Spanish. The Spanish, however—unlike English and French traders—generally refused to sell firearms to Indians, so the gun frontier moved in the opposite direction, from northeast to southwest. The two waves met and crossed along the upper Missouri during the first half of the eighteenth century. For the tribes

that possessed them, horses provided greater mobility, both for hunting bison and for fighting. Guns, too, conferred obvious advantages, and the arrival of these new elements inaugurated an extremely unsettled era for Plains Indian cultures.

The Sioux first moved onto the Minnesota prairie during the early 1700s to hunt beaver, whose pelts could be exchanged with European traders for manufactured goods. Having obtained guns in exchange for furs, the Sioux drove the Omahas, Otos, Cheyennes, and Missouris (who had not yet acquired guns) south and west. But by the 1770s their advantage in firepower had disappeared, and any further advance was blocked by powerful tribes such as the Mandans and Arikaras. These peoples were primarily horticultural, raising corn, beans, and squash and living in well-fortified towns. They also owned more horses than the Sioux; thus it was easier for them to resist attacks.

But the third frontier, disease, threw the balance of power toward the Sioux after 1779. That year, a continental smallpox pandemic struck the plains via New Mexico. The horticultural tribes were hit especially hard because they lived in densely populated villages, where the epidemic spread more easily. By the time Lewis and Clark came through in 1804, the Sioux firmly controlled the upper Missouri as far as the Yellowstone River. From an estimated 5,000 in 1804 they grew

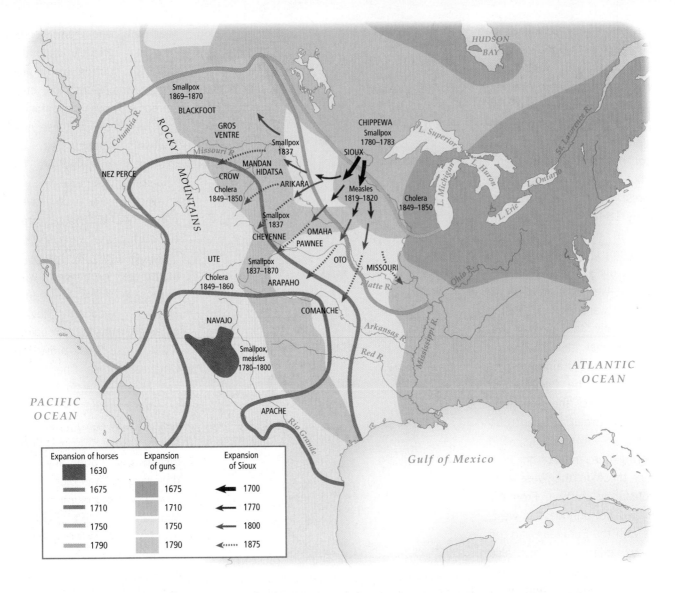

MAP 14.1: SIOUX EXPANSION AND THE HORSE AND GUN FRONTIERS

In 1710 the horse and gun frontiers had not yet crossed, but by 1750 the two waves began to overlap. The Sioux pushed west during the early eighteenth century thanks in part to firearms; they were checked from further expansion until the 1770s, when smallpox epidemics again turned the balance in their favor.

Why did smallpox prove more dangerous to Mandans, Arikaras, and Hidatsas than to Sioux communities?

to 25,000 in the 1850s. Indeed, the Sioux became the largest nation on the plains and was the only nation whose high birthrate approximated that of whites.

These shifting frontiers of animals, disease, firearms, and trade goods disrupted the political and cultural life of the Great Plains. And as white Americans moved westward, their own frontier lines produced similar disruptions, not only

between white settlers and Indians but also between Anglo-American and Hispanic cultures. The relations between Indian peoples and Mexico were also in flux, as many tribes across the plains began attacking Mexico during the 1830s. There would even be a frontier moving west to east, as thousands of Chinese were drawn, along with other immigrants, to gold fields discovered after 1848. Ironically,

perhaps the greatest instability created by the moving frontiers occurred within the United States. As the political system incorporated the new territories, the North and South fiercely debated whether they should become slave or free. Just as the Sioux's cultural identity was brought into question by moving frontiers, so, too, was the identity of the American Republic. <<

What's to Come

MANIFEST (AND NOT SO MANIFEST) DESTINY

"Make way . . . for the young American Buffalo—he has not yet got land enough," roared one U.S. politician in 1844. In the space of a few years, the United States acquired Texas, California, the lower half of the Oregon Territory, and the lands between the Rockies and California: nearly 1.5 million square miles in all. John L. O'Sullivan, a prominent Democratic editor in New York, struck a responsive chord when he declared that it had become the United States' "**manifest destiny**" to overspread the continent allotted by Providence for the free development of our yearly multiplying millions." The cry of Manifest Destiny soon echoed in other editorial pages and in the halls of Congress.

The Roots of the Doctrine >>

Many Americans had long believed that their country had a special, even divine, mission, which could be traced back to the Puritans' attempt to build a "city on a hill." Manifest Destiny also contained a political component, inherited from the ideology of the Revolution. In the mid–nineteenth century Americans spoke of extending democracy, with widespread suffrage among white males, no king or aristocracy, and no established church, "over the whole North American continent."

Americans believed that their social and economic system, too, should spread around the globe. They pointed to its broad ownership of land, individualism, and free play of economic opportunity as superior features of American life. More important, Manifest Destiny was about power, especially economic power. American business interests recognized the value of the fine harbors along the Pacific coast, which promised a lucrative trade with Asia, and they hoped to make those harbors American.

> **Manifest Destiny** mid-nineteenth-century political doctrine that argued the benefits of democracy would spread along with territorial expansion. Yet Manifest Destiny was also racist in its assumption of the inferiority of other peoples and cultures; and it encompassed a purely economic desire to expand the nation's commerce and power.

With the Star of Empire blazing from her forehead, the "Spirit of Progress" dominates this painting by John Gast. Indians and wild animals retreat in the face of Anglo-American settlers and farmers, railroads and other forms of transportation, telegraph lines, schools symbolized by a book, and, in the distance, cities. In reality, the movement of the frontier was hardly one-dimensional, as Hispanic, Indian, Asian, and Anglo-American cultures clashed over a destiny that was not so manifest as Gast thought.

⚡ Throughout the Spanish and Mexican periods, town life in California, New Mexico, and Texas revolved around central plazas and their churches. One of the first structures built in Santa Fe, the Mission Church of San Miguel (est. ca. 1610) is today the oldest church building in the present-day United States.

Mexican race "must amalgamate and be lost, in the superior vigor of the Anglo–Saxon race," proclaimed O'Sullivan's *Democratic Review*, "or they must utterly perish."

Before 1845 most Americans assumed that expansion would be achieved without international war. American settlement would expand westward, and when the time was right, neighboring provinces, like ripe fruit, would fall naturally into American hands: Texas, New Mexico, Oregon, and California. With time, American expansionists became less willing to wait patiently for the fruit to fall.

The Mexican Borderlands >> The heart

of Spain's American empire was Mexico City, where spacious boulevards spread out through the center of the city and the University of Mexico, the oldest university in North America, had been accepting students since 1553, a full 85 years earlier than Harvard. From the Mexican point of view, the frontier was 1,000 miles to the north, a four–week journey to Texas, another two weeks to New Mexico, and three months by land and sea to the missions of California. Being isolated, these Mexican provinces developed with little metropolitan supervision.

California's settlements were anchored by four coastal **presidios,** or forts, at San Diego, Santa Barbara, Monterey, and San Francisco. Between them lay 21 Catholic missions run by a handful of Franciscans (only 36 in 1821). The missions controlled enormous tracts of land on which grazed gigantic herds of cattle, sheep, and horses. These animals and irrigated fields were tended by about 20,000 Indians, who in certain ways lived and worked like slaves.

presidio Spanish military garrison.

When Mexico won its independence from Spain in 1821, little changed in California at first. But in 1833 the Mexican Congress stripped the Catholic Church of its vast landholdings. These lands were turned over to Mexican cattle ranchers, usually in massive grants of 50,000 acres or more. The new *rancheros* ruled their estates much as great planters of the Old South. Labor was provided by Indians, who again were forced to work for little more than room and board. Indeed, the mortality rate of Indian workers was twice that of southern slaves and four times that of nonnative Californians. By the 1830s the Mexican population of California stood at approximately 4,000. During the 1820s and 1830s Yankee traders set up shop in California in order to buy cattle hides for the growing shoe industry at Lynn and elsewhere. Still, in 1845 the American population amounted to only 700.

Finally, underlying the doctrine of Manifest Destiny was widespread racism. The same belief in racial superiority that had been used to justify Indian removal under Jackson, to uphold slavery in the South, and to excuse segregation in the North also proved useful in defending expansion westward. The United States had a duty to regenerate the backward peoples of America, declared politicians and propagandists. Their reference was not so much to Indians: the forced expulsion of assimilated Cherokees during Indian removal made clear what most American policy makers thought about Indian "regeneration." By the 1840s it was rather the Mexicans who had caught the attention of Manifest Destiny's prophets of progress. The

Spanish settlement of New Mexico was denser than that of California: the province had about 44,000 Spanish–speaking inhabitants in 1827. But as in California, great landowning families dominated, grazing large herds of sheep along the upper Rio Grande valley between El Paso and Taos. A few individuals controlled most of the wealth, while their workers eked out meager livings. Spain had long outlawed any commerce with Americans, but that all changed with independence. Caravans from the United States began making the long journey along the Santa Fe Trail starting in 1821. Although this trade flourished over the next two decades, developments in the third Mexican borderland, neighboring Texas, would all but wreck relations between Mexico and the United States.

The Texas Rebellion >> At first the new government in Mexico encouraged American emigration

to Texas, where only about 3,000 Mexicans, mostly ranchers, lived. In 1821 Moses Austin, an American, received a grant from the Spanish government to establish a colony. After his death his son Stephen took over the project, laying out the little town of San Felipe de Austin along the Brazos River and offering large grants of land at almost no cost. By 1824 the colony's population exceeded 2,000. Stephen Austin was only the first of a new wave of American land agents, or *empresarios*, who obtained permission from Mexican authorities to settle families in Texas. Ninety percent of the new arrivals came from the South. Many, intending to grow cotton, brought slaves.

Tensions between Mexicans and American immigrants grew with the Texas economy. Most settlers from the States were Protestant. Although the Mexican government passed no laws mandating Catholicism, it did officially bar Protestant churches. In

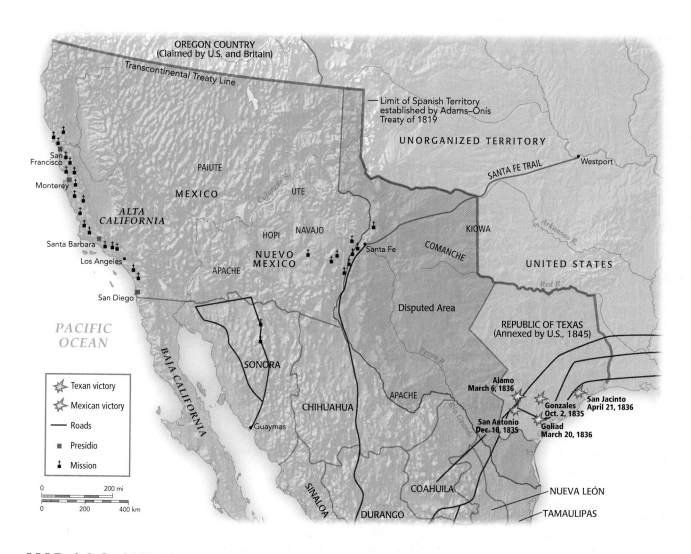

MAP 14.2: MEXICAN BORDERLANDS, 1821–1845

What factors explain the concentration of U.S. immigrants in east Texas?

1829 Mexico abolished slavery, then looked the other way when Texas slaveholders evaded the law. In the early 1830s the Mexican government began to have second thoughts about American settlement and passed laws prohibiting any new immigration. Austin likened the new anti–immigration laws to "trying to stop the Mississippi with a dam of straw." It was an apt metaphor: between 1830 and 1833, illegal American immigrants and their slaves flooded into Mexican Texas, nearly doubling its colonial population.

Admitting that the new regulations had served only to inflame Texans, Mexico repealed them in 1833. But by then colonial ill–will had soared. By mid–decade the American white population of 40,000 was nearly 10 times the number of **Tejanos.** Once again Mexico's government talked of abolishing slavery in Texas. Even more disturbing to the American newcomers, in 1834 President Antonio López de Santa Anna and his allies in the Mexican Congress passed legislation that took power away from the states and concentrated it in Mexico City. Texans had been struggling for more autonomy, not less. When Santa Anna brutally suppressed an uprising against the central government in the state of Zacatecas, Texans grew more nervous. Finally, when conflicts over taxes led Santa Anna to march soldiers north and enforce his new regime, a ragtag Texas army drove back the advance party and then captured Mexican troops in nearby San Antonio. A full–scale rebellion was under way.

Tejano Texan of Hispanic descent.

The Texas Republic >> As Santa Anna massed his forces, a provisional government on March 2, 1836, proclaimed Texan independence. The document was signed by a number of prominent Tejanos, Mexican residents of Texas. The constitution of the new Republic of Texas borrowed heavily from the U.S. Constitution, except that it explicitly prohibited the new Texas Congress from interfering with slavery. Meanwhile, Santa Anna's troops overran a Texan garrison at an old mission in San Antonio, known as the Alamo, and killed all its 187 defenders—including the famous backwoodsman and U.S. congressman, Davy Crockett. The Mexicans, however, paid dearly for the victory, losing more than 1,500 men. The massacre of another force at Goliad after it surrendered further inflamed American resistance.

But anger was one thing; organized resistance another. The commander of the Texas forces was Sam Houston, a former governor of Tennessee. Houston's intellectual ability and talent as a stump speaker thrust him to the forefront of the Texas independence movement. Houston knew his army needed seasoning, so he retreated steadily eastward, buying time in order to forge a disciplined fighting force. By late April he was ready. Reinforced by eager volunteers from the United States, Houston's men surprised the Mexican army camped along the San Jacinto River. Shouting "Remember the Alamo!" they took only 15 minutes to overwhelm the Mexicans (who had been enjoying an afternoon siesta) and capture Santa Anna.

Threatened with execution, the Mexican commander signed treaties recognizing Texan independence and ordering his remaining troops south of the Rio Grande. Texans would later claim that Santa Anna thereby acknowledged the Rio Grande as Texas's southern boundary. The Mexican Congress repudiated the agreement, especially the claim to the Rio Grande. Houston assumed office in October 1836 as president of the new republic, determined to bring Texas into the American Union as quickly as possible.

Houston assumed that the United States would quickly annex such a vast and inviting territory. But Andrew Jackson worried that any such move would revive sectional tensions and hurt Martin Van Buren's chances in the 1836 presidential election. Only on his last day in office did he extend formal diplomatic recognition to the Texas Republic. Van Buren, distracted by the economic panic that broke out shortly after he entered office, took no action during his term.

Rebuffed, the Texans went their own way. In the 10 years following independence, the Lone Star Republic attracted more than 100,000 immigrants by offering free land to settlers. Mexico refused to recognize Texan independence, and the vast majority of its citizens still wished to join the United States, where most of them had been born. There matters stood when the Whigs and William Henry Harrison won the presidency in 1840.

✓ REVIEW

How did Mexico lose Texas?

THE TREK WEST

As thousands of white Americans were moving into Texas, and increasingly bringing slaves with them, a much smaller trickle headed toward the Oregon country. Since 1818 the United States and Great Britain had occupied that territory jointly, as far north as latitude 54°4′. Although white settlement remained sparse, by 1836 American settlers outnumbered the British in the Willamette valley.

Pushed by the Panic of 1837 and six years of depression and pulled by tales of Oregon's lush, fertile valleys and the healthy, frost–free climate along Cali–fornia's Sacramento River, many American farmers struck out for the West Coast. Missouri was "cleaned" out of money, worried farmer Daniel Waldo, and his wife was even more adamant about heading west: "If you want to stay here another summer and shake your liver out with the fever and ague, you can do it," she announced to her husband, "but in the spring I am going to take the children and go to Oregon, Indians or no Indians." The wagon trains began rolling west.

The Overland Trail >> Only a few hundred emigrants reached the West in 1841 and 1842, but by 1844 thousands were following the Overland Trail across the mountains to Oregon. The migration was primarily a family enterprise, and many couples had only recently married. Most adults were between 20 and 50, since the hard journey discouraged the elderly.

Furthermore, a family of four needed about $600 to outfit their journey, an amount that excluded the poor.

Caravans of 20 to 30 wagons were common the first few years, but after 1845 parties traveled in smaller trains of 8 to 10 wagons. Large parties used up the grass quickly, disagreements were more likely, and breakdowns were more frequent. The trip lasted about 6 months.

Women on the Overland Trail >> The jour–ney west often placed a special strain on women. Few wives were as eager as Dan Waldo's to undertake the move. "Poor Ma said only this morning, 'Oh I wish we never had started,'" one daughter reported, "and she looks so sorrowful and dejected." In one study of Oregon–bound parties, three–fourths of the women did not want to head west.

At first, parties divided work by gender, as had been done back home. Women cooked, washed, sewed,

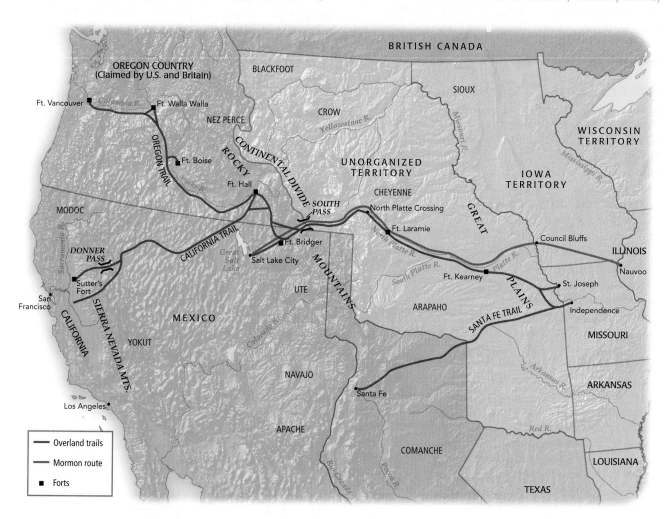

MAP 14.3: THE OVERLAND TRAIL

Beginning at several different points, the Overland Trail followed the Platte and Sweetwater Rivers across the plains to South Pass, where it crossed the Continental Divide. The trail split near Fort Hall. Between 1840 and 1860 more than a quarter of a million emigrants made the trek. *What would have been the most important considerations when planning an overland route across the West?*

and took care of the children, while men drove the wagons, cared for the stock, stood guard, and did the heavy labor. Necessity placed new demands on women, however, and eventually altered their roles. Within a few weeks, they found themselves helping to repair wagons and construct bridges. When men became exhausted, sick, or injured, women stood guard and drove the oxen. The change in work assignments proceeded only in one direction, however, for few men undertook "women's work."

As women strove to maintain a semblance of home on the trail, many experienced a profound sense of loss. Trains often worked or traveled on the Sabbath, which had been ladies' day back home and an emblem of women's moral authority. Women also felt the lack of close companions to whom they could turn for comfort. One woman, whose husband separated their wagon from the train after a dispute, sadly watched the other wagons pull away: "I felt that indeed I had left all my friends to journey over the dreaded plains without one female acquaintance even for a companion—of course I wept and grieved about it but to no purpose."

Indians and the Trail Experience >> The
peoples whose lands were crossed by white wagon trains reacted in a number of ways to the westward tide. The Sioux, who had long traded with whites, regularly visited overlanders to swap for blankets, clothes, cows, rifles, and knives. But the European migrants took a heavy toll on the Plains Indians' way of life: emigrant parties scared off game and reduced buffalo herds, overgrazed the grass, and depleted the supply of wood. Having petitioned unsuccessfully in 1846 for government compensation, some Sioux decided to demand payment from the wagon trains crossing their lands. Whether parties paid or not depended on the relative strength of the two groups, but whites complained bitterly of what seemed to them outright robbery.

Their fears aroused by sensational stories, overland parties were wary of Indians, but this menace was greatly exaggerated, especially on the plains. Few wagon trains were attacked by Indians, and less than 4 percent of deaths on the trail were caused by Native Americans. In truth, emigrants more often killed Indians. For overlanders the most aggravating problem posed by native peoples was theft of stock. Many parties received valuable assistance from Indians, who acted as guides, directed them to grass and water, and transported animals and wagons across rivers.

 REVIEW

What motivated Americans to migrate on overland trails, and how did the experiences of women and men differ on the journey?

THE POLITICAL ORIGINS OF EXPANSION

President William Henry Harrison came into office determined to undo some of Jackson's and Van Buren's key economic policies and eliminate the spoils system in government service. But the old Indian fighter had run out of time. He came down with pneumonia and died only one month after his inauguration.

For the first time in the nation's history, a vice president succeeded to the nation's highest office on the death of the president. John Tyler of Virginia had once been a Democrat and a strong supporter of states' rights. But after he quarreled with Jackson during the nullification controversy (see pages 216 and 217), Democrats refused to have anything to do with him, so Tyler joined the Whigs, who nominated him for vice president in 1840 in order to balance the ticket sectionally. During the rollicking campaign that followed, the Whigs sang all too accurately: "And we'll vote for Tyler, therefore, / Without a why or wherefore." Indeed, once in office, Tyler repeatedly vetoed bills passed by Henry Clay and his own party. Disgusted, the Whigs in Congress formally expelled their president from the party.

Tyler's Texas Ploy >> Although shunned by
most Whigs and Democrats, Tyler still believed that he might win another four years in the White House if only he latched onto the right popular issue. That issue, he came to believe, was the annexation of Texas. In April 1844 the president sent to the Senate for ratification a treaty he had secretly negotiated to bring Texas into the Union. He also decided to run for president as an independent.

Meanwhile, the frontrunners for the Whig and Democratic presidential nominations were Clay and Van Buren. Although rivals, they were both moderates who feared that the slavery issue would be injected into the campaign if Texas was annexed as a slave state. Apparently by prearrangement, both men issued letters opposing annexation on the grounds that it threatened the Union and would provoke war with Mexico.

As expected, the Whigs unanimously nominated Clay on a platform that ignored the expansion issue entirely. But Van Buren's Democratic opponents viewed the former president as an ineffective leader who had stumbled through a depression and in 1840 gone down in ignominious defeat. They persuaded the convention to adopt a rule requiring a two-thirds vote to nominate a candidate. That blocked Van Buren's nomination. On the ninth ballot the delegates finally turned to James K.

Polk of Tennessee, who favored annexation, as well as the "reoccupation" of Oregon, all the way to its north-ernmost boundary at 54°40′.

Angered by the convention's outcome, Van Buren's supporters in the Senate joined the Whigs in decisively defeating Tyler's treaty of annexation. Tyler eventually withdrew from the race, but the Texas issue would not go away. Seeking to shore up his support in the South, Clay announced that he would be glad to see Texas annexed if it would not lead to war. And in the North, a few antislavery Whigs turned to James G. Birney, running on the Liberty Party ticket.

In the end, Polk squeaked through by 38,000 votes out of nearly 3 million cast. If just half of Birney's 15,000 ballots in New York had gone to Clay, he would have carried the state and been narrowly elected president. Indignant Whigs charged that by refusing to support Clay, political abolitionists had made the annexation of Texas, and hence the addition of slave territory to the Union, inevitable. And indeed, in the new atmosphere following Polk's victory, Congress approved a joint resolution annexing Texas. On March 3, 1845, his last day in office, Tyler invited Texas to enter the Union.

To the Pacific >> Humorless, calculating, and often deceitful, President Polk pursued his objectives with dogged determination. Embracing a continental vision of the United States, he not only endorsed Tyler's offer of annexation but looked beyond, hoping to gain the three best harbors on the Pacific: Puget Sound, San Francisco, and San Diego. That meant wresting Oregon from Britain and California from Mexico.

Claiming that American title to all of Oregon was "clear and unquestionable," Polk convinced Congress to terminate the joint occupation. His blustering, which was intended to put pressure on Great Britain, gained weight by the fact that American settlers in Oregon outnumbered the British 5,000 to 750. However, Polk hardly wanted war with a nation as powerful as Great Britain. So when the British offered, in June 1846, to divide the Oregon Territory along the 49th parallel, he readily agreed (see Map 14.6). The arrangement gave the United States Puget Sound, which had been the president's objective all along.

Provoking a War >> The Oregon settlement left Polk free to deal with Mexico. In 1845 Congress admitted Texas

to the Union as a slave state, but Mexico had never formally recognized Texas's independence. Mexico insisted, moreover, that Texas's southern boundary was the Nueces River, not the Rio Grande, 130 miles to the south, as claimed by Texas. In reality Texas had never controlled the disputed region; the Nueces had always been Texas's boundary when it was a Mexican province; and if taken literally, the Rio Grande border incorporated most of New Mexico, including Santa Fe, Albuquerque, Taos, and other major towns. Few Texans had ever even been to these places. Indeed, the one time Texas tried to exert authority in the region, New Mexicans had to ride out onto the plains to save the lost and starving expedition. Nonetheless, Polk was already looking toward the Pacific and he supported the Rio Grande boundary.

As soon as Texas entered the Union, Mexico broke off diplomatic relations with the United States, and Polk sent American troops under General Zachary Taylor into the newly acquired state. At the same time, knowing that the unstable Mexican government desperately needed money, he attempted to buy territory to the Pacific. Sending John Slidell of Louisiana to Mexico as his special minister, Polk was prepared

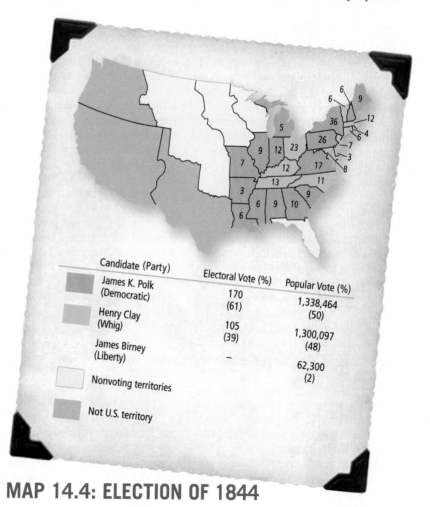

Candidate (Party)	Electoral Vote (%)	Popular Vote (%)
James K. Polk (Democratic)	170 (61)	1,338,464 (50)
Henry Clay (Whig)	105 (39)	1,300,097 (48)
James Birney (Liberty)	–	62,300 (2)
Nonvoting territories		
Not U.S. territory		

MAP 14.4: ELECTION OF 1844

IN WHAT COUNTRY DID THE U.S.-MEXICAN WAR BEGIN?

When President Polk insisted that Mexico had "shed American blood upon American soil," his critics demanded proof. Everyone acknowledged that the initial clash occurred just north of the Rio Grande. But did the boundary of Texas (and hence the boundary of the United States) extend to the Rio Grande, as Polk insisted, or only to the Nueces River, as had been internationally recognized before the Texas rebellion? Nearly all Mexicans believed that the fighting happened in Mexico, and some prominent Americans agreed. Among their number was a freshman member of Congress, Abraham Lincoln, whose "spot resolutions" took Polk to task. The dispute was motivated partly by politics: Lincoln, a Whig, happily criticized the Democratic Polk. Still, Lincoln's resolutions reflected genuine doubts about the war's legitimacy.

DOCUMENT 1
The War Began in the United States: President James K. Polk

The existing state of the relations between the United States and Mexico renders it proper that I should bring the subject to the consideration of Congress. . . . An envoy of the United States repaired to Mexico with full powers to adjust every existing difference. But though present on Mexican soil by agreement between the two Governments, invested with full powers, and bearing evidence of the most friendly dispositions, his mission has been unavailing. The Mexican Government not only refused to receive him or listen to his propositions, but after a long-continued series of menaces have at last invaded our territory and shed the blood of our fellow-citizens on our own soil. . . . In my message at the commencement of the present session I informed you that upon the earnest appeal both of the Congress and convention of Texas I had ordered an efficient military force to take a position "between the Nueces and Del Norte." This had become necessary to meet a threatened invasion of Texas by the Mexican forces, for which extensive military

preparations had been made. The invasion was threatened solely because Texas had determined, in accordance with a solemn resolution of the Congress of the United States, to annex herself to our Union, and under these circumstances it was plainly our duty to extend our protection over her citizens and soil. . . . Meantime Texas, by the final act of our Congress, had become an integral part of our Union. The Congress of Texas, by its act of December 19, 1836, had declared the Rio del Norte to be the boundary of that Republic. Its jurisdiction had been extended and exercised beyond the Nueces. The country between that river and the Del Norte had been represented in the Congress and in the convention of Texas, had thus taken part in the act of annexation itself, and is now included within one of our Congressional districts. Our own Congress had, moreover, with great unanimity, by the act approved December 31, 1845, recognized the country beyond the Nueces as a part of our territory by including it within our own revenue system, and a revenue

officer to reside within that district had been appointed by and with the advice and consent of the Senate. It became, therefore, of urgent necessity to provide for the defense of that portion of our country. . . . But no open act of hostility was committed until the 24th of April. On that day General [Mariano] Arista, who had succeeded to the command of the Mexican forces, communicated to General Taylor that "he considered hostilities commenced and should prosecute them." A party of dragoons of 63 men and officers were on the same day dispatched from the American camp up the Rio del Norte, on its left bank, to ascertain whether the Mexican troops had crossed or were preparing to cross the river, "became engaged with a large body of these troops, and after a short affair, in which some 16 were killed and wounded, appear to have been surrounded and compelled to surrender."

Source: Message to Congress, Washington, May 11, 1846. In James D. Richardson, ed., *A Compilation of the Messages and Papers of the Presidents,* Volume 4 (New York: Bureau of National Literature and Art, 1908), pp. 437–443.

DOCUMENT 2
The "Spot" Was beyond the U.S. Borders: Representative Abraham Lincoln

Whereas the President of the United States, in his message of May 11, 1846, has declared that "the Mexican Government not only refused to receive him, [the envoy of the United States,] or listen to his propositions, but, after a long-continued series of menaces, has at last

invaded *our territory* and shed the blood of our fellow-citizens on our *own soil:*"
　And again, in his message of December 8, 1846, that "we had ample cause of war against Mexico long before the breaking out of hostilities; but even then we forbore to take redress into our own hands

until Mexico herself became the aggressor, by invading *our soil* in hostile array, and shedding the blood of our citizens:"
　And yet again, in his message of December 7, 1847, that "the Mexican Government refused even to hear the terms of adjustment which he [our

minister of peace] was authorized to propose, and finally, under wholly unjustifiable pretexts, involved the two countries in war, by invading the territory of the State of Texas, striking the first blow, and shedding the blood of our citizens on *our own soil.*" And whereas this House is desirous to obtain a full knowledge of all the facts which go to establish whether the particular spot on which the blood of our citizens was so shed was or was not at that time *our own soil:* Therefore, *Resolved By the House of Representatives,* That the President of the United States be respectfully requested to inform this House—

1st. Whether the spot on which the blood of our citizens was shed, as in his messages declared, was or was not within the territory of Spain, at least after the treaty of 1819, until the Mexican revolution.

2d. Whether that spot is or is not within the territory which was wrested from Spain by the revolutionary Government of Mexico.

3d. Whether that spot is or is not within a settlement of people, which settlement has existed ever since long before the Texas revolution, and until its inhabitants fled before the approach of the United States army.

4th. Whether that settlement is or is not isolated from any and all other settlements by the Gulf and the Rio Grande on the south and west, and by wide uninhabited regions on the north and east.

5th. Whether the people of that settlement, or a majority of them, or any of them, have ever submitted themselves to the government or laws of Texas or the United States, by consent or compulsion, either by accepting office, or voting at elections, or paying tax, or serving on juries, or having process served upon them, or in any other way.

6th. Whether the people of that settlement did or did not flee from the approach of the United States army, leaving unprotected their homes and their growing crops, *before* the blood was shed, as in the messages stated; and whether the first blood, so shed, was or was not shed within the enclosure of one of the people who had thus fled from it.

7th. Whether our *citizens,* whose blood was shed, as in his message declared, were or were not, at that time, armed officers and soldiers, sent into that settlement by the military order of the President, through the Secretary of War.

8th. Whether the military force of the United States was or was not sent into that settlement after General Taylor had more than once intimated to the War Department that, in his opinion, no such movement was necessary to the defence or protection of Texas.

Resolutions introduced into the House of Representatives Dec. 22, 1847.

Source: http://teachingamericanhistory.org/library/index.asp?document=2463.

THINKING CRITICALLY

How does Polk justify Taylor's presence on the Rio Grande? How does Lincoln critique Taylor's presence on the Rio Grande? Do they disagree over facts, or over which facts matter? What more information would you need to decide who makes the more persuasive case?

to offer up to $32 million in return for clear title to the Rio Grande boundary, the remaining part of New Mexico, and California. But the Mexican public overwhelmingly opposed ceding any more territory to the land–hungry "Yankees," and the government refused to receive the proposal. "Depend upon it," reported Slidell, as he departed from Mexico in March 1846, "we can never get along well with them, until we have given them a good drubbing."

Blocked on the diplomatic front, Polk ordered Taylor, who had already crossed the Nueces with 4,000 troops, to proceed south to the Rio Grande. From the Mexican standpoint, the Americans had invaded their country and occupied their territory. For his part Polk hoped that, since he could not buy the territory he wanted, at least Taylor's position on the Rio Grande would provoke the Mexican army into starting a war.

By May 9 Polk and his cabinet had lost patience with the plan and decided to submit a war message to Congress without Mexican provocation. But on that day word arrived that two weeks earlier Mexican forces had crossed the Rio Grande and attacked some of Taylor's troops, killing 11 Americans. The president quickly rewrote his war message, placing the entire blame for the war on Mexico. "Mexico has passed the boundary of the United States, has invaded our territory, and shed American blood upon American soil," he told Congress on May 11. "War exists, and notwithstanding all our efforts to avoid it, exists by the act of Mexico herself." The administration sent a bill to Congress calling for volunteers and requesting money to supply American troops.

Indians and Mexicans
>> In battle, Mexican forces often outnumbered their American enemies. Even so, Mexico suffered from critical disadvantages in the U.S.–Mexican War. Chronic instability in its central government left the nation divided against itself in its moment of crisis. An empty national treasury fueled this instability and made it difficult to mobilize an effective response to the American invasion. Mexico was also at a disadvantage in terms of military technology. While Mexican forces relied on bulky, fixed cannons, the U.S. Army employed new light artillery that could be repositioned quickly as battles progressed. Light artillery tipped the balance in several crucial engagements.

Finally, much of Mexico had to fight two wars at once. While Mexico enjoyed formal diplomatic title to most of the present–day American West, Indians still controlled the vast majority of that territory, and

Mexico had seen its relations with these Indians collapse in the 15 years before the U.S. invasion. During the late eighteenth century Comanches, Navajos, Utes, and several different tribes of Apaches had made peace with Spanish authorities, ending decades of destructive war. Spaniards provided Indian leaders with gifts, guaranteed fair trade, and even handed out rations to minimize the animal thefts that could spark conflict.

This expensive and delicate system began to falter once Mexico achieved independence in 1821. Lacking the finances, the political unity, the stability, and the diplomatic resources of Spain, Mexican authorities watched the peace with northern Indians slip away. By the early 1830s native men were traveling hundreds of miles to raid Mexican ranches, haciendas, and towns, killing or capturing the people they found there, and stealing or destroying animals and other property. Whenever they were able, Mexicans did the same things to their Indian enemies. American markets helped drive the increasing violence, as Indian or white traders from the United States eagerly purchased horses and mules stolen from Mexico. These traders supplied Indian raiders with arms and ammunition in return. By the eve of the U.S. invasion of Mexico, the violence encompassed all or parts of nine Mexican states and had claimed thousands of Mexican and Indian lives.

Thus, when American troops invaded northern Mexico, they were literally marching in the footsteps of Navajos, Kiowas, Comanches, and Apaches, traversing territory that had already endured more than a decade of war. As Indian peoples pursued their own political, strategic, and economic goals, they made it far easier for the United States to achieve its objectives. Too few northern Mexicans were willing or able to resist the U.S. conquest—impoverished, divided, and exhausted as they were by ongoing Indian raids.

Opposition to the War

>> The war with Mexico posed a dilemma for Whigs. They were convinced (correctly) that Polk had provoked the conflict in order to acquire more territory from Mexico, and many northern Whigs accused the president of seeking to extend slavery. But they remembered, too, that the Federalist Party had doomed itself to extinction by opposing the War of 1812. Throughout the conflict,

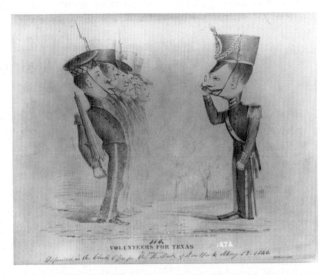

⌃ The U.S.-Mexican War was a divisive issue even at the outset, when this cartoon was published mocking early recruits. Note that one soldier holds a parasol instead of a rifle and that his prissy commander squints through a monocle.

they strenuously attacked the conduct of "Mr. Polk's War." But they could not bring themselves to cut off funding for it.

Prowar sentiment remained strongest in the Old Southwest and most of the Old Northwest. It was much weaker in the East, where antislavery "Conscience Whigs" were prominent. "If I were a Mexican," Senator Thomas Corwin of Ohio affirmed in the Senate, "I would tell you,…'we will greet you with bloody hands and welcome you to hospitable graves.'" With their party deeply divided over the issue of the expansion of slavery, Whigs opposed the acquisition of any territory from Mexico.

Victory and Its Price

>> Even before any word of hostilities arrived in California, a group of impetuous American settlers around Sacramento launched the "Bear Flag Revolt." In June 1846 they proclaimed California an independent republic. While Mexican Californians under former governor Pio Pico organized a determined resistance, by the following January California was safely in American hands.

Meanwhile, Taylor moved south from the Rio Grande and won several battles. At each town conquered or surrendered, he read statements provided in advance by President Polk and the War Department, promising to respect private property and protect the long-suffering residents from Indian attack. Taylor's campaign culminated in a narrow victory over General Antonio López de Santa Anna at Buena Vista in southern Coahuila. Polk had gained the territory he sought to reach the Pacific and wanted an end to the war. But Mexico refused to surrender, so the president ordered an invasion into the heart of the country.

After an American army led by General Winfield Scott captured Mexico City in September 1847, Mexico agreed to terms. The two nations ratified the Treaty of Guadalupe Hidalgo in 1848. The treaty transferred half of Mexico's territory—more than half a million square miles, including Texas—to the United States. In return the United States assumed all the outstanding claims that U.S. citizens had filed against Mexico and gave the Mexicans $15 million.

The war had cost the United States $97 million and 13,000 American lives, mostly as a result of disease. Yet the real cost was even higher. By bringing vast new territories into the Union, the war forced the explosive slavery issue to the center of national politics and threatened to upset the balance of power between North and South. Ralph Waldo Emerson had been prophetic: "The United States will conquer Mexico," he wrote when the war began, "but it will be as the man who swallows the arsenic which brings him down in turn. Mexico will poison us."

The Rise of the Slavery Issue >> From the start, the movement to annex Texas, where slavery flourished, increased suspicions between the North and the South. And President Polk did nothing to ease this problem. Polk was a politician to his bones: constantly maneuvering, promising one thing, doing another, making a pledge, taking it back—using any means to accomplish his ends.

Discontent over his double-dealing finally erupted in August 1846, when Polk requested $2 million from Congress, as he vaguely explained, to "facilitate negotiations" with Mexico. It was widely understood that the money was to be used to bribe the Mexican government

Opinion

Was the U.S.-Mexican War justified?

MAP 14.5: THE U.S.–MEXICAN WAR

How would the climate of the lands conquered by the United States be likely to affect the issue of slavery?

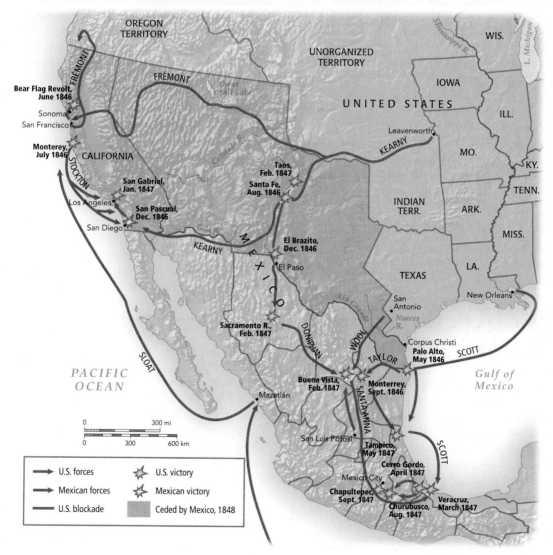

to cede territory to the United States. On August 8, David Wilmot, an obscure Pennsylvania congressman, startled Democratic leaders by introducing an amendment to the bill that barred slavery from any territory acquired from Mexico. The Wilmot Proviso, as the amendment became known, passed the northern-controlled House of Representatives several times, only to be rejected in the Senate, where the South had more power. As such, it revealed mounting sectional tensions.

Wilmot himself was hardly an abolitionist. Indeed, he hoped to keep not only slaves but all black people out of the territories. Denying any "morbid sympathy for the slave," he declared, "I would preserve for white free labor a fair country…where the sons of toil, of my own race and color, can live without the disgrace which association with negro slavery brings upon free labor." The Wilmot Proviso aimed not to destroy slavery in the South but to confine it to states where it already existed. Still, abolitionists had long contended that southern slaveholders—the "Slave Power"—were plotting to extend their sway over the rest of the country. The political maneuverings of slaveholders such as Tyler, and especially Polk, convinced growing numbers of northerners that the Slave Power did indeed exist.

The status of slavery in the territories became more than an abstract question once peace returned. The United States gained title to an immense territory, including all of what would become the states of California, Nevada, and Utah, nearly all of New Mexico, most of Arizona and Colorado, and parts of Wyoming, Kansas, and Oklahoma. With the United States in control of the Pacific coast from San Diego to Puget Sound, Polk's continental vision had become a reality. But slavery would once again dominate national politics.

 REVIEW

What factors best explain the cause and the outcome of the U.S.-Mexican War?

NEW SOCIETIES IN THE WEST

As Hispanic, Asian, Anglo–American, and dozens of different native cultures interacted, the patterns of development along the frontier varied widely. Some newcomers re-created the farm economies and small towns of the Anglo–American East; others continued the cattle-ranching life of the Hispanic West. In California the new settlements were overwhelmingly shaped by the rush for gold after 1848. And in the Great Basin around Salt Lake, the Mormons established a society whose sense of religious mission was as strong as that of the Puritans.

Farming in the West >> The overlanders expected to replicate the societies they had left behind. When a wagon train arrived at its destination, members had usually exhausted their resources and thus quickly scattered in search of employment or a good farm site. "Friday, October 27.—Arrived at Oregon City at the falls of the Willamette," read one pioneer diary. "Saturday, October 28.—Went to work."

In a process repeated over and over, settlers in a new area set up the machinery of government. Although violence was common on the frontier, farming communities tended to resolve problems by traditional means. Churches took longer to establish, because ministers were hard to recruit and congregations were often not large enough to support a church. As the population grew, however, a more conventional society evolved. Towns and a middle class developed, the proportion of women increased, schools were established, and the residents became less mobile.

Although opportunity was greater on the frontier and early arrivals had a special advantage, more and more the agricultural frontier of the West resembled the older society of the East. With the development of markets and transportation, wealth became concentrated, some families fell to the lower rungs of society, and those who were less successful left, seeking yet another fresh start.

The Gold Rush >> In January 1848, while constructing a sawmill along the American River, James Marshall noticed gold flecks in the millrace. More discoveries followed, and when the news reached the East, it spread like wildfire. The following spring some 55,000 emigrants jammed the Overland Trail as "forty–niners" on the way to California. Another 25,000 traveled by boat. In only two years, from 1848 to the end of 1849, California's population jumped from 14,000 to 100,000. By 1860 it stood at 380,000.

Among those who joined the rush was William Swain, a 27–year–old farmer in western New York. Bidding good–bye to his wife and daughter in 1849, he set off for the gold fields to make his fortune. On his arrival he entered a partnership and staked a claim along the Feather River, but months of backbreaking work in icy waters led only to the discovery that his claim was "worth nothing." He sold out and joined another company, but early rains soon forced a halt to the work. In October 1850, after less than a year in the diggings, Swain returned home, only a few hundred dollars richer. He counted himself one of the vast majority of miners who had seen "their bright daydreams of golden wealth vanish like the dreams of night."

Predictably, mining the miners offered a more reliable road to prosperity than digging for gold. Perhaps half the inhabitants of a mining town were shopkeepers, businesspeople, and professionals who provided services for prospectors. Also conspicuous were gamblers, card

↑ San Francisco in 1850. In this daguerreotype, the masts of hundreds of sailing ships along the wharves appear like a forest, hemming in the chaos and overcrowding of a city thrown up over a space of months.

sharks, and other outcasts, all bent on separating the miner from his riches.

More than 80 percent of the prospectors who poured into the gold country were Americans, including free blacks. Mexicans, Australians, Argentinians, Hawaiians, Chinese, French, English, and Irish also came. Observers praised the diggings' democratic spirit. Yet such asser—tions overlooked strongly held nativist prejudices: when frustrated by a lack of success, American miners directed their hostility toward foreigners. The miners ruthlessly exterminated the Indians in the area, sometimes hunt—ing them for sport. Mob violence drove Mexicans out of nearly every camp, and the Chinese were confined to claims abandoned by Americans as unprofitable. The state eventually enacted a foreign miners' tax that fell largely on the Chinese. Free African Americans felt the sting of discrimination as well, both in the camps and in state law. White American miners proclaimed that "colored men were not privileged to work in a country intended only for American citizens."

Only about 5 percent of gold rush emigrants were women or children; given this relative scarcity, men were willing to pay top dollar for women's domestic skills. Women supported themselves by cooking, sewing, and washing, as well as by running hotels and boardinghouses. "A smart woman can do very well in this country," one woman informed a friend in the East. "It is the only country I ever was in where a woman received anything like a just compensation for work." Women went to the mining frontier to be with their husbands, to make money, or to find adventure. But the class most frequently seen in the diggings was prostitutes, who numbered perhaps 20 percent of female Californians in 1850.

Before long the most easily worked claims had been played out, and large corporations moved in heavy equipment to get at hidden ore. Such techniques caused lasting environmental damage. Abandoned prospect holes and diggings pockmarked the gold fields and created piles of debris that heavy rains would wash down the valley, choking streams and ruining lands below. Excavation of hillsides, construction of dams to divert rivers, and the destruction of the forest cover to meet the heavy demand for lumber and firewood caused serious erosion of the soil and spring floods.

Instant City: San Francisco >> When the United States assumed control of California, San Fran—cisco had a population of perhaps 200. But thousands of emigrants took the water route west, passing through San Francisco's harbor on their way to the diggings. By 1856 the city's population had jumped to an astonishing 50,000. In a mere 8 years the city had attained the size New York had taken 190 years to reach.

San Francisco developed in helter—skelter fashion. Residents lived in tents or poorly constructed, half—finished buildings. Land prices soared, speculation was rampant, and commercial forces dominated. To enlarge the commercial district, hills began to be leveled, with the dirt used to fill in the bay (thereby creating more usable land). Since the city government took virtually no role in directing development, almost no land was reserved for public use. Property owners defeated a proposal to widen the streets, prompting the city's leading newspaper to complain, "To sell a few more feet of lots, the streets were compressed like a cheese, into half their width."

The Migration from China

>> The gold rush that swelled San Francisco's streets was a global phenomenon. Americans predominated in the mining population, but Latin Americans, Europeans, Australians, and Chinese flocked to California. An amazing assortment of languages could be heard on the city's streets: indeed, in 1860 San Francisco was 50 percent foreign–born.

The most distinctive ethnic group was the Chinese. They had come to Gum San, the land of the golden mountain. Those who arrived in California overwhelmingly hailed from the area of southern China around Canton (Guangdong)—and not by accident. Although other provinces also suffered from economic distress, population pressures, social unrest, and political upheaval, Canton had a large European presence, since it was the only port open to outsiders. That situation changed after the first Opium War (1839–1842), when Britain forced China to open other ports to trade. For Cantonese the sudden loss of their trade monopoly produced widespread economic hardship. At the same time, a series of religious and political revolts in the region led to fighting that devastated the countryside. Many residents concluded that emigration was the only way to survive, and Western ships in the harbors of Canton and nearby Hong Kong (a British possession since 1842) made it easier to migrate to California rather than to Southeast Asia.

Between 1849 and 1854 some 45,000 Chinese flocked to California. Like other gold seekers, Chinese immigrants were overwhelmingly young and male, and they wanted only to accumulate savings and return home to their families. (Indeed, only 16 Chinese women arrived before 1854.) Generally poor, Chinese immigrants arrived already in debt, having borrowed the price of their steamship ticket; they fell further into debt to Chinese merchants in San Francisco, who loaned them money to purchase needed supplies.

When the Chinese were harassed in the mines, many opened laundries in San Francisco and elsewhere, since little capital was required—soap, scrub board, iron, and ironing board. Other Chinese around San Francisco set up restaurants or worked in the fishing industry. In these early years they found Americans less hostile, as long as they stayed away from the gold fields. As immigration and the competition for jobs increased, however, anti–Chinese sentiment intensified.

Gradually, San Francisco took on the trappings of an orderly community. The city government established a public school system, erected streetlights, created a municipal water system, and halted further filling–in of the bay. Industry was confined to the area south of the city; several new working–class neighborhoods grew up near the downtown section. Fashionable neighborhoods sprouted on several hills, as high rents drove many residents from the developing commercial center, and churches and families became more common. By 1856 the ramshackle city of the gold rush had been replaced by an orderly metropolis whose stone and brick buildings gave it a sense of permanence.

California Genocide

>>Eager to possess native land, resources, and even Indian slaves; determined to avenge Indian thefts or attacks (real or imagined); or anxious about imagined Indian conspiracies, many white Californians attempted to exterminate the state's indigenous population.

In 1859 California's governor hired notorious Indian killer Walter S. Jarboe to kill or capture

<< With their distinctive clothing and bamboo hats, Chinese miners could be seen throughout the diggings. Chinese immigration reached a peak in 1852, when 20,000 arrived in California. In the heyday of the mining camp, perhaps 20 percent of the miners were Chinese. Confronted with intense hostility from other miners, they worked abandoned claims and unpromising sites with primitive and less expensive equipment.

any Yuki Indians found outside their newly established reservation, in northwestern California. After four months Jarboe boasted that he and his men had killed or captured nearly 500 Yuki. "However cruel it may be," Jarboe candidly explained, "nothing short of extermination will suffice to rid the Country of them." Some white Californians protested Jarboe's "deliberate, cowardly, brutal massacre of defenseless men, women, and children." But others celebrated, and the state legislature reimbursed Jarboe and men like him for their expenses. Washington encouraged extermination by rejecting treaties that might have provided Indians some land and security, ignoring the pleas of dismayed federal Indian agents. The federal government reimbursed California nearly $1.5 million for the costs of its ongoing Indian campaigns. Survivors lived to see the seizure of their historic territories, the destruction of the animals they relied upon, profound ecological transformation through overgrazing and hydraulic mining, and the dissolution of families through kidnapping and enslavement. In 1850 the California legislature passed the "Act for the Government and Protection of Indians." The measure legalized the seizure and forced labor of Indian children, as well as the capture of native men and women for loitering, begging, or leading "an immoral or profligate course of life." People seized on these counts were leased out to the highest bidder, for a four-month term of forced labor. By the late 1850s white observers reported Indian villages comprised almost totally of adults, most of the children "doubtless having been stolen and sold."

Though population estimates are imprecise, few historians doubt that California's Indians experienced a demographic, social, and spiritual catastrophe in the mid-nineteenth century. In the 20 years following the U.S.–Mexican War, homicide, displacement, captivity, forced labor, malnutrition, disease, and social trauma reduced the state's native population from perhaps 150,000 to some 30,000. That said, men like Jarboe and their patrons in state and national government failed to "exterminate" California's Indians. Native men, women,

and children employed a host of tactics to protect their families and preserve their cultures and values. Today hundreds of thousands of Californians self-identify as Native American, many of them descended from survivors of the California genocide.

The Mormons in Utah >> The makeshift, often chaotic society spawned by the gold rush was a product of largely uncontrolled economic forces. In contrast, the society evolving in the Great Basin of Utah exhibited an entirely different but equally remarkable growth. Salt Lake City became the center of a religious kingdom established by the Church of Jesus Christ of Latter-day Saints, also known as the Mormon Church.

After founder Joseph Smith's death in 1844, the Mormon Church was led by Brigham Young, who lacked Smith's religious mysticism but was a brilliant organizer. Young decided to move his followers to the Great Basin, an isolated area a thousand miles from the settled parts of the United States. In 1847 the first thousand settlers arrived, the vanguard of thousands more who extended Mormon settlement throughout the valley of the Great Salt Lake and the West. Church officials also held the government positions, and Young had supreme power in legislative, executive, and judicial matters as well as religious affairs. In 1849 the state of Deseret was officially established, with Brigham Young as governor. It applied for admission to the Union.

The most controversial church teaching was the doctrine of polygamy, or plural marriage, which Young sanctioned publicly in 1852. Visitors reported with surprise that few Mormon wives seemed to rebel against the practice. Some plural wives developed close friendships; indeed, in one sample almost a third of plural marriages included at least two sisters. Moreover, because polygamy distinguished Mormonism from other religions, plural wives saw it as an expression of their religious faith. "I want to be assured of *position in God's estimation*," one such wife explained. "If polygamy is the Lord's order, we must carry it out."

⌃ In 1847 about a thousand Mormons trekked across the Great Plains to the Great Salt Lake. Thousands more soon followed.

The Mormons connected control of water to their sense of mission and respect for hierarchy. Mormon settlements spread throughout the arid Salt Lake Valley, all connected to and dependent upon a centralized system of dams, aqueducts, and ditches. By 1850 there were more than 16,000 irrigated acres in what would eventually become the state of Utah.

Manipulation of water reinforced the Mormons' sense of hierarchy and group discipline. In a radical departure from American ideals, church leaders insisted that water belonged to the community, not individuals, and vested this authority in the hands of the local bishop. Control of scarce water resources reinforced the power of the church hierarchy over not just the faithful but dissidents as well. Community needs, as interpreted by church leaders, took precedence over individual rights. Thus irrigation did more than make the desert bloom. By checking the Jeffersonian ideal of an independent, self–sufficient farmer, it also made possible a centralized, well–regulated society under the firm control of the Mormon Church.

Mexican American Rights and Property >>

At the conclusion of the U.S.–Mexican War, some 100,000 Mexican citizens suddenly found themselves living inside the newly expanded United States. The Treaty of Guadalupe Hidalgo guaranteed them "the free enjoyment of their liberty and property." Mexican negotiators understood how critical that was: without land, their former citizens would enjoy neither economic security nor political influence in their new country. But the treaty said little about how Mexican Americans would prove their ownership of land. They rarely had the sort of documentation that American courts expected. Differences in legal culture, combined with racism and pervasive fraud, led to the dispossession and impoverishment of most Spanish–speaking property holders in the Southwest.

California's Land Act of 1851 required everyone with Spanish– or Mexican–era claims to document them within two years. Hundreds failed to file claims in the time allotted, and by the terms of the Land Act all their territories passed into the public domain. The board eventually confirmed three–quarters of the claims it did receive. But resolution often took years and proved to be enormously expensive. Property owners had to mortgage their lands to pay legal fees, and in the end the great majority lost everything. Claimants in New Mexico likewise lost vast tracts of lands to Anglo ranchers and, especially, to lawyers. The lengthy and expensive review process left Mexican and Pueblo Indian claimants holding only about 6 percent of the lands they had possessed before the U.S. invasion.

Tejanos faced similar pressures. Stigmatized and despised by whites as racial inferiors, they were the poorest group in free society. One response to this dislocation, an option commonly taken by persecuted minorities, was social banditry. An example was the folk hero Juan Cortina. A member of a displaced landed family in southern Texas, Cortina was driven into resistance in the 1850s by American harassment. He began stealing from wealthy Anglos to aid poor Mexicans, proclaiming, "To me is entrusted the breaking of the chains of your slavery." Cortina continued to raid Texas border settlements until finally he was imprisoned by Mexican authorities. While failing to produce any lasting change, Cortina demonstrated the depth of frustration and resentment among Hispanics over their abuse at the hands of the new Anglo majority.

 REVIEW

Who were the winners and the losers in the gold rush? Why?

^ South Carolina's senator John C. Calhoun insisted that slavery was legal in all territories.

ESCAPE FROM CRISIS

With the return of peace, Congress confronted the problem of whether to allow slavery in the newly acquired territories. David Wilmot, in his controversial proviso, had already proposed outlawing slavery throughout the Mexican cession. John C. Calhoun, representing the extreme southern position, countered that slavery was legal in all territories. The federal government had acted as the agent of all the states in acquiring the land, Calhoun argued, and southerners had a right to take their property there, including slaves. Only when the residents of a territory drafted a state constitution could they decide the question of slavery.

Two moderate positions softened these extremes. One proposed extending

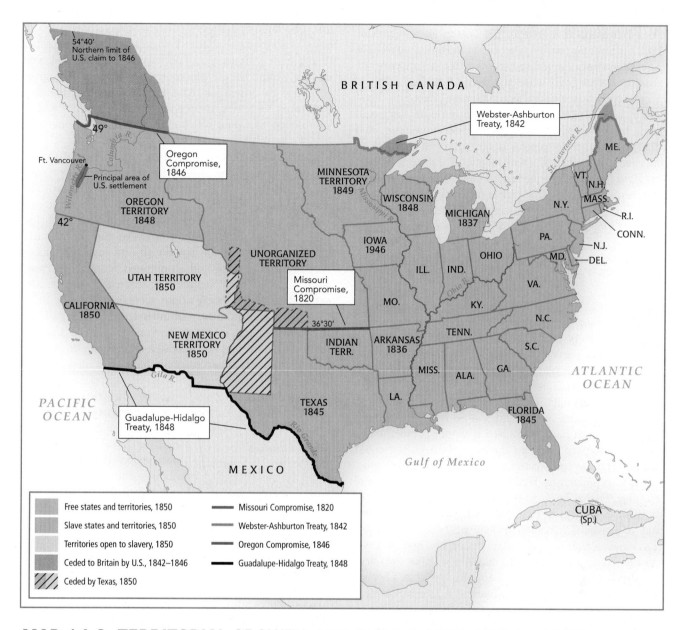

MAP 14.6: TERRITORIAL GROWTH AND THE COMPROMISE OF 1850

Why weren't slavery's champions in the 1850s content with the limits established in the Missouri Compromise?

the Missouri Compromise line of 36°30′ to the Pacific, which would have continued the earlier policy of dividing the national domain between the North and the South. The other proposal, championed by Senator Lewis Cass of Michigan and Senator Stephen A. Douglas of Illinois, was to allow the people of the territory rather than Congress to decide the status of slavery. This solution, which became known as *popular sovereignty*, was tactically ambiguous, since its supporters refused to specify whether the residents could make this decision at any time or only when drafting a state constitution, as Calhoun insisted.

When Congress organized the Oregon Territory in 1848, it prohibited slavery there, since even southerners admitted that the region was too far north to grow the South's staple crops. But this seemingly straightforward decision made it impossible to apply the Missouri Compromise line to the other territories. With Oregon already firmly committed to outlawing slavery, the greater part of the remaining land split by the Compromise line would be open to slavery. That included New Mexico, Arizona, and southern California. Northern members of Congress balked at that solution, especially since supporters of the Wilmot Proviso had wanted slavery barred from *all* territories acquired from Mexico. Almost inadvertently, one of the two moderate solutions had been discarded by the summer of 1848.

A Two-Faced Campaign >> In the election of 1848 both major parties tried to avoid the slavery issue. The Democrats nominated Lewis Cass, a supporter of popular sovereignty, while the Whigs bypassed all their prominent leaders and selected General Zachary Taylor, who had taken no position on any public issue and who remained silent throughout the campaign. The Whigs adopted no platform and planned instead to emphasize the general's war record.

But the slavery question would not go away. A new antislavery coalition, the **Free Soil Party,** brought

] **Free Soil Party** antislavery party formed in 1848 by northern Democrats disillusioned with southern Democratic support for slavery.

together northern Democrats who had rallied to the Wilmot Proviso, Conscience Whigs who disavowed Taylor's nomination because he was a slaveholder, and political abolitionists in the Liberty Party. To gain more votes, the Free Soil platform focused on the dangers of extending slavery rather than on the evil of slavery itself. Ironically, the party nominated Martin Van Buren—the man who for years had struggled to keep the slavery issue out of national politics.

Both the Whigs and the Democrats ran different campaigns in the North and the South. To southern audiences, each party promised it would protect slavery in the territories; to northern voters, each claimed it would keep the territories free. In this two-faced, sectional campaign, the Whigs won their second national victory. Taylor held on to the core of Whig voters in both sections. But in the South, where the contest pitted a southern slaveholder against two northerners, Taylor won many more votes than Clay had in 1844. As one southern Democrat complained, "We have lost hundreds of votes, solely on the ground that General Cass was a Northerner and General Taylor a Southern man." Furthermore, Van Buren polled five times as many votes as the Liberty Party had four years earlier. Increasingly, the two national political parties were being pulled apart along sectional lines.

The Compromise of 1850 >> Once he became president Taylor could no longer remain silent. The territories gained from Mexico had to be organized; furthermore, by 1849 California had gained enough residents to be admitted as a state. In the Senate the balance of power between North and South stood at 15 states each. California's admission would break the sectional balance.

Called "Old Rough and Ready" by his troops, Taylor was a forthright man of action, but politically inexperienced and prone to oversimplify complex problems. Since even Calhoun admitted that entering states had the right to ban slavery, Taylor naively proposed that the way to end the sectional crisis was to skip the territorial stage and admit the new lands directly as states. He suggested that the entire Mexican cession be split

into two huge states, New Mexico and California. Even more shocking to southern Whigs, he proposed to apply the Wilmot Proviso to the entire area, since he believed slavery would never flourish there. When Congress convened in December 1849, Taylor recommended that California and New Mexico be admitted as free states. The president's plan touched off the most serious sectional crisis the Union had yet confronted.

Into this turmoil stepped Henry Clay, now 73 years old and nearing the end of his career. A savvy card player all his life, Clay loved the bargaining, the wheeling and dealing, the late-night trade-offs eased along by a bottle of bourbon that were part of politics. Clay sought a grand compromise to end all disputes between the North and the South and save the Union. Already, Mississippi had summoned a southern convention to meet at Nashville to discuss the crisis, and extremists spoke openly about secession.

Clay's compromise, submitted in January 1850, addressed all the major controversies between the two sections. California, he proposed, should be admitted as a free state, which represented the clear wishes of most settlers there. The rest of the Mexican cession would be organized as two territories, New Mexico and Utah, under the doctrine of **popular sovereignty.** Thus slav-

popular sovereignty doctrine, devised by Senator Stephen A. Douglas of Illinois, that a territory could decide by vote whether or not to permit slavery within its boundaries.]

ery would not be prohibited in these regions. Clay also proposed that Congress abolish the slave trade but not slavery itself in the District of Columbia and that a new, more rigorous fugitive slave law be passed to enable southerners to reclaim runaway slaves. To reinforce the idea that both North and South were yielding ground, Clay combined those provisions that dealt with the Mexican cession (and several others adjusting the Texas–New Mexico border) into a larger package known as the Omnibus Bill. With the stakes so high, the Senate debated the bill for six months—and then rejected it.

With Clay exhausted and his strategy in shambles, Democrat Stephen A. Douglas assumed leadership of the pro-compromise forces. The sudden death in July of President Taylor, who had threatened to veto Clay's plan, aided the compromise movement. One by one Douglas submitted the individual measures for a vote. Northern representatives provided the necessary votes to admit California and abolish the slave trade in the District of Columbia, while southern representatives supplied the edge needed to organize the Utah and New Mexico territories and pass the new fugitive slave law. On the face of it everyone had compromised. But in truth only 61 members of Congress, a mere 21 percent of the membership, had not voted against some part of Clay's compromise.

By September 17 all the separate parts of the Compromise of 1850 had passed and been signed into law by the new president, Millard Fillmore. The Union, it seemed, was safe.

Away from the Brink >> The general public rallied to the Compromise of 1850. Still, most southerners felt that a firm line had been drawn. With California's admission, they were now outnumbered in the Senate, so it was critical that slaveholders be granted equal legal access to the territories. They insisted that any breach of the Compromise of 1850 would justify secession.

The North, for its part, saw the new fugitive slave law as politically necessary but ethically obscene. It denied accused runaways trial by jury, and it required that all citizens assist federal marshals in its enforcement. Harriet Beecher Stowe's popular novel *Uncle Tom's Cabin* (1852) presented a powerful moral indictment of the law—and of slavery itself. Despite sentimental characters, a contrived plot, and clumsy dialect, the book profoundly moved its readers. Emphasizing the duty of Christians toward the downtrodden, it reached a greater audience than any previous abolitionist work and stimulated moral opposition to the institution.

In reality, however, fewer than 1,000 slaves a year ran away to the North, and many of those failed in the attempt. Despite some cases of well–publicized resistance, the free states more or less enforced the 1850 fugitive slave law. Stephen Douglas spoke accurately enough when he boasted in 1851, "The whole country is acquiescing in the compromise measures—everywhere, North and South. Nobody proposes to repeal or disturb them."

And so calm returned. In the lackluster 1852 presidential campaign, both the Whigs and the Democrats endorsed the Compromise of 1850. Franklin Pierce, a little–known New Hampshire Democrat, soundly defeated the Whig candidate, Winfield Scott. Even more significant, the antislavery Free Soil candidate received only about half as many votes as Van Buren had four years before. With the slavery issue seemingly losing political force, it appeared that the Republic had weathered the storm unleashed by the Wilmot Proviso.

 REVIEW

What was the crisis of 1850, and how was it averted?

The moving frontier had worked many changes during the 1830s and 1840s, and many more upheavals awaited the decade ahead. From a continental point of view, political relations among the United States, Mexico, and the Indian peoples had shifted significantly. Indian attacks on Mexico in the 1820s and 1830s had weakened Mexico's ability to repel an invasion by the United States. And with the Treaty of Guadalupe Hidalgo, the United States gained over half a million square miles, as its frontier leaped from the Mississippi valley to the Pacific Ocean.

In between remained territory still unorganized and still controlled by formidable Indian peoples. And as the North became increasingly industrialized and the South more firmly committed to an economy based on cotton and slavery, the movement of Americans into those territories soon revived growing conflict between the two sections over slavery. The disputes would shatter the Jacksonian party system, reignite the slavery issue, and shake the Union to its foundation.

CHAPTER SUMMARY

In the 1840s the United States expanded to the Pacific, a development that required an aggressive war and that led to the rise of the slavery issue in national politics.

- In the 1840s Americans proclaimed that it was the United States' Manifest Destiny to expand across the North American continent.
- Americans in Texas increasingly clashed with Mexican authorities, and in 1835–1836 Texans revolted and established an independent republic.
- Americans headed for Oregon and California on the Overland Trail.
- The journey put special pressures on women as the traditional division of labor by gender broke down.
- It also put pressure on Plains Indians' grazing lands, wood supplies, and freedom of movement.
- The gold rush spawned a unique society that was overwhelmingly male, highly mobile, and strongly nativist and racist.
- Led by Brigham Young, the Mormons established a tightly organized, centrally controlled society in the Great Salt Lake basin.
- Throughout the Southwest, Hispanic residents suffered at the hands of the new Anglo majority, as did the Chinese immigrants in California.
- President James K. Polk entered office with a vision of the United States as a continental nation.
- He upheld President John Tyler's annexation of Texas and agreed to divide the Oregon country with Britain.
- Polk instigated a war with Mexico in order to obtain that country's northern territories.
- Divided, impoverished, and distracted by ongoing wars with Indians, the war forced Mexico to surrender more than half a million square miles of territory.
- The U.S.–Mexican War reinjected the slavery issue into American national politics.
- The Wilmot Proviso sought to prohibit slavery from any territory acquired from Mexico.
- The struggle over the Wilmot Proviso eventually disrupted both major parties.
- Congress momentarily stilled the sectional crisis with the Compromise of 1850.

Additional Reading

For the Sioux, see Richard White, "The Winning of the West: The Expansion of the Western Sioux in the Eighteenth and Nineteenth Centuries," *Journal of American History* (1978), pp. 319–343. See also Colin G. Calloway, *One Vast Winter Count: The Native American West before Lewis and Clark* (2003). David J. Weber, *The Mexican Frontier, 1821–1846* (1982), is a superb study of the Southwest prior to American control. For a transnational interpretation of the Texas Rebellion, see Andrés Reséndez, *Changing National Identities at the Frontier* (2005). For the Overland Trail, see John Mack Faragher, *Women and Men on the Overland Trail* (2001). *Mormonism: A Very Short Introduction* (2008), by Richard Bushman, is an elegant primer. For California's missions, see Steven W. Hackel's *Children of Coyote, Missionaries of St. Francis* (2005). Susan Lee Johnson's *Roaring Camp* (2001) explores social interaction during the California gold rush. For the environmental consequences of mining, see Andrew Isenberg's *Mining California* (2005). Robert V. Hine and John Mack Faragher, *Frontiers* (2008), is an excellent synthesis of the region's history.

The fullest treatment of American life in this period is Daniel Walker Howe's magisterial book *What Hath God Wrought* (2007). Thomas R. Hietala examines the social roots of expansionism in *Manifest Design* (1985). For Indians and the geopolitics of the era, see Brian DeLay, *War of a Thousand Deserts: Indian Raids and the U.S.–Mexican War* (2008). The drive to annex Texas is carefully untangled in Joel H. Silbey, *Storm over Texas* (2005). The best discussions of Polk's handling of the Oregon and Texas issues remain Charles G. Sellers Jr., *James K. Polk, Continentalist, 1843–1846* (1966); and David M. Pletcher, *The Diplomacy of Annexation* (1973). Amy Greenberg's *A Wicked War* (2012) is a marvelous study of American politics and the war in Mexico. Michael F. Holt powerfully analyzes the Whig Party's difficulties in *The Rise and Fall of the American Whig Party* (1999). For the California Indian genocide, see Benjamin Madley, "California's Yuki Indians: Defining Genocide in Native American History," *Western Historical Quarterly* 39, no. 3 (2008): 303–332; and Brendan C. Lindsay, *Murder State* (2012). Howard Lamar's classic account *The Far Southwest* (1966) explores political and economic power in the territories after conquest; and Richard Griswold del Castillo's *The Treaty of Guadalupe Hidalgo* (1990) examines that critical document. For more recent work on the region's postwar history, see Samuel Truett and Elliott Young, *Continental Crossroads* (2004). Holman Hamilton, *Prologue to Conflict* (new ed., 2005), is an excellent study of the Compromise of 1850.

Significant Events

1821
Mexico wins independence; Santa Fe trade opens

1823
First American settlers enter Texas

1831
Violence between northern Mexicans and Indians begins to increase dramatically

1836
Texas Republic established; Battle of the Alamo; Santa Anna defeated at San Jacinto

1843
Large-scale migration to Oregon begins

1844
Polk elected president

1845
United States annexes Texas; phrase *Manifest Destiny* coined

1846
War declared against Mexico; Bear Flag Revolt in California; Oregon Treaty with Britain ratified; Wilmot Proviso introduced

1847
Mormon migration to Utah; U.S. troops occupy Mexico

1848
Gold discovered in California; Treaty of Guadalupe Hidalgo ratified; Free Soil Part founded; Taylor elected president

1849
Gold rush

1850
Compromise of 1850 enacted

15 The Union Broken 1850–1861

During the 1850s Kansas became a battleground over whether slavery would expand into the new territories. Artist John Steuart Curry's mural *Tragic Prelude* places abolitionist John Brown at the center of the conflicts that led to civil war. What elements of the painting make the struggle seem mythic, almost biblical, in this mural done about 80 years after the event?

>> An American Story
THE SACKING OF A KANSAS TOWN

nto town they rode, several hundred strong, unshaven, rough-talking men, "armed . . . to the teeth with rifles and revolvers, cutlasses and bowie-knives." At the head of the procession flapped an American flag, alongside another featuring a crouching tiger emblazoned on black and white stripes, followed by banners proclaiming "Southern Rights" and "The Superiority of the White Race." At the rear rolled five artillery pieces. Watching intently from his office window, Josiah Miller, the editor of the *Kansas Free State,* predicted, "Well, boys, we're in for it."

Lawrence, Kansas, had been founded by the New England Emigrant Aid Company, a Yankee association that recruited settlers in an effort to keep Kansas Territory from becoming a slave state. Accepting Senator Stephen Douglas's idea that the people should decide the status of slavery, the town's residents intended to see to it that under this doctrine of "popular sovereignty" Kansas entered the Union as a free state. Emigrants from the neighboring slave state of Missouri were equally determined that no "abolition tyrants" would control the territory. Conflict erupted in Kansas almost immediately.

The federal government seemed to back the proslavery forces. In the spring of 1856 a U.S. district court indicted several of Lawrence's leading citizens for treason, and federal marshal Israel Donaldson led a posse, swelled by eager volunteers from across the Missouri border, to Lawrence on May 20 to make the arrest.

Meanwhile, Lawrence's "committee of safety" had agreed on a policy of nonresistance. Donaldson arrested two men without incident and, finding no one else on his list, dismissed his posse. But Sheriff Samuel Jones, who on his previous visit to Lawrence had been shot, had a score to settle. The irate sheriff took over the band and led the cheering, thoroughly liquored "army" into town at three o'clock in the afternoon. Ignoring the pleas of some leaders, the mob smashed the presses of Miller's *Kansas Free State* as well as that of the *Herald of Freedom*. Then the horde unsuccessfully tried to blow up the now-deserted Free State Hotel, which more closely resembled a fort, before finally putting it to the torch. When the mob rode off, it left the residents of Lawrence unharmed but thoroughly terrified.

Retaliation by free-state partisans was not long in coming. Hurrying north along a different road

to Lawrence, an older man with a grim face and steely eyes heard the news that the town had been attacked. "Old Man Brown," as everyone called him, was on his way with several of his sons to provide reinforcements. A severe, God-fearing Calvinist and staunch abolitionist, John Brown had once remarked to a friend that he believed "God had raised him up on purpose to break the jaws of the wicked."

Brooding over the failure of the free-staters to resist the "slave hounds" from Missouri, Brown headed toward Pottawatomie Creek on the night of May 24, with half a dozen others, including his sons. Announcing that they were "the Northern Army" come to serve justice, they burst into the cabin of James Doyle, a proslavery man from Tennessee, with cutlasses drawn. As Brown marched off Doyle and his three sons, Doyle's terrified wife, Mahala, begged him to spare her youngest, and the old man relented. The others were led no more than 100 yards down the road before Owen and Salmon Brown hacked them to death with broadswords. Old Man Brown then walked up to James Doyle's body and put a bullet through his forehead. Before the night was done, two more cabins had been visited and two more proslavery settlers

Startling News!
OUR BORDER IN DANGER!!
Missouri to be Invaded!

We have authority which will not admit of doubt, for stating that Lane, with 3000 lawless abolitionists, and 10 pieces of artillery, is about to march into Missouri, and sack the border towns of Lexington, Independence, Westport, and New Santa Fe. This is no idle rumor; and there can be no doubt of it. These desperadoes swear they wil carry everything before them, and spare nothing.

⌃ A proslavery newspaper—Missouri was never invaded.

brutally executed. Not one of the five murdered men owned a single slave or had any connection with the raid on Lawrence.

Brown's action precipitated a new wave of fighting in Kansas, and controversy throughout the nation. "Everybody here feels as if we are upon a volcano," remarked one congressman in Washington.

Indeed, that smoldering volcano did finally erupt in the spring of 1861, showering civil war, death, and destruction across the land. Popular sovereignty, the last remaining moderate solution to the controversy over the expansion of slavery, had failed dismally. The violence and disorder in Kansas provided a stark reply to Stephen Douglas's proposition: What could be more peaceable, more fair than the notion of popular sovereignty? <<

What's to Come

SECTIONAL CHANGES IN AMERICAN SOCIETY

The road to war was not straight or short. Six years elapsed between the Compromise of 1850 and the crisis in "Bleeding Kansas." Another four would pass before the first shot was fired. And the process of separation involved more than popular fears, ineffective politicians, and an unwillingness to compromise. As we have seen, Americans were bound together by a growing transportation network, by national markets, and by a national political system. Increasingly, however, the changes occurring in American society heightened sectional tensions. As the North continued to industrialize, its society came into conflict with that of the South. The coming of civil war, in other words, involved social and economic changes as well as political ones.

The Growth of a Railroad Economy >> By the time the Compromise of 1850 produced a lull in the tensions between North and South, the American economy had left behind the depression of the early 1840s and was booming again. Its basic structure, however, was changing. Cotton remained the nation's major export, but it was no longer the driving force for American economic growth. After 1839 this role was taken over by the construction of a vast railroad network covering the eastern half of the continent. By 1850 the United States possessed more than 9,000 miles of track; 10 years later it had over 30,000 miles, more than the rest of the world combined. Much of the new construction during the 1850s occurred west of the Appalachian Mountains—over 2,000 miles in Ohio and Illinois alone.

Because western railroads ran through less settled areas, they depended especially on public aid. State and local governments made loans to rail companies and sometimes exempted them temporarily from taxes. Federal land grants were crucial, too. By mortgaging or selling the land to farmers, the railroad raised construction capital and also stimulated settlement, which increased its business and profits. By 1860 Congress had allotted about 28 million acres of federal land to 40 different companies.

The effect of the new lines rippled through the economy. Nearby farmers began to specialize in cash crops and market them in distant locations. With the profits, they purchased manufactured goods. Before the railroad reached Athens, Tennessee, the surrounding counties produced about 25,000 bushels of wheat, selling at less than 50 cents a bushel. Once the railroad came, farmers near Athens grew 400,000 bushels and sold their crop at a dollar a bushel. Railroads also stimulated the mining and iron industries, which provided the bar and sheet iron needed for tracks, engines, and other equipment.

The new rail networks shifted the direction of western trade. In 1840 most northwestern grain was shipped down the Mississippi River to the bustling port of New Orleans. But low water made steamboat travel risky in summer, and ice shut down traffic in winter. Products such as lard, tallow, and cheese quickly spoiled if stored in New Orleans's sweltering warehouses.

With the new rail lines, traffic from the Midwest increasingly flowed west to east. Chicago became the region's hub, connecting the farms of the upper Midwest to New York and other eastern cities. The South's overall share of western trade dropped dramatically. The old political alliance between South and West, based on shared economic interests, was weakened by the new patterns of commerce.

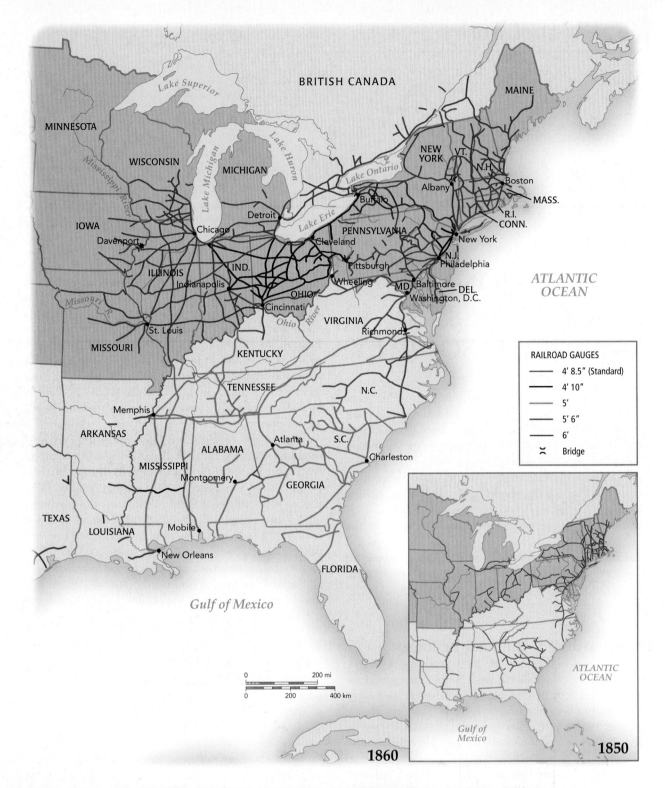

RAILROAD GAUGES

—— 4' 8.5" (Standard)
—— 4' 10"
—— 5'
—— 5' 6"
—— 6'
✕ Bridge

0   200 mi
0   200   400 km

1860

1850

MAP 15.1: GROWTH OF THE RAILROAD NETWORK, 1850–1860

Although a good deal of track mileage was laid during the 1850s, total track mileage is misleading because the United States lacked a fully integrated rail network in 1860. A few trunk-line roads had combined a number of smaller lines into a single system to make shipment of goods easier. The Pennsylvania Railroad, for example, linked Philadelphia and Pittsburgh. But the existence of five major track gauges (or widths) meant that passengers and freight often had to be transferred from one line to the next. And north-south traffic was further disrupted by the lack of bridges over the Ohio River.

How many changes in railroad cars does the map indicate would have to be made for freight to ship from Chicago to New York City? From St. Louis to New Orleans?

PROPORTION OF WESTERN EXPORTS SHIPPED VIA NEW ORLEANS, 1835–1860

In 1835 nearly 100 percent of western exports of corn, pork, and whiskey were being shipped via New Orleans. By 1860 only about 40 percent of pork and whiskey and 20 percent of flour and corn were. The change in shipping patterns weakened the political ties between the South and the Old Northwest.

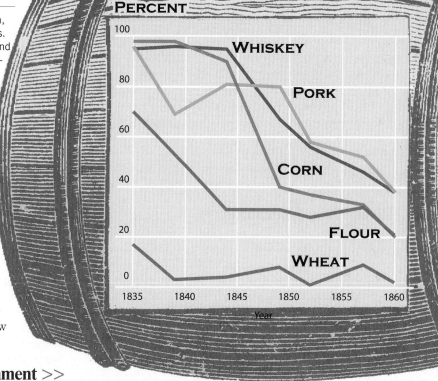

The growing rail network was not the only factor that led farmers in the Northeast and Midwest to become more commercially oriented. Another was the sharp rise in international demand for grain. Farmers responded by specializing in cash crops such as wheat and corn, and investing in equipment to increase productivity. "The power of cotton over the financial affairs of the Union has in the last few years rapidly diminished," the *Democratic Review* remarked in 1849, "and breadstuffs will now become the governing power."

Railroads and the Prairie Environment >>

As railroad lines fanned out from Chicago, farmers began to acquire open prairie land in Illinois and then Iowa, putting its deep black soil into production. Commercial agriculture transformed this remarkable treeless environment.

To settlers accustomed to woodlands, the thousands of square miles of grass taller than a person were an awesome sight. In 1838 Edmund Flagg gazed on "the tall grasstops waving in . . . billowy beauty in the breeze; the narrow pathway winding off like a serpent over the rolling surface, disappearing and reappearing till lost in the luxuriant herbage." Tallgrass prairies had their perils, too: year–round, storms sent travelers searching for the shelter of trees along river valleys, and stinging insects were thick in the summer.

Normal plows could not penetrate the densely tangled roots of prairie grass, until John Deere invented a sharp–cutting steel plow in 1837 that sliced through the sod without soil sticking to the blade. In addition, Cyrus McCormick refined a mechanical reaper that harvested 14 times more wheat with the same amount of labor. By the 1850s McCormick was selling 1,000 reapers a year and could not keep up with demand, and Deere turned out 10,000 plows annually.

The new commercial farming transformed the landscape and the environment. Indians had grown corn in the region for years, but never in fields as large as those of white farmers, whose surpluses were shipped east. Prairie farmers also introduced new crops that were not part of the earlier ecological system, notably wheat, along with fruits and vegetables. Native grasses were replaced by a small number of plants cultivated as commodities. Domesticated grasses replaced native grasses in pastures for making hay.

Western farmers altered the landscape by reducing the annual fires, often set by Indians, that had kept the prairie free from trees. In the fires' absence, trees reappeared on land not in cultivation and, if undisturbed, eventually formed woodlots. The earlier unbroken landscape gave way to independent farms, each fenced in the precise checkerboard pattern established by the Northwest Ordinance. It was an artificial ecosystem of animals, woodlots, and crops whose large, uniform layout made western farms more efficient than the more irregular farms in the East.

Railroads and the Urban Environment >>

Railroads transformed the urban environment as well. Communities soon recognized that their economic survival depended on creating rail links to the countryside and to major urban markets. Large cities feared they would be left behind in the struggle to be the dominant city in the region, and smaller communities saw their very survival at stake in the battle for rail connections.

Communities that obtained rail links found the new technology difficult to adjust to. Merchants in Jacksonville, Illinois, complained about the noise, dirt, and billowing smoke produced by the new locomotives passing through their business district. "The public square was filled with teams [of horses]," one resident recalled, "and whenever the engine steamed into the square making all the noise possible, there was such a stampede." After a few years the tracks were relocated to the outskirts of town. Increasingly, communities kept railroads away from fashionable neighborhoods and shopping areas. As the tracks became a physical marker of social and economic divisions in the town, the notion of living "on the wrong side of the tracks" became a way of defining the urban landscape.

Rising Industrialization >> The expansion of commercial agriculture, along with the shift from water power to steam, spurred the growth of industry. Out of the 10 leading American industries, 8 processed raw materials produced by agriculture, including flour milling and the manufacture of textiles, shoes, and woolens. (The only exceptions were iron and machinery.)

Most important, the factory system of organizing labor and the technology of interchangeable parts spread to other areas of the economy during the 1850s. Isaac Singer began using interchangeable parts in 1851

to mass—produce sewing machines, which made possible the ready—made clothing industry, while workers who assembled farm implements performed a single step in the process over and over again. By 1860 the United States had nearly a billion dollars invested in manufacturing, almost twice as much as in 1849. And for the first time, less than half the workers in the North were employed in agriculture.

Immigration >> The surge of industry depended on a large factory labor force. Natural increase helped swell the nation's population to more than 30 million by 1860, but only in part, since the birthrate had begun to decline. It was the beginning of mass emigration to America during the mid—1840s that kept population growth soaring.

In the 20 years from 1820 to 1840, about 700,000 newcomers had entered the United States. That figure jumped to 1.7 million in the 1840s, then to 2.6 million in the 1850s. Though even greater numbers arrived after the Civil War, as a percentage of the nation's total population, the wave from 1845 to 1854 was the largest influx of immigrants in American history. The great majority of newcomers were in the prime of life, between 10 and 40 years old. Certainly the booming economy and the lure of freedom drew immigrants, but they were also pushed by deteriorating conditions in Europe. In Ireland a potato blight beginning in

⌃ German immigrants enjoyed gathering for music and conversation in beer gardens. One of the most elegant and spacious of its day was New York City's German Winter-Garden in the Bowery neighborhood, shown in this watercolor by Fritz Meyer. "There are immense buildings," wrote one American, "fitted up in imitation of a garden. . . . Germans carry their families there to spend a day, or an evening."

1845 created a *Gorta Mór*—"Great Famine"—leaving potatoes rotting in the fields. The blight may well have spread from the United States and Canada, and it also infected Europe generally. But Ireland suffered more, because nearly a third of its population depended almost entirely on the potato for food. "They are all gone—clean gone," wrote a priest in the Irish town of Galway. "If travelling by night, you would know when a potato field was near by the smell." Out of Ireland's population of 9 million, as many as a million people perished, while a million and a half more emigrated, two–thirds to the United States.

The Irish tended to be poorer than other immigrant groups of the mid–nineteenth century. Although the Protestant Scots–Irish continued to emigrate, as so many had during the eighteenth century, the decided majority of the Irish who came after 1845 were Catholic. Because they were poor and unskilled, the Irish congregated in the cities, where the women performed domestic service and took factory jobs and the men did manual labor.

Germans and Scandinavians also had economic reasons for leaving Europe. They included small farmers whose lands had become marginal or who had been displaced by landlords, and skilled workers thrown out of work by industrialization. Some fled political and social oppression and came to live under the free institutions of the United States. Since arriving in America, wrote a Swede who settled in Iowa in 1850, "I have not been compelled to pay a penny for the privilege of living. Neither is my cap worn out from lifting it in the presence of gentlemen."

Unprecedented unrest and upheaval prevailed in Europe in 1848, the so–called year of revolutions. The famine that had driven so many Irish out of their country was part of a larger food shortage caused by a series of poor harvests. In this situation, middle–class reformers, who wanted civil liberty and a more representative government, joined forces with lower–class workers to overthrow several regimes. France, Austria, Hungary, Italy, and Prussia all witnessed popular uprisings. Yet though these revolts gained temporary success, they were all quashed by the forces of the old order. Liberal hopes for a more open, democratic society suffered a severe setback.

In the aftermath of this failure a number of hard–pressed German workers and farmers as well as disillusioned radicals and reformers emigrated to the United States, the symbol of democratic liberalism in the world. They were joined by the first significant migration from Asia, as thousands of Chinese joined the gold rush to California and other strikes. This migration was part of a century–long phenomenon, as approximately 50 million Europeans, largely from rural areas, would migrate to the Western Hemisphere.

Although many Germans and Scandinavians arrived in modest straits, few were truly impoverished, and many could afford to buy a farm or start a business. Unlike the Irish, Germans tended to emigrate as families, and wherever they settled, they formed social, religious, and cultural organizations to maintain their language and customs. Whereas the Scandinavians, Dutch, and English immigrants were Protestant, half or more of the Germans were Catholic.

Factories came more and more to depend on immigrant labor, including children, since newcomers would work for lower wages and were less likely to protest harsh working conditions. The shift to an immigrant workforce could be seen most clearly in the textile industry, where by 1860 over half the workers in New England mills were foreign–born.

The sizable foreign–born population in many American cities severely strained urban resources. Immigrants who could barely make ends meet were forced to live in overcrowded, unheated tenement houses, damp cellars, and even shacks. Urban slums became notorious for crime and drinking, which took a heavy toll on families and the poor. In the eyes of many native–born Americans, immigrants were to blame for driving down factory wages and pushing American workers out of jobs. Overshadowing these complaints was a fear that America might not be able to **assimilate** the new groups, with their unfamiliar languages and customs. These fears precipitated an outburst of political **nativism** in the mid–1850s.

> **assimilate** to absorb a culturally distinct group into the dominant culture.
>
> **nativism** outlook championing the supremacy of "native" cultural traits and political rights over those of immigrants from different backgrounds.

Southern Complaints

>> With British and northern factories buying cotton in large quantities, southern planters prospered in the 1850s. But instead of investing in machinery as northern commercial farmers had, white southerners invested in slaves. During the 1850s, the price of prime field hands reached record levels.

Despite southern prosperity the section's leaders repeatedly complained that the North had used its power over banking and commerce to convert the South into a colony. Storage and shipping charges, insurance, port fees, and commissions, which added some 20 percent to the cost of cotton and other commodities, went into the pockets of northern merchants, shippers, and bankers. The idea that the South was a colony of the North was inaccurate, but white southerners found it a convincing explanation of the North's growing wealth. More important, it reinforced their resistance to federal aid for economic development, which they were convinced would enrich the North at southern expense. This attitude further weakened the South's political alliance with the West, which needed federal aid for transportation.

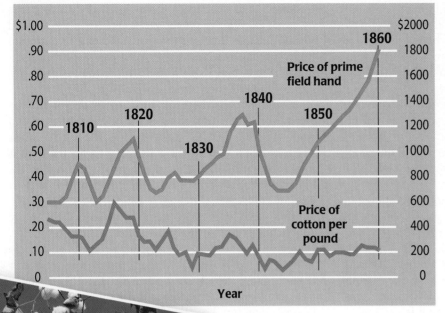

PRICES OF COTTON AND SLAVES

From 1815 to 1850 cotton and slave prices generally moved together, as southerners plowed their profits from growing cotton into buying more land and slaves. During the 1850s, however, the booming southern economy and bumper cotton crops drove the price of slaves steeply upward compared to cotton prices, squeezing slaveowners' profit margins and heightening southern anxieties about the future.

White south-erners also feared that the new tide of immigration would shift the sectional balance of power. Most immigrants shunned the South, not want-ing to compete with cheap slave labor. The lack of industry and the limited demand for skilled labor also shunted immigrants northward. As a result, the North surged even further ahead of the South in population, thereby strengthening its control of the House of Representatives and heightening southern concern that the North would rapidly settle the western territories.

 REVIEW

How did the new railroads affect urban and prairie environments? How did they increase sectional tensions?

THE POLITICAL REALIGNMENT OF THE 1850S

When Franklin Pierce (he pronounced it "Purse") assumed the presidency in 1853, he was only 48 years old, the youngest man yet to be elected president. He was also a supporter of the "Young America" movement of the Demo-cratic Party, which enthusiastically looked to spread democracy around the globe and annex additional territory to the United States.

The believers in Young America felt it idle to argue about slavery when the nation could be developing new resources. In 1853 Pierce did manage to conclude the Gadsden Purchase, thereby gaining control of about 45,000 square miles of Mexican desert, which contained the most practical southern route for a transcontinen-tal railroad. He had no success with his major goal, acquiring Cuba, the rich sugar–producing island where slavery had once been important. In any case, he soon had his hands full with the proposals of another Dem-ocrat of the Young America stamp, Senator Stephen A. Douglas of Illinois.

The Kansas-Nebraska Act >> Known as the Little Giant, Douglas was ambitious, bursting with energy, and impatient to get things done. As chairman of the Senate's Committee on Territories, he hoped to organize federal lands west of Missouri as part of his program for economic development. And as a citizen of Illinois, he wanted Chicago selected as the eastern terminus of the proposed transcontinental railroad. To do so, the rest of the Louisiana Purchase would have to be organized into territories, since any northern rail route would run through that region.

Under the terms of the Missouri Compromise of 1820, slavery was prohibited in this portion of the Louisiana Purchase. Stephen Douglas had tried once to organize the area while keeping a ban on slavery— only to have his bill voted down by southern opposi-tion in the Senate. In January 1854 he reintroduced the measure. This time, to obtain southern support, he omitted the prohibition on slavery that had been in effect for 34 years.

The bill created two territories: Kansas, directly west of Missouri, and a much larger Nebraska Territory,

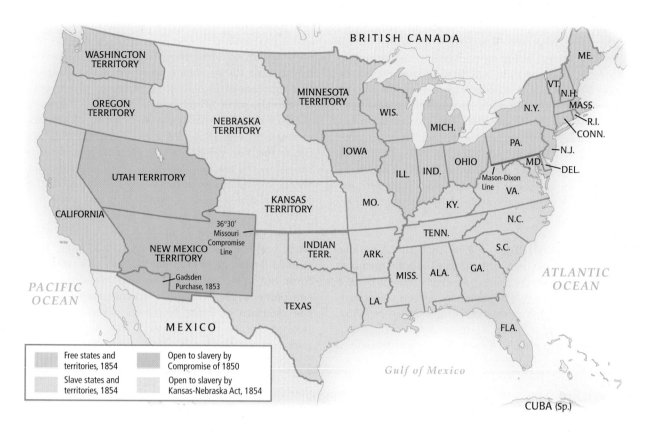

MAP 15.2: THE KANSAS-NEBRASKA ACT

When the Kansas-Nebraska Act of 1854 opened the remaining portion of the Louisiana Purchase to slavery under the doctrine of popular sovereignty, conflict between the two sections focused on control of Kansas, directly west of the slave state of Missouri.
Which part of the map indicates the unorganized portion of the Louisiana Purchase? How did the doctrine of popular sovereignty effectively repeal the Missouri Compromise?

located west of Iowa and the Minnesota Territory. The Missouri Compromise was explicitly repealed. Instead, Douglas's doctrine of popular sovereignty was to determine the status of slavery in both territories, though it was left unclear whether residents of Kansas and Nebraska could prohibit slavery at any time or only at the time of statehood, as southerners insisted. It was widely assumed that Kansas would be a slave state and Nebraska a free state.

The Kansas–Nebraska Act outraged northern Democrats, Whigs, and Free Soilers alike. Critics rejected Douglas's contention that popular sovereignty would keep the territories free. The bill, they charged, was meant to give slaveholders—the "Slave Power"— territory previously consecrated to freedom. Most northern opponents of the bill focused on the expansion of slavery and the political threat of a Slave Power rather than the moral evil of slavery. Indignation swept the North, but the Senate passed the bill easily. The real fight came in the House, where the North held a large majority. President Pierce put intense pressure on his fellow northern Democrats to come along, and

finally the bill passed by a narrow margin, 113 to 100. Pierce signed it on May 30, 1854.

The Collapse of the Second American Party System >> The furor over the Kansas–Nebraska Act laid bare the underlying tensions that had developed between the North and the South. These tensions put mounting pressure on the political parties, and in the 1850s the Jacksonian party system collapsed. Voters who had been loyal to one party for years, even decades, began switching allegiances. By the time the process of realignment was completed, a new party system had emerged, divided this time along clearly sectional lines.

In part, the old party system decayed because new problems had replaced the traditional economic issues of both Whigs and Democrats. The Whigs alienated many of their traditional Protestant supporters by openly seeking the support of Catholics and recent immigrants. Then, too, the growing agitation for the prohibition of alcohol divided both parties, especially the Whigs. Finally, both the Whigs and the Democrats were increasingly perceived as little more than corrupt engines of plunder. Many voters became disillusioned.

Thus the party system was already weak when the Kansas–Nebraska Act divided the two major parties along sectional lines. In such an unstable atmosphere, independent parties flourished. Antislavery veterans, who had earlier sparked the Liberty and Free Soil parties, united with Whigs and anti–Nebraska Democrats in the new antislavery Republican Party. Their calculations were derailed, however, when another new party capitalized on fears aroused by the recent flood of immigrants.

The Know-Nothings >> In 1854 the American Party, a secret nativist organization whose members were called Know–Nothings, suddenly emerged as a potent political force. (Its members, sworn to secrecy, had been instructed to answer inquiries by replying, "I know nothing.") Taking as their slogan "Americans should rule America," Know–Nothings denounced illegal voting by immigrants, the rising crime and disorder in urban areas, and immigrants' heavy drinking. They were also strongly anti–Catholic and were

convinced that the church's "undemocratic" hierarchy of bishops and archbishops was conspiring to undermine American democracy. Know–Nothings advocated lengthening the residency period for naturalization and ousting from office corrupt politicians who openly bid for foreign and Catholic votes.

The Know–Nothings won a series of remarkable victories in the 1854 elections. Their showing spelled doom for the Whigs, as party members deserted in droves to the Know–Nothings. With perhaps a million voters enrolled in its lodges in every state of the Union, Know–Nothing leaders confidently predicted in 1855 that they would elect the next president.

Yet only a year later—by the end of 1856—the party had collapsed as quickly as it had risen. Inexperienced leaders failed to enact the party's reform platform; but in the end, rising sectional tensions destroyed the party when it adopted a proslavery platform for the elections of 1856. Northern party members then flocked to the other new party, the Republicans. This party, unlike the Know–Nothings, had no base in the South. It intended to elect a president by sweeping the free states, which controlled a majority of the electoral votes.

⌃ As Kansas became a battleground over whether slavery would expand into the new territories, proslavery and antislavery factions armed themselves for open conflict. This free-state battery stands with its howitzer at the ready.

The Republicans and Bleeding Kansas >>

At first, the Republican Party made little headway in the North. Although it attracted a variety of Whigs, anti–Nebraska Democrats, and Free Soilers, many moderate Whigs and Democrats viewed the party as too radical.

Those attitudes changed on the heels of the alarming developments in Kansas. Most early settlers migrated to Kansas for the same reason other white Americans headed west: the chance to prosper in a new land. But Stephen Douglas's idea of popular sovereignty trans–formed the new settlement into a referendum on slav–ery in the territories. A race soon developed between northerners and southerners to settle Kansas first. To the proslavery residents of neighboring Missouri, free–state communities like Lawrence seemed ominous threats. "We are playing for a mighty stake," former senator David Rice Atchison of Missouri insisted. "If we win, we carry slavery to the Pacific Ocean; if we fail we lose Missouri, Arkansas and Texas and all the territories; the game must be played boldly."

When the first Kansas elections were held in 1854 and 1855, Missourians poured over the border, seized the polls, and stuffed the ballot boxes. This massive fraud tarnished popular sovereignty at the outset and greatly aroused public opinion in the North. It also pro–vided proslavery forces with a commanding majority in the Kansas legislature, where they enacted a strict legal code designed to intimidate antislavery settlers. This Kansas Code limited such time–honored rights as freedom of speech, impar–tial juries, and fair elec–tions. Mobilized into action, the free–staters in the fall of 1855 organized a separate government, drafted a state constitution prohibiting slavery, and asked Congress to admit Kansas as a free state. In such a polarized situation, violence quickly broke out between the two factions, which culminated in the raid on Lawrence in May 1856 (see the chapter introduction).

The Caning of Charles Sumner >>

Only a few days before the proslavery attack on Law–rence, Republican senator Charles Sumner of Massa–chusetts delivered a scath–ing speech, "The Crime against Kansas." Sumner passionately condemned slavery and deliberately insulted the state of South Carolina and one of its senators. Preston S. Brooks, a member of Congress from South Carolina, was outraged that Sumner had insulted his relative and mocked his state.

Several days later, on May 22, Brooks strode into the Senate after it had adjourned, went up to Sumner, who was seated at his desk, and proceeded to beat him over the head with a cane. The cane shattered into three pieces from the violence of the attack, but Brooks, swept up in the emotion of the moment, furiously continued hitting Sumner until the senator collapsed unconscious, drenched in blood.

Northerners were electrified to learn that a sena–tor of the United States had been beaten uncon–scious in the Senate chamber. What caused them even greater consternation was southern reaction—for in his own region, Preston Brooks was lionized as a hero. Instantly, the Sumner caning breathed life into the fledgling Republican Party. Its claims about "Bleeding Kansas" and the Slave Power now seemed credible.

The Election of 1856 >>

In the face of the storm over Kansas, the Democrats turned to James Buchanan of Pennsylvania as their presidential nominee. Buchanan's supreme qualification was having the good fortune to have been out of the country as minister to

SOUTHERN CHIVALRY — ARGUMENT VERSUS CLUB'S.

⚘ The caning of Senator Charles Sumner of Massachusetts by Representative Preston S. Brooks of South Carolina inflamed public opinion. In this northern cartoon the fallen Sumner, a martyr to free speech, raises his pen against Brooks's club. Rushing to capitalize on the furor, printmakers did not know what the obscure Brooks looked like and thus had to devise ingenious ways of portraying the incident. In this print, Brooks's face is hidden by his raised arm.

England when the Kansas–Nebraska Act was passed. The American Party, split badly by the Kansas issue, nominated former president Millard Fillmore.

The Republicans chose John C. Frémont, a western explorer who had helped liberate California during the Mexican War. The party's platform denounced slavery as a "relic of barbarism" and demanded that Kansas be admitted as a free state. Throughout the summer the party hammered away on Bleeding Sumner and Bleeding Kansas.

A number of basic principles guided the Republican Party, one of which was the ideal of free labor. Slavery degraded labor, Republicans argued, and would inevitably drive free labor out of the territories. Condemning the South as a stagnant, hierarchical, and economically backward region, Republicans praised the North as a fluid society of widespread opportunity where enterprising individuals could improve their lot. Stopping the expansion of slavery, in Republican eyes, would preserve this heritage of opportunity and economic independence for white Americans. Republicans also appealed to former Know–Nothings by criticizing the Catholic Church, particularly its political activity, and by being much more favorable to temperance.

Also important was the moral opposition to slavery, strengthened by such works as Harriet Beecher Stowe's *Uncle Tom's Cabin*. Republican speakers and editors stressed that slavery was a moral wrong, that it was incompatible with the ideals of the Republic and Christianity. "Never forget," Republican leader Abraham Lincoln declared on one occasion, "that we have before us this whole matter of the right and wrong of slavery in this Union, though the immediate question is as to its spreading out into new Territories and States."

More negatively, Republicans gained support by shifting their attacks from slavery itself to the Slave Power, or the political influence of the planter class. Pointing to the Sumner assault and the incidents in Kansas, Republicans contended that the Slave Power had set out to destroy the liberties of white northerners. Just as the nation's founders had battled against tyranny, aristocracy, and minority rule in the Revolution, so the North confronted the unrepublican Slave Power. "If our government, for the sake of Slavery, is to be perpetually the representative of a minority," argued the *Cincinnati Commercial*, "it may continue republican in form, but the substance of its republicanism has departed."

In the election Buchanan all but swept the South (losing only Maryland to Fillmore) and won enough free states to push him over the top. Still, the violence in Kansas and Sumner's caning nearly lofted Frémont into the presidency. Had he carried Pennsylvania plus one more free state, he would have been elected. For

the first time in American history, an antislavery party based entirely in the North threatened to elect a president and snap the bonds of union.

 REVIEW

What events led the political realignment of the 1850s to favor the Know-Nothings at first? What events led the Republicans to emerge as the more powerful party?

THE WORSENING CRISIS

James Buchanan was one of the most experienced men ever elected president: he had served in Congress, in the cabinet, and in the foreign service. Moderates in both sections hoped that the new president would thwart Republicans in the North and secessionists of the Deep South, popularly known as "fire–eaters." Throughout his career, however, Buchanan had taken the southern position on sectional matters, and he proved insensitive to the concerns of northern Democrats. Moreover, on March 6, 1857, only two days after Buchanan's inauguration, the Supreme Court rendered one of the most controversial decisions in its history.

The *Dred Scott* Decision >>The owner of a Missouri slave named Dred Scott had taken him to live for several years in Illinois, a free state, and in what is now Minnesota, where slavery had been banned by the Missouri Compromise. Eventually the owner returned with Scott to Missouri. Scott sued for his freedom on the grounds that his residence in a free state and a free territory had made him free, and his case ultimately went to the Supreme Court. Two northern justices joined all five southern members in ruling 7 to 2 that Scott remained a slave. The majority opinion was written by Chief Justice Roger Taney of Maryland.

Wanting to strengthen the judicial protection of slavery, Taney ruled that African Americans could not be and never had been citizens of the United States. Instead, he insisted that they were "regarded as beings of an inferior order" at the time the Constitution was adopted, "so far inferior that they had no rights which the white man was bound to respect." In addition, the Court ruled that the Missouri Compromise was unconstitutional. Congress, it declared, had no power to ban slavery from any territory of the United States.

While southerners rejoiced at this result, Republicans denounced the Court for rejecting their party's main principle, that Congress should prohibit slavery in all territories. "We know the court…has often over-ruled its own decisions," Abraham Lincoln observed, "and we shall do what we can to have it over—rule this." For Republicans, the decision foreshadowed the spread of slavery throughout the West and even the nation.

But the decision also was a blow to Stephen Douglas's moderate solution of popular sovereignty. If Congress had no power to prohibit slavery in a territory, how could it authorize a territorial legislature to do so? Although the Court did not rule on this point, the clear implication of the *Dred Scott* decision was that popular sovereignty was also unconstitutional. The Court, in effect, had endorsed John C. Calhoun's radical view that slavery was legal in all the territories. In so doing, the Court, which had intended to settle the question of slavery in the territories, instead pushed the political debate toward new extremes.

Although the nation grappled with the *Dred Scott* decision, an economic depression aggravated sectional conflict. The Panic of 1857 was nowhere near as severe as the depression of 1839–1843. But the psychological results were far—reaching, for the South remained relatively untouched. With the price of cotton and other southern commodities still high, southern secessionists hailed the panic as proof that an independent southern nation could survive economically. Insisting that cotton sustained the international economy, James Henry Hammond, a senator from South Carolina, boasted: "No, you dare not make war on cotton. No power on earth dares to make war on it. Cotton is king."

The Lecompton Constitution

>>Although the *Dred Scott* decision and economic depression weakened the bonds of the Union, Kansas remained at the center of the political stage. In June 1857, when the territory elected delegates to draft a state constitution, free—staters boycotted the election, giving pro-slavery forces control of the convention that met in Lecompton. The delegates promptly drafted a constitution that made slavery legal. Even more boldly, they scheduled a referendum in which voters could not vote against either the constitution or slavery. Once again, free—staters boycotted the election, and the Lecompton constitution was approved.

President Buchanan had pledged earlier that there would be a free and fair vote on the Lecompton constitution. But the outcome offered Buchanan the unexpected opportunity to create one additional slave state and thereby satisfy his southern supporters by pushing the Lecompton constitution through Congress. This was too much for Douglas, who broke party ranks and denounced the Lecompton constitution as a fraud. Although the administration prevailed in the Senate without Douglas's support, the House rejected the constitution. In a compromise, Congress returned the constitution to Kansas for another vote. This time it was decisively defeated, 11,300 to 1,788. No doubt remained that as soon as Kansas had sufficient population, it would come into the Union as a free state.

The attempt to force slavery on the people of Kansas drove many conservative northerners into the Republican Party. And Douglas now found himself assailed by the southern wing of his party. On top of that, in the summer of 1858, he faced a desperate fight for reelection to the Senate in his race against Republican Abraham Lincoln.

The Lincoln-Douglas Debates

>> "He is the strong man of his party…and the best stump speaker, with his droll ways and dry jokes, in the West," Douglas commented when he learned of Lincoln's nomination to oppose him. "He is as honest as he is shrewd, and if I beat him my victory will be hardly won." Tall (6 feet 4 inches) and gangly, Lincoln had an awkward manner as he spoke, yet his logic and sincerity carried the audience with him. His sentences had none of the oratorical flourishes common in that day. "If we could first know *where* we are, and *whither* we are tending, we could then better judge *what* to do, and *how* to do it," Lincoln began, in accepting his party's nomination for senator in 1858. He then commented on a proverb from the Bible:

"A house divided against itself cannot stand." I believe this government cannot endure, permanently half *slave* and half *free*. I do not expect the Union to be *dissolved*—I do not expect the house to *fall*—but I *do* expect it will cease to be divided. It will become *all* one thing, or *all* the other. Either the *opponents* of slavery, will arrest the further spread of it, and place it where the public mind shall rest in the belief that it is in the course of ultimate extinction; or its *advocates* will push it forward, till it shall become alike lawful in all the States, *old* as well as *new*—*North* as well as *South*.

The message echoed through the hall and across the pages of the national press.

Born in the slave state of Kentucky, Lincoln had grown up mostly in southern Indiana and central Illinois. Yet his intense ambition lifted him above the backwoods from which he came. He compensated for a lack of schooling through disciplined self—education, and he became a shrewd courtroom lawyer of respectable social standing. Known for his sense of humor, he was nonetheless subject to fits of acute depression.

Lincoln's first love was always politics. A fervent admirer of Henry Clay and his economic program, Lincoln became a Whig and then, after the party's collapse, joined the Republicans and became one of their key leaders in Illinois. He challenged Douglas to discuss the issues of slavery and the sectional controversy in a series of seven debates.

In the campaign Douglas sought to portray Lincoln as a radical who preached sectional warfare. The nation *could* endure half slave and half free, Douglas declared, as long as states and territories were left alone to regulate their own affairs. Lincoln countered by insisting that the spread of slavery was a blight on the Republic. Even though Douglas had voted against the Lecompton constitution, he could not be counted on to oppose slavery's expansion, for he admitted that he didn't care whether slavery was voted "down or up."

In the debate held at Freeport, Illinois, Lincoln asked Douglas how under the *Dred Scott* decision the people of a territory could lawfully exclude slavery before statehood. Douglas answered, with what became known as the **Freeport Doctrine,** that slaveowners would never bring their slaves into an area where slavery was not legally protected. Therefore, Douglas explained, if the people of a territory refused to pass a slave

⋏ Superb debaters, Douglas (*left*) and Lincoln (*right*) nevertheless had very different speaking styles. The deep-voiced Douglas was constantly on the attack, drawing on his remarkable memory and showering points like buckshot in all directions. Lincoln, who had a high-pitched voice, developed his arguments more carefully and methodically than Douglas, and he relied on his sense of humor and unmatched ability as a storyteller to drive his points home to the audience.

Freeport Doctrine Stephen A. Douglas's response to Lincoln (at Freeport, Illinois) that even though the *Dred Scott* decision forbade Congress from banning slavery in any territory, a territorial government might effectively do so by refusing to pass a slave code.

code, slavery would never be established there.

In a close race, the legislature elected Douglas to another term in the Senate.[1] But on the national scene, southern Democrats angrily repudiated him and condemned the Freeport Doctrine. And although Lincoln lost, his impressive performance marked him as a possible presidential contender for 1860.

The Beleaguered South >> While northerners increasingly feared that the Slave Power was conspiring

to extend slavery into the free states, southerners worried that the "Black Republicans" would hem them in and undermine their political power.

The very factors that brought prosperity during the 1850s stimulated the South's sense of crisis. As the price of slaves rose sharply, the proportion of southerners who owned slaves had dropped almost a third since 1830. At the same time, California and Kansas had been closed to southern slaveholders—unfairly, in their eyes. Finally, Douglas's clever claim that a territory could effectively outlaw slavery using the Freeport Doctrine seemed to negate the *Dred Scott* decision that slavery was legal in all the territories.

Several possible solutions to the South's internal crisis had failed. Agricultural reform to restore worn-out lands had made significant headway only in Virginia and Maryland. Elsewhere the rewards of a single-crop economy were too great to persuade southern farmers to adopt new methods. Another alternative—bringing industry to the South—had also failed to take root.

[1]State legislatures elected senators until 1913, when the Seventeenth Amendment was adopted. Although Lincoln and Douglas both campaigned for the office, Illinois voters actually voted for candidates for the legislature who were pledged to one of the senatorial candidates.

Finally, private military expeditions in Latin America, which were designed to strengthen the South by adding slave territory to the United States, came to naught.

The South's growing sense of isolation made this crisis more acute. By the 1850s slavery had been abolished throughout most of the Americas, and in the United States the South's political power was steadily shrinking. Only the expansion of slavery and the admission of new slave states held any promise of preserving the South's political power and protecting its way of life. "The truth is," fumed one Alabama politician, "the South is excluded from the common territories of the Union. The right of expansion John Brown claimed to be a necessity of her continued existence, is practically and effectively denied the South."

✓ REVIEW

How did the *Dred Scott* decision and Stephen A. Douglas's Freeport Doctrine affect the debate over whether slavery could exist in the territories?

THE ROAD TO WAR

In 1857 John Brown—the abolitionist firebrand—had returned to the East from Kansas, consumed with the idea of attacking slavery in the South itself. Financed by a number of prominent northern reformers, Brown gathered 21 followers, including 5 free blacks, in hope of fomenting a slave insurrection. On the night of October 16, 1859, his band seized the unguarded federal armory at Harpers Ferry in Virginia. But no slaves rallied to Brown's standard: few lived in the area to begin with. Before long the raiders found themselves surrounded and holed up in the town. Charging with

Opinion

Was the Civil War an "irrepressible conflict," as Senator William Seward of New York insisted, or could it have been avoided?

bayonets fixed, federal troops commanded by Colonel Robert E. Lee soon captured Brown and his raiders. On December 2, 1859, Virginia hanged Brown for treason.

Brown's raid at Harpers Ferry was yet another blow weakening the forces of compromise within the nation. Although the invasion itself was a dismal failure, the old man knew how to bear himself with a martyr's dignity. Republicans made haste to denounce Brown's raid, lest they be tarred as radicals, but other northerners were less cautious. Ralph Waldo Emerson described Brown as a "saint, whose martyrdom will make the gallows as glorious as the cross." While only a minority of northerners endorsed Brown, southerners were shocked by such displays of sympathy. "I have always been a fervid Union man," one North Carolina resident wrote, "but I confess the endorsement of the Harpers Ferry outrage has shaken my fidelity and I am willing to take the chances of every probable evil that may arise from disunion, sooner than submit any longer to Northern insolence and Northern outrage."

A Sectional Election >>When Congress convened in December, there were ominous signs everywhere of the growing sectional rift. Intent on destroying Douglas's Freeport Doctrine, southern radicals demanded a congressional slave code to protect slavery in the territories. To northern Democrats such a platform spelled political death. As one Indiana Democrat put it, "We cannot carry a single congressional district on that doctrine in the state."

At the Democratic National Convention in April, southern radicals boldly pressed their demand for a federal slave code. Instead the convention adopted the Douglas platform upholding popular sovereignty, whereupon the delegations from eight southern states walked out. The convention finally reassembled two months later and nominated Douglas. At this point most of the remaining southern Democrats departed and, together with those delegates who had seceded earlier, nominated Vice President John C. Breckinridge of Kentucky on a platform supporting a federal slave code. The last major national party had shattered.

The Republicans turned to Abraham Lincoln, a moderate on slavery who was strong in his home state of Illinois and the other doubtful states that the party had failed to carry in 1856. Republicans also sought to broaden their appeal by adding to their platform several economic planks that endorsed a moderately protective tariff, a homestead bill, and a northern transcontinental railroad.

The election that followed was really two contests in one. In the North, which had a majority of the electoral votes, only Lincoln and Douglas had any chance to carry a state. In the South the race pitted Breckinridge against John Bell of Tennessee, the candidate of the new Constitutional Union Party. Although Lincoln received less than 40 percent of the popular vote and had virtually no support in the South, he won 180 electoral votes, 27 more than needed for election. For the first time, the nation had elected a president who headed a completely sectional party and who was committed to stopping the expansion of slavery.

Secession >>Although the Republicans had not won control of either house of Congress, Lincoln's election struck many southerners as a blow of terrible finality. Lincoln had been lifted into office on the strength of the free states alone. It was not unrealistic, many fire—eaters argued, to believe that he

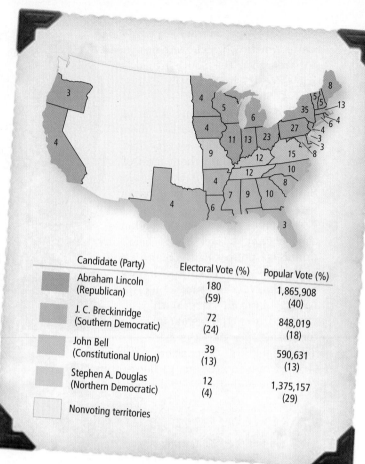

Candidate (Party)	Electoral Vote (%)	Popular Vote (%)
Abraham Lincoln (Republican)	180 (59)	1,865,908 (40)
J. C. Breckinridge (Southern Democratic)	72 (24)	848,019 (18)
John Bell (Constitutional Union)	39 (13)	590,631 (13)
Stephen A. Douglas (Northern Democratic)	12 (4)	1,375,157 (29)
Nonvoting territories		

MAP 15.3: ELECTION OF 1860

Although Lincoln did not win a majority of the popular vote, he still would have been elected even if the votes for all three of his opponents had been combined, because he won a clear majority in every state he carried except California, Oregon, and New Jersey (whose electoral votes he split with Douglas).

↑ In Iowa a somber young member of the Republicans' "Wide Awake" marching club shows his support for Lincoln in the 1860 election.

would use federal aid to encourage the border states to free their slaves voluntarily. Once slavery disappeared there, and new states were added, the necessary three—fourths majority would exist to approve a constitutional amendment abolishing slavery. Or perhaps Lincoln might send other John Browns into the South to stir up more slave insurrections. The *Montgomery* (Alabama) *Mail* accused Republicans of intending "to free the negroes and force amalgamation between them and the children of the poor men of the South."

Secession seemed the only alternative left to protect southern rights. South Carolina, which had challenged federal authority in the nullification crisis of the 1830s, was determined to force the other southern states to act. On December 20, 1860, a popular convention unanimously passed a resolution seceding from the Union. The rest of the Deep South followed, and on February 7, 1861, the states stretching from South

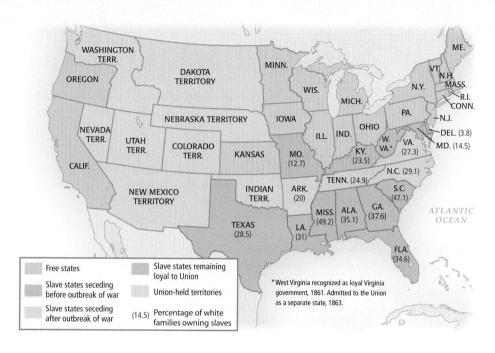

MAP 15.4: THE PATTERN OF SECESSION

Led by South Carolina, the Deep South seceded between Lincoln's election in November and his inauguration in March. The Upper South did not secede until after the firing on Fort Sumter. The four border slave states never seceded and remained in the Union throughout the war. As the map indicates, secession sentiment was strongest in states where the highest percentage of white families owned slaves.
What factors explain the hesitation of the Upper South to secede?

Carolina to Texas organized the Confederate States of America and elected Jefferson Davis president.

But the Upper South and the border states declined to secede, hoping that once again Congress could patch together a settlement. Senator John Crittenden of Kentucky proposed extending to California the old Missouri Compromise line of 36°30′. Slavery would be prohibited north of this line and given federal protection south of it in all territories, including any acquired in the future. Furthermore, Crittenden proposed an "unamendable amendment" to the Constitution, forever safeguarding slavery in states where it already existed.

But the Crittenden Compromise was doomed for the simple reason that the two groups who were required to make concessions—Republicans and secessionists—had no interest in doing so. "We have just carried an election on principles fairly stated to the people," Lincoln wrote in opposing the compromise. "Now we are told in advance, the government shall be broken up, unless we surrender to those we have beaten, before we take the offices. If we surrender, it is the end of us, and of the government."

The Outbreak of War

>>As he prepared to become president, Lincoln pondered what to do about secession. In his inaugural address on March 4, he sought to reassure southerners that he did not intend,

"directly or indirectly, to interfere with the institution of slavery in the States where it exists." But echoing Andrew Jackson in the nullification crisis, he maintained that "the Union of these states is perpetual," and he announced that he intended to "hold, occupy and possess" federal property and collect customs duties under the tariff. He closed by calling for a restoration of the "bonds of affection" that united all Americans.

The new president hoped for time to work out a solution, but on his first day in office he was given a dispatch from Major Robert Anderson, commander of the federal garrison at Fort Sumter in Charleston harbor. Sumter was one of the few remaining federal outposts in the South. Anderson informed the government that he was almost out of food and that, unless resupplied, he would have to surrender. For a month Lincoln looked for a way out, but he finally sent a relief expedition. As a conciliatory gesture, he notified the governor of South Carolina that supplies were being sent and that if the fleet were allowed to pass, only food, and not men, arms, or ammunition, would be landed.

The burden of decision now shifted to Jefferson Davis. From his point of view, secession was a constitutional right, and the Confederacy was not a bogus but a legitimate government. To allow the United States to hold property and maintain military forces

Dueling DOCUMENTS

SLAVERY AND SECESSION

The two highest officials of the Confederacy provide contrasting opinions on slavery's relation to the Civil War. The first, Alexander Stephens, delivered his remarks (which came to be known as the "Cornerstone Speech") in Savannah, Georgia, shortly after being elected vice president of the new government. Jefferson Davis, president of the Confederacy, published his reflections after the war.

DOCUMENT 1
Alexander Stephens: Slavery Is the Cornerstone

The new Constitution [of the Confederate States of America] has put at rest forever all the agitating questions relating to our peculiar institutions—African slavery as it exists among us—the proper *status* of the negro in our form of civilization. *This was the immediate cause of the late rupture and present revolution.* JEFFERSON, in his forecast, had anticipated this, as the "rock upon which the old Union would split." He was right. What was conjecture with him, is now a realized fact. But whether he fully comprehended the great truth upon which that rock stood and stands, may be doubted. *The prevailing ideas entertained by him and most of the leading statesmen at the time of the formation of the Old Constitution were, that the enslavement of the African was in violation of the laws of nature; that it was wrong in principle, socially, morally and politically.* It was an evil they knew not well how to deal

with but the general opinion of the men of that day was that, somehow or other, in the order of Providence, the institution would be evanescent and pass away. This idea, though not incorporated in the Constitution, was the prevailing idea at the time. . . . *Those ideas, however, were fundamentally wrong. They rested upon the assumption of the equality of races. This was an error.* It was a sandy foundation, and the idea of a Government built upon it—when the "storm came and the wind blew, it fell."

Our new Government is founded upon exactly the opposite ideas; its foundations are laid, its cornerstone rests, upon the great truth that the negro is not equal to the white man; that slavery, subordination to the superior race, is his natural and moral condition. This, our new Government, is the first, in the history of the world, based upon this great physical philosophical and moral truth. . . .

It is the first Government ever instituted upon principles in strict conformity to nature, and the ordination of Providence, in furnishing the materials of human society. Many Governments have been founded upon the principles of certain classes; but the classes thus enslaved, were of the same race, and in violation of the laws of nature. Our system commits no such violation of nature's laws. The negro by nature, or by the curse against Canaan, is fitted for that condition which he occupies in our system. . . . The substratum of our society is made of the material fitted by nature for it, and by experience we know that it is the best, not only for the superior but for the inferior race, that it should be so.

Source: Alexander Stephens speech delivered March 21, 1861. Savannah, Georgia. Frank Moore, ed., *The Rebellion Record* (New York, 1861–1866), pp. 45–46.

DOCUMENT 2
Jefferson Davis: Slavery Did Not Cause the Civil War

The reader of many of the treatises on these events, which have been put forth as historical . . . might naturally enough be led to the conclusion that the controversies which arose between the States, and the war in which they culminated, were caused by efforts on the one side to extend and perpetuate human slavery, and on the other to resist it and establish human liberty. The Southern States and Southern people have been sedulously represented as "propagandists" of slavery,

and the Northern as the defenders and champions of universal freedom. . . .

I have not attempted, and shall not permit myself to be drawn into any discussion of the merits or demerits of slavery as an ethical or even as a political question. It would be foreign to my purpose, irrelevant to my subject and would only serve—as it has invariably served in the hands of its agitators—to "darken counsel" and divert attention from the genuine issues involved. . . .

As a mere historical fact, we have seen that African servitude among us—confessedly the mildest and most humane of all institutions to which the name "slavery" has ever been applied—existed in all the original States, and that it was recognized and protected in the fourth article of the Constitution. Subsequently, for climatic, industrial, and economical—not moral or sentimental—reasons, it was abolished in the Northern, while it continued to exist in the Southern States. . . . Eleven years after the agitation on the

Missouri [Compromise of 1820], when the subject first took a sectional shape, the abolition of slavery was proposed and earnestly debated in the Virginia Legislature, and its advocates were so near the accomplishment of their purpose, that a declaration in its favor was defeated only by a small majority. . . . At a still later period, abolitionist lecturers and teachers were mobbed, assaulted, and threatened with tar and feather in New York, Pennsylvania, Massachusetts, New Hampshire, Connecticut, and other States. . . .

These facts prove incontestably that the sectional hostility which exhibited itself in 1820, on the application of Missouri for admission into the Union, which again broke out on the proposition for the annexation of Texas in 1844, and which reappeared after the Mexican war . . . was not the consequence of any difference on the abstract question of slavery. It was the offspring of sectional rivalry and political ambition. It would have manifested itself just as certainly if slavery had existed in all the States, or if there had not been a negro in America. . . . It was not slavery that threatened a rupture in 1832 [during the nullification crisis], but the unjust and unequal operation of a protective tariff. . . .

The truth remains intact and incontrovertible, that the existence of African servitude was in no wise the cause of the conflict, but only an incident. In the later controversies that arose, however, its effect in operating as a lever upon the passions, prejudices, or sympathies of mankind, was so potent that it has been spread, like a thick cloud, over the whole horizon of historical truth.

Source: Jefferson Davis, *The Rise and Fall of the Confederate Government* (New York, 1881), pp. 77–80.

THINKING CRITICALLY

What does Stephens mean by "the curse against Canaan"? How do Davis and Stephens differ in discussing the underlying causes of the Civil War? Does the date when each man delivered his opinion suggest a reason for the attitudes toward slavery and the reasons for secession? What evidence would you seek to decide the question of whether the dispute over slavery was the primary motivation for seceding?

within the Confederacy would destroy its claim of independence. Davis therefore instructed the Confederate commander at Charleston to demand the immediate surrender of Fort Sumter and, if refused, to open fire. When Anderson declined the ultimatum, Confederate batteries began shelling the fort on April 12 at 4:30 a.m. Some 33 hours later Anderson surrendered. A wave of indignation swept across the North in response. When Lincoln called for 75,000 volunteers to put down the rebellion, four states in the Upper South, led by Virginia, also seceded. Matters had passed beyond compromise.

The Roots of a Divided Nation

>>And so the Union was broken. After 70 years, the forces of sectionalism and separatism had finally outpulled the ties binding "these United States." Why did affairs come to such a pass?

In some ways, the revolution in markets, improving transportation networks, and increasingly sophisticated systems of credit and finance all served to tie the nation together. The cotton planter who rode the steamship *Fashion* along the Alabama River ("Time's money! Time's money!") was wearing ready-made clothes manufactured in New York from southern cotton. Chauncey Jerome's clocks from Connecticut were keeping time not only for commercial planters but also for Lowell mill workers such as Mary Paul, who learned to measure her lunch break in minutes. Farmers in both Tennessee and Iowa were interested in the price of wheat in New York, for it affected the profits that could be made shipping their grain by the new railroad lines. American society had become far more specialized and far more interdependent since the days of Hector St. John de Crèvecoeur's self-sufficient farmer of the 1780s.

But a specialized economy had not brought unity. For the North, specialization meant more factories, more cities and towns, and a higher percentage of urban workers. Industry affected midwestern farmers as well, for their steel plows and McCormick reapers allowed them to farm larger holdings and required greater capital investment in the new machinery. For its part, the South was transformed by the Industrial Revolution too, as textile factories made cotton the booming mainstay of its economy. But for all its growth, the region remained largely a rural society. Its prosperity stemmed from expansion westward into new areas of cotton production, not new forms of production or technology.

Above all, the intensive labor required to produce cotton, rice, and sugar made slavery an inseparable part of the southern way of life—"so intimately mingled with our social conditions," as one Georgian admitted, "that it would be impossible to eradicate it." An increasing number of northerners viewed slavery as evil, not so much out of high-minded sympathy toward slaves but as a labor system that threatened the republican ideals of white American society.

It fell to the political system to try to resolve sectional conflict, through a system of national parties that represented various interest groups and promoted democratic debate. But the political system had critical weaknesses. The American process of electing a president gave the winning candidate a state's entire electoral vote, regardless of the margin of victory.

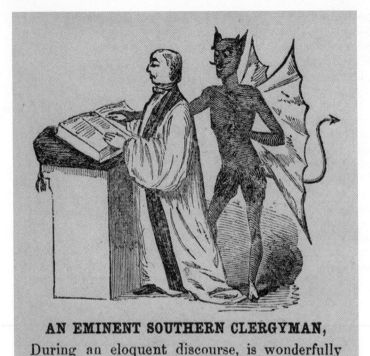

AN EMINENT SOUTHERN CLERGYMAN,
During an eloquent discourse, is wonderfully assisted in finding scriptural authority for Secession and Treason, and the divine ordination of Slavery.

<< Both northerners and southerners believed that political conspiracies were being put in motion by their opponents. In the North, letter envelopes could be bought that suggested who was the ultimate conspirator behind southern secession.

That procedure made a northern sectional party possible, since the Republicans could never have carried an election on the basis of a popular vote alone. In addition, since 1844 the Democratic Party had required a two–thirds vote to nominate its presidential candidate. Unintentionally, this requirement made it difficult to pick any truly forceful leader and gave the South a veto over the party's candidate. Yet the South, by itself, could not elect a president.

The nation's republican heritage also contributed to the political system's vulnerability. Ever since the Revolution, when Americans accused the king and Parliament of deliberately plotting to deprive them of their liberties, Americans were on the watch for political conspiracies. For their part, Republicans emphasized the existence of the Slave Power bent on eradicating northern rights. Southerners, however, accused the Black Republicans of conspiring to destroy southern equality. Each side viewed itself as defending the country's republican tradition from an internal threat.

 REVIEW

Why did Lincoln's election cause some southern states to secede from the Union? Which southern states did not secede until later, and why?

But in the end the threat to the Union came not from within but from beyond its borders. As the United States expanded in the 1840s it incorporated vast new territories, becoming a truly continental republic. And that forced the Union, in absorbing new lands, to define itself anew. If the American frontier had not swept so quickly toward the Pacific, the nation might have been able to postpone the day of reckoning on slavery until some form of gradual emancipation could be adopted. But the luxury of time was not available. The new territories became the battlegrounds for two contrasting ways of life, with slavery at the center of the debate. Elsewhere in the world the push toward abolition grew louder, whether of serfdom in eastern Europe or of slavery across the globe. Americans who saw the issue in moral terms joined that chorus. They saw no reason why the abolition of slavery should be postponed.

In 1850 supporters and opponents of slavery were still willing to compromise on how "the peculiar institution" could expand into the new territories. But a decade later, many Americans both North and South had come to accept the idea of an irrepressible conflict between two societies, one based on freedom, the other on slavery, in which only one side could ultimately prevail. At stake, it seemed, was control of the nation's future. Four years later, as a weary Abraham Lincoln looked back to the beginning of the conflict, he noted, "Both parties deprecated war, but one of them would make war rather than let the nation survive, and the other would accept war rather than let it perish, and the war came."

CHAPTER SUMMARY

In the 1850s the slavery issue reemerged in national politics and increasingly disrupted the party system, leading to the outbreak of war in 1861.

- Fundamental economic changes heightened sectional tensions in the 1850s.
  - The construction of a vast railroad network reoriented western trade from the South to the East.

- ▶ A tide of new immigrants swelled the North's population (and hence its political power) at the expense of the South, thereby stimulating southern fears.
- The old Jacksonian party system was shattered by the nativist movement and by renewed controversy over the expansion of slavery.
  - ▶ In the Kansas–Nebraska Act, Senator Stephen A. Douglas tried to defuse the slavery debate by incorporating popular sovereignty (the idea that the people of a territory should decide the status of slavery there). This act effectively repealed the Missouri Compromise.
  - ▶ Popular sovereignty failed in the Kansas Territory, where fighting broke out between proslavery and antislavery partisans.
  - ▶ Sectional violence reached a climax in May 1856 with the proslavery attack on Lawrence, Kansas, and the caning of Senator Charles Sumner of Massachusetts by Representative Preston S. Brooks of South Carolina.
- Sectional tensions sparked the formation of a new antislavery Republican Party, and the party system realigned along sectional lines.
  - ▶ The Supreme Court's *Dred Scott* decision, the Panic of 1857, the congressional struggle over the proslavery Lecompton constitution, and John Brown's attack on Harpers Ferry in 1859 strengthened the two sectional extremes.
- In 1860 Abraham Lincoln became the first Republican to be elected president.
  - ▶ Following Lincoln's triumph, the seven states of the Deep South seceded.
  - ▶ When Lincoln sent supplies to the Union garrison in Fort Sumter in Charleston harbor, Confederate batteries bombarded the fort into submission.
  - ▶ The North rallied to Lincoln's decision to use force to restore the Union, and in response the four states of the Upper South seceded.

Additional Reading

The problem of the coming of the Civil War has attracted considerable historical attention over the years. John Ashworth, *The Republic in Crisis* (2012), is a lucid, recent interpretation. The political aspects of the conflict also take center stage in Michael F. Holt's brief and incisive work, *The Fate of Their Country: Politicians, Slavery Extension, and the Coming of the Civil War* (2004). Holt stresses the self-interest of the political leaders and plays down the larger structural economic and social factors. A contrasting and similarly brief study can be found in Don E. Fehrenbacher, *Sectional Crises and Southern Constitutionalism* (1995).

The heavy immigration during these years is explored in Raymond L. Cohn, *Mass Migration under Sail* (2009). For slavery's mounting implications for American politics, see Eric Foner, *The Fiery Trial* (2010).

Paul Quigley's *Shifting Grounds* (2012) puts the idea of southern nationalism in a broad spatial context. The most thorough examination of the blend of factors that produced the Republican Party is William E. Gienapp, *The Origins of the Republican Party, 1852–1856* (1987). Eric Foner's classic *Free Soil, Free Labor, Free Men* (1970) focuses on the ideas of Republican Party leaders. For the turbulent history of Kansas in this period, see Nicole Etcheson, *Bleeding Kansas* (2006). The critical events of 1857 are the focal point of Kenneth M. Stampp's *America in 1857* (1990). William W. Freehling's two-volume work *The Road to Disunion* (1991, 2007) offers a broad perspective on the secessionist project; and Charles B. Dew provides a regional view by examining the role of the Secession Commissioners appointed by the Confederacy to persuade wavering southerners in *Apostles of Secession* (2001). Adam Goodheart's *1861: The Civil War Awakening* (2011) presents a rich portrait of the war's beginnings. For a discussion of the broader issues of why the South chose secession and fought the Civil War, see Gary W. Gallagher and Alan T. Nolan, eds., *The Myth of the Lost Cause and Civil War History* (2000).

Significant Events

1834
McCormick patents mechanical reaper

1840–1860
Expansion of railroad network

1846–1854
Mass immigration to United States

1854
Kansas-Nebraska Act passed; Republican Party founded

1854–1855
Height of Know-Nothings' popularity

1856
"Sack of Lawrence"; caning of Charles Sumner; Pottawatomie massacre

1857
Dred Scott decision; Lecompton constitution drafted

1857–1861
Panic and depression

1858
Lincoln-Douglas debates

1859
John Brown's raid on Harpers Ferry

1860
Democratic Party ruptures; Lincoln elected president; South Carolina secedes

1861
Confederate States of America established; war begins at Fort Sumter

16 Total War and the Republic

1861–1865

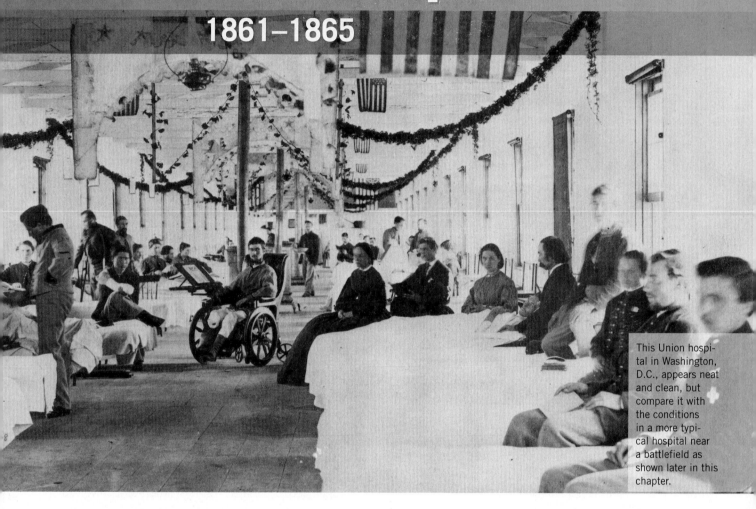

This Union hospital in Washington, D.C., appears neat and clean, but compare it with the conditions in a more typical hospital near a battlefield as shown later in this chapter.

>> An American Story

A ROUT AT BULL RUN

"The war won't last sixty days!" Of that Jim Tinkham was confident. With dreams of a hero's return, Tinkham enlisted for three months in a Massachusetts regiment. Soon he was transferred to Washington, D.C., as part of the Union army being assembled by General Irvin McDowell to crush the rebellion. Tinkham was elated when in mid-July 1861 he was finally ordered to march toward the Confederates concentrated at Manassas Junction, 25 miles away.

The battle began at dawn on July 21, with McDowell commanding 30,000 troops against General Pierre Beauregard's 22,000. Tinkham did not arrive on the field until early afternoon. As his regiment pushed toward the front, he felt faint at his first sight of the dead and wounded,

↥ The Civil War was the first conflict whose major battles routinely involved more than 100,000 troops, and casualties soared beyond the scale Americans experienced in the U.S.-Mexican War. The Battle of Antietam, fought in 1862, produced almost 23,000 casualties, the bloodiest single day of the war. A group of Confederate soldiers are shown where they fell along the Hagerstown Pike. Said one Union officer of the fighting: "Men, I cannot say fell; they were knocked out of the ranks by dozens."

some mangled horribly. But he was soon caught up in the excitement of battle as he charged up Henry Hill. Suddenly the Confederate ranks broke, and exuberant Union troops shouted: "The war is over!"

The arrival of fresh troops, however, enabled the Confederates to regroup. Among the reinforcements who rushed to Henry Hill was 19-year-old Randolph McKim of Baltimore. A student at the University of Virginia, McKim joined the First Maryland Infantry as a private when Abraham Lincoln imposed martial law in his home state. "The cause of the South had become identified with liberty itself," he explained. The arrival of the First Maryland and other reinforcements in the late afternoon turned the tide of battle. The faltering Confederate line held, and Union troops began to withdraw.

But with retreat came confusion. Discipline dissolved and the army degenerated into a stampeding mob. As they fled, terrified troops threw away their equipment, shoved aside officers who tried to stop them, and raced frantically past the wagons and artillery pieces that clogged the road. All the next day in a drizzling rain, mud-spattered troops straggled into the capital in complete disorder. William Russell, an English reporter, asked one pale officer where they were coming from. "Well, sir, I guess we're all coming out of Virginny as far as we can, and pretty well whipped too," he replied. Joining the stampede was Jim Tinkham, who confessed he would have continued on to Boston if he had not been stopped by a guard in Washington.

The rout at Bull Run sobered the North. Gone were dreams of ending the war with one glorious battle. Gone was the illusion that 75,000 volunteers serving three months would be sufficient. As one perceptive observer noted, "We have undertaken to make war without in the least knowing how." Having cast off his earlier misconceptions, a newly determined Jim Tinkham reenlisted for a three-year hitch.

Still, it was not surprising that both sides underestimated the magnitude of the conflict. Warfare as it had evolved in Europe consisted largely of maneuverings that took relatively few lives, respected private property, and left civilians largely unharmed. The Civil War, however, was the first war whose major battles routinely involved more than 100,000 troops. So many combatants could be equipped only through the use of factory-produced weaponry, they could be moved and supplied only with the help of railroads, and they could be sustained only through the concerted efforts of civilian society as a whole. The morale of the population, the quality of political leadership, and the use of industrial and economic might were all critical to the outcome. Quite simply, the Civil War was the first total war in history. <<

What's to Come

THE DEMANDS OF TOTAL WAR

When the war began the North had an enormous advantage in manpower and industrial capacity. The Union's population was 2.5 times larger; it contained more railroad track and rolling stock and possessed more than 10 times the industrial capacity.

From a modern perspective the South's attempt to resist against such odds seems hopeless. But the South enjoyed definite strategic advantages. To be victorious it did not need to invade the North—only to defend its own land and prevent the North from destroying its armies. Southern soldiers knew the topography of their home country better than Yankees, and a friendly population regularly supplied them with intelligence about Union troop movements.

The North, in contrast, had to invade and conquer the Confederacy and destroy the southern will to resist. To do so it would have to deploy thousands of soldiers to defend long supply lines in enemy territory, a situation that significantly reduced the northern advantage in manpower. Yet by 1865 Union forces had penetrated virtually every part of the 500,000 square miles of the Confederacy and were able to move almost at will. The Civil War demonstrated the capacity of a modern society to overcome the problems of distance and terrain with technology.

Political Leadership >> To sustain a commitment to total war required effective political leadership. This task fell on Abraham Lincoln and Jefferson Davis, presidents of the rival governments.

Jefferson Davis grew up in Mississippi accustomed to life's advantages. Educated at West Point, he fought in the U.S.–Mexican War, served as Franklin Pierce's secretary of war, and became one of the South's leading advocates in the Senate. Although hardworking and committed, he was quarrelsome, resented criticism, and refused to work with those he disliked. "He cannot brook opposition or criticism," one member of the Confederate Congress testified, "and those who do not bow down before him have no chance of success with him."

Yet for all Davis's personal handicaps, he faced an institutional one even more daunting. The Confederacy had been founded on the ideology of states' rights. But to meet the demands of total war, Davis would need to increase the authority of the central government beyond anything the South had ever experienced.

When Lincoln took the oath of office, his national experience consisted of one term in the House of Representatives. But Lincoln was a shrewd judge of character and a superb politician. To achieve a common goal, he willingly overlooked withering criticism and personal slights. He was not easily humbugged, overawed, or flattered, and he never allowed personal feelings to blind him to his larger objectives. "No man knew better how to summon and dispose of political ability to attain great political ends," commented one associate.

"This is essentially a People's contest," Lincoln asserted at the start of the war, and few presidents have been better able to communicate with the average citizen. He regularly visited Union troops in camp, in the field, and in army hospitals. "The boys liked him," wrote Joseph Twichell, from a Connecticut regiment, "in fact his popularity with the army is and has been universal." Always Lincoln reminded the public that

	Union	Confederacy	Union advantage
Total population	23,300,000	9,100,000*	**2.5 to 1**
White male population (18–45 years)	4,600,000	1,100,000	**4.2 to 1**
Bank deposits	$207,000,000	$47,000,000	**4.4 to 1**
Value of manufactured goods	$1,730,000,000	$156,000,000	**11 to 1**
Railroad mileage	22,000	9,000	**2.4 to 1**
Shipping tonnage	4,600,000	290,000	**16 to 1**
Value of textiles produced	$181,000,000	$10,000,000	**18 to 1**
Value of firearms produced	$2,290,000	73,000	**31 to 1**
Pig iron production (tons)	951,000	37,000	**26 to 1**
Coal production (tons)	13,680,000	650,000	**21 to 1**
Corn and wheat production (bushels)	698,000,000	314,000,000	**2.2 to 1**
Draft animals	5,800,000	2,900,000	**2 to 1**
Cotton production (bales)	43,000	5,344,000	**1 to 124**

Slaves accounted for 3,300,000, or 40 percent.

RESOURCES OF THE UNION AND THE CONFEDERACY, 1861

(Source: U.S. Census 1860 and E. B. Long, *The Civil War Day by Day* [New York: Doubleday, 1971], p. 723.)

the war was being fought for the ideals of the Revolution and the Republic. It was a test, he remarked in his famous address at Gettysburg, of whether a nation "conceived in Liberty, and dedicated to the proposition that all men are created equal" could "long endure."

He also proved the more effective military leader. Jefferson Davis took his title of commander in chief literally, constantly interfering with his generals, but he failed to formulate an overarching strategy. In contrast, Lincoln clearly grasped the challenge confronting

the Union. He accepted General Winfield Scott's proposal to blockade the Confederacy, cut off its supplies, and slowly strangle it into submission, just as an anaconda snake squeezes its prey. But unlike Scott, Lincoln realized that this "anaconda plan" was not enough: the South would also have to be invaded and defeated on at least two fronts. The first was the eastern theater in Virginia. A second front was in the West, where Union control of the Mississippi River would divide the Confederacy. Lincoln understood that the Union's superior

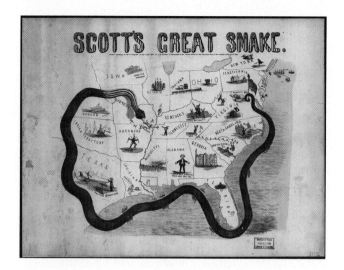

General Winfield Scott's "anaconda plan" called for a naval blockade to squeeze the Confederacy, like an anaconda snake. Ships are sketched in around the snake in this cartoon from 1861. But Lincoln realized that the war would have to be taken to the interior of the Confederate States, in the eastern theater of battle (Virginia, the Carolinas, and Georgia) as well as in the western theater, beyond the Appalachian Mountains.

manpower and matériel would become decisive only when the Confederacy was simultaneously threatened at many points. It took time before the president found generals able to execute this novel strategy.

The Border States >>
When the war began, only Delaware of the border slave states was certain to remain in the Union. Lincoln's immediate political challenge was to retain the loyalty of Maryland, Kentucky, and Missouri. Maryland especially was crucial, for if it was lost, Washington itself would have to be abandoned.

Lincoln moved vigorously—even ruthlessly—to secure Maryland. He suppressed pro-Confederate newspapers and suspended the writ of **habeas corpus,** the right under the Constitution of an arrested person either to be charged with a specific crime or to be released. That done, he held without trial prominent Confederate sympathizers. Under these conditions Unionists won a complete victory in the fall state election.

> **habeas corpus** the right that ensures the government cannot arbitrarily arrest and imprison a citizen without giving grounds for doing so.

As for Kentucky, which had proclaimed itself neutral, Lincoln forbid Union generals from occupying the state, preferring to wait for Unionist sentiment to assert itself. After Unionists won control of the legislature in the summer election, a Confederate army entered the state, giving Lincoln the opening he needed. He quickly sent in troops, and Kentucky stayed in the Union.

In Missouri, guerrilla warfare raged between Union and Confederate sympathizers throughout the war. But a Union victory in the state in March 1862 kept Missouri within the Union. In Virginia internal divisions led to the creation of a new border state, because the hilly western counties where slavery was weak refused to support the Confederacy. After adopting a congressionally mandated program of gradual emancipation, West Virginia was formally admitted to the Union in June 1863.

The Union scored an important triumph in holding the border states. The population of all five equaled that of the four states of the Upper South that had joined the Confederacy, and their production of military supplies—food, animals, and minerals—was greater. Furthermore, Maryland and West Virginia contained railroad lines critical to the defense of Washington, while Kentucky and Missouri gave the Union army access to the major river systems of the western theater, down which it launched the first successful invasions of the Confederacy.

✔ **REVIEW**

How was Lincoln's leadership demonstrated in the opening months of the war? What leadership qualities did Jefferson Davis lack?

OPENING MOVES

After the Confederate victory at Bull Run, Congress authorized a much larger army of long-term volunteers, and Lincoln named 34-year-old George McClellan, a West Point graduate and former railroad executive, to be the new commander. Energetic and ambitious, he spent the next eight months directing the much-needed task of organizing and drilling the Army of the Potomac.

Blockade and Isolate >>
Although the U.S. Navy began the war with only 42 ships available to blockade 3,550 miles of Confederate coastline, by the spring of 1862 it had taken control of key islands off the

Opinion

Was Lincoln justified in suspending habeas corpus? Was the Bush administration justified in doing so in the war on terror?

coasts of the Carolinas and Georgia, to use as supply bases. The navy also began building powerful gunboats to operate on the rivers. In April 1862 Flag Officer David G. Farragut ran a gauntlet of Confederate shore batteries to capture New Orleans, the Confederacy's largest port. Memphis, another important river city, fell to Union forces in June.

Small, fast ships continued to slip through the blockade, but southern trade suffered badly nonetheless. As a countermeasure the Confederacy converted the wooden USS *Merrimack* (rechristened the *Virginia*) into an ironclad gunboat. In March 1862 a Union ironclad, the *Monitor*, battled it to a standoff, and the Confederates scuttled the *Virginia* when they evacuated Norfolk in May. After that, the Union's naval supremacy was secure.

The Confederacy looked to diplomacy as another means to lift the blockade. With cotton so vital to European economies, especially Great Britain's, southerners believed Europe would formally recognize the Confederacy and come to its aid. Indeed, the governments of France and Great Britain both seemed to favor the South. Leaders in the two countries dismissed the notion that this was a war to end slavery; after all, Lincoln himself denied it. Stripped of that larger purpose, the conflict seemed to many observers across the Atlantic only a futile and increasingly savage effort to force southerners back into a union they abhorred. Most concretely, the war crippled the global distribution of cotton, something French and British industry remained

desperately dependent upon. The two powers contemplated intervention, or at least formal recognition of the Confederacy—prospects that terrified Lincoln and thrilled Davis. But France and Britain hesitated to act until Confederate armies demonstrated that they could win the war. Meanwhile, new supplies of cotton from Egypt and India enabled the British textile industry to recover. In the end, Europe's great powers refused to recognize the Confederacy, and the South was left to stand or fall on its own resources.

Grant in the West >> In the western war theater the first decisive Union victory was won by a short, shabbily dressed, cigar-chomping general named Ulysses S. Grant. An undistinguished student at West Point, Grant eventually had resigned his commission. He had failed at everything he tried in civilian life, and when the war broke out, he was a store clerk in Galena, Illinois. Almost 39, he promptly volunteered, and two months later became a brigadier general.

Grant's quiet, self-effacing manner gave little indication of his military ability or iron determination.

MAP 16.1: THE WAR IN THE WEST, 1861–1862

Grant's push southward stalled after his costly victory at Shiloh; nevertheless, by the end of 1862 the Union had secured Kentucky and Missouri, as well as most of Confederate Tennessee and the upper and lower stretches of the Mississippi River.
How did Grant use the geography of the South to plan his campaign in the West?

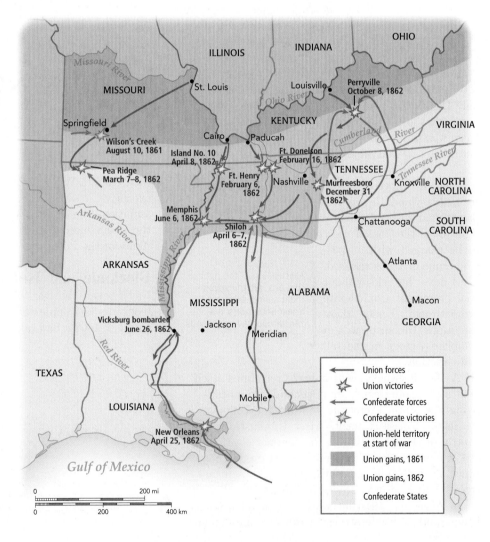

He had a flair for improvising, was alert to seize any opening, and remained extraordinarily calm and clear-headed in battle. Most important, Grant grasped that hard fighting, not fancy maneuvering, would bring victory. "The art of war is simple," he once explained. "Find out where your enemy is, get at him as soon as you can and strike him as hard as you can, and keep moving on."

Grant realized that rivers were avenues into the interior of the Confederacy, and in February 1862, supported by Union gunboats, he captured Fort Henry on the Tennessee River and Fort Donelson on the Cumberland. These victories forced the Confederates to withdraw from Kentucky and middle Tennessee. Grant continued south with 40,000 men, but he was surprised on April 6 by General Albert Johnston at Shiloh, just north of the Tennessee–Mississippi border. Johnston was killed in the day's fierce fighting, but by nightfall his army had driven the Union troops back to the Tennessee River, where they huddled numbly as a cold rain fell. William Tecumseh Sherman, one of Grant's subordinates, found the general standing under a dripping

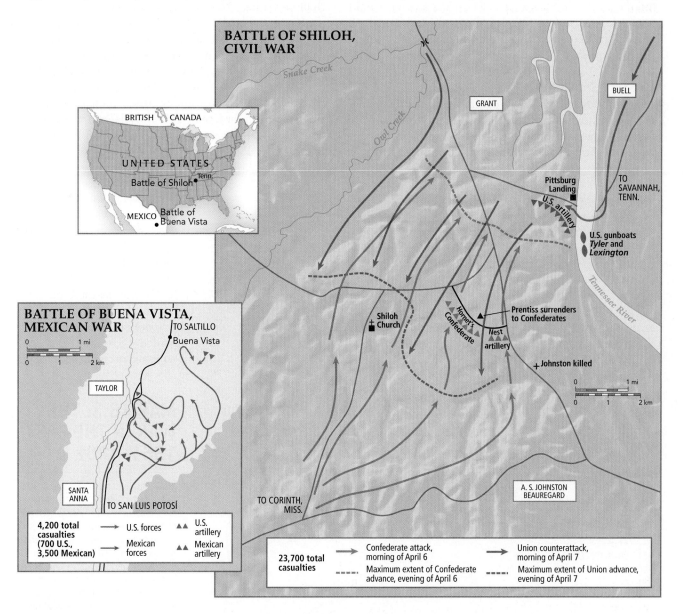

MAP 16.2: THE CHANGING MAGNITUDE OF BATTLE

During the Mexican War at Buena Vista, the American army of 4,800 men was overextended to defend a two-mile line against 15,000 Mexicans. At Shiloh, in contrast, battle lines stretched almost six miles. (The maps are drawn to the same scale.) Against 40,000 Confederates Grant galloped back and forth, rallying some 35,000 troops organized under five subordinates and coordinating the overnight reinforcement of 25,000 troops. The size of the armies, the complexity of their organization, the length of the battle lines, and the number of casualties all demonstrate the extent to which the magnitude of battle had changed.

tree, his coat collar drawn up against the damp, puffing on a cigar. Sherman was about to suggest retreat, but something in Grant's eyes, lighted by the glow of his stogie, made him hesitate. So he said only, "Well, Grant, we've had the devil's own day, haven't we?" "Yes," the Union commander replied quietly. "Lick 'em tomorrow, though." And he did. With the aid of reinforcements, which he methodically ferried across the river all night, Grant counterattacked the next morning and drove the Confederates from the field.

But victory came at a high price, for Shiloh inflicted more than 23,000 casualties. The Confederacy would not yield easily. "At Shiloh," Grant wrote afterward, "I gave up all idea of saving the Union except by complete conquest."

Eastern Stalemate >> Grant's victories did not silence his critics, who charged that he drank too much. But Lincoln was unmoved. "I can't spare this man. He fights." That was a quality in short supply in the East, where General McClellan directed operations.

McClellan looked like a general, but beneath his arrogance and bravado lay a self-doubt that rendered him excessively cautious. As the months dragged on and McClellan did nothing but train and plan, Lincoln's frustration grew. "If General McClellan does not want to use the army I would like to *borrow* it," he remarked sarcastically. Where McClellan was cautious and defensive, the aristocratic Lee was daring and ever alert to assume the offensive. His first name, one of his colleagues commented, should have been Audacity: "He will take more chances, and take them quicker than any other general in this country."

In the Seven Days' battles, McClellan successfully parried the attacks of Lee and Thomas "Stonewall" Jackson, a deeply religious Calvinist whose rigorous discipline honed his troops to a hard edge. But McClellan, ever cautious, pulled the Union army back until it was under the protection of Union gunboats. Frustrated, Lincoln ordered the Peninsula campaign abandoned and formed a new army under John Pope. After Lee mauled Pope at the Second Battle of Bull Run in August, Lincoln restored McClellan to command.

Now Lee looked to strike a decisive victory for the Confederacy. He invaded the North, hoping to detach Maryland and isolate Washington. By good fortune McClellan learned of Lee's battle plan when two Union soldiers stumbled on a discarded "Special Order 191" wrapped around three cigars.

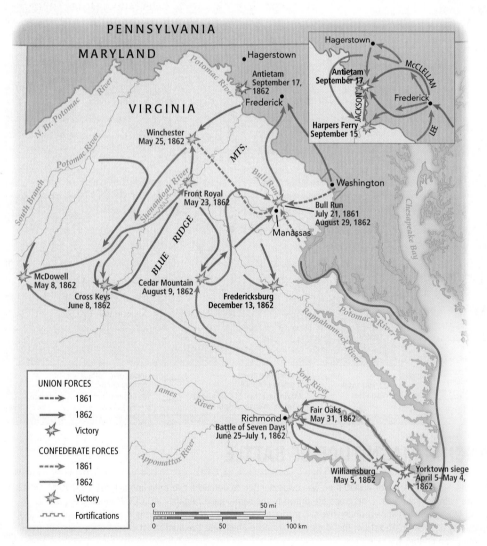

MAP 16.3: THE WAR IN THE EAST, 1861–1862

McClellan's campaign against Richmond failed when Joseph Johnston surprised him at Fair Oaks. Taking command of the Army of Northern Virginia, Lee drove back McClellan in the Seven Days' battles, then won a resounding victory over Pope in the Second Battle of Bull Run. He followed this up by invading Maryland. McClellan checked his advance at Antietam. The Army of the Potomac's devastating defeat at Fredericksburg ended a year of frustration and failure for the Union in the eastern theater.

What does this map tell us about the relative naval power of the two sides?

But even with this advantage McClellan managed only to launch a series of badly coordinated assaults near Antietam Creek on September 17. Lee repulsed the attack—barely—but his daring plan to invade the North had been blocked, and he retreated back to Virginia. Nearly 5,000 soldiers were killed and another 18,000 wounded, making it the bloodiest single day in American history. When McClellan allowed Lee's army to escape back into Virginia, an exasperated Lincoln permanently relieved him of command.

In the winter of 1862 Union morale sank to an all-time low. General Ambrose Burnside, who assumed McClellan's place, took little more than a month to demonstrate his utter incompetence at the Battle of Fredericksburg. The Union's disastrous defeat there prompted Lincoln to put "Fighting Joe" Hooker in charge. In the West, Grant had emerged as the dominant figure, but the Army of the Potomac still lacked a capable commander, the deaths kept mounting, and no end to the war was in sight.

 REVIEW

How did Grant's strategies in the western theater of the war contrast with McClellan's in the eastern theater?

EMANCIPATION

In 1858 Abraham Lincoln had proclaimed that the United States must eventually become either all slave or all free. When the war began, however, the president refused to make emancipation a Union war aim. He feared the social upheaval that such a revolutionary step would cause, and he did not want to alarm the wavering border slave states.

Republican radicals such as Senator Charles Sumner and newspaper editor Horace Greeley pressed Lincoln to adopt a policy of emancipation. Slavery had caused the war, they argued; its destruction would hasten the war's end. Lincoln, however, placed first priority on saving the Union. "My paramount object in this struggle is to save the Union, and is not either to save or to destroy slavery," he wrote Greeley in 1862. "If I could save the Union without freeing any slave I would do it, and if I could save it by freeing all the slaves I would do it, and if I could save it by freeing some and leaving others alone, I would also do that." For the first year of the war, this remained Lincoln's policy.

Moving toward Freedom >> As the Union army began to occupy Confederate territory, slaves flocked to the Union lines. In May 1861 the army adopted the policy of declaring runaway slaves "**contraband** of war" and refused to return them to their rebel owners. In the Confiscation Act of August 1861, Congress provided that slaves used for military purposes by the Confederacy would become free if they fell into Union hands. For a year Lincoln accepted that position but would go no further. When two of his generals, acting on their own authority, abolished slavery in their districts, he countermanded their orders.

> **contraband** goods seized by a government during wartime, when the goods were being used by an enemy nation or being shipped to an enemy nation by a neutral nation. The term was also applied during the Civil War to escaped slaves who fled behind Union lines.

By 1862 opinion was clearly shifting. In July Congress passed the Second Confiscation Act, which declared that the slaves of anyone who supported the rebellion would be freed if they came into federal custody. Unlike with the first act, it did not matter whether the slaves had been used for military purposes. Lincoln signed this bill, then proceeded to ignore it. Instead, he encouraged the border states to undertake programs of gradual emancipation, warning them that the war was likely to destroy slavery of its own momentum.

When Lincoln's efforts were rebuffed, on July 22 he presented to his cabinet a proposed proclamation freeing the slaves in the Confederacy. He was increasingly confident that the border states would remain in the Union, and he wanted to strike a blow that would weaken the Confederacy militarily. By making the struggle one of freedom versus slavery, such a proclamation would also undermine Confederate efforts to obtain diplomatic recognition. But Lincoln decided to wait for a Union military victory, so that his act would not seem like one of desperation.

The Emancipation Proclamation >> On September 22, 1862, in the aftermath of the victory at Antietam, Lincoln announced that all slaves within rebel lines would be freed unless the seceded states returned to their allegiance by January 1, 1863. When that day came, the Emancipation Proclamation went into effect. Excluded from its terms were the Union slave states and areas of the Confederacy that were under Union control. In all, about 830,000 of the nation's 4 million slaves were not covered by its provisions. Since Lincoln justified his actions on strictly military grounds, he believed he had no legal right to apply the measure to areas not in rebellion.

After initial criticism of the Proclamation, European public opinion swung toward the Union. Within the Union popular reaction was mixed. Even so, the Emancipation Proclamation had immense symbolic importance, for it redefined the nature of the war. The

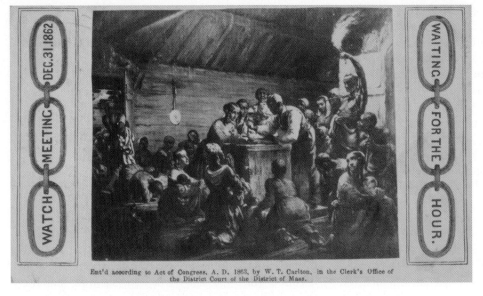

DEC. 31. 1862

WATCH MEETING

WAITING FOR THE HOUR.

Ent'd according to Act of Congress, A. D. 1863, by W. T. Carlton, in the Clerk's Office of the District Court of the District of Mass.

⌃ Many African American churches held "watch night meetings" every New Year's Eve, to welcome in the new year. With the Emancipation Proclamation set to go into effect January first, these sessions took on special significance in December 1862.

North was fighting, not to save the old Union, but to create a new nation. The war had become, in Lincoln's words, "remorseless revolution."

African Americans' Civil War >> Under the pressure of war, slavery disintegrated. Well before federal troops entered an area, slaves undermined the institution by openly challenging white authority and claiming greater personal freedom. One experienced overseer reported in frustration that the "slaves will do only what pleases them, go out in the morning when it suits them, come in when they please, etc."

Early in the conflict slaves concluded that emancipation would be one consequence of a Union victory. Perhaps as many as half a million—one-seventh of the total slave population of the Confederacy—fled to Union lines. The ex-slaves, called "freedmen," ended up living in refugee or contraband camps that were overcrowded and disease-ridden and provided only the most basic shelter and food.

Convinced that freed slaves would not work on their own initiative, the U.S. government put some contrabands to work assisting the army. Their wages were well below those paid white citizens for the same work. In the Mississippi valley, where two-thirds of the freedpeople under Union control were located, most were forced to work on plantations leased or owned by loyal planters. They worked for little more than room and board, and the conditions often approximated slavery.

Black Soldiers >> In adopting the policy of emancipation, Lincoln also announced that African

⌃ Black men, including runaway slaves, joined the Union army and navy beginning in 1863. As soldiers, former slaves developed a new sense of pride and confidence. At his first roll call, recruit Elijah Marrs recalled, "I felt freedom in my bones."

Americans would be accepted into the navy and, more controversially, the army. Resistance to accept—ing black volunteers in the army remained especially strong in the Midwest. Black northerners themselves were divided over whether to enlist, but Frederick Douglass spoke for the vast majority when he argued that once a black man had served in the army, there was "no power on earth which can deny that he has earned the right of citizenship in the United States."

In the end, nearly 200,000 black Americans served in the Union forces, about 10 percent of the Union's total military manpower. Some, including two of Dou—glass's sons, were free, but most were former slaves who enlisted after escaping to Union lines. As a concession to the racism of white troops, blacks served in segregated units under white officers. Not until June 1864 did Congress grant equal pay to African American soldiers.

Assigned at first to the most undesirable duties, black soldiers successfully lobbied for the chance to fight. They deeply impressed white troops with their courage under fire. "I have been one of those men, who never had much confidence in colored troops fighting," one Union officer admitted, "but these doubts are now all removed, for they fought as bravely as any troops in the Fort." In the end 37,000 African American servicemen gave their lives, a rate of loss about 40 percent higher than that among white soldiers. Black recruits had good reason to fight fiercely: they knew that the freedom of their race hung in the balance, they hoped to win civil rights at home by their performance on the battlefield, they resented racist sneers about their loyalty and ability, and they knew that capture might mean death.

 REVIEW

What steps took the North along the path from a war to save the Union to a war in which emancipation became a central goal?

THE CONFEDERATE HOME FRONT

"How shall we subsist this winter?" John Jones won—dered in the fall of 1862. A clerk in the War Depart—ment in Richmond, Jones found it increasingly difficult to make ends meet. "I cannot afford to have more than an ounce of meat daily for each member of my family of six," he recorded in 1864. By the end of the year inflation had taken such a toll that a month's supply of food and fuel was costing him $762, a sum sufficient to have supported his family for a year in peacetime. "This is war, terrible war!" The conflict's privations fell most heavily on the Confederacy, where the demands of war fundamentally transformed the southern economy, society, and government.

The New Economy >> With the Union blockade tightening, the production of foodstuffs became cru—cial. More and more plantations switched from cotton to raising grain and livestock. Even so, food production declined. In the last two years of the war the shortage was serious.

The Union blockade also made it impossible to rely on European manufactured goods. So the Confeder—ate War Department built and ran factories, took over the region's mines, and regulated private manufac—turers so as to increase the production of war goods. Although the Confederacy never became industrially self—sufficient, its accomplishments were impressive. In fact, the Confederacy sustained itself far better in industrial goods than it did in agricultural produce. It was symbolic that when Lee surrendered, his troops had sufficient guns and ammunition to continue, but they had not eaten in two days.

New Opportunities for Southern Women >> Southern white women took an active role in the war. Some gained notoriety as spies; others smuggled

⌃ Southern women aided the war effort in a variety of ways, but in addition to the often unexpected jobs they performed the shadow of death was never far away. This Confederate woman wears a black mourning dress and a brooch showing a Confederate soldier (her dead husband?) and holds her son in her lap.

Face Value?

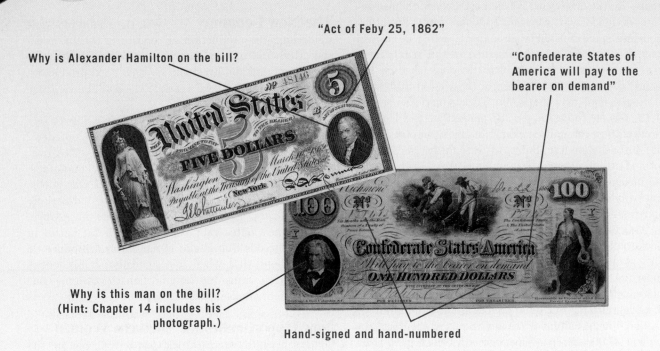

"Act of Feby 25, 1862"

Why is Alexander Hamilton on the bill?

"Confederate States of America will pay to the bearer on demand"

Why is this man on the bill? (Hint: Chapter 14 includes his photograph.)

Hand-signed and hand-numbered

A government at war can survive only if it maintains its credit—not only with its bankers but with its citizens. Both the Union and the Confederacy issued paper money to finance the war, and by examining the bills' designs, historians can appreciate the efforts to portray the issuers as creditworthy. The Union note uses Alexander Hamilton to vouch for its reliability—the republic's first treasury secretary, who during the 1790s stabilized the nation's shaky finances. It announces the act of Congress that allows the government to issue the notes: the Legal Tender Act, passed February 25, 1862. And the intricate engraving and red treasury seal made the bill harder to counterfeit. The Confederacy had more difficulty issuing bills because few skilled engravers lived in the South. To help prevent counterfeiting, the Confederacy followed the older tradition of signing each bill individually, employing as many as 200 secretaries to do the tedious work. (The Union's signatures were printed.) But by war's end so many Confederate notes had been issued that they were carted about in wheelbarrows to pay the hugely inflated prices for goods. In the end mere symbols of credit could not obliterate the realities on the ground.

THINKING CRITICALLY

The fine print located above the Confederate promise to "pay on demand" reads "Six months after a ratification of a Treaty of Peace between The Confederate States & The United States of America." What effect does this condition have? Who are the people portrayed at the center of the Confederate bill? Why choose to include them?

---

military supplies into the South. Many knitted and sewed clothes for soldiers. Perhaps most important, with so many men fighting, women took charge of agricultural production. On plantations the mistress often supervised the slaves as well as the wrenching shift from cotton to foodstuffs. "All this attention to farming is uphill work with me," one South Carolina woman confessed to her army husband.

One such woman was Emily Lyles Harris, the wife of a small slaveowner in upcountry South Carolina. When her husband joined the army in 1862, she was left to care for her seven children as well as supervise the slaves and manage the farm. Despite the disruptions of wartime, she succeeded remarkably, one year producing the largest crop of oats in the neighborhood and always making enough money for her family to live decently. She took little pride, however, in her achievements. "I shall never get used to being left as the head of affairs at home," she confessed. "The burden is very heavy." Although she pushed on, by 1865 she openly hoped for defeat.

Confederate Finance and Government >>

The most serious domestic problem the Confederate government faced was finance, for which officials at Richmond never developed a satisfactory program. Only in 1863 did the government begin levying a **graduated income tax** (from 1 to 15 percent) and a series of excise taxes. Most controversial, the government resorted to a tax—in—kind on farmers that, after

> **graduated income tax** tax based on a percentage of an individual's income, the percentage increasing as total income increases.

exempting a certain portion, took one—tenth of their crops. Even more unpopular was the policy of impress—ment, which allowed the army to seize private property for its own use, often with little or no compensation.

Above all, the Confederacy financed the war effort simply by printing paper money not backed by spe—cie, some $1.5 billion, which amounted to three times more than the federal government issued. The result was runaway inflation, so that by 1865 a Confeder—ate dollar was worth only 1.7 cents in gold and prices had soared to 92 times their prewar base. Prices were highest in Richmond, where flour sold for $275 a barrel by early 1864 and coats for $350 each. Shortages led to widespread suffering, and even looting.

In politics even more than finance, the Confederacy exercised far greater powers than those of the federal government before 1861. Indeed, Jefferson Davis strove to meet the demands of total war by transforming the South into a centralized, national state. He sought to limit state authority over mili—tary units, and in April 1862 the Confederacy passed the first national **conscription** law in American history.

> **conscription** act of compul—sory enrollment for military service, as opposed to a voluntary enlistment.

The same year, the Confed—erate Congress authorized Davis to invoke martial law and suspend the writ of habeas corpus.

Critics protested that Davis was destroying states' rights, the driving principle of the Confederacy. Intent on preserving states' traditional powers, Confederate governors obstructed the draft and retained military supplies. When President Davis suspended the writ of habeas corpus, his own vice president, Alexander H. Stephens, accused him of aiming at a dictator—ship. Davis used those powers for a limited time and only with the permission of Congress, yet in practice it made little difference whether the writ was suspended or not. With disloyalty a greater problem than in the Union, the Confederate army arrested thousands of civilians.

But the Confederate draft, more than any other measure, produced an outcry. As one Georgia leader complained, "It's a notorious fact if a man has influ—ential friends—or a little money to spare—he will never be enrolled." Most controversially, the draft exempted from service one white man on every plantation with 20 or more slaves (later reduced to 15). This law was designed to preserve control of the slave population, but more and more non—slaveholders complained that it was a rich man's war and a poor man's fight.

 REVIEW

In what ways did the Confederacy, which championed states' rights, become a more centralized, national government?

THE UNION HOME FRONT

Since the war was fought mostly on southern soil, northern civilians rarely felt its effects directly. Yet to be effective, the North's economic resources had to be organized and mobilized.

Government Finances and the Economy >>

To begin with, the North required a comprehensive system to finance its massive campaign. Taxing the populace was one obvious means, and taxes paid for 21 percent of Union war expenses, compared with only 1 percent of the Confederacy's. In August 1861 Con—gress levied the first federal income tax, of 3 percent on all incomes over $800 a year. When that, along with increased tariff duties, proved insufficient, Congress enacted a comprehensive tax law in 1862 that for the first time brought the tax collector into every northern household.

The government also borrowed heavily, through the sale of $2.2 billion in **bonds.** It financed the rest of the war's cost by issu—ing paper money. In all, the Union printed $431 million in greenbacks (so named

> **bonds** certificates of debt issued by a government or corporation promising to repay the buyers of the bonds their original invest—ment, plus interest, by a specified date of maturity.

because of their color on one side). Congress also insti—tuted a national banking system, allowing nationally chartered banks to issue notes backed by U.S. bonds. By taxing state bank notes out of circulation, Congress for the first time created a uniform national currency.

During the war the Republican—controlled Con—gress encouraged economic development. Tariffs to protect industry from foreign competition rose to an average rate of 47 percent, compared to 19 percent in 1860. To encourage development of the West, the Homestead Act of 1862 granted 160 acres of pub—lic land—the size of the traditional American family farm—to anyone (including women) who settled and improved the land for five years. In addition, the Land Grant College Act of 1862 donated the proceeds from certain land sales to finance public colleges and uni—versities. This aid was especially crucial in promoting higher education in the West.

A Rich Man's War >> Over the course of the war the government purchased more than $1 billion worth of goods and services. In response to this heavy demand, the economy boomed and business and agriculture prospered. Since prices rose faster than wages, workers' real income dropped almost 30 percent, which meant that the working class paid a disproportionate share of financing the war.

The Republican belief that government should play a major role in the economy also fostered a cozy relationship between business and politics inviting corruption. In the rush to profit from government contracts, some suppliers sold inferior goods at inflated prices. Uniforms made of "shoddy"—bits of unused thread and recycled cloth—were fobbed off in such numbers that the word became an adjective describing inferior quality.

Stocks and dividends rose with the economy, speculation during the last two years of the war became particularly feverish, and the fortunes made went toward the purchase of showy luxuries. Like Richmond, Washington became the symbol of this moral decay. Prostitution, drinking, and corruption reached epidemic proportions in the capital, and social festivities became the means to shut out the numbing horror of the casualty lists.

Women and the Workforce >> Even more than in the South, the war opened new opportunities for northern women. Countless wives ran farms while their husbands were away at war. One traveler in Iowa reported, "I met more women driving teams on the road and saw more at work in the fields than men." The war also stimulated the shift to mechanization: by 1865 three times as many reapers and harvesters were in use as in 1861. Beyond the farm, women filled approximately 100,000 new jobs in industry. As in the South, they also worked as clerks in the expanding government bureaucracy.

↑ This anti-Republican cartoon from Philadelphia expresses the fears of many Copperhead Democrats that the war for the Union had been subverted by becoming a war on slavery. A caricatured black soldier tries to prevent a legless Union veteran from voting for General McClellan, Lincoln's opponent in the election of 1864. The election clerk beside the stuffed ballot box is told to "pretend you see nothing" of the ballot stuffing.

The war allowed women to enter and eventually dominate the profession of nursing. Led by Drs. Emily and Elizabeth Blackwell, Dorothea Dix, and Mary Ann Bickerdyke, women fought the bureaucratic inefficiency of the army medical corps. Their service in the hospital wards reduced the hostility to women in medicine.

One nurse was Clara Barton, who later founded the Red Cross. During the Battle of Fredericksburg, she worked in a battlefield hospital. She later recalled that as she rose from the side of one soldier, "I wrung the blood from the bottom of my clothing, before I could step, for the weight about my feet." She steeled herself at the sight of amputated arms and legs casually tossed in piles outside the front door as the surgeons cut away. Sleeping in a tent nearby, she drove herself to the brink of exhaustion until the last patients were transferred to permanent hospitals.

Civil Liberties and Dissent >>

In mobilizing the northern war effort, Lincoln did not hesitate to curb dissenters. Shortly after the firing on Fort Sumter, he suspended the writ of habeas corpus in specified areas, which allowed the indefinite detention of anyone suspected of disloyalty or activity against the war. Although the Constitution permitted such suspension in time of rebellion or invasion, Lincoln did so without consulting Congress (unlike President Davis), and he used his power far more broadly, expanding it in 1862 to cover the entire North for cases involving antiwar activities. The president also decreed that those arrested under its provisions could be tried in a military court. Eventually more than 20,000 individuals were arrested, most never brought to trial.

Democrats attacked Lincoln as a tyrant bent on destroying the Constitution. After the war the Supreme Court, in *Ex parte Milligan* (1866), struck down the military conviction of a civilian accused of plotting to free Confederate prisoners of war. The Court ruled that as long as the regular courts remained open, civilians could not be tried by military tribunals.

Republicans labeled northern Democrats who opposed the war **Copperheads,** conjuring up the image of a venomous snake waiting to strike the Union. Copperheads constituted the extreme peace wing of the Democratic Party. They condemned the draft as an attack on individual freedom and an instrument of special privilege. According to the provisions enacted in 1863, a person would be exempt from the present draft by paying a commutation fee of $300, about a year's wages for a worker or an ordinary farmer. Or those drafted could hire a substitute, the cost of which was beyond the reach of all but the wealthy. In July

> **Copperheads** derogatory term used by Republicans to label northern Democrats who opposed the war policies of the Lincoln administration and advocated a negotiated peace.

1863 largely Irish workers in New York City rose in anger against the draft. By the time order was restored four days later, at least 105 people had been killed, the worst loss of life from any riot in American history.

 REVIEW

How did the war affect women in the workforce? How were civil liberties compromised?

GONE TO BE A SOLDIER

Marcus Spiegel, the son of a rabbi, came to the United States after the German revolution of 1848 failed. A naturalized citizen when the war began, Spiegel considered it his duty to preserve the Union for his children, so he enlisted and eventually rose to the rank of colonel. He did not go to war to end slavery and flatly proclaimed that black people were not "worth fighting for." But after seeing slavery firsthand, his views changed, and by 1864 he was "in favor of doing away with the institution of Slavery." He assured his wife that "this is no hasty conclusion but a deep conviction." A few weeks later Spiegel died while fighting in Louisiana.

By war's end about 2 million men had served the Union cause and another million the Confederate. They were mostly young, with almost 40 percent of entering soldiers 21 years of age or younger. They were not drawn disproportionately from the poor, and in both North and South, farmers and farm laborers accounted for the largest number of recruits.

Camp Life >>

The near–holiday atmosphere of the war's early months soon gave way to dull routine. While discipline remained lax by modern standards, Union and Confederate soldiers alike chaffed under supervision. Men from rural areas, accustomed to the freedom of the farm, complained about the endless recurrence of reveille, roll call, and drill. "When this war is over," one Rebel promised, "I will whip the man that says 'fall in' to me." Troops in neither army cared for the spit and polish of regular army men. "They keep us very strict here," noted one Illinois soldier. "It is the most like a prison of any place I ever saw."

On average, soldiers spent 50 days in camp for every day in battle. Camp life was often unhealthy as well as unpleasant. Poor sanitation, miserable food, exposure, and primitive medical care contributed to widespread sickness and disease. It was a common belief that if a fellow went to the hospital, "you might as well say

⌃ Reveille rouses drowsy Union soldiers on a wintry morning as a drummer boy warms his hands. Instead of the glory they expected, reveille, roll call, and drill constituted Civil War soldiers' usual camp routine. A hired black laborer is already at work as the troops awaken.

good bye." Conditions were even worse in the Confederate hospitals, for the Union blockade produced a shortage of medical supplies. Twice as many soldiers died from dysentery, typhoid, and other diseases as from wounds.

The boredom of camp life, the horrors of battle, and the influence of an all–male society all loosened morals. Swearing and heavy drinking were common and gambling was pervasive, especially immediately after payday. Prostitutes flooded the camps of both armies. Yet with death so near, some soldiers also sought solace in religion, especially in Confederate camps. A wave of revivals swept their ranks during the last two winters of the war, producing between 100,000 and 200,000 conversions. Significantly, the first major revivals occurred after the South's twin defeats at Vicksburg and Gettysburg. Then, too, as battle after battle thinned Confederate ranks, the prospect of death loomed increasingly large.

Carnage at the Front >> Most obviously, Americans at the front produced death and bore witness to it on a staggering scale. Upwards of three-quarters of a million men died in the war. The conflict lasted 1,458 days, claiming more than 500 lives each day on average. But of course the war's carnage did not unfold gradually. The scale of the violence increased as the conflict ground on, and much of the dying came in staggering, appalling surges at places thereafter synonymous with death—places like Bull Run, Shiloh, Antietam, Gettysburg.

Technological advances in the tools of destruction helped account for staggering losses. Smoothbore muskets, which at first served as the basic infantry weapon, gave way to the rifle, so named because of the grooves etched into the barrel to give a bullet spin. A new bullet, the minié ball, allowed the rifle to be easily loaded, and the invention of the percussion cap rendered it serviceable in wet weather. More important, the new weapon had an effective range of 400 yards—up to four times greater than that of the old musket. As a result, soldiers fought each other from greater distances and hit their targets far more frequently. Battles took much longer to fight and produced vastly more casualties. Under such conditions, the defense became a good deal stronger than the offense. The larger artillery pieces also adopted rifled barrels, but they lacked good fuses and accurate sighting devices and could not effectively support attacking troops at distance. Artillery remained a deadly defensive weapon, however, one that devastated advancing infantry at close range. More than 100 regiments on both sides suffered in excess of 50 percent casualties in a single battle.

Soldiers struggled to convey to those back home the gruesome truths of combat. "No tongue can tell, no mind can conceive, no pen portray the horrible sights I witnessed this morning," a Union soldier wrote after Antietam. And still they tried. An Indiana soldier at Perryville (7,600 casualties): "It was an awful sight to see there men torn all to pieces with cannon balls and bom shells[.] [T]he dead and wounded lay thick in all directions." An Ohio soldier at Antietam (23,000 casualties), two days after the fighting: "The smell was offul...there was about 5 or 6,000 dead bodes decaying over the field....I could have walked on the bodees all most from one end too the other." A Georgian, the day after Chancellorsville (30,000 casualties): "It looked more like a slaughter pen than anything else....

Field hospitals were often makeshift, like this house where the surgeon operates in front on a table. The only anesthetic is to the right of the patient's head: a bottle of whiskey. Often, wounded soldiers lay untended or waited so long for help that their open wounds teemed with maggots "as though a swarm of bees had settled" on them. Confederate Walter Lenoir had his wounded leg sawn off below the knee and then endured a 20-mile ride in a rude farm wagon, every jolt causing "a pang which felt as if my stump was thrust into liquid fire."

The shrieks and groans of the wounded...was heart rending beyond all description." A Maine soldier who fought at Gettysburg (50,000 casualties): "I have Seen...men rolling in their own blood, Some Shot in one place, Some another...our dead lay in the road and the Rebels in their hast to leave dragged both their baggage wagons and artillery over them and they lay mangled and torn to pieces so that Even friends could not tell them. You can form no idea of a battlefield."

Surrounded by the wreckage of war, amid the sounds and smells and sight of thousands of dead or dying men, soldiers who fell on the battlefield struggled to die as they thought they should. If they made it to a camp hospital, they might look to exhausted nurses, doctors, or aides to stay with them in their final moments. They might give comrades or outright strangers messages for kin—parents, wives, siblings, and children they knew they would never see again. Many tens of thousands simply died where they fell; some immediately, others more slowly, and some others granted final moments with treasured photographs or with letters from people they loved. Survivors became hardened through horror. "The daily sight of blood and mangled bodies," observed a Rhode Island soldier, "so blunted their finer sensibilities as almost to blot out all love, all sympathy from the heart."

The Business of Grief >> This multitude of war dead forced immense tasks upon the living. Millions of people across the country would spend years and lifetimes grieving as a consequence of the war. They wanted to know how their loved ones died, wanted to know where their bodies were, and, increasingly, wanted to retrieve those bodies and bury them closer to home. The railroad network and the new practice of embalming made this heartfelt desire possible for the first time in the history of warfare. Volunteers like Clara Barton organized to help grieving families locate the bodies of their fallen soldiers. A feverish alliance of shipping agents and undertakers emerged to meet demand. Embalmers propped up the preserved corpses of unknown dead in shop windows to advertise their services. Responding to popular pressure, the U.S. government pledged to help in the task of identification and recovery—eventually spending $4 million to identify the resting places of half the Union's fallen soldiers and to reburying most of them. Not until 1906 would the national government assume the same responsibilities for Confederate dead. Instead, such tasks fell to state governments and, after the war, to civic organizations like the Daughters of the Confederacy.

 REVIEW

How did the experience of battle evolve during the war?

THE UNION'S TRIUMPH

In the spring of 1863 matters still looked promising for Robert E. Lee, the general who had so ably led the Confederates in Virginia. At the battle of Chancellorsville, he won another brilliant victory. But during the fighting Stonewall Jackson was accidentally shot by his own men and died a few days later—a grievous setback for the Confederacy. Determined to invade the North and take the offensive, Lee invaded Pennsylvania in June with an army of 75,000. Lincoln's newest general, George Gordon Meade, warily shadowed the Confederates. On the first of July, advance parties from the two armies accidentally collided at the town of Gettysburg, and the war's greatest battle ensued.

The Battle of Gettysburg >> The iconic battle unfolded over the course of three bloody days, July 1–3. Confederate forces enjoyed some successes at first,

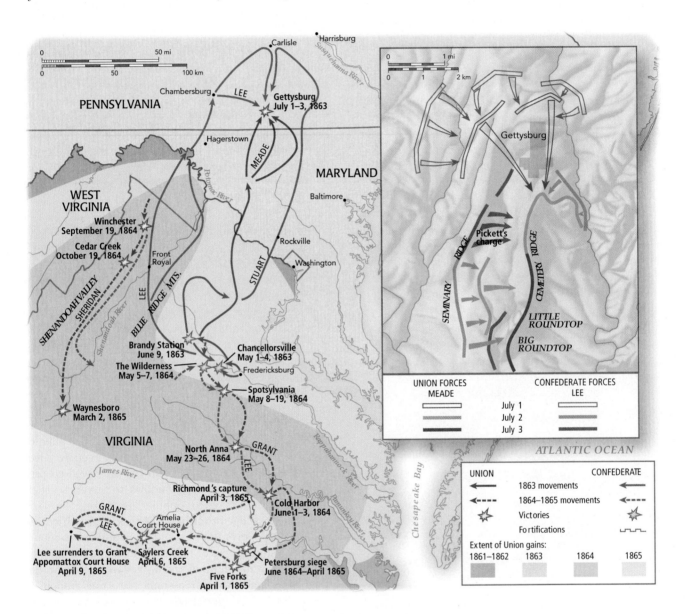

MAP 16.4: THE WAR IN THE EAST, 1863–1865

Lee won his most brilliant victory at Chancellorsville, then launched a second invasion of the North, which ended in defeat at Gettysburg. In 1864 Grant delivered a series of blows against Lee's outnumbered forces in Virginia. Despite staggering losses, Grant pressed on in a ruthless demonstration of total war. (Note the casualties listed from mid-May to mid-June of 1864; Grant lost nearly 60,000 men, equal to Lee's total strength.) In April 1865, too weak to defend Richmond any longer, Lee surrendered at Appomattox Court House.
Which battles showed the steepest losses for Grant?

before either side had all its troops in position, and these successes left Lee emboldened. He instructed General Richard Ewell, in command of Stonewall Jackson's corps, to seize a critical Union position called Cemetery Ridge, "if practicable." Jackson would have taken this for an order and charged his men up the hill. But Ewell, far more cautious, took Lee's wording as a suggestion rather than a command and decided against an attack. Some historians point to this inaction as the critical missed opportunity in the battle.

By day two most Union and Confederate troops had reached Gettysburg. Northern forces arrayed themselves in a formidable defensive line—so formidable that Lee's top subordinate urged him to withdraw and find a more defensible position somewhere to the east.

Lee refused, and desperate fighting raged for a second day. The rebels won some close–fought engagements, but failed to consolidate them for lack of coordination. By dusk both sides had endured great casualties, but the robust Union lines held. Again Lee was urged to withdraw. Again he refused. Convinced that he had left Union men bloodied and demoralized, he decided to mass his forces for a coordinated attack on Meade's center the following day. It would prove to be the costliest mistake of his military career.

Day three opened with some surprising Union victories, including one led by a dashing 23–year–old General named George Armstrong Custer. Not until early afternoon did Lee's plan become clear. Around 1 p.m. he gave the order and the sky exploded as massed

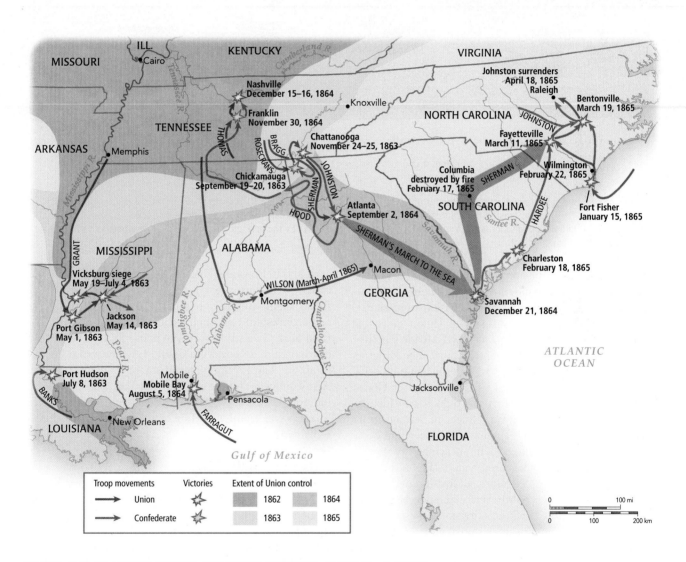

MAP 16.5: THE WAR IN THE WEST, 1863–1865

The Union continued its war of mobility in the western theater, bringing more Confederate territory under its control. After Grant captured Vicksburg, the entire Mississippi River lay in Union hands. His victories at Lookout Mountain and Missionary Ridge, near Chattanooga, ended the Confederate threat to Tennessee. In 1864 Sherman divided the Confederacy by seizing Atlanta and marching across Georgia; then he turned north. When Joseph Johnston surrendered, several weeks after Lee's capitulation at Appomattox, the war was effectively over.

U.S. Gunboat Cimerone   Steamer landing troops from Harrison

"U.S TROOPS BURNING "The COLE HOUSE" and PLANTATION. OPPOSITE HARRISON'S
LANDING JAMES RIVER on the night of 1st August 1862

⌃ General William Sherman demonstrated the tactics of total war in the autumn of 1864. "Destroyed all we could not eat . . . burned their cotton and gins . . . burned and twisted their railroads," wrote one of Sherman's soldiers. This drawing, done by a Union private, depicts a similar destructive raid on a plantation along Virginia's James River in 1862, and by the spring of 1865 Confederate armies were increasingly unable to resist Union might.

Confederate artillery blasted away at the Union center. Meade responded in kind, and for an hour Gettysburg was a deafening furnace of explosions and shattering bodies. Then, one by one, the Union guns fell silent. Convinced that he had disabled Meade's artillery and believing victory was at hand, Lee ordered three Confederate divisions to take the Union positions. Remembered as "Pickett's Charge," after General George Pickett, the effort started off confidently with some 12,500 Confederate soldiers marching up to Cemetery Ridge. But the silencing of artillery had been a ruse; once the Confederate infantrymen were well advanced, union cannons roared back to life and began blasting them to pieces. Meade's soldiers poured musket and rifle fire into the cratering Confederate charge, with horrible results. "Pickett's division just seemed to melt away in the blue musketry smoke which now covered the hill," one Confederate officer wrote. "Nothing but stragglers came back."

Indeed, only half of the men in the charge returned to Lee's lines, leaving the great general distraught. "It's all my fault," he exclaimed. "You must help me. All good men must rally." But there would be no rally. Lee managed to get most of his surviving men back across the Potomac, barely. Lincoln implored Meade to throw his army at the retreating Confederates and finish them. But Meade's men were battered, bloody, and exhausted; and their general would do little more than harry Lee's retreat. "We had only to stretch forth our hands and they were ours," Lincoln wrote, inconsolably. "And nothing I could say or do could make the Army move." Gettysburg did not end the war. But it did rob Lee of more than 25,000 men—a third of his force. Never again would he be in a position to take the fight to the North.

Lincoln Finds His General >> To the west,
Grant had been trying for months to capture Vicksburg, a Rebel stronghold on the Mississippi. In a daring maneuver, he left behind his supply lines and marched inland, feeding his army from the produce of Confederate farms. These were the tactics of total war, and seldom had they been tried before. On July 4 the city surrendered. With the fall of Port Hudson, Louisiana, four days later, the Mississippi was completely in Union hands, thus dividing the Confederacy.

Grant followed up this victory by rescuing Union forces holed up in Chattanooga. His performance confirmed Lincoln's earlier judgment that "Grant is my man, and I am his the rest of the war." In March 1864 Lincoln brought Grant east and placed him in command of all the Union armies.

Grant recognized that in the past Union forces had "acted independently and without concert, like a balky team, no two ever pulling together." He intended to change that. While he launched a major offensive against Lee in Virginia, William Tecumseh Sherman, who replaced Grant as commander of the western army, would drive a diagonal wedge through the Confederacy from Tennessee across Georgia. Grant instructed Sherman to "get into the interior of the enemy's country so far as you can, inflicting all the damage you can against their war resources."

In May and June 1864 Grant tried to maneuver Lee out of the trenches and into an open battle. But Lee was too weak to win head-on, so he opted for a strategy of attrition, hoping to inflict such heavy losses that the northern will would break. It was a strategy that nearly worked, for Union casualties were staggering. In a month of fierce fighting, the Army of the Potomac lost 60,000 men. Yet at the end of the campaign Grant's reinforced army was larger than when it started, whereas Lee's was significantly weaker.

Unable to break Lee's lines, Grant settled into a siege of Petersburg, which guarded Richmond's last remaining rail link to the south. In the west, meanwhile, the gaunt and grizzled Sherman fought his way by July to the outskirts of Atlanta, which was heavily defended and gave no sign of capitulating. "Our all depends on that army at Atlanta," wrote Mary Chesnut in August, based on her conversations with Confederate leaders in Richmond. "If that fails us, the game is up."

War in the Balance >>

As the Union war machine swept more and more northerners south to their death, and with Grant and Sherman bogged down in Virginia and Georgia, Lincoln's chances for reelection in 1864 seemed slim. Yet the president rejected any suggestion to postpone the election, an act that he believed would be to lose democracy itself. At the Republican National Convention, he made certain that the Republican platform called for adoption of a constitutional amendment abolishing slavery. To balance the ticket he selected Andrew Johnson, the military governor of Tennessee and a prowar Democrat, as his running mate. The two men ran under the label of the "Union" party.

The Democrats nominated George McClellan, the former Union commander. Their platform called for an armistice and a peace conference. Warned that a cessation of fighting would lead to disunion, McClellan partially repudiated this position, insisting that "the Union is the one condition of peace—we ask no more." In private he made it clear that if elected he intended to restore slavery. Late in August, Lincoln was still gloomy about his prospects, as well as those of the Union. But Admiral David Farragut won a dramatic victory

⌃ The war's greatest generals, Ulysses S. Grant (*left*) and Robert E. Lee (*right*), confronted each other in the eastern theater during the last year of the war. A member of a distinguished Virginia family, the tall, impeccably dressed Lee was every inch the aristocratic gentleman. Grant, a short, slouched figure with a stubby beard, dressed indifferently, but his determination is readily apparent in this picture, taken at his field headquarters in 1864.

at Mobile Bay, and in early September, Sherman captured Atlanta. As Secretary of State Seward gleefully noted, "Sherman and Farragut have knocked the bottom out of the Chicago [Democratic] nominations."

Polling an impressive 55 percent of the popular vote, Lincoln won 212 electoral votes to McClellan's 21. Eighteen states allowed soldiers to vote in the field, and Lincoln received nearly 80 percent of their ballots. One lifelong Democrat described the sentiment in the army: "I had rather stay out here a lifetime (much as I dislike it) than consent to a division of our country." Jefferson Davis remained defiant, but the last hope of a Confederate victory was gone.

Equally important, the election of 1864 ended any doubt that slavery would be abolished in the reconstructed Union. The Emancipation Proclamation had not put an end to the question, for its legal status remained unclear. Lincoln argued that as a war measure, it would have no standing once peace returned; and in any case, it had not freed slaves in the border states or those parts of the Confederacy already under Union control.

In 1864 the Senate approved an amendment to the Constitution that freed all slaves without compensating their owners. The measure passed the House on January 31, 1865. By December enough states had ratified the Thirteenth Amendment to make it part of the Constitution.

The Twilight of the Confederacy

>> For the Confederacy the outcome of the 1864 election had a terrible finality. In March 1865 the Confederate Congress authorized recruiting 300,000 slaves for military service. When he signed the bill, Davis announced that freedom would be given to those who volunteered and to their families. That same month he offered through a special envoy to abolish slavery in exchange for British diplomatic recognition. A Mississippi paper denounced this proposal as "a total abandonment of the chief object of this war." The British rejected the offer, and the war ended before any slaves were mustered into the Confederate army, but the demands of total war had forced Confederate leaders to forsake the Old South's most important values and institutions.

In the wake of Lincoln's reelection the Confederate will to resist disintegrated. As Sherman pushed deeper into the Confederacy, the war came home to southern civilians as never before. "We haven't got nothing in the house to eat but a little bit o meal," wrote the wife of one Alabama soldier in December 1864. "Try to get off and come home and fix us all up some and then you

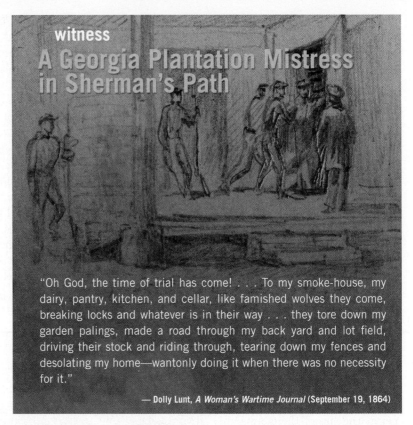

can go back. . . . If you put off a—coming, 'twont be no use to come, for we'll all . . . [be] in the grave yard." He deserted. In the last months of the fighting, over half the Confederacy's soldiers were absent without leave.

After the fall of Atlanta, Sherman gave a frightening demonstration of the meaning of total war. He imitated Grant's strategy by abandoning his supply lines for an audacious 300—mile march to the sea. The goal was to deprive Lee's army of the supplies it desperately needed to continue and to break the southern will to resist. Or as he bluntly put it, "to whip the Rebels, to humble their pride, to follow them to their recesses, and make them fear and dread us."

Moving in four columns, Sherman's army covered about 10 miles a day, cutting a path of destruction 50 miles wide. Sherman estimated that his men did $100 million in damage, of which $20 million was necessary to supply his army and the rest was wanton destruction. After he captured Savannah, he turned north and wreaked even greater havoc in South Carolina.

By December the interior of the Confederacy was essentially conquered. Only Lee's army remained, entrenched around Petersburg. As Grant extended his lines, Lee's troops were forced to evacuate Richmond. Westward Grant doggedly pursued the Army of Northern Virginia, until the weary gentleman from Virginia finally asked for terms. On April 9, 1865, Lee surrendered at Appomattox Court House. As the vanquished foe mounted his horse, Grant saluted by raising

 Lincoln's funeral procession.

his hat; Lee raised his respectfully and rode off at a slow trot. The guns were quiet.

Remaining resistance throughout the Confederacy collapsed within a matter of weeks. Visiting the captured city of Richmond on April 4, Lincoln was enthusiastically greeted by the black population. He looked "pale, haggard, utterly worn out," noted one observer. The lines in his face showed how much the war had aged him in only four years. Often his friends had counseled rest, but Lincoln had observed that "the tired part of me is inside and out of reach." The burden, he confessed, was almost too much to bear.

Back in Washington the president received news of Lee's surrender with relief. The evening of April 14,

Lincoln, seeking a welcome escape, went to a comedy at Ford's Theater. In the midst of the performance John Wilkes Booth, a famous actor and Confederate sympathizer, slipped into the presidential box and shot him. Lincoln died the next morning. As he had called on his fellow citizens to do in his Gettysburg Address, the sixteenth president had given his "last full measure of devotion" to the Republic.

✔ REVIEW

What decisions by Grant and Lincoln led the Union to victory?

The assassination left a tiredness in the nation's bones—a tiredness "inside" and not easily within reach. In every way the conflict had produced fundamental changes. There was, of course, the carnage. Historians now believe that upwards of 800,000 men lost their lives, as many or more than as in all the other wars the nation has fought from the Revolution through Vietnam combined. In material terms, the conflict cost an estimated $20 billion, more than 11 times the total amount spent by the federal government from 1789 to 1861. Even without adding the market value of freed slaves, southern wealth declined 43 percent, transforming what had been the richest section in the nation (on a white per–capita basis) into the poorest.

The Civil War reordered not only the national economy but also economic relations worldwide. Manufacturers were forced to supply the army on an unprecedented scale over great distances. One consequence was the creation of truly national industries in flour milling, meatpacking, clothing and shoe manufacture, and machinery making.

People across the globe felt the effects of the war, particularly because of changes in the cotton trade. In 1860 the South was supplying more than three-quarters of all cotton imported by Britain, France, Germany, and Russia. When the war cut off that supply, India, Egypt, and Brazil all opened new cotton fields. The effect of the trade on Egypt was so great, historians of that nation rank the American Civil War along with the construction of the Suez Canal as the most crucial events in its nineteenth–century history.

Politically, the war dramatically changed the balance of power. The South lost its substantial influence, as did the Democratic Party, while the Republicans emerged in a dominant position. The Union's military victory also signaled the triumph of nationalism. The war destroyed the idea that the Union was a voluntary confederacy of sovereign states, as John C. Calhoun and others had argued, and that the states had the right to secede.

In the short run, the price was disillusionment and bitterness. The war's corrosive effect on morals corrupted American life and politics, destroyed idealism, and severely crippled humanitarian reform. Millennialism and perfectionism were victims of the war's appalling slaughter, forsaken for a new emphasis on practicality, order, materialism, and science.

The remorseless logic of war did push to the fore one ideal of the previous decades: the abolition of slavery. In 1865 the United States joined the ranks of those nations that had embraced emancipation: Britain in 1833, Portugal (1836), Sweden (1847), Denmark and France (1848), and Holland (1863). (Spain would not relent until 1886.) Without war to force the issue, slavery in the United States might have continued for decades.

George Ticknor, a prominent critic of the day, reflected on the changes that had shaken the nation. The war, it seemed to him, had left "a great gulf between what happened before it in our century and what has happened since.... It does not seem to me as if I were living in the country in which I was born."

CHAPTER SUMMARY

As the first total war in history, the Civil War's outcome depended not just on armies but also on the mobilization of society's human, economic, and intellectual resources.

- Confederate president Jefferson Davis's policy of concentrating power in the government at Richmond, along with the resort to a draft and impressment of private property, provoked strong protests from many southerners.
- Abraham Lincoln's suspension of habeas corpus and interference with civil liberties were equally controversial, but Lincoln skillfully kept the border states in the Union.
- Lincoln at first resisted pressure to make emancipation a Union war aim, but he eventually issued the Emancipation Proclamation, which transformed the meaning of the war.
- African Americans helped undermine slavery and contributed vitally to the Union's military victory.
- On the home front, women confronted new responsibilities and enjoyed new occupational opportunities.
- Confederate financial and tax policies and the tightening Union blockade increased hardships within the Confederacy.
- Technology, particularly the use of rifles and rifled artillery, revolutionized the tactics of warfare.
- The Union victory at Gettysburg and Lincoln's choice of Grant to lead Union forces marked the turning point of the war. Union success relied in part on the strategy of attacking the civilian population of the South.

Additional Reading

A good single–volume history of the Civil War remains James M. McPherson's *Battle Cry of Freedom* (1988). Some historians have questioned whether the conflict should be considered a "total war." McPherson argues that it should in *Drawn with the Sword* (1996); Mark Neely makes the opposite case in *The Civil War and the Limits of Destruction* (2007). For the evolution of the Union's strategy toward southern civilians, see Mark Grimsley, *The Hard Hand of War* (1995).

The best biography of Lincoln is David Donald, *Lincoln* (1995). William E. Gienapp, *Abraham Lincoln and Civil War America* (2002), is concise and focuses on the presidential years. The president's complex thinking on slavery is the subject of Eric Foner's masterful book *The Fiery Trial* (2010). For the contradictions of the southern project, see Stephanie McCurry, *Confederate Reckoning* (2010). Drew Gilpin Faust, *Mothers of Invention* (1996), is an imaginative study of slaveholding women; Edward Ayers, *In the Presence of Mine Enemies* (2003), examines the consequences of war in Virginia and Pennsylvania. For the northern home front, see J. Matthew Gallman, *The North Fights the Civil War* (1994). Chandra Manning, in *What This Cruel War Was Over* (2007), argues that Union rank and file widely believed in emancipation as early as the end of 1861. Drew Gilpin Faust, *This Republic of Suffering* (2008), brilliantly explores how death, grieving, and belief were changed by this most deadly of wars. For Britain's critical role in the diplomacy of the Civil War, see Amanda Foreman's *A World on Fire* (2011).

Significant Events

1861
Border states remain in the Union; Battle of Bull Run

1862
Forts Henry and Donelson captured; Battle of Shiloh; New Orleans captured; McClellan's Peninsula campaign fails; Battle of Antietam; Lincoln suspends writ of habeas corpus throughout the Union; Battle of Fredericksburg

1863
Emancipation Proclamation issued; Union institutes conscription; Confederacy enacts general tax laws, initiates impressment; bread riots in the Confederacy; Battle of Gettysburg; Vicksburg captured; New York City draft riots

1864
Grant becomes Union general in chief; Grant's Virginia offensive; siege of Petersburg; fall of Atlanta; Lincoln reelected; Sherman's march to the sea

1865
Sherman's march through the Carolinas; Lee surrenders; Lincoln assassinated; Thirteenth Amendment ratified

17 Reconstructing the Union

1865–1877

"Men stood speechless, haggard . . . gazing at the desolation," reported one journalist in Richmond at war's end. Many residents must have felt that way, though newly freed African Americans were jubilant.

>> **An American Story**

A SECRET SALE AT DAVIS BEND

J oseph Davis had had enough. Well on in years and financially ruined by the war, he decided to sell his Mississippi plantations Hurricane and Brierfield to Benjamin Montgomery and his sons in November 1866. Such a sale was common enough after the war, but this transaction was bound to attract attention, since Joseph Davis was the elder brother of Jefferson Davis. Indeed, before the war the ex–Confederate president had operated Brierfield as his own plantation, even though his brother retained legal title to it. But the sale was unusual for another reason—so unusual that the parties involved agreed to keep it secret. The plantation's new owners were black, and Mississippi law prohibited African Americans from owning land.

Though a slave, Benjamin Montgomery had been the business manager of the two Davis plantations before the war. He had also operated a store on Hurricane Plantation with his own line of credit in New Orleans. In 1863 Montgomery fled to the North, but when the war was over, he returned to Davis Bend, where the federal government had confiscated the Davis plantations and was leasing plots of the land to black farmers. Montgomery quickly emerged as the leader of the African American community at the Bend.

Then, in 1866, President Andrew Johnson pardoned Joseph Davis and restored his lands. Davis was now over 80 years old and lacked the will and stamina to rebuild, yet unlike many ex-slaveholders, he felt bound by obligations to his former slaves. Convinced that with encouragement African Americans could succeed in freedom, he sold his land secretly to Benjamin Montgomery. Only when the law prohibiting African Americans from owning land was overturned in 1867 did Davis publicly confirm the sale to his former slave.

For his part, Montgomery undertook to create a model society at Davis Bend based on mutual cooperation. He rented land to black farmers, hired others to work his own fields, sold supplies on credit, and ginned and marketed the crops. The work was hard indeed: Davis Bend's farmers faced the destruction caused by the war, several disastrous floods, insects, droughts, and declining cotton prices. Yet before long, cotton production exceeded that of the prewar years. The Montgomerys eventually acquired 5,500 acres, which made them reputedly the third-largest planters in the state, and they won national and international awards for the quality of their cotton. Their success demonstrated what African Americans, given a fair chance, might accomplish.

The experiences of Benjamin Montgomery were not those of most black southerners, who did not own land or have a powerful white benefactor. Yet all African Americans shared Montgomery's dream of economic independence. As one black veteran noted: "Every colored man will be a slave, and feel himself a slave until he can raise him own bale of cotton and put him own mark upon it and say this is mine!" Blacks could not gain effective freedom simply through a proclamation

↑ African American soldiers greeting loved ones after being mustered out of the army in Arkansas. The war's end brought both joy and uncertainty about what was to come.

of emancipation. They needed economic power, including their own land that no one could unfairly take away. And political power too, if the legacy of slavery was to be overturned.

How would the Republic be reunited, now that slavery had been abolished? War, in its blunt way, had roughed out the contours of a solution, but only in broad terms. The North, with its industrial might, would be the driving force in the nation's economy and retain the dominant political voice. But would African Americans receive effective power? How would North and South readjust their economic and political relations? These questions lay at the heart of the problem of Reconstruction. <<

What's to Come

PRESIDENTIAL RECONSTRUCTION

Throughout the war Abraham Lincoln had considered Reconstruction his responsibility. Elected with less than 40 percent of the popular vote in 1860, he was acutely aware that once the states of the Confederacy were restored to the Union, the Republicans would be weakened unless they ceased to be a sectional party. By a generous peace, Lincoln hoped to attract former Whigs in the South, who supported many of the Republicans' economic policies, and build up a southern wing of the party.

Lincoln's 10 Percent Plan >> Lincoln outlined
his program in a Proclamation of **Amnesty** and Reconstruction, issued in December 1863. When a minimum of 10 percent of the qualified voters from 1860 took a **loyalty oath** to the Union, they could organize a state government. The new state constitution had to abolish slavery and provide for black education, but Lincoln did not insist that high-ranking Confederate leaders be barred from public life.

amnesty general pardon granted by a government, usually for political crimes.

loyalty oath oath of fidelity to the state or to an organization.

Lincoln indicated that he would be generous in granting pardons to Confederate leaders and did not rule out compensation for slave property. Moreover, while he privately advocated limited black suffrage in the disloyal southern states, he did not demand social or political equality for black Americans. In Louisiana, Arkansas, and Tennessee he recognized pro-Union governments that allowed only white men to vote.

The Radical Republicans found Lincoln's approach much too lenient. Strongly antislavery, Radical members of Congress had led the struggle to make emancipation a war aim. Now they led the fight to guarantee the rights of former slaves, or freedpeople. The Radicals believed that it was the duty of Congress, not the president, to set the terms under which states would regain their rights in the Union. Though the Radicals often disagreed on other matters, they were united in a determination to readmit southern states only after slavery had been ended, black rights protected, and the power of the planter class destroyed.

Under the direction of Senator Benjamin Wade of Ohio and Representative Henry Winter Davis of Maryland, Congress formulated a much stricter plan of Reconstruction. The Wade–Davis bill required half the white adult males to take an oath of allegiance before drafting a new state constitution, and it restricted

political power to the hard-core Unionists. Lincoln vetoed this approach, but as the war drew to a close, he appeared ready to make concessions to the Radicals, such as placing the defeated South temporarily under military rule. Then Booth's bullet found its mark, and Lincoln's final approach to Reconstruction would never be known.

Reconstruction under Andrew Johnson >>
In the wake of defeat, the immediate reaction among white southerners was one of shock, despair, and hopelessness. Some former Confederates were openly antagonistic. A North Carolina innkeeper remarked bitterly that Yankees had stolen his slaves, burned his house, and killed all his sons, leaving him only one privilege: "To hate 'em. I got up at half-past four in the morning, and sit up till twelve at night, to hate 'em." Most Confederate soldiers were less defiant, having had their fill of war. Even among hostile civilians the feeling was widespread that the South must accept northern terms. A South Carolina paper admitted that "the conqueror has the right to make the terms, and we must submit."

This psychological moment was critical. To prevent a resurgence of resistance, the president needed to lay out in unmistakable terms what white southerners had to do to regain their old status in the Union. Perhaps even a clear and firm policy would not have been enough. But with Lincoln's death, the executive power came to rest in far less capable hands.

Andrew Johnson, the new president, had been born in North Carolina and eventually moved to Tennessee, where he worked as a tailor. Barely able to read and write when he married, he rose to political power by portraying himself as the champion of the people against the wealthy planter class. "Some day I will show the stuck—up aristocrats who is running the country," he vowed as he began his political career. Although he accepted emancipation as one consequence of the war, Johnson lacked any concern for the welfare of African Americans. "Damn the negroes," he said during the war, "I am fighting these traitorous aristocrats, their masters." After serving in Congress and as military governor of Tennessee following its occupation by Union forces, Johnson, a Democrat, was tapped by Lincoln in 1864 as his running mate on the rechristened "Union" ticket.

The Radicals expected Johnson to uphold their views on Reconstruction, and on assuming the presidency he spoke of prosecuting Confederate leaders and breaking up planters' estates. Unlike most Republicans, however, Johnson strongly supported states' rights, and his political shortcomings sparked conflicts almost immediately. Scarred by his humble origins, he became tactless and inflexible when challenged or criticized, alienating even those who sought to work with him.

Johnson moved to return the southern states to the Union quickly. He prescribed a loyalty oath that most white southerners would have to take to regain their civil and political rights and to have their property, except for slaves, restored. High Confederate officials and those with property worth over $20,000 had to apply for individual pardons. Once a state drafted a new constitution and elected state officers and members of Congress, Johnson promised to revoke martial law and recognize the new state government. Suffrage was limited to white citizens who had taken the loyalty oath. This plan was similar to Lincoln's, though more lenient. Only informally did Johnson stipulate that the southern states were to renounce their ordinances of secession, repudiate the Confederate debt, and ratify the Thirteenth Amendment abolishing slavery, which had been passed by Congress in January 1865 and was in the process of being ratified by the states. (It became part of the Constitution in December.)

The Failure of Johnson's Program >> The

southern delegates who met to construct new governments were in no mood to follow Johnson's recommendations. Several states merely repealed instead of repudiating their ordinances of secession, rejected the Thirteenth Amendment, or refused to repudiate the Confederate debt.

Nor did the new governments allow African Americans any political rights or provide in any effective way for black education. In addition, each state passed a series of laws, often modeled on its old slave code, that applied only to African Americans. These **"black codes"** did give African Americans some rights that had not been granted to slaves. They legalized marriages from slavery and allowed black southerners to hold and sell property and to sue and be sued in state courts. Yet their primary intent was to keep African Americans as propertyless agricultural laborers with inferior legal rights. The new freedpeople could not serve on juries, testify against whites, or work as they pleased. Mississippi prohibited them from buying or renting farmland, and most states ominously provided that black people who were vagrants could be arrested and hired out to landowners. Many northerners were incensed by the restrictive black codes, which violated their conception of freedom.

black codes laws passed by southern states in 1865 and 1866, modeled on the slave codes in effect before the Civil War. The codes did grant African Americans some rights not enjoyed by slaves, but their primary purpose was to keep African Americans as propertyless agricultural laborers.

Southern voters under Johnson's plan also defiantly elected prominent Confederate military and political leaders to office. At this point, Johnson could have called for new elections or admitted that a different program of Reconstruction was needed. Instead, he caved in. For all his harsh rhetoric, he shrank from the prospect

⌃ Andrew Johnson was a staunch Unionist, but his contentious personality and inflexibility masked a deep-seated insecurity, which was rooted in his humble background. As a young man, he worked and lived in this rude tailor shop in Greeneville, Tennessee.

of social upheaval, and as the lines of ex–Confederates waiting to see him lengthened, he began issuing special pardons almost as fast as they could be printed. Publicly Johnson put on a bold face, announcing that Reconstruction had been successfully completed. But many members of Congress were deeply alarmed, and the stage was set for a serious confrontation.

Johnson's Break with Congress >> The new Congress was by no means of one mind. A small number of Democrats and a few conservative Republicans backed the president's program of immediate and unconditional restoration. At the other end of the spectrum, a larger group of Radical Republicans, led by Thaddeus Stevens, Charles Sumner, Benjamin Wade, and others, was bent on remaking southern society in the image of the North. Reconstruction must "revolutionize Southern institutions, habits, and manners," insisted Representative Stevens, "or all our blood and treasure have been spent in vain."

As a minority the Radicals needed the aid of the moderate Republicans, the largest bloc in Congress. Led by William Pitt Fessenden and Lyman Trumbull, the moderates had no desire to foster social revolution or promote racial equality in the South. But they wanted to keep Confederate leaders from reassuming power, and they were convinced that the former slaves needed federal protection. Otherwise, Trumbull declared, the freedpeople would "be tyrannized over, abused, and virtually reenslaved."

The central issue dividing Johnson and the Radicals was the place of African Americans in American society. Johnson accused his opponents of seeking "to Africanize the southern half of our country," while the Radicals championed civil and political rights for African Americans. The only way to maintain loyal governments and develop a republican party in the South, Radicals argued, was to give black men the ballot. Moderates agreed that the new southern governments were too harsh toward African Americans, but they feared that too great an emphasis on black civil rights would alienate northern voters.

In December 1865, when southern representatives to Congress appeared in Washington, a majority in Congress voted to exclude them. Congress also appointed a joint committee, chaired by Senator Fessenden, to look into Reconstruction.

The growing split with the president became clearer when Congress passed a bill extending the life of the Freedmen's Bureau. Created in March 1865, the bureau provided emergency food,

 Thaddeus Stevens, Radical leader in the House.

clothing, and medical care to war refugees (including white southerners) and took charge of settling freedpeople on abandoned lands. The new bill gave the bureau the added responsibilities of supervising special courts to resolve disputes involving freedpeople and establishing schools for black southerners. Although this bill passed with virtually unanimous Republican support, Johnson vetoed it.

Johnson also vetoed a civil rights bill designed to overturn the more flagrant provisions of the black codes. The law made African Americans citizens of the United States and granted them the right to own property, make contracts, and have access to courts as parties and witnesses. (The law did not go so far as to grant freedpeople the right to vote.) For most Republicans Johnson's action was the last straw, and in April 1866 Congress overrode his veto. Congress then approved a slightly revised Freedmen's Bureau bill in July and promptly overrode the president's veto. Johnson's refusal to compromise drove the moderates into the arms of the Radicals.

The Fourteenth Amendment >> To prevent unrepentant Confederates from taking over the reconstructed state governments and denying African Americans basic freedoms, the Joint Committee on Reconstruction proposed an amendment to the Constitution, which passed both houses of Congress with the necessary two–thirds vote in June 1866.

The amendment guaranteed repayment of the national war debt and prohibited repayment of the Confederate debt. To counteract the president's wholesale pardons, it disqualified prominent Confederates from holding office. Because moderates balked at giving the vote to African Americans, the amendment merely gave Congress the right to reduce the representation of any state that did not have impartial male suffrage. The practical effect of this provision, which Radicals labeled a "swindle," was to allow northern states to retain white suffrage, since unlike southern states they had few African Americans in their populations and thus would not be penalized.

The amendment's most important provision, Section 1, defined an American citizen as anyone born in the United States or naturalized, thereby automatically making African Americans citizens. Section 1 also prohibited states from abridging "the privileges or immunities" of citizens, depriving "any person of life, liberty, or property, without due process of law," or denying "any person . . . equal protection of the laws." The framers of the amendment probably

SCENES IN MEMPHIS, TENNESSEE, DURING THE RIOT—BURNING A FREEDMEN'S SCHOOL-HOUSE.

ʌ In 1866 white mobs in Memphis and New Orleans attacked African Americans in two major riots. Here rioters set fire to a schoolhouse used by freedpeople.

intended to prohibit laws that applied to one race only, such as the black codes, or that made certain acts felonies when committed by black but not white people, or that decreed different penalties for the same crime when committed by white and black lawbreakers. The framers probably did not intend to prevent segregation (the legal separation of the races) in schools and public places.

Johnson denounced the amendment and urged southern states not to ratify it. Ironically, of the seceded states only the president's own state ratified the amendment, and Congress readmitted Tennessee with no further restrictions. The telegram sent to Congress by a longtime foe of Johnson officially announcing Tennessee's approval ended: "Give my respects to the dead dog in the White House."

The Election of 1866 >>When Congress blocked his policies, Johnson undertook a speaking tour of the East and Midwest in the fall of 1866 to drum up popular support. But the president found it difficult to convince northern audiences that white southerners were fully repentant. Only months earlier white mobs in Memphis and New Orleans had attacked black residents and killed nearly 100 in two major race riots. "The negroes now know, to their sorrow, that it is best not to arouse the fury of the white man," boasted one Memphis newspaper. When the president encountered hostile audiences during his northern campaign, he made matters only worse by trading insults and proclaiming that the Radicals were traitors.

Not to be outdone, the Radicals vilified Johnson as a traitor aiming to turn the country over to former rebels.

Resorting to the tactic of "waving the **bloody shirt**," they appealed to voters by reviving bitter memories of the war. In a classic example of such rhetoric, Governor Oliver Morton of Indiana proclaimed that "every bounty jumper, every deserter, every sneak who ran away from the draft calls himself a Democrat. Every 'Son of Liberty' who conspired to murder, burn, rob arsenals and release rebel prisoners calls himself a Democrat. In short, the Democratic party may be described as a common sewer."

> **bloody shirt** political campaign tactic of "waving the bloody shirt," used by Republicans against Democrats; it invoked the deaths and casualties from the Civil War as a reason to vote for Republicans as the party of the Union, rather than the Democrats, who had often opposed the war.

Voters soundly repudiated Johnson, as the Republicans won more than a two–thirds majority in both houses of Congress. The Radicals had reached the height of their power, propelled by genuine alarm among northerners that Johnson's policies would lose the fruits of the Union's victory. Johnson was a president virtually without a party.

✓ **REVIEW**

What were Lincoln's and Andrew Johnson's approaches to Reconstruction, and why did Congress reject Johnson's approach?

CONGRESSIONAL RECONSTRUCTION

With a clear mandate in hand congressional Republicans passed their own program of Reconstruction, beginning with the first Reconstruction Act in March 1867. Like all later pieces of Reconstruction legislation, it was repassed over Johnson's veto.

Placing the 10 unreconstructed states under military commanders, the act provided that in enrolling voters, officials were to include black adult males but not former Confederates, who were barred from holding office under the Fourteenth Amendment. Delegates to the state conventions were to frame constitutions that provided for black suffrage and disqualified prominent ex–Confederates from office. The first state legislatures to meet under the new constitution were required to ratify the Fourteenth Amendment. Once these steps were completed and Congress approved the new state constitution, a state could send representatives to Congress.

White southerners found these requirements so insulting that officials took no steps to register voters. Congress then enacted a second Reconstruction Act, also in March, ordering the local military commanders to put the machinery of Reconstruction into motion. Johnson's efforts to limit the power of military commanders produced a third act, passed in July, that upheld their superiority in all matters. When the first election was held in Alabama to ratify the new state constitution, whites boycotted it in sufficient numbers to prevent a majority of voters from participating. Undaunted, Congress passed the fourth Reconstruction Act (March 1868), which required ratification of the constitution by only a majority of those voting rather than those who were registered.

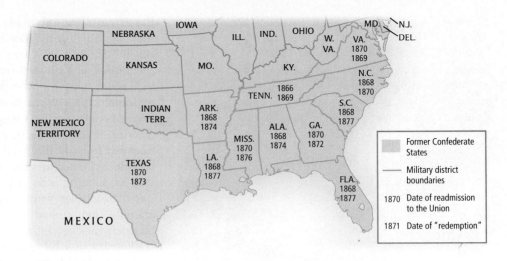

MAP 17.1: THE SOUTHERN STATES DURING RECONSTRUCTION

By June 1868 Congress had readmitted the representatives of seven states. Texas, Virginia, and Mississippi did not complete the process until 1869. Georgia finally followed in 1870.

Post-Emancipation Societies in the Americas

>> With the exception of Haiti's revolution (1791–1804), the United States was the only society in the Americas in which the destruction of slavery was accomplished by violence. But the United States, uniquely among these societies, enfranchised former slaves almost immediately after the emancipation. Thus, in the United States, former masters and slaves battled for control of the state in ways that did not occur in other post–emancipation societies. In most of the Caribbean, property requirements for voting left the planters in political control. Jamaica, for example, with a population of 500,000 in the 1860s, had only 3,000 voters.

Moreover, in reaction to political efforts to mobilize disenfranchised black peasants, Jamaican planters dissolved the assembly and reverted to being a Crown colony governed from London. Of the sugar islands, all but Barbados adopted the same policy, thereby blocking the potential for any future black peasant democracy. Nor did any of these societies have the counterparts of the Radical Republicans, a group of outsiders with political power that promoted the fundamental transformation of the post–emancipation South. These comparisons highlight the radicalism of Reconstruction in the United States, which alone saw an effort to forge an interracial democracy.

The Land Issue

>> While the political process of Reconstruction proceeded, Congress debated whether land should be given to former slaves to foster economic independence. At a meeting with Secretary of War Edwin Stanton near the end of the war, African American leaders declared: "The way we can best take care of ourselves is to have land, and till it by our own labor." The Second Confiscation Act of 1862 had authorized the government to seize and sell the property of supporters of the rebellion. In June 1866, however, President Johnson ruled that confiscation laws applied only to wartime.

After more than a year of debate, Congress rejected all proposals to give land to former slaves. Given Americans' strong belief in self–reliance, little sympathy existed for the idea that government should support any group. In addition, land redistribution represented an attack on property rights, another cherished American value. "A division of rich men's lands amongst the landless," argued the *Nation*, a Radical journal, "would give a shock to our whole social and political system from which it would hardly recover without the loss of liberty." By 1867 land reform was dead.

Impeachment

>> Throughout 1867 Congress routinely overrode Johnson's vetoes, but the president undercut congressional Reconstruction in other ways. He interpreted the new laws narrowly and removed military commanders who vigorously enforced them. Congress responded by restricting his power to issue orders to military commanders in the South. It also passed the Tenure of Office Act, which forbade Johnson to remove any member of the cabinet without the Senate's consent. The intention of this law was to prevent him from firing Secretary of War Edwin Stanton, the only remaining Radical in the cabinet.

When Johnson tried to dismiss Stanton in February 1868, the House of Representatives angrily approved articles of impeachment. The articles focused on the violation of the Tenure of Office Act, but the charge with the most substance was that Johnson had acted to systematically obstruct Reconstruction legislation. In the trial before the Senate, his lawyers argued that a president could be impeached only for an indictable crime, which Johnson clearly had not committed. The Radicals countered that impeachment applied to political offenses, not merely criminal acts. In May 1868 the Senate voted 35 to 19 to convict, one vote short of the two-thirds majority needed. The seven Republicans who joined the Democrats in voting for acquittal were uneasy about using impeachment as a political weapon.

 REVIEW

What was Congress's approach to Reconstruction, and why did it not include a provision for giving land to former slaves?

RECONSTRUCTION IN THE SOUTH

As the power of the Radicals in Congress waned, the fate of Reconstruction increasingly hinged on developments in the southern states themselves. Power in these states rested with the new Republican parties, representing a coalition of black and white southerners and transplanted northerners.

Black and White Republicans >> Once African Americans received the right to vote, black men constituted as much as 80 percent of the Republican voters in the South. They steadfastly opposed the Democratic Party with its appeal to white supremacy. But during Reconstruction, African Americans never held office in proportion to their voting strength. No African American was ever elected governor. And only in South Carolina, where more than 60 percent of the population was black, did they control even one house of the legislature. Between 15 and 20 percent of the state officers and 6 percent of members of Congress (2 senators and 15 representatives) were black. Only in South Carolina did black officeholders approach their proportion of the population.

Those who held office came from the top levels of African American society. Among state and federal officeholders, perhaps 80 percent were literate, and over a quarter had been free before the war, both marks of distinction in the black community. Their occupations also set them apart: many were professionals (mostly clergy), and of the third who were farmers, nearly all owned land. In their political and social values, African American leaders were more conservative than the rural black population, and they showed little interest in land reform.

Black citizens were a majority of the voters only in South Carolina, Mississippi, and Louisiana. Thus in most of the South the Republican Party had to secure white votes to stay in power. Opponents scornfully labeled white southerners who allied with the Republican Party **scalawags,** yet an estimated quarter of white southerners at one time voted Republican. They were primarily Unionists from the upland counties and hill areas and largely yeoman farmers. Such voters were attracted by Republican promises to rebuild the South, restore prosperity, create public schools, and open isolated areas to the market with railroads.

> **scalawags** white southerners who supported the Republican Party.

The other group of white Republicans in the South were known as **carpetbaggers.** Originally from the North, they allegedly had arrived with all their worldly possessions stuffed in a carpetbag, ready to loot and plunder the defeated South. Some did, certainly, but northerners moved south for a variety of reasons. Though carpetbaggers made up only a small percentage of Republican voters, they controlled almost a third of the offices in the South. More than half of all southern Republican governors and nearly half of Republican members of Congress were originally northerners.

> **carpetbaggers** northern white Republicans who came to live in the South after the Civil War. Most were veterans of the Union army; many were teachers, Freedmen's Bureau agents or investors in cotton plantations.

The Republican Party in the South had difficulty maintaining unity. Scalawags were especially susceptible to the race issue and social pressure. "Even my own kinspeople have turned the cold shoulder to me because I hold office under a Republican administration," testified a Mississippi white Republican. As black southerners pressed for greater recognition, white southerners increasingly defected to the Democrats. Carpetbaggers, in contrast, were less sensitive to race, although most felt that their black allies should be content with minor offices. The animosity between scalawags and carpetbaggers, which grew out of their rivalry for party honors, was particularly intense.

Reforms under the New State Governments >> The new southern state constitutions enacted several significant reforms. They devised fairer systems of legislative representation and made many previously appointive offices elective. The Radical state governments also assumed some responsibility for social welfare and established the first statewide systems of public schools in the South.

All the new constitutions proclaimed the principle of equality and granted black adult males the right to vote. On social relations they were much more cautious. No state outlawed segregation, and South Carolina and Louisiana were the only ones that required integration in public schools (a mandate that was almost universally ignored). Sensitive to status, mulattoes pushed for prohibition of social discrimination, but white Republicans refused to adopt such a radical policy.

Economic Issues and Corruption >> With the

southern economy in ruins at the end of the war, problems of economic reconstruction were severe. The new Republican governments encouraged industrial development by providing subsidies, loans, and even temporary exemptions from taxes. These governments also largely rebuilt the southern railroad system, offering lavish aid to railroad corporations. In the two decades after 1860, the region doubled its manufacturing establishments, yet the South steadily slipped further behind the booming industrial economy of the North.

The expansion of government services offered temptations for corruption. Southern officials regularly received bribes and kickbacks for awarding railroad charters, franchises, and other contracts. The railroad grants and new social services such as schools also left state governments in debt, even though taxes rose in the 1870s to four times the rate in 1860.

Corruption, however, was not only a southern problem but a national one. During these years, the Democratic Tweed Ring in New York City alone stole more money than all the southern Radical governments combined. Moreover, corruption was hardly limited to southern Republicans: many Democrats and white business leaders participated. Louisiana governor Henry Warmoth, a carpetbagger, told a congressional committee: "Everybody is demoralizing down here. Corruption is the fashion."

Corruption in Radical governments existed, but southern Democrats exaggerated its extent for partisan purposes. They opposed honest Radical regimes just as bitterly as notoriously corrupt ones. In the eyes of most white southerners, the real crime of the Radical governments was that they allowed black citizens to hold some offices and tried to protect the civil rights of black Americans. Race was white conservatives' greatest weapon. And it would prove the most effective means to undermine Republican power in the South.

SAML. DOVE wishes to know of the whereabouts of his mother, Areno, his sisters Maria, Neziah, and Peggy, and his brother Edmond, who were owned by Geo. Dove, of Rockingham county, Shenandoah Valley, Va. Sold in Richmond, after which Saml. and Edmond were taken to Nashville, Tenn., by Joe Mick; Areno was left at the Eagle Tavern, Richmond
Respectfully yours,
SAML. DOVE.
Utica, New York., Aug. 5, 1865–3m.

⌃ During the decades before the Civil War, many slave families were split when individual slaves were sold to new masters. This Tennessee newspaper advertisement shows one way that freedpeople sought to deal with the consequences.

 REVIEW

What roles did African Americans, southern whites, and northern whites play in the Reconstruction governments of the South?

BLACK ASPIRATIONS

Emancipation came to slaves in different ways and at different times. Betty Jones's grandmother was told about the Emancipation Proclamation by another slave while they were hoeing corn. Mary Anderson received the news from her master near the end of the war when Sherman's army invaded North Carolina. Whatever the timing, freedom meant a host of precious blessings to people who had been in bondage all their lives.

Experiencing Freedom >> The first impulse was to think of freedom as a contrast to slavery. Emancipation immediately released slaves from the most oppressive aspects of bondage—the whippings, the breakup of families, the sexual exploitation. Freedom also meant movement, the right to travel without a pass or white permission. Above all, freedom meant that African Americans' labor would be for their own benefit. One Arkansas freedman, who earned his first dollar working on a railroad, recalled that when he was paid, "I felt like the richest man in the world."

Freedom included finding a new place to work. Changing jobs was one concrete way to break the psychological ties of slavery. Even planters with reputations for kindness sometimes saw most of their former hands depart. The cook who left a South Carolina family, despite the offer of higher wages than her new job's, explained: "I must go. If I stays here I'll never know I'm free."

Symbolically, freedom meant having a full name. African Americans now adopted last names, most commonly the name of the first master in the family's oral history as far back as it could be recalled. Most, however, retained their first name, especially if the name had been given to them by their parents (as most often had been the case). Whatever the name, black Americans insisted on making the decision themselves.

The Black Family >> African Americans also sought to strengthen the family in freedom. Since slave marriages had not been recognized as legal, thousands of former slaves insisted on being married again by proper authorities, even though this was not required by law. Those who had been forcibly separated in slavery and later remarried confronted the dilemma of which spouse to take. Laura Spicer, whose husband had been sold away in slavery, wrote him after the war seeking to resume their marriage. In a series of wrenching letters, he explained that he had thought her dead, had remarried, and had a new family. "You know it never was our wishes to be separated from each other, and it never was our fault. I had rather anything to had happened to me most than ever have been parted from you and the children," he wrote. "As I am, I do not know which I love best, you or Anna." Declining to return, he closed, "Laura, truly, I have got another wife, and I am very sorry."

As in white families, black husbands deemed themselves the head of the family and acted legally for their wives. They often insisted that their wives would not work in the fields as they had in slavery. "The [black] women say they never mean to do any more outdoor work," one planter reported, "that white men support their wives and they mean that their husbands shall support them." In negotiating contracts, a father also demanded the right to control his children and their labor. All these changes were designed to insulate the black family from white control.

⋏ After living for years in a society in which teaching slaves to read and write was usually illegal, freedpeople viewed literacy as a key to securing their newfound freedom. Blacks were not merely "anxious to learn," a school official in Virginia reported, they were "crazy to learn."

The Schoolhouse and the Church

>> In freedom, the schoolhouse and the black church became essential institutions in the black community. "My Lord, Ma'am, what a great thing learning is!" a South Carolina freedman told a northern teacher. "White folks can do what they likes, for they know so much more than we." At first, northern churches and missionaries, working with the Freedmen's Bureau, set up black schools in the South. Tuition at these schools represented 10 percent or more of a laborer's monthly wages, yet these schools were full. Eventually, states established public school systems, which by 1867 enrolled 40 percent of African American children.

Black adults, who often attended night classes, had good reasons for seeking literacy. They wanted to be able to read the Bible, to defend their newly gained civil and political rights, and to protect themselves from being cheated. Both races saw that education would undermine the servility that slavery had fostered.

The teachers in the Freedmen's Bureau schools were primarily northern middle-class white women

sent south by northern missionary societies. "I feel that it is a precious privilege," Esther Douglass wrote, "to be allowed to do something for these poor people." Many saw themselves as peacetime soldiers, struggling to make emancipation a reality. Indeed, hostile white southerners sometimes destroyed black schools and threatened and even murdered white teachers. Then there were the everyday challenges: low pay, run-down buildings, few books, classes of 100 or more children. By 1869 most teachers in these Freedmen's Bureau schools were black, trained by the bureau.

Most slaves had attended white churches or services supervised by whites. Once free, African Americans quickly established their own congregations led by black preachers. Mostly Methodist and Baptist, black churches were the only major organizations in the African American community controlled by blacks themselves. A white missionary reported that "the Ebony preacher who promises perfect independence from White control and direction carried the colored heart at once." Just as in slavery, religion offered African Americans a place of refuge in a hostile white world and provided them with hope, comfort, and a means of self-identification.

New Working Conditions

>> As a largely propertyless class, blacks in the postwar South had no choice but to work for white landowners. Except for

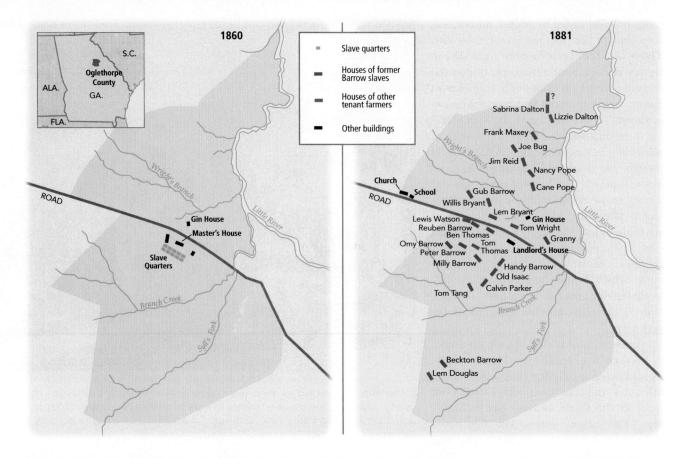

MAP 17.2: GEORGIA PLANTATION AFTER THE WAR

After emancipation, sharecropping became the dominant form of agricultural labor in the South. Black families no longer lived in the old slave quarters but dispersed to separate plots of land that they farmed themselves. At the end of the year, each sharecropper turned over part of the crop to the white landowner.

What accounts for the difference between where slave families lived before the war and where the families of freedpeople lived by 1881?

paying wages, whites wanted to retain the old system of labor, including close supervision, gang labor, and physical punishment. Determined to remove all emblems of servitude, African Americans refused to work under these conditions, and they demanded time off to devote to their own interests. Because of shorter hours and the withdrawal of children and women from the fields, blacks' output declined by an estimated 35 percent in freedom. They also refused to live in the old slave quarters located near the master's house and instead erected cabins on distant parts of the plantation. Wages initially were $5 or $6 a month plus provisions and a cabin; by 1867, they had risen to an average of $10 a month.

These changes eventually led to the rise of sharecropping. Under this arrangement African American families farmed discrete plots of land and then at the end of the year divided the crop, normally on an equal basis, with the white landowner. Sharecropping had higher status and offered greater personal

freedom than being a wage laborer. "I am not working for wages," one black farmer declared in defending his right to leave the plantation at will, "but am part owner of the crop and as [such,] I have all the rights that you or any other man has." Although black per-capita agricultural income increased 40 percent in freedom, sharecropping was a harshly exploitative system in which black families often sank into perpetual debt.

The task of supervising the transition from slavery to freedom on southern plantations fell to the Freedmen's Bureau, a unique experiment in social policy supported by the federal government. Assigned the task of protecting freedpeople's economic rights, approximately 550 local agents regulated working conditions in southern agriculture after the war. The racial attitudes of Bureau agents varied widely, as did their commitment and competence.

Most agents required written contracts between white planters and black laborers, specifying wages and the conditions of employment. Although agents sometimes intervened to protect freedpeople from unfair treatment, they also provided important help to planters. They insisted that black laborers not leave at harvesttime, they arrested those who violated their contracts or refused to sign new ones at the beginning of the year, and they preached the need to be orderly and respectful. Because of such attitudes, freedpeople increasingly complained that Bureau agents were mere tools of the planter class. One observer reported: "Doing justice seems to mean seeing that the blacks don't break contracts and compelling them to submit cheerfully."

The primary means of enforcing working conditions were the Freedmen's Courts, which Congress created in 1866 in order to avoid the discrimination African Americans received in state courts. These new courts functioned as military tribunals, and often the agent was the entire court. The sympathy black laborers received varied from state to state. But since Congress was opposed to creating any permanent welfare agency, it shut down the Freedmen's Bureau, and by 1872 it had gone out of business. Despite its mixed record, it was the most effective agency in protecting blacks' civil and political rights. Its disbanding signaled the beginning of the northern retreat from Reconstruction.

Planters and a New Way of Life >> Planters and other white southerners faced emancipation with dread. "All the traditions and habits of both races had been suddenly overthrown," a Tennessee planter recalled, "and neither knew just what to do, or how to accommodate themselves to the new situation." Slavery had been a complex institution that welded black and white southerners together in intimate relationships. The old ideal of a paternalistic planter, which required blacks to act subservient and grateful, gave way to an emphasis on strictly economic relationships. Only with time did planters develop new norms to judge black behavior.

After the war, however, planters increasingly embraced the ideology of segregation. Since emancipation significantly reduced the social distance between the races, white southerners sought psychological separation and kept dealings with African Americans to a minimum. By the time Reconstruction ended, white planters had developed a new way of life based on the institutions of sharecropping and segregation, and undergirded by a militant white supremacy.

While most planters kept their land, they did not regain the economic prosperity of the prewar years. Cotton prices began a long decline, and southern per-capita income suffered as a result. By 1880 the value of southern farms had slid 33 percent below the level of 1860.

 REVIEW

In what ways were the church and the school central to African American hopes after the Civil War?

THE ABANDONMENT OF RECONSTRUCTION

On Christmas Day 1875 a white acquaintance approached Charles Caldwell in Clinton, Mississippi, and invited him to have a drink. A former slave, Caldwell was a state senator and the leader of the Republican Party in Hinds County. But the black leader's fearlessness made him a marked man. Only two months earlier, Caldwell had fled the county to escape an armed white mob. Despite threats against him, he had returned home to vote in the November state election. Now, as Caldwell and his "friend" raised their glasses in a holiday toast, a gunshot exploded through the window and Caldwell collapsed, mortally wounded. He was taken outside, where his assassins riddled his body with bullets. He died alone in the street.

Charles Caldwell shared the fate of a number of black Republican leaders in the South during Reconstruction. Resorting to violence and terror, white southerners challenged the commitment of the federal government to sustaining Reconstruction. After Andrew Johnson was acquitted in May 1868 at his impeachment trial, the crusading idealism of the Republican Party began to wane. Ulysses S. Grant was hardly the cause of this change, but he certainly came to symbolize it.

The Grant Administration >> In 1868 Grant was elected president—and Republicans were shocked. Their candidate, a great war hero, had won by a margin of only 300,000 votes. Furthermore, with an estimated 450,000 black Republican votes cast in the South, a majority of whites had voted Democratic. The election helped convince Republican leaders that an amendment securing black suffrage throughout the nation was necessary.

If the North won the war, how well did it win the peace?

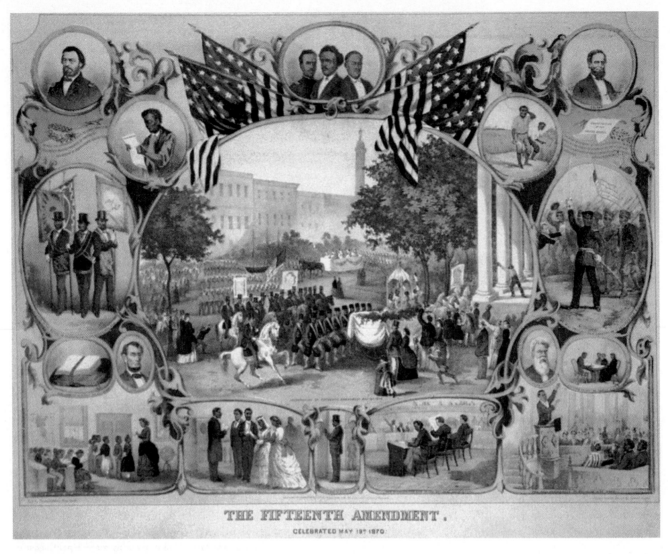

︿ The Fifteenth Amendment, ratified in 1870, secured the right of African American males to vote as free citizens. In New York, black citizens paraded in support of Ulysses S. Grant for president (*center*). But citizenship was only one component of what African Americans insisted were central aspects of their freedom. What other features of a free life does the poster champion?

In February 1869 Congress sent the Fifteenth Amendment to the states for ratification. It forbade any state to deny the right to vote on grounds of race, color, or previous condition of servitude. It did not forbid literacy and property requirements, as some Radicals wanted, because the moderates feared that only a conservative version of the amendment could be ratified. As a result, when the amendment was ratified in March 1870, loopholes remained that eventually allowed southern states to **disfranchise** African Americans.

disenfranchisement denial of a citizen's right to vote.

Advocates of women's suffrage were bitterly disappointed when Congress refused to outlaw voting discrimination on the basis of sex as well as race. The Women's Loyal League, led by Elizabeth Cady Stanton and Susan B. Anthony, had pressed for first the Fourteenth and then the Fifteenth Amendment to recognize that women had a civic right to vote. But even most Radicals were unwilling to back women's suffrage, contending that black rights had to be ensured first. As a result, the Fifteenth Amendment divided the feminist movement. Although disappointed that women were not included in its provisions, Lucy Stone and the American Woman Suffrage Association urged ratification. Stanton and Anthony, however, denounced the amendment and organized the National Woman Suffrage Association to work for passage of a new amendment giving women the ballot. The division hampered the women's rights movement for decades to come.

When Ulysses S. Grant was a general, his quiet manner and well-known resolution served him well. As president he proved much less certain of his goals and therefore less effective at corralling politicians than at maneuvering troops.

A series of scandals wracked his administration, so much so that "Grantism" soon became a code word in American politics for corruption, cronyism, and venality. Although Grant did not profit personally, he remained loyal to his friends and displayed little zeal to root out wrongdoing. Nor was Congress immune from the lowered tone of public life. In such a climate ruthless state machines, led by men who favored the status quo, came to dominate the party.

As corruption in both the North and the South worsened, reformers became more interested in cleaning up government than in protecting black rights. Congress in 1872 passed an amnesty act, allowing many more ex-Confederates to serve in southern governments. That same year, liberal Republicans broke with the Republican Party and nominated for president Horace Greeley, the editor of the New York *Tribune*. A one-time Radical, Greeley had become disillusioned with Reconstruction and urged a restoration of home rule in the South as well as adoption of civil service reform. Democrats decided to back the Liberal Republican ticket. The Republicans renominated Grant, who, despite the defection of a number of prominent Radicals, won an easy victory.

Growing Northern Disillusionment >> During Grant's second term Congress passed the Civil Rights Act of 1875, the last major piece of Reconstruction legislation. This law prohibited racial discrimination in public accommodations, transportation, places of amusement, and juries. At the same time, Congress rejected a ban on segregation in public schools, which was almost universally practiced in the North as well as the South. The federal government made little attempt to enforce the law, however, and in 1883 the Supreme Court struck down its provisions, except the one relating to juries.

Despite passage of the Civil Rights Act, many northerners were growing disillusioned with Reconstruction. They were repelled by the corruption of the southern governments, they were tired of the violence and disorder that accompanied elections in the South, and they had little faith in black Americans. William Dodge, a wealthy New York capitalist and an influential Republican, wrote in 1875 that the South could never develop its resources "till confidence in her state governments can be restored, and this will never be done by federal bayonets." It had been a mistake, he went on, to make black southerners feel "that the United States government was their special friend, rather than those . . . among whom they must live and for whom they must work. We have tried this long enough," he concluded. "Now let the South alone."

^ Grant swings from a trapeze while supporting a number of associates accused of corruption. Secretary of the Navy George M. Robeson (*top center*) was accused of accepting bribes for awarding Navy contracts; Secretary of War William W. Belknap (*top right*) was forced to resign for selling Indian post traderships; and the president's private secretary, Orville Babcock (*bottom right*), was implicated in the Whiskey Ring scandal. Although not personally involved in the scandals, Grant was reluctant to dismiss from office supporters accused of wrongdoing.

As the agony of the war became more distant, the Panic of 1873, which precipitated a severe four-year depression, diverted public attention to economic issues. Battered by the panic and the corruption issue, the Republicans lost a shocking 77 seats in Congress in the 1874 elections, and along with them control of the House of Representatives for the first time since 1861.

"The truth is our people are tired out with the worn out cry of 'Southern outrages'!!" one Republican concluded. "Hard times and heavy taxes make them wish the 'ever lasting nigger' were in hell or Africa." More and more, Republicans spoke about cutting loose the unpopular southern governments.

The Triumph of White Supremacy >>

Meanwhile, southern Democrats set out to overthrow the remaining Radical governments. Already, white Republicans in the South felt heavy pressure to desert their party. To poor white southerners who lacked social standing, the Democratic appeal to racial solidarity offered special comfort. The large landowners and other wealthy groups that led southern Democrats objected less to black southerners voting, since they were confident that if outside influences were removed, they could control the black vote.

Democrats also resorted to economic pressure to undermine Republican power. In heavily black counties, newspapers published the names of black residents who cast Republican ballots and urged planters to discharge them. But terror and violence provided the most effective means to overthrow the radical regimes. A number of paramilitary organizations broke up Republican meetings, terrorized white and black Republicans, assassinated Republican leaders, and prevented black citizens from voting. The most notorious of these organizations was the Ku Klux Klan, which along with similar groups functioned as an unofficial arm of the Democratic Party.

In the war for supremacy, contesting control of the night was paramount to both southern whites and blacks. Before emancipation masters regulated the nighttime hours, with a system of passes and patrols that chased slaves who went hunting or tried to sneak a visit to a family member at a neighboring plantation. For slaves the night provided precious free time: to read, to meet for worship, school, or dancing. During Reconstruction African Americans actively took back

the night for a host of activities, including torchlight political parades and meetings of such organizations as the Union League. Part of the Klan's mission was to recoup this contested ground and to limit the ability of African Americans to use the night as they pleased. When indirect threats of violence were not enough (galloping through black neighborhoods rattling fences with lances), beatings and executions were undertaken—again, facilitated by the dark of night.

What became known as the Mississippi Plan was inaugurated in 1875, when Democrats decided to use as much violence as necessary to carry the state election. Local papers trumpeted, "Carry the election peaceably if we can, forcibly if we must." Recognizing that northern public opinion had grown sick of repeated federal intervention in southern elections, the Grant administration rejected the request of Republican governor Adelbert Ames for troops to stop the violence. Bolstered by terrorism, the Democrats swept the election in Mississippi. Violence and intimidation prevented as many as 60,000 black and white Republicans from voting, converting the normal Republican majority into a Democratic majority of 30,000. Mississippi had been "redeemed."

The Disputed Election of 1876 >>

The 1876 presidential election was crucial to the final overthrow of Reconstruction. The Republicans nominated Ohio governor Rutherford B. Hayes to oppose Samuel, governor New York. Once again violence prevented an estimated quarter of a million Republican votes from being cast in the South. Tilden had a clear majority of 250,000 in the popular vote, but the outcome in the Electoral College was in doubt because both parties claimed South Carolina, Florida, and Louisiana, the only reconstructed states still in Republican hands.

To arbitrate the disputed returns, Congress established a 15–member electoral commission. By a straight party vote of 8 to 7, the commission awarded the disputed electoral votes—and the presidency—to Hayes.

When angry Democrats threatened a filibuster to prevent the electoral votes from being counted, key Republicans met with southern Democrats and reached an informal understanding, later known as the Compromise of 1877. Hayes's supporters agreed to withdraw federal troops from the South and not oppose the new Democratic state governments. For their part, southern Democrats dropped their opposition to Hayes's election and pledged to respect African Americans' rights.

Without federal support, the last Republican southern governments collapsed, and Democrats took control of

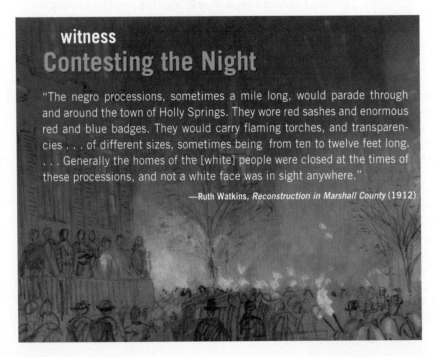

witness
Contesting the Night

"The negro processions, sometimes a mile long, would parade through and around the town of Holly Springs. They wore red sashes and enormous red and blue badges. They would carry flaming torches, and transparencies . . . of different sizes, sometimes being from ten to twelve feet long. . . . Generally the homes of the [white] people were closed at the times of these processions, and not a white face was in sight anywhere."

—Ruth Watkins, *Reconstruction in Marshall County* (1912)

Dressed to Kill

Klan members drawn for *Harper's Weekly* magazine.

These three Klansmen were arrested in Tishomingo County, Mississippi, for attempted murder.

Why wear a hooded mask? Might there be more than one reason?

The costumes of Ku Klux Klan night riders—pointed hoods and white sheets—have become a staple of history books. But why use such outlandish disguises? To hide the identity of members, according to some accounts, or to terrorize freedpeople into thinking they were being managed by Confederate ghosts. Historian Elaine F. Parsons has suggested that KKK performances took their cues from American popular culture the costumes of Mardi Gras and similar carnivals, as well as minstrel shows. In behaving like carnival revelers, KKK members may have hoped to fool northern authorities into viewing the night rides as humorous pranks, not a threat to Radical rule. For southern white Democrats the theatrical night rides helped overturn the social order of Reconstruction, just as carousers at carnivals disrupted the night. The ritual garb provided seemingly innocent cover for what was truly a campaign of terror and intimidation that often turned deadly.

THINKING CRITICALLY

In what ways do these disguises affect the people who wear them? Assess how the combination of horror and jest might have worked in terms of the different groups perceiving the Klan's activities: white northerners, white southerners, and African American southerners. In terms of popular culture, do modern horror films sometimes combine both terror and humor?

---

the remaining states of the Confederacy. By 1877 the entire South was in the hands of the **Redeemers,** as they called themselves. Reconstruction and Republican rule had come to an end.

> **Redeemers** southerners who came to power in southern state governments from 1875 to 1877, claiming to have "redeemed" the South from Reconstruction. The Redeemers looked to undo many of the changes wrought by the Civil War.

Racism and the Failure of Reconstruction >> Reconstruction failed for a multitude of reasons. The reforming impulse behind the Republican Party of the 1850s had been battered and worn down by the war. The new materialism of industrial America inspired a jaded cynicism in many Americans. In the South, African American voters and leaders inevitably lacked a certain amount of education and experience;

elsewhere, Republicans were divided over policies and options.

Yet beyond these obstacles, the sad fact remains that the ideals of Reconstruction were most clearly defeated by a deep—seated racism that permeated American life. Racism stimulated white southern resistance, undercut northern support for black rights, and eventually made northerners willing to write off Reconstruction, and with it the welfare of African Americans. Although Congress could pass a constitutional amendment abolishing slavery, it could not overturn at a stroke the social habits of two centuries.

 REVIEW

What factors in the North and the South led the federal government to abandon Reconstruction in the South?

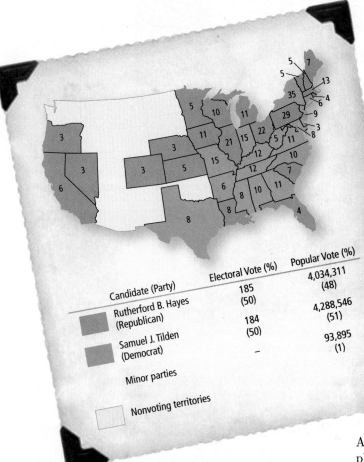

Candidate (Party)	Electoral Vote (%)	Popular Vote (%)
Rutherford B. Hayes (Republican)	185 (50)	4,034,311 (48)
Samuel J. Tilden (Democrat)	184 (50)	4,288,546 (51)
Minor parties	–	93,895 (1)
Nonvoting territories		

MAP 17.3: ELECTION OF 1876

With the overthrow of Reconstruction, the white South had won back some of the power it had lost in 1865—but not all. In the longer term, the political equations of power had been changed. Even under Redeemer governments, African Americans did not return to the social position they had occupied before the war. They were no longer slaves, and black south—erners who walked dusty roads in search of family members, sent their children to school, or worshiped in their own black churches knew what a momentous change this was. Even under the exploitative share—cropping system, black income rose significantly in freedom. Then, too, the guarantees of "equal protec—tion" and "due process of law" had been written into the Constitution and would be available for later generations to use in championing once again the Radi—cals' goal of racial equality.

But this was a struggle left to future reformers. For the time being, the clear trend was away from change or hope—especially for former slaves like Benjamin Montgomery and his sons, the owners of the old Davis plantations in Mississippi. In the 1870s bad crops, lower cotton prices, and falling land values undermined the Montgomerys' financial position, and in 1875 Jefferson Davis sued to have the sale of Brierfield invalidated. Following the overthrow of Mississippi's Radical government, a white con—servative majority of the court awarded Brierfield to Davis in 1878. The Montgomerys lost Hur—ricane as well.

The waning days of Reconstruction were times filled with such ironies: of governments "redeemed" by violence, of Fourteenth Amend—ment rights being used by conservative courts to protect not black people but giant corpo—rations, of reformers taking up other causes. Increasingly, the industrial North focused on an economic task: integrating both the South and the West into the Union. In the case of both regions, northern factories sought to use southern and western raw materi—als to produce goods and to find national markets for those products. Indeed, during the coming decades European nations also scrambled to acquire natural resources and markets. In the onrushing age of imperialism, Western nations would seek to dominate newly acquired colonies in Africa and Asia, with the same disregard for their "subject peo—ples" that was seen with African Americans, Latinos, and Indians in the United States.

Disowned by its northern supporters and unmourned by public opinion, Reconstruction was over.

CHAPTER SUMMARY

Presidents Abraham Lincoln and Andrew Johnson and the Republican–dominated Congress each developed a program of Reconstruction to quickly restore the Confederate States to the Union.

- Lincoln's 10 percent plan required that 10 percent of qualified voters from 1860 swear an oath of loyalty to begin organizing a state government.
- Following Lincoln's assassination, Andrew Johnson changed Lincoln's terms and lessened Reconstruction's requirements.
- The more radical Congress repudiated Johnson's state governments and eventually enacted its own program of Reconstruction, which included the principle of black suffrage.
  - ▶ Congress passed the Fourteenth and Fifteenth Amendments and also extended the life of the Freedmen's Bureau, a unique experiment in social welfare.
  - ▶ Congress rejected land reform, however, which would have provided the freedpeople with a greater economic stake.
  - ▶ The effort to remove Johnson from office through impeachment failed.
- The Radical governments in the South, led by black and white southerners and transplanted northerners, compiled a mixed record on matters such as racial equality, education, economic issues, and corruption.
- Reconstruction was a time of both joy and frustration for former slaves.
  - ▶ Former slaves took steps to reunite their families and establish black–controlled churches.
  - ▶ They evidenced a widespread desire for land and education.
  - ▶ Black resistance to the old system of labor led to the adoption of sharecropping.
  - ▶ The Freedmen's Bureau fostered these new working arrangements and also the beginnings of black education in the South.
- Northern public opinion became disillusioned with Reconstruction during the presidency of Ulysses S. Grant.
- Southern whites used violence, economic coercion, and racism to overthrow the Republican state governments.
- In 1877 Republican leaders agreed to end Reconstruction in exchange for Rutherford B. Hayes's election as president.
- Racism played a key role in the eventual failure of Reconstruction.

Additional Reading

Historians' views of Reconstruction have dramatically changed over the past half century. Modern studies offer a more sympathetic assessment of Reconstruction and the experience of African Americans. Indicative of this trend is Eric Foner, *Reconstruction* (1988), and his briefer treatment (with photographic essays by Joshua Brown) *Forever Free: The Story of Emancipation and Reconstruction* (2005). Michael Les Benedict treats the clash between Andrew Johnson and Congress in *The Impeachment and Trial of Andrew Johnson* (1973). Political affairs in the South during Reconstruction are examined in Dan T. Carter, *When the War Was Over* (1985); and Thomas Holt, *Black over White* (1977), an imaginative study of black political leadership in South Carolina. Hans Trefousse, *Thaddeus Stevens: Nineteenth–Century Egalitarian* (1997), provides a sympathetic reassessment of the influential Radical Republican. Mark W. Summers, *A Dangerous Stir* (2009), deftly examines the ways in which fear and paranoia shaped Reconstruction.

Leon Litwack, *Been in the Storm So Long* (1979), sensitively analyzes the transition of enslaved African Americans to freedom. Heather Andrea Williams, *Self–Taught: African American Education in Slavery and Freedom* (2005), illustrates the black drive for literacy and education. James L. Roark, *Masters without Slaves* (1977), discusses former slaveholders' adjustment to the end of slavery. The dialectic of black–white relations is charted from the antebellum years through Reconstruction and beyond in Steven Hahn, *A Nation under Our Feet: Black Political Struggles in the Rural South from Slavery to the Great Migration* (2003). Two excellent studies of changing labor relations in southern agriculture are Julie Saville, *The Work of Reconstruction* (1995); and John C. Rodrigue, *Reconstruction in the Cane Fields* (2001). For contrasting views of the Freedmen's Bureau, see George R. Bentley, *A History of the Freedmen's Bureau* (1955)—favorable—and Donald Nieman, *To Set the Law in Motion* (1979)—critical. William Gillette, *Retreat from Reconstruction, 1869–1879* (1980), focuses on national politics and the end of Reconstruction; while Michael Perman, *The Road to Redemption* (1984), looks at developments in the South. Heather Cox Richardson explores the postwar context in the North in *The Death of Reconstruction* (2004) and considers Reconstruction in the West in *West from Appomattox* (2008).

Significant Events

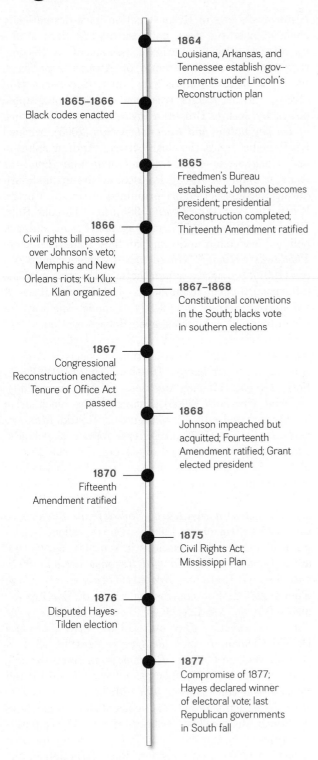

1864
Louisiana, Arkansas, and Tennessee establish gov--ernments under Lincoln's Reconstruction plan

1865–1866
Black codes enacted

1865
Freedmen's Bureau established; Johnson becomes president; presidential Reconstruction completed; Thirteenth Amendment ratified

1866
Civil rights bill passed over Johnson's veto; Memphis and New Orleans riots; Ku Klux Klan organized

1867–1868
Constitutional conventions in the South; blacks vote in southern elections

1867
Congressional Reconstruction enacted; Tenure of Office Act passed

1868
Johnson impeached but acquitted; Fourteenth Amendment ratified; Grant elected president

1870
Fifteenth Amendment ratified

1875
Civil Rights Act; Mississippi Plan

1876
Disputed Hayes-Tilden election

1877
Compromise of 1877; Hayes declared winner of electoral vote; last Republican governments in South fall

Appendix

- The Declaration of Independence

- The Constitution of the United States of America

The Declaration of Independence

IN CONGRESS, JULY 4, 1776

The Unanimous Declaration of the Thirteen United States of America

When, in the course of human events, it becomes necessary for one people to dissolve the political bands which have connected them with another, and to assume, among the powers of the earth, the separate and equal station to which the laws of nature and of nature's God entitle them, a decent respect to the opinions of mankind requires that they should declare the causes which impel them to the separation.

We hold these truths to be self—evident, that all men are created equal; that they are endowed by their Creator with certain unalienable rights; that among these, are life, liberty, and the pursuit of happiness. That, to secure these rights, governments are instituted among men, deriving their just powers from the consent of the governed; that, whenever any form of government becomes destructive of these ends, it is the right of the people to alter or to abolish it, and to institute a new government, laying its foundation on such principles, and organizing its powers in such form, as to them shall seem most likely to effect their safety and happiness. Prudence, indeed, will dictate that governments long established, should not be changed for light and transient causes; and, accordingly, all experience hath shown, that mankind are more disposed to suffer, while evils are sufferable, than to right themselves by abolishing the forms to which they are accustomed. But, when a long train of abuses and usurpations, pursuing invariably the same object, evinces a design to reduce them under absolute despotism, it is their right, it is their duty, to throw off such government and to provide new guards for their future security. Such has been the patient sufferance of these colonies, and such is now the necessity which constrains them to alter their former systems of government. The history of the present King of Great Britain is a history of repeated injuries and usurpations, all having, in direct object, the establishment of an absolute tyranny over these States. To prove this, let facts be submitted to a candid world:

He has refused his assent to laws the most wholesome and necessary for the public good.

He has forbidden his governors to pass laws of immediate and pressing importance, unless suspended in their operation till his assent should be obtained; and, when so suspended, he has utterly neglected to attend to them.

He has refused to pass other laws for the accommodation of large districts of people, unless those people would relinquish the right of representation in the legislature; a right inestimable to them, and formidable to tyrants only.

He has called together legislative bodies at places unusual, uncomfortable, and distant from the depository of their public records, for the sole purpose of fatiguing them into compliance with his measures.

He has dissolved representative houses repeatedly for opposing, with manly firmness, his invasions on the rights of the people.

He has refused, for a long time after such dissolutions, to cause others to be elected; whereby the legislative powers, incapable of annihilation, have returned to the people at large for their exercise; the state remaining, in the meantime, exposed to all the danger of invasion from without, and convulsions within.

He has endeavored to prevent the population of these States; for that purpose, obstructing the laws for naturalization of foreigners, refusing to pass others to encourage their migration hither, and raising the conditions of new appropriations of lands.

He had obstructed the administration of justice, by refusing his assent to laws for establishing judiciary powers. He has made judges dependent on his will alone, for the tenure of their offices, and the amount and payment of their salaries.

He has erected a multitude of new offices, and sent hither swarms of officers to harass our people, and eat out their substance.

He has kept among us, in time of peace, standing armies, without the consent of our legislatures.

He has affected to render the military independent of, and superior to, the civil power.

He has combined, with others, to subject us to a jurisdiction foreign to our Constitution, and unacknowledged by our laws; giving his assent to their acts of pretended legislation:

For quartering large bodies of armed troops among us:

For protecting them by a mock trial, from punish—ment, for any murders which they should commit on the inhabitants of these States:

For cutting off our trade with all parts of the world:

For imposing taxes on us without our consent:

For depriving us, in many cases, of the benefit of trial by jury:

For transporting us beyond seas to be tried for pretended offences:

For abolishing the free system of English laws in a neighboring province, establishing therein an arbi—trary government, and enlarging its boundaries, so as to render it at once an example and fit instrument for introducing the same absolute rule into these colonies:

For taking away our charters, abolishing our most valuable laws, and altering, fundamentally, the powers of our governments:

For suspending our own legislatures, and declar—ing themselves invested with power to legislate for us in all cases whatsoever.

He has abdicated government here, by declaring us out of his protection, and waging war against us.

He has plundered our seas, ravaged our coasts, burnt our towns, and destroyed the lives of our people.

He is, at this time, transporting large armies of foreign mercenaries to complete the works of death, desolation, and tyranny, already begun, with circum—stances of cruelty and perfidy scarcely paralleled in the most barbarous ages, and totally unworthy the head of a civilized nation.

He has constrained our fellow citizens, taken captive on the high seas, to bear arms against their country, to become the executioners of their friends, and brethren, or to fall themselves by their hands.

He has excited domestic insurrections amongst us, and has endeavored to bring on the inhabitants of our frontiers, the merciless Indian savages, whose known rule of warfare is an undistinguished destruction of all ages, sexes, and conditions.

In every stage of these oppressions, we have peti—tioned for redress, in the most humble terms; our repeated petitions have been answered only by repeated injury. A prince, whose character is thus marked by every act which may define a tyrant, is unfit to be the ruler of a free people.

Nor have we been wanting in attention to our British brethren. We have warned them, from time to time, of attempts made by their legislature to extend an unwarrantable jurisdiction over us. We have reminded them of the circumstances of our emigra—tion and settlement here. We have appealed to their native justice and magnanimity, and we have conjured them, by the ties of our common kindred, to disavow these usurpations, which would inevitably interrupt our connections and correspondence. They, too, have been deaf to the voice of justice and consanguinity. We must, therefore, acquiesce in the necessity which denounces our separation, and hold them as we hold the rest of mankind, enemies in war, in peace, friends.

We, therefore, the representatives of the United States of America, in general Congress assembled, appealing to the Supreme Judge of the world for the rectitude of our intentions, do, in the name, and by the authority of the good people of these colonies, solemnly publish and declare, that these united colonies are, and of right ought to be, free and independent states: that they are absolved from all allegiance to the British Crown, and that all political connection between them and the state of Great Britain is, and ought to be, totally dissolved; and that, as free and independent states, they have full power to levy war, conclude peace, contract alliances, establish commerce, and to do all other acts and things which independent states may of right do. And, for the support of this declara—tion, with a firm reliance on the protection of Divine Providence, we mutually pledge to each other our lives, our fortunes, and our sacred honor.

The foregoing Declaration was, by order of Congress, engrossed, and signed by the following members:

NEW HAMPSHIRE
Josiah Bartlett
William Whipple
Matthew Thornton

MASSACHUSETTS BAY
Samuel Adams
John Adams
Robert Treat Paine
Elbridge Gerry

RHODE ISLAND
Stephen Hopkins
William Ellery

CONNECTICUT
Roger Sherman
Samuel Huntington
William Williams
Oliver Wolcott

NEW YORK
William Floyd
Philip Livingston
Francis Lewis
Lewis Morris

NEW JERSEY
Richard Stockton
John Witherspoon
Francis Hopkinson
John Hart
Abraham Clark

PENNSYLVANIA
Robert Morris
Benjamin Rush
Benjamin Franklin
John Morton
George Clymer
James Smith
George Taylor
James Wilson
George Ross

DELAWARE
Caesar Rodney
George Read
Thomas M'Kean

MARYLAND
Samuel Chase
William Paca
Thomas Stone
Charles Carroll, of
Carrollton

VIRGINIA
George Wythe
Richard Henry Lee
Thomas Jefferson
Benjamin Harrison
Thomas Nelson, Jr.
Francis Lightfoot Lee
Carter Braxton

NORTH CAROLINA
William Hooper
Joseph Hewes
John Penn

SOUTH CAROLINA
Edward Rutledge
Thomas Heyward, Jr.
Thomas Lynch, Jr.
Arthur Middleton

GEORGIA
Button Gwinnett
Lyman Hall
George Walton

Resolved, That copies of the Declaration be sent to the several assemblies, conventions, and committees, or coun‐
sils of safety, and to the several commanding officers of the continental troops; that it be proclaimed in each of
the United States, at the head of the army.

The Constitution of the United States of America[1]

We the People of the United States, in Order to form a more perfect Union, establish Justice, insure domestic Tranquility, provide for the common defence, promote the general Welfare, and secure the Blessings of Liberty to ourselves and our Posterity, do ordain and establish this CONSTITUTION for the United States of America.

ARTICLE I

SECTION 1. All legislative Powers herein granted shall be vested in a Congress of the United States, which shall consist of a Senate and House of Representatives.

SECTION 2. The House of Representatives shall be composed of Members chosen every second Year by the People of the several States, and the Electors in each State shall have the Qualifications requisite for Electors of the most numerous Branch of the State Legislature. No Person shall be a Representative who shall not have attained to the Age of twenty—five Years, and been seven Years a Citizen of the United States, and who shall not, when elected, be an Inhab— itant of that State in which he shall be chosen.

[Representatives and direct Taxes[2] shall be appor— tioned among the several States which may be included within this Union, according to their respective Num— bers, which shall be determined by adding to the whole Number of free Persons, including those bound to Service for a Term of Years, and excluding Indians not taxed, three fifths of all other Persons.][3] The actual Enumera— tion shall be made within three Years after the first Meeting of the Congress of the United States, and within every subsequent Term of ten Years, in such Manner as they shall by Law direct. The Number of Representa— tives shall not exceed one for every thirty Thousand, but each State shall have at Least one Representative; and until such enumeration shall be made, the State of New Hampshire shall be entitled to chuse three, Massachu— setts eight, Rhode— Island and Providence Plantations one, Connecticut five, New York six, New Jersey four, Pennsylvania eight, Delaware one, Maryland six, Virginia ten, North Carolina five, South Carolina five, and Georgia three. When vacancies happen in the Representation from any State, the Executive Authority thereof shall issue Writs of Election to fill such Vacancies. The House of Representatives shall chuse their Speaker and other Officers; and shall have the sole Power of Impeachment.

SECTION 3. The Senate of the United States shall be composed of two Senators from each State, chosen by the Legislature thereof, for six Years; and each Senator shall have one Vote.

Immediately after they shall be assembled in Con— sequence of the first Election, they shall be divided as equally as may be into three Classes. The Seats of the Senators of the first Class shall be vacated at the Expi— ration of the second Year, of the second Class at the Expiration of the fourth Year, and of the third Class at the Expiration of the sixth Year, so that one—third may be chosen every second Year; and if Vacancies hap— pen by Resignation, or otherwise, during the Recess of the Legislature of any State, the Executive thereof may make temporary Appointments until the next Meeting of the Legislature, which shall then fill such Vacancies. No Person shall be a Senator who shall not have attained to the Age of thirty Years, and been nine Years a Citizen of the United States, and who shall not, when elected, be an Inhabitant of that State for which he shall be chosen.

The Vice President of the United States shall be President of the Senate, but shall have no vote, unless they be equally divided.

The Senate shall chuse their other Officers, and also a President pro tempore, in the absence of the Vice President, or when he shall exercise the Office of President of the United States.

The Senate shall have the sole Power to try all Impeachments. When sitting for that purpose they shall be on Oath or Affirmation. When the President of the United States is tried, the Chief Justice shall preside: And no person shall be convicted without the Concurrence of two thirds of the Members present.

Judgment in Cases of Impeachment shall not extend further than to removal from Office, and disqualifica— tion to hold and enjoy any Office of honor, Trust, or Profit under the United States: but the Party convicted shall nevertheless be liable and subject to Indictment, Trial, Judgment, and Punishment, according to Law.

---

1 This version follows the original Constitution in capitalization and spelling. It is adapted from the text published by the United States Department of the Interior, Office of Education.

2 Altered by the Sixteenth Amendment.

3 Negated by the Fourteenth Amendment.

SECTION 4. The Times, Places and Manner of holding Elections for Senators and Representatives, shall be prescribed in each State by the Legislature thereof; but the Congress may at any time by Law make or alter such Regulations, except as to the Places of Chusing Senators. The Congress shall assemble at least once in every Year, and such Meeting shall be on the first Monday in December, unless they shall by Law appoint a different Day.

SECTION 5. Each House shall be the Judge of the Elections, Returns and Qualifications of its own Members, and a Majority of each shall constitute a Quorum to do Business; but a smaller number may adjourn from day to day, and may be authorized to compel the Attendance of absent Members, in such Manner, and under such Penalties, as each House may provide.

Each House may determine the Rules of its Proceedings, punish its Members for disorderly Behaviour, and, with the Concurrence of two thirds, expel a Member. Each House shall keep a Journal of its Proceedings, and from time to time publish the same, excepting such Parts as may in their Judgment require Secrecy; and the Yeas and Nays of the Members of either House on any question shall, at the Desire of one fifth of those Present, be entered on the Journal.

Neither House, during the Session of Congress, shall, without the Consent of the other, adjourn for more than three days, nor to any other Place than that in which the two Houses shall be sitting.

SECTION 6. The Senators and Representatives shall receive a Compensation for their Services, to be ascertained by Law, and paid out of the Treasury of the United States. They shall in all Cases, except Treason, Felony, and Breach of the Peace, be privileged from Arrest during their Attendance at the Session of their respective Houses, and in going to and returning from the same; and for any Speech or Debate in either House, they shall not be questioned in any other Place.

No Senator or Representative shall, during the Time for which he was elected, be appointed to any civil Office under the Authority of the United States, which shall have been created, or the Emoluments whereof shall have been increased, during such time; and no Person holding any Office under the United States shall be a Member of either House during his continuance in Office.

SECTION 7. All Bills for raising Revenue shall originate in the House of Representatives; but the Senate may propose or concur with Amendments as on other bills. Every Bill which shall have passed the House of Representatives and the Senate, shall, before it become a Law, be presented to the President of the United States; If he approve he shall sign it, but if not

he shall return it, with his Objections, to that House in which it shall have originated, who shall enter the Objections at large on their Journal, and proceed to reconsider it. If after such Reconsideration two thirds of that House shall agree to pass the bill, it shall be sent, together with the objections, to the other House, by which it shall likewise be reconsidered, and if approved by two thirds of that House, it shall become a Law. But in all such Cases the Votes of both Houses shall be determined by Yeas and Nays, and the Names of the Persons voting for and against the Bill shall be entered on the Journal of each House respectively. If any Bill shall not be returned by the President within ten Days (Sundays excepted) after it shall have been presented to him, the Same shall be a Law, in like Manner as if he had signed it, unless the Congress by their Adjournment prevent its Return, in which Case it shall not be a Law. Every Order, Resolution, or Vote to which the Concurrence of the Senate and House of Representatives may be necessary (except on a question of Adjournment) shall be presented to the President of the United States; and before the Same shall take Effect, shall be approved by him, or being disapproved by him, shall be repassed by two thirds of the Senate and House of Representatives, according to the Rules and Limitations prescribed in the Case of a Bill.

SECTION 8. The Congress shall have Power To lay and collect Taxes, Duties, Imposts and Excises, to pay the Debts and provide for the common Defence and general Welfare of the United States; but all Duties, Imposts and Excises shall be uniform throughout the United States;

To borrow money on the credit of the United States;

To regulate Commerce with foreign Nations, and among the several States, and with the Indian Tribes;

To establish an uniform rule of Naturalization, and uniform Laws on the subject of Bankruptcies throughout the United States; To coin Money, regulate the Value thereof, and of foreign Coin, and fix the Standard of Weights and Measures;

To provide for the Punishment of counterfeiting the Securities and current Coin of the United States;

To establish Post Offices and post Roads; To promote the Progress of Science and useful Arts, by securing for limited Times to Authors and Inventors the exclusive Right to their respective Writings and Discoveries;

To constitute Tribunals inferior to the Supreme Court;

To define and punish Piracies and Felonies committed on the high Seas, and Offenses against the Law of Nations;

To declare War, grant Letters of Marque and Reprisal, and make Rules concerning Captures on Land and Water;

To raise and support Armies, but no Appropriation of Money to that Use shall be for a longer Term than two Years;

To provide and maintain a Navy;

To make Rules for the Government and Regulation of the land and naval forces;

To provide for calling forth the Militia to execute the Laws of the Union, suppress Insurrections and repel Invasions;

To provide for organizing, arming, and disciplining the Militia, and for government such Part of them as may be employed in the Service of the United States, reserving to the States respectively, the Appointment of the Officers, and the Authority of training the Militia according to the discipline prescribed by Congress;

To exercise exclusive Legislation in all Cases whatsoever, over such District (not exceeding ten Miles square) as may, by Cession of particular States, and the acceptance of Congress, become the Seat of the Government of the United States, and to exercise like Authority over all Places purchased by the Consent of the Legislature of the State in which the Same shall be, for the Erection of Forts, Magazines, Arsenals, Dockyards, and other needful Buildings;—And

To make all Laws which shall be necessary and proper for carrying into Execution the foregoing Powers, and all other Powers vested by this Constitution in the Government of the United States, or in any Department or Officer thereof.

SECTION 9. The Migration or Importation of such Persons as any of the States now existing shall think proper to admit, shall not be prohibited by the Congress prior to the Year one thousand eight hundred and eight, but a tax or duty may be imposed on such Importation, not exceeding ten dollars for each Person.

The privilege of the Writ of Habeas Corpus shall not be suspended, unless when in Cases of Rebellion or Invasion the public Safety may require it.

No bill of Attainder or ex post facto Law shall be passed.

No capitation, or other direct, Tax shall be laid unless in Proportion to the Census or Enumeration herein before directed to be taken.

No Tax or Duty shall be laid on Articles exported from any State.

No Preference shall be given by any Regulation of Commerce or Revenue to the Ports of one State over those of another: nor shall Vessels bound to, or from, one State, be obliged to enter, clear, or pay Duties in another.

No Money shall be drawn from the Treasury, but in Consequence of Appropriations made by Law; and a regular Statement and Account of the Receipts and Expenditures of all public Money shall be published from time to time.

No Title of Nobility shall be granted by the United States: And no Person holding any Office of Profit or Trust under them, shall, without the Consent of the Congress, accept of any present, Emolument, Office, or Title, of any kind whatever, from any King, Prince, or foreign State.

SECTION 10. No State shall enter into any Treaty, Alliance, or Confederation; grant Letters of Marque and Reprisal; coin Money; emit Bills of Credit; make any Thing but gold and silver Coin a Tender in Payment of Debts; pass any Bill of Attainder, ex post facto Law, or Law impairing the Obligation of Contracts, or grant any Title of Nobility.

No State shall, without the Consent of the Congress, lay any Imposts or Duties on Imports or Exports, except what may be absolutely necessary for executing its inspection Laws; and the net Produce of all Duties and Imposts, laid by any State on Imports or Exports, shall be for the use of the Treasury of the United States; and all such Laws shall be subject to the Revision and Control of the Congress.

No state shall, without the Consent of Congress, lay any duty of Tonnage, keep Troops, or Ships of War in time of Peace, enter into any Agreement or Compact with another State, or with a foreign Power, or engage in War, unless actually invaded, or in such imminent Danger as will not admit of delay.

ARTICLE II

SECTION 1. The executive Power shall be vested in a President of the United States of America. He shall hold his Office during the Term of four years, and, together with the Vice President, chosen for the same Term, be elected, as follows:

Each State shall appoint, in such Manner as the Legislature thereof may direct, a Number of Electors, equal to the whole Number of Senators and Representatives to which the State may be entitled in the Congress: but no Senator or Representative, or Person holding an Office of Trust or Profit under the United States, shall be appointed an Elector.

[The Electors shall meet in their respective States, and vote by Ballot for two persons, of whom one at least shall not be an Inhabitant of the same State with themselves. And they shall make a List of all the Persons voted for, and of the Number of Votes for each; which List they shall sign and certify, and transmit sealed to the Seat of the Government of the United States, directed to the President of the Senate. The President of the Senate shall, in the Presence of the Senate and House of Representatives, open all the Certificates, and the Votes shall then be counted. The Person having the greatest Number of Votes shall be the President, if such Number be a Majority of the whole Number of Electors appointed; and if there be more than one who have such Majority, and have an equal Number of Votes, then the House of Representatives shall immediately chuse by Ballot one of them for President; and if no Person have a Majority, then from the five highest on the List the said House shall in like Manner chuse the President. But in chusing the President, the Votes shall be taken by States, the Representation from each State having one Vote; a quorum for this Purpose shall consist of a Member or Members from two—thirds of the States, and a Majority of all the States shall be necessary to a Choice. In every Case, after the Choice of the President, the Person having the greatest Number of Votes of the Electors shall be the Vice President. But if there should remain two or more who have equal votes, the Senate shall chuse from them by Ballot the Vice President.][4]

The Congress may determine the Time of chusing the Electors, and the Day on which they shall give their Votes; which Day shall be the same throughout the United States.

No person except a natural—born Citizen, or a Citizen of the United States, at the time of the Adoption of this Constitution, shall be eligible to the Office of President; neither shall any Person be eligible to that Office who shall not have attained to the Age of thirty—five years, and been fourteen Years a Resident within the United States.

In Case of the Removal of the President from Office, or of his Death, Resignation, or Inability to discharge the Powers and Duties of the said Office, the same shall devolve on the Vice President, and the Congress may by Law provide for the Case of Removal, Death, Resignation, or Inability, both of the President and Vice President, declaring what Officer shall then act as President, and such Officer shall act accordingly, until the disability be removed, or a President shall be elected.

The President shall, at stated Times, receive for his Services a Compensation, which shall neither be increased nor diminished during the Period for which he shall have been elected, and he shall not receive within that Period any other Emolument from the United States, or any of them.

Before he enter on the execution of his Office, he shall take the following Oath or Affirmation:—"I do solemnly swear (or affirm) that I will faithfully execute the Office of President of the United States, and will, to the best of my Ability, preserve, protect, and defend the Constitution of the United States."

4 Revised by the Twelfth Amendment.

SECTION 2. The President shall be Commander in Chief of the Army and Navy of the United States, and of the Militia of the several States, when called into the actual Service of the United States; he may require the Opinion, in writing, of the principal Officer in each of the executive Departments, upon any subject relating to the Duties of their respective Offices, and he shall have Power to Grant Reprieves and Pardons for Offenses against the United States, except in Cases of Impeachment.

He shall have Power, by and with the Advice and Consent of the Senate, to make Treaties, provided two—thirds of the Senators present concur; and he shall nominate, and by and with the Advice and Consent of the Senate, shall appoint Ambassadors, other public Ministers and Consuls, Judges of the supreme Court, and all other Officers of the United States, whose Appointments are not herein otherwise provided for, and which shall be established by Law: but the Congress may by Law vest the Appointment of such inferior Officers, as they think proper, in the President alone, in the Courts of Law, or in the Heads of Departments.

The President shall have Power to fill up all Vacancies that may happen during the Recess of the Senate, by granting Commissions which shall expire at the End of their next Session.

SECTION 3. He shall from time to time give to the Congress Information of the State of the Union, and recommend to their Consideration such Measures as he shall judge necessary and expedient; he may, on extraordinary occasions, convene both Houses, or either of them, and in Case of Disagreement between them, with respect to the Time of Adjournment, he may adjourn them to such Time as he shall think proper; he shall receive Ambassadors and other public Ministers; he shall take care that the Laws be faithfully executed, and shall Commission all the Officers of the United States.

SECTION 4. The President, Vice President and all civil Officers of the United States, shall be removed from Office on Impeachment for, and Conviction of, Treason, Bribery, or other high Crimes and Misdemeanors.

ARTICLE III

SECTION 1. The judicial Power of the United States, shall be vested in one supreme Court, and in such inferior Courts as the Congress may from time to time ordain and establish. The Judges, both of the supreme and inferior Courts, shall hold their Offices during good Behaviour, and shall, at stated Times, receive for their Services, a Compensation, which shall not be diminished during their Continuance in Office.

SECTION 2. The judicial Power shall extend to all Cases, in Law and Equity, arising under this Constitution, the Laws of the United States, and Treaties made, or which shall be made, under their Authority;—to all Cases affecting ambassadors, other public ministers and consuls;—to all cases of admiralty and maritime Jurisdiction;— to Controversies to which the United States shall be a Party;—to Controversies between two or more States;—between a State and Citizens of another State;[5]—between Citizens of different States—between Citizens of the same State claiming Lands under Grants of different States, and between a State, or the Citizens thereof, and foreign States, Citizens, or Subjects. In all Cases affecting Ambassadors, other public Ministers and Consuls, and those in which a State shall be Party, the supreme Court shall have original Jurisdiction. In all the other Cases before mentioned, the supreme Court shall have appellate Jurisdiction, both as to Law and Fact, with such Exceptions, and under such Regulations as the Congress shall make.

The trial of all Crimes, except in Cases of Impeachment, shall be by Jury; and such Trial shall be held in the State where the said Crimes shall have been committed; but when not committed within any State, the Trial shall be at such Place or Places as the Congress may by Law have directed.

SECTION 3. Treason against the United States, shall consist only in levying War against them, or in adhering to their Enemies, giving them Aid and Comfort. No Person shall be convicted of Treason unless on the Testimony of two Witnesses to the same overt Act, or on Confession in open Court.

The Congress shall have power to declare the Punishment of Treason, but no Attainder of Treason shall work Corruption of Blood, or Forfeiture except during the Life of the Person attainted.

ARTICLE IV

SECTION 1. Full Faith and Credit shall be given in each State to the public Acts, Records, and judicial Proceedings of every other State. And the Congress may by general Laws prescribe the Manner in which such Acts, Records and Proceedings shall be proved, and the Effect thereof.

5 Qualified by the Eleventh Amendment.

SECTION 2. The Citizens of each State shall be entitled to all Privileges and Immunities of Citizens in the several States.

A Person charged in any State with Treason, Felony, or other Crime, who shall flee from Justice, and be found in another State, shall on demand of the executive Authority of the State from which he fled, be delivered up, to be removed to the State having Jurisdiction of the crime. No Person held to Service or Labour in one State, under the Laws thereof, escaping into another, shall, in Consequence of any Law or Regulation therein, be discharged from such Service or Labour, but shall be delivered up on Claim of the Party to whom such Service or Labour may be due.

SECTION 3. New States may be admitted by the Congress into this Union; but no new State shall be formed or erected within the Jurisdiction of any other State; nor any State be formed by the Junction of two or more States, or parts of States, without the Consent of the Legislatures of the States concerned as well as of the Congress. The Congress shall have Power to dispose of and make all needful Rules and Regulations respecting the Territory or other Property belonging to the United States; and nothing in this Constitution shall be so construed as to Prejudice any Claims of the United States, or of any particular State.

SECTION 4. The United States shall guarantee to every State in this Union a Republican Form of Government, and shall protect each of them against Invasion; and on Application of the Legislature, or of the Executive (when the Legislature cannot be convened) against domestic Violence.

ARTICLE V

The Congress, whenever two–thirds of both Houses shall deem it necessary, shall propose Amendments to this Constitution, or, on the Application of the Legislatures of two–thirds of the several States, shall call a Convention for proposing Amendments, which, in either Case, shall be valid to all Intents and Purposes, as part of this Constitution, when ratified by the Legislatures of three–fourths of the several States, or by Conventions in three–fourths thereof, as the one or the other Mode of Ratification may be proposed by the Congress; Provided that no Amendment which may be made prior to the Year One thousand eight hundred and eight shall in any Manner affect the first and fourth Clauses in the Ninth Section of the first Article; and that no State, without its Consent, shall be deprived of its equal Suffrage in the Senate.

ARTICLE VI

All Debts contracted and Engagements entered into, before the Adoption of this Constitution, shall be as valid against the United States under this Constitution, as under the Confederation.

This Constitution, and the Laws of the United States which shall be made in Pursuance thereof; and all Treaties made, or which shall be made, under the Authority of the United States, shall be the supreme Law of the Land; and the Judges in every State shall be bound thereby, any Thing in the Constitution or Laws of any State to the Contrary notwithstanding.

The Senators and Representatives before mentioned, and the Members of the several State Legislatures, and all executive and judicial Officers, both of the United States and of the several States, shall be bound by Oath or Affirmation to support this Constitution; but no religious Tests shall ever be required as a qualification to any Office or public Trust under the United States.

ARTICLE VII

The Ratification of the Conventions of nine States shall be sufficient for the Establishment of this Constitution between the States so ratifying the same.

Done in Convention by the Unanimous Consent of the States present the Seventeenth Day of September in the Year of our Lord one thousand seven hundred and Eighty seven, and of the Independence of the United States of America the Twelfth. In Witness whereof We have hereunto subscribed our Names.[6]

GEORGE WASHINGTON
PRESIDENT AND DEPUTY FROM VIRGINIA

NEW HAMPSHIRE
John Langdon
Nicholas Gilman

MASSACHUSETTS
Nathaniel Gorham
Rufus King

CONNECTICUT
William Samuel Johnson
Roger Sherman

NEW YORK
Alexander Hamilton

NEW JERSEY
William Livingston
David Brearley
William Paterson
Jonathan Dayton

PENNSYLVANIA
Benjamin Franklin
Thomas Mifflin
Robert Morris
George Clymer
Thomas FitzSimons
Jared Ingersoll
James Wilson
Gouverneur Morris

DELAWARE
George Read
Gunning Bedford, Jr.
John Dickinson
Richard Bassett
Jacob Broom

MARYLAND
James McHenry
Daniel of St. Thomas Jenifer
Daniel Carroll

VIRGINIA
John Blair
James Madison, Jr.

NORTH CAROLINA
William Blount
Richard Dobbs Spaight
Hugh Williamson

SOUTH CAROLINA
John Rutledge
Charles Cotesworth
Pinckney
Charles Pinckney
Pierce Butler

GEORGIA
William Few
Abraham Baldwin

Articles in Addition to, and Amendment of, the Constitution of the United States of America, Proposed by Congress, and Ratified by the Legislatures of the Several States, Pursuant to the Fifth Article of the Original Constitution[7]

[AMENDMENT I]

Congress shall make no law respecting an establishment of religion, or prohibiting the free exercise thereof; or abridging the freedom of speech, or of the press; or the right of the people peaceably to assemble, and to petition the Government for a redress of grievances.

[AMENDMENT II]

A well regulated Militia, being necessary to the security of a free State, the right of the people to keep and bear Arms shall not be infringed.

6 These are the full names of the signers, which in some cases are not the signatures on the document.

7 This heading appears only in the joint resolution submitting the first ten amendments, known as the Bill of Rights.

[AMENDMENT III]

No Soldier shall, in time of peace, be quartered in any house, without the consent of the Owner, nor in time of war, but in a manner to be prescribed by law.

[AMENDMENT IV]

The right of the people to be secure in their persons, houses, papers, and effects, against unreasonable searches and seizures, shall not be violated, and no Warrants shall issue, but upon probable cause, supported by Oath or affirmation, and particularly describing the place to be searched, and the persons or things to be seized.

[AMENDMENT V]

No person shall be held to answer for a capital or otherwise infamous crime, unless on a presentment or indictment of a Grand Jury, except in cases arising in the land or naval forces, or in the Militia, when in actual service in time of War or public danger; nor shall any person be subject for the same offence to be twice put in jeopardy of life or limb; nor shall be compelled in any criminal case to be a witness against himself, nor be deprived of life, liberty, or property, without due process of law; nor shall private property be taken for public use, without just compensation.

[AMENDMENT VI]

In all criminal prosecutions, the accused shall enjoy the right to a speedy and public trial, by an impartial jury of the State and district wherein the crime shall have been committed, which district shall have been previously ascertained by law, and to be informed of the nature and cause of the accusation; to be confronted with the witnesses against him; to have compulsory process for obtaining witnesses in his favour, and to have the Assistance of Counsel for his defence.

[AMENDMENT VII]

In suits at common law, where the value in controversy shall exceed twenty dollars, the right of trial by jury shall be preserved, and no fact tried by a jury, shall be otherwise reexamined in any Court of the United States, than according to the rules of the common law.

[AMENDMENT VIII]

Excessive bail shall not be required, nor excessive fines imposed, nor cruel and unusual punishments inflicted.

[AMENDMENT IX]

The enumeration of the Constitution, of certain rights, shall not be construed to deny or disparage others retained by the people.

[AMENDMENT X]

The powers not delegated to the United States by the Constitution, nor prohibited by it to the States, are reserved to the States respectively, or to the people. [Amendments I–X, in force 1791.]

[AMENDMENT XI][8]

The Judicial power of the United States shall not be construed to extend to any suit in law or equity, commenced or prosecuted against one of the United States by Citizens of another State, or by Citizens or Subjects of any Foreign State.

[AMENDMENT XII][9]

The Electors shall meet in their respective States and vote by ballot for President and Vice–President, one of whom, at least, shall not be an inhabitant of the same State with themselves; they shall name in their ballots the person voted for as President, and in distinct ballots the person voted for as Vice–President, and they shall make distinct lists of all persons voted for as President, and of all persons voted for as Vice–President, and of the number of

8 Adopted in 1798.
9 Adopted in 1804.

votes for each, which lists they shall sign and certify, and transmit sealed to the seat of the government of the United States, directed to the President of the Senate;—The President of the Senate shall, in the presence of the Senate and House of Representatives, open all the certificates and the votes shall then be counted;—The person having the greatest number of votes for President, shall be the President, if such number be a majority of the whole number of Electors appointed; and if no person have such majority, then from the persons having the highest numbers not exceeding three on the list of those voted for as President, the House of Representatives shall choose immediately, by ballot, the President. But in choosing the President, the votes shall be taken by states, the representation from each state having one vote; a quorum for this purpose shall consist of a member or members from two–thirds of the states, and a majority of all the states shall be necessary to a choice. And if the House of Representatives shall not choose a President whenever the right of choice shall devolve upon them, before the fourth day of March next following, then the Vice–President shall act as President, as in the case of the death or other constitutional disability of the President.— The person having the greatest number of votes as Vice–President, shall be the Vice–President, if such number be a majority of the whole number of Electors appointed, and if no person have a major– ity, then from the two highest numbers on the list, the Senate shall choose the Vice–President; a quo– rum for the purpose shall consist of two–thirds of the whole number of Senators, and a majority of the whole number shall be necessary to a choice. But no person constitutionally ineligible to the office of President shall be eligible to that of Vice–President of the United States.

[AMENDMENT XIII] [10]

SECTION 1. Neither slavery nor involuntary servitude, except as a punishment for crime whereof the party shall have been duly convicted, shall exist within the United States, or any place subject to their jurisdiction.

SECTION 2. Congress shall have power to enforce this article by appropriate legislation.

10 Adopted in 1865.
11 Adopted in 1868.

[AMENDMENT XIV] [11]

SECTION 1. All persons born or naturalized in the United States, and subject to the jurisdic– tion thereof, are citizens of the United States and of the State wherein they reside. No State shall abridge the privileges or immunities of citizens of the United States; nor shall any State deprive any person of life, liberty, or property, without due process of law; nor deny to any person within its jurisdiction the equal protection of the laws.

SECTION 2. Representatives shall be apportioned among the several States according to their respec– tive numbers, counting the whole number of persons in each State, excluding Indians not taxed. But when the right to vote at any election for the choice of electors for President and Vice–President of the United States, Representatives in Congress, the Executive and Judi– cial officers of a State, or the members of the Legisla– ture thereof, is denied to any of the male inhabitants of such State, being twentyone years of age, and citizens of the United States, or in any way abridged, except for participation in rebellion, or other crime, the basis of representation therein shall be reduced in the pro– portion which the number of such male citizens shall bear to the whole number of male citizens twenty–one years of age in such State.

SECTION 3. No person shall be a Senator or Representative in Congress, or elector of President and Vice– President, or hold any office, civil or military, under the United States, or under any State, who, having previously taken an oath, as a member of Con– gress, or as an officer of the United States, or as a member of any State legislature, or as an executive or judicial officer of any State, to support the Con– stitution of the United States, shall have engaged in insurrection or rebellion against the same, or given aid or comfort to the enemies thereof. But Congress may by a vote of two–thirds of each House, remove such disability.

SECTION 4. The validity of the public debt of the United States, authorized by law, including debts incurred for payment of pensions and bounties for services in suppressing insurrection or rebellion, shall not be questioned. But neither the United States nor any State shall assume or pay any debts or obligation incurred in aid of insurrection or rebellion against the United States, or any claim for the loss or emancipa– tion of any slave; but all such debts, obligations, and claims shall be held illegal and void.

SECTION 5. The Congress shall have the power to enforce, by appropriate legislation, the provisions of this article.

[AMENDMENT XV][12]

SECTION 1. The right of citizens of the United States to vote shall not be denied or abridged by the United States or by any State on account of race, color, or previous condition of servitude.

SECTION 2. The Congress shall have power to enforce this article by appropriate legislation.

[AMENDMENT XVI][13]

The Congress shall have power to lay and collect taxes on incomes, from whatever source derived, without apportionment among the several States, and without regard to any census or enumeration.

[AMENDMENT XVII][14]

The Senate of the United States shall be composed of two Senators from each State, elected by the people thereof, for six years; and each Senator shall have one vote. The electors in each State shall have the quali-fications requisite for electors of the most numerous branch of the State legislatures.

When vacancies happen in the representation of any State in the Senate, the executive authority of such State shall issue writs of election to fill such vacancies: Provided, That the legislature of any State may empower the executive thereof to make tempo-rary appointments until the people fill the vacancies by election as the legislature may direct. This amendment shall not be so construed as to affect the election or term of any Senator chosen before it becomes valid as part of the Constitution.

12 Adopted in 1870.
13 Adopted in 1913.
14 Adopted in 1913.
15 Adopted in 1918.

[AMENDMENT XVIII][15]

SECTION 1. After one year from the ratification of this article the manufacture, sale, or transportation of intoxicating liquors within, the importation thereof into, or the exportation thereof from the United States and all territory subject to the jurisdiction thereof for beverage purposes is hereby prohibited.

SECTION 2. The Congress and the several States shall have concurrent power to enforce this article by appropriate legislation.

SECTION 3. This article shall be inoperative unless it shall have been ratified as an amendment to the Constitution by the legislatures of the several States, as provided in the Constitution, within seven years from the date of the submission hereof to the States by the Congress.

[AMENDMENT XIX][16]

The right of citizens of the United States to vote shall not be denied or abridged by the United States or by any State on account of sex.

Congress shall have power to enforce this article by appropriate legislation.

[AMENDMENT XX][17]

SECTION 1. The terms of the President and Vice—President shall end at noon on the 20th day of January, and the terms of Senators and Representa—tives at noon on the 3d day of January, of the years in which such terms would have ended if this article had not been ratified; and the terms of their successors shall then begin.

SECTION 2. The Congress shall assemble at least once in every year, and such meeting shall begin at noon on the 3d day of January, unless they shall by law appoint a different day.

16 Adopted in 1920.
17 Adopted in 1933.

SECTION 3.
If, at the time fixed for the beginning of the term of the President, the President elect shall have died, the Vice—President elect shall become President. If a President shall not have been chosen before the time fixed for the beginning of his term or if the President elect shall have failed to qualify, then the Vice—President elect shall act as President until a President shall have qualified; and the Congress may by law provide for the case wherein neither a President elect nor a Vice—President elect shall have qualified, declaring who shall then act as President, or the manner in which one who is to act shall be selected, and such person shall act accordingly until a President or Vice—President shall have qualified.

SECTION 4.
The Congress may by law provide for the case of the death of any of the persons from whom the House of Representatives may choose a President whenever the right of choice shall have devolved upon them, and for the case of the death of any of the persons from whom the Senate may choose a Vice—President whenever the right of choice shall have devolved upon them.

SECTION 5.
Sections 1 and 2 shall take effect on the 15th day of October following the ratification of this article.

SECTION 6.
This article shall be inoperative unless it shall have been ratified as an amendment to the Constitution by the legislatures of three—fourths of the several States within seven years from the date of its submission.

[AMENDMENT XXI] [18]

SECTION 1.
The eighteenth article of amendment to the Constitution of the United States is hereby repealed.

SECTION 2.
The transportation or importation into any State, Territory, or possession of the United States for delivery or use therein of intoxicating liquors, in violation of the laws thereof, is hereby prohibited.

SECTION 3.
This article shall be inoperative unless it shall have been ratified as an amendment to the Constitution by conventions in the several States,

18 Adopted in 1933.

as provided in the Constitution, within seven years from the date of the submission hereof to the States by the Congress.

[AMENDMENT XXII] [19]

No person shall be elected to the office of the President more than twice, and no person who has held the office of President, or acted as President, for more than two years of a term to which some other person was elected President shall be elected to the office of the President more than once.

But this Article shall not apply to any person holding the office of President when this Article was proposed by the Congress, and shall not prevent any person who may be holding the office of President, or acting as President, during the term within which this Article becomes operative from holding the office of President or acting as President during the remainder of such term.

This article shall be inoperative unless it shall have been ratified as an amendment to the Constitution by the legislatures of three—fourths of the several states within seven years from the date of its submission to the states by the Congress.

[AMENDMENT XXIII] [20]

SECTION 1.
The District constituting the seat of Government of the United States shall appoint in such manner as the Congress may direct:

A number of electors of President and Vice—President equal to the whole number of Senators and Representatives in Congress to which the District would be entitled if it were a State, but in no event more than the least populous State; they shall be in addition to those appointed by the States, but they shall be considered, for the purpose of the election of President and Vice—President, to be electors appointed by a State; and they shall meet in the District and perform such duties as provided by the twelfth article of amendment.

SECTION 2.
The Congress shall have power to enforce this article by appropriate legislation.

19 Adopted in 1951.
20 Adopted in 1961.

[AMENDMENT XXIV][21]

SECTION 1. The right of citizens of the United States to vote in any primary or other election for President or Vice- President, for electors for President or Vice-President, or for Senator or Representative in Congress, shall not be denied or abridged by the United States or any state by reason of failure to pay any poll tax or other tax.

SECTION 2. The Congress shall have the power to enforce this article by appropriate legislation.

[AMENDMENT XXV][22]

SECTION 1. In case of the removal of the President from office or of his death or resignation, the Vice-President shall become President.

SECTION 2. Whenever there is a vacancy in the office of the Vice President, the President shall nominate a Vice President who shall take office upon confirmation by a majority vote of both Houses of Congress.

SECTION 3. Whenever the President transmits to the President Pro Tempore of the Senate and the Speaker of the House of Representatives his written declaration that he is unable to discharge the powers and duties of his office, and until he transmits to them a written declaration to the contrary, such powers and duties shall be discharged by the Vice-President as Acting President.

SECTION 4. Whenever the Vice-President and a majority of either the principal officers of the executive departments or of such other body as Congress may by law provide, transmit to the President Pro Tempore of the Senate and the Speaker of the House of Representatives their written declaration that the President is unable to discharge the powers and duties of his office, the Vice President shall immediately assume the powers and duties of the office as Acting President.

Thereafter, when the President transmits to the President Pro Tempore of the Senate and the Speaker of the House of Representatives his written declaration that no inability exists, he shall resume the powers and duties of his office unless the Vice President and a majority of either the principal officers of the executive departments or of such other body as Congress may by law provide, transmit within four days to the President Pro Tempore of the Senate and the Speaker of the House of Representatives their written declaration that the President is unable to discharge the powers and duties of his office. Thereupon Congress shall decide the issue, assembling within forty-eight hours for that purpose if not in session. If the Congress, within twenty-one days after receipt of the latter written declaration, or, if Congress is not in session, within twenty-one days after Congress is required to assemble, determines by two-thirds vote of both Houses that the President is unable to discharge the powers and duties of his office, the Vice President shall continue to discharge the same as Acting President; otherwise, the President shall resume the powers and duties of his office.

[AMENDMENT XXVI][23]

SECTION 1. The right of citizens of the United States, who are eighteen years of age or older, to vote shall not be denied or abridged by the United States or by any State on account of age.

SECTION 1. The Congress shall have power to enforce this article by appropriate legislation.

[AMENDMENT XXVII][24]

No law, varying the compensation for the services of the Senators and Representatives, shall take effect, until an election of Representatives shall have intervened.

21 Adopted in 1964.
22 Adopted in 1967.
23 Adopted in 1971.
24 Adopted in 1992.

Credits

Text Credits

Chapter 2 Page 25: Bernal Díaz, *The True History of the Conquest of New Spain*, excerpted in *Victors and Vanquished: Spanish and Nahua Views of the Conquest of Mexico*, Stuart B. Schwartz, ed. Boston, MA: Bedford/St. Martin's, 2000, pp. 85–90. p. 25: Fray Bernardino de Sahagún, *Florentine The Codex*, excerpted in *Victors and Vanquished: Spanish and Nahua Views of the Conquest of Mexico*, Stuart B. Schwartz, ed. Boston, MA: Bedford/St. Martin's, 2000, pp. 91–99.

Chapter 4 Pages 70–71: Sarah Bibber, Ann Putnam and Mary Warren, "The Accusations." http://etext.virginia.edu; p. 71: John Procter, "The Defense." http://wtext.virginia.edu.

Chapter 6 Page 112: "Deposition of Captain Thomas Preston, March 1770." www.law.umkc.edu; p. 112: "Deposition of Robert Goddard, March 1770." www.law.umkc.edu.

Chapter 9 Page 171: "'The Female Advocate' on the Virtues of an Educated Wife," from *The Female Advocate, Written by a Lady*. New Haven, CT: Thomas Green and Son, 1801; p. 171: Samuel K. Jennings, "On the Virtues of a Submissive Wife," *The Married Lady's Companion, or Poor Man's Friend*. New York, NY: Lorenzo Dow, 1808.

Chapter 10 Page 200: Frances Wright, "Equality Secures Liberty," *Views of Society and Manners in America*. London, England: E. Bliss and E. White, 1821; pp. 200–201: Alexis de Tocqueville, "Equality Promotes Anxiety," *Democracy in America*. 1840.

Chapter 11 Page 215: Henry Clay, "Speech at the Annual Meeting of the American Colonization Society, Washington, January 30, 1827," in *The Works of Henry Clay*, Calvin Colton, ed. New York, NY: G. P. Putnam's and Sons, 1904; pp. 215–216: David Walker, *Appeal to the Coloured Citizens of the World*. 1829.

Chapter 14 Page 272: James K. Polk, "Message to Congress, Washington, May 11, 1846," in *A Compilation of the Messages and Papers of the Presidents*, Vol. 4, James D. Richardson, ed. New York, NY: Bureau of National Literature and Art, 1908, pp. 437–443; pp. 272–273: "The 'Spot' Was Beyond the U.S. Borders: Representative Abraham Lincoln," December 22, 1847. http://teachingamericanhistory.org.

Chapter 15 Page 302: Alexander Stephens, "Speech Delivered March 21, 1861. Savannah, Georgia," in *The Rebellion Record*, Frank Moore, ed. New York, NY: G. P. Putnam, 1868, pp. 45–46; pp. 302–303: Jefferson Davis, "Slavery Did Not Cause the Civil War," *The Rise and Fall of the Confederate Government*. New York, NY: D. Appleton and Co., 1881, pp. 77–80.

Chapter 16 Page 310: U.S. Census Bureau 1860 and E. B. Long, *The Civil War Day by Day*. New York, NY: Doubleday, 1971, p. 723; p. 328: Dolly Lunt, *A Woman's Wartime Journal*, September 19, 1864.

Chapter 17 Page 346: Ruth Watkins, *Reconstruction in Marshall County*. 1912.

Photo Credits

Feature Design Elements (repeated throughout)

Pen and Quill: © DNY59/iStock; Pencil: © Torsten Stahlberg/iStock; Blotter and Fountain Pen: Lars/© Christensen/Cutcaster; Ink Bottle and Pen: ©Nataliya Hora/iStock; Pen: © Olivier Blondeau/iStock; Ballpoint Pen and Post-its: ©Floortje/iStock; Sword: © Civil War Archive/Bridgeman Images.

Frontmatter

Page ii: © Paramount Pictures/Photofest; pg. iv © Corbis; pg. v: Historicus, Inc.; pg. ix: Private Collection/©Peter Newark American Pictures/Bridgeman Images; pg. x (top): © Richard A. Cooke/Corbis; (bottom): © Valls Gallery, London, UK/Bridgeman Images; pg. xi: © MedioImages/Corbis (RF); pg. xii: Private Collection/©Peter Newark American Pictures/Bridgeman Images; pg. xiii (left): Segesser II. © Courtesy Palace of Governors (MNM/DCA) 158345.; (right): American Pictures/Bridgeman Images; pg. xiv: Private Collection/© Peter Newark American Pictures/Bridgeman Images; pg. xv: © Winterthur Museum; pg. xvi: © Collection of New-York Historical Society/Bridgeman Images; pg. xvii: © Collection of the New-York Historical Society, USA/Bridgeman Images; pg. xviii (left): © Collection of the New-York Historical Society, USA/Bridgeman Images; (right): The Library of Congress; pg. xix: © Private Collection/Bridgeman Images; pg. xx: The Library of Congress; pg. xxi: Historicus, Inc.; xxii: The Library of Congress; pg. xxiv: The McGraw-Hill Companies.

Text

Chapter 1 Page 1: © Richard A. Cooke/Corbis; p. 2: © Heritage Images/Corbis; p. 4: © Werner Formans/HIP/Image Works; p. 6: Photo by Karl Kernberger/© Solstice Project; p. 9: Service Historique de la Marine, Vincennes, France/© Giraudon/Bridgeman Images; p. 10:© Raymond Gehman/Corbis; p. 11:© Free Library, Philadelphia/Bridgeman Images.

Chapter 2 Page 17: © Rafael Valls Gallery, London, UK/Bridgeman Images; p. 21(top): © Everett Collection Inc/Alamy; (bottom): © Walters Art Museum, Baltimore, USA/Bridgeman Images; p. 26 (right): The Library of Congress; (left): © The Art Gallery Collection/Alamy; p. 28: © Dorling Kindersley/Getty Images (RF); p. 30: De Agostini Picture Library/© G. Costa/Bridgeman Images; p. 32: © Private Collection/Bridgeman Images.

Chapter 3 Page 37: © MedioImages/Corbis RF; p. 38(left): The Library of Congress (LC-USZ62-8104); (right) © Walt Disney Pictures/Photofest; p. 40 © Kevin Fleming/Corbis; p. 43: Private Collection/© Peter Newark American Pictures/Bridgeman Images; p. 44: © Courtesy of APVA Preservation Virginia; p. 46: Photo © Virginia Historical Society/Xanterra Corporation; p. 48 (top): Gabinetto dei Disegni e Stampe, Galleria Degli Uffizi, Florence, Italy/© Alinari/Bridgeman Images; (bottom): © The Granger Collection, New York; p. 49 (top): Private Collection/© Michael Graham-Stewart/Bridgeman Images; (bottom left): © The Granger Collection, New York; (bottom right) *Blacks Working on the James River* by Benjamin Henry Latrobe, 1798–99. Courtesy of The Library of Virginia; p. 50: © Corbis; p. 53: Private Collection/Photo © Christie's Images/Bridgeman Images; p. 56: *View of Mulberry, House and Street, 1805* by Thomas Coram (American, 1756–1811), Oil on paper. © Gibbes Museum of Art/Carolina Art Association, 1968.18.01.

Chapter 4 Page 59: Private Collection/© Peter Newark American Pictures/Bridgeman Images; p. 61: © Historic Collection/Alamy; p. 62(top): World Health Organization/Images From the History of Medicine Collection, The National Library of Medicine; p. 65: Universal History Archive/© UIG/Bridgeman Images; p. 68: © Steve Dunwell; p. 72: The Library of Congress (cph3b42346); p. 75: © The Granger Collection, New York; p. 76: © Bristol City Museum and Art Gallery, UK/Bridgeman Images.

Chapter 5 Page 79: *Segesser II*. © Courtesy Palace of Governors (NMHM/DCA) 158345.; p. 83 (top): © De Agostini Pictures/Getty Images; (bottom): Courtesy of the Private Collection of Mrs. Janis Lyon/Photo © Phoenix Art Museum; p. 84: National Library of Australia; p. 86: Courtesy Vermillionville/Photo James West Davidson; p. 89: © The Granger Collection, New York; p. 90: © Shelburne Museum, Shelburne, Vermont; p. 92: © Abby Aldrich Rockefeller Folk Art Museum, Williamsburg, VA; p. 94(left): © North Wind Picture Archives/Image Works; (right): © Francis G. Mayer/Corbis; p. 95: © British Museum, London, UK/Bridgeman Images.

Chapter 6 Page 99 (background): Fort Necessity Battlefield, National Park Service; (foreground): Private Collection/© Peter Newark American Pictures/Bridgeman Images; p. 102 (left): Private Collection/Photo © Christie's Images/Bridgeman Images; (right): Library of Congress; p. 107: © Philadelphia History Museum at the Atwater Kent,/Courtesy of Historical Society of Pennsylvania Collection,/Bridgeman Images; p. 109: © Corbis; p. 110: © North Wind Picture Archives/Alamy; p. 111: © Bettmann/Corbis; p. 113: The Library of Congress; p. 117: © The Granger Collection, New York.

Chapter 7 Page 120: Private Collection/© Peter Newark American Pictures/Bridgeman Images; p. 123: © Atwater Kent Museum of Philadelphia/Courtesy of Historical Society of Pennsylvania Collection,/Bridgeman Images; p. 128:

Index